D0026634

Creative and Critical Thinking

Creative and Critical Thinking

Second Edition

W. Edgar Moore
Emeritus
University of Florida

Hugh McCann
Texas A & M University

Janet McCann
Texas A & M University

Houghton Mifflin Company
Boston

Dallas   Geneva, Illinois
Hopewell, New Jersey   Palo Alto

Acknowledgment is made to Houghton Mifflin Company for permission to reprint material from *The Riverside Shakespeare*: William Shakespeare's *Julius Caesar, The First Part of Henry the Fourth*, and *Hamlet*. Copyright © 1974 by Houghton Mifflin Company. Used with permission.

Copyright © 1985 by Houghton Mifflin Company. All Rights Reserved. No part of this work may be reproduced or transmitted in any form or by any means, electronic or mechanical, including photocopying and recording, or by any information storage or retrieval system, except as may be expressly permitted by the 1976 Copyright Act or in writing by the Publisher. Requests for permission should be addressed to Permissions, Houghton Mifflin Company, One Beacon Street, Boston, MA 02108.

Printed in the U.S.A.
Library of Congress Catalog Number: 84-81047
ISBN: 0-395-35780-2

ABCDEFGHIJ-H-8987654

Contents

Part Six   **The Argumentative Essay**

Preface

Purpose

Creative and Critical Thinking is a text on the development of thinking skills. It is designed for courses whose primary goal is to teach students how to solve problems using practical reasoning. Although the text's coverage is rooted in applied logic, it covers those subjective factors that influence decision-making. We believe that a course devoted to the development of effective thinking is as necessary as a basic course in English or mathematics. While students can and do improve their thinking through the study of such courses as English, mathematics, physical science, and social science, they also need to study the techniques of effective thinking directly. Many studies in psychology reveal that the study of those techniques—the development of metacognitive skills—improves thinking and learning abilities. Sound thinking is too complex a process to be adequately treated as an adjunct to a course devoted primarily to other matter and is too important to be relegated to spare moments.

Audience

The text was written for students at the undergraduate level and should serve for students in any curriculum. No previous training in logic is presupposed, and many of the examples were designed for students who are in the early stages of their college curriculum.

Previous Editions

This text has a long history. The first version, *Applied Logic*, by Winston W. Little, W. Harold Wilson, and W. Edgar Moore, was published in 1955. Their purpose was to present a text that would enable students to develop their intellectual skills for practical use in problem-solving. For this purpose the content of the traditional logic text was changed, more categories of informal logic were added, and the traditional treatment of deduction was simplified and streamlined to make it more applicable to everyday problems. The standard principles of induction and probability were presented with an emphasis on applications. From the behavioral sciences were taken materials that would provide insight into the operation of such factors as emotion and cultural influence and their impact on sound thinking.

In 1967, the book was revised by W. Edgar Moore. Its scope was altered to focus on decision-making, the most practical application of effective thinking techniques. The material on subjective factors was enlarged and updated, and chapters were added to show how techniques in effective thinking could be used to help create a consistent system of values to live by. Material was included on the theory of creativity, and this information too was put in practical form. Reflecting this last addition, the title of the text was changed to *Creative and Critical Thinking*.

The Present Edition

In this revision, we have kept in mind the book's original goal: to teach students the specific skills necessary for selecting and using information to solve problems and make decisions. Thus we have tried to retain the book's practical approach and its involvement in student concerns while at the same time thoroughly updating both theory and example. The changes we have made include the following:

Chapter 2 (a new chapter) now introduces the fundamental logical concepts employed in the text;

Two new chapters apply the skills developed throughout the text to the writing of argumentative essays;

The text is now organized into six parts, which may be used as units in the course;

The chapters on informal fallacies, which were previously distributed throughout the text, now form a complete unit;

The Exercises which appear at the end of each chapter have been revised and updated, and, in many cases, additional problems are provided.

Like the previous revision of the text, this one has drawn heavily on the experiences and suggestions of instructors and students who have used earlier editions. With the exception of some historical material and a few incidents that are public knowledge, the subject matter of illustrations and exercises is completely fictitious.

Acknowledgments

We are grateful above all to W. Edgar Moore, both for providing an excellent foundation and for trusting us to build upon it. The manuscript was reviewed by:

Harold Alderman, California State University at Sonoma, CA

John M. Barbee, National College of Education, Evanston, IL

John A. Barker, Southern Illinois University at Edwardsville, IL

Linda A. Bell, Georgia State University, Atlanta, GA

Dion K. Brown, Polk Community College, Winter Haven, FL

Their suggestions did much to shape and improve the book. We also benefitted greatly from numerous discussions with our colleagues at Texas A & M University. Special thanks are due to Mary Johnson and Melissa Meyer for their patient and unflagging dedication in preparing the manuscript. Finally, we must thank our children, Stephanie, Hugh, Paul, and Peter, for their understanding and tolerance in enduring the hardship of having both parents at work on a book.

Hugh McCann

Janet McCann

Creative and
Critical Thinking

Part One

Decision Making and Problem Solving

Chapter 1

Decision Making

- **Creative and Critical Thinking**
- **Phases of Decision Making**
- **The Personal Point of View**
- **Objectivity**
- **Improving Thinking**

On Saturday, October 27, 1962, President John F. Kennedy sat with his advisers in the White House faced with a difficult and potentially apocalyptic decision. All week long the world had stood at the brink of all-out nuclear war. The Soviet Union was in the process of installing medium and intermediate range ballistic missiles in Cuba, and the United States wanted them out. On Monday President Kennedy had announced a blockade of the island, and when it went into effect on Wednesday, all Soviet cargo ships other than tankers had turned for home. But construction of launching sites for the missiles already in Cuba had proceeded without interruption and was now nearly complete. On Friday evening a long and rambling message had been received from Soviet Premier Nikita Krushchev—a man U.S. intelligence had described as "unstable." It was essentially conciliatory and suggested that if only the United States would guarantee not to invade Cuba, the Soviet missiles could be removed. This would be a satisfactory arrangement, and Kennedy's staff was ac-

cordingly relieved. But now new and more ominous developments were occurring. On Saturday morning, a new message was received, more formal and more demanding: if the United States wanted the Soviet Union to remove its missiles from Cuba, it would have to remove its own missiles from Turkey, which borders the Soviet Union. That same morning a United States reconnaissance plane was shot down over Cuba by a Soviet missile; the pilot was killed. Finally, the FBI was reporting that Soviet personnel in New York City were preparing to burn all sensitive documents, a procedure reserved only for the most serious circumstances. Clearly, the situation was deteriorating.

Faced with an escalating crises, President Kennedy had numerous options to consider. One was to take further military action. The air force had urged from the beginning that the missile sites be bombed, and it now appeared that this might be the only way to get the missiles out. If necessary, air strikes could be followed by an invasion of Cuba, for which a force was being assembled. The danger of this course was obvious: it would almost certainly force some sort of Soviet military response with potentially devastating consequences. On the diplomatic side were several options. Premier Krushchev's first message was taken by many as a sign of weakness. Perhaps it was time to back the Soviets into a corner: to tell them that the entire Soviet presence in Cuba had to be removed, with no guarantees whatever. On the other hand, the United States missiles in Turkey were obsolete, and there had been plans to remove them anyway. Perhaps the United States should accept the trade-off proposed in the second Soviet message, even though to do so would be perceived as backing down. Finally, one could opt for a cooling-off period. The secretary general of the United Nations, U Thant, had suggested this earlier in the week: the Soviet Union would stop shipping weapons to Cuba, and the United States would lift its blockade, with negotiations to follow later.

As often happens when momentous decisions must be made, President Kennedy was caught in a dilemma. If he acted too forcefully, he could trip the most colossal disaster in history. All through the crisis he had sought to avoid this by trying not to cause the Soviets any unnecessary loss of face. On the other hand, he would be acting too weakly if he accepted the missile trade proposed in the latest Soviet message. Acceptance would mean paying a price for having the missiles removed from Cuba, and he had been adamant that no price would be paid, for that would reward Soviet adventurism and invite more of it. Neither, finally, could he accept the cooling-off period U Thant had proposed. If he did, he would be caught in the pitfall of **decision by indecision**, that is, delaying a decision until it is

made by time or events. For to dismantle the blockade would be to accept the Soviet missiles already in Cuba. By the time negotiations could begin, the missiles would be an established fact, and it might no longer be possible to remove them. Clearly, a decisive move had to be made, but what should it be?

It was in this situation that Attorney General Robert Kennedy, the president's brother and one of his most trusted advisers, suggested what proved to be a brilliant tactic for resolving the dilemma. Throughout the crisis, the United States had maintained both formal and informal contacts with the Soviet Union, seeking any information it could get about Soviet intentions. Part of the problem on Saturday was that clear information regarding those intentions was lacking. The United States had received conflicting proposals from the Soviet Union, and it was not clear which one represented its final position. Presumably, it would be the more recent one, which insisted that the missiles in Turkey be removed. Informal sources indicated, however, that Premier Krushchev's proposal of Friday night, which had asked only that the United States guarantee not to invade Cuba, might still be open. If so, it might be possible to ignore the demand in the message of Saturday morning that the United States get its missiles out of Turkey. Robert Kennedy thought it was worth a chance. In effect, he suggested that the United States reply to the first Soviet proposal rather than the more recent one. The advantage would be that such a reply would be positive: it would say yes to one Soviet offer rather than no to the other. And rather than continuing the crisis, it would offer Premier Krushchev a chance to extricate himself from it on terms the United States could accept. President Kennedy agreed, and the message was sent: if the Soviet Union would remove the missiles, the United States would not invade Cuba. It worked. The next morning, Sunday, the Soviet Union agreed to dismantle the missiles and take them home.[1]

The decision that President Kennedy made with the aid of his advisers was an excellent example of **effective thinking**. It was based on the best information available, even though that information was not complete; it was creative; and it avoided the peril of decision by indecision. You may never have to make a decision so fateful for so many people as President Kennedy's. But the complex and rapidly changing society in which you live will force you to make many difficult decisions as important for you as his was for the world. Your decisions will be vital to both your own and other people's health, success, and happiness. And you, like President Kennedy, will be forced to choose between the perils of decision by indecision and making decisions without adequate information. How well your decisions turn out will depend in part on the procedures of thinking you use.

The importance of methods of thinking is amply illustrated by the history of science. Until the seventeenth century, science progressed quite slowly. In the last three centuries, however, a number of procedures of thinking have evolved that are now known as the scientific method. Their use has been responsible to a large degree for the impressive success of modern science in discovering the secrets of the universe, as well as in developing solutions to technological problems. Many of our most serious problems can be lessened or even solved by the application of these techniques.

Outside the context of scientific investigation, however, we tend to commit repeatedly the same blunders in thinking that seriously retarded science until the development of effective procedures. Consequently, progress in solving most human problems has lagged far behind progress in science. Most human problems cannot, of course, be taken to the laboratory and subjected to rigorous controls, and some aspects of the scientific method may not apply to these problems. Nevertheless, a large body of evidence gives us ample reason to believe that effective methods of thinking can be of great value in solving everyday human problems.

This textbook presents a comprehensive set of procedures of thinking designed to help not only the scientist but also the layperson dealing with everyday affairs. These procedures are based directly on the philosophy and methods of science, but other elements have been added to make them useful in a wide range of situations.

Creative and Critical Thinking

The procedures described in this text require two distinctly different kinds of thinking, **creative thinking** and **critical thinking**. Creative thinking may be defined as the formation of possible solutions to a problem or possible explanations of a phenomenon; critical thinking is the testing and evaluation of these proposed solutions.

Effective thinking is both creative and critical. Indeed, both kinds of thinking are essential in all areas of human activity. To put a new product on the market, a manufacturer must first create the

---

[1] For details of this decision, see David Detzer, *The Brink* (New York: Crowell, 1979).

idea for the product. But if the manufacturer has good business sense, he or she will not market the product until it has been thoroughly criticized by testing and evaluation. In solving a crime, a good detective formulates possible explanations and tests them with all the evidence available. If the detective fails to think of the right explanations, he or she cannot possibly solve the crime. If the detective is careless in criticizing the explanations, the resulting "solution" of the crime may be the wrong one. In diagnosing an illness, a physician first develops possible diagnoses that seem to fit the symptoms and then evaluates them by further examination of the patient or by laboratory tests. The final diagnosis cannot be right unless the possible diagnoses include the right one. Even when the possible diagnoses do include the right one, the physician may still make a mistake by being careless in criticizing them and settling on the wrong one.

The methods of modern science are both creative and critical. In trying to explain a phenomenon, a well-trained scientist first tries to formulate many tentative explanations. Then the scientist subjects each possible explanation to rigorous tests. Often all the explanations fail to pass the tests, but in the process more information about the phenomenon under investigation is acquired. The scientist then proceeds to create and criticize other possible explanations until one that withstands rigorous testing is found.

Outside the context of the laboratory, however, scientists and laypersons alike tend to be careless about both creative and critical aspects of thinking. When our feelings are aroused, we are likely to act first and think only after it is too late. We tend to seize upon the first course of action that occurs to us without bothering to

criticize it or to look for better courses of action. The blunders we make are the natural consequences of our failure to create and criticize.

Create and **criticize**, then, are the twin watchwords of the effective thinker.

Phases of Decision Making

The general procedure for applying creative and critical thinking to any problem can be described as a cycle with five phases. This cycle should not be treated as a rigid procedure in which each phase must be completed before the next is begun. In practice, you may go back to an earlier phase or work on several phases simultaneously. But if you are to have any real assurance that your ultimate decision is sound, all phases must be completed. The details of each phase will vary with the problem, but the general principles apply to all situations.

The details of each phase are too complex to permit more than a brief description of them at this point. Even so, you should begin immediately to practice using this cycle with your own problems. Merely reading or talking about effective thinking is not enough. Only through practice can we acquire the skills we need.

Phase 1. Recognizing and Defining the Problem. A typical process of decision making begins with the recognition of a problem. In this book the word "problem" is used in a broad sense: one has a problem when one has a need or a question but no obvious answer to it. One may have the problem of how to deal with a threat to safety or psychological well-being, or how to take advantage of an opportunity, or to discover what happened, or to predict what is going to happen, or to find the cause of some phenomenon, or to find the answer to a philosophical question, or to decide whether something one has read or heard is correct. Many problems are never solved because they are not recognized soon enough or not recognized at all. For example, some freshmen fail in college because they do not recognize soon enough that their study habits are inadequate or that they are in an unsuitable curriculum.

Once a problem has been recognized, it should be carefully defined. If you do not correctly define your problem, you are not likely to solve it. You may solve some problem but not the one you should have been trying to solve. Suppose, for example, that you are the sort of person who is constantly running out of money and unable to meet expenses. You may react in characteristically human fashion—by resenting your employer or those responsible for your financial support for being stingy. And you may, without realizing it, define your problem as how to get even with these people. You may succeed in solving *this* problem only to realize too late that the real problem was how to reduce your expenditures.

In many situations defining the problem will be the most difficult phase; once you have correctly defined the problem, the rest will be relatively easy. Often you will start with the wrong definition. The thinking you do in the last four phases can help you realize that your original definition was wrong. In this event you should start over at the beginning of the cycle. Sometimes you will find it helpful to use the entire five-phase cycle to define the problem.

You will find it helpful in defining problems to follow three rules. The first

is that **the definition should not be too general.** The definition sets the guidelines for the succeeding phases of the cycle. If it is too broad, the guidelines for a solution will be too broad, and the investigation may flounder. Suppose that, in response to the missiles in Cuba, President Kennedy had defined his problem to be one of eliminating all Soviet threats to American security. The strategies for doing this would likely have been either too radical to be acceptable or too long-range to do anything about the missiles. In any case, the investigation would have led in so many directions that the result would have been confusion and delay at a time when quick action was needed. Large problems can be very real, but their solution usually requires breaking them down into smaller, clearly defined ones to be solved one at a time.

The second rule for defining problems addresses the opposite danger: **the definition should not be too specific.** A definition of a problem is too specific when it unnecessarily restricts alternative solutions. Suppose Kennedy had defined his problem as one of how to destroy the missiles in Cuba. If so, invasion, bombing, or sabotage would have been the only options, and a blockade would never have been tried. Moreover, this would not have led to any meeting of minds with the Soviets but only raised tensions and increased the risk of war. Of course destroying the missiles would have produced a temporary solution to part of the problem, but this "solution" would have ignored most of the significance of the missile crisis for international affairs.

Finally, **the definition should not in itself constitute a "solution" to the problem.** Suppose President Kennedy had defined his problem as one of what trade to make with the Soviets to get the missiles out of Cuba. If so, his definition would in itself have contained the "solution" that he should negotiate a trade-off, and other solutions would have been ruled out of consideration. For this kind of definition of the problem to be acceptable, one would first have to solve another problem: that of whether to negotiate a trade at all. Very often definitions of problems that are themselves solutions also have the fault of being too specific. As definitions become more specific, alternative answers tend increasingly to be ruled out, until at last only one remains. But not all definitions that are too specific get as far as dictating only one conclusion, and we will do better at defining problems if we keep these two rules separate.

Phase 2. Gathering Information. Once you have defined your problem, you should begin to gather information about it. The information may be of many kinds. The detective may call his or her information "clues"; the doctor may speak of "symptoms"; the scientist, of "data"; the layperson or government leader, of "facts." Adequate and accurate information is essential to sound decisions. In general, the more information you have on which to base your decision, the more likely it is that the decision will be sound.

Phase 3. Forming Tentative Conclusions. The next phase is to form tentative conclusions, which represent solutions to the problem. You can begin doing this as soon as you have enough information to suggest some possible answers, but you must remember that solutions at this stage can only be tentative. The objective in this phase is not to settle on one conclusion but rather to formulate as many plausible ones as possible. The more we produce, the more likely we are to include

a sound one. Furthermore, forming several tentative conclusions is the best safeguard against the dangers of accepting or acting upon a proposed conclusion without adequate evidence.

In this phase your thinking must be primarily creative. You should give freedom to your imagination and postpone critical thinking until the next phase. If you look for flaws in tentative conclusions while forming them, you may choke off a sound one before it can be born. In this phase, it is desirable to give attention to every idea that comes to mind. Sometimes, ideas you might impatiently reject as wild or irrelevant turn out to be solutions of problems or important clues to solutions. For example, people first noted centuries ago that malaria epidemics are frequently accompanied by swarms of mosquitoes, but it was not until the nineteenth century that Sir Ronald Ross investigated the connection and found out how malaria is transmitted.

Phase 4. Testing Tentative Conclusions. The objective of the fourth phase is to "criticize" all tentative conclusions by assessing their *reliability*.

All tentative conclusions are reached through some kind of **inference**, a process of reasoning by which they are derived from evidence or available facts. Suppose, for example, that a young man of seventeen reads this statement in a newspaper: "All males must register for the draft when they reach the age of seventeen." If he concludes that he is about to be drafted and put in the army, his conclusion is the result of an inference. He combines two pieces of evidence, the statement in the newspaper and the fact that he is seventeen, and infers that he is soon to be inducted. If he immediately charges down to a recruiting office to volunteer so that he can choose his branch of the service, he has violated two cardinal rules of effective thinking: he has formed only one tentative conclusion, and he has acted on it without testing it for reliability. Although his conclusion could prove to be true, it is not reliable. A conclusion is **completely reliable** only when it is *known* to be true. In order to know that a conclusion is true you must know that (1) the evidence used is in itself completely reliable, that is, known to be true; and that (2) all inferences involved are logically flawless. The young man's conclusion fails to meet either test. He does not know yet whether the statement in the newspaper is true; newspaper statements are often false. Furthermore, his inference is faulty: even though registration for the draft might be required, it does not follow that anyone is presently being drafted. The young man's inference is therefore not reliable at all; he has jumped to a conclusion. Although a *completely* reliable conclusion that he was about to be drafted would be difficult, if not impossible, to reach—even an order to report for induction could possibly be in error—he should have investigated the situation more fully before acting so he could consider all the relevant evidence.

Throughout human history we have been notoriously careless in testing our conclusions. Consequently, we have made countless blunders and accumulated a vast amount of misinformation that has led to more blunders. Ideally, *all* conclusions should be tested for reliability. If you test some but not others, you may be protecting your cherished beliefs by testing only the tentative conclusions that displease you.

Phase 5. Evaluation and Decision. The objective of the fifth phase of the cycle is to determine whether you have found any workable solutions to your problem and, if so, to select the best of them. Thus this phase involves assessing the reliability of solutions based on the testing done in phase 4. When you begin testing tentative conclusions by appropriate methods, you will soon discover that completely reliable conclusions are rare. Usually there will be some weakness either in the evidence or in the inferences or in both. In practical matters, the best we can hope for is a high degree of reliability. If we delayed making a decision until we reached absolute reliability, we would dwell forever in the limbo of decision by indecision.

The minimum degree of reliability you should have before accepting or acting on a conclusion varies with the circumstances. A juror in a murder case who believes that convicting an innocent defendant of murder would be a tragic error should demand the high degree of reliability known as **true beyond reasonable doubt**. A person trying to decide which is the better of two boxes of cereal can afford to settle for a much lower degree of reliability since relatively little is at stake. The purchasing agent of a college cafeteria trying to make the same decision should demand a higher degree of reliability because more is at stake. The various degrees of reliability will be discussed in Chapter 5.

When evaluation of your tentative conclusions shows that none of them is sufficiently reliable, you should repeat the whole cycle. Each time we repeat the cycle we are likely to discover new information that may suggest new and more promising tentative conclusions. The process should be repeated until you have a conclusion with a degree of reliability sufficient for your purpose.

But how do we know when the degree of reliability is sufficient for our purpose? This question is not easy to answer, and much of this book is devoted to examining it.

Phases of Decision Making

1. Recognizing and Defining the Problem
2. Gathering Information
3. Forming Tentative Conclusions
4. Testing Tentative Conclusions
5. Evaluation and Decision

The Personal Point of View

Every phase of decision making is strongly affected by the fact that we each see both ourselves and the world from our own unique point of view. This personal point of view can be described under three headings.

Frame of Reference. One component is the **frame of reference**, that is, the organized body of knowledge, belief, and experience with which we interpret and understand new experiences. One's frame of reference includes all that one believes or knows to be true of the world: the sorts of things that are in it, both animate and inanimate, and how they behave; what has happened in the past; and what is likely to happen in the future. One makes use of one's frame of reference both in gaining new information and in deciding what actions to take to get on in the world.

Because each of us is human, no one's frame of reference is either complete or totally accurate. Rather, we all have vast gaps in our fund of knowledge—things we simply don't understand in the least. Worse still, some of what each of us takes to be knowledge is in fact not knowledge

at all but error. We all make mistakes. Because of these shortcomings, our frame of reference limits us in various ways.

The frame of reference limits perception, the process by which we give meaning to sensory stimuli. We do not "see" automobiles or "hear" music; we "see" light waves and "hear" sound waves. We *perceive* automobiles and music. Perception is strongly influenced by the content of one's frame of reference. Everyone has had the experience of searching for some article—a set of keys, for example—and failing to see it even though it was in plain view all the time. The reason is in the frame of reference: when we suppose something to be lost or hidden, we do not expect to see it, and that limits our perception. It is also possible to see things but interpret them wrongly. A child who expects all fire engines to be red might, upon seeing a green one, decide it must be something else. And the history of science is replete with possibilities for discovery that went unrealized because observers failed to understand what they saw. You can realize how essential your frame of reference is to perception by recalling experiences you could not understand as a child because you lacked the necessary knowledge.

A second way in which our frame of reference limits us is in the ability to recognize problems. Serious problems often go unrecognized because the necessary knowledge is lacking. A man who has just bought his first boat and whose frame of reference does not include any knowledge of Coast Guard regulations or the knowledge that gasoline fumes are heavier than air might be unable to realize the significance of gasoline spilled on the hatch covering the engine. If he starts his engine without thoroughly airing the engine compartment, he has failed to recognize a serious problem. His frame of reference is inadequate for this particular situation. His next problem may be more easily recognized.

Likewise, the frame of reference limits ability to interpret or use evidence in solving any kind of problem. For example, before identification by fingerprinting was developed, police were handicapped in gathering evidence. The evidence was frequently there—the police simply lacked the knowledge to use it.

The frame of reference also limits the acquisition of new knowledge, for knowledge is necessary to acquire knowledge. Even the most intelligent student who knows no chemistry would be helpless at first in a rigorous course in organic chemistry. Many students in their first year in college have falsely concluded that they are not bright enough for college because their frames of reference were not yet adequate for the demands of their courses.

False information in one's frame of reference can be worse than no information at all. Doctors would have little chance of dealing with flu epidemics if they believed, as was widely believed well into the nineteenth century, that they are caused by meteorological influences. Today we know that these "influenzas" have other causes and we can do more about them. In the same way, there would be no science of astrophysics today if astronomers had continued to believe, as they did in the Middle Ages, that the earth is the center of the universe.

Every college student is faced with the problem of developing a rich and accurate frame of reference. In part, the problem stems from the sheer bulk of information and experience available, which makes selection necessary. The library of a fair-sized university may contain more than a million bound volumes and hundreds of current newspapers and magazines. Assuming that the bound volumes average 200,000 words each and that a student reads 500 words a minute for 12 hours a day, 360 days a year, in his or her 4 college years, it would be possible to read less than .3 of one percent of the bound volumes alone! Since you can read only a tiny fraction of the books available to you, whenever you read a particular book you prevent yourself from reading some other. Likewise, when you select one experience, you automatically exclude other experiences. You cannot afford to stock your frame of reference with trivia.

The problem of developing a good frame of reference also stems in part from concern with career preparation, which often leads students into narrowly conceived courses of study aimed at gaining the technical knowledge needed to make a living. And certainly many people need such knowledge to get launched in a successful career. But if we wish to be a successful citizen and human being, as well as an expert in some specialized field, it is logical to add to our frame of reference at least the fundamentals of what is known as a "general" or "liberal" education. Such an education includes knowledge of the social sciences, the physical and biological sciences, and the humanities. Knowledge of the social sciences is necessary if we are to understand and deal with the powerful forces society and culture exert on how we think and behave. Without it, we are apt to be tossed about by those forces like a rudderless boat in a stormy sea. Knowledge of the physical and biological sciences is necessary as well. No citizen who is ignorant in these areas can make informed judgments about the usefulness of new technologies and their effect on his or her well-being and environment. Last, but hardly least, a sound education must attend to the humanities. Language skills are fundamental both to acquiring knowlege and to communicating with others. Knowledge of literature and of history provides a vast casebook of human behavior through which you can sample and evaluate experience without going through it yourself. And the study of philosophy will introduce you to the most fundamental and far-reaching concepts of the world that humans have devised, as well as the value systems that can guide our lives. To be sure, no one can be expert in all of these areas, and most of them have little cash value. But they are necessary to sound decision making; to ignore them is to impoverish one's frame of reference and risk the unhappiness of the unwise choices that may result.

Values. The second major component of the personal point of view is one's **system of values**. Whereas the frame of reference has to do with the way we think things *are*, our values have to do with how we feel they *ought to be*. They are the standards by which we judge the worth of objects, experiences, ideas, and actions. Values having to do with actions are perhaps the most important, since it is these that we use to guide our own conduct and hence to run our lives. We also inculcate standards of conduct in our children, encourage them in our friends, and embody them in our laws. But values pervade our thought about many other things as well, which may be seen from our language. The difference between a weed and a flower, between a predator or pest and a beneficial animal, or between a beautiful river and a raging torrent is often a difference in the value we place on these things. At other times we are more explicit: we discuss good cars, nice weather, bright ideas, and fine clothing all the time. In all such cases, our thinking involves **value judg-ments**, judgments of the worth of the things we are talking about.

Whether we know it or not, the value judgments we make affect our decisions, for we cannot help but choose among things in terms of the way we value them. Thus, because we have values about so many things, value judgments are involved in most, if not all, of the decisions we make. The soldier who decides to advance into heavy enemy fire instead of retreating, the citizen who decides to pay her taxes instead of lying about the amount owed, the student who decides to do some extra studying instead of going out—all are basing their decisions on judgments of the value of the things involved. Perhaps in part because values are so important, we often have trouble agreeing about them, especially when they concern human conduct. More than others, disputes about values tend to threaten us and to rouse our emotions. But they cannot be avoided, and neither can the influence of values on decisions. Thus we will be devoting more attention to values in later chapters.

The Self-concept. A part of the personal point of view worthy of special mention is the **self-concept**, the picture each of us has of the kind of person he or she is. Our self-concept is not independent of our frame of reference or our value system. It includes our beliefs about our abilities, special talents, strengths, and weaknesses and our notion of the role we play in the world and the responsibilities that go with it. Most of all, it includes our sense of personal worth: whether we feel important and capable enough to be treated with dignity and respect or inadequate and fit to be ignored. For each of us, it is important to maintain a satisfactory self-concept, and the need to do so frequently influences our decisions. At times, this can be helpful. But it can also interfere with objectivity, which is crucial to effective thinking.

Objectivity

How effective our thinking is depends in part on how **objective** we are, on the degree to which we can view ourselves and the world without distortion. Because we can observe reality only through the lens of our own point of view, absolute objectivity is impossible. A person might be reasonably objective in one area and highly prejudiced in another because his or her frame of reference is inadequate; new theories in science often have difficulty gaining acceptance at first simply because they are not well understood. Prejudice can often result from a system of values that distorts reality. Much racial prejudice involves unquestioning disvalue of others: "they" are viewed as inferior, and this negative attitude serves as a filter, allowing in "information" that confirms the prejudice but screening out all contradictory evidence. Finally, prejudiced viewpoints can and often do arise because one's self-concept is endangered. Frequently, accepting the solution to a problem involves admitting, at least implicitly, that one has been wrong in the past, and that can be very hard to do.

For example, suppose a student who has been working hard is threatened with failing grades in her major, yet her grades in some difficult electives are excellent. Very probably, she ought to consider changing fields. Unfortunately, however, that could involve a reassessment of her own talents and the kind of profession she is suited for, not to mention difficulties with family and friends, all of which are a threat to her sense of personal worth. In such a case, she can all too easily deceive herself into believing that grades are not important. Or she can deceive herself into believing that low grades are not really her own fault by convincing herself that the instructor is unfair, that her courses are too hard, or that there is too much noise in her dormitory. Such self-deception eases the pain of the threat for the moment, but only at a price. For the problem with self-deception is always that it embeds errors in the frame of reference, so that one's perception of reality becomes distorted. And that is exactly what prejudice is all about: one begins to see the world not as it is but as one would like it to be. Further self-deception then becomes necessary in order to protect this distorted view. The more distorted one's view of reality, the more difficult it is to deal directly and constructively with threats to the self-concept.

As the above case illustrates, one's frame of reference and one's values are tightly intertwined. For this reason, one tends always to defend one's personal point of view as a whole. A threat to an important idea in one's frame of reference can be as much a threat to one's sense of worth as a personal insult. And the more threatening a new idea is, the more it tends to be resisted, even to the point of violence. The history of science is full of examples of such resistance. Galileo's astronomical treatise, the *Dialogue on the Two Chief Systems of the World*, published in 1632, was a defense of the new theory of astronomy begun by Copernicus. It included a skillful and devastating attack on the older Ptolemaic view, which placed the earth at the center of the universe and which was accepted by most scholars and scientists of the time. Thus not only the frames of reference but also the self-concepts of these authorities were seriously threatened. They reacted violently and they had an easy target. For in addition to writing a book that could be interpreted as a challenge to the authority of the church, Galileo had dealt in the *Dialogue* with some of the views of Pope Urban, who until then had been his friend and supporter. Unfortunately, the pope's views were expressed in the *Dialogue* by a character named Simplicio, who defends the old theory and is made to appear every bit as simple as his name implies. Galileo's enemies had little trouble convincing Pope Urban that Simplicio was intended as a caricature of himself. The pope was deeply insulted, and it appears to have been partly for this reason that he ordered Galileo to appear before the Inquisition, where he was forced to deny ever having held the views of Copernicus. His book was banned, he was forbidden to publish further, and he was compelled to spend the rest of his life confined to his country estate near Florence.[2]

The progress of modern science is due in large part to the fact that scientists have become more and more objective in their investigations. Objectivity in science stems from a number of factors, the chief of which is the development of sound procedures of thinking. Another contributing factor has been that in many areas of scientific investigation, human emotions are not heavily involved. But objectivity in interpreting reality is just as important in human affairs as in science, and human problems tend to be heavily laden with emotions. The procedures of thinking presented in this text are designed to promote objectivity. But procedures alone are not sufficient. If they were, it would be reasonable to assume that scientists would be significantly more objective outside the laboratory

than laypersons. The truth appears to be that they are not. Rather, the scientist outside the laboratory is as prone to failures of wisdom as the rest of us. Moreover, methods for effective thinking are like any tool in that they can be used well or poorly. Used properly, they will uncover errors and distortions in our views of reality and lead to greater knowledge. Misused, they will perpetuate the errors and magnify the distortions. If you apply your critical skill to ideas you dislike and fail to apply it with equal care to ideas you like, your critical skill can create barriers that hide the truth from you.

The problem of using the procedures for effective thinking in an objective way is discussed in later chapters. In the meantime, two essentials for objectivity should be kept in mind. The first is to concentrate on the pursuit of truth in all the problems we take up, no matter how unpleasant or threatening it may be. This trait is fostered in scientific settings by the system of values of science itself, which punishes failures of objectivity. A scientist who sticks to a favored theory in the face of mounting evidence to the contrary is quite likely to be ignored and forgotten and thus to lose professional standing. In the human setting, we have no group of professional peers to impose disciplined thought on us, so we must develop our own sense of discipline.

The second essential is to develop a kind of objectivity about our own feelings. Many people mistakenly try to be objective by eliminating their feelings. This is a dangerous course because much of our thinking takes place below the conscious level. When we try to eliminate our feelings, we merely drive them underground, where they continue to exert powerful and often disruptive influences on our thinking.

A much better way is to be tolerant of

2 For more on the case of Galileo, see Arthur Koestler, *The Sleepwalkers* (New York: Grosset and Dunlap, 1963).

and open to our feelings, so that they can come more easily to the surface. When we know what they are, we can deal with them much more effectively. When we are trying to make a decision about what has happened or is happening in the world outside us, our feelings are irrelevant and should not be permitted to affect our decisions. But when we are trying to decide how outside reality affects us personally, our feelings are quite relevant. And to conceal them from ourselves violates the principles of effective thinking as much as concealing evidence about outside reality. The second element in objectivity, then, is to be open to our feelings, to exclude them when they are not relevant, to include them when they are, and to be able to discern the difference.

Improving Thinking

It should now be clear that perfection in thinking is unattainable, and a satisfactory solution to every problem is too much to expect. The person who expects to solve every problem and make the right decision every time is as unrealistic as the baseball player who expects to hit a home run every time at bat. We should therefore strive for **effective thinking** rather than perfect thinking. In this book we shall consider thinking effective when it meets two criteria: (1) when sound procedures are followed reasonably well, and (2) when the information used is as complete and accurate as can reasonably be expected.

Effective thinking, like playing a musical instrument, requires practice; practice is essential both for understanding the techniques fully and for developing skill in applying them. Opportunities for practice are provided by the numerous exercises in this book. You should give them careful attention. You should also practice the procedures of effective thinking in making simple decisions. Otherwise you may fail to use these procedures when the issue is important. The rewards for learning to think effectively are great. There are many new frontiers left to conquer, but they are as much intellectual as geographical. Learning to think effectively is important enough to be your central purpose in college.

Exercise 1

1. It is 8:30 p.m. of the first day of classes in the fall semester at Wysacki University. Mary Smythe, a beginning freshman, has been studying her Chemistry 101 assignment since 7:30 p.m. Curious to know how much she has left to study, she looks quickly at the rest of the assignment. She discovers that at the rate she has been going she will need six more hours to complete it. She has three other assignments to prepare for tomorrow. What phase of the decision-making cycle has Mary reached?

_____

Problems 2–5. Below are four definitions of Mary's immediate problem. For each definition, state the rule or rules, if any, for defining problems that this definition violates.

2. To make room in her next semester's schedule for Chemistry 101.

_____

3. To find a method of completing her chemistry assignment in four hours.

_____

4. To learn how to make every minute count in all her activities.

_____

5. To estimate the average amount of study time per week all her assignments will require.

_____

6. Mary estimates that at her present rate of study her assignments will require sixty hours each week. Classes and labs require twenty-two hours. What phase of the decision-making cycle is she working on? _____

7. What should Mary do next?

_____

8. List three tentative conclusions she might form.

_____

_____

_____

9. Which of these tentative conclusions should Mary act on?

_____

10. Suppose Mary now defines her problem to be to find out why it takes her so long to complete her assignments. Form a tentative conclusion that would be likely to threaten Mary's self-concept.

_____

Problems 11–14. Consider the following statements:

    a. The average student at Wysacki is expected to study at least two hours per week per credit.

    b. Mary Smythe is a beginning freshman.

    c. Mary's courses total fourteen credits.

    d. Mary is average among Wysacki students.

11. Write the numbers of the above statements that can be combined to make an inference.

_____

12. What conclusion can be inferred from these statements?

_____

13. Is this conclusion reliable? _____

14. If so, why? If not, why not? _____

15. During her senior year in high school, Mary decided to study engineering in college because she had heard that graduates in engineering receive relatively high starting salaries. State the value judgment apparently involved in Mary's decision.

_____

16. What is your opinion of this value judgment?

_____

17. Mary's twin brother, Joe, is having trouble removing stains from his cotton sports slacks. He forms the tentative conclusion that a mixture of ammonia and chlorine bleach will work better than either chemical alone. In deciding whether to act on this tentative conclusion, what knowledge should Joe Smythe have in his frame of reference?

_____

Chapter 2

Propositions and Arguments

- **Propositions**
- **Arguments**
- **Premises and Conclusions**
- **Induction and Deduction**
- **Validity**
- **Arguments and Decision Making**

In order to develop into effective thinkers, we need to learn how to evaluate the procedures of thinking that we and others use in decision making. The principles for evaluating thinking are the same whether our own or someone else's reasoning is at stake. As we have seen, however, decision making can at times be a lengthy and complex process. Thus, in order to evaluate thinking accurately, we have to be able to break down complex thought processes into constituents that lend themselves to logical analysis.

Propositions

Each of us has in his frame of reference and value system innumerable **propositions**, or statements that are either true or false. These are the elements of thought that carry the information we have gathered and developed in the past. The most obvious examples of propositions are those signified by simple declarative sentences, such as "It is raining" or "There are mice in the attic." Sometimes, though, smaller propositions can be combined into larger ones, as in "Either it is raining or there are mice in the attic." All these statements are either true or false; hence all are propositions. By contrast, commands ("Shut the door!") and questions ("Is it the 29th or the 30th today?") are not propositions, for they are neither true nor false. The position of statements about things that do not exist is less clear. Can it be true or false that Hamlet was Prince of Denmark? Any analysis of Hamlet's actions in the play would assume that he was. Moreover, an instructor who included as a true or false question "Hamlet was Prince of Norway" would expect the answer "False!" and would not settle for a refusal to answer on the ground that, since Hamlet did not exist, we cannot talk about whether he was prince of anything. Therefore, such statements are propositions because there are contexts in which they are true or false. It is also clear that while questions and commands are not themselves propositions, they may communicate information and thus imply that certain propositions are true. For example, to say "Shut the door!" is to imply that the door is open. The question "Should a spendthrift Congress be allowed to waste more of your tax money by setting up these useless and inefficient committees?" presupposes a number of assumptions. It assumes that Congress is spendthrift, that the committees are useless and inefficient, and that the money spent in setting them up would be wasted.

Arguments

Sentences, of course, usually occur in groups, in which they are combined according to the rules of language so that they elucidate one another in a meaningful way. Such combinations of sentences are called **discourse**. And while discourse often involves sentences expressing questions or commands, sentences that express propositions are by far its most numerous components. At times, but not always, discourse is argumentative. Whether this is so depends on how the propositions it includes are related.

What exactly is an argument? In ordinary language, we usually use the word *argument* to refer to any kind of dispute from a debate to a fight. ("They carried on an argument all night about the existence of God, so I didn't get any sleep at all"; "Honestly, Officer, we were just having a little argument about who was supposed to pay for the beer, and. . . . ") In the study of reasoning, however, we use the logician's meaning of the word. In logic, an ar-

gument embodies an **inference**, that is, an implicit or explicit claim that something follows from something else. An example is Descartes's famous inference: "I think; therefore I am." The second proposition, "I am," is supposed to follow from the first proposition, "I think."

Most arguments are longer than that of Descartes, for they state more than one proposition as the basis from which the inference is drawn. For example, one might say "Either it is raining or there are mice in the attic, and it is not raining, so there are mice in the attic." Here two propositions are asserted as the basis for the conclusion, and in other cases there are many more. An **argument**, then, is a set of propositions related in such a way that one of them is claimed to follow from the other or others. A great deal of discourse is argumentative, for arguments are used whenever a person tries to prove something: to show that it is true by supporting it with reasons. For example, much of the discourse in textbooks is composed of arguments because most textbooks, including this one, have a great deal to prove.

The first skill you must develop in dealing with arguments is to recognize when an argument occurs. At times this is not hard because, as in the above examples, the person giving the argument will use words such as *so* and *therefore*, which make it clear that an argument is intended. At other times, however, arguments are presented in such a way that they are difficult to spot. For instance, one of the following weather reports is an argument while the other is not.

Tomorrow will be fair and sunny, with a high in the low nineties and a low in the mid-seventies. However, there is a 20 percent chance of thundershowers.

A cold front is headed our way from the Rockies, bringing with it high winds and thunderstorms. If you were planning to go sailing on the Gulf this weekend, you'd better think about some indoor sports instead.

The first report states facts that are related only in that they are all about the weather. Such discourse as this we call **exposition**. Exposition is simply a matter of setting forth information in a coherent and unified way. The propositions it contains are *claimed* to be true, but no effort is made to *show* that they are true. The first report is expository in that it seeks simply to describe the weather, without trying to prove any of the propositions stated.

By contrast, the second of the above weather reports contains an argument. This report seeks to establish a conclusion concerning what you should do today, based on facts about the weather. Thus, it implies a logical relationship between propositions—that one is supposed to follow from the others. Moreover, not all of the propositions required for the argument are explicitly stated. One of them, that thunderstorms and high winds make sailing dangerous, is only implied. Formally structured and explicitly stated, the complete argument would read something like this:

Whenever sailing is dangerous, it should be avoided.

High winds and thunderstorms make sailing dangerous.

This weekend will be a time of high winds and thunderstorms.

Therefore this weekend will be a time when sailing should be avoided.

What makes the second report an argument, then, is that rather than simply giving information it uses the information it contains to support a further claim, namely, that sailing should be avoided this weekend. It is the effort to demonstrate the truth of one proposition based on information provided by others that distinguishes argument from strictly expository discourse. Of course, some discourse that is mostly expository will contain a few inferences, and argumentation will contain exposition. With practice, however, you will learn to disentangle the two. The key question is always whether the speaker or writer is trying only to provide information or trying to prove something. The former is exposition; the latter is argument.

Premises and Conclusions

Once we identify discourse as argumentative, we face a second task which can be difficult: we need to analyze its structure so that we can decide exactly what the argument is getting at. Only if we know precisely what is being argued, can we effectively counter or support the conclusion. The first step in evaluating an argument is to identify its evidence or reasons, which logicians call its **premises**, and its **conclusion**, which is the proposition inferred from those premises. This identification is often aided by words like *so* and *therefore*, which serve to indicate not only that an argument is being given but also the argument's structure. Such words are called **logical connectors**, and they are found in many arguments. They tell us what the conclusion of the argument is or what the premises are. In the argument "I think; therefore I am," the word *therefore* makes a straightforward announcement that what follows is the conclusion and that the preceding statement is the premise. On the other hand, Descartes might have said, "I am, since I think." If he had, he would still have given exactly the same argument: "I am" would still be the conclusion, and "I think" would still be the premise. The difference is that here the word *since* announces that what follows is a premise and that what went before is the conclusion. In this connection, it is important to remember that the conclusion need not come last in an argument. Rather, the conclusion is whatever proposition the argument is trying to prove. It may appear at the beginning, in the middle, or at the end of the argument.

The most common words for indicating the conclusion are *so* and *therefore.* Less common ones are *hence, thus, consequently, as a result, it must be, indicating that (which indicates that), suggesting that (which suggests that), proving that, showing that, demonstrating that,* and so on. The most common words or phrases identifying premises, or reasons, are *because, since,* and *for*; among the many others are *for the reason that, as shown by, as demonstrated by, inasmuch as,* and *as.* In a two-premise argument, often one premise will be identified by one of the reason indicators above, and the premise will be identified by *and.* An example would be "Since sailing will be dangerous this weekend and you should not sail when it is dangerous, you should not go sailing this weekend."

When arguments contain logical connectors, it is usually easy to tell which propositions are premises and which is the conclusion. But many arguments do not contain any logical connectors. Moreover, as we have seen, it may be that not all the propositions in the argument are explicitly stated; some may be only implied. When this happens, we have to pay attention to the context to determine the structure of the argument. An example

would be "How can you take that third piece of pie? You told me you were on a diet." This argument could be interpreted as having either of two possible conclusions:

Premises:	If you are on a diet, you should not take that pie. You are taking that pie.
Conclusion:	Therefore you are not on a diet.

Premises:	If you are on a diet, you should not take that pie. You are dieting.
Conclusion:	Therefore you should not take that pie.

Which would be the more accurate diagnosis of the original argument? Most likely the second, for the person giving the argument would usually believe that the listener is truly on a diet. Thus, he would be trying to convince the listener that he ought to refuse the pie rather than give in to temptation. There are, however, circumstances in which the first diagnosis would be correct: for example, if the speaker thought the other person was only kidding about being on a diet. By and large, the context in which an argument occurs will tell you how it should be understood. If not, you should choose the most likely interpretation, since it has the best chance of being correct.

Another important clue to the structure of an argument is the evidential relationships that obtain among the propositions themselves. "Hey, don't touch that dog! He'll take your arm off!" clearly implies that a proposition implied by the command (that you shouldn't touch the dog) is the conclusion. You should not touch the dog, because he will take your arm off. It would not be sensible to recast the argument, "Because you should not touch that dog, he will take your arm off." Similar considerations apply to this argument:

> I cannot be blamed for shooting down Korean Air Lines Flight 007; I was only following orders. The person who issued the orders is the one who should be held responsible.

Although this argument contains no logical connectors, there are still logical relationships among its propositions. The third proposition clearly implies that only those who issue orders can be held responsible. This, together with the claim that the speaker was only following orders, supports the assertion that the speaker was not responsible for the plane crash. The argument then becomes something like this:

Premises: Only those who issue orders can be blamed.
             I did not issue orders.

Conclusion: Therefore (whatever I did), I cannot be blamed.

The process of rewriting arguments in this way, with implied premises made explicit, the premises in some reasonable order, and the conclusion clearly indicated, is extremely useful for making the structure of an argument obvious. Once this is done, we can see better whether to accept or reject the argument and how to counter it. If the premises do not really support the conclusion, we would want to point that out. If they do, we would want to examine whether they are true. Is it true that only those who issue orders can be held responsible? Is it true that the speaker did not issue any orders?

Writing out arguments in clearer form is especially helpful when, as is often the case, they occur in chains or sequences. The terms *premise* and *conclusion* are relative. A proposition that is the conclusion of one argument can quickly become a premise in another. Elaborate sequences of argument may then result, and they may require detailed structural analysis, in which each step of the reasoning process is identified. Consider the following argument, in which the sentences have been numbered for ease of reference.

> 1. Recently, three textbooks were dropped from the sixth-grade curriculum because a group of parents complained that the books presented evolution as a fact rather than as a theory. 2. Another group complained that several texts in current use promoted racial and sexual stereotypes, but these books were not dropped. 3. Clearly, parent groups have no right to influence text choices. 4. The parents don't know enough about the issues and have no training in evaluating the books. 5. The parents have no clear or consistent criteria for their judgments. 6. Moreover, their positions may be used by those in power within the educational system as an endorsement for their own biases.

The argument above may be analyzed with slight difficulty, even though it contains little in the way of transitional phrases that would guide us to the conclusion. The purpose of the passage is clearly to argue for the proposition in sentence 3; sentences 1, 2, 4, and 5 are all used in some way to support the conclusion that parent groups should not be permitted to influence text choices. The relationships among the other propositions are less clear. The first two propositions describe an example which seems to support the sixth sentence. That is, the passage suggests that the educational authorities chose to accept one group's objections and reject the other's for reasons of their own—quite possibly, to support a reactionary bias. The first two sentences may also be considered as evidence for statement 5; since these two groups were quite obviously not evaluating on the basis of the same criteria, it might be claimed that "parent groups" are not consistent. There may be a logical fallacy involved here, but we won't worry about it now, as we are concerned only with the structure of the argument. An overall view of the argument looks something like this:

> *Premises:* One parent group's objections were accepted while another group's were disregarded.
> Therefore
>
> *Conclusions:* Parents aren't consistent; educational authorities can use parent groups to endorse biases.
>
> *Conclusions Used as Premises:* Because of inconsistency and the use of parent groups by authorities and
>
> *Additional Premise:* Because of parents' lack of knowledge and training,
>
> *Final Conclusion:* Parents should not influence text choices.

Now that we have a clear sense of the structure of the argument, we can begin to evaluate it, and we can better attack or support it as we choose. We have finished a first and vitally important step in argumentation.

It should be clear by now that there can be many subtleties involved in determining the structure of an argument, and no simple set of rules will be adequate in every case. Nevertheless, there are still some very useful guidelines for analyzing the structure of an argument. We should begin by reading the passage carefully and asking if, in fact, some of the propositions are being offered as evidence for the truth of others. If there is no such relationship, of course, we have exposition rather than argument. If we do have an argument, then we must ask what the overall purpose of the piece is. Most of all, what is the author or speaker trying to prove? Is there a clearly stated conclusion for the entire passage? If not, is there a clearly implied conclusion? Once we have determined the overall goal of the passage, we look for the logical connectors and use them to see how the parts are linked. Where connectors are omitted, we will need to take into account the context and the relations among the propositions. These instructions may seem backward—why not look for the logical connectors first? But in analysis, it helps a great deal to begin with an overall sense of what the passage is about since there may not be enough logical connectors to tell the whole story. On the other hand, it may sometimes turn out that analysis of the logical connectors indicates we were wrong about the overall gist of the passage. When this happens, we will need to look at it again. Occasionally, we may not be able to figure out what the writer is getting at, and the logical connectors may lead us in this case to our first clear view of the drift of the argument.

Words and Phrases Used to Indicate Conclusions

Therefore	It must be
So	Indicating that
Hence	Suggesting that
Thus	Proving that
Consequently	Showing that
As a result	Demonstrating that

Words and Phrases Used to Indicate Premises

Since	For the reason that
For	As shown by
Because	As demonstrated by
As	Inasmuch as

Induction and Deduction

You may have noticed that the arguments we have been discussing vary drastically. This difference is partly due to the fact that there are basically two reasoning processes or types of argument, traditionally called induction and deduction. Whether an argument is inductive or deductive determines the form and direction of the argument and alters completely the way we go about evaluating it. The complex argument discussed above is basically **inductive**; its conclusion intentionally goes beyond the information cited in the premises. The argument starts from a specific instance in which parental influence is held to have bad consequences on textbook choice and ends with a general conclusion based in part on that instance, that parental influence should never occur. There is a great difference between that passage and an argument such as this one:

Premises: If you're on a diet, you
             shouldn't eat pie.
             You are on a diet.

Conclusion: Therefore you shouldn't eat
             pie.

This argument is **deductive**. The first premise makes a statement about the absolute relationship between two classes of people: dieters and people who may eat pie. It claims that these two classes are mutually exclusive—that no one can be in both classes at once. Thus if you are in the class of dieters, as the second proposition asserts, it follows that you are not in the class of people who may eat pie. Here the conclusion is not intended to go beyond the information contained in the premises. Unlike the case with induction, the premises here are intended to *guarantee*

the truth of the conclusion. And that is the difference between deduction and induction. In a **deductive argument**, the premises are intended to make the conclusion inevitable, in the sense that if they turn out to be true, it will not be possible for the conclusion to be false. In an **inductive argument**, the premises are meant only to provide significant support for the conclusion, in the sense that if they are true, the conclusion becomes more probable, though it still might be wrong.

Because deductive arguments make such a strong claim about the relationship between their premises and conclusions, it is necessary to evaluate them according to rigorous standards, which would be inappropriate for inductive arguments. Thus it is important to recognize whether we have a deductive argument or an inductive argument before evaluating it. This is not always easy since the intention of the writer or speaker partially determines whether the argument is inductive or deductive. A good guideline to follow is to consider the area covered by the premises and by the conclusion. In deduction, the conclusion covers no more ground than the premises. For example, consider the deductive argument below:

Premises: All athletes are people with
             well-toned muscles.
             All professional tennis players
             are athletes.

Conclusion: Therefore all professional
             tennis players are people
             with well-toned muscles.

There are no individuals covered by the conclusion who are not mentioned in the premises. However, if two pickup trucks cut in front of you on your way to school and if you then conclude that drivers of pickup trucks are careless and rude, you are obviously going far beyond the evidence to make a statement about a much wider group than the drivers you observed. You can see that this conclusion could never be guaranteed completely by your evidence, as deductive conclusions are supposed to be. Rather, like other inductive conclusions, it can at best be made more probable. You cannot test the potentially infinite number of cases it involves; you cannot observe the driver of every pickup truck. And even if you could, you have not. Your evidence includes only two cases. Thus your conclusion must make an "inductive leap" from the evidence to a wider group. This "leap" from evidence to a conclusion that goes beyond it is always present in induction, even when the evidence for the conclusion is voluminous and thoroughly researched. There may have been millions of instances counted to establish that smoking contributes to the development of cancer, but there is always the possibility that it does not.

In other cases, inductive arguments go from evidence gathered in one case to a conclusion about another or from a given set of facts to a possible hypothesis explaining those facts. Besides looking at the area covered by the premises and conclusion, therefore, you might also ask whether it makes sense if you insert the word "probably" or "certainly" before the conclusion. It doesn't make much sense to say "All collies are dogs, and all dogs are animals; therefore probably all collies are animals." The premises given here make it certain that all collies are animals, so that a deductive argument is called for. On the other hand, it would be quite sensible to say "These cherries from Kroger's are good, so probably those will be, too." This is an inductive argument, and probability is all we can expect, given the evidence. To substitute "certainly" for "probably" would be to make too strong a claim.

The difference between induction and deduction is often oversimplified. It is sometimes stated that a deductive argument moves from the general to the specific and an inductive argument from the specific to the general. But this way of making the distinction does not always work. It is true that the inductive argument about drivers of pickup trucks goes from specific cases to a general conclusion and that the typical example of deduction (All men are mortal; John is a man; therefore John is mortal) goes from general to specific. However, some arguments go from general to general, or from particular to particular. Consider the following:

> No dogs are cats; therefore no cats are dogs.

This argument is a deduction, though its premise and conclusion are equally general. By contrast, consider:

> These cherries, which I bought at Kroger's, are good. Therefore those cherries, which you bought at Kroger's, will be good.

This is an inductive argument whose conclusion is no more general than its premise. Therefore the "general-to-specific" and "specific-to-general" guideline is not reliable.

Validity

Because the purpose of a deductive argument is to provide evidence from which the conclusion follows inevitably, it is possible to evaluate deductive arguments partly on the basis of whether they succeed in achieving this goal. Success or failure in this regard is strictly determined by the **structure** of the argument. Either its parts fit together in such a way that the premises, if true, guarantee the truth of the conclusion, or they do not. If an argument does have this type of organization, it will not be possible for the premises to be true and the conclusion false. An argument that has this character is called **valid**. By contrast, a deductive argument in which the structure is such that it is even *possible* for the premises to be true and the conclusion false is **invalid**.

The argument that if you are on a diet you should not eat pie, and you are on a diet, therefore you should not eat pie, is an example of a deductive argument that is valid. This argument is correctly structured, for its conclusion follows necessarily from its premises. That is, if it is always and unequivocally true that if you're on a diet you should not eat pie, and if you are indeed on a diet, then you should not eat pie. You may deny either of the premises—you may claim that dieters may sometimes eat pie or that perhaps only for the duration of the dessert, you are not on a diet. But if you accept the premises, you must accept the conclusion. Moreover, since validity is strictly a structural matter, the same would go for any argument that has this form, regardless of what the propositions it contains assert. By contrast, the following is an invalid deductive argument:

Premises: All dogs are animals.
                  All cats are animals.

Conclusion: Therefore all dogs are cats.

This argument is incorrectly structured. It places dogs and cats within the larger class of animals, but makes no statement about the relationship between the two smaller classes. The premises are true, but the conclusion is false. Moreover, even if it happened to be true that all dogs are cats, the argument would still be invalid, for this conclusion would still not be guaranteed by the premises given. Thus

some deductive patterns guarantee valid arguments, and others do not. Part of our task in this book will be to learn which are which.

In the preceding chapter, we noted that a conclusion is completely reliable only when the evidence used is known to be true and the inferences have no loopholes. In valid arguments the second of these conditions is satisfied: there are no loopholes. But the careful thinker must never forget that **validity has nothing to do with the truth or falsity of the evidence**. It is not necessary to know that a proposition is true in order to use it as a premise. Many arguments use premises that are only uncertain assumptions. For example, to deal with a specific action of a hostile foreign government, the State Department must make an assumption about the intent and significance of the action before deciding how to deal with it. The student deciding what courses to take next term must make assumptions about the grades he or she will make this term. The particular assumptions the student makes may prove false, but it is impossible to avoid making any assumptions at all.

A conclusion may be validly inferred from false or questionable premises:

Premises: Only those who issue orders
                  can be blamed.
                  I did not issue orders.

Conclusion: Therefore I cannot be blamed.

The conclusion in this example follows validly, for there is no loophole in the structure of the argument; if the premises are true, the conclusion must be true. Yet the conclusion is hardly reliable, for the implication of the first premise—that those who only follow orders can evade responsibility by placing it all on their superiors—is unacceptable. Thus we can reject the conclusion as unproved, not because the inference is invalid, but because the first premise is unreliable.

Just as valid inferences will not always produce true conclusions, invalid inferences will not always produce false ones. The fact that the argument is invalid means only that the premises are not sufficient to guarantee that the conclusion is true. Thus we may have the following combinations of premises, inferences, and conclusions.

Premises	*Inference*	*Conclusion*
Known to be true	valid	known to be true
Known to be true	invalid	in doubt
One or more known to be false	valid	in doubt
One or more known to be false	invalid	in doubt
One or more in doubt	valid	in doubt
One or more in doubt	invalid	in doubt

When we have tested an argument and found it valid, we have eliminated doubt about the correctness of the inference, but *we have done nothing to demonstrate the truth of the premises*. In order to evaluate the argument fully we must check the reliability of the premises themselves. The propositions we use as premises can be evaluated for reliability by deductive reasoning from other premises. We can in turn evaluate these premises by deductive reasoning from still other premises, and so on. Ultimately, however, we must reach a premise which we must either assume to be true without sufficient proof or which we must establish by methods other than deductive reasoning. The chief among these other methods is induction.

Obviously, it would be inappropriate to evaluate an inductive argument according to the standards for a deductive one. This is because the standard of validity is a high one, which inductive arguments are not even intended to meet. Even when the premises of an inductive argument are true, its conclusion is at best probably true. If you eat three times at The Greasy Cow and the food is terrible, you are likely to conclude inductively that the food there is always terrible and not go back. However, the evidence might be quite true and the conclusion false. Perhaps you always ordered hamburgers and only the hamburgers are terrible while everything else is delicious. Perhaps they fired the cook right after your third visit and hired a good one. There are all kinds of possibilities, and acceptance of the evidence in no way necessitates acceptance of the conclusion. Inductive arguments are, then, harder than deductive ones to evaluate. Of course, the more and better evidence you have, the more reliable your conclusion becomes. But how many bad meals must one eat at a restaurant before deciding that the food there is bad? Obviously, far fewer than the number of supporters of a presidential candidate one needs to find in order to conclude that the candidate will win the election. Thus not just the size of the evidence but also its appropriateness to the case at hand need to be considered. Inductive arguments are not, however, to be evaluated as valid or invalid; rather, their conclusions are to be rated as more or less probable, depending on the weight of the evidence.

Arguments and Decision Making

The study of arguments dates back at least to the time of Aristotle, who wrote the first formal treatises on logic in the fourth century B.C. Traditional logic, which reached its height during the Middle Ages, was largely concerned with deductive argument, and for good reason. The principles that govern the validity of arguments constitute one of the most secure forms of truth we have. They are, in fact, every bit as certain as the principles of mathematics, and techniques for determining validity tend to be clear and precise. In the last century, too, deductive logic has seen dramatic advances, including the development of computer logics, whose impact we increasingly feel. By contrast, progress on the logic of induction has been more difficult to achieve. Yet the study of induction cannot be ignored, for induction is crucial to our finding out about the world and thus extending our frames of reference. Indeed, induction is often identified with the "scientific method," though the truth is that scientific inquiry employs both deductive and inductive methods of reasoning.

For our purposes, it will be necessary to study carefully both induction and deduction, since both are important to decision making. Indeed, although the importance of simply collecting available information should not be underestimated, the fact is that decision making is above all a process of argument, and arguments of both kinds may turn up in any of its phases. In particular, we use arguments whenever we form tentative conclusions from the information we have gathered about a problem, and when we test those conclusions. Indeed, part of the business of testing tentative conclusions is to evaluate the arguments by which they were reached. Much of the information in the chapters that follow, therefore, will be concerned with recognizing and evaluating various types of inductive and deductive arguments.

Exercise 2

Problems 1–10. Identify each of the following examples of discourse as either argument or exposition.

1. He was talking to the rubber tree in the dining room. Nobody in his right mind would talk to a rubber tree. He must be crazy. _____

2. He was talking to the rubber tree in the dining room. Then he went outside and had a long discussion with the azalea bush. _____

3. Since it's going to rain and Bill will have trouble finding a taxi, we ought to meet him at the station. _____

4. Since the end of World War II, this committee has been in existence. _____

5. But, Officer, you shouldn't give me a ticket. I was only going five miles over the speed limit. _____

6. This late Picasso has the style but not the life of his best work. The angles and forms are there, but the vibrancies and resonances are missing. It is as though he were an inept imitator of himself. The painting is a very poor one. _____

7. This late Picasso is not a good painting. Neither are the Matisses on this wall what I would call excellent. _____

8. If you can't find the widget that goes on top of this woozle, you'll have to go down to the hardware store and buy another one. _____

9. Joe Smythe couldn't have committed the crime. He was sitting with me in The Plastic Pig when the crime was committed. _____

10. The better cuts of beef will soon be scarce. So will lobster, shrimp, and other luxury foods. _____

Problems 11–19. Identify the conclusions of the following arguments. If they are not explicitly stated, state them.

11. The bigger the burger, the better the burger; the burgers are bigger at Burger City.

_____

12. I know you're a vegetarian, but you can eat the hot dogs here at The Plastic Pig because they're nothing but soybeans.

_____

13. A woman without a man is like a fish without a bicycle.

_____

14. Liquor provides relaxation and entertainment. Eighteen-year-olds need relaxation and entertainment. Therefore, eighteen-year-olds need liquor.

_____

15. Let me have men about me that are fat,
Sleek-headed men and such as sleep a-nights;
Yond Cassius has a lean and hungry look;
He thinks too much; such men are dangerous.

—Shakespeare, _Julius Caesar_

_____

16. Studies have shown that in many patients even a small dose of aspirin will increase clotting time. It is possible that taking aspirin on a regular basis may help prevent those strokes that are caused by blood clots.

_____

17. The butler must have committed the murder. He is the one with the key to the potting shed, where the strychnine was kept.

_____

18. In Switzerland, every male citizen is required to have a gun, and there is hardly any violent crime in Switzerland. Clearly, gun ownership has nothing to do with the rising crime rate! If anything, more guns would bring the crime rate down.

_____

19. I smell smoke. Help! Fire!

_____

Problems 20–28. Identify each of the following arguments as induction or deduction. For each inductive argument, state how the conclusion goes beyond the evidence.

20. These cans of peaches are two for a dollar, so you owe me fifty cents for one.

---

21. Sylvia Plath, Mark Vonnegut, and Robert Pirsig all wrote sophisticated and insightful books after undergoing shock therapy, so it is clear that shock therapy does not significantly impair mental capability.

---

22. If someone is thinking of you, your ear itches. I'm thinking about you, so your ear must itch.

---

23. The cancer patients had far more whorls in their fingerprints than the control group had. Therefore, investigating fingerprints may be a way of diagnosing cancer, or at least of establishing susceptibility to cancer.

---

24. If American health care were the best possible, then our prenatal and neonatal death rates would be lower than those of other advanced countries. But in fact our rates are much higher than those of other countries—Norway, Sweden, and Holland, for instance. Therefore, our health care is not the best possible.

---

25. Either the gas tank is empty, or there is something seriously wrong with this car. The gas tank is not empty, so there is something seriously wrong with the car.

---

26. His fingerprints are on the gun. Hence he must be the murderer.

---

27. She is loyal, hardworking, honest, and intelligent. You could not go wrong in hiring her as a supervisor.

---

28. No other planet in our solar system has the conditions that would support life. Therefore earth must be the only inhabited planet in the solar system.

Chapter 3

The Hypothetical Syllogism

- **The Hypothetical Proposition**
- **Structure of the Hypothetical Syllogism**
- **Affirming the Antecedent**
- **Denying the Antecedent**
- **Affirming the Consequent**
- **Denying the Consequent**

- **Uncertain Relationship Between Premises**
- **Non Sequitur**
- **Hypothetical Syllogisms in Extended Reasoning**
- **Interpreting Hypothetical Propositions**
- **Logical Shorthand**

If the hundreds of decisions we must make every day were as complex and difficult as President Kennedy's decision about the missiles in Cuba, most of us would never finish breakfast. The fact that most of us do finish breakfast and do manage to make the decisions required of us indicates that there are patterns of reasoning that facilitate reasonably quick decisions. For the most part, these patterns of reasoning are relatively simple forms of deductive argument, which enable us to organize our experience so as to make simple decisions in an effective way. The purpose of this chapter is to examine one of the simplest forms of deductive argument, the hypothetical syllogism, and to illustrate some of the ways in which various forms of the hypothetical syllogism function in decision making.

Suppose you are searching for a park-ing space. You see enough space for your car near the corner ahead, but when you get there you see that the space is next to a fire hydrant. You must now decide whether to park in this space. You have completed phase 1 of the decision-making process by defining your problem. In a situation like this, phase 2 of the cycle, gathering information, consists simply of searching your frame of reference for propositions that fit. One such proposition may be that it is not your policy to park by fire hydrants; another may be that you do not wish to get a ticket. These propositions can be joined with others in your frame of reference to reach a quick conclusion, thus getting you to phase 3. These other propositions represent beliefs about what will happen if you park in this space. For example, it is an obviously correct belief that if you park in this space you will park next to a fire hydrant. This, together with the proposition that you do not park by fire hydrants, leads by a deductive inference to the conclusion that you will not park in this space. Given that you do not wish to get a ticket, you might reach the same conclusion based on the proposition that if you park here you will get one. On the other hand, you may choose to act on the dubious belief that if you park here you will *not* get a ticket. If so, parking in the space will be a test (phase 4) of your conclusion to park here. Unless you are lucky, phase 5, evaluation and decision, will probably lead you to park elsewhere in the future.

The Hypothetical Proposition

All the above ways of deciding whether to park in the space by the hydrant involve the hypothetical syllogism. A **syllogism** is a deductive argument that has two premises and a conclusion. What distinguishes a hypothetical syllogism from syllogisms of other sorts is its major premise, which is a hypothetical proposition. A **hypothetical proposition** consists of two parts, the **antecedent** and the **consequent**, which are joined in a conditional relationship. The antecedent describes a condition or situation that is said to precede or cause or be accompanied by another condition or situation described in the consequent. Thus your belief that parking by the fire hydrant will lead to your getting a ticket can be represented as follows:

Antecedent	*Consequent*
If I park in this space	*then* I will get a ticket.

If and *then* are here italicized because,

strictly speaking, they are not part of the antecedent and consequent. *If* introduces the antecedent, and *then* introduces the consequent, and together express the hypothetical relationship.

It is important to understand that a hypothetical proposition makes no claim that either the antecedent or the consequent is true. The above proposition does not say that you will park in this space or that you will get a ticket; neither does it say that either of these things is false. Rather, it states a conditional relationship between the antecedent and consequent: that the consequent is true *if* the antecedent is true. Whether the hypothetical proposition as a whole is true depends only on whether this conditional relationship holds. Thus, if you were to park in the space by the hydrant and not get a ticket, the claim that if you park there you will get a ticket would be false, for the conditional relationship it asserts would not in fact exist.

Structure of the Hypothetical Syllogism

A hypothetical syllogism consists of a major premise in hypothetical form, a minor premise, and a conclusion inferred from the two premises. In simple cases, the minor premise is a straightforward factual statement to the effect that something is true or not true. It must declare that some specific situation, object, or idea meets or fails to meet the conditions described either in the antecedent or in the consequent. It may or may not repeat the words used in the antecedent or consequent, but it must establish something about its subject (not necessarily the grammatical subject) definitely, not hypothetically.

Typical everyday decisions begin with the minor premise, which describes the situation about which a decision must be made. The major premise states an important principle for dealing with it, often a law or policy. For example, when the traffic officer observes your car parked by a fire hydrant, this observation starts his or her reasoning and forms the minor premise. The law the officer is obliged to enforce forms the major premise. His or her deductive reasoning can be fully stated in the hypothetical syllogism below.

	Antecedent
Major Premise:	*If* a car is parked by a fire hydrant,
	Consequent
	then I must give it a ticket.
Minor Premise:	This car is parked by a fire hydrant.
Conclusion:	I must give it a ticket.

The officer may not consciously think of the major premise, but it is part of his or her reasoning nonetheless.

In a hypothetical syllogism, the conclusion is derived by deductive inference. In the example above the inference is the recognition that the minor premise states that if the condition described in the antecedent of the major premise is true in this specific situation, then the condition described in the consequent of the major premise must also be true in this specific situation.

Affirming the Antecedent

The minor premise may **affirm** the antecedent. That is, it may declare that the conditions described in the antecedent of the major premise are true in the particular situation involved. The argument of the traffic officer in the example above is an example of affirming the antecedent.[1] Here is another:

	Antecedent	*Consequent*
Major Premise:	*If* it rains,	*then* there are clouds
Minor Premise:	It is raining.	
Conclusion:	There are clouds.	

Here the minor premise affirms the antecedent, for it states that the condition described by the antecedent is true now. The argument is valid, for the major premise declares that there are always clouds when it rains, and it is raining now. Unless one of the premises is false, there must be clouds in the sky.

Affirming the antecedent is, then, a *valid* form of argument, for it is impossible for arguments of this kind to have true premises yet yield a false conclusion. It is important to realize, though, that not just any conclusion will do. Given the premises above, you are not entitled to conclude that the sky is free of clouds, or that it is raining in Australia. The only conclusion you can validly infer is that there are clouds. When the minor

---

[1] This type of argument is often called by its Latin name, *modus ponens,* which means "the method of affirming."

premise affirms the antecedent, the conclusion, to follow validly, must declare that the conditions of the consequent are true of the subject of the minor premise.

Denying the Antecedent

The minor premise may **deny** the antecedent by declaring that the conditions stated in the antecedent are not true in the particular situation involved.

	Antecedent	*Consequent*
Major Premise:	*If* it rains	*then* there are clouds.
Minor Premise:	It is not raining.	
Conclusion:	There are no clouds.	

Many people would find this conclusion tempting, given the evidence cited in the premises. In fact, however, this argument is invalid, for the hypothetical premise does not say that clouds are present *only* when it rains. It describes what is the case if it does rain but says nothing whatever about situations where it is not raining. We cannot determine from these premises whether there are clouds or not. Indeed, it would be invalid to infer any definite conclusion about clouds.

Denying the antecedent is thus an *invalid* form of argument. Showing in the minor premise that the antecedent is not true of a particular situation proves nothing about whether the consequent is true of the situation. There may be—in fact, there often are—other conditions under which the consequent will be true in addition to those described by the antecedent. For example, there are also clouds when it snows.

It may have been a logical fallacy of this type that encouraged the Soviet Union to install missiles in Cuba. Early in the Kennedy administration, an invasion of Cuba by Cuban exiles at the Bay of Pigs had failed, in part because the administration, secretly supporting the invasion but wishing to avoid involving the air force, had failed to provide air cover. The Soviet Union appears to have interpreted this to mean that President Kennedy was irresolute about risking war over Cuba. The Soviets may have reasoned as follows:

> If the United States had fully supported the Bay of Pigs invasion, then it would be willing to risk war over conditions in Cuba. But the United States did not provide full support. Therefore it will not risk war over conditions in Cuba.

Affirming the Consequent

The minor premise may affirm the consequent by stating that the conditions the consequent describes are true. Suppose you get a letter from a friend saying he is seriously ill, but that if he can obtain a scarce serum he will recover. You later receive a card from him saying that he is well. Can you conclude that he got the serum? The answer is no, for you would have to argue as follows:

	Antecedent	*Consequent*
Major Premise:	*If* he gets the serum	*then* he recovers.
Minor Premise:	He recovered.	
Conclusion:	He got the serum.	

Once again, the argument may be tempting, but a little reflection will show you that it is invalid. The major premise does not state that getting the serum is the *only* condition under which your friend can recover. There may be other conditions. Hence affirming the consequent is an *invalid* form.

Denying the Consequent

Suppose that instead of a card from your sick friend you get a telegram saying that he died of his illness. You wonder whether he got the serum. A hypothetical syllogism will tell you.

Major Premise:	If he had gotten the serum, then he would have recovered.
Minor Premise:	He did not recover.
Conclusion:	He did not get the serum.

Since the minor premise flatly contradicts the consequent of the major premise, you can validly conclude that the antecedent is also false—your friend did not get the serum. Should you later learn that he did get the serum and died anyway, blame the major premise, not the inference.

Denying the consequent is a *valid* form.[2] Assuming that the hypothetical premise is true, any situation that does not fit the consequent cannot fit the antecedent. But note again that only one conclusion will do. You cannot conclude from the premises that your friend got the serum too late, or that it hastened his death. To be validly inferred, the conclusion must declare that the conditions described in the antecedent are not true of the specific situation. Nothing else will do.

The minor premise need not be nega-

tive to deny an antecedent or consequent. The minor premise below is a positive statement, but it denies the consequent by stating that the conditions described by the consequent are not true.

	Antecedent	Consequent
Major *Premise:*	*If* one is diligent	*then* he will not fail.
Minor Premise:	Smythe failed.	
Conclusion:	Smythe is not diligent.	

The point here is that the condition described by the consequent of the major premise is itself a negative one. Thus the minor premise, by being affirmative, effectively denies that the condition holds. Hence the argument is valid.

The rules for validity of hypothetical syllogisms are summarized below.

If the minor premise	**The argument is**
Affirms the antecedent	valid if the conclusion affirms the consequent
Denies the antecedent	invalid
Affirms the consequent	invalid
Denies the consequent	valid if the conclusion denies the antecedent

Uncertain Relationship Between Premises

You may have noticed that in the last chapter and this one, we have begun to speak of **fallacies**. In logic, a fallacy is an

---

[2] The Latin name for denying the consequent is *modus tollens*, which means "the method of denying."

error in reasoning. The study of fallacies is especially valuable for developing effective procedures of thinking, since certain types of fallacies occur frequently when poor procedures are followed. Studying fallacies helps us learn to avoid them and the unreliable conclusions to which they lead. This does not mean that the conclusion of an argument that commits a fallacy will always be false. For example, the conclusion of an argument in which the antecedent is denied may still be true. But a fallacious argument can never guarantee the reliability of its conclusion, in the strong sense at which deductive argument aims.

Fallacious arguments can be recognized either by their logical form or by their content—that is, their strategy or the sort of information they employ. Denying the antecedent and affirming the consequent are both formal fallacies: their structure is such that they cannot lead to reliable conclusions. A fallacy more easily recognized by looking at the content of the argument is that of **uncertain relationship between premises**. It is not enough for a minor premise to *seem* to affirm an antecedent or deny a consequent. A valid syllogism requires that one of these relationships be stated clearly and unequivocally. The following argument fails to observe this requirement.

	Antecedent	*Consequent*
Major Premise:	*If* it rains,	the game will be postponed.
Minor Premise:	The Weather Bureau predicts rain.	
Conclusion:	The game will be postponed.	

The conclusion of this argument does not follow validly from the premises given, nor would any similar conclusion, for the minor premise only appears to affirm the antecedent. Saying that the Weather Bureau predicts rain is not the equivalent of saying that there will certainly be rain. Thus the relationship between the premises is too unclear to permit any validly drawn conclusion. The words used in the two premises do not, of course, have to be exactly the same, but it must be clear from a reasonable interpretation of the premises whether they are related so as to make a valid inference possible. If information not stated in the premises is needed in order to establish such a relationship, the syllogism should be ruled invalid.

Non Sequitur

In the two valid forms of hypothetical syllogism, affirming the antecedent and denying the consequent, we noted that not just any conclusion is permissible. The only validly inferred conclusion following an affirmed antecedent states that the consequent is true. The only validly inferred conclusion following a denied consequent states that the antecedent is not true. A conclusion cannot go even a hair's breadth beyond the evidence in the premises and still be validly drawn. Consider the following example.

> If one has an accident while violating the law, then he is legally responsible. You were violating the law by exceeding the speed limit when you had your accident. Therefore you are legally and morally responsible.

The premises of this syllogism could have been used to make a valid argument, for they yield the conclusion that you are legally responsible. But the above conclusion goes beyond the consequent by adding the element of moral responsibility. This argument is thus invalid because the truth of the conclusion is not guaranteed by the premises given.

We call this fallacy a **non sequitur**.[3] In a non sequitur the fault is in the conclusion. In the other fallacies in hypothetical syllogisms (affirmed consequent, denied antecedent, and uncertain relationship), the fault is in the premises.

It is of the essence of validity that the conclusion go only as far as the evidence justifies. An argument in which the conclusion does not go as far as the evidence is still valid. Suppose that the hypothetical premise in the example above had read: "If one has an accident while violating the law, he is both legally and morally responsible." Given the same minor premise, the conclusion "You are legally responsible" could be validly inferred, even though this conclusion does not include the element of moral responsibility. In short, a validly drawn conclusion need not necessarily state everything that follows from the premises, but it must never state anything that does not follow.

Hypothetical Syllogisms in Extended Reasoning

Thus far, we have emphasized the use of hypothetical syllogisms in relatively simple cases of reasoning and decision. But hypothetical syllogisms can and often do occur in the process of thinking through complex decisions. When they do, it is important that they be used carefully, avoiding fallacies and testing premises as well as possible. Faulty hypothetical syllogisms may seem like small mistakes,

but in some circumstances their effects can be devastating.

For example, on June 17, 1972, a group of burglars were arrested at the headquarters of the Democratic National Committee, in the Watergate Hotel, in Washington, D.C. In their possession were telephone-bugging equipment and cameras for photographing documents. It was soon learned that the burglars were employed by the Committee to Reelect the President, the campaign organization of President Nixon. This created an obvious problem for the president and his advisers: with the election only a few months away, a scandal could be very damaging. Moreover, the potential for scandal was great, for those who had planned and approved the Watergate break-in—a group that included some of the top officials in the Nixon administration—had been involved in a number of other illegal activities as well. As a result, President Nixon and his staff committed one of the worst blunders in American political history: in the weeks that followed, an elaborate cover-up developed, the discovery of which would eventually force Richard Nixon to resign the presidency in disgrace.

Besides involving acts that were illegal, the Watergate cover-up involved poor thinking, some of which can be captured in hypothetical syllogisms. First, consider some of the facts that were available.

1. The break-in was only one of many illegal activities that had occurred.

2. The illegal activities involved several high administration officials.

3. The Watergate burglars expected to have their legal and family expenses paid by those who had approved the break-in.

---

[3] *Non sequitur* is Latin for "it does not follow."

4. Money could be raised to pay the burglars.

Not all of the thinking in the White House that led to the cover-up was logically inept. Propositions 1 and 2 above do indeed suggest that the potential for scandal was great. But the effort to protect the president and others by concealing the facts was completely misconceived. Propositions 3 and 4 suggest a strategy: the burglars were to be paid in an effort to keep them from talking. Perhaps the reasoning was as follows:

Major Premise: If the burglars are paid off, then they will keep silent.

Minor Premise: The burglars will be paid off.

Conclusion: They will keep silent.

This is a valid syllogism, since its minor premise affirms the antecedent. But its major premise turned out to be false. When Judge John J. Sirica threatened to impose extended prison terms on those found guilty of the break-in, one of them cracked, and the whole scandal began to unravel.

If, on the other hand, one looks in this situation for arguments that involve true premises, the arguments turn out to be invalid. Given the extent of the illegal activity that had already occurred, those who perpetrated the cover-up might have argued in this way:

Major Premise: If the president is to be protected from the effects of Watergate, then there must be a cover-up.

Minor Premise: There will be a cover-up.

Conclusion: The president will be protected from the effects of Watergate.

There is reason to think both premises here are true. But this argument is a case of affirming the consequent. The conclusion does not follow, and of course it turned out to be false.

Moreover, it is almost certain that the creative thinking of those involved in the cover-up was at fault. No one seems to have seriously considered that if the cover-up itself was discovered, the situation for both the president and his staff would be far worse than one of simply losing an election. Nor does the problem of keeping so many people quiet in the White House itself seem to have been recognized, or the dangers involved in the Nixon administration opening itself up to blackmail on the part of the burglars by paying to keep them quiet. Why these problems were not seen to be serious is not clear. Certainly, subjective factors such as ambition and misguided loyalty were involved. In any case, had these problems been given the consideration they deserved, the solution of engaging in cover-up activities might well have received a different evaluation than it did, and another, less tragic, decision could have resulted.

Interpreting Hypothetical Propositions

It is obvious from the examples we have seen thus far that the most common logical connector used to express hypothetical propositions is **if . . . then**. Also, when hypothetical propositions are stated, the antecedent is usually given first, followed by the consequent. This order need not always be observed, however. Like the premises and conclusion of an argument, an antecedent and consequent may be given in either order, according to the preference of the speaker or writer. The following two sentences express exactly the same hypothetical proposition:

If you cannot make it in the morning, then I will schedule the meeting later.

I will schedule the meeting later if you cannot make it in the morning.

The important point to remember is that whether a proposition counts as the antecedent or consequent of a hypothetical depends not on its position, but on the logical connectors.

In addition to *if . . . then,* there are several other logical connectors that can be used to express hypothetical propositions. Some important and relatively easy ones are *to* or *in order to,* and *given that*, which introduce the antecedent of a hypothetical proposition. Consider these examples:

In order to pass, you will have to study hard.

You will have to hurry to catch the bus.

Given that it is raining, you will need an umbrella.

Using *if . . .then*, these may be expressed as follows:

If you are to pass, then you must study hard.

If you catch the bus, then you will have hurried.

If it is raining, then you will need an umbrella.

Two logical connectors that are especially troublesome are **only if** and **unless.** Regarding the first, *only if* does not mean the same as *if*. Whereas *if* is used to introduce antecedents in hypothetical propositions, *only if* is used to introduce con-

sequents. The statement

Only if you stop smoking will you live a long life.

does not mean that quitting smoking will guarantee a long life. Rather, it means that if the hearer is to have a chance at a long life, he or she must quit smoking. The correct translation therefore is

If you are to live a long life, then you must stop smoking.

As for *unless*, its meaning is basically negative in hypothetical propositions. In effect, *unless* attaches itself to the negated form of the antecedent. Consider the following argument.

Unless I hurry, I will be late.
I will not hurry.
Therefore I will be late.

This syllogism is valid, for it is in effect a disguised form of affirming the antecedent. Its major premise translates to

If I do not hurry, then I will be late.

Finally, there are some occasions when we wish to express a reciprocal conditional relationship between two propositions. That is, we wish to say that if either one of them is true, then the other is true, and if either is false, then the other is false. The logical connector used for this purpose is **if and only if**. Consider the following:

Major Premise:	If and only if it rains, our crops will be saved.
Minor Premise:	It will not rain.
Conclusion:	Our crops will not be saved.

Given these premises, we can validly conclude that our crops will not be saved, even though the minor premise denies the first component of the major premise. The reason is that the words *if and only if* indicate a relationship of mutual implication between the two sides. Fully expressed, the premise means: If it rains our crops will be saved, and if our crops will be saved, then it will rain. Thus, unlike the case with *if . . . then,* the use of *if and only if* expresses a symmetrical conditional relationship, one which runs in both directions. As a result, we can affirm either antecedent or deny either consequent and still get a validly drawn conclusion.

Logical Shorthand

Since we will be analyzing many hypothetical propositions, we can save trouble by adopting a shorthand for writing them. Also, it will be helpful to have a way of indicating quickly the conclusions of arguments. From symbolic logic let us borrow the symbols below and substitute them for the logical connectors indicated.

Logical Connector	*Symbol*
If . . . then . . .	⊃
Therefore . . .	∴

We noted above that in ordinary English, either the antecedent or the consequent of a hypothetical proposition can come first, depending on how the logical connectors are used. By adopting the horseshoe to represent hypothetical propositions, however, we rule out this kind of complication. When the horseshoe is used, the antecedent of a hypothetical proposition must be written to the left of the symbol and the consequent to the right. Otherwise the meaning will be changed. **The hypothetical relationship itself is not reversible.**

The use of our logical shorthand is illustrated below (the example is invalid).

Full Statement

If beef prices are controlled, then shortages will occur.
Beef prices will not be controlled.
Therefore shortages will not occur.

Shorthand Statement

Beef prices are controlled ⊃ shortages will occur.
Beef prices will not be controlled.
∴ Shortages will not occur.

As we have noted, the hypothetical syllogism is one of the simplest forms of deduction; in Part Three of this book, we will return to deduction and examine some of its more complex forms.

Exercise 3A

Problems 1–7. These items refer to the syllogism below.

If Jones studied faithfully, then she passed the course.
Jones passed the course.
Therefore Jones studied faithfully.

1. What is the antecedent of the major premise?

_____

2. What is the consequent?

_____

3. What is the relationship between the minor premise and the major premise?

_____

4. What is the relationship between the conclusion and the major premise?

_____

5. Is the argument valid?

_____

6. If so, why? If not, why not?

_____

7. Write the syllogism in logical shorthand.

_____

_____

_____

Problems 8–15. For each of the following arguments,

    a. using Key List A, state the relationship between the premises.

    b. state whether the argument is valid or invalid.

c. if you say it is invalid, state which fallacy from Key List B the argument commits.

Key List A
1. The antecedent is affirmed.
2. The antecedent is denied.
3. The consequent is affirmed.
4. The consequent is denied.
5. The relationship is uncertain.

Key List B
1. Denied antecedent
2. Affirmed consequent
3. Uncertain relationship
4. Non sequitur

8. If the victim was murdered, then there would be water in his lungs.
There is no water in his lungs.
Therefore the victim was not murdered.

_____

_____

_____

9. If a student is late to Dr. Wiltmore's class, then he is marked absent.
John was marked absent today.
Therefore he must have been late to class.

_____

_____

_____

10. If the temperature is below 80 degrees, then Carla will refuse to go swimming.
The temperature is 75 degrees this afternoon.
Therefore Carla will not go swimming this afternoon.

_____

_____

_____

11. If our sentries remain alert at their posts, then the enemy cannot infiltrate our lines.
Enemy troops have infiltrated our lines.
Therefore our sentries must have fallen asleep at their posts.

_____

_____

_____

12. If a chapter is assigned, then questions on it will be included in the examination.
There were two questions on Chapter 5 in the exam.
Therefore Chapter 5 was assigned.

_____

_____

_____

13. If one is to be successful in business, then he has to be clever.
Higgins was entirely unsuccessful in business.
Therefore he must not have been a clever man.

_____

_____

_____

14. If the ship can maintain a speed of twenty knots, then it can outrun the storm.
The *South Seas* can easily maintain a speed of twenty knots.
Therefore the *South Seas* will reach port on time.

_____

_____

_____

15. If killing is evil, then capital punishment should be abolished.
The prisoner was found guilty of first-degree murder.
Therefore he should not be executed.

_____

_____

_____

Exercise 3B

Problems 1–7. These items refer to the syllogism below.

> If Barry has a poor teacher, then he will never learn the subtleties of his profession.
> His teacher is Mr. Cowan, who is considered the foremost authority in his field.
> Barry no doubt will learn the subtleties of his profession.

1. What is the antecedent of the major premise?

_____

2. What is the consequent?

_____

3. What is the relationship between the minor premise and the major premise?

_____

4. What is the relationship between the conclusion and the major premise?

_____

5. Is the argument valid?

_____

6. If so, why? If not, why not?

_____

7. Write the syllogism in logical shorthand.

_____

_____

_____

Problems 8–17. For each of the following pairs of premises, if they yield a valid conclusion, state what it is. If the premises do not yield a valid conclusion, state the fallacy they commit.

8. To be eligible for medical school, a student must have excellent grades.
Ruth was accepted by the top medical school in the country.

---

9. If we pick up intelligible radio signals from outer space, then we will know that other intelligent beings exist out there.
We have not picked up any intelligible signals from outer space.

---

10. Given that the wrecked car had been speeding, it would have overturned.
The car skidded off the road but did not overturn.

---

11. When a poem is interesting, it is not unpopular among people of good taste.
The distinguished Great Poems Society judged Myrick's poem technically flawless.

---

12. If a police officer believes that alibi, he or she must be quite suggestible.
Inspector Carmody believes every word of it.

---

13. To think effectively one must have a rich frame of reference.
Davis is a college graduate.

---

14. If at times emotions interfere with objectivity in thinking, then one cannot know the whole truth about reality.
It is clearly impossible to know the whole truth about reality.

---

15. If the seller neglects to get the contract notarized, it is not binding.
My lawyer informs me that the contract is not binding.

---

16. In order to win the election, Johnson must carry the large cities.
But she has lost every large city.

---

17. Even though it might involve great sacrifice, if one is able to obtain a college education he or she will never regret it.
A large number of high school graduates are unable to get a college education.

Exercise 3C

Problems 1–6. For each of the following sentences,

    a. express the sentence as a hypothetical statement using **if . . . then.**

    b. write the statement using logical shorthand.

1. The mission will be scrubbed unless all components function perfectly.

_____

_____

2. Only if you meet all requirements will you receive your degree.

_____

_____

3. No student is a failure if he or she is learning to think more effectively.

_____

_____

4. Unless you repent, you will all likewise perish.

_____

_____

5. Given these conditions, you can expect an explosion.

_____

_____

6. You can have my cattle, pilgrim, but only if you shoot me first.

_____

_____

Problems 7–10. State whether each of the following syllogisms is valid or not. If it is invalid, state what fallacy it commits.

7. Unless I hurry, I will be late. But I will hurry, so I will not be late.

_____

_____

8. A student can graduate from Wysacki only if he or she passes the English proficiency requirement. Clark graduated from Wysacki. Therefore he must have passed the English proficiency requirement.

_____

_____

9. Unless you are a dangerous driver, you will not be guilty of many moving violations. But Eleanor has never been guilty of a moving violation. Hence she is not a dangerous driver.

_____

_____

10. The anaconda would have escaped if and only if you left the cage door open. You did not leave it open. Therefore the anaconda did not escape.

_____

_____

Chapter 4

Forming Hypotheses

- **The Problem of Induction**
- **The Nature of Hypotheses**
- **Guidelines for Forming Hypotheses**
- **Adding and Testing Consequents**
- **Priorities in Testing Hypotheses**
- **Repeating the Cycle**

Early one autumn evening, Lauren Stewart, inspector for the Civil Aeronautics Board, answered her telephone and heard her chief say: "United Airlines Flight 629 has crashed west of Denver. I'm putting you in charge of the investigation—find out why the plane crashed."[1]

Information given Stewart by her chief included the following propositions:

1. All forty-four persons aboard were killed.

2. Flight 629 left Denver twenty-two minutes late.

3. The crash occurred within eleven minutes after takeoff.

4. The plane was a DC 6B.

Note that no two of these propositions could form the premises of a valid syllogism as to why Flight 629 crashed. Each of them is an independent, particular piece of information concerning the plane or its passengers. Any one of them might serve as a minor premise, but none will do as a major premise. Nor would it be reasonable at this point for Stewart to try to extract from her frame of reference any premise with which one or more of these propositions could be combined to tell her the cause of the crash. While deductive inferences will prove useful in the investigation, they will not suffice. For Stewart's problem is new in the sense that its solu-

---

[1] The character Stewart and her role in the investigation are fictitious. The crash actually occurred (late in 1955) and received intensive coverage in the news media at the time.

tion cannot be derived from premises she already has. Inductive inferences are necessary in situations like this.

The Problem of Induction

In all except the simplest of decisions, we are likely to use both deductive and inductive inferences and to shift quickly from one to the other. An understanding of the nature of both types is essential for effective thinking because the methods for testing each type are very different. As we have seen, an important part of the evaluation of a deductive argument consists in determining whether it is valid. If it is, the inference itself cannot be successfully challenged, for the conclusion is inherent, though not stated, in the premises. The only way the argument can be refuted is by attacking the premises. Thus, if your insurance agent explains that he must charge a higher rate to insure your car because you are eighteen years old and all drivers in your age bracket must pay a higher rate because they have more accidents, he is making a deductive inference. If you wish to disagree with the agent, it is useless to challenge his inference, for it is valid. If there is a weakness in his argument, it must be in the premises, for the conclusion of a valid deductive argument never goes beyond the information stated in the premises.

By contrast, as we saw in Chapter 2, the conclusion of an inductive argument does go beyond the evidence contained in the premises. Thus the conclusion of an inductive inference can never have been fully verified by observation. Officials of the insurance company made an inductive inference when they put together thousands of facts about accidents and the ages of the drivers involved and concluded that younger drivers should be charged higher premiums because they are more likely to have accidents. They went beyond the evidence by drawing a conclusion about drivers in the future on the basis of information about drivers in the past. Here, if you wish to disagree, there are two ways in which the argument can be attacked. As with deductive arguments, you could challenge the evidence, though in this case you would probably find that it had been carefully collected. Or you may challenge the inference itself, on the ground that the accident rate for the past will not necessarily continue into the future.

When we challenge an inductive argument in this second way, we are exploiting the fact that in inductive arguments it is always possible for the premises to be true and the conclusion false. What philosophers of science call the **problem of induction** consists in the fact that no matter how carefully it is constructed, an inductive argument is always open to this sort of challenge. This does not mean, however, that inductive arguments should be avoided. They cannot be, for precisely because inductive inferences go beyond the evidence in hand, they are our primary tool for solving new problems, finding new solutions to old problems, and developing new premises. Indeed, even the conclusion of a deductive argument is no more reliable than its premises, and the premises of many deductive arguments are derived by other arguments that are inductive. Instead of avoiding inductive inferences, then, we must deal with the problem of induction by making the conclusions we get by this sort of inference as reliable as possible.

In this chapter and the next, we will concentrate on inductive arguments that try to account for a particular event or fact, such as the crash of Flight 629. Essentially, we explain such events by forming various hypotheses as to what the cause may be and then testing them until the best hypothesis emerges. We will concentrate first on forming hypotheses and then on testing them and judging their reliability. In fact, however, the operations of forming and testing hypotheses cannot be completely separated because testing some hypotheses often leads us to form new and better ones. Hence some of the concepts introduced in this chapter will reappear in the next. We will also see that although identifying the correct hypothesis to explain an event is an inductive process, arguments by which mistaken hypotheses are eliminated are frequently deductive.

The Nature of Hypotheses

The term *hypothesis* is often used in a general sense to refer to any theoretical speculation or unproved assumption. In this book we will use it in a more restricted sense: by a **hypothesis**, we will mean a tentative conclusion that relates and explains a group of different items of information.

Let us clarify our definition with examples. Suppose it is the first day of the fall semester and that after a long day of classes you return to your dormitory. When you get there you observe that (1) the door to your room has been left open, (2) the furniture is not where you remember it as being, and (3) a lot of clothes are scattered about, some of which you do not recognize. Your observations give you a set of three different propositions. They are not necessarily related. You could have mistakenly packed some clothes belonging to a brother or sister; perhaps there is a new custodial service, and the custodian rearranged the furniture; an official from the housing office could have left the door open.

If, however, you had not even had a chance to unpack yet, you would probably be disturbed by your observations. Almost before entering the room you would make a guess to account for them. Depending on your experience, you might make any or all of the following guesses: "I have been robbed"; "Someone else has been mistakenly assigned to my room"; "Somebody already has a grudge against me." These guesses are hypotheses. Each of them relates and explains the different items of information by linking them to a common cause. For example, the hypothesis "Someone else has been mistakenly assigned to my room" explains why the door has been left open, the furniture is arranged differently, and strange clothing is scattered about, for it is reasonable to suppose a new occupant might be responsible for these changes. All three hypotheses can be confirmed only inductively, however, for they go beyond the evidence you have to supply an explanation of it. And of course all three could be wrong. If closer observation on your own part discloses that in fact none of the items in the room belong to you and that the view from the window is not as you remember it, it might begin to dawn on you that in fact this is not your room at all, that you have entered someone else's room by mistake.

The decision-making cycle with the hypothesis as the basic type of tentative conclusion is helpful in a wide variety of situations. It is used by historians reconstructing the past, by doctors making diagnoses, by detectives investigating crimes, by lawyers pleading cases, by newspaper reporters piecing together stories, by military strategists interpreting intelligence reports, by economists predicting future market conditions, by counselors helping students solve their problems, and by students solving their problems. It is used in combination with other techniques by scientists unraveling the secrets of the universe.

In using hypotheses we should begin phase 3 (forming tentative conclusions) as soon as a few items of information have been gathered. For there is a reciprocal relationship between hypotheses and information: information is the substance from which hypotheses are formed, and forming hypotheses guides the search for further information.

A hypothesis adds meaning to a group of propositions that the individual propositions do not have. For example, consider Joe Smythe's semester grade report shown below.

Course	Credits	Grade
English 101	3	C
Sociology 101	3	A
Mathematics 101	3	D
Chemistry 101	3	D
Biology 101	3	F

Different people would form different hypotheses about these grades according to their frames of reference. Joe's parents might form the hypothesis that Joe did not study much during the semester. Joe's rival for the affections of a certain girl might form the hypothesis that Joe is not very bright. Joe's academic counselor, who advises all the premedical students at Wysacki, might form the hypothesis that medicine is not a suitable profession for Joe. Note that all these hypotheses, though formed from different points of view, add meaning to the grades. Any particular meaning might not be correct, of course, but meaning has been added nevertheless.

By adding meaning to the propositions at hand, a hypothesis serves as a guide to what information is relevant. Suppose your problem is to find out why Joe made poor grades in three courses. Without one or more hypotheses, you would have no basis for deciding what kind of information to seek. You might gather vast quantities of data about Joe, such as his weight, height, or taste in food, without including any information of use in solving your problem. On the other hand, suppose you formed the hypothesis that Joe made bad grades in these courses because he was not really interested in medicine. This hypothesis gives you a clear sense of direction in seeking more information. Even if the hypothesis eventually proves to be wrong, your investigation of it is likely to turn up useful information.

Now let us return to the case of Flight 629. Lauren Stewart had hardly hung up her telephone before she had formed the following hypotheses to guide her investigation.

A. The crash was caused by a storm.

B. The crash was caused by engine failure.

C. The crash was caused by fire aboard the plane.

D. The crash was caused by structural failure.

Forming hypotheses is the essence of creative thinking. In a sense it is like guessing what picture a jigsaw puzzle will make before you put it together. When you have taken only a few pieces from the box, your imagination has few clues to help; on the other hand, your imagination is virtually unlimited because the picture could be of almost anything. Later, as you begin to assemble some of the pieces, your imagination has more clues, but it is more limited because fewer pictures will fit the pieces you have assembled. Even when you have many of the pieces assembled, your imagination must fill in the gaps.

At this stage in her investigation, Stewart had only a few clues to help her imagination fill in the picture of what caused Flight 629 to crash. Proposition 1 makes her investigation important but does little to suggest what caused the crash. Propositions 2 and 3 suggest that the plane might have been delayed in Denver by some kind of mechanical trouble, which might later have caused the crash. Proposition 4 would be helpful only if other planes of the type had crashed before. Because she had few clues, Stewart's imagination was almost unrestricted, for the only causes of the crash eliminated by the evidence so far in hand are those connected with the takeoff.

Guidelines for Forming Hypotheses

Three general guidelines should be followed in forming hypotheses.

The Hypotheses Should Solve or Help to Solve the Problem as Defined. Since Stewart's problem is to discover why the plane crashed, she would be wasting time forming hypotheses about the effects of the crash on the families of the passengers or about the cost to the airline.

In General, the More Hypotheses Formed, the Better. We must be extremely careful not to limit ourselves to one hypothesis, for if we do, the probability is high that we will exclude the very information that will provide the key to the problem. Also, if we begin with only one hypothesis, we are likely to develop a liking for it and unconsciously search only for evidence to support it. We must avoid trying to establish any particular hypothesis. Darwin remarked that it was so easy to

pass over facts contrary to a favorite hypothesis that he found it necessary to write down these facts, or he was almost sure to forget them. The preventive is to form several hypotheses. The more hypotheses we form, the more likely we are to include the correct one.

It is, of course, important not to carry this guideline too far. The number of hypotheses that might account for a given phenomenon is theoretically limitless, and far-fetched ones can impede the investigation. For instance, it would not be reasonable for Stewart to spend a lot of time exploring the hypothesis that Flight 629 was shot down by a World War II fighter pilot lost in a time warp. However, hypotheses that at first seem unlikely often prove fruitful when familiar avenues of investigation fail. Inductive investigations are more apt to be impeded by a shortage of hypotheses than by an overabundance of them. The ability to come up with a number of hypotheses to explain a phenomenon is valuable and worth developing.

Extra Effort Should Be Made to Form Unpalatable Hypotheses. As we form hypotheses, our self-concept may hamper effective thinking, for we tend to restrain the imagination from forming hypotheses that threaten it in any way. If Stewart believed, for example, that her knowledge of airplane engines was inadequate for this investigation, she would have been far less likely to form the hypothesis that the crash of Flight 629 was caused by engine failure.

Adding and Testing Consequents

Although we can start testing a single hypothesis as soon as we have formed one, it is better to form a number of hypotheses before we begin extensive testing. We thereby lessen the risk of becoming attached to a single hypothesis. We may also save time, since it is often possible to proceed by testing a number of hypotheses simultaneously. Since any hypothesis that correctly explains a phenomenon goes beyond the evidence in hand, it will not be possible to show that the hypothesis is true by a valid argument. It is possible at times, however, to use valid arguments to eliminate incorrect hypotheses. Moreover, the evidence by which incorrect or unlikely hypotheses are eliminated often helps lead us to the correct hypothesis.

We test hypotheses by asking ourselves what else would be true if the hypothesis is true and then checking to see if the further proposition holds. The first step, then, is to form a hypothetical proposition by using the hypothesis in question as the antecedent and then adding a consequent that was or is or will be true if the hypothesis is true. Shown below are Stewart's first four hypotheses, to each of which a consequent has been added:

Hypothesis		*Consequent Added*
A. The crash was caused by a storm	⊃	weather reports would show bad flying weather in the area of the crash.
B. The crash was caused by engine failure	⊃	one or more engines may have been running badly when Flight 629 took off from Denver.
C. The crash was caused by fire	⊃	the wreckage would show signs of fire.

Hypothesis		*Consequent Added*
D. The crash was caused by structural failure	⊃	evidence might be found in the wreckage of the plane.

The second step is to test the consequents by any practicable means. Note that the consequents themselves point like the needle of a compass to sources of relevant information. Note also that Stewart can save time and trouble by testing several hypotheses simultaneously: she can test consequents A and B by calling the airport and C and D by inspecting the wreckage.

Stewart's call to the airport yielded the information in the following propositions.

5. Flying conditions in the area of the crash were excellent.

6. All engines were functioning normally at takeoff.

The next step is to assess the significance of the evidence gathered by testing consequents. The significance of such evidence can be seen by completing a hypothetical syllogism, using the evidence gathered as the minor premise. Consider proposition 5 in relation to hypothesis A.

The crash was caused by a storm ⊃ weather reports would show bad flying weather in the area of the crash.

Weather reports show that flying conditions were excellent.

∴ The crash was not caused by a storm.

This syllogism shows that proposition 5 is a **diverging proposition**, that is, a proposition that reduces the probability that a hypothesis is true. Diverging propositions reduce the probability of a hypothesis because they run counter to what we would expect if it were true. In this case, the probability of the hypothesis is reduced to zero, for in Stewart's frame of reference the consequent of the major premise in the above syllogism would have to be true if the hypothesis were true. Proposition 5 directly denies the consequent, producing a valid argument that the hypothesis is false. Thus Stewart discarded hypothesis A.

In other cases, diverging propositions do not directly deny the consequent attached to a hypothesis and hence do not lead to the conclusion that the hypothesis is false. Nevertheless, they have enough negative impact to reduce the probability that the hypothesis is true. Consider proposition 6 in relation to hypothesis B.

The crash was caused by engine failure	$\supset$	one or more engines may have been running badly when Flight 629 took off from Denver.

All engines were functioning normally at takeoff.

Proposition 6 is also a diverging proposition, but it is not as significant as proposition 5. Since the consequent of the major premise is qualified by the word *may,* we would be guilty of a *non sequitur* if we concluded that the plane crash was not caused by engine failure. Even so, the proposition does reduce the probability that the hypothesis is true, for it asserts that one thing we might expect if the crash was caused by engine failure did not in fact occur.

The next morning, Stewart was on the scene of the crash testing consequents C and D. A quick inspection of the wreckage yielded two surprising facts.

7. Wreckage from the plane showed no signs of fire.

8. Debris from the plane was widely scattered.

Proposition 7 clearly diverges from hypothesis C. Proposition 8 diverges from hypothesis D, for in plane crashes caused by structural failure the debris is not normally as widely scattered as the debris from Flight 629. Thus, as often happens in complex investigations, Stewart has partially tested her original four hypotheses and found no supporting evidence for any of them. Even so she has made progress, for proposition 8 suggests a new hypothesis.

E. The crash was caused by an explosion aboard the plane.

Proposition 8 not only suggests hypothesis E but also provides a **converging proposition**, a proposition that increases the probability that a hypothesis is true. Converging propositions accord with what we would expect if a hypothesis is true. The significance of a converging proposition can be seen by putting it into a hypothetical syllogism.

The crash was caused by an explosion aboard the plane	$\supset$	debris from the plane would be widely scattered.

Debris from the plane was widely scattered.

∴ The crash was caused by an explosion aboard the plane.

As you can see, this argument is deductively invalid because the consequent is affirmed. From an inductive point of view, however, proposition 8 increases the probability that hypothesis E is true by eliminating all possible causes of the crash that would not result in widely scattered debris. Another consequent with which to test hypothesis E is obvious: someone may have seen the explosion. Eyewitnesses were quickly found, and all of them agreed that the plane exploded in midair. This evidence strongly confirmed hypothesis E.

In adding and testing consequents three general guidelines should be followed.

Consequents Should Bear on the Truth or Falsity of the Hypothesis Being Tested. Consider hypothesis E, to which a consequent has been added.

The crash was caused by an explosion aboard the plane	⊃	the airline is liable for damages.

This consequent does not bear on the truth or falsity of the hypothesis in question, because it cannot be determined whether the airline is liable for damages until the cause of the crash is known.

The Consequents Should Be Worth Testing. Whether or not a consequent is worth the time and expense of testing depends on its significance to the truth or falsity of the hypothesis and the importance of the issue.

For example, it is a consequent of hypothesis E that someone connected either with Flight 629 or with one of its passengers might have had training in the use of high explosives at some time in the past. But the number of people to whom this consequent applies, along with the time span it covers, would make a test both expensive and time-consuming. Furthermore, the results would prove little. That one or another of the people referred to in the consequent did have such training would not significantly increase the probability that there was an explosion, nor would the absence of such training show that no explosion had occurred.

When There Is Doubt That the Consequent Would Certainly Be True if the Hypothesis Is True, the Consequent Should Be Appropriately Qualified. The consequents added to hypotheses B and D are qualified by the words *may have been* and *might,* respectively. Failure to so qualify a consequent may lead us to attach too much significance to it.

Priorities in Testing Hypotheses

The order in which we test hypotheses is sometimes important. Four principles are useful in deciding which hypothesis to test first.

One of these is the principle of **urgency**. Sometimes we should test first the hypothesis that, if true, would require the most immediate attention. Suppose you smell smoke in your house and these hypotheses occur to you: (1) your house is on fire, and (2) your neighbor is burning trash. A prudent person would first test the hypothesis that the house is on fire.

If no hypothesis in our list requires immediate attention, then the principle of **economy** should prevail, and we should begin with the hypothesis that can be tested with the least expenditure of time or money. If your car stops dead in front of a filling station, you could test the hypothesis that your ignition system has burned out, but it would be both easier and quicker to test first the hypothesis that you have run out of gasoline.

A third principle is **likelihood**. If you are studying and the light on your desk suddenly goes out, you would be wiser to check the bulb first, rather than taking the lamp apart. If you are typing a paper at a computer terminal and the margins come out wrong, you would be better advised to make sure you entered the correct commands before having the printer checked. The reason is not just that in each case the first test is easier to perform, but also that the most common cause of light failure is a burnt-out bulb, and the most common cause of computer difficulty is operator error. When it is known that one hypothesis is by far the more likely explanation of some event, it is only sensible to test that hypothesis before less likely ones.

Finally, it is important to consider **bias**. When we have strong feelings about some of the hypotheses in our list, we would do well to check early the ones we like least. If we permit ourselves to give priority to the one we like best, we may unconsciously search for evidence to support it, and not test it fairly.

Repeating the Cycle

By testing hypotheses and assessing the results, we carry out phase 4 of the decision-making cycle. As we have seen, doing so often leads us to form new and better hypotheses. In complex investigations, however, it is sometimes necessary to repeat the five-phase cycle many times before a satisfactory solution can be found. Each repetition of the cycle usually produces new information that suggests new or revised hypotheses and narrows the investigation by eliminating other hypotheses.

At this point Stewart repeated the cycle. She returned to phase 1 and redefined her problem: to find the cause of the apparent explosion aboard Flight 629. To guide her search for additional information she skipped to phase 3 and formed two more specific versions of hypothesis E.

F. A fuel tank exploded.

G. Gasoline fumes seeped into a compartment of the plane and exploded.

Stewart added the same consequent to both hypotheses: evidence would be found in the wreckage. She then proceeded with a closer inspection of the wreckage, and added a new and startling proposition to her information.

9. Debris from the plane was scattered over six square miles.

In Stewart's frame of reference, proposition 9 diverged strongly from hypothesis F because she did not believe that the explosion of a fuel tank would scatter debris so widely.

To test hypothesis G, she added this consequent: the debris from a particular compartment would be more widely scattered than other debris. Stewart now had to consider the second guideline for adding and testing consequents. To test this consequent conclusively would require collecting and assembling much of the debris. Would testing this consequent be worth the enormous cost? While she pondered this question, Stewart continued to examine the wreckage and added a new proposition.

10. Some of the wreckage had an acrid odor like burned-out fireworks.

This proposition suggested a revision of

hypothesis G, as well as a consequent by which to test it.

H. An explosion was caused by high explosives in a compartment of the plane ⊃ residue from the explosives *might be* found in the debris.

Note that Stewart has observed the third guideline for adding and testing consequents. At this point she could not be certain that residue from high explosives could be found, because the debris was so widely scattered. She therefore qualified her consequent with *might be*. If she had not done so, and if she also failed to find any residue from high explosives, she might have rejected the hypothesis.

To test this consequent she continued to examine bits of the wreckage and added another proposition.

11. There was a grayish residue on some bits of debris.

Stewart thought the residue was from high explosives, but to be certain she had it examined by an explosives expert. The expert's report provided proposition 12.

12. The grayish residue in question was from dynamite.

Proposition 12 both suggested and strongly converged on a new hypothesis concerning the cause of the crash.

I. The crash was caused by an explosion of dynamite aboard the plane.

Although Stewart has added and tested many consequents, note that she has not yet completed phase 4 (testing tentative conclusions), for an essential part of this phase is an assessment of the degree of reliability demonstrated for her hypotheses. On the basis of the evidence in propositions 1–12, Stewart judged hypothesis I to be highly probable.

Stewart now proceeded to phase 5, the function of which is to decide whether the reliability of any tentative conclusion, as judged in phase 4, is sufficient in the circumstances. For Stewart the question was whether she should now make a formal report to her chief. She decided that the degree "highly probable" was sufficient, and made her report. The problem now belonged to officials of the Civil Aeronautics Board, who had to judge for themselves the degree of reliability of hypothesis I and decide whether it was sufficient to justify calling in the Federal Bureau of Investigation. They too judged hypothesis I to be highly probable and decided that this degree of reliability was sufficient.

Procedures for judging the reliability of hypotheses are discussed in the next chapter, in which the case of Flight 629 is continued. Before reading it, however, you should complete the following exercise, which contains further information about the case and will give you some practice in forming hypotheses and adding and testing consequents.

Exercise 4

Problems 1–3. This exercise continues the case of Flight 629. Complete each item before reading beyond it.

1-2. Write two hypotheses to account for a dynamite explosion aboard Flight 629.

(a.) _____

(b.) _____

3. Write a third hypothesis, one that would be unpalatable to the president of the airline.

_____

Problems 4–8. These items refer to the following hypotheses.

J. Neither passengers nor crew were aware that dynamite was aboard the plane.

K. The dynamite came aboard the plane in a passenger's baggage.

4. Criticize hypothesis J in terms of the guidelines for forming hypotheses.

_____

5. Criticize hypothesis K in the same terms.

_____

6. Criticize the following as a consequent of hypothesis K: The baggage would have been put aboard in Denver.

_____

7. Criticize this consequent in the same terms: Collecting the fragments of the plane and fitting them into a mock-up would show that the explosion occurred in the compartment where baggage from Denver was carried.

_____

8. Criticize this consequent in the same terms: The passenger may have intended to blow open a bank vault.

_____

Problems 9–11. These items refer to the following new propositions.

13. A crew of forty collected fragments from the plane and took them to Denver, where experts fitted them into a mockup of the plane.

14. The general manager of engineering of United Air Lines examined the mockup and said that the center of the explosion was in Pit 4, where baggage was carried.

9. Which of these propositions is itself a hypothesis? _____

10. What is the effect of proposition 13 on the reliability of proposition 14?

_____

11. On which hypothesis (J or K) does proposition 14 converge?

_____

Problems 12–13. These items refer to proposition 15 below.

15. Two hundred FBI agents searched the area of the crash and found a piece of an Eveready battery and a cog from a clock that might have been used as a timing device.

12. What revision in hypothesis K does proposition 15 suggest?

_____

13. Write a hypothesis to explain proposition 15 that would make it irrelevant to hypothesis K.

_____

Problems 14–16. The following propositions were brought to light by FBI agents who investigated the lives of the victims of the crash and their relatives.

16. Mrs. Daisy E. King boarded Flight 629 in Denver.

17. Mrs. King was going to Alaska to visit a married daughter.

18. Mrs. King's baggage weighed eighty-seven pounds, thirty-seven pounds over the limit.

19. Mrs. King was taken to the airport by John Gilbert Graham, her son by a former marriage.

20. At the airport Graham bought six air travel insurance policies on his mother.

14. Add an appropriate consequent to hypothesis L below.

    L. Graham put a bomb in Mrs. King's ⊃ _____

       baggage.

                                               _____

15. Which of the propositions above converge on hypothesis L?_____

16. Write a hypothesis that accounts for all the evidence so far presented without involving Mrs. King or John Graham in a crime.

Chapter 5

Testing Hypotheses

- **Rival Hypotheses**
- **Reliability and Probability**
- **Converging Propositions**
- **Diverging Propositions**
- **Criteria**
- **Evaluation and Decision**

Two weeks after the crash of Flight 629, the FBI accused John Gilbert Graham of murder. The FBI's accusation can be expressed as hypothesis M.

M. The crash of Flight 629 was caused by a bomb placed in the baggage of Mrs. Daisy E. King by John Gilbert Graham.

Was hypothesis M sufficiently reliable to justify this accusation? Let us examine the evidence and judge for ourselves.

Rival Hypotheses

When we judge the reliability of hypotheses, we confront the problem of induction. In order to explain the phenomenon under investigation, a hypothesis must go beyond the evidence at hand. Thus the evidence cannot be used to provide a deductive proof for the hypothesis; it can only make the hypothesis more or less

probable. And there is always the danger that some other hypothesis may in fact be the correct one. Consider some of the evidence for hypothesis M.

1. About eleven minutes after takeoff, Flight 629 exploded in midair and crashed.

2. All forty-four persons aboard were killed.

3. In the opinion of experts, the crash was caused by an explosion aboard the plane.

4. A grayish residue was found on fragments from the inside of the plane.

5. Experts identified the residue as the by-product of an explosion of dynamite.

6. FBI agents who searched the area of the crash found a part of a battery and a cog from a clock, both of which could

have been used in a timing device for a bomb.

7. Mrs. King was taken to the Denver airport by John Gilbert Graham, her son by a former marriage.

Hypothesis M goes beyond the evidence in these propositions, which contain no direct evidence that Graham put a bomb in Mrs. King's baggage. Yet hypothesis M puts these propositions into a picture that explains them. It explains why the plane crashed, why a grayish residue was found on fragments from the inside of the plane, why part of a battery and a cog from a clock were found in the area of the crash, and how Graham could have put the bomb in his mother's baggage. The question at issue is whether hypothesis M is the *true* explanation of the evidence now in hand. Perhaps there are other hypotheses that would explain the evidence as well or better.

This question leads us to one of two essential steps in judging the reliability of a hypothesis. We should always form as many **rival hypotheses** as possible that might reasonably explain the relevant facts. Hypotheses are rivals when at most one of them can be true. Hypotheses M and N (below) are rivals: both could be false, but only one can be true.

N. The bomb that destroyed the plane was put in an engine compartment by an employee who was angry with the airline.

Hypotheses are not rivals merely because they differ. Hypothesis M–1 (below) and hypothesis M are not rivals: both could be true, for M–1 is a more specific version of M.

M–1. The crash of Flight 629 was caused by a time bomb made of dynamite and placed in the baggage of Mrs. Daisy E.

King by John Gilbert Graham before Mrs. King left for the airport.

Rival hypotheses formed for the purpose of testing hypotheses should bear on the main issue. Since the main issue for the FBI at this point is whether Graham is guilty of murder, as many rival hypotheses as possible should be formed to explain the crash of Flight 629 without involving Graham in murder. If we consider only the evidence in propositions 1–7, it is easy to think of another rival for M and N.

O. The crash of Flight 629 was caused by a time bomb placed in the baggage of a passenger other than Mrs. King by someone other than Graham or an employee of the airline.

We now have three rival hypotheses: M, N, and O.

The second essential step is to assess the relative reliability of the rival hypotheses. It is neither necessary nor desirable to perform each step separately, but both steps must be completed.

Reliability and Probability

Especially in inductive contexts, the concept of reliability is closely related to that of probability. The word *probable* signifies an intricate concept having to do with the nature of evidence. As we will use it, the term **probability** means the degree of likelihood that a proposition is true, based on the evidence in hand. In many cases, the probability that a statement is true is also an assessment of the reliability of the statement, that is, the degree to which we may trust it. We will see later that it is sometimes possible to calculate mathematically the degree of probability that a statement is true. In most practical circumstances, however, this is not possible; we have to be content with a rough estimate of probability rather than a mathematically precise one. Even so, it is easy to distinguish nine different degrees of reliability that a proposition may have.

1. **Certain.** This term is reserved for propositions and conclusions about which there can be no possible doubt, as with the truths of deductive logic and mathematics. This degree of reliability never occurs with inductive arguments. When an argument is deductive and valid, however, its conclusion is to be regarded as certain relative to the evidence in the premises. In other words, if the premises are true, then the conclusion must be true.

2. **True beyond reasonable doubt.** All reasonable doubt is eliminated. Suppose that when you go out in the yard to get the morning paper the newsboy is just passing on his bicycle and throws one that lands right at your feet. The dateline on the paper reads "Saturday." You turn on the radio and hear the announcer finish a commercial about a sale at a supermarket which "will continue through today, Saturday." Your mother seems to think it is Saturday, as does the mail carrier, and a check with the telephone operator and the local police indicates they are of the same view. There is still room for doubt. All of the sources could have combined to perpetrate a hoax by convincing you that it is Saturday when it is really Friday. But such a doubt is not reasonable.

3. **Highly probable.** The evidence is strong but does not eliminate all reasonable doubt. It would be highly probable that it was Saturday if you had only the first two pieces of evidence cited above. This is the degree of reliability Lauren Stewart assessed for the hypothesis that the crash of Flight 629 was caused by an explosion of dynamite aboard the plane.

4. **Probable.** The weight of evidence is favorable but not as strong as 3. Suppose that you have only the evidence of the newspaper. It's still probably Saturday, although the newsboy may have thrown yesterday's paper by mistake.

5. **Indifferent.** Our ignorance as to whether the statement in question is true is complete, since the evidence we have is as strong for the statement as against it.

6. **Improbable.** The weight of the evidence is negative in about the same degree as 4 above (probable) is positive.

7. **Highly improbable.** The weight of the evidence is strongly negative, but not sufficient to eliminate any reasonable doubt that the proposition is false.

8. **False beyond reasonable doubt.** The weight of the evidence is sufficient to eliminate any reasonable doubt that the hypothesis is false.

9. **Certainly false.** This phrase is reserved for cases where there is no possibility that the proposition is true.

Clearly, matters of judgment will be involved in deciding which of these degrees of reliability attaches to a hypothesis. This does not mean, however, that the matter is an arbitrary one, for various considerations may aid us in the assessment. For example, other factors being equal, the more general a hypothesis, the more likely it is to be true. Hypothesis M is specific, for it accuses John Gilbert Graham. N and O are general. N accuses an unidentified employee of the airline, and O accuses an unidentified person who could be anybody except Graham or an employee. But although general hypotheses are more likely to be true than specific ones, they are usually less useful. Hypotheses N and O would not solve the FBI's problem. If our evidence were limited to propositions 1–7, we should rate hypothesis O to be indifferent, N to be improbable, and M to be highly improbable. Fortunately for the soundness of our decisions, we can usually find evidence that raises the reliability of some hypotheses and lowers the reliability of others.

Converging Propositions

As we noted in Chapter 4, one such form of evidence is a converging proposition, or a proposition that raises the reliability of a hypothesis by being in line with what we would expect if the hypothesis is true. Converging propositions vary widely in **significance**, that is, in their effect on the reliability of the hypothesis in question. In situations like that of Flight 629, the degree to which a converging proposition increases the reliability of a hypothesis cannot be calculated exactly. The best we can do is make a reasoned guess based on knowledge in our frame of reference. Since no two persons have identical frames of reference, some disagreement must be expected.

The significance of a converging proposition can always be brought into focus in the way shown in the last chapter—by using it as both the consequent and the minor premise of a hypothetical syllogism, the antecedent of which is the hypothesis in question. Once we have become thoroughly familiar with the hypothetical syllogism, we can take a short cut simply by constructing a hypothetical proposition in which the antecedent is the converging proposition and the consequent is a statement that the hypothesis in question is true. Consider proposition 3 in relation to hypothesis M.

Converging Proposition		*Hypothesis True*
In the opinion of experts the crash was caused by an explosion aboard the plane	⊃	Hypothesis M is true.

The reliability of the hypothetical proposition thus formed is a measure of the significance of the converging proposition. Actually proposition 3 converges equally on all three rival hypotheses. It raises the reliability of all three rivals by making it less likely that some other hypothesis is the true explanation, but it does nothing to change the relative reliability of M, N, and O.

The number as well as the significance of converging propositions is important, for the effect of converging propositions is cumulative to the extent that the propositions do not overlap. It is ordinarily not the weight of a single proposition that demonstrates any high degree of reliability for a hypothesis, but rather the weight of a number of converging propositions. Converging propositions are somewhat like the threads with which the Lilliputians tied Gulliver. Gulliver could have broken any single thread with a twitch of his little finger, but the network of threads rendered him helpless. Consider the following group of propositions.

7. Mrs. King was taken to the Denver airport by John Gilbert Graham, her son by a former marriage.

8. Mrs. King boarded Flight 629 in Denver.

9. Mrs. King's baggage weighed eighty-seven pounds, thirty-seven pounds over the limit.

10. At the airport Graham bought six air travel insurance policies on his mother.

The significance of each of these propositions, considered individually, is low. Collectively, however, they begin to form a network of circumstantial evidence. Propositions 7 and 8 suggest that Graham had an opportunity to put a bomb aboard the plane, proposition 9 suggests that the bomb was in Mrs. King's baggage, and proposition 10 suggests a motive.

Diverging Propositions

Considerable differences in the reliability of rival hypotheses are apt to result from diverging propositions, which, as we have seen, fail to accord with what we might expect if one or another hypothesis is true. Diverging propositions, like converging ones, vary widely in significance. Consider proposition 11, which diverges from hypothesis N.

11. The explosion occurred in Pit 4 (a baggage compartment).

The significance of a diverging proposition can be brought into sharp focus by constructing a hypothetical proposition with the antecedent the diverging proposition and the consequent a **null hypothesis**—a statement that the hypothesis in question is false. The reliability of the resulting proposition is the measure of the significance of the diverging proposition.

Diverging Proposition		*Null Hypothesis*
The explosion occurred in Pit 4	⊃	it is *not true* that the bomb that destroyed the plane was put in an engine compartment by an employee who was angry with the airline.

The significance of proposition 11 can now be seen to be high, for it seems highly improbable that the bomb was moved from an engine compartment to Pit 4.

A hazard in interpreting diverging propositions should be carefully avoided. Hypothesis N, like many hypotheses, is composed of several subhypotheses: (1) the plane was destroyed by a bomb, (2) the bomb was placed aboard the plane by an employee who was angry with the airline, and (3) the employee placed the bomb in an engine compartment. Proposition 11 virtually demolishes the third subhypothesis, for it is difficult to think of any way the explosion could have occurred in Pit 4 if the bomb had been placed in an engine compartment. Proposition 11 does not diverge at all from the subhypothesis that an angry employee placed the bomb aboard the plane, for he or she could have put it in Pit 4. It would therefore be a mistake to abandon this subhypothesis because of proposition 11. When a proposition diverges mainly from a subhypothesis, the other subhypotheses should be salvaged by excising the questionable element.

N-1. The bomb that destroyed the plane was put aboard by an employee who was angry with the airline.

The number, as well as the significance, of diverging propositions must be considered, for the effect of diverging propositions, like that of converging ones, may be cumulative. Consider propositions 12 and 13, which diverge from hypothesis O that someone other than Graham or an employee placed the bomb.

12. The FBI investigated the lives of all passengers boarding the plane in Denver and, except for Mrs. King, found nothing to incriminate them or their relatives.

13. Pit 4 contained only mail and baggage put aboard in Denver.

These propositions in combination reduce the reliability of hypothesis O to a low level. Proposition 12 tends to eliminate all the passengers who boarded the plane in Denver except Mrs. King, and proposition 13 tends to eliminate all the others. Note that the same proposition may converge on one hypothesis and diverge from another. Proposition 13 diverges from hypothesis O and converges on hypothesis M.

Criteria

Suppose we could be certain that we had formed all the rival hypotheses that could reasonably explain the phenomenon we are investigating and that we had available full and completely reliable information for testing all of them. If so, we could be certain which hypothesis is the right explanation, for our set of hypotheses would have to include the correct one, and the evidence would eliminate all the others. Obviously, these conditions can never be completely fulfilled. Our inability to think of another hypothesis that explains the relevant facts does not prove that there is none. In situations like the case of Flight 629, there is no way to know the number of possible hypotheses. Consider hypothesis O. We could form many

specific versions of O for the thirty-nine passengers aboard, for their relatives and acquaintances, and even for people not connected with the passengers. The problem of uncertainty about whether all reasonable rival hypotheses have been formed points up the fact that failures in creative thinking can thwart a correct assessment of rival hypotheses as easily as failures in critical thinking. For example, a person who lacks skill in creative thinking might accept hypothesis M with less evidence, simply because he or she cannot think of rivals.

As for the information we use to test hypotheses, it is of course subject to error and inaccuracy, as we will see more fully in the next chapter. But even when our evidence is excellent, its significance can be wrongly assessed. Human judgment is always involved when we assess the reliability of conclusions. When the reliability of a hypothesis is at issue, one's judgment is particularly subject to influence from the personal point of view. For example, a loyal employee of the airline would be inclined to rate hypothesis M higher than would a relative of a passenger: if M is true, the airline is blameless; if N–1 is true, the airline may be liable for heavy damages. Thus individuals can be expected to differ in rating the reliability of hypotheses. Careful attention to the following criteria increases our objectivity and thereby improves the soundness of our decisions.

The Number and Significance of Converging Propositions. Propositions converging on a hypothesis raise its reliability and lower the reliability of its rivals. Suppose the evidence supporting hypotheses M, N–1, and O is equal in significance. If so, each hypothesis would have the same chance of being true. A converging proposition that raises the probability that hypothesis M is correct would correspondingly lower the reliability of the others. Furthermore, the greater the number and significance of converging propositions, the more difficult it is to form rival hypotheses. Propositions 11 (The explosion occurred in Pit 4) and 13 (Pit 4 contained only mail and baggage put aboard in Denver) limit the suspects to those who could have put a bomb in baggage or mail put aboard in Denver. Thus the number and significance of converging propositions is an indirect indicator of how close we have come to forming all reasonable rival hypotheses.

The Number and Significance of Diverging Propositions. In proportion to their total significance, diverging propositions not only lower the reliability of the hypotheses from which they diverge but also raise the reliability of rival hypotheses.

The Reliability of Evidence. Any doubt about the reliability of a converging or diverging proposition reduces its significance. The reliability of propositions must be judged by appropriate standards. Most of the propositions used as evidence in the crash of Flight 629 were reports of observations made by investigators. Others recorded the opinions of experts as to various facts of the case. Standards for judging the reliability of both these types of evidence will be described in the next chapter.

Note that doubt about the reliability of a converging or diverging proposition affects the reliability of a hypothesis in proportion to the significance of the proposition. Consider proposition 14 in relation to hypothesis M.

14. In the opinion of a chemist, the dynamite was manufactured by Du Pont.

If we learned that proposition 14 is false, the effect on hypothesis M would be negligible, for the maker of the dynamite is not significant. In contrast, if we learned that proposition 13 (Pit 4 contained only baggage and mail put aboard in Denver) is false, the effect would be much greater, for this proposition is an important strand in the evidence supporting hypothesis M.

Completeness of the Evidence. As we have noted, a hypothesis may be composed of subhypotheses. These subhypotheses may be like links in a chain in that the hypothesis as a whole is no stronger than the weakest subhypothesis. Thus the evidence cannot be considered complete unless all subhypotheses are adequately supported. Hypothesis M is a case in point, as it is composed of three subhypotheses: (1) the crash was caused by a bomb, (2) the bomb was in the baggage of Mrs. Daisy E. King, and (3) the bomb was placed in Mrs. King's baggage by John Gilbert Graham. On the basis of the evidence now in hand, the first subhypothesis can be rated true beyond reasonable doubt. It has neither rival hypotheses nor diverging propositions, and the converging propositions are numerous and significant. In contrast, the third element should not be rated higher than probable. It has two rival hypotheses (N–1 and O), and the total significance of its converging propositions is low. Thus at this point hypothesis M as a whole should not be rated higher than probable.

Precision of the Evidence. One of the reasons why proposition 11 (the explosion occurred in Pit 4) is so significant is that it specifies an exact location in the baggage storage area of Flight 629 in which the explosion occurred. This kind of precision in the information by which we test hypotheses is invaluable, both in eliminating rival hypotheses and in prompting more accurate formulations of hypotheses with which it converges. Precise evidence is especially important in scientific contexts, where the consequents by which hypotheses are tested are frequently quantitative predictions about phenomena. For example, in formulating his laws of planetary motion, the astronomer Johannes Kepler made use of the observations of Tycho Brahe, which he knew to be exceedingly exact. Eventually, Kepler was led to the correct hypothesis that the planets move in elliptical orbits rather than circular ones, as had previously been supposed. But for the confidence he was able to place in the evidence Brahe had provided, such a result would have been impossible.[1]

Unexplained Evidence. Hypotheses should be formed to account for all possibly relevant items of evidence because a proposition carelessly ignored as irrelevant may be the key to the problem. Once the truth has been established beyond a reasonable doubt, it is easy enough to determine whether a proposition is relevant. Until then, however, there is no positive test for relevance, for a proposition is relevant or irrelevant only in terms of a hypothesis. Consider proposition 15.

15. Flight 629 waited twelve minutes in Denver for a late passenger.

The only way to test this proposition for relevance is to form and test a hypothesis to which it is relevant. One such hypothesis is that someone delayed the passenger in order to get an opportunity to put a bomb in his baggage. The FBI investigated the late passenger and added another proposition.

16. No evidence was found to connect the late passenger with the bomb.

Thoroughness of the Investigation. The more thorough the investigation the more likely it is that all relevant evidence has come to light. More than two hundred FBI agents investigated all aspects of the crash of Flight 629. It is unlikely that significant evidence remained undiscovered. The thoroughness of the investigation is the primary criterion in judging the significance of propositions stating that no evidence of something was found. Proposition 16 is a case in point. If the investigation of the late passenger had been cursory, this proposition would have had little significance. As it happened, however, the investigation of the late passenger was thorough enough to make it unlikely that he was connected with the bomb.

Possibility of Unformed Rival Hypotheses. Any doubt that all reasonable rival hypotheses have been formed reduces the reliability of at least one rival. For until we are certain that we have formulated the correct hypothesis, we cannot have full confidence that one or another of the alternatives known to us is correct. Suppose, then, that we are working with hypotheses M, N–1, and O. If there is reasonable doubt that these three are the only possible rivals, we must reduce the reliability of at least one of them to account for this doubt. Most likely, we will reduce the reliability of all three, since we do not yet know what the unformulated hypothesis is. The number and significance of both converging and diverging propositions, the completeness of the evidence, unexplained evidence, and the thoroughness of the investigation are all indicators of whether all reasonable rival hypotheses have been formed. In the case of Flight 629, all these indicators are posi-

---

[1] For more on this case, see Arthur Koestler, *The Sleepwalkers* (New York: Grosset and Dunlap, 1963).

tive. The probability is very high that one of the three rival hypotheses, M, N–1, and O, is true.

Reliability of Rival Hypotheses. The reliability of any hypothesis should be judged in terms of its rivals. It would be theoretically possible to prove a hypothesis to be true beyond reasonable doubt without a single converging proposition, if we could prove beyond reasonable doubt that we had formed and eliminated all possible rivals. By the same token, no rival hypothesis should be rated true beyond reasonable doubt as long as a single rival remains with a rating higher than false beyond reasonable doubt. On the basis of the evidence presented so far, including that in the previous chapter, hypothesis M is weak only with respect to the completeness of the evidence implicating Graham. Unfortunately for Graham's longevity, there was more evidence.

17. Mrs. King was the only Denver resident who boarded Flight 629 in Denver.

18. According to his wife, Graham said that he had surreptitiously placed a "Christmas present" in Mrs. King's baggage.

19. According to an employee of an electrical supply company in Denver, Graham bought a timing device a few days before the crash.

20. According to a merchant who knew Graham when he was a boy, Graham bought twenty sticks of dynamite three days before the crash.

21. Graham had no legitimate reason for having dynamite.

22. Graham had an impressive criminal record.

23. Graham lied about a number of details when he was being questioned by the FBI.

All these propositions converge on hypothesis M and only on M. Even though the investigation was thorough, no propositions that diverged from M came to light. No unexplained items of information remained. There was no reason to question the reliability of the propositions converging on M. There are no propositions that converge on rivals N–1 and O that do not also converge on M. We are now justified in rating hypotheses N–1 and O false beyond reasonable doubt and hypothesis M true beyond reasonable doubt.

This outcome may seem surprising inasmuch as the evidence we have considered is for the most part circumstantial rather than direct. We have no testimony from eyewitnesses who saw Graham construct a time bomb or place it in his mother's baggage. Yet this case serves to demonstrate just how strong a case can be constructed from evidence that is largely circumstantial. The testimony of witnesses is not always reliable. They can err in identifying a person or lie about an identification because they are already convinced of the person's guilt or innocence and want to see a corresponding verdict. Moreover, courtroom experience indicates that when witnesses do decide to lie they often prefer a big lie to a little one. An intelligent witness may be afraid to lie about details, especially when unaware of how much is known about them, lest he or she be charged with perjury. An unintelligent witness may tell a big lie and still tell the truth about details because he or she does not realize their significance. Thus, when circumstantial evidence is extensive and sound procedures are employed to determine its significance, the case that results may be more reliable even than one based on eyewitness testimony.

Evaluation and Decision

A few months later Graham was tried for murder in the first degree. The primary problem facing the jury was to decide whether to find him guilty. To reach a solution they had first to complete phase 4 and judge for themselves the reliability of the state's hypothesis that he committed the crime. Presumably the jury completed phase 5 (evaluation and decision) deductively. The law in effect provides two major premises: (1) if the evidence is judged sufficient to remove any reasona-

ble doubt that the state's hypothesis is true, then the defendant must be found guilty; (2) if there is a reasonable doubt, the defendant must be acquitted. The jury judged the state's hypothesis to be true beyond reasonable doubt and found Graham guilty. The sentence was death. Graham's attorney appealed the verdict to the Supreme Court of Colorado, which upheld the verdict and ordered the execution of the sentence.

Phase 5 is often more complex than in the Graham case. We must often act in situations in which our hypotheses have only a low degree of reliability and in which there are many actions we can take. We shall discuss procedures for dealing with such situations in Chapter 12.

Exercise 5

Problems 1–5. In May of 1927, Charles Lindbergh made aviation history when he flew nonstop from New York to Paris in his monoplane, *Spirit of St. Louis*. But the great fame and wealth he gained from this flight led to personal tragedy. In March 1932 Lindbergh's two-year-old son was kidnaped from the Lindbergh home in New Jersey and murdered; only after a ransom of $50,000 had been paid was the child's body found. The kidnap-murder and the trial of Bruno Richard Hauptmann, who was executed for the crime in 1936, may have received more publicity than any other crime of the thirties. To this day not everyone is convinced Hauptmann was guilty. Suppose that you are foreman of the jury. According to the instructions of the judge, Hauptmann is guilty of murder in the first degree if he participated in the crime, even though he may not have killed the child himself. The state's hypothesis is that Hauptmann did participate in the crime. The jury's problem is deciding whether the evidence presented in the trial is sufficient to justify rating the state's hypothesis true beyond reasonable doubt. The following evidence has been introduced by the prosecution.

1. A wood technologist testified that a ladder found under the nursery window was made by a skilled carpenter (which Hauptmann was). **2.** The technologist testified further that wood in the ladder was dressed by a plane found in Hauptmann's garage.

3. He testified further that a piece of wood in the ladder was cut from a board in the floor of Hauptmann's attic.

4. Another expert testified that nails in the ladder were made by the same machine as nails in a box in Hauptmann's garage.

1. Which of the above propositions converges most significantly on the hypothesis that Hauptmann made the ladder?

   _____

2. Write a rival for the above hypothesis that also explains propositions 1–4.

   _____

   _____

3. Rate the reliability of your rival hypothesis, using the terminology defined in Section 2 of this chapter.

   _____

4. Write a rival hypothesis that explains propositions 1–4 without involving Hauptmann in the crime.

   _____

   _____

5. According to which criteria is the evidence (propositions 1–4 only) weak with respect to the state's hypothesis?

_____

_____

Problems 6–7. Additional evidence introduced by the prosecution included:

    5. Prints of feet wrapped in some kind of cloth were found on the ground near the foot of the ladder. Hauptmann's feet were small enough to have made these prints.

    6. A rung on the ladder was broken.

    7. Marks on the ground indicated that the kidnaper might have injured his leg.

    8. Hauptmann was walking with a cane some weeks after the crime.

6. How significant is the combination of propositions 5–8 for the subhypothesis that Hauptmann used the ladder in the crime?

_____

_____

7. Write a rival for the state's hypothesis that explains propositions 1–8 without involving Hauptmann in the crime.

_____

_____

Problems 8–11. As the trial progressed, additional evidence was introduced.

    9. The ransom notes were apparently written by a German.

    10. Hauptmann was born and reared in Germany.

    11. Paper found in Hauptmann's home was identical to paper used in the ransom notes.

    12. Handwriting in the ransom notes appeared to be disguised. A sample of Hauptmann's handwriting appeared to be disguised in the same way.

    13. The following words misspelled in the ransom notes were similarly misspelled in Hauptmann's diary: "tit" for "did," "ouer" for "our," "note" for "not," and "boad" for "boat."

    14. Two handwriting experts testified that Hauptmann wrote the ransom notes.

    15. A handwriting expert introduced by the defense testified that Hauptmann did not write the ransom notes.

8. Which propositions in this group diverge from the subhypothesis that Hauptmann wrote the ransom notes?

                                         _____

9. Rate the reliability of the subhypothesis that Hauptmann wrote the ransom notes.

_____

10. What effect would rating this subhypothesis false beyond reasonable doubt have on the state's hypothesis?

_____

_____

11. What effect would rating this subhypothesis true beyond reasonable doubt have on the state's hypothesis?

_____

_____

Problems 12–14. Evidence presented by the defense included the following proposition.

    16. The baby's nurse committed suicide a few weeks after the kidnaping.

12. Write a hypothesis to which proposition 16 is relevant that is a rival for the state's hypothesis.

_____

_____

13. Write a subhypothesis to which this proposition is relevant that would converge on the state's hypothesis.

_____

_____

14. Write a hypothesis explaining this proposition that makes it irrelevant to the case.

_____

_____

Problems 15–16. Still further evidence presented included the following.

    17. Dr. J.F. Condon, who acted as intermediary, testified that he sat on a bench in a cemetery and talked with a man who presented the baby's nightgown as evidence that he was the kidnaper.

    18. Dr. Condon testified that at a later meeting in the cemetery he gave this man $50,000 in bills, the serial numbers of which had been recorded.

    19. Dr. Condon identified Hauptmann as the man he met in the cemetery.

20. A taxi driver testified that Hauptmann was the man who gave him a dollar to deliver a note to Dr. Condon.

21. Lindbergh testified that Hauptmann's voice was that of the man in the cemetery.

22. Dr. Condon testified that he gave his address and a privately listed telephone number to the man in the cemetery.

23. This address and telephone number were found scribbled on the back of a closet in Hauptmann's house.

24. Hauptmann said he found the address and number in a newspaper ad.

25. The address and number had not been published either in a newspaper or in the telephone directory.

26. Nearly $15,000 of the ransom money was found under a board in Hauptmann's garage.

27. After the ransom money was delivered, Hauptmann lost about $9,000 in the stock market, bought a new car, went on expensive trips, and quit his job (federal agents estimated that about $35,000 was spent in these and other ways).

28. Hauptmann testified that a man named Fisch gave him the money.

29. Hauptmann testified that he loaned Fisch $2,000.

15. Which of the propositions in this group (17–29) converge on a subhypothesis that Hauptmann was the man in the cemetery?

_____

16. Which of the propositions in this group diverge from this subhypothesis?

_____

17. Write a rival for the state's hypothesis that explains all evidence presented without involving Hauptmann in the crime.

_____

_____

18. With respect to which criteria is the state's hypothesis now weak?

_____

19. Rate the reliability of the state's hypothesis based on the evidence presented.

_____

20. Rate the reliability of this hypothesis: No one but Hauptmann was involved in the crime.

_____

Chapter 6

Evaluating Evidence

- **Physical Conditions**
- **Sensory Acuity**
- **Technical Knowledge**
- **Degree of Objectivity**

- **Effects of Memory**
- **Corroboration**
- **Degree of Precision Required**
- **Evidence from Authorities**

We have now had a first look at both deductive and inductive contexts of thinking and at some of the important types of inferences that are employed in each context. As we have seen, one role of critical thinking is to evaluate these inferences. When we encounter a deductive argument, we must ascertain that the argument is valid—that the premises, if true, will guarantee the truth of the conclusion. When a conclusion is reached by induction, we must use critical thinking to determine the degree of probability conferred on the conclusion by the evidence contained in the premises. But critical thinking is not used only to assess the relationship between the premises and conclusions of arguments. Whether an argument is deductive or inductive, we must also consider the reliability of the evidence itself. For however satisfactory the relationship between the premises and the conclusion of an argument may be, no conclusion is

reliable if the evidence presented in the premises is itself unreliable. For years, for instance, scientists accepted theories about heredity that were based on the evidence of certain famous studies of resemblances between twins. Recently, however, the evidence of these studies has been determined to be fraudulent. As a result, the theories are open to question, not because they were reached by faulty reasoning, but because the evidence used as premises in the reasoning was fraudulent.

Let us consider, then, the problems of judging evidence. In so doing, we must bear in mind that, as in the case of judging conclusions for reliability, the practical question of the reliability of evidence is how much confidence we are justified in placing in it. As we will see, a number of factors need to be taken into account in answering this question.

The basic type of evidence that enters into arguments consists in what we may call **observation statements**, which are propositions that record or report perceptions. Whenever a scientist weighs something or takes its temperature, he or she is making an observation. When the scientist records the observed data, he or she is making an observation statement. In the same way, when a witness testifies in court that he or she saw the defendant leave the scene of a crime, the witness is making an observation statement, that is, reporting a perception he or she claims to have experienced. Observation requires more than the use of the sense organs; it demands also the interpretation of the sensory data. An observation begins with **sensation**, a complex process in which sensory stimuli are received by the sense organs and transmitted to the brain. If you look at the vapor trail of a jet plane, the light waves from the sky are received by the retinas of your eyes, and signals are transmitted to the brain. The image produced is a sensation. The next stage is the **interpretation** of sensation by the mind in terms of experience stored in the frame of reference. You **sense** the visual stimuli in the sky; you **perceive** or **observe** the vapor trail of a jet plane. You take a further step if you formulate your observation in an observation statement. When you do so, you express your interpretation of your sensation in words or other symbols. This step is necessary in order to communicate your observations to others, and it is also invaluable for putting observations to use in reasoning.

Though we may like to think our own observation statements are always reliable, we all know this is not the case. Errors may creep into observation at either of its two stages and they may also occur in reporting observations. Sensations may be inaccurate because of imperfections in sensory equipment. A witness to an auto-mobile accident who lacks normal depth perception may give a very misleading report of what happened, simply because he did not "see," or perceive, what would have been very apparent to another person standing in his shoes. A person with a certain type of colorblindness may not be able to tell by its color that the light is green and will have to look for other cues, such as the position of the light, to tell him when it is safe to enter the intersection. A person who says she has a "tin ear" may simply dislike music, but she may be unable to sense the harmonics and overtones of musical instruments.

We also make errors in interpreting what is sensed. Sensation can be interpreted only in terms of the frame of reference. When our frame of reference does not contain the knowledge necessary to perceive something for what it is, we are likely to perceive it to be something it resembles. If your frame of reference contained no knowledge of the vapor trails of planes, you would probably perceive the trail to be only a straight, narrow cloud. At the beginning of the space program, some psychologists feared that a moon landing would have a traumatic effect on the first astronauts to achieve it because the sensations might be so alien to the human frame of reference that they would be uninterpretable and the astronauts would be overcome by the barrage of incoherent data assaulting their senses. Fortunately, enough in the moon environment was similar to what the astronauts had experienced that they were able to interpret adequately. Another problem is that perceptions are often shaped by what we are looking for or thinking about. The sparkle of dew in the grass becomes the dime we are looking for. Deer hunters may perceive the movement of another hunter in the brush as that of the deer they are waiting for and fire away.

The verbalization of perceptions is also subject to error, because language is not an absolutely accurate vehicle for communicating observations. Moreover, our own ability with language may well be inadequate, especially when we encounter new experiences. If the language we use in describing a perception is vague, ambiguous, or inaccurate, then the observation statement will not be sharp and precise, no matter how accurate the perception may have been. A young child might witness a robbery and have a very accurate perception of the robber and the robber's clothing, but the child might lack the vocabulary to describe the perception clearly to the police.

Many of the problems of evaluating observation statements can be seen in a trial at law, where the testimony of witnesses may constitute all or most of the evidence. When a witness testifies that he or she saw the defendant leaving the scene of the crime carrying a smoking revolver, an intelligent jury will not accept the claim as truth without considering the possibilities that the witness might be lying and that the witness might not be capable of making the observation he or she claims to have made. Good lawyers are always careful to ensure that an inference by the witness does not slip into what is supposed to be an observation statement. The courts have evolved an elaborate code to guard against false or improper testimony. The code determines what kinds of testimony are acceptable as evidence, who may testify as a witness, how and when witnesses may testify, and how their testimony may be attacked through cross-examination. Most courts will not admit **hearsay evidence**—testimony based on what the witness heard others say—because such evidence is often unreliable.

The judge acts as referee in enforcing the rules of evidence, and he or she must be very careful since a questionable decision on the admissibility of a piece of evidence may be made the basis of an appeal for a new trial. The rules of evidence take volumes to cover, and even a superficial study of them will show that the courts have long been concerned with the problems of evaluation discussed here.

In evaluating the reliability of evidence, it is essential to distinguish observations from inferences. Editors have this distinction in mind when they tell new reporters to get the facts and leave the editorializing or interpretation to those who write the editorial page. In Chicago in 1982, a number of people were poisoned by Tylenol capsules that had been laced with cyanide and then placed on drugstore shelves. A reporter describing this case would be stating the facts if she gave the locations around Chicago where the poisoned capsules were found, the names and ages of the victims, and so on. But if she added that the poisoner was probably a Chicagoan with some grievance against a firm or a drugstore, she would be making inferences. The reliability of discourse that involves both observation statements and inferences must be judged by the standards of both. Henceforth, in discussing evidence of any kind we shall reserve the word **fact** for a proposition that has been demonstrated to be true beyond a reasonable doubt.

The degree to which we are justified in being confident that an observation statement is true depends on the conditions under which the observation was made and the ability of the observer. Before we accept *any* observation as correct, even our own, we should ask the following questions about it.

Physical Conditions

The first question is whether the physical conditions under which the observation took place were favorable. If you are sitting in the grandstand well to one side of home plate, your location is not as favorable for calling balls and strikes as is the umpire's. The coach at a football game is not in a good position to observe some aspects of the action, and he therefore stations an observer in the press box high above the field. The farther you are from an accident, the less reliable your perceptions of it will probably be. We should not expect to make reliable observations under unfavorable conditions.

Lawyers often use cross-examination to show that reliable perception was unlikely under the prevailing conditions. A famous anecdote describes how Abraham Lincoln won his first defense at a murder trial by this technique. The prosecution's case rested mainly on the testimony of a witness who swore he saw the defendant fire the fatal shot and then run away. In cross-examining this witness, Lincoln led him to testify to a number of details: that he was standing twenty feet or more from the defendant at the time of the shooting, that the shooting occurred in a wooded area, that he could see how the pistol was pointed, that the shooting occurred at night, that the nearest lights were candles three quarters of a mile away, that he saw the shooting by moonlight. Producing an almanac, Lincoln then demonstrated that the moon did not rise until several hours after the shooting. The witness broke down and confessed he had fired the fatal shot himself. Readers (and watchers) of Perry Mason stories know innumerable examples of dramatic cross-examinations showing why the witness could not have made the observation reported. Such ex-

amples are not rare in real life either.

Sensory Acuity

The second question is whether the observer had the sensory acuity necessary for the observation. What one individual sees sharply at a hundred feet another will see only as a blur. What one hears distinctly another will not hear at all. When unusual sensory acuity is necessary for an observation, an attorney will often ask his or her own witness questions designed to convince the jury that the witness really could see or hear what happened.

Of course, in scientific procedures where precise measurement is essential, instruments are used to aid the senses. A laboratory technician cannot estimate temperature and weight by feel or length by sight. In evaluating the reliability of scientific investigations that require exact measurements of weight, length, volume, and the like, the accuracy of the instruments used, as well as the sensory acuity of the observer, sometimes needs to be evaluated.

Technical Knowledge

The third question is whether the observer has the knowledge necessary to make his or her perceptions trustworthy. As we noted earlier, perception is affected by the frame of reference. A person with 20–20 vision watching a football game under ideal physical conditions cannot determine whether the linemen are charging properly unless his or her frame of reference includes the necessary technical knowledge of football.

As our world becomes more diversified and as knowledge expands so fast that we can keep up in only a very few areas at once, we depend more and more on specialists for observations that we cannot make ourselves. Laypersons cannot determine for themselves whether a tumor is cancerous but instead must rely on a pathologist's observation and judgment. Courts of law rely increasingly on expert witnesses as crime detection becomes more and more technical. Physicians, psychiatrists, ballistics experts, fingerprint experts, and handwriting experts are frequently called to give testimony. Without their assistance, the average person sitting on the jury would be unable to determine whether the defendant is insane, whether the fatal bullet came from the defendant's gun, whether the ransom note was written by the defendant, or whether the prints left at the scene were made by the defendant or the plumber. Often these experts are aided in their observations and inferences by instruments. The problem of evaluating evidence becomes increasingly complex.

Degree of Objectivity

The fourth question is whether the observer is objective. We noted in Chapter 1 that certain factors decrease our objectivity; these factors also may affect our observations.

Prejudice is one factor that affects the accuracy of observations. Racial prejudice or prejudice against members of a particular nationality may cause an individual to see things that are not there. He or she may even interpret a simple greeting as a threat. Sexual stereotyping may cause an observer to expect certain behavior patterns in the opposite sex so strongly that words and actions are automatically understood as examples of the expected behavior.

The accuracy of observations is also affected adversely by **emotion**. To a person who is afraid, a snake looks bigger than it is; in rough, open water, the skiff seems smaller than it is. A jealous lover continually misreads his or her partner's behavior. Much of this misreading will be faulty inference, but some misperception may also be involved. Under emotional stress a person is more susceptible to suggestion. If the stress is strong enough, the individual may become subject to hallucinations and delusions.

Our focus of **attention** also affects our observations. We do not perceive all the elements in a situation but tend to notice only those that interest us or attract our attention somehow. A holdup victim might notice only that the gunman took his or her valuable gold watch, and not that the robber had taken equally valuable items from the two patrons standing only a few feet away. A group of students walking into a dormitory room would all notice a blazing wastebasket, but, after the fire was put out, there might be no agreement among the observers as to what else they had seen.

Effects of Memory

A fifth question is whether the observer is likely to remember his or her perception accurately. We should never forget that memory is selective: we tend to remember some things and forget others.

The personal point of view is a strong factor in this selectivity. We tend to remember on the basis of how relevant the information is to us personally. Moreover, we tend to remember things that seem to support the self-concept and to forget instances that threaten it. As Nietzsche put it, "My memory says that I did it, my pride says that I could not have done it, and in the end, my memory yields." Thus an encounter with an authority figure in which we felt humiliated or "put down" may magically transform itself in memory into a session in which we gently but firmly told the policeman, or the dean, just what was what. Even if the stored information is nonthreatening, we may quickly forget it if we have no use for it. A student may cram for an examination and forget the material immediately thereafter, especially if the course is not in his or her major and the student doesn't at the moment see a future need for the information. Courses that you take in college will be of more benefit to you if you try to find a relevance to your life in the data or skills they cover.

Other things being equal, we tend to retain best the information we encounter most frequently. Propagandists and advertisers take advantage of this tendency; a one-minute television commercial may contain twenty repetitions of the product's name. When you go to the store to buy products you may not have purchased before—your first mops, brooms, cleansers, for example—you may choose brands whose names you remember simply because you have heard them frequently.

Again, other things being equal, we are likely to retain best the instances we have encountered most recently. Thus the spot just before the last five minutes of the television show is the most desirable time for a commercial. Political propagandists sometimes use this principle of recency by reserving for the day before the election some argument particularly damning to the opposition in the hope that the undecided voters will go to the polls with this argument fresh in mind.

Additionally, other things being equal, we tend to remember instances that were vivid, either in their content or in their language. For this reason advertisers and propagandists do their best to come up with vivid, memorable slogans. When Winston first came out with "Winston tastes good like a cigarette should," grammarians were irate because the line used *like* for *as*. But even their pique was good for Winston because it made an already memorable slogan stick even more firmly in the public mind. When Adlai Stevenson lost the Presidential election to Dwight Eisenhower in 1956, one commentator theorized that among uninformed voters the names contributed to the outcome. "Everybody had 'I like Ike' buttons. What could poor Stevenson come up with? 'I'm madly for Adlai?' "

We should never forget another human tendency—to imagine that we remember what we have forgotten or never perceived. Because both memory and perception are selective, we can rarely recall accurately all the details of an episode. When we try to recall them, imagination tends to fill in the gaps. Witnesses to an accident who are unable to remember important details may supply them from their imagination. They remember what *should* have happened in terms of their dominant impression of the episode, even when it did not happen that way. This tendency helps to explain why eyewitness accounts often conflict.

The vagaries of memory help us in our tendency to romanticize the past, to think of it as "the good old days." We remember that there were fewer cars on the road and that the local merchants knew our names. We forget polio epidemics and the dangers of all contagious diseases before antibiotics. Especially in the area of economics, we tend to idealize the past. Those of us who remember when a Coke cost a nickel forget how hard we had to work to get that nickel.

Corroboration

The sixth question is whether the observation has been sufficiently corroborated by other observers. The chance of error in observation is so great that, even though an observation seems to meet all of the tests we have so far discussed, it usually should not be accepted as true beyond reasonable doubt unless it has been corroborated by other observers.

In general, when the observations of two or more persons correspond, two principles apply: (1) the higher the reliability of each observer, judged by the criteria discussed above, the higher the reliability of the observation; and (2) within limits, the larger the number of observers, the higher the reliability. These principles, although useful, must be applied with caution. An unknown factor in the situation or a common error in the frames of reference of the observers could make a thousand seemingly reliable witnesses wrong whereas one seemingly unreliable witness could be right.

Degree of Precision Required

We saw in the last chapter that precise evidence can be especially valuable in testing and refining hypotheses. By the same token, insufficiently precise evidence may have little bearing on the reliability of the propositions it is used to support or attack. When we use observation statements in making decisions, therefore, we must consider the degree of precision required for the observation to have legitimate bearing on our conclusions. In some situations, a rough approximation is sufficient. For example, suppose a witness in a jury trial testifies that he saw the defendant put around fifty drops of poison in food later eaten by the deceased. Suppose, further, that ten drops of this poison is lethal. In this situation it doesn't matter much whether the defendant actually put forty-five or fifty-five drops of poison into the food, since the issue is whether the amount put into the food was lethal.

In other situations, a very high degree of precision in observation is essential. For example, the Greeks believed (correctly) the following hypothetical premise:

The earth moves $\supset$ a closer star would show
through space,   parallax[1] with respect
 to a more distant star.

But they wrongly assumed that they would perceive parallax if it were present. Because their equipment for stellar observation was inadequate, the Greeks were unable to detect parallax between stars of different distances from the earth. Therefore they concluded (by a valid argument) that the earth does not move through space. For this and other reasons, Ptolemy's geocentric theory prevailed for centuries. Even after Copernicus advanced the heliocentric theory in the six-

---

[1] Parallax is the apparent movement of other objects that is perceived when you yourself are moving. The closer the object, the more pronounced the effect. That is why when you are driving the trees closest to the road appear to go by more quickly than those further away. In astronomy, the earth's movement makes the stars appear to move slightly during the course of the year, and again the effect is more pronounced for the nearer ones. In general, parallax is measured by determining the difference in the angle at which a star appears in the sky at six-month intervals. But it is easier to measure the angle for a nearby star simply by observing how it changes position relative to a more distant, relatively motionless one.

teenth century, the great Danish astronomer Tycho Brahe rejected the idea that the earth moves because he was unable to measure any parallax of the stars in spite of the fact that his instruments were capable of measuring angles to within one minute of arc. It was not until 1838, over two hundred years after Galileo first used the telescope for astronomical purposes, that the telescope and accessories were sufficiently refined to enable Friedrich Bessel to measure stellar parallax. The angle he measured was about one seven-thousandth of a degree!

Evidence from Authorities

If a person has serious heart disease and must decide between a bypass operation and drug treatment, the choice he makes may be a crucial one. But he probably won't be able to base it on the evidence in medical journals as to the relative effectiveness of the two methods, for he will lack the technical knowledge this requires. Instead, he will have to rely on the advice of his doctors. When we lack the expertise to interpret and judge the primary evidence ourselves, we are forced to rely on authorities. We decide our stand on whether to have surgical procedures, whether to support antipollution legislation, whether to fight a proposed nuclear dumping site, and other important issues on the basis of the opinions of others. Some authorities, however, are more trustworthy than others. Therefore, we must learn how to evaluate authorities as well as evidence. Three questions may help determine whether or not to accept an authority's opinion.

1. How Much Does the Individual Know About the Specific Questions at Issue? We are likely to assume that, because someone has achieved renown as an authority in one field, he or she must be competent in other fields as well. But however recognized a nuclear physicist may be in the field of nuclear physics, it would be foolish to accept his or her opinion in another area—politics, for instance—as being more reliable than that of another person with comparably little political knowledge. Advertisers often take advantage of our respect for the famous by trying to convince us that a product tastes better or cleans better or makes a car run more smoothly because some well-known sports hero says it does. When we consult an authority, it is his or her competence in the field in question that matters. Although there is no completely reliable rule for determining competence, there are some helpful clues. A list of the individual's publications on the issue is useful; if one has published widely and in reputable places, one should be granted some credibility. Degrees held and institutions granting them may be clues. A Ph.D. degree from a reputable institution is not a guarantee of competence in the field of the degree, but it is evidence of competence. Sometimes membership in learned or professional societies, such as the American College for Surgeons, confers some credibility. For a really careful analysis of an authority's reliability, we might look to see what other authorities in the field think about his or her research.

2. Is the Individual Objective About the Matter in Question? Courts of law long ago recognized that the testimony of a witness is less reliable if the witness has a financial or emotional interest in the matter under discussion. If personal interest may make factual testimony unreliable, it may have an even more adverse effect on the reliability of opinions. In important matters, it is well to try to discover the authority's own peculiar interest, if any, and weigh this factor in with others in deciding how much to value his or her opinion. Civilian and military authorities, for example, may differ on how much money is needed for national defense. It cannot be concluded that either gives a deliberately false image of the situation in order to promote a point of view, but as human beings they tend to see what they want to see. They may automatically pick up the facts that support their position and overlook the facts that weaken it. Emotional interests may be even more powerful than financial interests. For example, an authority who gains fame for a certain conclusion may be reluctant to give up his or her position should further research weaken its reliability.

3. What Do Other Authorities Conclude About the Matter? Suppose your doctor tells you that the disc trouble which is causing your severe back pain can be alleviated only by surgery. Without extensive medical knowledge you cannot yourself evaluate fully either the reliability of the doctor's observations or the inferences involved in the diagnosis. You should, of course, consult other physicians—not, as many people do, to find one who will give you a more palatable diagnosis but to help you determine the reliability of the original one. Experts often reach different conclusions from the same evidence. In such cases, the best criterion of reliability is a majority opinion of qualified authorities. Clearly, a conclusion reached independently by three medical specialists is a

sounder basis for decision than the conclusion of only one.

Generally, we should not accept the views of authorities uncritically, for authorities are not infallible. The history of science shows that many theories once accepted universally have now been demonstrated to be false beyond a reasonable doubt. Many propositions we now accept as true beyond a reasonable doubt will eventually meet the same fate. We are constantly subjected to a barrage of theories presented as "information." Often the best way to evaluate such material is to trace it back to its original source and then try to weigh both the credibility of the authority and the evidence itself.

For instance, in a supermarket checkout line, you might pick up a tabloid and read, "Marijuana Smoking Causes Males to Grow Breasts!" This "information" might interest you, but you might have doubts, especially since the tabloid might also have recently announced the invention of the perpetual motion machine and the landing of Martians in Grosse Point, Michigan. If the article makes reference to a specific medical journal, you might track down the article through the journal's index, and read it. When you do, it is important to pay careful attention to the strength of the claims the author is making. Often you will find that the author is claiming only that the conclusion of the article is probably true, not that it is a fact. You should consider the evidence and conclusions according to the appropriate criteria and find out what you can about the investigator. Then you will have more solid grounds for accepting or rejecting the conclusion.

Exercise 6

Problems 1–5. Classify the italicized passages according to the key list below.

Key List

A. Sensation   **B.** Observation

C. Observation Statement   **D.** Inference

1. As Professor Thomas peered through his telescope at the night sky, he *saw a light source* he could not identify in the constellation Gemini.

2. He saw it again the next night but at a slightly different location relative to the stars of Gemini. The thought dawned on him: *a new planet!*

3. Unable to contain his excitement, he rushed to the phone and called his wife. *"I've discovered a new planet!"* he shouted into the receiver.

4. The next morning, Professor Thomas read in the college newspaper that *the comet Zwilling was presently visible in the constellation Gemini.*

5. *"What I saw must have been the comet,"* he thought dejectedly.

6. Describe an instance of erroneous perception from your own experience.

Problems 7–15. Use Key List A below to indicate all grounds on which there is reason to question the italicized observation statement. Assume that the observers are not deliberately lying. Use Key List B to rate the reliability of the observation statement. Exclude your personal opinion of the issue and base your judgment solely upon the criteria in Key List A.

Key List A
1. Physical conditions were not favorable.
2. The observer lacked the necessary sensory acuity.
3. The observer lacked the necessary technical knowledge.
4. The observer was not objective.
5. The observer is not likely to have remembered the observation.
6. There is insufficient corroboration.
7. The observation is not sufficiently accurate.

Key List B
1. Certainly true
2. True beyond reasonable doubt
3. Highly probable
4. Probable
5. Indifferent
6. Improbable
7. Highly improbable
8. False beyond reasonable doubt
9. Certainly false

7. Spectator, who was sitting in the end zone, speaking of a play which occurred at midfield: *"I clearly saw Smythe,* who was playing left tackle, *deliberately break the arm of our quarterback* during that pileup."

A. _____

B. _____

8. American, aged twenty, who has never been in a foreign country: "I saw the man yesterday when he came into the room. *He was a Korean, about forty years old."*

A. _____

B. _____

9. Ph.D. in physics: *"The painting which was sold to the plaintiff is not a genuine Rembrandt."*

A. _____

B. _____

10. Man who wears a hearing aid: "I was sitting on my front porch, and the defendant was sitting in his car at the curb. *I heard him whisper to his companion, 'Here's where we pick up some fast bread.'* "

A. _____

B. _____

11. Mechanic: "When I lubricated the defendant's car about a month ago, *I noticed that the tire on the left front wheel was not new."*

A. _____

B. _____

12. Palmist: "I was looking out of my window, across the street from the defendant's house. I happened to be watching his window. *I saw him put a .32 automatic in his pocket.* I never approved of his doings. Always thought he had bad vibes."

        A. _____

        B. _____

13. Medical examiner, testifying in a murder trial in which the defendant could not have been at the scene of the crime earlier than 11:00 P.M.: *"My examination showed that the deceased was shot sometime between 10:30 P.M. and midnight."*

        A. _____

        B. _____

14. Unidentified radio commentator: *"The convention was a farce from beginning to end. The platform and candidates were picked in advance by the bosses, and the delegates were mere puppets on a stage, moved by strings pulled by the fat cats."*

        A. _____

        B. _____

15. Prison barber: "When I gave Joey his haircut, *I noticed that his hair had recently been bleached."*

        A. _____

        B. _____

Part Two

Probability and Induction

Chapter 7

Calculating Probabilities

In Chapters 4 and 5 we discussed one type of inductive inference, the purpose of which is to find a hypothesis that correctly explains a particular event or fact. Our chief purpose here in Part Two will be to examine some further types of inductive inference, which have in common the feature that instead of covering just one case they generalize from relatively few cases to cover many. In dealing with these types of induction, it is helpful to be familiar with the basic elements of the mathematical theory of probability. The aim of this chapter, therefore, is to introduce you to some simple ways of calculating the probability that an event or combination of events will occur or be found to have occurred.

If those investigating the crash of Flight 629 had delayed their decision until they could infer by a valid argument from completely reliable premises that

John Gilbert Graham was responsible for the explosion, Graham would never have been indicted. Instead they had to use inductive methods and settle for a conclusion judged to be true beyond reasonable doubt. The great majority of the decisions we all must make are like that of the investigators, since we must base them on conclusions that are not completely reliable. Indeed, even an assessment of a conclusion as true beyond reasonable doubt is available only in relatively few cases. It is rare, for example, that a college student can judge it to be true beyond reasonable doubt that he or she will succeed in a certain curriculum. One's choice of a major usually has to be made on the basis of lower assessments of reliability. There is nothing irrational about this sort of choice, provided the fourth phase of the decision-making cycle (testing tentative conclusions) includes a reasonable method for assessing the reliability of tentative conclusions.

We have already seen one way of making such assessments. If we understand the reliability of a proposition as the probability that it is true, careful procedures like those followed by the investigators of the crash of Flight 629 will often permit confident assessments of reliability. So far, however, we have only considered assessments that take the form of estimates, or reasoned guesses that the degree of confirmation conferred on a proposition by the evidence falls within one of nine categories ranging from certainly true to certainly false. Let us now consider a case where it is possible to be a lot more precise than this and provide a mathematical measure of reliability. You will remember from Chapter 5 that probability is defined as the degree of likelihood that a proposition is true, based on the evidence in hand. We will first consider the second part of this definition—"based on the evidence in hand."

Suppose we toss a silver dollar behind the sofa, where we cannot see it, and we hear it settle to the floor. For all practical purposes it is a fact that the dollar is resting heads up or tails up, but which? Without crawling behind the sofa and looking, what evidence do we have in hand? Let us assume that we tossed the coin without skill or intention to make it fall in any certain way and that the dollar is balanced. These two assumptions constitute our "evidence in hand."

With this evidence, what is the *degree of likelihood* for the proposition "The coin fell heads up?" The two assumptions constituting our evidence in hand give us no reason whatever for thinking that the dollar is any more likely to fall heads up than tails up. Our proposition, then, is equally likely to be true or false. In point of fact, of course, it is either true or false, and if we

could only see the coin, we would know which. But in that case we would be using different "evidence in hand."

Theoretical Probability

When we assess the probability of an event in the above manner, we determine its **theoretical probability.** Determining theoretical probability is actually a deductive procedure: the probability of the event is reached through deductive reasoning from relevant assumptions made *before* experience. Theoretical probability is to be distinguished from **empirical probability**, which is determined by inductive reasoning *from* experience. We will have more to say about empirical probability below. Here, it is important to note that when theoretical probability is being decided the results are no better than the assumptions used as premises. In the above case, for example, one of the assumptions is that the coin is balanced, so that there is not more reason to think it will come up heads than tails, or vice versa. Had this assumption been incorrect, the conclusion that the two results were equally probable would have been mistaken.

In general, the more specific the assumptions we are able to make in determining the theoretical probability of an event, the more closely our conclusion will conform to the actual probability of the event in question. Suppose three persons are sitting around a table on which there is a deck of cards. What is the probability that the top card in the deck is the ace of spades? The answer will differ according to each person's knowledge of the deck. Suppose the first person has just come into the room and knows nothing about the deck except that it appears to be a standard one. On the basis of this evidence in hand, he can only assume that the deck is standard and that the ace of spades is as likely as any other of the fifty-two cards to be on top. Thus to him there is one chance in fifty-two that the ace of spades is on top. Suppose that the second person has been playing with the deck and knows that all twenty-six black cards are on top but does not know which of these is the ace of spades. On the basis of her evidence in hand, she can assume that the ace of spades is as likely to be on top as any of the twenty-six black cards and that the chances are one in twenty-six that it is on top. Suppose, further, that the third person saw the top two cards placed on the deck and noticed that both were black, and both were aces. For this person, there is one chance in two that the top card is the ace of spades.

Each of the three people in this example reaches a different conclusion as to the likelihood that the ace of spades is the top card in the deck. Each is justified in the conclusion he or she draws, for each conclusion is based on the most accurate assumptions the particular individual could reasonably make about how the deck is arranged. But the third person's conclusion—that there is an even chance that the top card is the ace—most accurately approximates the true state of affairs. Thus theoretical probability is commonly determined on the basis of assumptions, and the results achieved are no more reliable than the assumptions themselves.

The Master Formula

Theoretical probability is usually expressed in terms of the following formula:

$$\text{theoretical probability} = \frac{\text{number of favorable possibilities}}{\text{total possibilities}}$$

When we toss our silver dollar, the total possibilities are two: heads up and tails up. By **favorable possibilities** we do not necessarily mean possibilities to be desired but rather the possibilities whose probability we are trying to determine. In calculating the probability that the dollar fell heads up, there is only one favorable possibility, heads up, and the theoretical probability would therefore be expressed by the fraction $\frac{1}{2}$. When we draw a card from a standard deck, the total possibilities are the number of cards in the deck, fifty-two. If we are calculating the probability of drawing the ace of spades, there is only one "favorable" possibility; thus the probability of drawing this card would be expressed by the fraction $\frac{1}{52}$.

Single Events

The theoretical probability for any single event, such as tossing *one* coin or drawing *one* card, is computed by filling in the master fraction: favorable possibilities divided by total possibilities.

What is the probability, for example, of drawing an ace purely by chance from a standard deck? The total possibilities are the fifty-two cards. The favorable possibilities are the four aces. Thus the probability is $\frac{4}{52}$, or $\frac{1}{13}$.

What is the probability of rolling an even number with one die? The total possibilities are the six sides of the die. The favorable possibilities are the three sides with an even number of dots. Thus the probability is $\frac{3}{6}$, or $\frac{1}{2}$.

Conjunctions of Independent Events

Once we know the probability for single events, the mathematical theory of probability enables us to calculate the likelihood that they will occur in conjunction. Thus if we know the probability of getting heads when we toss one coin, we can calculate the likelihood of getting two heads if we toss two coins or toss the same coin twice. To compute the probability that two or more events will occur in conjunction, we use the **rule of multiplication:** the probability that two or more events will occur together is the product of the fractions expressing the probability of each event.

In order to apply this rule correctly, however, we need to ascertain whether the occurrence of one of the favored events would affect the probability of the other or others. If so, then the fractions used in the multiplication have to be varied to account for the change. In the case of a pair of coin tosses, this is not a problem. Whether either of the tosses results in heads has no bearing whatever on whether the other toss will have the same result. Events like this are said to be **independent:** the occurrence of either one has no effect on the probability that the other will occur.

Suppose then that we toss both a penny and a nickel. What is the chance of both falling heads up? You will find it easier to see how the rule of multiplication applies to this case if you first consider a list of all the **permutations** for the pair of events, that is, all the possible combinations of outcomes that may occur.

Table 7.1

Penny	Nickel
Heads	Heads
Heads	Tails
Tails	Heads
Tails	Tails

As you can see, each of the two possible outcomes for the penny must be considered twice, because whether the penny comes up heads or tails, the nickel can still go either way. Thus there are four cases to be considered. In only one of them, however, do both coins come up heads, so there is only one chance in four that the outcome for the **conjunction** of events will be favorable. That is, the probability of two heads is ¼.

This is exactly the result achieved by the rule of multiplication. To apply it, first visualize tossing the penny, and count the total possibilities. There are two: heads up and tails up. Now write this as the denominator of a fraction, as shown below.

(Total possibilities:)
$$\frac{}{2}$$

Now ask yourself how many of these total possibilities are favorable, that is, meet the requirements of the problem. In this case only one (heads up) will do. Now write in *1* as the numerator of the fraction. Thus the probability that the penny will fall heads up is ½. Now repeat the procedure for the nickel. There are two possibilities, heads up and tails up, only one of which will do. Thus the probability that the nickel will fall heads up is also ½. The two events must both happen if the requirements of the problem are to be satisfied. The next step in the procedure, then, is to multiply the two fractions.

1st Event *(Penny Heads Up)*		*2d Event* *(Nickel Heads Up)*		*Both Events*
½	×	½	=	¼

As you can see, this is just the result we got above by considering all possible outcomes for the conjunction of events. Multiplying the fractions produces the correct answer because in only half the cases where we toss a penny will it come up heads, and in only half of those cases will we get another heads by also tossing a nickel. The probability of two heads is therefore one-half of one-half, or one-fourth.

Now test your understanding so far by computing the probability of guessing the correct answers on the first two questions of an objective test purely by chance. Assume that each question has five answers, only one of which is correct. Fill in the blanks below and then check the answer at the end of this chapter.

1st Question Right		*2d Question Right*		*Both Questions Right*
No. right answers:		No. right answers:		
———————	×	———————	=	———————
Total possible answers:		Total possible answers:		

Conjunctions Involving Dependent Events

Suppose we have a bag containing three white marbles and two black ones. If we draw a marble from the bag, the probability that it will be black is ⅖, since that is the ratio of favorable cases to the total number of possibilities. Suppose also that, after withdrawing one marble, we place it back in the bag, shake the contents thoroughly, and draw again. What is the probability of getting a black marble on this draw? The answer is again ⅖, for these events are independent, just as those studied above. But now suppose that

instead of replacing the first marble we lay it aside and draw again. Clearly, the probability of getting a black marble on the second draw is now different, for there are now only 4 marbles in the bag, and only one of them is black. In this case, the two events are not independent. Rather, the second is dependent on the first, for the chances of getting a black marble on the second draw depend on what color the first marble turned out to be. An event is **dependent** on one or more prior events when its probability is affected by them. In computing probabilities for combinations that involve dependent events, we must observe the **rule of dependency**: when events are dependent, the fractions expressing their probability must be adjusted for the effect of previous events.

Keeping this in mind, let us compute the probability that two marbles drawn by chance from the bag described above will be black. First, we must write the probability fraction for the first marble drawn. As mentioned above, it is ⅖. The five marbles in the bag represent the total number of cases and of these two are favorable, that is, black.

As for the fraction representing the probability for the second event, it is easy to see that its denominator must be 4, since once the first marble has been removed only four possibilities will remain. But what about the numerator? If the first marble chosen was favorable, it will be 1, since only one black marble remains. But can we assume that the first draw was favorable? The answer is not only that we can but that we *must*, for we are interested only in the case where the combination of draws produces two black marbles. This can only occur if the first draw is favorable, leaving only one black marble available for the second draw. Thus we observe the **rule of favorability:** in adjusting the numerator for a dependent event, always assume the events on which it depends were favorable. The numerator for the second fraction is therefore 1, and the probability that the second marble drawn will be black is ¼. Since both events must occur for the overall outcome to be favorable, the two fractions are multiplied, as shown below.

1st Event *(Black Marble)*		*2d Event* *(Black Marble)*		*Both Events*
⅖	×	¼	=	2/20

Thus the probability for a combination of two black marbles is 2/20 or 1/10. A table of all possible outcomes of the two draws will bear this out. In this case constructing the table of all of the permutations is more difficult since we must remember that there are not just two possible outcomes for each draw but five for the first and four for the second. Moreover, the four possibilities for the second draw differ for each possibility on the first draw. If we label the white marbles W1, W2, and W3, and the black B1 and B2, the full range of possibilities is as follows:

Table 7.2

First Draw	Second Draw
B1	B2
B1	W1
B1	W2
B1	W3
B2	B1
B2	W1
B2	W2
B2	W3
W1	B1
W1	B2
W1	W2

First Draw	Second Draw
W1	W3
W2	B1
W2	B2
W2	W1
W2	W3
W3	B1
W3	B2
W3	W1
W3	W2

You can see that there are exactly twenty possible combinations, of which only the first and fifth are favorable. However, tables like this are of use only for determining theoretical probabilities and they become more difficult to construct as more complex problems are encountered. Thus the method of multiplication is to be preferred, and should be mastered.

Now test your understanding by computing the solution to this problem. Suppose you have seven cigars, three of which contain small charges of black powder that will explode when the cigar is smoked. What is the probability that you can select purely by chance two cigars that are not explosive? Fill in the blanks below and then check the answer at the end of this chapter.

1st Event		*2d Event*		*Both Events*
Nonexplosive cigars:		Nonexplosive cigars:		
———————	×	———————	=	———————
Total cigars:		Total cigars:		

Now try another problem. Suppose a mail order catalogue offers slacks in three colors, red, yellow, and blue, but specifies that the customer cannot choose the color. On a different page the catalogue offers sweaters in the same colors but with no choice. Suppose you would like to order a sweater and a pair of slacks, but you abhor the combination of red slacks and a yellow sweater. What is the probability that you would get this particular combination? Write out the fractions before peeking at the answer at the end of the chapter.

Now try a subtle problem using the same situation. What is the probability that slacks and sweater will be of the same color?

Alternative Possibilities

We have already seen that situations involving probability are frequently such that more than one possible outcome is considered favorable. Thus if we wish to determine the probability of getting an even number in a single throw of a die, there are three favorable possibilities out of a total of six, for three of the six faces of a die have even numbers. The three even-numbered faces represent alternative possibilities for a favorable outcome of the throw. They need not all come up, and indeed only one face can come up in a single throw of the die. Rather, the three favorable possibilities count as alternatives in that the outcome of the throw will be favorable provided the die stops with one or another of the even-numbered faces up. We have also seen that when more than one possible outcome is considered favorable for a single event, the probability that the event will be favorable can be determined by filling in the master fraction with the sum of favorable possibilities as the numerator and the total of all possibilities as the denominator. The proba-

bility of getting an even number in one throw of a die is $\frac{3}{6}$ or $\frac{1}{2}$.

When we employ this procedure, we reach the same result that would be achieved by following a general principle for dealing with alternative possibilities, the **rule of addition**: the probability that one or another of a set of alternative possibilities will occur is the sum of the fractions expressing the probability of each alternative. It is easy to see that the result of following this rule is the same as the one reached above by filling in the master fraction. The probability for each favorable alternative, that is, each even-numbered face of the die, is $\frac{1}{6}$. Thus the calculation is as follows.

Face	*Probability*
two	$\frac{1}{6}$
four	$\frac{1}{6}$
six	$\frac{1}{6}$
Total	$\frac{3}{6} = \frac{1}{2}$

Determining the probability of a favorable outcome for a single event by filling in the master fraction is, then, equivalent to calculating the result using the rule of addition. Simply filling in the fraction is, of course, the easier procedure for single events, but it is usually necessary to rely on the rule of addition when we are concerned with alternative possibilities for conjunctions of events, which require a more complex calculation. For example, what is the probability that if we toss two coins both would land with the same face up? Here too we are concerned with alternative possibilities, for there are two favorable outcomes: both heads or both tails. The difference is that each favorable outcome concerns a conjunction of two events. When this is the case, we must first determine the likelihood of each favorable outcome and then add the fractions together. The calculation is as follows.

Favorable outcome	*Penny*		*Nickel*	*Probability*
Two heads	½	×	½	= ¼
Two heads	½	×	½	= ¼
Total				2⁄4 = ½

The procedure for solving problems involving alternative possibilities for conjunctions of events, then, is to **compute the probability for each favorable possibility and then add the probabilities**. This procedure is not completely divorced from that of filling in the master fraction. Its effect is the same as what we would achieve by filling in the fraction with the number of favorable permutations for the conjunction of events as the numerator and the total number of permutations as the denominator. Shown below is the full set of permutations for tossing two coins, with the probability for each. You will notice that the total of the probabilities is 1. This signifies that it is certain that one or another of the permutations in the table will occur.

Table 7.3

Penny	Nickel	Probability
Heads	Heads	¼
Heads	Tails	¼
Tails	Heads	¼
Tails	Tails	¼
Total		4⁄4 = 1

Were it not for the inconvenience of constructing tables of permutations for all complex cases, we could handle alternative possibilities for conjunctions of events simply by filling in the master fraction with the favorable permutations di-

vided by the total of permutations. In many cases, however, this procedure is too complicated to warrant the effort. Suppose you are in a Binomian jail. The jailer hands you a die and offers you a deal: you give him all your valuables in return for two rolls of the die; if on either roll you get a six, he will allow you to escape; otherwise you stay in jail without your valuables.

It is easier to deal with this case if we assume that, instead of rolling one die twice for the jailer, you roll two dice once. The problem then is simply to determine the probability of your getting at least one six. We could use a table of permutations, but that would be both inconvenient (there are thirty-six possible outcomes) and unnecessary. Instead, let us consider the alternative types of outcome that are relevant to your problem. Essentially, there are four, of which three are favorable. You will win if you get a six on both dice, a six on the first only, or a six on the second only; and you will lose if you get no sixes. The probabilities for these four alternatives are given in the table below.

Table 7.4

Outcome	First Die		Second Die		Probability
1. Six on both dice	⅙	×	⅙	=	1⁄36
2. Six on first only	⅙	×	⅚	=	5⁄36
3. Six on second only	⅚	×	⅙	=	5⁄36
4. No sixes	⅚	×	⅚	=	25⁄36
				Total	36⁄36

The effect of this table is to summarize, in terms relevant to your problem, what a complete table of permutations would show. The first line gives the probability of getting two sixes. Each of the next two lines gives the probability of getting a six on exactly one of the two dice, and having one of the other five numbers turn up on the other. The last line gives the probability that a number other than six will turn up on both dice. All the possibilities are covered, as the total probability of $^{36}/_{36}$ shows. Since Outcomes 1, 2, and 3 give you at least one six, they are the favorable alternatives. The probability of getting at least one six then, is the total of the probabilities for each of these three patterns: $^1/_{36} + {}^5/_{36} + {}^5/_{36} = {}^{11}/_{36}$. Thus, by using the rule of addition for this example, we are able to solve the problem in installments. Different kinds of favorable outcomes are considered separately and their probabilities calculated; totaling the probabilities gives the correct result.

In dealing with alternative favorable possibilities for conjunctions of events, then, we must first determine the probability of each favorable alternative and then add the probabilities. In determining the probability for each alternative, we must of course remember to adjust probabilities for single events that are dependent on others. The problems considered above all involve independent events, but adjustments must always be made when particular events are dependent. Once they have been made, however, the probabilities of each favorable alternative for the conjunction of events can safely be added together; no further adjustment is needed.

Now test your understanding by computing the probability of getting two heads and one tails (not necessarily in that order) by tossing three coins. Write out your computation for all the alternative favorable outcomes and add them together before checking the answer at the end of the chapter.

Now try this problem. What is the probability of getting at least two heads by tossing three coins?

Applications

The principles of theoretical probability have innumerable applications in practical situations. An especially interesting one is in measuring the practical value, or utility, of proposed actions. For example, suppose you are offered a ticket in a charity raffle of an automobile worth $10,000. The ticket costs five dollars and four thousand of them are to be sold. What is the probable worth of the ticket? We can apply theoretical probability, for it is reasonable to assume that the raffle is honest and that is all we need in order to assign a theoretical value to each ticket. Using this assumption as our evidence in hand, we can assign each ticket the same value, since each ticket has an equal chance of winning. The theoretical value of each ticket, then, will be $^1/_{4000}$ of $10,000, or $2.50. Under these circumstances, if you buy a ticket with the idea of investing $2.50 in a business proposition and donating $2.50 to charity, your reasoning is sound. But if you buy a ticket on the assumption that you are investing five dollars in a business proposition, your thinking is unsound, even if you should win the automobile, for on the basis of the evidence in hand your ticket is worth only $2.50.

Value can be assigned to actions in any situation where we can make reasonable assumptions about the likelihood of events. But we must be careful in making our assumptions. Suppose, for example, you operate a factory that cans orange juice. You have lost a gold watch worth $500, and you believe it has been "canned" somewhere in a batch of ten thousand cans of juice. You estimate the cost of opening these cans, including destruction of the product, to be 75 cents per can. Assuming that your watch is in one of the cans and that it is as likely to be in one can as another, what is the probable cost of recovering it by opening cans? You might find it in the first can you open, but to be certain of finding it, you would have to be prepared to open all the cans. On the basis of the evidence in hand, the watch is as likely to be in the last as in the first can. If it is in the first can, the cost is 75 cents. If it is in the last can, the cost is $7,500. The average of the two is slightly over $3,780. Thus, on the basis of your assumptions, it would be cheaper to buy a new watch. But before you do so, you had better examine your assumptions. First of all, you should not assume the cost of *not* finding the watch would be limited to the $500 for a replacement. If an irate consumer sues your company, the cost could be a lot higher. Moreover, there may be some method by which you could determine that the watch is more likely to be in one can than another. Perhaps shaking or weighing the cans would determine its location. Then only one can would have to be opened.

Though it is useful to be able to assess the value of an action in monetary terms, we can often get some idea of its value in terms of probabilities alone. Suppose, for example, that you are faced with a short test composed of five five-choice objective questions. The value of studying is obvious, for there are 3,125 permutations for the five answers on the test, only one of which is correct. Suppose you study well, and when you take the test you find that you know four of the answers, guaranteeing you a score of 80. You are, however, unable to decide between the five possible answers for the remaining question. Obviously, it is to your advantage to guess,

provided there is no penalty for doing so. For guessing gives you one chance in five of raising your score to 100. Suppose, on the other hand, that you do not study well, and find yourself knowing only two of the answers. Here, guessing is even more likely to be of *some* use, for the probability that you will miss all three of the remaining answers is $4/5 \times 4/5 \times 4/5 = 64/125$. This leaves a slightly less than even chance that you will get at least one of the three answers right. But guessing only one answer correctly gives you the undistinguished score of 60, and the probability of making more than one correct guess is quite slim. There are three combinations for two correct answers, the probability for each of which (ignoring the order of the answers) is $1/5 \times 1/5 \times 4/5 = 4/125$. The probability for guessing all three answers correctly is $1/5 \times 1/5 \times 1/5 = 1/125$. Adding the probabilities for all four alternatives yields a likelihood of only $13/125$ that you will guess more than one answer correctly, and it must be remembered that the chance of even one correct guess is less than $1/2$. Clearly, the best course of action in preparing for tests is to leave as little to chance as possible.

The Gambler's Fallacy

In applying the principles of probability to practical circumstances, it is important to avoid a common mistake. Many people seem to believe that there is something akin to a law of atonement in probability, whereby if a coin tossed 20 times has "misbehaved" by falling heads up only 6 times, it will sooner or later atone for its misbehavior by falling heads up more often than tails up. While coins might do this often enough to give an unwary thinker some instances to support his or her belief in such a law of atonement, there is no sound basis for it. A coin has no memory, no conscience, no desire to please. The explanation for the fact that coins, dice, and the like do seem to atone for their "misbehavior" is to be found in the tendency for disparities to be swallowed by large numbers. When a coin "misbehaves" by producing only 6 heads in 20 tosses, the disparity seems large; but if the coin "behaves" for the next 980 tosses, the total result would be 496 heads and 504 tails, at which point the disparity is small. No matter how often a coin has fallen heads up, the probability that it will fall heads up on the next toss is still ½—unless something other than chance is operating.

Empirical Probability

Computing the theoretical probability of events is actually a process of deductive inference. In it, the premises, which constitute our evidence in hand, consist of assumptions about events of the kinds in question. The computation itself is the inference, and the resultant probability is the conclusion. As with any inference, our aim in calculating theoretical probability is to produce a conclusion that is as reliable as possible. In this case, reliability consists in the resultant probability being the same as what we may call the "true" probability—the actual frequency with which favorable cases will be found in experience. Thus, if we calculate that the probability of rolling a twelve with a certain pair of dice is $\frac{1}{36}$, our conclusion will be reliable if a long series of rolls with the pair of dice in question will produce a twelve in an average of one out of 36 cases. And this frequency of favorable cases will in fact occur, provided the assumptions about the dice that were used as premises are complete and accurate and the computation is accurate.

In theoretical probability calcula-tions, the most important premise is usually an assumption that one possibility is as likely as any other. In the case of the dice, our conclusion that the probability of a twelve is $\frac{1}{36}$ is based on the assumption that each face of a die is as likely as any other to be on top when the dice come to rest after a roll. With most dice, this is a correct assumption to make. But unfortunately, especially for amateur gamblers, the assumptions of theoretical probability do not always apply to a given case. Dice have been known to be loaded, and card sharks have been known to stack the deck. When this happens, the frequency with which favorable cases actually occur over the long run will differ from what theoretical calculations call for. One's assumptions may have seemed reasonable and the calculations may have been accurate, but the theoretical probability turns out to differ from the true probability.

When computations of theoretical probability prove unreliable, empirical probabilities are often of use. Empirical probability differs from theoretical probability only in the kind of evidence used. In determining theoretical probability, our evidence in hand consists of assumptions about the likelihood of events that are made prior to experience with those events, such as the assumption that one face of a die is as likely to come up as any other, or that a coin is as likely to fall heads up as tails up. In determining empirical probability, the evidence in hand is experience with the events in question. Suppose, for example, that in a series of five thousand rolls with the pair of dice in our example, twelve comes up five hundred times. If so, then the empirical probability of getting a twelve on the next roll would be $\frac{500}{5000}$, or $\frac{1}{10}$. Given the large number of rolls on which this result is based, the conclusion that the dice are loaded would have to be considered highly reliable.

When we work with empirical probabilities, the interpretation of the master fraction changes slightly: instead of dealing with possibilities, we deal with actual cases drawn from past experience. In any given setting, the empirical probability of an event is determined by the number of favorable cases divided by the total number of cases included in our evidence in hand. Aside from this adjustment, the methods of computation for empirical probabilities are the same as those for theoretical probabilities. Once we have determined empirical probabilities for particular events, the probabilities for conjunctions of events and alternative events are calculated by the rules already given.

When we determine the empirical probability of an event, we must rely on a form of inductive inference in which we generalize from past experience. Thus when we conclude on the basis of five thousand throws that the probability of getting a twelve with a pair of dice is actually $\frac{1}{10}$, we are taking the five thousand cases constituting our evidence in hand as a reliable guide to what will happen in all future rolls of the same pair of dice. Obviously, there is an inductive leap here, and we will have more to say about the hazards of generalizing in the chapter that follows. Clearly, however, we want our conclusions about the empirical probability of events to be based on evidence that is likely to reflect the true frequency with which favorable events are likely to occur in the future. In particular, we want the cases that constitute our evidence in hand to be numerous enough for the true probability to emerge. For example, if you toss a coin ten times and it falls heads up eight of the ten times, the theoretical probability that it will fall heads up the next time is still $\frac{1}{2}$, on the assumption that heads up is

as likely as tails up. If, however, you use only your experience with the ten tosses as your evidence in hand, the empirical probability that on the next toss the coin will fall heads up is $\frac{8}{10}$. In a case like this, you would do better to trust the theoretical probability rather than the empirical probability.

Empirical probabilities are not used only to check the results of calculations of theoretical probability; indeed, that is not even their main use. There are many situations in which reliable assumptions about the likelihood of events are unavailable, and decisions must be based on empirical probability. Consider, for example, some of the decisions the promoter of a football bowl game must make. Suppose the bowl game is a new one, to be played in a stadium seating 100,000, and a week before the game only 10,000 tickets have been sold. Bad weather is likely to reduce the sale of tickets drastically. The promoter can, for a price, purchase rain insurance. To decide intelligently whether to buy the insurance, he cannot avoid estimating the probability that enough rain will fall at a time that will seriously reduce the sale of tickets. There are, however, no reliable theoretical assumptions on which to base the estimate. The best he can do is rely on weather forecasts as to the probability of rain or, if he wishes, attempt to assess the probability himself.

In either case the promoter will be relying ultimately on empirical probability. Computation of the probabilities of events like rain, illness, accidents, and victories in elections is nearly always based on empirical experience indicating the frequency of such events in the past, and the assumption that this experience accurately reflects the true probability of the events and hence will provide a reliable guide for the future. The assumption that empirical probabilities can be trusted in this way is, of course, often less reliable than assumptions of theoretical probabilities. First, past experience is rarely either complete or accurate. The most reliable fund of past experience for weather forecasting is provided by the records of the United States Weather Bureau, founded in 1891. But accurate records of rainfall going back another hundred years might well indicate different probabilities of rain for some situations. Second, some factor in the total situation may change and thereby change the probability that an event will occur. Many meteorologists believe, for example, that the large amount of carbon dioxide being released into the atmosphere from automobile exhausts and other sources is changing the climate of the world.

All the same, our promoter's best course of action would be to use a weather forecast based on empirical probabilities. Theoretical probabilities are simply unavailable in this case, and an intuitive guess as to the likelihood of rain would be far less trustworthy than a forecast based on past experience. Indeed, the use of empirical probabilities has done much to improve weather forecasting in recent years. Empirical probabilities are also used with great success by insurance companies in setting their rates. By surveying the frequency with which persons in various age groups will live, say, to age seventy, a company can determine how much it should charge as a monthly premium on a life insurance policy in order both to meet its responsibilities and to make a profit. The great advantage of empirical probabilities in this context is that they are responsive to new experience. If people in one generation tend to live longer than their parents, the charge for insurance can be adjusted accordingly. And if experience indicates that smokers are apt to live less long than nonsmokers, smokers can be charged a higher rate.

Intuitive Estimates of Probability

Both theoretical and empirical probabilities are meant as estimates of true probability, the latter being the actual frequency with which favorable cases will be found to occur in long-run experience. They are by far the most reliable means of assessing true probabilities. In certain cases, however, neither means is available. For example, suppose that near the middle of your first term in college you are incapacitated for two weeks by illness. Your problem is to decide whether to drop out for the remainder of the term. Suppose further that if you drop out now you can start afresh next term, but if you finish this term you must pass all four of your courses to stay in school. The danger that completing the term will put you out of school is certainly a relevant factor in your decision. But how great is the likelihood of this occurring? Theoretical means of telling are unavailable, and you probably do not have access to any empirical information as to the failure rate for students in your situation. In this sort of case, it might be worth your while simply to make intuitive estimates about true probabilities. A guess as to the overall probability of your passing all four courses would have little reliability. But you can take a more reasoned approach by estimating the probability that you will pass each course and then multiplying the fractions for each course. The result is still a guess, but it is likely to be more reliable than a simple, overall guess because the procedure forces you to take into account some of the separate factors involved.

It is a natural human tendency to overestimate the likelihood of combinations of events. For example, people asked to estimate the probability that their favorite football teams will win every game tend to rate the probability much higher if they merely make a single guess than if they estimate the probability of each game and multiply the fractions. Even when computing probabilities is not practical, it is helpful to remember the rule that the probability of two or more independent events occurring together is the product of the fractions expressing the probability of each event. The lower the probability of each event, the greater will be the difference between the probability of the single event and the probability of the combined events. For example, if the probability that you will pass each course is $\frac{1}{2}$, the probability that you will pass all four is $\frac{1}{16}$; but if the probability that you will pass each course is only $\frac{1}{4}$, the probability that you will pass all four is only $\frac{1}{256}$.

Degrees of Reliability

The introduction of mathematical probabilities, then, makes for considerably greater precision in assessing the reliability of statements than the simple intuitive use of the nine degrees of reliability discussed in Chapter 5. Even when mathematical probabilities are used, however, it helps to be able to speak of a statement as highly improbable or true beyond reasonable doubt. In the chapters to come, therefore, we will understand the nine degrees of reliability to reflect the ranges of probability indicated below. You should bear in mind that the particular ranges of probability given are somewhat arbitrary and

intended only for practical purposes.

Degree of reliability	*Probability range*
Certain	1
True beyond reasonable doubt	$\frac{999}{1000}$ up to but not including 1
Highly probable	$\frac{9}{10}$ to $\frac{998}{1000}$ inclusive
Probable	$\frac{501}{1000}$ to $\frac{899}{1000}$ inclusive
Indifferent	1/2
Improbable	$\frac{499}{1000}$ to $\frac{101}{1000}$ inclusive
Highly improbable	$\frac{1}{10}$ to $\frac{2}{1000}$ inclusive
False beyond reasonable doubt	$\frac{1}{1000}$ down to but not including 0
Certainly false	0

Answers to Self-Check Questions

Page 101. Two questions right: $\frac{1}{5} \times \frac{1}{5} = \frac{1}{25}$.

Page 102. Two nonexplosive cigars: $\frac{4}{7} \times \frac{3}{6} = \frac{12}{42}$ or $\frac{2}{7}$

Page 103. Red slacks and yellow sweater: $\frac{1}{3} \times \frac{1}{3} = \frac{1}{9}$. (Since you have no knowledge of the colors in stock, you have no reason for thinking that one color is more likely than another.)

Slacks and sweater of matching color: $\frac{3}{3} \times \frac{1}{3} = \frac{1}{3}$. (Since the problem does not state which color, all three colors are favorable. Thus it does not matter what color the slacks are, provided the sweater is of the same color.)

Page 105. Two heads and one tails: there are three alternatives.

Heads-Heads-Tails: $\frac{1}{2} \times \frac{1}{2} \times \frac{1}{2} = \frac{1}{8}$
Heads-Tails-Heads: $\frac{1}{2} \times \frac{1}{2} \times \frac{1}{2} = \frac{1}{8}$
Tails-Heads-Heads: $\frac{1}{2} \times \frac{1}{2} \times \frac{1}{2} = \frac{1}{8}$
$$\text{Total} \quad \frac{3}{8}$$

At least two heads: there is one additional alternative.

Three Heads: $\frac{1}{2} \times \frac{1}{2} \times \frac{1}{2} = \frac{1}{8}$
Two heads and one tails: $= \frac{3}{8}$
$$\text{Total} \quad \frac{4}{8} = \frac{1}{2}$$

Suggested Supplementary Reading

David S. Moore, *Statistics: Concepts and Controversies* (San Francisco: W.H. Freeman and Company, 1979), Chapter 7.

Exercise 7

Problems 1–11. These items refer to an objective test. Each question on the test has three choices, one and only one of which is correct.

1. What is the probability that choice three is the *correct* answer to question *one*?

   _____

2. What assumption was involved in your answer to the question above?

   _____

3. What is the probability that you can guess *correctly* the *first two* questions purely by chance?

Problems 4–11. Compute the probabilities of the events described. Assume that only chance is involved.

4. Guessing the *first* question *right* and the *second* question *wrong*. _____

5. Guessing *both* of the *first two* questions *wrong*. _____

6. Guessing the *first three* questions *right*. _____

7. Guessing the *first* question *right*, the *second wrong,* and the *third right*.

   _____

8. Answering *exactly one* of the *first two* questions *right*. _____

9. Answering *exactly one* of the *first two* questions *wrong*. _____

10. Answering *at least one* of the *first two* questions *right*. _____

11. Answering *at least one* of the *first two* questions *wrong*. _____

Problems 12–19. A playful friend has changed the labels on seven cans of the same size on your kitchen shelf. Compute the probability for each item below on the assumption that you select the cans you open purely by chance. The cans contain

Tomato juice	Creamed chicken
Prune juice	Beef stew
Orange juice	Lamb stew
Grapefruit juice	

12. The *first* can opened will contain *tomato juice*. _____

13. The *first* can opened will contain *juice*. _____

14. The *first* can opened will contain *tomato juice* and the *second* can *lamb stew*.

_____

15. The *first* can opened will contain *juice* and the *second* can *meat*. _____

16. The *first two* cans opened will contain *citrus juice*. _____

17. *Neither* of the *first two* cans opened will contain *citrus juice*. _____

18. The *first* can *but not the second* will contain *citrus juice*. _____

19. The *first* can opened will contain *either citrus juice or meat*. _____

20. Suppose you answer ten true-false questions purely by chance. According to the principles of probability, what is your most likely total score?

_____

21. Suppose that on a true-false test of one hundred items you guess the answers purely by chance. When you check your answers against the key, you find that you guessed the first ten right. Based on the principles of probability, what is your most likely total score?

_____

Chapter 8   Generalization

- **The Function of Generalization**
- **Hasty Generalization**
- **Defining the Problem**
- **Selecting the Sample**
- **Forming General Conclusions**
- **Testing General Conclusions**
- **Evaluation and Decision**

In everyday discourse, the word *generalization* is normally used to refer to propositions in which all members of a group are said to have a common characteristic. An example would be, "All wolves are carnivores." In this book we will call such propositions *general statements, general propositions,* or, when they occur as the conclusions of arguments, *general conclusions.* The term *generalization* will be used to refer to a particular type of inductive reasoning. We make a **generalization** whenever we make an inference to a conclusion about a group of instances without observing all instances in the group. By **instances** we mean things of a kind. Instances may be objects, people, ideas, or actions that have some factor in common. Automobiles, freshmen at Wysacki University, political philosophies, and felonies are groups of instances.

The process of generalization should not be confused with that of **enumeration**. If you taste every apple in a crate and then conclude that all these apples are sour, you have made an enumeration. Your conclusion is based on observation of *all* instances in the group. But if you taste only a few apples and then conclude that all or most apples in the crate are sour, you have made a generalization, for you have made an inductive leap from the apples tasted to those not tasted. Conclusions based on enumeration are reached by a deductive process whereas generalization is inductive. Note, too, that although conclusions reached through generalization frequently attribute the characteristic at issue to all instances in the group, they need not. Thus your sampling of the apples may lead you to conclude that most or a certain percentage—

rather than all—of them are sour. However, you will still have generalized, in the logical sense.

The Function of Generalization

The process of generalization is indispensable to thinking. Without it our personal points of view would be extremely meager, for the only empirical information they would contain would relate merely to specific events of past experience. Generalization allows us to go beyond particular experiences. Figuratively speaking, it enables us to extend our knowledge from the red-hot stoves that have burned us to all the hot objects there are and will be. If we could not do this, innumerable decisions we make by deductive inference would have to be made some other way, for most of the premises we use about people, places, actions, things, ideas, and values result from generalization. Without generalization modern science would be impossible.

Generalization makes it much easier to gather the information necessary for reaching some kinds of decisions. Suppose that a television producer must decide whether to continue a certain show. To make the right decision, she should find out approximately how many people watch the show. The cost of an enumeration would be prohibitive; she is therefore likely to form a general conclusion based on data provided by a rating service, and use it as the basis for her decision.

Generalization has yet another indispensable function in thinking, for it enables us to predict the future from the past. When an insurance company sets its rates for automobile accident policies, it is predicting the cost of accidents in the year to come. Even if the company makes an enumeration of the cost of past accidents involving its own policyholders, any prediction about future costs requires generalizing, for it involves an inductive leap from past conditions and policyholders to future conditions and policyholders.

Hasty Generalization

Although generalization is a type of inference we cannot do without, it also involves dangers. The chief of them is the fallacy of **hasty generalization**, that is, generalizing from insufficient or biased evidence, and failing to test the conclusion for reliability. Suppose an instructor finds that the first student he questions in class is unprepared and concludes without further thought that the class as a whole is unprepared. The instructor's conclusion is reached by generalization, for his reasoning involves an inductive leap from the one student observed to the class as a whole. The conclusion is reached by hasty generalization because the instructor has made no effort to determine whether the one student observed is typical of the whole class.

Hasty generalization is a tempting fallacy because of our human tendency to do things the easy way. It is usually much easier to generalize quickly than to make the effort reliable conclusions require: it is easier to make a general statement based on evidence about one student than to question a number of students and judge how typical they are. Our love of the dramatic adds to the temptation: it is much more dramatic to condemn a whole class than to generalize that half the class is unprepared. Above all, our tendency to protect our personal points of view can make hasty generalization irresistible. Prejudices against minorities and other groups virtually live on this fallacy. So long as we can point to a few overly emotional women, a few blacks or Hispanics who are criminals, or a few dishonest merchants, we find it easy to condemn or look down on the whole group. When we want to believe we are better than others, we recklessly embrace such conclusions and forget about testing them. It is important to realize, by the way, that the term *hasty generalization* refers to a type of *argument,* not a type of proposition. Someone who simply states uncritically that all lawyers are thieves may be guilty of overstatement but is not guilty of hasty generalization. But if he or she makes this general statement as the conclusion of an argument based on a small or biased group of instances, then the fallacy is committed.

The hazards of hasty generalization should not make us avoid all general statements, however. The consequences of never generalizing can be as bad as those of generalizing too hastily. If you get food poisoning twice after eating in a certain restaurant, you would be foolish to eat there again before forming and testing the general conclusion that the food served in this restaurant is unsafe. The point is that we should never accept such a conclusion as truth until we have tested it for reliability.

The five-phase cycle of decision making applies to the process of generalization as well as to other forms of inference. The five phases should not be followed in rigid sequence, but each phase should be completed.

Defining the Problem

In phase 1 our purpose in generalizing should be clearly defined, because the purpose affects the procedures in the other four phases. Two guidelines should be followed.

1. The Definition Should Indicate Whether the Conclusion We Reach by Generalizing Is to Be Descriptive or Predictive. When the conclusion is a *descriptive* general statement, the inductive leap is restricted to the time span of the sample. When the conclusion is a *predictive* general statement, the leap extends to the future. A statement about current Wysacki freshmen is descriptive; one about future Wysacki freshmen is predictive.

2. The Definition Should Accurately Limit the Group About Which We Are to Generalize. When the conclusion is to be descriptive, the definition should describe precisely the group to be included. Generalizing about the opinions of Wysacki freshmen concerning a certain course, for example, would require significantly different procedures from those needed to generalize about the students themselves. When the conclusion is to be predictive, the definition should describe the time span as well as the group to be covered.

Selecting the Sample

The objective of phase 2 (gathering information) is to select and observe a sample of the instances that will be representative of the entire group. Because of the expense of observing instances, it is often desirable to observe the smallest sample that will yield the necessary level of reliability. For example, sampling voter opinion is an expensive process, and a political pollster could easily spend more money on a sample than the results of the study she is conducting will earn. Thus a small sample is necessary. But if the pollster is prudent, she will take pains to make the sample representative of the total group of voters.

The great danger in taking a sample is that it may be *loaded*—that the manner of selection will include a disproportionate number of instances of one kind. A spectacular illustration of the danger in loaded samples can be seen in the *Literary Digest*'s prediction of the outcome of the 1936 presidential election. Until then the *Digest* had an enviable record of accuracy. Its method of polling was to send sample ballots to persons listed in telephone books and city directories all over the country. The last issue of the *Digest* before the election listed a total of 2,266,566 ballots, approximately 4.6 per cent of the number of votes actually cast—a very large sample for political polls. Tabulations indicated a total of 370 electoral votes for Alfred M. Landon and only 161 for Franklin D. Roosevelt. The actual results, however, gave Roosevelt 523 electoral votes and Landon only 8. The *Digest* never recovered from the blow to its prestige, and within a few months it ceased publication.

Apparently the *Digest* sample was loaded in two ways. By sending ballots mainly to people listed in telephone books and city directories, the *Digest* unwittingly introduced a strong socioeconomic bias into its sample. Furthermore, the *Digest* counted only the ballots that were returned. Experience indicates that ballots or questionnaires that are returned voluntarily very likely constitute a loaded sample. Returning a questionnaire requires effort; therefore, those with an interest in the outcome are more likely to return the questionnaire.

Whether a sample is loaded or not depends in part on our purpose in generalizing. A sample may be loaded because instances irrelevant to the purpose are included. Suppose, for example, that Congress commissions a study to determine whether the hospital costs of Medicare patients are higher than those of others. Presumably, the purpose of such a study would be to determine whether the availability of government support for these patients encourages more and longer hospital stays, more expensive procedures, inflated rates, and so on. Clearly, those conducting the study will have to survey patients who do not receive Medicare support as well as those who do. They should not, however, include in the group not receiving support people who would be too young to qualify for it, since people in lower age groups tend to have fewer medical expenses anyway. With regard to the *Literary Digest* sample, since the purpose was to predict an election, all classes of voters were relevant. The sample was loaded because the lower socioeconomic classes were not adequately represented in the sample.

Three types of samples are commonly used to reduce the likelihood of loading and other errors.

1. Random Sample. One method of reducing the probability of loading is to select the sample at **random**, that is, in such a way that nothing but chance determines the instances selected. Selecting a purely random sample is not as easy as one might suppose. If a television rating service selected every tenth person passing the corner of Main and First streets during school hours, the sample would obviously be loaded: the number of children would be disproportionately small. How close a sample comes to being random depends in part on the purpose of the sample. A sample composed of every tenth name on an alphabetic roster of registered voters would presumably be close to random for predicting an election; but it would be heavily loaded for the purpose of rating the popularity of television programs since it would exclude all people below voting age.

A sample chosen haphazardly is not necessarily random. Suppose an instructor wishes to examine a sample of ten students in her class to determine how well the class as a whole has prepared an assignment. If she selects the sample by letting her eyes roam the class, the sample is haphazard but not necessarily random. Elements in her personal point of view could easily influence the selection. If she is annoyed with the class, she could select the students least likely to be prepared without realizing her bias. One method of selecting a random sample would be to assign each student a number and then select the sample by numbers. Statisticians have found, however, that even the selection of numbers can be influenced by the personal point of view. One method of avoiding this kind of bias is to use a book of random numbers selected by chance by a computer.

2. Stratified Sample. Another method of reducing the probability of loading is to identify the relevant strata in the group and select a random sample from each stratum in proportion to the number of instances in each stratum. To the television rating services, the relevant strata are determined by the characteristics of people that could influence their preferences in programs, such as age, sex, region, and educational level. To take a **stratified sample**, three steps are necessary: (1) identify the strata relevant to the sample, (2) ascertain the number of instances in each stratum, and (3) select at random the same proportion from each stratum.

3. Time-Lapse Sample. In many situations samples become unreliable because of changes in the relevant characteristics of the group. Political polls are a case in point. A reliable sample of voter opinion taken in June may not be reliable in July because many voters may have changed their minds. Several respected political polls went wrong in the 1948 national election because the pollsters stopped taking samples in mid-summer and failed to detect the shift in sentiment late in the campaign that resulted in the election of Harry S. Truman.

A **time-lapse sample** consists of two or more samples taken with a significant lapse of time between them and compared for changes in the characteristics being studied. The time between samples and the number of samples needed vary with the situation. The time lapses need not be identical. In a national election, samples taken every two months could be sufficient before the national conventions; between the conventions and the elections, however, the samples should be taken more frequently to detect the effects of the campaign.

The individual samples within a time-lapse sample may be random or stratified. But since the object is to determine changing trends, each sample in the series should be taken in the same way in order to minimize other variables. If in sampling voter opinion, we take one sample on Main Street at noon and another in front of a theater in the evening a month later, any difference in the samples may be due to a difference in loading factors rather than to changing opinions.

Time-lapse samples are essential when generalization is used for predictive purposes. If we know the college board scores of 99 per cent of current Wysacki freshmen, we can generalize to a highly reliable descriptive conclusion, but unless we also have a sample of the scores of at least one freshman class from the past, we have no basis for a predictive conclusion that the scores of future freshman classes will either rise or fall.

Forming General Conclusions

In the early stages of an investigation, it is usually desirable to begin with a small preliminary sample in order to learn more about the characteristics of the group. Otherwise we may waste time and money observing a large number of instances only to find that our method of sampling was unsatisfactory. Suppose you have been commissioned by the *Wysacki Reporter* to survey the opinions of the ten thousand Wysacki students about a new rule, to go into effect next year, requiring seniors to pass a comprehensive examination on all subjects studied in order to graduate. It is now Sunday, and your deadline for completing the survey and writing your story is 1:00 p.m. on Friday.

You could begin by asking a small number of students whether they favor the examinations. But if you recorded only the answers to this one question, your sample would give you relatively lit-tle information to guide you in selecting your next sample. A better method would be to form tentative conclusions about the relevant strata in the group before you take your preliminary sample. It seems reasonable to suppose that class (freshman, sophomore, etc.), sex, major field, and grade averages might affect opinions on the issue under investigation. In interviewing students in your preliminary sample, you should, therefore, ascertain and record the information relevant to these strata.

Suppose that you begin by interviewing students entering the library Sunday night. For the purpose of illustration, we will confine the sample to ten students, although for most purposes this would actually be too few even in a preliminary sample; twenty or thirty would be more adequate. The data you obtain are shown in Table 8.1.

Your next step is to form preliminary general conclusions based on the data in your sample. Some of the many conclusions you might form are stated below.

A. The majority of Wysacki students oppose the examinations.

B. More underclassmen than seniors oppose the examinations.

Table 8.1

Class	Sex	Grade Average	Major	Favor	Oppose	Undecided
Sr.	F	3.1	liberal arts	x		
Sr.	M	3.3	engineering	x		
Jr.	F	2.5	education		x	
Jr.	M	2.1	business		x	
Soph.	F	3.8	liberal arts	x		
Soph.	M	2.5	engineering		x	
Soph.	M	2.1	business		x	
Fresh.	F	3.4	liberal arts	x		
Fresh.	F	2.3	business		x	
Fresh.	M	3.5	architecture			x

C. More men than women oppose the examinations.

D. Students in business and education are more likely to oppose the examinations than those in liberal arts and engineering.

E. Students with low averages are more likely to oppose the examinations.

Your preliminary sample is so small that none of these preliminary conclusions has any significant degree of reliability. Even so, they are useful in guiding your next step.

Testing General Conclusions

General conclusions based on small, preliminary samples should be tested (phase 4) by taking a larger sample designed to correct any faults observed in the original sample. Your preliminary sample suggests that Wysacki students are heterogeneous with respect to their opinions of comprehensive examinations. Your sample also suggests that class, sex, major, and grade averages are possible loading factors. Ideally, you should now take a stratified sample designed to control these factors. You would need to know the total number of Wysacki students, as well as the number in such strata as men, women, freshmen, engineering students, and so forth. Since grade averages range on a continuum, you should divide students into categories, such as 3.0 and below, and above 3.0. Additional data needed would include the number of students in such substrata as sophomore female liberal arts students with grade averages above 3.0.

It often happens that generalization involves a conflict between the values of reliability and economy. Your problem is a case in point, for with only five days left to finish your survey and write your story, you would probably not have time to take a stratified sample. Consequently, you might have to settle for a relatively small random type of sample.

A useful procedure would be to take another sample by interviewing ten students entering the gymnasium on Monday night for a basketball game. If the number of students who oppose the examinations is significantly higher in this sample than in your original one, it is probable that the place you take your sample is a loading factor.

You now have a total sample of twenty. You could test this sample by taking another sample of twenty at a different place and time, such as the cafeteria at noon. The more closely this sample matches your first two samples, the higher the reliability of your total sample of forty. Suppose your total sample of forty shows the following:

Category	Favor	Oppose	Undecided
Seniors	5	0	0
Underclassmen	5	25	5
Men	4	14	2
Women	6	11	3
Grade averages above 3.0	9	0	1
Grade averages 3.0 and below	1	25	4

To complete phase 4, you must assess the reliability of your conclusions. Because conclusions reached by generalization are based on samples, we can never be sure that they accurately represent the total group. When absolute accuracy is required, enumerations must be made. The practical problem in testing conclusions reached by generalization, therefore, is to judge the degree of reliability conferred on the conclusion by the evidence of the sample. In making this judgment, we must consider the length of the inductive leap. If you taste twenty-four of the fifty Winesap apples in a crate and find them sour and conclude that most of the apples in the crate are sour, your inductive leap is very short. If from this sample you conclude that most Winesap apples from a particular orchard are sour, you have made a longer leap. If you conclude that most apples are sour you have made a tremendous leap. There is no foolproof method for judging the degree to which the sample justifies the leap, but there are a number of helpful criteria.

A Conclusion Reached by Generalization Is No More Reliable than the Observations on Which It Is Based. The observations of instances in the sample should be judged for reliability according to the criteria described in Chapter 6. When the instances are responses to questions, as in your survey of student opinion on comprehensive examinations, the conclusions based on them will not be reliable unless the questions asked are phrased in neutral language. Obviously your question should not be, "You don't want to take comprehensive examinations, do you?" A neutral question would be, "Do you favor or oppose final comprehensive examinations?"

In General, the More Heterogeneous the Group, the More Carefully the Sample Must Be Selected. You know from experience that a very small sample from a well-shaken bottle of milk will show whether the whole bottle is sour. But an accurate estimate of the size of the stones in a carload of gravel will require samples from several parts of the car, in-

cluding at least one from the bottom. For when gravel is shaken, as it is in transportation, the smaller stones tend to settle to the bottom. A well-shaken bottle of milk is homogeneous in sourness, but a well shaken carload of gravel is heterogeneous in size of stones.

People are heterogeneous in many respects. A drug that is beneficial to many people may be poisonous to others. Opinions on such matters as television programs, politics, examinations, and professors often range on a continuum from one extreme to the other.

In General, the Larger the Number of Instances Observed, the More Reliable Is the Conclusion Because of the Tendency of Large Numbers to Follow Fixed Laws. You can demonstrate this tendency by tossing pennies. In one experiment, ten tosses produced only three heads, or 40 per cent below expectations. But a hundred tosses yielded fifty-one heads, or 2 per cent above expectations, while a thousand tosses yielded 501 heads, almost exactly the expected result.

In General, the More Nearly the Number of Instances in the Sample Approaches Enumeration, the More Reliable Is the Conclusion. You can demonstrate this criterion for yourself by considering situations in which the probability of one event is dependent on another. Suppose you wish to generalize about the proportion of freshmen who pass Chemistry 101. To keep the arithmetic simple, suppose that there are only ten freshmen in the course, of whom half will pass and half fail. The smallest possible sample that would include both a passing and a failing freshman would be two, or 20 per cent of the total. The probability that a random sample of two (20 per cent of the group) would mislead you completely by including no failing freshman is $\frac{5}{10} \times \frac{4}{9}$, or $\frac{2}{9}$. But the probability that a sample of five (50 per cent) would mislead you completely by including no failing freshmen is $\frac{5}{10} \times \frac{4}{9} \times \frac{3}{8} \times \frac{2}{7} \times \frac{1}{6}$, or only $\frac{1}{252}$. A sample of six (60 per cent) would have to include at least one failing freshman. In effect, then, the principle of dependency is an automatic corrective factor, for the less representative a sample is, the greater the probability that increasing it will make it more representative.

In General, a Stratified Sample of a Heterogeneous Group Is More Reliable than a Strictly Random Sample of the Same Size. Suppose that the five freshmen who pass chemistry plan to major in the subject and that the five who fail do not. If you took a stratified sample of two by selecting at random one major (20 per cent of this stratum), and one non-major (20 per cent of this stratum), the probability that your sample would be perfectly representative is 1. The probability that a strictly random sample would be perfectly representative is only $\frac{5}{9}$. The difference in reliability between strictly random and stratified samples decreases as the difference between strata decreases. Now suppose that four of the passing freshmen are majors and one is a non-major. The probability that a strictly random sample of two would be exactly representative is $\frac{5}{9}$. The probability that a stratified sample would be exactly representative is $\frac{17}{25}$.

In General, the Greater the Margin for Error, the More Reliable Is the Conclusion. Consider conclusion A (The majority of Wysacki students oppose comprehensive examinations) in the light of the evidence in your sample of forty. If we ignore the undecided, those who oppose outnumber those who favor by a ratio of five to two. Since only a majority is required, the sample has a substantial margin for error. In contrast, the margin for error in conclusion C (More men than women oppose the examinations) is small, for the ratio of men to women is only fourteen to eleven.

All criteria considered, none of your preliminary general conclusions should be rated higher than probable. Since the Wysacki student body is apparently a heterogeneous group, a stratified sample would have been more reliable. You cannot even be certain that your sample is random, since the places and times you took your partial samples could be loading factors. The number of instances in your total sample is very small both in raw size and in proportion to the total group of ten thousand.

Evaluation and Decision

When you have tested and assessed your general conclusions for reliability, the decision-making process should shift to phase 5 (evaluation and decision), in which you decide whether your conclusions are sufficiently reliable for your purpose. If you had time, you should increase your sample since none of your conclusions deserves a rating higher than probable. But suppose you do not have time. You could write a story presenting your conclusions as truth, or you could abandon the project altogether.

A better decision would be to write your story but make it clear that your conclusions have a low degree of reliability. Procedures for deciding what to do about conclusions rated lower in reliability than

true beyond reasonable doubt are discussed in Chapter 13.

Suggested Supplementary Reading

David S. Moore, *Statistics: Concepts and Controversies* (San Francisco: W.H. Freeman and Company, 1979), Chapter 1.

Exercise 8

Problems 1–11. You are a counselor at Wysacki University, where 3,000 freshmen enroll each year. A number of entering freshmen have expressed anxiety because they have not made a definite choice of career. You define your problem to be to determine whether students who have made a definite career choice when they enter Wysacki are more likely to graduate. You decide to study a sample of the freshman class of six years ago.

1. How should you select a random sample?

   _____

   _____

2. How should you select a stratified sample?

   _____

3. Would a sample composed of one hundred graduates who entered Wysacki six years ago be satisfactory for your purpose?

   _____

4. Why or why not?

   _____

   _____

5. You begin your investigation by selecting a random sample of one hundred from the freshman class of six years ago. Official records reveal the following data.

Choices	Number in Group	Number Graduated
Definite	35	15
Not definite	65	45

   On the basis of this evidence alone, rate the reliability of this general conclusion: Students who have not made a definite career choice when they enter college have a better chance of graduating.

   _____

6. You now take a stratified sample of one hundred and obtain the following data.

Career Choices	Number in Group	Number Graduated
Definite	33	16
Not definite	67	50

   Does this sample indicate that your sample was significantly loaded?

   _____

7. Considering both samples, rate the reliability of this general conclusion: Freshmen entering Wysacki six years ago were more likely to graduate if they had not made definite career choices.

_____

8. On the basis of both samples, rate the reliability of this conclusion: Wysacki freshmen have a better chance of graduation if they have not made a definite career choice.

_____

9. Rate the reliability of this conclusion: College freshmen have a better chance of graduating if they have not made a definite choice of a career.

_____

10. Would you be justified in reassuring freshmen that not having made a definite choice of a career will not necessarily reduce their chances of graduation?

_____

11. Would you be justified in urging high school students not to make a definite choice of a career before entering college?

_____

Problems 12–13. Which of the statements in the key list below apply to the samples described in these items? Assume that all observations involved are accurate.

Key List
1. The population from which the sample is drawn is relatively heterogeneous.
2. There is good reason for believing that the sample is loaded.
3. The number of instances in the sample is too small for the degree of accuracy required.
4. The instances sampled are too small a percentage of the total group for the degree of accuracy required.
5. A time-lapse sample should have been taken.
6. The sample is not reliable enough for the decision based on it.
7. The sample is larger than necessary.

12. You manufacture electrical components for computers. Your contract specifies that you receive $10 for each component and pay a penalty of $1,000 for each one that proves defective. Each component costs you $8 to manufacture. Rigorous testing of a component costs $5 and makes the component unsalable. You subject to rigorous testing a random sample of five components, none of which proves defective. You decide that the quality is satisfactory.

_____

13. You subject to rigorous testing every fifth component coming off the assembly line. Only one component per thousand proves defective. You decide that the quality is satisfactory.

_____

Chapter 9

Statistical Concepts

- **Selecting the Sample**
- **Frequency Tables**
- **Frequency Polygons and Curves**
- **Averages**
- **Percentile Ranks**
- **Measures of Dispersion**

Many problems of modern life require the analysis of vast amounts of quantitative data. In medicine, testing a new vaccine requires that it be tried on a large number of people and that the results be carefully analyzed. People in business have learned that they can increase the reliability of their decisions in such matters as the location of new branches by collecting and analyzing data about population, economic trends, and the like. Educators rely on quantitative data in making all sorts of decisions, from determining the passing mark on a certain test to locating a new school or making changes in curricula. Something of the importance, as well as the amount and variety, of the quantitative data available to us can be seen from thumbing through *The World Almanac*, which contains tables of information on such varied matters as batting averages, raw sugar production, and the earnings of corporations. In short, we can solve a great variety of problems more easily if we generalize on the basis of quantitative data.

The primary tool used in making such generalizations is statistics. The importance of statistics in modern life has been greatly increased by computers, which enable statisticians to analyze data with incredible speed. Before the age of computers, business executives, government leaders, and university administrators had to make many vital decisions with little evidence because the relevant data could not be collected and analyzed soon enough. With the aid of computers, they can base decisions on analyses of vast amounts of data.

It is not our purpose to make an extended study of statistical procedures. So important have they become, however, that the educated layperson needs to understand at least the basic concepts. Perhaps the most effective means of acquiring an understanding of these concepts is to make a few elementary statistical analyses. In doing so, we shall emphasize only the most important concepts and keep the mathematics as simple as possible.

Selecting the Sample

When extreme accuracy is required and when the amount of data involved is relatively small, statisticians work from enumerations rather than samples. But often enumerations are impractical, even when using computers, and a carefully selected sample will yield information accurate enough for many purposes. Thus, when we studied sampling in Chapter 8, we were dealing with one of the fundamental problems of statistics. Suppose we wish to analyze the performance of eleven hundred students on a logic test in order to judge such matters as the difficulty of the test and the effectiveness of the course. If the test scores were already recorded in a computer, there would be little advantage in working with only a sample, for the machine could perform the necessary computations on all eleven hundred scores in seconds. But since many of us do not yet own computers, and since absolute accuracy is unnecessary in this situation, let us see how we can reduce the computation at little sacrifice of accuracy by working from a sample. A relatively small but representative sample can be obtained simply by arranging the scores in order, from high to low or vice versa, and then selecting every eleventh score.

Frequency Tables

Listed below is a sample of one hundred scores from a logic test taken by eleven hundred students. The sample was se-

lected from scores arranged in order, but they are listed in Table 9.1 as they might have looked had they been selected at random from the alphabetical roll.

Table 9.1 Haphazard Array of a Sample of 100 Scores on a Logic Test

30	53	13	32	30	43	24	28	23	42
10	48	49	35	32	37	29	38	26	34
14	32	19	24	39	20	40	22	37	33
19	36	19	15	20	28	21	34	33	40
61	6	28	49	37	24	41	38	27	42
54	27	34	31	28	45	30	33	36	25
0	43	21	27	38	34	30	30	43	25
58	23	38	36	17	26	29	29	23	24
20	11	29	17	46	19	33	26	31	18
22	51	25	47	39	23	21	44	35	44

It is easy enough to see from these scores that the lowest is 0 and the highest 61. Beyond this, the array looks meaningless, even though only 100 scores are listed. The difficulty of interpreting an array of 10,000 scores in haphazard order can easily be imagined.

After the sample is selected, the next step is to arrange the scores in some kind of systematic order. If we simply arranged them from low to high, they would make considerably more sense. But we would still have to count to find the number of scores that are alike. For statistical purposes, it would be much better to arrange the scores in a **frequency table** by dividing them into **intervals** (also called *classes*) and counting the number of scores in each interval. Table 9.2 below shows the logic scores divided into intervals of twenty.

Table 9.2 Frequency Table of Logic Scores with Interval of 20

Scores	Frequency
0–19	14
20–39	65
40–59	20
60–79	1

It can be seen at a glance, however, that this arrangement is too crude because important details are obscured. We cannot tell with any precision what the average is, and well over half the scores are clustered in one interval. On the other hand, if we arranged the scores in intervals of two, we would have thirty-one intervals, and although such a table would yield more exact analyses, the details would tend to hide significant features. As we shall see, increasing the number of intervals also increases the necessary computation. Statisticians, therefore, usually prefer to use intervals of a size that avoids both extremes. Table 9.3 shows the logic scores in intervals of five, an appropriate arrangement that reveals important details without excessive computation.

Table 9.3 Frequency Table of Logic Scores with Interval of 5

Interval	Frequency	Cumulative Frequency
0– 4	1	1
5– 9	1	2
10–14	4	6
15–19	8	14
20–24	16	30
25–29	17	47
30–34	18	65
35–39	14	79
40–44	10	89
45–49	6	95
50–54	3	98
55–59	1	99
60–64	1	100

In this frequency table, the column headed "Interval" lists the classes in which we have grouped our scores. The column headed "Frequency" gives the number of students making scores in each class, or interval, and the column headed "Cumulative Frequency" provides a running total of the number of students making scores *within or below* each interval.

For example, the sixth line in the table shows that seventeen students made scores between 25 and 29, inclusive, and forty-seven students made scores *in this interval or lower*, that is, between 0 and 29, inclusive.

Once our data have been arranged in a suitable frequency table, we can at a glance make a number of generalizations. We can tell, for example, that the great majority of the students clustered between scores of 20 and 44. We can also see that the students were almost symmetrically and rather widely spread out between scores of 0 and 64. And we can see that the best student did about thirty times as well as the poorest student.

Frequency Polygons and Curves

The information contained in a frequency table may be presented in readily understandable form by drawing a picture. The simplest picture is obtained by piling up blocks to indicate the different frequencies. The frequency table of our logic scores (Table 9.3), thus pictured, would look like the diagram in Figure 9.1 on the next page.

The same information can be shown by drawing connecting lines through the midpoints of the tops of the columns of blocks. The picture thus obtained is called a **frequency polygon.** Another type of picture, called a **frequency curve,** is obtained by drawing a smooth curve that follows the frequency polygon closely. By eliminating some of the sharp fluctuations of the polygon, the frequency curve theoretically approximates more nearly the way the distribution would have looked had the number of instances been much larger. Thus the frequency curve represents a generalization from the instances actually observed to a much larger group of instances. Figure 9.2 on page 131 shows a frequency curve sketched over a frequency polygon for the data in Table 9.3.

Averages

Because of its great convenience, the frequency table is basic to many types of statistical analyses. The purpose of many of these is to determine the distinguishing characteristics of the group being studied. For example, a manufacturer of automobiles or air conditioners may need an analysis of the incomes of potential customers in order to decide in which price range to design his or her product. A teacher may wish specific information about the aptitude and achievement of a class so that he or she may fit assignments and discussions to its needs.

The first step in analyzing the distinguishing characteristics of a group is to locate a starting point, or center, by which the representative core of the group may be specified and from which its boundaries or limits may be measured. The "center" needed for this purpose is some kind of measure of the average performance of the group, or, as it is often called, a "measure of central tendency."

Figure 9.1 Column Diagram of Logic Scores

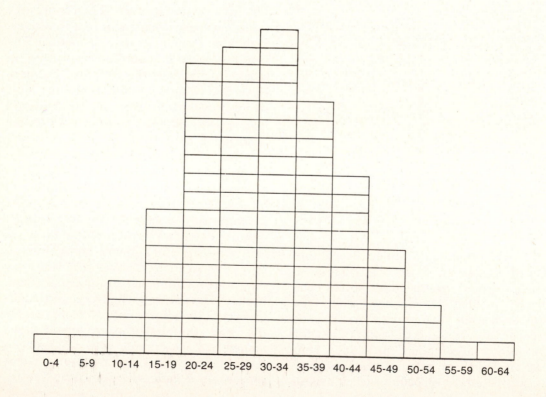

0-4   5-9   10-14   15-19   20-24   25-29   30-34   35-39   40-44   45-49   50-54   55-59   60-64

Figure 9.2 Frequency Polygon and Curve for Logic Scores

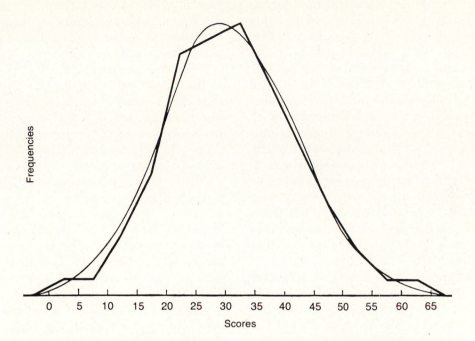

One such measure commonly used is the familiar arithmetic average, or **mean**, computed simply by adding all the items and dividing the sum by the number of items. Thus we could get the average of the scores in Table 9.1 simply by adding the hundred scores and dividing by one hundred. But this calls for a lot of adding, and we would shudder at the thought of adding ten thousand scores. Consequently, statisticians have developed a so-called "short method" of computing the mean from the frequency table, a description of which can be found in any text on statistics.

Even without using this somewhat complicated method, we can save considerable work by taking a **weighted average** from the data shown in Table 9.3. Since the individual scores in each interval cannot be identified, we must make an assumption about their average value. The most reasonable assumption is that the scores are evenly distributed through the range of the interval. On this assumption the average of the scores in an interval is the **midvalue** of the interval, that is, halfway between the lowest and highest possible scores in the interval. In determining the midvalue of an interval, we must consider the nature of the data. In this distribution, we are dealing with test scores in which fractions of less than half, if any, were dropped and fractions of one half or larger werer counted as the next highest number. Thus the interval 5–9 actually covers scores from 4.5 up to, but not including, 9.5. Thus the true midvalue of this interval is the average of the two, which is 7.

We cannot get our average, however, merely by adding the midvalues of each interval, for the number of students in the different intervals varies. We must therefore **weight** each interval by multiplying its midvalue by its frequency. Thus for the third interval, 10–14, we would multiply the midvalue, 12, by the frequency in that interval, 4. We would then add the products for the intervals and divide by 100, the total number of scores. Note that an average obtained from a frequency table would probably not coincide exactly with the average obtained by adding the individual scores, for the average of the scores in an interval is not necessarily the midvalue. Usually, however, a weighted average taken from a frequency table is close enough to the mean for practical purposes. The weighted average is another instance of how statistical procedures save work at a small sacrifice in accuracy.

Another common measure of central tendency is the **median**, which is simply the middle number when the numbers have been arranged in order. To get the median of the numbers 1, 4, 2, 6, 9, we must first arrange them in order: 1, 2, 4, 6, 9. The middle number, or median, in this group is 4. Where there is an even number of items in the group, the median is taken to be the average of the two in the middle. Thus the median of the numbers 1, 2, 4, 6, 8, 9 is 5.

When we are working from a frequency table, the median must be approximated. Look at Table 9.3. Since there are one hundred scores in the distribution, the median is the average of the fiftieth and fifty-first scores. A glance at the column headed "cumulative frequency" will show that these two scores occur in the interval 30–34. But the median set at the midvalue of this interval, 32, would be too high, for there are eighteen scores in this interval, and the fiftieth and fifty-first are the third and fourth scores, respectively, in this interval. Statisticians use a more precise method for calculating the median, but for our purpose it is sufficient to estimate that it is low in this interval, or roughly 31. We make this estimate on the assumption that the scores are distributed evenly throughout the interval.

A third measure of central tendency is the **mode**, which is simply the value that occurs most frequently. Thus for the numbers 1, 2, 4, 4, 4, 5, 6, 8, the mode is 4. In working from a "frequency table" we do not know what the individual scores are. Although statisticians have better methods, for our purpose it is sufficient to guess the mode to be the midvalue of the interval having the highest frequency. Thus in Table 9.3 we would guess the mode to be the midvalue of the interval 30–34, or 32. (Actually, the mode taken from the individual scores in this table is 30.)

Each of these measures of central tendency has particular advantages, as we shall see in Chapter 10.

Percentile Ranks

A statistical measure frequently used in characterizing the performance of an individual on a test is the **percentile rank**, which is often defined as the percentage of the scores that the given score equals or exceeds. Percentile ranks can be computed easily from a frequency table. To get the percentile rank of a score in any interval, simply divide the cumulative frequency of that interval by the total number of scores and multiply by 100. For example, turn back to the distribution in Table 9.3. To get the percentile rank of a score in the interval 50–54, divide the cumulative frequency for that interval, 98, by the number of scores, 100, which gives .98. Then multiply by 100 (to remove the decimal point), and you get 98. Actually this procedure yields the percentile rank for the top score of the interval, but it is satisfactory for most purposes, especially if the group is large. Note that the percentile ranks would have been more precise if the intervals had been smaller. Thus the fewer intervals, the less precise the percentile rank is.

Percentile ranks have certain advantages over grades and scores in evaluating the performance of an individual on tests and examinations. In the first place, grades and scores tell us little about the performance of an individual with respect to his or her competition unless we know the grades or scores of the other individuals in the group. A grade of A or a score of 90 may mean that the individual is near the top of the group, or it may mean merely that he or she met a certain standard that most or all of the competitors also met. Percentile ranks, on the other hand, give a specific measure of the individual's competitive position with respect to the group. In the second place, it is difficult to compare an individual's grades or scores on tests in different subjects. A grade of D or a score of 30 on one test may actually represent higher achievement than a grade of A or a score of 90 on another test. On the other hand, where the groups taking the different tests are large and reasonably comparable, percentile ranks give grades and scores a definite meaning in terms of the performance of the group as a whole. Thus, when the groups are reasonably comparable, as would probably be the case with a large freshman class taking two different required courses, the same percentile rank on two different tests would probably represent roughly comparable achievement in the two tests.

Measures of Dispersion

Once a center, or average, has been found, another step in analyzing the characteristics of a group is to determine the **dispersion**, that is, the extent to which the group is spread. Wide dispersion indicates heterogeneity in the characteristic being measured. Dispersion is one indication of the worth of a test as a grading device: the more widely scores are spread, the easier it is to separate students by grades.

One measure of dispersion is called the **range**, which is the difference between the lowest and highest figures. Thus the range of our logic scores is 61, since the lowest score is 0 and the highest 61. In working from a frequency table, where we do not know the individual scores, the range is usually taken to be the difference between the midvalues of the lowest and highest intervals. Thus the range for the data in Table 9.3 is the difference between 2 and 62, or 60, which closely approximates the range computed from the individual scores, which is 61.

For many purposes, however, the range is too crude a measure. In the first place, it may be strongly influenced by a single instance. In the scores of our logic test, had the student who made the lowest score been absent, the range would have been reduced from 61 to 55. Furthermore, for many purposes we are not interested in the extreme cases, whether high or low. Thus, in deciding how much to charge, the manufacturer of a medium-priced air conditioner is not concerned with people whose income is so low that they cannot buy the product anyway or with those so rich that price is not a major factor. Instead, he or she is concerned with the large central core of potential buyers. For this purpose, some measure of dispersion other than the range would be more suitable.

One measure of dispersion the manufacturer might use, which would leave the extremes out of consideration, is the **10–90 interpercentile range.** It is computed by disregarding 10 percent of the individual items at each end of the distribution and taking the range of the remainder. For example, consider the following scores: 1, 12, 13, 13, 15, 16, 17, 18, 18, 19. Since there are ten scores, 10 percent of the scores is one score. Thus we would disregard the lowest score, 1, and the highest score, 19. The 10–90 interpercentile range is simply the difference between the highest and lowest scores remaining, or 18 minus 12, which is 6. We can, of course, use other interpercentile ranges, such as the 25–75 interpercentile range.

Probably the most frequently used measure of dispersion is the **standard deviation**, which is a kind of average of the amounts by which the instances in a group differ from the mean of the group. It is defined technically as *the square root of the arithmetic average of the squares of the deviations from the mean.* Actually, this measure is not as complicated as it sounds. The standard deviation, usually symbolized by a small Greek sigma (σ), is computed in Table 9.4 for a group of ten test scores.

The first step in computing the standard deviation is to determine the mean, since we are trying to measure how much the scores differ from the mean. With only ten scores, it is easy to add the separate scores, which total 90, and divide by 10, the number of scores, as shown in the first column of Table 9.4. Thus the mean is 9.

The second step is to determine how much each score differs, that is, deviates, from the mean of 9. This is done in the column headed "Deviation from Mean." Since a score of 2 deviates from 9 by -7, -7 is entered in this column for the first score.

The third step is to square these deviations, as shown in the column headed "Squares of the Deviations." The next step is to find the average of all the squared deviations. There are 10 scores, with squared deviations totaling 160. Thus the average of the squared deviations is 16. To get the standard deviation, we have only to take the square root of 16, which is 4.

Table 9.4 Computation of Standard Deviation

Scores	Deviations from Mean	Squares of the Deviations
2	-7	49
4	-5	25
6	-3	9
9	0	0
9	0	0
9	0	0
9	0	0
13	4	16
14	5	25
15	6	36
Sum 90		Sum 160

Mean of scores $= \dfrac{90}{10} = 9$

Mean of squares of deviations $= \dfrac{160}{10} = 16$

Standard deviation (σ) = square root of $16 = 4$.

Note that in the example we computed, the standard deviation turned out to be a certain number of score points that represented a unit of measurement of the extent to which all the scores differed from the mean. Actually, the standard deviation would be nothing more than an average of the deviations except that the process of squaring the deviations and then taking the square root of the mean of the squares of the deviations results in a figure slightly larger than the straight average would be. This is illustrated by Table 9.4. Disregarding minus signs, the average of the deviations is 30 divided by 10, or 3, whereas the standard deviation is 4. We shall see more of the significance of standard deviations in Chapter 10.

Suggested Supplementary Reading

David S. Moore, *Statistics: Concepts and Controversies* (San Francisco: W.H. Freeman and Company, 1979), Chapter 5.

Exercise 9

Problems 1–16. All problems in this exercise refer to the following data showing the number of vacuum cleaners sold by thirty salespersons in a ninety-day period.

39	29	28	25	42	40
31	26	25	32	21	27
07	18	16	21	03	21
17	21	26	24	14	16
23	49	31	41	17	11

1. Compile a frequency table for these sales records, using an interval of five.

Interval	*Frequency*	*Cumulative Frequency*
_____	_____	_____
_____	_____	_____
_____	_____	_____
_____	_____	_____
_____	_____	_____
_____	_____	_____
_____	_____	_____
_____	_____	_____
_____	_____	_____
_____	_____	_____

2. Draw a frequency polygon for the frequency table. Sketch over it a frequency curve.

3. What is the mean, computed from the individual sales records? _____

4. What is the weighted average, computed from the frequency table? _____

5. What is the median, taken from the individual sales records? _____

6. Estimate the median from the frequency table. _____

7. What is the mode, taken from the individual sales record? _____

8. Estimate the mode, from the frequency table.   _____

9. Why do the mean, median, and mode computed from the individual records differ from those estimated from the frequency table?

_____

10. Draw and label vertical lines on the frequency polygon (problem 2) to show the mean, median, and mode.

11. Estimate the range from the frequency table.   _____

12. What is the 10–90 interpercentile range taken from the individual sales records?

                                                                    _____

13. Would the range or the 10–90 interpercentile range be more truly representative of the salespersons' performance? Why?

_____

_____

14. What is the percentile rank of the salesperson who sold fourteen vacuum cleaners?

                                                                    _____

15. Compute the standard deviation for the following records of the ten salespersons in a single district.

Values	Deviations	Squares of Deviations
19	_____	_____
21	_____	_____
22	_____	_____
23	_____	_____
24	_____	_____
25	_____	_____
26	_____	_____
27	_____	_____
30	_____	_____
33	_____	_____

$$\sigma \;=\; \text{_____}$$

16. If each salesperson in the district received a $10 bonus for each vacuum cleaner he or she sold in excess of one standard deviation above the mean, how much would be the total bonus paid in the district?

                                                                    _____

Chapter 10

Reasoning from Statistics

- **The Normal Probability Curve**
- **Inferences from Normal Distributions**
- **Inferences from Irregular Distributions**

- **Interpreting Averages**
- **Hazards in Interpreting Statistics**
- **Misuse of Statistics**

The results of statistical studies are often used in decision making. When you were accepted into college, statistical studies probably formed part of the basis for the admission officer's judgment that it was possible for you to succeed in college work. When a traffic signal is installed at an intersection, statistical information about the flow of traffic through the intersection is likely to constitute part of the reason. Indeed, statistically based reasoning on the part of some person or other is apt to be responsible for everything from the thickness of the shelves in your college library to the amount of time the bread you buy at the store stays fresh. Moreover, a number of our decisions in life—whether to smoke cigarettes, for example, or whether to buy a particular type of automobile—will probably be based in part on statistical information. Because this is so, it is important to consider some of the ways in which statistics can be utilized to make effective decisions, as well as some of the ways they can be misunderstood or misused.

The Normal Probability Curve

Suppose we were to compute the theoretical probability for every conjunction of heads and tails possible with ten coins. The results we would achieve are shown in Table 10.1.

Table 10.1

Combination	Probability
10 heads	1/1,024
9 heads, 1 tail	10/1,024
8 heads, 2 tails	45/1,024
7 heads, 3 tails	120/1,024
6 heads, 4 tails	210/1,024
5 heads, 5 tails	252/1,024
4 heads, 6 tails	210/1,024
3 heads, 7 tails	120/1,024
2 heads, 8 tails	45/1,024
1 head, 9 tails	10/1,024
10 tails	1/1,024

Now suppose we were to translate these probabilities into a frequency polygon, and then "smooth" the polygon into a curve by statistical procedures. The curve that would result is shown in Figure 10.1 below.

This curve is often called the **normal curve of distribution** because it delineates the distribution we would expect when nothing but chance is affecting the distribution. A normal curve has several distinguishing characteristics. Note that it is symmetrical. From this it follows that mean, median, and mode all fall at the midpoint. The rate at which frequencies decrease on either side of this midpoint can be expressed in multiples of the standard deviation, which are called "first standard deviation," "second standard deviation," and so on. The territory defined by the first standard deviation below the mean includes 34.13 percent of the population. Note further that the rate of decrease in frequencies is not uniform, for the territory defined by the second standard deviation below the mean includes only 13.59 percent of the population, while the territory of the third standard deviation below the mean includes only 2.145 percent. Since a normal curve is symmetrical, the standard deviations above and below the mean include the same percentages. Thus the territory covered between one standard deviation to the left and one standard deviation to the right of the mean includes 68.26 percent of the population, a large but relatively uniform central core. Two standard deviations on both sides include 95.44 percent, a larger group but twice as diverse. Three standard deviations on both sides include 99.73 percent. The remaining .27 percent (27 out of 10,000) of the population unaccounted for would be included in additional standard deviations.

Inferences from Normal Distributions

It is unlikely that any actual distribution would have the exact characteristics of a normal probability curve. But interestingly enough, distributions of all manner of things, from scores on intelligence tests to the wing spread of pigeons, resemble such a curve. The resemblance is so strong that the normal probability curve is useful as a standard of comparison in analyzing empirical distributions.

First let us look at the significance of our three measures of dispersion—range, 10–90 interpercentile range, and standard deviation—in terms of the normal probability curve. Suppose you are planning to manufacture a new automobile and you have made a survey of the horsepower potential buyers prefer. Your survey shows an approximately normal distribution.

Figure 10.1 Normal Probability Curve

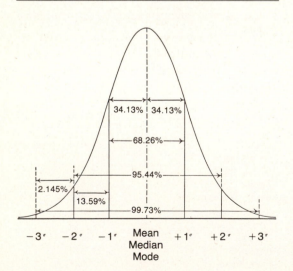

34.13% | 34.13%
68.26%
95.44%
2.145%
13.59%
99.73%

−3′ −2′ −1′ Mean Median Mode +1′ +2′ +3′

Horsepower	
Range	150
10–90 interpercentile range	40
Mean	175
Standard Deviation	15

The large size of the range compared to the 10–90 interpercentile range tells you that it is hopeless to try to please everybody with one engine. You must therefore content yourself with trying to please a central core of the population.

The mean, together with the 10–90 interpercentile range, tells you that an engine of 175 horsepower will come within 20 horsepower of satisfying the middle 80 percent of your potential customers. The mean and the standard deviation, together with the characteristics of a normal curve, tell you that an engine of 175 horsepower will come within 15 horsepower of satisfying 68 percent of your potential customers and within 30 horsepower of satisfying about 95 percent. But suppose the standard deviation had been 40 instead of 15. You would then know that your customers' preferences vary widely. An engine of 175 horsepower would then come only within 40 horsepower of satisfying 68 percent of the market you want to reach, and you had better consider offering different engines.

Thus the size of the standard deviation has a significance of its own. Suppose that the standard deviation on a test of 100 items is 15. If the distribution is normal, 68 percent of the students would be spread out over a total of two standard deviations, or 30 score points, which is a wide spread for a test of 100 items. But suppose the standard deviation had been only 2. This would mean that 68 percent of the students are clustered within a range of only 4 score points. One would be jus-

tified in suspecting that the test did not distinguish very well between poor and good students, or that the students taking the test were very much alike in ability, or both. On the other hand, when the standard deviation is relatively large, one is justified in forming a tentative conclusion that the test differentiated among the students rather well, or that the students varied a great deal, or both.

Inferences about the significance of an individual instance can also be drawn by comparison with the normal probability curve. For example, let us suppose that you have taken a college aptitude test given to thousands of college students all over the country. You know that the distribution was approximately normal, the maximum possible score 100, the mean 50, and the standard deviation 15. If your score is 50, you would be exactly in the middle, with half of the students on either side of you. If your score is 65, you would be exactly one standard deviation better than the mean, and you would be as good as or better than approximately 84 percent of your competition. You might now be said to be at the top of the great middle class. A score of 80 would put you two standard deviations above the mean, and in select company—as good as or better than approximately 98 percent of the competition. A score of 95 would put you out almost by yourself, as good as or better than 99.865 percent of the competition. But note that each standard deviation covered the same number of score points, so that it took three times as many points above the mean to get out by yourself as it did to get to the top of the middle class. Thus one moral of standard deviations might be that it is wise to think twice before going into a highly competitive occupation—for example, professional baseball or acting—unless your aptitude for it is at least two standard deviations above the mean for the total population eligible for that occupation.

Many nationally administered tests are scored in terms of standard deviations and normal distributions. The Scholastic Aptitude Test given by the College Entrance Examination Board is a case in point. Each form of this test is given to a fairly large sample of students, and the mean and the standard deviations of their scores are computed. The mean is then arbitrarily assigned a score of 500. Each hundredth of a standard deviation is assigned a value of one point. Thus, if your score on this test is 497, it is three hundredths of a standard deviation below the mean of the sample group. If your score is 600, it is exactly one standard deviation above the mean.

This system has several advantages. The scores are easily interpreted by anyone with an elementary knowledge of statistics, whereas the raw scores on the test cannot be interpreted without studying the distribution. Furthermore, with this system scores on different versions of the test are readily compared. If raw scores were used, comparison would be much more difficult, since the mean on one version of the test might differ considerably from the mean on another.

Inferences from Irregular Distributions

When a distribution is irregular, that is, when its characteristics differ significantly from those of a normal distribution, we can draw certain inferences about the population covered, according to the type of irregularity.

Sharp fluctuations in a distribution are usually an indication of an inadequate sample. The frequency polygon below, which has been sketched over a normal probability curve, shows the distribution of heads and tails obtained by shaking ten pennies in a jar and pouring them out thirty-two times. We would not expect the polygon for so small a number of instances to follow the normal probability curve very closely, and indeed this one does not. Polygons plotted for a small number of instances, whether of tossed coins or the weight of cabbage heads, are likely to look jagged, like the one shown in Figure 10.2.

Figure 10.2 Polygon Showing Distribution of Heads and Tails in 32 Pourings of 10 Coins

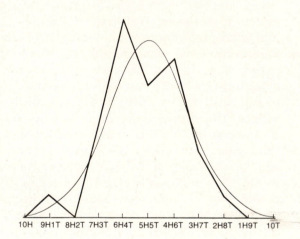

10H 9H1T 8H2T 7H3T 6H4T 5H5T 4H6T 3H7T 2H8T 1H9T 10T

When the number of instances in a distribution is large enough to make a smooth curve, the variations from the normal curve may be due to the operation of some factor other than chance. To introduce such an element into the tossing of coins, a drop of solder was affixed to Lincoln's head on ten pennies. These coins were then placed in a jar, shaken well, and poured out 256 times. The frequency polygon in Figure 10.3, sketched over a normal curve, shows the distribution obtained.

Figure 10.3 Polygon Showing Distribution of Heads and Tails in 256 Pourings of 10 "Loaded" Coins

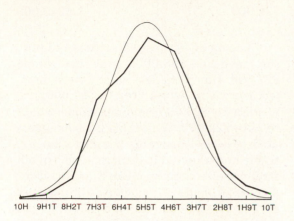

10H 9H1T 8H2T 7H3T 6H4T 5H5T 4H6T 3H7T 2H8T 1H9T 10T

The fact that this polygon follows the normal probability curve more closely than the one in Figure 10.2 is presumably due to the larger number of instances. All the combinations in which heads and tails are equal or heads are in the majority, with the exception of the combination of seven heads and three tails, fall below the expected frequencies, while all the combinations in which tails are in the majority exceed the expected frequencies. The unexpectedly large frequency for the combination of seven heads and three tails is presumably due to a freak of the distribution, since the number of tails exceeds theoretical expectations everywhere else in the distribution. The excess number of tails could itself be a freak of the distribution, since 256 instances is not a large number, but the presence of solder on the coins provides the most reasonable explanation.

When instances involving dice, coins, and the like deviate significantly and consistently from the theoretical expectations, a search for a factor other than chance is indicated.

The curves for some distributions are **skewed**, that is, stretched out on one side or the other. Curves stretched out to the right are said to be **positively skewed**, while those stretched out to the left are **negatively skewed**. The curve in Figure 10.4 is positively skewed. In this curve the mode, median, and mean are not in the same position, as would be true of a normal probability curve. Both mean and median have been pulled to the right of the mode by a relatively small number of extremely high values.

Figure 10.4   Positively Skewed Curve

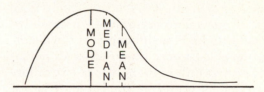

Skewness may be an indication of the operation of some factor other than chance. For example, the salaries of professional actors are determined not by chance, but by such factors as the size of the roles they play, the size of the audience that sees their performance, and the frequency with which they are able to find work. Since there are far more struggling actors than stars, there are many more low salaries than high ones, and the distribution curve (at least for those who are working at all) would probably look something like the one in Figure 10.4. Skewness in scores on standardized tests, such as tests of intelligence or college aptitude, usually indicates some factor other than chance in the selection of the individuals taking the test since standardized tests are designed to yield an approximately normal distribution. Skewness in scores where the test has not been standardized usually indicates that the test is not suited to the abilities or knowledge of the students.

Sometimes distributions are **bimodal**, that is, the instances cluster around two centers instead of one. A bimodal curve is shown in Figure 10.5

Figure 10.5 Bimodal Distribution

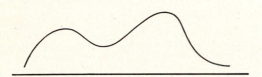

If our manufacturer of automobiles should find a bimodal curve in the distribution of customer preferences in horsepower, two different engines or two different models would be indicated. When a teacher finds a bimodal distribution in a class, he or she has in effect two classes in one, and what would be intelligible to the lower group would probably be dull to the upper group.

Interpreting Averages

In normal distributions, mean, median, and mode all have the same significance. In irregular distributions, however, especially where there is strong skewness, each of these measures has a different significance, and it is important to use the measure appropriate for the purpose at hand.

To illustrate, let us take a hypothetical example that will keep the arithmetic simple. Suppose you are considering philosophy as a profession and you have the following list of salaries of American philosophers.

$12,000	$ 28,000
$19,000	$ 32,000
$22,000	$ 34,000
$22,000	$ 36,000
$22,000	$240,000

The mean of these salaries is $45,000, the median $28,000, and the mode $22,000. But if the last salary were omitted, the mean would drop to $25,000, the median to $25,000, and the mode would remain $22,000. While this is an exaggerated case, it illustrates the fact that extreme and unusual instances have a much stronger effect on the mean than on either median or mode. If you choose philosophy as a profession on the ground that you would probably earn a salary of $45,000, you would be using the wrong average, for you would be using the mean as an indication of the typical salary whereas you should have used the median or the mode. Assuming that you can become a philosopher but know nothing else about your aptitude for the profession, the probability of your earning the median salary or more is $6/11$, whereas the probability of your earning as much as the mean salary is only $1/11$.

To summarize the characteristics of the three measures of central tendency, the mean takes all instances into full account. It should be used in situations where every item is equally important to the whole. Computation of averages on scholastic aptitude tests is an example. The median and the mode take into account the relative positions and frequencies of the various instances in relation to the whole, but they are not distorted by the extreme instances. They are measures that one would consider with respect to the probable income in a career one is contemplating. The median would be the "middle income" of those working in the field, and the mode would be the income that is most frequently earned. If the median and mode differ appreciably, the distribution of incomes may be skewed somewhat, like the salaries of professional actors, and this will be important. This skewness is likely to reflect keen competition and an extraordinary demand for ability at the high end of the scale, and, as we have said, unless one has evidence that one will be very good in the field, one's chances of achieving success may be better in some other area of work.

When the issue is important and the data are available, the frequency distribution and its curve should be studied carefully. Choosing a career is one of many situations that demonstrate the importance of gathering and studying all the evidence we can find. To draw conclusions without knowing a great deal about salaries in the particular field, about our qualifications for a career, and about our probable achievements compared with the achievements of others in that field, is to run the risk of deceiving ourselves disastrously.

Hazards in Interpreting Statistics

The basic statistical concepts we have been discussing are invaluable in decision making—provided certain hazards in interpretation are avoided.

A fundamental hazard in all statistical analysis lies in selecting the sample on which the analysis is based. Conclusions drawn from statistical analyses, like any others, are no more reliable than the evidence on which they are based. Since they are based on observations of a sample of the total group, **conclusions drawn from statistical analyses are reliable only to the degree that (1) the observations themselves are accurate, and (2)** **the sample is representative of the total group.**

Careful application of statistical techniques can easily lure us into a false sense of security by causing us to forget that the sample is only a sample and not a complete enumeration. We then become prone to the fallacy of hasty generalization by extending inferences about the sample to groups not represented in the sample at all.

We are particularly vulnerable to hasty generalization when we attempt to predict the future on the basis of a single sample from the present or the past. No matter how accurate the sample at the time it was taken, it is not necessarily an accurate indication of the future characteristics of the group. This is not to say that we should avoid predicting the future on the basis of samples from the past, for evidence from the past is often the only evidence we can get. But **wherever the passage of time may even remotely affect the situation, time-lapse samples should be used in predictions.**

Insurance companies are making predictions when they base their charges for a given kind of insurance on past experience with the particular kind of risk involved. They protect themselves from some of the hazards of prediction by collecting vast amounts of data. Furthermore, the data are in effect time-lapse samples. Thus their predictions are more reliable because of the tendency of large numbers of instances to remain relatively stable and because time-lapse samples reveal changes in trends. A glance at the vital statistics provided by the National Safety Council will illustrate this tendency.[1] For example, Table 10.2, based on some of these figures, gives the death rate per hundred thousand population for the

---

[1] *Accident Facts 1983 Edition*. National Safety Council (Chicago, IL, 1983), pp.13–15.

principal types of accidental deaths for the years 1975–1978.

This table shows that rates of accidental deaths do change, but they usually change slowly enough for the companies to make necessary adjustments in premium rates. Even so, the companies carry large reserves and in effect pool their resources by insuring one another.

Another hazard lies in applying a statistical statement to an individual. If, using the data in Table 10.2, you compute the probability that you will die an accidental death within the next twelve months at $47.5/100,000$, the sample you are using is large enough, but you would be assuming that you are as likely to die accidentally as any other of the millions of persons on whom the rate is based. And this is a hazardous assumption, for the probability will be raised or lowered by many factors, such as your age and physical condition, your type of work, how

Table 10.2 Accidental Death Rates per 100,000

Type of Accidental Death	1975	1976	1977	1978
All types	47.8	46.3	47.0	47.5
Motor vehicle	21.3	21.6	22.5	23.6
Falls	6.9	6.5	6.3	6.2
Burns	2.8	2.9	2.9	2.8
Drowning	3.7	3.1	3.2	3.2
Firearms	1.1	0.9	0.9	0.8
Poison gases	0.7	0.7	0.7	0.8
Other poisons	2.2	1.9	1.5	1.4

much you ride in automobiles, or how carefully you drive.

Insurance companies must face this problem too. If they charged all applicants the same rate for life insurance, a selective factor would enter, for the old and infirm would tend to take out more insurance than the young and healthy. Insurance companies deal with the problem by dividing the population into strata according to age, sex, occupation, physical condition, and the like, and they vary their rates accordingly.

Even if you had the statistics of the insurance companies available, it would still be difficult to compute your own probability, for there may be great variation among the instances within the several strata. If the death rate for your stratum happened to be two per 100,000, your probability might still range from near zero to near certainty because of your individual characteristics. **The more heterogeneous the group covered by a statistical statement, the more precarious is the prediction of individual behavior.**

A related hazard is involved in comparing two or more sample groups. Suppose the alumni office at Wysacki announces that its graduates are earning a mean salary of $22,000, while the alumni office at State University announces that its graduates are earning a mean salary of $28,000. It would be extremely hazardous to conclude from this evidence that State alumni earn more than Wysacki alumni. Presumably both averages were derived from samples, and the samples might not be comparable at all. Suppose that the Wysacki sample was taken at random and that every graduate included in the sample was interviewed. Suppose that the State sample was taken from questionnaires voluntarily returned by alumni. This latter sample is highly likely to be loaded since alumni who are making low salaries are not as likely to return the questionnaires as those who are proud of the fact that they are making high salaries. **Inferences should not be drawn by comparing samples unless we know that the samples are representative.**

Another hazard lies in attaching undue significance to small differences in averages, for small differences are likely to be due to chance. It would surely be imprudent to believe, for example, that women are better students than men on the ground that the mean grade-point average of the women at Wysacki was 2.3333 whereas that of the men was 2.3331.

Both students and faculty are prone to certain hazards in interpreting percentile ranks. It is hazardous to conclude, because you made a percentile rank of 55 in English and 45 in chemistry, that your performance was better in English. It is altogether possible that the group taking chemistry studied harder and learned more than the group taking English, and that the percentile rank of 45 in chemistry actually represents significantly higher achievement than the 55 in English. It should never be forgotten that percentile ranks have meaning only in terms of the group from which they were computed.

Nor is it safe to conclude, since you made percentile ranks of 0 and 5 on your first and second tests in English, and percentile ranks of 45 and 55 on your first and second tests in chemistry, that you made more progress in chemistry than in English. For differences in percentile rank near the middle of a distribution mean much less than differences of the same magnitude near the extremes. On the logic test for which scores were given in Table 9.3, raising your score from the interval 0–4 to the interval 5–9 would raise your percentile rank only one point, whereas raising your score from the interval 25–29 to the interval 30–34 would raise your percentile rank eighteen points.

Although standard deviations are somewhat more reliable than percentile ranks (since each standard deviation represents the same spread), they also must be used with caution. It is hazardous to

conclude that your performance was better in chemistry than in English on the ground that your score in English was only average, whereas your score in chemistry was a standard deviation above the mean. For it is altogether possible that the group taking English was so superior in ability and effort to the group taking chemistry that your score in English represents higher achievement.

Thus measures of dispersion should be applied to individuals only with great care, for they are meaningless except in terms of the particular group on which they are based.

Misuse of Statistics

It has been said that figures never lie, but liars figure. While statistics can be an important tool in discovering the truth and in making sound decisions, statistics can also be misused by propagandists, advertisers, and others to distort the truth and to lead us into making unsound decisions.

One method of using statistics to deceive is to deliberately exaggerate the significance of small differences in averages. A company manufacturing potato peelers might arrange a perfectly fair test of the efficiency of its own and rival brands in which its gadget peeled a few more potatoes per hour. The difference might not be any greater than would occur between two peelers of the same model. But the company could make the difference seem much greater by using in its advertising a graph like this:

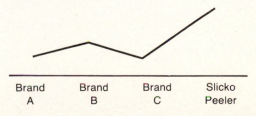

Note that this graph does not show how many potatoes any brand peeled. It is well to be suspicious of any graph in which frequencies and quantities are not specifically shown.

Another method is the use of deliberately loaded samples. We should be suspicious of statements like this fictitious one: "Eighty-seven percent of the doctors interviewed reported that they prescribed 'Painstop.'" This statement could be literally true and yet misleading. Suppose "Painstop" is a brand of aspirin, and that free samples were distributed to one hundred doctors shortly before these doctors were asked whether they ever prescribed "Painstop." Note that the fictitious statement above does not indicate how many doctors were interviewed or how often they prescribed "Painstop" or how the doctors interviewed were selected.

There are other methods too numerous to describe. Suffice it to say at this point that we should distrust statements based on statistical evidence unless we are given the information necessary for judging the reliability of the statements.

Exercise 10

Problems 1–12. Suppose you find a paper labeled "Distribution of Grade Points Earned by Selected Group of Wysacki Freshmen in Their First Semester," showing the frequency table below.

Interval	Frequency	Cumulative Frequency
0– 4	1	1
5– 9	4	5
10–14	7	12
15–19	11	23
20–24	16	39
25–29	9	48
30–34	4	52
35–39	2	54
40–44	3	57
45–49	5	62
50–54	8	70
55–59	14	84
60–64	10	94
65–69	5	99
70–74	1	100

1. What is the mean computed from this table? _____

2. What is the percentile rank for the interval 35–39? _____

3. What is the median? _____

4. The standard deviation of the distribution is approximately 19.5. About how many instances fall within one standard deviation on either side of the mean?

   _____

5. How many honor points were earned by a freshman who stood one standard deviation above the mean?

   _____

6. Had the distribution been normal, approximately how many freshmen would have fallen within one standard deviation on both sides of the mean?

7. Approximately what is the 10–90 interpercentile range? _____

8. Describe the distribution (that is, "approximately normal," "positively skewed," etc.)

9. Which of the following statements are *probably true* of the distribution? (1) Some factor other than chance entered into the selection of the cases included. (2) The character of the distribution is mainly due to the small number of instances. (3) The group included within the distribution is in effect two groups in one. (4) The group is heterogeneous. (5) The group would be easy to teach. (6) The group does not have a well-defined central core.

_____

10. Suppose you plan to enter Wysacki. You make the following assumptions: (a) the frequency table you found accurately represents the performance of all Wysacki freshmen during the semester covered; (b) the distribution is an accurate prediction of the performance of future Wysacki freshmen; (c) you have no knowledge of how you will compare with Wysacki freshmen. On the basis of these assumptions, what is the probability that you will earn no fewer than twenty or more than twenty-four grade-points?

_____

11. Which assumptions in the question above are hazardous?   _____

12. Suppose you know that the rules require a freshman to earn at least thirty grade points to be initiated into a fraternity or sorority, and you learn that Mary Smythe was initiated at the end of her first semester. Assuming that Mary is included in the above distribution, what is the probability that she earned at least forty grade points?

_____

Problems 13–17. These items concern the three curves shown below.

Curve A   Curve B   Curve C

13. Describe curve A.   _____

14. Describe curve B.   _____

15. Describe curve C.   _____

16. In which of the three curves would there be the greatest difference between range and 10–90 interpercentile range?

_____

17. How could curves A, B, and C be used to deceive?

Chapter 11

Forming Causal Principles

- **Finding Common Factors**
- **Types of Causal Relationships**
- **Guidelines for Forming Causal Principles**
- **Refining Causal Principles**
- **Preliminary Testing**
- **Controls**
- **Statistical Procedures**

We turn now to perhaps the most important of inductive techniques. People in all walks of life constantly search for the causes of phenomena in order to understand and control their physical and social environment and to repeat desirable experiences and avoid undesirable ones. A student who makes an unexpectedly high grade on a test tries to find the cause, and his or her professor tries to learn what teaching techniques help students learn more effectively. A thinking citizen tries to learn what causes the community or nation to be a good or a bad place to live in so that he or she can preserve the good qualities and eliminate the bad ones. A social scientist tries to discover the causes of "good" and "bad" social phenomena.

The search for causes can take two forms. If you are wondering why you did well or poorly on a particular examination, you are looking for the cause of a **single event**. The procedures for this were discussed in Chapters 4 and 5. Stewart solved the case of Flight 629 by forming and testing hypotheses. A similar situation is likely to arise when a doctor diagnoses an illness. At times, deductive procedures can be used, for it may be known that the patient's pattern of symptoms is caused by only one disease. If so, it can be validly inferred that this disease is the cause. More commonly, however, a given pattern of symptoms is associated with several diseases. When this is so, the procedure must be inductive. The doctor forms rival hypotheses that each disease is the cause and proceeds, perhaps by laboratory tests, to try to determine which hypothesis is correct.

There are other cases, however, that

are unlike any of the above. At times, we seek the cause of **multiple instances** of a phenomenon, such as malaria, cancer, automobile accidents, aging, economic depressions, poverty, or war. Here, the aim is not to infer a particular cause for a particular event, but to develop a **causal principle**—a statement as to what causes a whole set of phenomena. While still inductive, the search for causal principles is apt to be considerably more difficult than the search for particular causes. When we are looking for a particular cause, we are usually aided by the fact that the kinds of events likely to have produced the phenomenon we are trying to explain are already known with some precision. The problem is simply to sort out the correct cause in the specific case at hand. Where causal principles are sought, however, knowledge about types of causes is precisely what we lack. Thus, arriving at correct causal principles often requires that new phenomena be discovered and new concepts developed. This in turn requires creative thinking on the investigator's part, tempered with the diligence of long study and careful preparation. When successful, the search for causal principles can have profound and far-reaching consequences, for arriving at such principles is the first step toward developing comprehensive **theories**, which include many causal principles and hence explain many sorts of phenomena. Such developments as Newton's theory of motion or the atomic theory of matter occur only as the culmination of a long process, in which many types of phenomena are investigated and many causal principles are found. Once developed, however, theories lend meaning and organization to whole areas of human experience, enable the development of new technologies, and pro-

vide wide-ranging guides to further research.

But if the search for causal principles is exciting, it is also treacherous. Indeed, the very concept of causation is complex and elusive. A given phenomenon can usually be held to have many causes, and which one we select as "the" cause will depend on our point of view and our purpose. Consider, for example, the disease of malaria. A laboratory technician may claim that malaria is caused by the presence of certain parasites in the blood, while a public health officer may insist that malaria is caused by the bite of anopheles mosquitoes. An epidemiologist might attribute malaria to anopheles mosquitoes that bite persons infected with malaria and then transmit the parasites by biting other people. A sanitation engineer might blame bad drainage that leaves pools of stagnant water in which the mosquitoes breed. A climatologist might point to heavy rainfall that provides the water. A sociologist might blame the lack of a social conscience in a community that permits the mosquitoes to thrive. An educator might point to the ignorance of the community. An economist might blame the lack of economic resources needed to rid the community of breeding places for the mosquitoes. Each point of view is at least partially correct, for malaria has been eliminated in many regions by simultaneous attacks on most of these causes.

In addition to the complexity of causes themselves, the search for causal explanations can be hampered by the fact that forming causal principles involves two kinds of inductive leap. Consider the situation when the principle that malaria is caused by parasites transmitted by the bites of anopheles mosquitoes was first formed. The first inductive leap involved was one of generalization. Although only relatively few of the countless cases of malaria that had occurred throughout history had been investigated, it was claimed that all people who contract malaria have been bitten by anopheles mosquitoes that have previously bitten people with malaria parasites in their blood. The second leap was to a special kind of hypothesis: these mosquito bites cause malaria. At the time, this hypothesis was a long leap in the dark. Millions of people have scratched billions of mosquito bites, but no one has ever actually seen malaria parasites pass from the bloodstream of one person into the mosquito and then to the bloodstream of another person. Inferences involving a long leap in the dark need not frighten us if we follow certain procedures. A high quality of both creative and critical thinking will be required, but the rewards are commensurate with the task.

We can see some of the importance, the problems, and the methods of finding causes if we look at a more recent case from the history of medicine. From July 21 through 24, 1976, the Pennsylvania Department of the American Legion held its fifty-eighth annual convention at the Bellevue-Stratford Hotel in Philadelphia. It was attended by some forty-four hundred delegates, members of their families, and others, and included a parade, meetings, and a number of social activities. When the convention ended, the legionnaires and their families returned to their homes throughout Pennsylvania. Within two weeks more than 150 of them developed a mysterious illness, characterized by fever, coughing, and pneumonia, and nearly 20 died. Because the conventioneers were now dispersed throughout the state, it was not immediately apparent what was happening, but by August 2 the problem had been recognized: a deadly epidemic associated with the convention

was under way. The illness, which came to be called Legionnaires' disease, quickly became the subject of one of the largest and most intensive investigations in the history of medical science.[1] The investigation was directed from the Center for Disease Control in Atlanta, and credit for its eventual success belongs to many. Indeed, as scientific investigations go, this one produced astonishingly quick results. By January 1977, the causative agent of Legionnaires' disease had been isolated and identified, an accomplishment that would not have been possible but for the teamwork involved. Even so, this success came only after numerous lines of investigation had failed and the search for the cause of Legionnaires' disease had all but been declared a failure.

Finding Common Factors

As we have seen, the kind of information we should search for in phase 2 varies with the problem. When we are trying to explain single events, we seek different facts or observations that might suggest useful hypotheses about the cause. When we wish to make a generalization, we seek observations or instances of the same kind. When the problem is to find the cause of multiple instances of a phenomenon, our procedure in phase 2 should com-

---

[1] Numerous treatments of the attempt to track down the cause of Legionnaires' disease exist. For an excellent summary see David W. Fraser and Joseph E. McDade, "Legionellosis," *Scientific American*, 241, No. 4 (October 1979), 82–99. See also Melvin Berger, *Disease Detectives* (New York: Crowell, 1978), and Gary L. Lattimer and Richard A. Ormsbee, *Legionnaires' Disease* New York: Dekker, 1981).

bine these two techniques. Our chief objective should be to discover common factors—that is, similarities among cases in which the phenomenon has occurred or common differences between cases where the phenomenon has occurred and cases where it has not. In following this procedure, we should be especially attentive to factors that changed just prior to the appearance of the phenomenon. Once recognized, common factors should suggest tentative conclusions about the cause of the phenomenon.

The first efforts to find common factors associated with Legionnaires' disease were carried out by a team of specialists in the study of epidemics from the Center for Disease Control, under the direction of Dr. David W. Fraser. Among other things, the epidemiologists conducted extensive interviews with victims of Legionnaires' disease and their families. These people were questioned as to their whereabouts and movements during the convention, what functions they attended, where they dined, and so on. In conducting this survey, the epidemiologists limited their investigation in an important way. An illness similar to Legionnaires' disease had been observed in several people who, though not associated with the convention, were in the vicinity of the Bellevue-Stratford while it was going on. These cases of so-called Broad Street pneumonia were excluded from the survey, even though as it turned out, this too was Legionnaires' disease. Excluding these cases may seem an arbitrary step, and in some ways it was. Yet when nothing is known about the cause or causes of a phenomenon, it is important to limit the information gathered in phase 2 to only those cases that are obviously pertinent. Besides reducing the sheer amount of data to be analyzed, thus eliminating wasted

effort, this procedure confined the epidemiologists' investigation to clear-cut instances of Legionnaires' disease, lessening the danger of confusion with other types of sickness.

Nonetheless, the epidemiological investigation proved disappointing in several ways. For one thing, the obvious possibility that the disease arose from food or drink was ruled out. Among the conventioneers who had become ill, no pattern of eating at particular restaurants emerged. Nor were there any differences between victims and others in attending functions where food or drinks were served, drinking the water at the hotel, or using hotel ice. The disease did not appear to be spread from person to person, for the only members of the legionnaires' families to become ill had themselves been in Philadelphia for the convention. The investigators did, however, uncover some suggestive similarities and differences. Incidence of the disease increased with the age of the conventioneers, and men were more likely to have contracted it than women. In addition, the sickness was more frequent among those who stayed overnight at the Bellevue-Stratford than among those staying at other hotels. Especially suggestive was the fact that on the average, legionnaires who became afflicted with the disease had spent about 60 percent more time in the lobby of the Bellevue-Stratford than those who escaped infection. A similar correlation obtained between contracting the disease and spending time on the sidewalk in front of the hotel. Thus one common factor associated with Legionnaires' disease can be expressed by this proposition:

1. Victims of Legionnaires' disease tended to spend time in or near the lobby of the Bellevue-Stratford.

Types of Causal Relationships

In searching for causes, we can begin phase 3 as soon as a common factor is discovered. As in other inductive contexts, the five-phase cycle should not be used rigidly in searching for causal principles. As soon as a common factor is discovered, a tentative conclusion should be formed about it. Meanwhile, the search for other common antecedents should continue. Proposition 1 above provides enough information to begin phase 3 by forming a tentative conclusion. When we are seeking the cause of multiple instances of a phenomenon, the tentative conclusions formed are **causal principles**. On the basis of the common factor described in proposition 1, we might form the following causal principle:

A. Legionnaires' disease was caused by one's being in or near the lobby of the Bellevue-Stratford.

Note that this causal principle is a hypothesis since it aims to explain the cases of the disease that the epidemiologists were investigating. As such, it involves an inductive leap, from the fact that contracting the disease was *correlated* with being in a certain location to the tentative conclusion that being in that location *caused* the disease. Note also that causal principle A involves generalizing from some to all cases. Not all of those who were afflicted with the disease spent a lot of time in or near the lobby of the Bellevue-Stratford. Yet it is suggested that even those who spent little time there contracted the illness in that location.

Causal principles may involve four different relationships between cause and effect.

Necessary Cause. A necessary cause is a condition that must be present if the effect is to occur. Electricity is a necessary cause of light in a bulb, for the light will not occur without the electricity. In other words, if A is a **necessary cause** of B, then B will not occur without A.

Sufficient Cause. A sufficient cause is any condition that will bring about the event alone and by itself. If A is a **sufficient cause** of B, then B will always occur when A occurs. A blown fuse is a sufficient cause for the light to go out, for the light will go out whenever the fuse blows. But a blown fuse is not a necessary cause for the darkness, since the light will go out for other reasons. The bulb might burn out or the current go off.

Necessary and Sufficient Cause. A necessary and sufficient cause is any condition that will bring about the event alone and of itself and without which the event cannot occur. If A is a **necessary and sufficient cause** of B, then B will occur when and only when A occurs. Necessary and sufficient causes are rare. One may be tempted to say "If and only if the current is turned on will the lights burn," but other conditions are also necessary, such as the correct voltage for the bulbs, satisfactory wiring, and bulbs in working order.

Contributory Cause. A contributory cause is a factor that helps to create the total set of conditions necessary or sufficient for an effect. Exposure is thought to be a contributory cause of the common cold, for it helps create the conditions that cause the cold, but we can have a cold with or without exposure. If A is a **contributory cause** of B, then B is more likely to occur when A occurs than when A does not occur. Contributory causes often present problems to investigators. An error we frequently make is to search for too simple a cause. Many times the real cause is a combination of contributory causes.

Guidelines for Forming Causal Principles

Three guidelines should be followed in forming causal principles.

At least in the early stages of an investigation, it is a good idea for the statement of a causal principle to contain the words "something connected with." Our first understanding of what causes a certain phenomenon is apt to be only vague and approximate. Causal principle A, for example, can at best be an approximation. Strictly speaking, being in the lobby of a hotel cannot cause a disease; rather, it must have been some factor to which conventioneers in the lobby of the Bellevue-Stratford were exposed that caused Legionnaires' disease. Thus causal principle A should be revised as shown below.

A-1. Something connected with being in or near the lobby of the Bellevue-Stratford caused Legionnaires' disease.

Adding these words to the statement of the causal principle has two advantages. First, it stimulates creative thinking. Without such a qualifier, we are likely to discard the causal principle as false beyond reasonable doubt instead of searching for common factors connected with being in the lobby of the hotel. Second, these qualifying words help to protect us

from accepting a false causal principle. For example, a comparison of the death rates of people admitted to hospitals and people not admitted might look like good evidence for the causal principle that being admitted to a hospital is a contributory cause of death—if we fail to realize that many people are already seriously ill when admitted.

The statement of the causal principle should indicate the type of causal relationship. For example, causal principle A-1 is shown below, revised to indicate a specific type of causal relationship.

A-2. Something connected with being in or near the lobby of the Bellevue-Stratford was a *necessary* cause of Legionnaires' disease.

Stating the type of cause involved helps indicate the type of testing required.

There is a small advantage in beginning with a necessary or a sufficient causal relationship. If we begin with the weakest relationship, the contributory cause, we may overlook the possible existence of a stronger relationship. Necessary or sufficient causal principles will often fail to stand up under testing, but they can easily be revised. For example, once we are certain that "Broad Street pneumonia" is actually Legionnaires' disease, we can easily revise causal principle A-2 by limiting it to the contributory relationship.

Causal principles should be formed for all plausibly relevant common factors. Failure to follow this guideline can be as costly as failure to form all reasonable rival hypotheses in explaining particular events. For example, one common factor in the cases studied by Dr. Fraser's epidemiological team was that all the victims had contracted the disease at a convention of a highly visible patriotic organization, the American Legion, of which they were either members or relatives of members. Was this common antecedent relevant? The epidemiologists had no way of knowing at first, and in the atmosphere of near-hysteria attending the first discovery of the epidemic, many people suggested it was. Some suspected that the conventioneers had been poisoned, perhaps by terrorists using a substance designed for chemical or biological warfare. No evidence to support this causal claim was ever found. Nevertheless, attention was given to the possibility that a chemical or biological warfare agent might be involved. This was sound procedure, for even when a causal principle proves to be entirely false, the process of testing it often uncovers clues that lead to the true cause. In short, when a common antecedent has any reasonable possibility of being relevant, a causal principle should be formed and tested. Failure to do so may prove costly.

Refining Causal Principles

It is characteristic of causal investigations that as they progress the exact nature of the cause comes to be more and more accurately understood. This increased understanding is reflected in the causal principles that are formed and tested as the investigation proceeds. As investigators close in on the cause of a phenomenon, the causal principles they form as tentative conclusions become more precise. Causal principles can be refined at any stage of the five-phase procedure. Doing so is a matter of creative thinking, based on a careful appreciation of the information available. Thus, based on the information they had gathered from the conventioneers, the investigators of Legionnaires' disease were able to focus on the area around the lobby of the Bellevue-Stratford as the precise location where the sickness appeared to have been transmitted to the victims. Moreover, it was possible to exchange causal principle A-2 for a principle considerably more precise. One factor common to the conventioneers in and near the lobby of the Bellevue-Stratford is that all of them were breathing pretty much the same air, circulated through the hotel's ventilation system. Knowing that respiratory diseases are frequently contracted by breathing air contaminated with either microbes or toxic substances, the investigators refined causal principle A-2 to A-3 below.

A-3. An airborne microbe or toxic substance, present in and around the lobby of the Bellevue-Stratford, was a necessary cause of Legionnaires' disease.

What might this unknown disease-causing agent be? Perhaps it was some sort of bacterium, for bacteria frequently cause pneumonia. Another possibility was a virus. An outbreak of infection from swine flu virus had been predicted for 1976. Perhaps this was it. Still another possibility was that the disease was caused by a rickettsia—a very small, bacterium-like organism, which, unlike bacteria, will grow only in a living host and not on a synthetic culture medium as most bacteria do. As for toxic chemicals that might have been in the air, any number of substances could have been the culprit. Overall, one might say that the possibilities were legion. At this point, therefore, the investigators had to follow the third guideline for forming causal principles and form a principle for each possible cause. Each of these was in turn more precise than A-3. For bacteria, for example, the relevant causal principle was:

A-4. An airborne bacterium, present in and around the lobby of the Bellevue-Stratford, was a necessary cause of Legionnaires' disease.

Preliminary Testing

Preliminary testing of causal principles should begin as soon as possible, for, as with hypotheses about the cause of single events, testing a causal principle often adds new and significant information. The principles of priority in testing hypotheses discussed in Chapter 5 apply to causal principles too. In this respect, the investigators of Legionnaires' disease were in a fortunate position. The search for the cause of the epidemic could now shift to the Center for Disease Control in Atlanta, where the staff and facilities were large enough to make it possible to proceed on a broad front, with different investigators testing the various causal principles simultaneously. This was the best procedure, given the urgency of the situation, in which lives were being lost and there was immense public pressure to solve the problem. Thus numerous members of the center's staff, all specialists in the particular fields involved, went to work testing different tentative conclusions about the cause of Legionnaires' disease.

Since the disease-causing agent was considered to be a necessary cause of contracting the illness, signs of its presence should be found in the bodies of those af-

flicted. Accordingly, samples of the tissues, blood, and waste products of victims were collected by field workers and sent to the center, where they were subjected to numerous tests. The specialists who tested the hypothesis that the disease was caused by bacteria attempted to grow the suspected bacteria in cultures prepared from the samples and grown on artificial media. Staining and microscopic examination should disclose the infectious agent if it were present. Those who tested for rickettsiae and viruses had to follow a different procedure: they injected living organisms with fluids prepared from the contaminated samples, hoping the disease-causing microbe would grow in the experimental animals. The tissues of these animals could then be subjected to various tests, again including staining and viewing under a microscope, in an effort to detect the cause. Finally, specialists in inorganic toxins examined tissue samples from the conventioneers in an effort to detect residues of any poisonous substance. In all, the tests conducted at the Center for Disease Control were extensive and thorough—enough, it was hoped, to uncover the cause of the disease, hitherto unknown.

Controls

Two basic procedures for testing causal principles are in use today. The first of these involves experiments in which the relevant factors are controlled as far as practicable. To take a simple example, if we wanted to test the effectiveness of a certain gasoline additive in prolonging engine life, we would set up an experiment in which two engines were run under carefully controlled conditions so that the only difference in their operation was the presence or absence of the additive in the gasoline used. At least one other test should be run to eliminate the possibility that the difference in the life of the two engines was due to the engines themselves rather than to the additive. Even then, an additional test should be arranged involving cars run on the road under normal conditions.

Careful controls are especially important in medical investigations. The complexity of the human organism is so great that it is impossible to list all the factors that might affect its well-being; and these factors must be kept constant as far as possible in any experiment. For example, unless kept in an antiseptic environment from birth, the body of almost any human being will be found to shelter all kinds of bacteria, viruses, and other microorganisms, some harmful and some not. Accordingly, the scientists at the Center for Disease Control had to set up controls in all their experiments. They took samples from people not infected with Legionnaires' disease, as well as from victims of it. The first set of samples was the **control** group, and the latter the **experimental** group. Both sets had to be subjected to the same tests and then compared. There was never any question that all sorts of microorganisms and toxic residues would show up in the samples from the afflicted conventioneers. The question was whether these would differ in any consistent way from what was found in the control group.

Another important use of control groups occurs in the testing of drugs. The experimental group is given the drug to be tested, and the control group is given a placebo, a harmless and inert substance that resembles the drug in appearance. The reason for this procedure is that in testing with human subjects it is extremely important to control psychologi-

cal factors. Suppose, for example, that we were testing a new formula to determine whether it will help to prevent the common cold. If we give the medicine to the experimental group, telling them that it will prevent colds, and give nothing to the control group, we have not controlled an important psychological factor—the experimental group know that they got the formula, and the control group that they did not. Experience has shown that under such conditions the experimental group is likely to report significant reduction in the number, duration, and severity of colds even when the supposed "formula" is itself a placebo, containing nothing more powerful than sterile sawdust. Most of us would like to believe that three capsules of something a day would help ward off common colds, and we tend to require less evidence for what we want to believe. Psychological factors like this can be controlled by giving the control group a placebo, and by administering placebo and formula under identical conditions so that no individual can know which of the two he or she took.

In using control groups, it is important that all relevant factors other than the one being tested be kept the same for both groups. A test of antihistamines, for example, would be of little value if the experimental group were to include only workers in a factory and the control group only people outside the factory. If the factory group were shown to suffer less from allergic reactions than the outsiders, it might be because of the air conditioning in the factory rather than because of the antihistamines. Such a procedure would not control all important relevant factors.

Since it is seldom possible to control all relevant factors in human beings, it is desirable to run the test with a large sample of individuals, on the assumption that with a large group chance tends to equalize factors that cannot be controlled.

When the medicine or object being tested is intended for diverse groups of people, the sample should obviously be diverse. If we were testing a certain food substance to see whether it increased energy and we tested it only with mail carriers, we could not conclude without further testing that it would also increase the energy of college athletes. For we would not have controlled such relevant factors as diet, age, and training. Thus we should be careful in extending conclusions about causal connections to groups not included within the sample tested.

The technique of controls should be applied as far as possible when you try to test any causal principle about yourself. Suppose you are trying to determine whether caffeine keeps you awake. The truth about caffeine seems to be that its effect varies widely with different individuals. The problem, therefore, is to determine its effect on you. It will not suffice to drink coffee every other night, for this will not control the psychological factors. It will be necessary to devise a way to get coffee with caffeine some nights and without caffeine other nights, without knowing which is which. One method would be to buy jars of the instant types and get someone to remove the labels but identify the jars by symbols known only to him or her. You could find out what the symbols meant after you had recorded the results. To get a reliable test, it would be necessary to record a large number of instances in order to offset factors you cannot control, such as diet, emotion, and fatigue.

Statistical Procedures

The second basic procedure for testing causal principles is statistical. Statistical procedures are necessary whenever it is impossible to establish satisfactory controls. Statistical procedures are widely used in studies of cause and effect in education. Suppose we wished to learn what causal relationship, if any, exists between studying calculus in college and success in medical school. It would not be practical to work with an experimental group of premedical students who study calculus and a control group who do not. Such an experiment would take too long, and there would be too many uncontrolled variables.

A more practical procedure would be to analyze a sample selected to include dropouts as well as graduates. A relatively large sample should be used in order to offset the fact that it is impossible to control all the possibly relevant factors. Some criteria, such as grades or the percentages of those graduating, would have to be adopted for determining success in medical school. If grades are used as the criterion, measures of central tendency could be computed for those who studied calculus and for those who did not. A comparison of these measures would yield evidence—though not necessarily conclusive—as to whether studying calculus is a contributory cause of success in medical school.

Causal relationships are not necessarily all-or-nothing, and we often need to know the degree of causal relationship between two variables. For example, when a new drug is discovered, it is necessary to establish the correct dosage, for many drugs are beneficial in certain quantities and harmful in others. In testing the effects of gasoline additive on the performance of automobiles, it is desirable to determine the effects of different amounts of the additive.

When we need to determine the degree of relationship between two or more variables, such as vocabulary and success, a statistical tool known as **correlation** can be extremely useful. Suppose our problem is to determine the degree of relationship between vocabulary and success. Our first step is to find a satisfactory method of measuring both success and vocabulary. Many satisfactory tests of vocabulary are available. To measure success, we would have to set up criteria. Income could be one criterion, but we should use others as well, lest we come out with a correlation between vocabulary and income rather than vocabulary and success.

Our next step would be to select an adequate sample. It would not do to select a group of highly successful people with excellent vocabularies and another group of unsuccessful people with poor vocabularies, for our sample would be loaded in favor of a high degree of correlation. On the other hand, if we selected our sample purely at random, a very large sample would be required to provide sufficient range in the two variables to represent the true picture. Thus the most economical method of getting a reliable sample might be to take a stratified sample on the basis of one, but not both, of the variables. It would probably be easier to select a sample on the basis of success, stratified to represent typical occupations and grades of success.

With our sample selected, the next step would be to administer a vocabulary test to as many members of the sample as possible. If a significant number of the individuals in the sample refused to take the test, we should suspect our results of being loaded, on the grounds that people who thought they had poor vocabularies would be more likely than others to refuse to take the test. In this event we should seek some method of persuading the reluctant ones.

With our data in hand, the next step is to determine the correlation between our variables. A practical method for doing so is to construct a **scatter diagram,** as shown in Figure 11.1. A study of the diagram will show how it was constructed. The measures of vocabulary and success were arranged in intervals, as in a frequency table, except that the number of instances in each interval is not shown. The same principles about the size and number of intervals apply. The x marks represent the position of each individual with respect to both variables. For an illustration, look at the x mark identified by the arrow, showing the standing of an individual named Smythe. Note that he or she is in the interval 0–10 on success and in the interval 10–20 on vocabulary.

Figure 11.1 Supposed Scatter Diagram Showing Moderate Positive Correlation

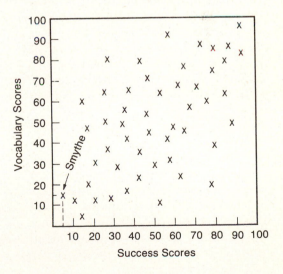

Figure 11.1 illustrates that if we were to draw a diagonal line from the lower left part of the diagram to the upper right the

x marks would tend to cluster on either side of the line. This indicates a **positive correlation** between the two variables. That is, the success scores of the individuals in our sample tend to increase as their vocabulary scores do. Cases of other kinds show a **negative correlation**, that is, one in which the values for one variable tend to decrease as those for another increase. Suppose, for example, that we wished to examine the relationship between the final grades students receive in their courses at Wysacki and the number of classes they miss. Figure 11.2 shows how the results of a survey might look on a scatter diagram.

Figure 11.2. Scatter Diagram Showing High Negative Correlation

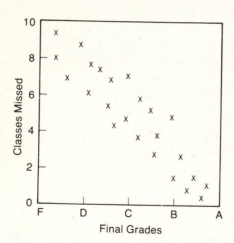

Here, the two factors show a negative correlation, for as the number of classes missed increases, the grades tend to decrease. The x marks cluster about an imaginary line running from the upper left to the lower right.

The degree of correlation between the two variables shown in a scatter diagram is determined by how closely the x marks

cluster about a diagonal line. The extent of clustering can be measured and expressed precisely by a number known as the **coefficient of correlation,** usually symbolized by the small letter r. The method for calculating a coefficient of correlation is a little complicated and need not detain us here. A description of the procedure can be found in any standard text in statistics. Since such coefficients are widely used, however, it is worth knowing a little bit about them. Coefficients of correlation always fall on a scale from $+1$ to -1. The number $+1$ indicates a **perfect positive** correlation. When this obtains, each individual represented in the scatter diagram falls exactly on the diagonal running from lower left to upper right, and the increases in one variable are directly proportional to increases in the other. In a **perfect negative** correlation, expressed as -1, each individual falls exactly on the diagonal running from upper left to lower right, increases in one variable being directly proportional to decreases in the other.

Perfect correlations are rare, especially with data involving human beings; most correlations turn out to fall between -1 and 0 or between 0 and $+1$. The scatter diagram in Figure 11.1 shows a moderate positive correlation of about $+.5$. Actually, the coefficient of correlation for vocabulary and success would vary according to how success is defined. A correlation of this strength suggests, but does not prove, that (1) there is a significant causal relation between the variables, and (2) one variable is not the sole cause of the other. The scatter diagram of Figure 11.2 shows a coefficient of about $-.9$. Here the agreement between the variables is even stronger, but it is strongly negative. The causal relationship suggested is that missing classes has a bad effect on grades. Finally, consider Figure 11.3, which seeks to correlate the heights of wives with the IQs of their husbands. Here, there is little or no agreement between the variables. The coefficient is roughly 0, suggesting no causal relationship whatever.

Although the investigators of Legionnaires' disease used some statistical methods in their epidemiological survey, the most important part of their investigation centered on the controlled experiments aimed at isolating the cause. The results of these tests will be outlined in the following chapter, where procedures for judging the reliability of causal principles are discussed.

Figure 11.3. Scatter Diagram Showing Negligible Correlation

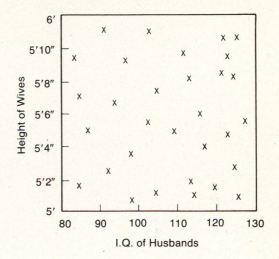

Exercise 11

Problems 1–15. To preserve the learning value of this exercise, complete each item before reading beyond it.

You are a member of the Peace Corps, assigned to a remote island in Micronesia. You expect to be the only Westerner on the island, but when you arrive, you find you have been preceded by another, one Gaston Smythe. In an effort to attract the tourist trade, Smythe has opened a gourmet restaurant featuring local dishes. Business is not good, but you sympathize with the project since it employs local people. You resolve to dine at Chez Smythe every Sunday evening.

1. On the Sunday night after your first dinner at the restaurant, you are awakened by a violent attack of coughing and wheezing. You have to sit up the rest of the night in order to breathe. You have never had these symptoms before, but you remember reading in a medical book that coughing and wheezing are symptoms of bronchial asthma. You form the tentative conclusion that you had an attack of bronchial asthma. Is your tentative conclusion (1) a causal principle, (2) a hypothesis about a single event, or (3) the product of a deductive inference?

   _____

2. On the second Sunday night you suffer another attack. You remember reading that bronchial asthma is believed to result from the inhalation or ingestion of certain substances termed *allergens* to which the patient is sensitive. Have you remembered (1) a hypothesis about a single event, or (2) a causal principle?

   _____

3. You define your problem as finding the allergen or allergens causing your asthma. Using only the data given above, list the common factors that may be relevant.

   _____

4. Write an appropriate causal principle based on the observation that both of your attacks came shortly after dining at Chez Smythe.

   _____

5. On the third Sunday evening you dine at Chez Smythe as usual, but you do not have an attack of asthma. Rate the reliability of the principle that dining at the restaurant is a sufficient cause of your asthma.

   _____

6. Revise the causal principle you wrote for problem 4 to conform to the evidence stated in problem 5.

   _____

7. Devise a procedure for testing this revised causal principle.

_____

8. On the fourth Sunday night you have a violent attack of asthma after your usual dinner at Chez Smythe. Since you must sit up to breathe anyway, you prepare the following table showing as much as you can remember about what you ate and drank on the four previous Sunday nights.

Date	Foods and Beverages	Symptoms
1st Sunday	Rice, boiled lobster, quemolia	Severe
2nd Sunday	Rice, boiled crabs, quemolia	Severe
3rd Sunday	Yams, oysters, water	None
4th Sunday	Rice, fried shrimp, quemolia	Severe

List three common foods and beverages in your table.

(1) _____ (2) _____ (3) _____

9. Which of these are possible necessary causes? _____

10. Which are possible sufficient causes? _____

11. On the fifth Sunday evening you drink quemolia (the local fermented beverage) and eat only yams and oysters. That night you have a severe attack. What substance can be eliminated as a necessary cause?

_____

12. On the sixth Sunday evening you eat yams and oysters, and drink only water. That night you sleep peacefully. On the basis of your evidence in hand, which substance is most likely to be the offending allergen?

_____

13. Considering the evidence in hand and following the guidelines stated in this chapter, fill in the blanks in this causal principle.

_____ is a _____ cause of my asthma.

14. On the next five Sunday nights you eat nothing but yams and oysters and vary the amount of quemolia you drink. You obtain the data below.

Date	Ounces of Quemolia	Hours Kept Awake by Asthma
7th Sunday	0	0
8th Sunday	3	1
9th Sunday	6	2
10th Sunday	9	4
11th Sunday	12	8

On a separate sheet of paper, construct a scatter diagram for the data.

15. Describe the correlation shown in this scatter diagram (high positive, low negative, etc.).

_____

Chapter 12

Testing Causal Principles

- **Repeating the Cycle**
- **The Fallacy of Questionable Cause**
- **Sources of Doubt**
- **Types of Evidence**
- **Criteria**

Throughout this book we have emphasized the importance of both creative and critical thinking. If we are not imaginative in forming tentative conclusions, we may miss the truth; if we do not carefully test and evaluate conclusions before accepting them, we may accept falsehood. We should be quick to form tentative hypotheses but slow to accept them as truth. The same point and counterpoint are true of causal principles. If we are not quick to notice common factors and form causal principles about them, we may fail to discover the cause. But if we accept causal principles as truth without completing phase 4, we may be inviting disaster by adopting solutions that are not only mistaken, but lead to greater harm. Both these points applied with special force to the investigation of Legionnaires' disease. It took a special dose of creativity even to find the microbe responsible for the sickness. Moreover, once it was found,

the investigators had to make doubly sure that this microbe was in fact the cause so that future outbreaks of the disease could be quickly recognized and controlled.

Repeating the Cycle

As with the process of forming hypotheses to explain single events, it may be necessary to repeat the decision-making cycle numerous times in the search for causal principles. The obstacles to quick success can be many, ranging from insufficient information in the frame of reference to inadequate test procedures to the complexity of the phenomena themselves. The investigation of Legionnaires' disease was remarkably thorough. Voluminous information had been collected, and tests for the various causative agents that had been hypothesized were thorough and careful. Yet within a few weeks after laboratory tests had begun, the investigation appeared headed for a dead end. With regard to bacteria, for example, no satisfactory results were produced. As expected, examination of the cultures that had been grown on artificial media turned up lots of bacteria. But comparison with control groups indicated that none of these bacteria was responsible. Causal principle A-5 seemed, then, to be false: no bacteria had been implicated as causing the illness. With rickettsiae and viruses the results were the same. The slides that had been prepared from the tissues of the laboratory animals were carefully stained and examined, but no guilty rickettsia was found, nor was there evidence that an infectious virus was responsible.

With the failure to find a biological cause, attention turned to the possibility that some inorganic toxin was responsible. But despite some initial positive indications, this line of investigation also failed to find the cause. In all, the results were completely disappointing, but Dr. Fraser had to respond to the public clamor that had surrounded the investigation from the beginning. In a talk at the annual meeting of the American Public Health Association in October, almost three months to the day from the start of the legion convention in Philadelphia, he reported that the cause of Legionnaires' disease was undiscovered and would probably remain so. Returning to Atlanta, he and other scientists prepared a lengthy summary report, as was usual at the conclusion of investigations. It was ready by December, and copies were delivered to all the laboratories at the Center for Disease Control that had been involved in the investigation. Among these was the laboratory of Dr. Joseph E. McDade.

As a specialist in rickettsiae, Dr. McDade had been involved in the phase of the investigation aimed at determining whether a rickettsia was responsible for Legionnaires' disease. The results of his investigation were negative, and like other scientists at the center, he suspected that the cause of the illness was some previously unknown microbe. The summary report contained a large amount of information gathered from various investigations. One of these bits of information was suggestive: the blood of the disease victims had consistently shown high levels of an enzyme called SGOT. This is indicative of liver damage, which can be caused by rickettsiae. That suggested the following causal principle:

A-5. A hitherto unknown rickettsia, probably present in the air at the Bellevue-Stratford, was a necessary cause of Legionnaires' disease.

If causal principle A-5 was correct, the disease-causing microbe might have been overlooked in earlier tests. Accordingly, Dr. McDade began to re-examine slides of stained tissue from laboratory animals that had been inoculated with material from victims of the disease. On one, which contained cells from the spleen of a guinea pig, he noticed a bundle of rod-like microbes, made to appear red by the stain used on the slide. They looked too large to be rickettsiae. In fact, similar rods had been observed before and dismissed as bacterial contamination. But those had been single rods; a bundle might mean something important. Still uncertain as to exactly what kind of organism this was, Dr. McDade undertook a new test. Materials from the spleens of the guinea pigs used in the earlier test were injected into fertilized chicken eggs. Within a week, all of the embryos in the eggs had died. Examination of stained cells from the yolk sacs of the eggs disclosed numerous bundles of the rod-shaped organism. Whether they were large rickettsiae or small bacteria, it had begun to appear that these organisms were the cause of Legionnaires' disease. This was only one of many repetitions of the cycle that had occurred in the investigation of the disease. Unlike others, however, this one appeared to have produced success.

The Fallacy of Questionable Cause

But success was not yet assured. Had the investigation of Legionnaires' disease concluded at this point, there would have been danger of committing the inductive fallacy of **questionable cause**. We commit this fallacy whenever we conclude that one event or condition causes another simply on the ground that the two events or conditions are associated in our experience. The questionable cause fallacy may be the most expensive of all errors in reasoning. It costs the human race untold amounts of time, money, and discomfort.

One version of this fallacy is often called by the Latin expression **post hoc, ergo propter hoc** (after this, therefore because of this). Here a causal relationship is held to obtain simply because the events or conditions in question occur in temporal sequence. Suppose a superstitious baseball player has been in a batting slump. Then he suddenly breaks out of the slump by hitting two home runs in one game. He would be less than conscientious if he did not want to know the cause of his success so that he could repeat it. He therefore thinks back over the hours since the last game, in which he struck out three times, looking for some factor that was different. He is likely to pounce on the first event or condition he thinks is different and treat it as the cause of his two home runs. The different factor could be anything he remembers, such as entering the field through a different gate. The logical fallacy is that the only ground he has for attributing his success to entering a different gate is that this event preceded the home runs. Yet there were probably many other factors with as good or better claim to be the cause of his success. Perhaps something in his personal life that had been causing anxiety had changed for the better. Perhaps he had a relaxing evening and a good night's sleep before his good game. Or perhaps the pitcher was having a bad day.

In other cases, the fallacy of questionable cause is committed on the ground that two factors tend to be regularly associated. At times the results can be quite pernicious. Suppose, for example, that based on differences in IQ test scores between blacks and whites, we were to conclude that blacks were genetically inferior to whites, having less native intelligence. Such an inference would commit the fallacy of questionable cause by treating a mere correlation between genetic heritage and IQ test performance as a causal relation. To do so is to ignore a host of historical and environmental factors that might account for the difference.

The fallacy of questionable cause is responsible for much of the distortion in our frames of reference. Suppose Mr. Smythe has had a hard day at the office. When he reaches home his nerves are frayed and he craves a few minutes of peace and comfort. But his son Algernon, aged three, has been lonesome all day and yearns for his father's attention. Algernon's efforts to get his father's attention could easily lead to a severe scolding. Algernon is then likely to blame the scolding entirely on his own behavior.

Especially if the incident is repeated later, it is only natural for Algernon to conclude that seeking his father's attention causes scolding. Unable to get attention at home, Algernon may try to get it at school and get scolded again. It would be natural for him to compound his error by concluding that seeking attention causes scolding. Little Al may retain this false conclusion in his frame of reference long after he has forgotten the incidents that led to it. He may also derive a value judgment from this fallacy: seeking attention is bad.

The way to avoid the fallacy of questionable cause is to carefully test all causal claims, in order to eliminate the possibility that other factors might be responsible for the phenomenon under investigation. Suppose you do unusually well on a test and afterward examine your procedures in an effort to identify the factor that was responsible. And suppose you recall that on the night before this test you went to a movie, whereas usually you studied for tests until very late in the evening. If, with no other evidence, you conclude that going to a movie causes better performance on tests, you have committed the questionable cause fallacy. Even on this slender evidence, there is nothing wrong with forming a tentative conclusion that going to a movie the night before is a contributory cause of better performance on tests, for this is creative thinking. But if you skip phase 4 and accept this causal principle as truth, you have committed the fallacy. Among the other possible explanations you would have to eliminate are that this test was unusually easy or the grading unusually lenient.

A final caution: even if you succeed in establishing beyond reasonable doubt that going to a movie contributes to successful performance on examinations in your own case, this would not show that the same relationship holds in the case of other students or of students generally. Thus to conclude that seeing a movie the night before an examination would be beneficial to all students, would be to commit the fallacy of hasty generalization. The same causal relationship might hold for some others but not for all. Some students who see movies the night before an exam could become bored or sedated by them or experience greater anxiety over the loss of study time. The result could be a worse performance rather than a better one.

Sources of Doubt

Let us set aside the difficulty of hasty generalization in the present discussion since it has been considered elsewhere. Establishing the reliability of causal principles can then be broken down into two tasks. It must be demonstrated that (1) a relationship between the phenomenon under investigation and the alleged cause does indeed exist, and (2) this relationship is the particular type of causal relationship alleged to exist. Despite the apparent success of Dr. McDade's experiment with the fertilized eggs, the investigation of Legionnaires' disease still left room for doubt on both points. Before continuing, you might pause for a moment and see if you can think of some reasons for doubting that the rod-shaped organism found in the yolk sacs was indeed the cause of Legionnaires' disease.

Consider first the question whether there was any relationship at all between these organisms and the disease. Similar rods had been observed in the lung tissue of the conventioneers and dismissed as bacterial contamination. Perhaps this was actually the case. Bacteria are notorious for their ability to survive even in the harshest environments, and they can as easily be found in scientific laboratories as elsewhere—sometimes more easily. It was at least possible that these organisms did not come from the legionnaires at all but instead had gotten introduced into Dr. McDade's cultures by accident at some other point in the test procedures. This possibility was strengthened by the fact that the materials injected into the eggs came not directly from the conventioneers but from guinea pigs that had in turn been inoculated with materials from disease victims. Perhaps the guinea pigs were already infected from some other source.

Second, even if the microbes in the yolk sacs did originate with the legionnaires, there was still a question as to just how they were related to the disease. Perhaps the relationship was not causal at all but one of mere correlation. More than one kind of microbe was undoubtedly present in the air at the Bellevue-Stratford, and the fact that one of them had proven deadly to chicken embryos hardly showed that it was the cause of Legionnaires' disease. Moreover, even if there were a causal relationship, it might have been merely contributory: perhaps this organism only weakened the conventioneers' resistance to illness from some other source, which was in turn fatal. There were, then, a number of reasons for doubting whether this organism was related to Legionnaires' disease and whether it was the necessary cause that had been postulated. Such doubts are especially important in medical investigations, where lives depend on care and accuracy. Dr. McDade had more testing to do.

Fortunately, it was possible to deal with both types of doubt at the same time. One of the chief mechanisms by which the human body fights infection is the production of antibodies to combat the invading organism and the toxins it produces. An important fact about antibodies is that they are highly disease-specific: the presence of a given microbe in the body will stimulate the production of antibodies targeted against that microbe and no other. The concentration of these antibodies in the blood increases as the body mobilizes its resources, reaching its peak during the stage of convalescence, when the victim is regaining health and strength. It is possible to test for the presence of antibodies to a particular microbe by adding serum from convalescing patients to cultures of the microbe suspected of causing their illness and then determining whether antibodies in the serum attach themselves to the microbe. Dr. McDade's next step was to perform this test.

Types of Evidence

The search for causal relationships is aided by four kinds of information. When we are forming causal principles, information of these kinds is useful in suggesting new hypotheses to us. When we are testing them, the information forms the evidence in terms of which we judge their reliability.

Agreement. One kind is derived from John Stuart Mill's classic method of agreement: "If two or more instances of the phenomenon under investigation have *only one circumstance in common*, the circumstance in which alone all the instances agree is the cause (or effect) of the given phenomenon."[1]

The essence of Mill's method of agreement is **the elimination of all but one**

---

[1] John Stuart Mill, *A System of Logic* (London: Longmans, 1967), p. 255.

common antecedent. It was this method that the epidemiologists employed when they searched for common factors among the victims of Legionnaires' disease. The method was also an important feature of Dr. McDade's test of serum from convalescing patients of the disease. More than 90 percent of the serum specimens tested were found to contain antibodies specific to the newly discovered microbe. By contrast, earlier serological tests had disclosed in these patients no consistent pattern of presence of antibodies to other organisms known to cause pneumonia. The table below illustrates what a partial summary of the results of these tests might look like.

These results go a long way toward eliminating one of the sources of doubt discussed in the last section. The consistent presence of antibodies to the new microbe in the legionnaires' blood makes it highly unlikely that the microbe originated anywhere except with the sick conventioneers. It also greatly strengthens the probability of the causal generalization that this microbe was responsible for the disease. In this respect, however, the evidence fails to satisfy Mill's rule in two important ways. First, the last case listed reflects the fact that in about 10 percent of

the serum specimens tested, antibodies to the new organism were not detected. There are a number of ways to explain the failure. Perhaps the time at which these specimens were collected was not ideal, or these patients actually had some other disease. Nevertheless, the ideal of Mill's rule is violated, for the rule requires that all instances agree as regards the factor thought to be the cause. Second, even if the agreement were total, the possibility that the disease might have some other cause would still not be completely eliminated; a more thorough study might reveal other common antecedents that have not been eliminated.

Such shortcomings are extremely common, for in practical circumstances we are rarely able to achieve what the ideal rules for a causal investigation demand. Even when the cause of a phenomenon has been found, complete agreement in the cases under investigation may not result, because of the complexity of the cases themselves and of the procedures used in testing. Strong positive correlations must often be accepted in lieu of complete agreement. Also, we are usually unable to demonstrate that there is only one possibly relevant common factor in an adequate sample of instances of a phe-

Table 12.1 Presence of Antibodies

Case	Legionnaires' Disease	New Microbe	Microbe A	Microbe B	Microbe C
1	Yes	Yes	No	No	No
2	Yes	Yes	No	Yes	No
3	Yes	Yes	Yes	No	No
4	Yes	Yes	No	No	No
5	Yes	Yes	No	No	No
6	Yes	Yes	No	No	No
7	Yes	Yes	No	Yes	No
8	Yes	Yes	No	No	Yes
9	Yes	Yes	No	No	No
10	Yes	No	No	No	No

nomenon. We cannot be sure that there are no undiscovered common factors even in the relatively few situations where we can find only one. In this regard, Mill's rule is too idealistic, for it is based on the assumption that the analysis of common antecedents is exhaustive. If this were the case, we would be involved in deduction rather than induction, for we would know all the possibilities and eliminate all but one. Yet even if we had covered all the possibilities, we would not know that we had done so. Thus it must always be assumed that other, as yet unknown, common factors might arise.

To deal with these practical difficulties, Mill's notion of agreement needs to be modified. Let us therefore define **agreement** as the existence of a common factor in at least two instances of a phenomenon. Also, we have to remember that this form of evidence has little significance when the number of instances examined is small. Actually, Dr. McDade tested serum from a lot more than ten patients, and future investigations of Legionnaires' disease were to examine many other cases as well.

Difference. Another type of evidence is derived from Mill's rule of **difference**: "If an instance in which the phenomenon under investigation occurs, and an instance in which it does not occur, have every circumstance in common save one, that one occurring only in the former; the circumstance in which alone the two instances differ is the effect, or the cause, or an indispensable part of the cause, of the phenomenon."[2] Note that Mill's rule of difference requires a comparison of at least one case in which the phenomenon occurred with at least one in which it did

_____
[2] Mill, *Logic*, p. 256.

not occur. Note further that the essence of the rule is **the elimination of all except one difference** between instances in which the phenomenon occurred and those in which it did not.

The rule of difference is what is responsible for the use of control groups, which also figured importantly in Dr. McDade's tests. If the suspect microbe was indeed the cause of Legionnaires' disease, then not only should antibodies to it be consistently present in victims of the disease, but they should also *not* appear consistently in those not afflicted. Thus the control group should show no consistent presence of antibodies. A small group of cases illustrating this application of the rule of difference might look like those summarized below.

Case	Legionnaires' Disease	Antibodies to New Microbe
1	Yes	Yes
2	Yes	Yes
3	Yes	Yes
7	Yes	Yes
8	Yes	Yes
11	No	No
12	No	No
13	No	No
14	No	Yes
15	No	No

Like the rule of agreement, the rule of difference reflects an ideal, and the evidence above does not fully satisfy the rule. As before, the group of cases is small and is for illustration only. A larger sample would be needed to make more certain that the experimental group differed consistently from the control group in having antibodies to the new microbe. Even then, it would be impossible to be absolutely certain that no further, as yet undetected difference was present between the two groups. The evidence does, however, support the hypothesis that the newly discovered microbe caused the disease outbreak at the Bellevue-Stratford, for the control group, unlike the victims of the disease, shows no consistent presence of antibodies. Antibodies do show up in case 14, but in fact this is consistent with the causal claim that was being tested, namely, that the microbe was a necessary cause of the disease outbreak at the hotel. Someone who was infected by the microbe at some earlier time might already have developed an immunity to it, as evidenced by the presence of antibodies, and hence not have become ill when exposed to it during the convention. In fact, this suggests an answer to a question that had puzzled investigators of Legionnaires' disease from the beginning, namely, why employees of the Bellevue-Stratford seemed to be unaffected by the sickness. Perhaps they had been infected at an earlier time and had already developed an immunity to the disease. This suspicion was confirmed in later tests of blood serum from employees and long-time residents of the hotel, in which antibodies to the microbe turned up with considerable frequency.

Because of the difficulty of being sure that all possibly relevant factors have been controlled in testing, Mill's rule of difference needs to be modified for practical purposes. Let us define **difference**, therefore, as a factor that tends to be present in instances where a phenomenon has occurred and absent where the phenomenon has not occurred.

Concomitant Variations. So far, the evidence considered raises the probability of the causal principle that the newly discovered microbe caused the disease outbreak. Antibodies to the microbe tended to be present in victims of Legionnaires' disease and absent in nonvictims. Nor was there any indication that the microbe was only a contributory cause, for no consistent presence of antibodies to other pneumonia-causing agents had been discovered. There was, however, still one source of doubt. Could it be that the legionnaires and their families had actually come into contact with this microbe at some earlier time, perhaps at an earlier meeting of the Legion? This was only a remote possibility, but if it were true, then in spite of the evidence so far, the new microbe would not in fact be the cause of the disease. The clinching argument against this possibility and in favor of the hypothesis that this microbe was the cause of Legionnaires' disease illustrates another of Mill's rules. It is called the rule of **concomitant variations**: "Whatever phenomenon varies in any manner whenever another phenomenon varies in some particular manner is either a cause or an effect of that phenomenon, or it is connected with it through some fact of causation."[3]

The rule of concomitant variations had been used earlier by the epidemiologists investigating Legionnaires' disease, when they determined that the conventioneers who were afflicted with the illness had tended to spend more time in or near the lobby of the Bellevue-Stratford than those who escaped it. Time spent in the lobby area had been found to be positively correlated with the disease: the longer people stayed in this area, the more likely they were to be afflicted. Dr. McDade's use of the rule concerned a negative correlation. In the course of an infectious disease, the disease-causing organism grows and multiplies in the body,

---

[3] Mill, *Logic*, p. 263.

having more and more serious effects. In response, the victim's immune system manufactures antibodies to fight the disease. During the period of convalescence, the concentration of antibodies in the bloodstream increases while the numbers of the disease-causing organism decline. By the rule of concomitant variations, this negative correlation indicates a causal relation, which in this case is well known to immunology: the decline in numbers of the infecting organism is caused by the increase in the attacking antibodies, which was in turn caused by the increasing numbers of the organism during the onset of the disease. Moreover, since antibodies are so highly disease-specific, it was possible for Dr. McDade to determine whether this concomitant variation had occurred simply by testing for an increase in antibodies to the new microbe in the serum of the conventioneers during the period of their recovery. If this phenomenon—known as "seroconversion"—could be detected, any lingering doubts as to whether the new microbe was the cause of Legionnaires' disease would be resolved. For although antibodies to a microbe may be found in a patient long after he or she has recovered from an illness, the concentration is low and does not vary. An increase could only mean that the new microbe had indeed infected the legionnaires during the convention.

Testing for seroconversion requires more than one serum specimen from each patient, and the specimens must be collected at suitable times during convalescence. Suitably timed specimens were available from more than 50 percent of the patients whose serum Dr. McDade examined. In most of them, he was able to show that seroconversion had occurred.

Scatter diagrams often help in the search for concomitant variations. A scatter diagram for some of the serum speci-

mens Dr. McDade tested for seroconversion might look something like the one below. The numbers on the left side of the diagram reflect the concentration of antibodies in the serum tested.

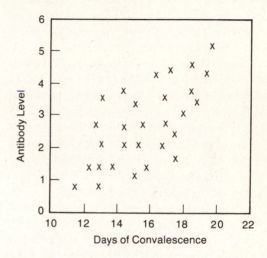

As you can see, the level of antibodies tends to rise as the period of convalescence proceeds. As with the other rules we have seen, however, it must be remembered that Mill's rule of concomitant variations represents an ideal. There are several ways in which the pattern this diagram illustrates does not completely satisfy the rule. The test is only an indirect one, for it measures antibody level over time, whereas the actual correlation being sought is between antibody increase and a decline in the numbers of the microbe in the patients. Only with the aid of well-established theories of disease and the immune mechanisms of the body is it possible to interpret the diagram as indicating that the suspected concomitant variation actually occurred. Also, it must be remembered that Mill's rule contains the word *whenever*. The fact that this scatter diagram indicates the occurrence of seroconversion in the patients studied does not prove that the same phenomenon would occur in *all* persons recovering from Legionnaires' disease. Another scatter diagram prepared for another group of patients might show no correlation at all, or even a negative one. Many a medical researcher has been encouraged by a positive correlation only to have the correlation disappear or even reverse itself in later experiments.

Furthermore, a correlation between two variables does not show which causes which. A positive correlation between grades in calculus and success in medical school would not prove that success in calculus causes success in medical school. It might be that success in medical school causes success in calculus, or both might be caused by some other factor.

Finally, even when the sample is adequate, a significant correlation shows only that there is a relationship between the two variables. The relationship may or may not be causal. Only a thorough understanding of the phenomenon being examined, usually requiring long and careful study by many researchers, can enable us to be sure that a suspected causal relationship actually obtains.

Converging Causal Principles. Converging propositions may support causal principles as well as hypotheses about causes of single events. For example, Dr. McDade's causal principle that the microbe he had found had caused the sickness of the legionnaires would gain support if it could be shown that the same microbe had been responsible for similar disease outbreaks at earlier times the cause of which had never been discovered. This line of research was also pursued at the Center for Disease Control, and with very positive results. To cite just one case, an unexplained outbreak of fever had occurred in a single building of the Oakland County Health Department in Pontiac,

Michigan, in 1968. Though the exact cause was never found, serum specimens from thirty-seven victims of "Pontiac fever" had been preserved at the Center for Disease Control. In tests conducted in 1977, nine years after the outbreak, seroconversion to the new microbe was demonstrated to have occurred during convalescence in thirty-one of these cases. An added bonus was that in the Pontiac outbreak it had been shown that the disease was spread by way of the air-conditioning system of the building in which the victims had contracted the illness. This evidence supported causal principle A-4, according to which the cause of Legionnaires' disease at the Bellevue-Stratford was an airborne agent.

It was becoming clear that this microbe was new only to the investigators. Indeed it was soon to develop that it had even been isolated previously. When a report on the characteristics of the "new" organism was published, Dr. F. Marilyn Bozeman, a scientist working with the U.S. Food and Drug Administration, noticed that it was similar to four rickettsia-like microbes that she had worked with nearly thirty years before and that had since been stored in a deep freeze. Tests undertaken on these four organisms in 1978 showed that indeed one of them was the same as the microbe that caused the Bellevue-Stratford outbreak. It had been isolated by Dr. Bozeman in 1947, from a patient with an illness characterized by fever and respiratory infection.

Criteria

As with other types of inductive conclusions, there are no foolproof methods of assessing the reliability of causal principles. The judgment of even the most careful investigator is influenced by his or her personal point of view. Insufficient or false information in one's frame of reference may prevent a correct interpretation of the evidence. One's self-concept or values may induce one to favor one causal principle and resist another. Lack of skill in creative thinking may prevent the formation of the one correct causal principle. Individuals can therefore be expected to differ in their judgments of the reliability of causal principles. Careful attention to the following criteria will increase both objectivity and skill.

Reliability of Observations. A causal principle is no more reliable than the observations on which it is based. Many promising causal principles have failed when subjected to rigorous testing that neutralized or eliminated bias in the observations.

Representativeness of Samples. Since causal principles are usually reached by generalizing from cases observed to cases not observed, the evidence for causal principles should meet the requirements for sampling discussed in Chapter 8.

Degree of Correlation. We should be particularly wary of causal principles based on low correlations computed from small samples. Low correlations in small samples may be accidental, or the two variables may be fluctuating in response to a third variable. It is likely, for example, that a comparison of distance of place of birth from Australia and the incidence of Legionnaires' disease would have shown a low positive correlation. Even with an adequate sample, a high degree of correlation between two variables proves only that a relationship exists between them—it does not prove that the relationship is causal. The high correlation between the incidence of Legionnaires' dis-

ease and time spent in or near the lobby of the Bellevue-Stratford was not in itself enough to pin the blame on conditions in the lobby, but it was more than enough to suggest that other causal principles should be formed and tested for all relevant factors that might have been connected with being in the lobby.

Adequacy of Controls. The closer we can come to establishing controls that eliminate all except one difference, the more likely it is that the factor that differs is a causal factor. Had Dr. McDade been able to perform serum tests in which he knew that the only difference between the experimental group and the control group was that the former had suffered from Legionnaires' disease, a high degree of correlation would have proved beyond reasonable doubt that the suspect microbe was the cause. But with human beings it is usually impossible to control all factors and always impossible to know that we have. Moreover, even if we could completely control physical conditions, subjective factors would vary.

Since subjective factors affect observers as well as the observed, medical researchers frequently use double-blind experimental procedures. The technique is so called because both subjects and observers are "blind" in the sense that they do not know which subjects are in the experimental and which in the control group.

A classic example of the double-blind procedure was the experiment conducted in 1952 by the National Foundation for Infantile Paralysis to determine whether gamma globulin was of any value in preventing or reducing the severity or damage of poliomyelitis. Houston, Texas, was selected for the experiment because a polio epidemic was in progress there. Since parents could not be compelled to have their children injected with the serum, the foundation had to depend on volunteers. To reduce the possibility that the volunteers would constitute a loaded sample, the foundation set out to test the serum with thirty-five thousand children. The large sample reduced the probability that the volunteers constituted a loaded sample and made it more likely that chance would equalize such possibly relevant factors as social and health conditions, which could not be controlled. To eliminate any possible psychological factors, both in children and parents, and in the doctors who would appraise the results, each child was injected with an individually numbered syringe. Half the syringes contained gamma globulin, and half contained a harmless and presumably ineffective gelatin. The syringe numbers were locked in the safe of the company that made the serum, so that no interested person could know which child was injected with which substance until the results were appraised and recorded.

In situations where it is impossible to control all possibly relevant factors, a large and representative sample should be used, on the theory that the "laws" of probability will tend to compensate for the lack of adequate controls.

Time Factors. You need not stick a pin into your finger many times to prove that sticking a pin into your finger causes pain because the relationship between cause and effect is immediately obvious. The greater the time lapse between the occurrence of the alleged cause and the appearance of the phenomenon, the greater is the number of other factors that might be causes. Proving that water you drank on a vacation in the Caribbean caused your typhoid fever would be a different matter because the symptoms might not appear for a month after you returned. During

this time you doubtless drank many beverages from many sources, and many of them must be suspect until tested. In general, then, the greater the lapse of time between cause and effect, the stronger the evidence must be.

Thoroughness of the Investigation. The weakness in evidence from agreement is the difficulty of demonstrating that the instances in which the phenomenon under investigation has occurred have *only one* factor in common. Similarly, the weakness in evidence from difference is the difficulty of demonstrating that the instances in which the phenomenon did and did not occur are different in *only one* respect. The weakness in evidence from concomitant variations is the difficulty of demonstrating that there are no other concomitant variations that would explain the phenomenon in question. Only by a thorough investigation can we eliminate reasonable doubt that there may be another common factor.

By all of these criteria, the investigation of Legionnaires' disease had by now progressed from apparent failure to unqualified success. The evidence of the seroconversion experiments made it clear that the surviving victims of the disease had recovered from an infection by the microbe Dr. McDade had isolated, and no indication had been found that any other disease-causing agent was involved. Accordingly, the investigators evaluated the conclusion that this microbe was the cause of Legionnaires' disease as true beyond reasonable doubt. The microbe was given the name *Legionella pneumophila*, and a public announcement that the cause of the disease had been found was made on January 18, 1977. This time, in contrast to the announcement of the previous October, the atmosphere was triumphant.

The investigators had reason to be proud, for it is rare that the search for a causal principle succeeds so quickly. Even so, the investigation very nearly failed, and it is instructive to see why. Dr. McDade had been set on the track of his discovery when he decided to look for evidence for causal principle A-5, according to which a rickettsia was responsible for the disease. Even upon finding the offending organism, however, he was not sure A-5 was true, and in fact it was false. *Legionella pneumophila* is a bacterium, as was proven by Robert E. Weaver, another scientist at the Center for Disease Control, who succeeded in growing the organism on a specially prepared artificial medium enriched with other substances, including hemoglobin. That the organism would grow outside a living organism proved it was a bacterium and hence that causal principle A-4, which said a bacterium was responsible, had been correct all along. The earlier bacteriological tests had failed to detect the organism because it does not grow on standard media. Indeed, it was in part a stroke of luck that Dr. McDade found the organism at all. Slides that are being examined for rickettsiae are usually disinfected to kill any contaminating bacteria. The particular slide on which Dr. McDade found the bacterium had not been treated in this way; otherwise he would probably have found nothing at all.

There are innumerable instances in the history of science of investigators who, like Dr. McDade, looked for one sort of solution to a problem only to find that another was correct. In many other cases solutions have been missed simply because investigators were not open to the unexpected and hence were either too inflexible in their methods of investigation or unable to interpret correctly what they saw. *Legionella pneumophila* presents an excellent case in point because, given its unusual growth characteristics, conventional means for detecting bacteria were almost doomed not to find it. It had to be found by someone who was not looking for it, like Dr. McDade. Even so, he could have dismissed what he saw as unimportant on the grounds that it looked like a bacterium and would surely have been isolated in other phases of the investigation had it been the cause. In cases like this, it almost appears that nature conspires to deceive us. But such a belief is strictly an artifact of the personal point of view. Nature is complex but not conspiratorial. At times the sheer mass of information at hand masks the truth. More commonly, however, the problem is the one Hamlet describes to Horatio: that there are more things in heaven and earth than are dreamt of in our philosophies. If Dr. McDade and others at the Center for Disease Control had not been open to new possibilities—an important part of creative thinking—Legionnaires' disease would very probably be the same mystery today that it was in 1976.

Exercise 12

Problems 1–15. These problems continue the case begun in Exercise 11. Again, for the full value of this exercise, complete each problem before reading beyond it.

1. Consider the following causal principle in the light of all evidence accumulated in Exercise 11: Drinking quemolia is a sufficient cause of your asthma. With respect to which criteria is the evidence weak?

   _____

2. For which common factors have causal principles not yet been formed and tested?

   _____

3. Rate the reliability of the causal principle above.   _____

4. What type of evidence does the table in Exercise 11, problem 8, provide?

   _____

5. Consider this causal principle: Something in the air you breathe on the way to Chez Smythe is a contributory cause of your asthma. What type of evidence do you have for this principle?

                                                                 _____

6. With respect to what criteria is this evidence weak?

   _____

7. Rate the reliability of this principle.   _____

8. Devise a procedure for testing this principle more thoroughly.

   _____

9. On the twelfth Sunday Chez Smythe is closed for a local religious festival, and you stay at home and limit your evening meal to American canned goods. That night you have no attack. What is the effect of this evidence on the causal principle stated in problem 5 above?

   _____

10. You remember reading in a medical book that airborne fungi and pollens are among the allergens that cause asthma. What type of evidence does this provide for the causal principle stated in problem 5 above?

_____

11. On the thirteenth Sunday night you have a violent attack. As you struggle to breathe, you try to recall the possibly relevant differences between this and other weekends. You recall that on your way to Chez Smythe you picked some exotic yellow flowers. If you conclude that the yellow flowers caused your asthma, what fallacy would you commit?

_____

12. If you warn the local people that picking these flowers will give them asthma, what additional fallacy would you commit?

_____

13. You recall two other unusual factors: you spent Saturday night drinking American beer with Gaston, and you drank about seven ounces of quemolia on Sunday evening. Write the causal principle that best fits all your evidence in hand.

_____

14. Rate the reliability of this principle. _____

15. What action should you take?

_____

16. As the Wysacki track coach, you wish to test a new vitamin compound alleged to increase endurance. You decide to measure the endurance of your athletes in September by having them ride a machine that measures their output of energy, administer the vitamin compound during the season, and measure endurance again at the end of the season. Describe three of the controls you should use in your experiment.

_____

_____

_____

17. Suppose you first measure the energy your athletes are capable of exerting. Then you feed half of them the compound for a week, meantime trying to give all athletes the same diet and training. At the end of the week you again measure the energy they are capable of exerting. Which type of evidence are you using?

_____

Chapter 13

Evaluation and Decision

- **Deductive Decisions**
- **Inductive Decisions**
- **Proposals for Action**
- **Predicting Consequences**

- **Evaluating Consequences**
- **Revising Proposals for Action**
- **Acting on Unreliable Conclusions**

Thus far we have concentrated on the first four phases of the decision-making cycle. Let us now turn our attention to phase 5, evaluation and decision.

Sometimes our only problem in phase 5 is to decide whether to accept any of the tentative conclusions formed in phase 3 and tested for reliability in phase 4. This situation occurs when, as in some academic contexts, our primary aim is simply to learn the truth about things. At other times phase 5 is more complicated because, depending on what conclusion we accept, we may wish to take some sort of practical action. In either sort of case, however, it is important to observe this principle: **tentative conclusions should never be accepted as fact until tested by the appropriate procedures and judged to be true beyond reasonable doubt.** This policy applies to *all* tentative conclusions, no matter what type of inference is used to reach them.

This principle may seem too strict. After all, if we exclude from our frames of

reference all beliefs except those tested and judged true beyond reasonable doubt, we are likely to have few beliefs indeed. Moreover, we often must act on beliefs of which we are uncertain. If we were always to wait until tentative conclusions were shown to be true beyond reasonable doubt, we would be guilty of decision by indecision through most of our lives. But the crucial words in the above principle are the words *as fact*. There is nothing wrong with accepting a tentative conclusion as probable or highly probable when the evidence in hand shows it to be so and acting on the conclusion as needed. The difference is that when we do this, we must remain especially sensitive to the fact that we may be wrong, adjust our actions accordingly if we can, and be prepared to test the conclusion further when the occasion requires it. Only in this way is it possible to keep our frames of reference from being dominated by beliefs that arise more from habit and prejudice than from critical thinking.

Deductive Decisions

In most situations, we must decide not only whether to believe our tentative conclusions, but also what to do about them. Sometimes this decision can be made by a relatively simple deductive inference. Thus we saw in Chapter 6 that the jury in the trial of John Gilbert Graham reached its verdict by deductive inference from premises provided by the law. The effect of the law in criminal cases is to provide a policy for dealing with them once the evidence has been evaluated. In the same way, the scientists at the Center for Disease Control have policies for the course of action to be taken when the investigation of a disease is concluded. One of the most important is that information gathered in the course of investigating a disease is to be set forth in a report, available to the scientific community and the general public. Dr. Fraser was following this principle when he prepared the report containing the hint that led Dr. McDade to his work with *Legionella pneumophila*. The same policy was followed in January 1977, when a special report detailing the success that had finally been achieved was published by the Center for Disease Control. Since then, the scientific literature on Legionnaires' disease has grown to voluminous proportions.

Inductive Decisions

When we have no rule, policy, or law to use as a premise for deductive decisions, phase 5 requires the use of inductive techniques. To see how we should proceed in this sort of case, imagine that you are a doctor working in a large city hospital in 1978. In the past week there has been an increase of pneumonia cases admitted to the hospital, and more patients are still arriving. Your problem is first to determine the exact nature of the patients' illnesses and then to decide how they should be treated.

The mere fact that all these patients have pneumonia does not even indicate that the treatment should be the same for all of them, much less what the preferred treatment should be, for the cause of the pneumonia could differ from case to case. Nevertheless, the marked rise in pneumonia cases suggests to you that an epidemic due to a single disease-causing agent may be under way. Furthermore, information about your patients' backgrounds suggests the same tentative conclusion. Of the pneumonia cases presently in the hospital, 60 percent work in the IRS building downtown, and another 30 percent have recently spent a considerable amount of time there having their income tax returns audited. For 90 percent of your patients, then, a common cause of their disease is indicated. The question is, what is the cause?

If you follow the procedures of effective thinking, you would now form a number of tentative conclusions about the cause of the illness of the patients connected with the IRS building. Among them, you would be wise to include the hypothesis that these patients are suffering from Legionnaires' disease, the cause of which had recently been discovered. You would then proceed to test your tentative conclusions in an effort to determine which one is correct. Let us assume your tests indicate that Legionnaires' disease is indeed the cause of your patients' illness, and you conclude that this hypothesis is true beyond a reasonable doubt.

Note that so far you have used the five-phase cycle only to interpret your problem situation. You now have a reliable causal principle, but you still must decide how to treat your patients. The difficulty, however, is that since Legionnaires' disease is still new to the medical profession there are as yet no settled policies for dealing with it. How should you proceed? You might, as we all sometimes do, act on impulse. You might decide to administer penicillin to your patients, on the grounds that penicillin is a broad-spectrum antibiotic, effective against a great many organisms known to cause pneumonia. This, it may seem to you, offers the best chance of easing your patients' suffering. But even if this assumption were to prove correct, you would be violating a cardinal rule of effective thinking, as we shall see.

Proposals for Action

When we must decide what to do about a situation, and neither precedent nor policy gives us satisfactory premises, **the five-phase cycle should be used twice, once to interpret the situation and once to find the best course of action.** In using the cycle to find the best course of action, the phases need not be followed in rigid sequence, but each should be completed.

In this use of the cycle, the tentative conclusions formed are **proposals for action**. In your situation at the hospital, you already have one proposal for action: to use penicillin. But there are other proposals you might form, for there are a number of drugs that, though not effective against as many types of infection as penicillin, could prove to be especially effective against Legionnaires' disease. Here would be a chance for some creative thinking on your part. You might recall, for example, that the bacterium that causes Legionnaires' disease was found by

using techniques designed to isolate rickettsiae and that this bacterium is similar to rickettsiae in some of its effects. Perhaps, then, a drug that is especially effective against rickettsial infections would be the best treatment. One such drug is erythromycin. While not useful against as many types of disease as penicillin, erythromycin is highly effective in combatting rickettsial infections. Thus you now have two proposals for action:

A. Treat the patients with penicillin.

B. Treat the patients with erythromycin.

There are, of course, a number of proposals involving other drugs that you should form as well. But for purposes of simplicity let us confine our attention to these two.

Predicting Consequences

When our purpose in reasoning is to reach the truth, tentative conclusions are tested for reliability. When our purpose is to decide on a course of action, a different approach is needed. **We test proposals for action by predicting their consequences and evaluating those consequences as solutions to our problem.** At this point, therefore, you should try to predict as accurately as possible what the consequences of your two proposals for action are likely to be. Suppose that in order to do so, you consult reports on the treatments that were tried by various physicians during the Philadelphia outbreak of Legionnaires' disease. You find that, among a number of other drugs, penicillin and erythromycin both were tried and with markedly different results. Some of the patients treated with penicillin responded, for the death rate among patients treated with penicillin was lower than that occurring with a number of other drugs. Nevertheless, these patients still showed a mortality rate of 20 percent. By contrast, the patients treated with erythromycin had a mortality rate of only 11 percent. Not all were saved, but erythromycin had proved to be as effective as any treatment used on the Philadelphia victims and more effective than most.

Our old friend the hypothetical proposition is perfectly suited to the purpose of representing the advantages and disadvantages of a course of action. The procedure consists of forming a hypothetical proposition by making the proposed action the antecedent and adding a consequent that states the **consequences**, that is, the advantages and disadvantages that will or may ensue.

Proposal for Action		Advantages	Disadvantages
A. Treat the patients with penicillin	⊃	Some patients will be saved	The mortality rate *may* be 20 percent.
B. Treat the patients with erythromycin	⊃	More patients will be saved	The mortality rate *may* be 11 percent.

Three guidelines for adding consequents should be observed.

1. When there is doubt that the predicted consequence will follow from the action, the consequent should be appropriately qualified. Note that the consequents for proposals A and B are qualified by *may*. The circumstances among your patients are not likely to be exactly the same as those of the Philadelphia victims of Legionnaires' disease. Average age, resistance to disease, and other factors could vary. Hence you cannot be sure the mortality rates for the two treatments will be precisely the same.

2. Long-term as well as short-term consequences should be predicted. Suppose a mathematics professor is debating whether to give a freshman a passing grade that she does not deserve. Obviously the short-term consequences would be pleasing to the student. But the long-term consequences may be quite different. A failing grade would probably force the student to repeat the course; a passing grade might permit her to take a more advanced course without being prepared. Another possible long-term consequence of a passing grade is that the student might continue in a curriculum for which she is unsuited instead of finding a better one.

3. Equal attention should be given to desirable and undesirable consequences.

Evaluating Consequences

When the cycle is being used to find the best course of action, one objective of phase 5 is to evaluate each proposal for action by weighing the predicted advantages against the disadvantages. When there is no reasonable doubt that the predicted consequences will follow, we need only weigh the predicted advantages and disadvantages of each proposal.

In this respect, your position with regard to proposals A and B is a good one.

For although there is some question as to what the exact mortality rate among your patients will be, there is no reasonable doubt that it will be lower if you administer erythromycin than if you use penicillin. *So far*, then, proposal B represents the best course of action for you to take. All the same, you should not yet be completely satisfied, as we shall see in the next section.

When there is some degree of doubt that the predicted consequences will follow, both advantages and disadvantages should be discounted according to the concepts of probability. Suppose a gambler makes this offer: you pay him twenty-five cents for one roll of a pair of dice; he will pay you five dollars if you roll two sixes, and nothing if you roll any other combination. If you accept his offer on the grounds that your possible loss is twenty-five cents and your possible net gain is $4.75, you would be oversimplifying the problem. The advantage of accepting his offer should be discounted by multiplying the advantage (winning $4.75) by the probability that this result will happen (1/36). Thus the theoretical advantage is worth only about thirteen cents. Similarly the disadvantage (losing twenty-five cents) should be discounted by the probability that this will happen (35/36). Thus the theoretical disadvantage is the loss of twenty-four cents.

Although in most situations, the probabilities cannot be calculated so precisely, the principle applies nonetheless. For example, suppose you were dealing with just a single case of Legionnaires' disease. You might well decide to begin treatment by administering erythromycin to your patient. Yet the statistics from the Philadelphia outbreak would force you to resist the conclusion that this treatment is certain to succeed. Based on that evidence in hand, your patient has only an 89-percent chance of surviving even with this treatment. For dealing with the epidemic at the IRS building, the relevant statistics for discounting probabilities would concern outbreaks of the disease other than the one in Philadelphia. Your decision that erythromycin is a better treatment than penicillin for the IRS patients is based on the fact that in Philadelphia there was a 9-percent differential in the mortality rates for the two treatments, favoring erythromycin. At the same time, however, you know that due to a number of factors, the mortality rates need not be exactly the same in the IRS epidemic. Suppose, then, that you had access to statistics regarding three other outbreaks of Legionnaires' disease, and that in these outbreaks the difference in the effectiveness of penicillin and erythromycin was not as great. If so, you should discount the advantage of treating your patients with erythromycin. It may still be the better of the two treatments, but you would have to consider it less probable that erythromycin would be significantly better than penicillin.

Revising Proposals for Action

We have already seen that in interpreting problem situations effective thinking requires being prepared to revise our tentative conclusions as more information comes to light. The same principle applies in the phase of evaluation and decision: **proposals for action should be revised as necessary based on assessments of their consequences**.

It is not uncommon for us to deal with our problems by halfway measures or to choose inferior solutions when better ones are available. Often we do so because we fail to revise proposals for action after considering their consequences. We can be so pleased at having found a proposal that promises some help with our problem that we overlook the possibility of doing better still by revising the proposal. Consider again your situation after evaluating proposals A and B. Clearly, proposal B is the better of the two since erythromycin will save more lives among your Legionnaires' disease patients than penicillin. But what about the 11 percent who can still be expected to die? If you were satisfied with this outcome, you would not be much of a physician.

When no proposal for action is evaluated as satisfactory, additional proposals or revisions of existing ones should be formed. Usually, the process of predicting and evaluating the consequences of the proposals we have already formed aids us in this task. In the present case, for example, a better course of action would be to begin by treating your patients with erythromycin, but to plan a back-up treatment for any patients who fail to respond. Experience with Legionnaires' disease since the Philadelphia outbreak has indicated that patients not responding to erythromycin alone are sometimes helped if a drug called rifampin is added to the treatment. Accordingly, physicians dealing with the disease today are advised to follow a revised version of proposal B: administer erythromycin and supplement the treatment with rifampin for patients who fail to respond.

Acting on Unreliable Conclusions

Ideally, we should take no action until we are reasonably certain that we have accurately interpreted the situation. Often, however, the threat of decision by indecision forces us to act before we can be sure what the situation is. In other words, we must act before we can be sure that the tentative conclusions we have formed to interpret the situation are true. Consider the case of Joe Smythe, who is typical of many students in this era of pressure to get into and graduate from college. Joe was the valedictorian of his graduating class in a small high school. Upon entering Wysacki University, he had his choice of fields to pursue. But the Smythes (unaccountably, it seems) have never been a prosperous clan, and like many students from less-privileged backgrounds, Joe was attracted to a career in one of the professions. He settled on the premedical curriculum, with high hopes of making the dean's list. But at midterm Joe received a warning from the dean's office that if his grades did not improve he would be put on probation at the end of the semester. Since this is a new experience for Joe, his first step in dealing with it should be to use the five-phase cycle to interpret his situation. In phase 1, he should define his problem as the discovery of the causes of his unsatisfactory performance at Wysacki. In phase 2, he should gather information relevant to his problem as defined in phase 1. Let us suppose that the information he gathers includes the following propositions.

1. There are many high school valedictorians at Wysacki.

2. The premedical curriculum is especially difficult.

3. He is studying only ten hours a week, which is well below average for Wysacki students.

4. His College Board scores are below the average for Wysacki students.

These propositions contain sufficient information to enable Joe to move to phase 3 and form hypotheses. The hypotheses he forms should include the two listed below.

A. His aptitude for medicine is insufficient.

B. Though his aptitude is sufficient, he is not studying enough and his background and study skills are not adequate.

Since hypotheses A and B are rivals, their combined probabilities cannot exceed one. Let us suppose, however, that after testing them Joe is unable to rate either hypothesis as even highly probable. He is inclined to consider hypothesis A slightly probable, and hypothesis B slightly improbable, but beyond this he cannot judge.

It might seem that Joe's puzzlement is too great for him to be able to proceed further. In fact, however, he should still go on to use the five-phase cycle to decide on a course of action. In phase 2 of this use of the cycle, he should gather information relevant to actions he might take. Essential information would include Wysacki's rules governing suspension, probation, and graduation. To complete this phase, Joe should consult his academic advisor, who is likely to have information he could not secure himself. In phase 3, the objective should be to form proposals for action. The more proposals he forms, the more likely he is to include a satisfactory one. Much human folly can be traced to a failure in creative thinking at this point. There is usually more than one way to solve a problem, and the first solution that comes to mind is not always the best.

If Joe Smythe had found a hypothesis about the cause of his poor grades that he could rate as true beyond reasonable doubt, he would need to form and evaluate proposals for action only in terms of this hypothesis. But he has two rival hypotheses about his grades, either of which could be true.

When we have two or more rival tentative conclusions about the problem situation, proposals for action should be formed for each rival. Thus Joe should form proposals for action for both his hypotheses.

Stated below are two of the many proposals for action he might form for hypothesis A (His aptitude for medicine is insufficient).

1. Change to a less rigorous curriculum next semester.

2. Withdraw from Wysacki and join the army.

Joe should also form proposals such as the two listed below for hypothesis B (Though his aptitude is sufficient, he is not studying enough and his background and study skills are inadequate).

3. Drop out and work on his background and study skills are inadequate.

4. Transfer to a less difficult college.

Joe could, of course, test one of the four proposals pragmatically by putting it into action and then evaluating the results. But pragmatic testing of proposals for action can be expensive in both money and suffering. He is far less likely to rue his decision if he carefully predicts and evaluates the consequences of each proposal.

Since Joe has two rival hypotheses about the cause of his problem, he must predict and evaluate the consequences for each. Shown below are some of the consequences he might predict for proposal 2 that take into account both of his hypotheses.

Proposal for Action		*Consequences if A is true*
Withdraw from Wysacki and join the army	⊃	avoid flunking out.

risk washing out of boot camp.

risk possibly severe limitations on career.

Consequences if B is true

Unnecessary loss of educational opportunity.

risk washing out of boot camp.

When we use this procedure we can often think of proposed actions whose probable consequences will be satisfactory for all tentative conclusions about the situation. For example, Joe Smythe might consider studying twenty hours a week for the rest of the semester and employing a tutor to help him improve his study habits. This action would have advantages whichever hypothesis is true. If hypothesis A is true, additional study should improve his grades, and better study habits will be valuable in any curriculum. If hypothesis B is true, this action may solve his problem. Furthermore, this action should yield additional evidence about his two hypotheses. If his grades in chemistry and biology improve, he will have a converging fact for hypothesis B. If they do not improve, he will have a converging fact for hypothesis A and he can then seriously consider changing to a less rigorous curriculum.

Note that Joe should be as objective as possible both in interpreting his situation and in predicting consequences of proposals for action. His feelings about medicine or low grades are completely ir-

relevant, and he should not let them influence either his interpretation of his situation or his predictions of consequences. If, because his self-concept is threatened by poor grades or the prospect of failure in medicine, he deceives himself about his academic situation or the consequences of his actions, he may persist in a direction that will prove disastrous. But note also that his feelings are quite relevant in *evaluating* the predicted consequences of his actions—in fact, his feelings are an essential part of the evidence. If he deceives himself into believing that medicine is not important to him and shifts to a different curriculum, he may be making the wrong decision.

Deciding whether to act on a proposal usually involves some kind of value judgment. If Joe Smythe places a high value on a career in medicine, the proposal that he study twenty hours a week is probably a good one. If he places a high value on earning a college degree and if the kind of degree is relatively unimportant to him, then changing to a less rigorous curriculum could be his best action.

Many decisions involve values that oppose one another. There are two ways that this can happen. Some decisions involve **competing values**—values both of which are acceptable but interfere with each other because our time, energy, and money are limited. A college football player who plans to study medicine may have a problem with competing values because football and his premedical studies compete for his time and energy, especially during the football season. If he is to be reasonably successful in both, he must budget his time and energy according to the relative demands of both activities. Other decisions involve **conflicting values** or values that are rivals in the sense that two hypotheses are rivals: if one is right, the other is wrong. A cadet at the U.S. Air Force Academy might have a problem if she discovered that another cadet was cheating on examinations. Out of loyalty, it might seem wrong to inform on a fellow cadet under any circumstances. At the same time, she may believe strongly in the academy honor code, since people who are to be entrusted with the lives of others should have a strong sense of honor. The code states: "We will not lie, steal, or cheat, or tolerate among us anyone who does." Procedures for resolving conflicts in values are discussed in Chapter 31.

Exercise 13

Problems 1–10. You are the commander of the Coast Guard station at Norfolk, Virginia. At 3:15 p.m. on February 7, you receive a telephone call from the president of Marine Tanker Lines saying that the Marine *Sulphur Queen* is overdue and unreported.

1. Define your problem.

_____

_____

Your routine questions elicit the following information from the president.

1. The *Queen* left Beaumont, Texas, at 8:00 a.m., February 2, with a cargo of molten sulphur.

2. The *Queen* carried a crew of thirty-nine.

3. The *Queen* was due to dock at Norfolk, Virginia, at noon, February 7.

4. The *Queen* carried a marine telephone and two high-frequency radio transmitters, all operated by separate sets of batteries.

5. The last radio message received from the *Queen* was a personal marine telephone call made by a crew member at 8:25 p.m. on February 3. The ship's position given at this time was 230 miles southeast of New Orleans.

6. Under normal procedure, the *Queen* would have sent radio messages to Norfolk forty-eight hours and twenty-four hours before her estimated time of arrival at Norfolk. No such messages were received.

7. The *Queen* did not respond to radio calls sent by marine telephone stations in New Orleans, Miami, Jacksonville, Charleston, and Norfolk on February 7.

On the basis of the evidence now in hand, you form the following two hypotheses.

    A. The *Queen's* delay is due to minor difficulties that can be corrected without assistance from the Coast Guard.

    B. The *Queen* has had a disaster at sea.

2. Are these two hypotheses rivals?　　　　　　　　　　_____

3. Rate the reliability of hypothesis A.　　　　　　　　_____

4. Suppose you rate hypothesis B as improbable. The regulations governing your performance in office state: "It is the duty of the commander of a Coast Guard station to take appropriate action when a boat or ship of any size is reported overdue, no matter how unlikely it is that the boat or ship is in trouble." You define your next problem to be to decide what action to take. Describe the reasoning used in deciding to redefine your problem.

_____

_____

5. This proposal for action occurs to you: Order all available cutters and planes to launch an immediate search of the area from New Orleans to Norfolk. Predict a consequence of this action if hypothesis A is true.

_____

6. Revise, in accordance with the guidelines in this chapter, the following predicted consequence of this action: The crew of the *Queen* will be saved.

_____

7. You form a second proposal for action: Alert all Coast Guard stations between New Orleans and Norfolk. Predict the consequences if hypothesis A is true.

_____

8. Predict the consequences of this action if hypothesis B is true.

_____

9. You form a third proposal for action: Delay launching a search for a few minutes while you form and test hypotheses as to the probable position of the *Queen*. Predict the consequences of this action if hypothesis B is true.

_____

10. Which of the three proposals for action should you execute? _____

Problems 11–16. You are a student at Wysacki, where a hundred students major in chemistry. You have a blind date with a chemistry major and find him or her dull. You form a tentative conclusion that most chemistry majors are dull.

11. Rate the reliability of your tentative conclusion. _____

12. Another chemistry major, whom you do not know, writes you a note asking if you would like to go to the annual chemistry department chili cookoff. You consider this proposal for action: Ignore the note. Predict the consequences of this action if your tentative conclusion about chemistry majors is true.

_____

13. Predict the consequences of this action if your tentative conclusion is false.

_____

14. You then consider a second proposal for action: Accept the date. Predict the consequences of this action if your tentative conclusion about chemistry majors is true.

_____

15. Predict the consequences of this action if your tentative conclusion is false.

_____

16. Write a third proposal for action that is likely to be satisfactory whether your tentative conclusion about chemistry majors is true or false.

_____

Part Three

Meaning and Deduction

Chapter 14

Classification and Definition

- **Utilitarian Systems of Classification**
- **Explanatory Systems of Classification**
- **Meaning**

- **Definition**
- **Genus and Difference**
- **Evaluation and Decision**

In Chapter 3 we examined one of the most important types of deductive inference, the hypothetical syllogism. Here in Part Three we will return to the subject of deductive reasoning to examine and evaluate other important kinds of argument used in it. You will remember that when we assess the reliability of a conclusion reached by a deductive argument, an important part of the assessment is to determine whether the argument is valid. We will soon be considering a number of types of argument whose validity can be assessed in terms of relationships between classes. In order to deal with these arguments, it is helpful to have some familiarity with the subject of classification and the closely related subject of definition. Thus the present chapter is devoted to these topics. They are, however, important in their own right. As we will see, skillfully developed systems of classification and clear definitions are indispensable aids to effective thinking.

An essential part of all learning is **classification**, or the organization of our experience and the items it contains into various categories. From earliest childhood, we learn that the things in our environment belong in different groups: there are people and animals, hot things and cold things, things we are allowed to play with and things we are not. As we grow in experience, the categories we use to classify things increase in both number and sophistication. We learn, for example, to classify automobiles into Chevrolets, Fords, Dodges, Toyotas, Volkswagons, and so on. Cutting across these categories are others having to do with engine size, whether the engine is cooled by air or water, whether the transmission is standard or automatic, the type of fuel required, and so on. Of course, some people have a much more elaborate system of classification for automobiles than others; but even the average person's represents no mean achievement. And this is only a tiny part of the full set of categories with which we order our experience. We can also classify events, qualities, ideas, facts—anything we can put a noun or noun phrase on. And that is virtually everything.

An accurate system of classification is essential to a good frame of reference and hence to sound thinking. One of the most important advances in scientific classification came in the late eighteenth and early nineteenth centuries with the development of the periodic table of the elements. Before this time substances that we now know to be compounds, such as water, were mistakenly thought to be elements; substances that we know to be elements, such as the metals, were falsely taken to be compounds. There were numerous systems for classifying chemical substances, and all were in error. The result was that chemists were unable to communicate effectively with one another, and advances in chemistry were slow and painful. Only when a better system of classification was devised was it possible for the field of chemistry to enter fully the age of modern science. The problem of poor systems of classification can also afflict college students. Consider, for example, the harmful way in which courses are often categorized. To some people, a "useful course" can only be one that fits neatly into a narrowly conceived career specialization, without any attention to how a course might prepare a person for the nonprofessional aspects of life. Other courses may be "interesting" or "fun" or "easy," but unless they fit into the "useful" category, they are less valued. The result can be an impoverished educational experience. A better-conceived system of classification helps avoid this problem.

Closely related to classification is **definition**, or the articulation of the meanings of words. Language itself is based on classification. For example, all common nouns are names of classes of objects, actions, qualities, or ideas. The use of linguistic symbols to designate classes is made possible by the fact that linguistic symbols have meanings. Thus the meaning of a noun like *father* consists of the characteristics by which we recognize items as belonging in the class of fathers, that is, the characteristics of being male and a parent. Once we know what these characteristics are, two reciprocal results occur. First, when we learn of something or someone that is both male and a parent, we can correctly classify it as a father in our frame of reference. Second, when we learn of an item in our experience that is a father, we can validly infer that it is both male and a parent. Simple though these two operations are, they are indispensable both to ordering and to making use of our frame of reference. If we could not describe classes with defined symbols and use these symbols in reasoning processes, our frame of reference would be of relatively little value. It would be like a vast library in which the books are shelved in haphazard and superficial order and which has no card catalog. Locating the information we need to bring to bear on a particular problem would be so difficult that we could only rarely reach informed and effective decisions.

Throughout our lives, we encounter many situations in which we need to develop for ourselves a system of classification. The five-phase cycle, with modifications, applies to working out systems of classification as well as to other tasks of reasoning. As with all other uses of the cycle, the phases should not be followed in rigid sequence. The objective of phase 3 is (1) to find a satisfactory basis for division and (2) to name and define the necessary classes and subclasses. In other words, the tentative conclusions formed are systems of classification, with names and definitions for each class and subclass. The items in one's frame of reference can be divided into classes according to many different bases or principles. The manager of a grocery store might divide merchandise into classes according to such bases as brand, container, size, shape, or quality. A student might divide literature according to author, type, period, or theme. How good a given system of classification is will depend on how well it serves the purposes it is designed to achieve.

Utilitarian Systems of Classification

The purpose of a **utilitarian** system of classification is to facilitate finding, handling, or putting to practical use the material classified. Suppose you have accumulated such a mass of class notes, college records, correspondence, and the like that you have trouble finding things. The time has come to set up a filing system based on a classification of this material. Your purpose is utilitarian—you want to store your papers so that you can find them readily.

In a utilitarian system of classification, the basis for division into classes and subclasses can be purely arbitrary, according to the needs or even the whims of the classifier. If you wish, you can divide your papers into classes according to any number of bases, such as size and subject, so that you can file your class notes in three-ring notebooks and your correspondence in an alphabetical filing case. Grocery store managers may arrange their goods on shelves according to such classifications as bread, soups, cookies, canned vegetables, fresh vegetables, and meats. Any item that does not fit one of these classes can be put into a miscellaneous class.

Systems of classification cannot be tested for reliability as can hypotheses or causal principles. A classificatory system is a kind of structure imposed on items in our experience. Obviously, a useful structure will have to reflect the actual nature of those items closely, but strictly speaking, a structure cannot be said to be either true or false. The test of a system of classification, then, is the degree to which it serves the purpose for which it was constructed. Utilitarian systems of classification are tested **pragmatically**, that is, by putting them to practical use. You can test your filing system simply by using it. As you use the system, you will doubtless discover flaws, but you can correct them as you go.

When the quantity of material to be classified is large, a preliminary test with a sample is in order. Suppose you have just become the manager of a large office with hundreds of filing cabinets full of records. After studying the files, you conclude that the records have outgrown the system, with the result that finding items in the files resembles a scavenger hunt. Therefore you devise a new system of classification. You could, of course, test it by having your clerks refile all records according to your new system. If it is sound, you may get a raise in salary; if it is not, the office may get a new manager. A better procedure would be to have a clerk try your new system on a sample of your files. You can then correct the flaws before applying the system to all the files. If you follow this procedure, your office is less likely to get a new manager.

Explanatory Systems of Classification

The purpose of an **explanatory** system of classification is quite different. Consider the problem facing a doctor who wishes to learn as much as possible about allergies, a field in which our knowledge is far from complete. Her purpose in classifying available information would be explanatory—to help her understand the causes, symptoms, and treatment of allergies. Explanatory systems of classification may also serve utilitarian purposes. The classificatory systems used by zoologists, for example, aid not only in understanding the fauna of the world but also in storing specimens and arranging exhibits. Since the basic purpose of an explanatory system of classification is to facilitate understanding the essential nature of the material classified, an explanatory system must be much more precise than a utilitarian one.

When explanatory systems of classification are constructed, phase 2 consists in collecting relevant information about whatever is to be classified. Relevant information for our allergist would include general statements and causal principles about allergies, as well as case studies of allergy victims. When the things to be classified are complex and heterogeneous, such as the causes, symptoms, and methods of treatment of allergies, much trial and error is likely to be required before a satisfactory system of classification is found. It is therefore advisable to begin with a sample of the material to be classified.

The objective in phase 3 is to construct a tentative system of classification by dividing the material into classes and subclasses. Our allergist might begin with the following classes.

I.   Allergens (substances causing allergic reactions)

II. Symptoms

III. Treatment

The next step (phase 4) would be to test the tentative system by placing some items in each category and assessing the results. Explanatory systems of classification may be judged by the following five criteria.

Significant Differences. Classes should be subdivided into as many levels as necessary to reveal significant differences. If our allergist classified all allergens under one main class, with no subdivisions, the classification would reveal very little about the essential nature of the allergens. She should therefore search for significant differences in allergens, and subdivide them as necessary to reveal these differences. It might, for example, be helpful to subdivide allergens on the basis of how they reach the body, as shown below.

I. Allergens
   A. Substances inhaled
   B. Substances ingested

The allergist might subdivide each of the second-level classes on the basis of differences in the nature of the substance, as shown below for substances inhaled.

I. Allergens
   A. Substances inhaled
      1. Pollens
      2. Fungi

She should continue the process of subdividing classes until the significant differences are exhausted.

Consistency. Whenever possible the basis for division into classes should be consistent within each given level. The third-level division below violates this criterion.

I. Allergens

    A. Substances inhaled

        1. Sawdust

        2. Dust

        3. House dust

The class *substances inhaled* has not been divided on one consistent basis. "Dust" is a general category including both sawdust and house dust. "Dust" should be a third-level class, along with "pollens" and "fungi," while "sawdust" and "house dust" should be fourth-level classes under "dust."

I. Allergens

    A. Substances inhaled

        1. Pollens

        2. Fungi

        3. Dust

            a. Sawdust

            b. House dust

Comprehensiveness. There should be enough classes and subclasses to provide a place for every item in the material to be classified. The second-level classes of allergens are insufficient, for they do not yet include a place for substances such as cosmetics that cause allergic reactions through contact with the skin. Usually, a fault like this one can be remedied simply by adding another subclass. Sometimes, however, it may be necessary to change the basis of division, even at the first level.

Essential Properties. Classes and subclasses should be divided on the basis of the essential properties of the things being classified. The color of an auto-mobile is not an essential property; the fact that it has wheels is. Most objects have many different essential properties, and the one chosen as the basis for division should be relevant to the particular explanatory purpose of the system of classification. Consider the following division.

    B. Substances ingested

        1. White bread

        2. Vitamin B-1

        3. Beer

Since our allergist's purpose is to identify the substances that cause allergic reactions, this division is unsatisfactory because it is not based on relevant essential properties. It gives no information about why these substances are allergens. Yet all three of these substances have a common element that is a relevant and essential property: all three contain yeast. If the allergist used this set of categories, she might needlessly prohibit a patient from eating bread when the offending substance was something in beer other than yeast. The following division would be better.

    B. Substances ingested

        1. Substances containing yeast cells

            a. Bread

            b. Vitamin B-1

            c. Beer

Unity. As far as possible, the entire system of classification should have a single, unified basis. Consider the allergist's first-level set of classes. Allergens, symptoms, and treatment are three very diverse categories, which are not themselves grouped under any unified heading. To make her system of classification fully useful, the allergist should unify the three elements as far as possible by showing some explicit connection among them. Our present knowledge of allergies indicates that specific symptoms are more likely to be caused by certain allergens than by others and that some symptoms respond better to certain treatments. Thus the three first-level categories can be unified to some extent by ordering them as indicated below.

Allergen	*Symptoms*	*Effectiveness of Treatment*
Fungi	Nasal congestion (probable) Nausea (improbable)	Injections (high) Antihistamines (moderate) Avoidance (low)

The next step would be to try to find a single, overall description for this system of classification. *Causes and Treatment of Allergies* might be a good candidate.

One might suppose that producing a system of classification is a purely mechanical process, with little or no creative thinking required. Actually, developing a satisfactory explanatory system of classification is often the culmination of a number of creative breakthroughs, in which new concepts are evolved, new causal relationships discovered, and new patterns of organization discerned in the subject matter under study. Finding a satisfactory basis for division is much like forming and testing hypotheses. The relevant information about the material to be classified is the evidence to be "explained." It may be necessary to develop and test systems of classification founded on a number of different bases before a satisfactory one is found. In short, when a subject is complex and poorly understood, finding a satisfactory basis for an explanatory system of classification

may prove to be the ultimate creative breakthrough.

Meaning

In developing systems of classification, an essential part of phase 3 is to define the terms used to refer to the classes. We define a term when we state its meaning. It is important that the terms used in classificatory systems have clear meanings, for systems of classification are to our experience as maps are to geographical territory. Their purpose is to help us find our way around in our experience. The meaning of a term sets the limits of the class to which it refers and thus determines which uses of the term are correct and which are not. And just as a map is of no value to us if we do not understand the meanings of the symbols it employs, so also a system of classification is of no use to us if we do not understand the meanings of the terms in which it is expressed. Indeed, this is a point of fundamental importance to all effective thinking, for language itself can usefully be viewed as one vast system of classification.

Language consists of sounds or other symbols organized into sequences that have meaning for a community that uses them; it is a means of communicating through agreed-upon symbols. The ability to think symbolically is what distinguishes the mental processes of humans from those of other animals. All the higher animals use signs, but only humans use symbols. **Signs** have a primitive sort of meaning in that they are natural indicators of the *presence* of something. The first robin is a sign of spring, for instance, and an abnormally yellow skin may be a sign of liver disorder. When we observe the sign, we may be led to think of the thing it signifies. In each case, however, the thing signified is something present, a part of ourselves or our environment. The meaning of a **symbol** is not limited in this way; symbols can be used to signify things that are not present, even things that do not exist at all. In addition, symbols can be used to signify abstractions, such as the gravitational constant or the figures of Euclidean geometry. Thus the effect of symbols is to help liberate our thinking from an exclusive concern with our immediate environment and to enable us to think in general and systematic terms about all of our experience rather than just small segments of it at a time.

The development of language deserves to be regarded as the most significant of human achievements. Without it, most of the others would have been impossible, for it is the symbolic nature of language that enables us to think abstractly, as well as to communicate abstractions to others. The vocabulary of any language is nothing more or less than a set of symbols that, by virtue of the meanings attached to them, serve as a device for classifying and understanding our experience and passing that understanding on to others. Thus verbs stand for actions and events, adjectives and adverbs for the qualities and characteristics of things and events, and nouns for virtually any object, event, quality, or idea. To manipulate the symbols of language effectively, we must understand and be sensitive to meaning.

Words have two kinds of meanings: denotation and connotation. The **denotation** of a word is its central, or core, meaning—the main concept that the word is used to signify. Thus the word *father* denotes a male parent, and the denotation of *triangle* is a closed, plane, three-sided figure. Words in established usage always have at least one standard denotation and sometimes have many. Thus the word *green* may denote (among other things) a color, a part of a golf course, or the state of being inexperienced. Which of these denotations it has on a given occasion of use depends on the context and the intentions of the user. When it is not clear which denotation is intended, the word is said to be used **ambiguously.** Although there are exceptions, such as poetry, we should avoid ambiguous uses of language in most contexts.

The purpose of a dictionary is to describe the various denotations words have in established usage. A dictionary meaning is, of course, merely a kind of consensus description of the way most educated people use the word, and this can change with time. Uses of a word that for years were considered incorrect or substandard are often accepted eventually as part of the language. *Silly,* for example, once meant "blessed"; and when Shakespeare wrote of "mice and rats and such small deer," his audiences did not imagine tiny Rudolphs prancing around the baseboards. Furthermore, it is possible for a speaker or writer to assign a denotation to a word arbitrarily if he or she wishes, for any combination of sounds or letters can be made to stand for anything. That is why it is possible to use words in secret codes and to develop new terminology to classify new areas of experience. But though the standard denotations of words are far from sacred, dictionary meanings are to be respected. If, like Humpty Dumpty in *Alice in Wonderland,* we claim to be able to use a word to mean exactly what we want it to mean, we must make it clear how our own usage differs from the standard one and have good reasons for the change. Otherwise we will needlessly confuse both ourselves and others.

The **connotations** of a word are the suggested meanings that it picks up by association with the various contexts in which it is used. Though not part of the dictionary meaning of the word, connotations can be extremely important. Color words, for example, have strong connotations. *Red* suggests passion or violence; *green,* the color of spring, often suggests renewal or youth. The same word may have very different connotations for different people. The word *home* suggests to most people a place of happiness and security, but not to the juvenile offender who has been confined in an institution called the "home." The word *book* may have approximately the same denotation but very different connotations to a Phi Beta Kappa and a student who has flunked out of college.

The connotations of a word can at times have compelling effects in contexts of reasoning, as we shall see in Part Four when we discuss ways in which language can be misused in arguing for or against a conclusion. For the present, however, we will concentrate on denotative meaning, for denotative meaning is what is most important in systems of classification and what most definitions are intended to articulate.

Definition

Definitions of a term are of two basic types. A **stipulative definition** is given when a denotation is arbitrarily assigned to a term. Often, the term involved is a new one, such as a name for a new drug or breakfast cereal. At other times, old terms are given new meanings, as when the term *hardware* came to be used to refer to computer equipment. But the essential feature of a stipulative definition lies in its arbitrariness—in the fact that when this sort of definition is given, the denotation of the term is set by the decision of the person framing the definition. Nothing need be new, so long as it is made clear that the previous meanings a term might have had make no difference to the discussion. Thus, if the author of an article on intelligence writes, "By intelligence I shall mean the ability to understand and to reason," he is giving a stipulative definition, even though many dictionaries would define intelligence in a way similar, if not identical, to this. The purpose of such a procedure is simply to focus attention away from other denotations or connotations the term might have in the reader's mind and upon the meaning the term is to have in the discussion that follows. This technique is especially useful when the meaning of a term is difficult to specify precisely or the subject at issue is a controversial one.

The second basic type of definition is a **lexical definition**, or a definition describing the denotation a term has in established usage. Obviously, one cannot be arbitrary in reporting the lexical meaning of a term. Rather, the definition has to conform to the actual meaning with which the term is ordinarily used. Where a term has more than one established meaning, a good dictionary will give a separate lexical definition for each one. In ordinary contexts of discussion, it suffices to focus on whatever particular meaning is relevant to the issue at hand.

Whether stipulative or lexical, any definition should be as clear and precise as possible. Otherwise neither we nor our listeners or readers will be able to use the term accurately. It would not do, for example, for a logic book to define as "valid" any argument that is "logically reliable."

This definition is correct as far as it goes, but it would be of little use to the student since it says nothing about what logical reliability consists in. Something about the essential attribute of a valid argument—that if its premises are true its conclusion must be true as well—has to be stated. Also, it is important in giving a definition to let the reader or listener know that this is your intention. Consider the following two statements.

Father means male parent.

A father is a male parent.

The first of these statements is obviously a definition, for it refers to the term *father* and reports what the term means. The second is not as obvious, since it refers to fathers, instead of the word *father*. Yet it still gives the defining characteristics of all members of the class, and hence can be used to define the term *father*. It is important to make it clear when statements of this second type are intended as definitions. A lot of needless verbal disputes arise because statements intended as definitions are mistaken for simple reports of facts and quarreled with unnecessarily. Finally, a good definition, whether stipulative or lexical, should be suitable for the purpose at hand. In giving a lexical definition for a term with more than one meaning, we have to make sure that the particular meaning we choose is right for our purposes. In giving stipulative definitions, we have to make sure the meaning we assign to a term will accomplish what we intend. Suppose, for example, that you are the guidance counselor at a high school and you are asked to produce a set of standards for determining what students should be put in a program for the "gifted." In producing your standards, you are in effect defining the term *gifted student* for this program and thereby deciding the class of students to which the term will refer. Accordingly, you would want to make sure that the standards you devise are neither so high that students who could do well in the program are excluded nor so low that students who cannot handle the demands of the program are admitted.

Genus and Difference

In a definition, the term that is being defined is called the **definiendum**; the expression that states the meaning is the **definiens**. The definiens could consist of anything from a one-word synonym to a paragraph or more. The ideal is somewhere in between. Reasonable brevity in a definition contributes to clarity and ease of understanding. One-word synonyms, on the other hand, often tend to be somewhat inaccurate and have the disadvantage of failing to spell out the meaning of the definiendum in any detail. To define *cat* as meaning "feline" is accurate enough, but does little to elaborate on the essential features of cats. Moreover, synonyms are often less known to the hearer than the words they are intended to define. Someone who did not know the meaning of *cat* could hardly be expected to know what *feline* means.

Perhaps the most common and effective type of definition is known as **definition by genus and difference**. In this type, the class signified by the definiendum is stated to belong to a larger class (the genus) and then differentiated from other members of the genus. The characteristics by which the differentiation is accomplished are known as the **differentia**. Here is an example:

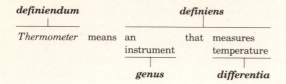

As you can see, this definition proceeds by first placing thermometers in the larger class, or genus, of instruments and then differentiating them from other instruments by citing the differentia, namely, the function of measuring temperature.

To be entirely satisfactory, definitions by genus and difference should conform to five rules.

The Definiens Should State Essential Attributes. In a stipulative definition, the essential attributes are simply whatever features are to be used to identify members of the class of items to which the definiendum is intended to refer. For example, in defining the term *gifted*, you might wish to make it an essential attribute of giftedness that a student have an IQ of at least 120. In a lexical definition, the essential attributes are those expressed in the **conventional meaning** of the definiendum. Consider the following lexical definition:

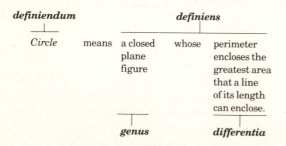

This definition is accurate in that only figures that are circles will satisfy the definiens. But the differentia cited here is not part of the conventional meaning of *circle*. A better definition would be this one:

Circle means a closed plane figure every point on the perimeter of which is equidistant from the center.

Definitions that proceed by citing examples or origins always violate this rule. It is not an essential feature of democracy, for instance, that it is a government of the sort found in the United States. And if we define *special relativity* as the physical theory set forth by Albert Einstein in 1905, we will have said nothing whatever about the essential attributes of this theory, which would be what they are whether Einstein had stated them or not.

The Definition Should Not Be Circular. A definition is circular when the definiens contains the definiendum or words that cannot be understood precisely without knowing the meaning of the definiendum. Consider the example below.

This definition is circular because a key word in the definiens is the adjective form of the definiendum. Figuratively speaking, this definition moves in a circle, for it begins with fallacy and proceeds to *fallacious*. If a person does not know what *fallacy* means, he or she will not be helped by this definition. It is little better than saying that a fallacy is a fallacy. Circular definitions are unsatisfactory because they do little to clarify the denotation of the definiendum.

The Definiens Should Be Neither Too Broad Nor Too Narrow. Although definitions by genus and difference cannot employ one-word synonyms, it is nevertheless important that the definiendum and definiens have the same meaning, and hence refer to exactly the same class of things. When the definiens fails to have the same meaning as the definiendum, it may refer to things to which the definiendum does not refer or fail to refer to things to which the definiendum does refer. In the first case, the definiens will be too broad, and in the second too narrow. As an example in which the definiens is too broad, consider the following definition.

A square is a closed plane figure with four sides and four right angles.

In this example the definiens refers to some items to which the definiendum does not. While it is true that all squares are closed plane figures with four sides and four right angles, it is not true that all closed plane figures with four sides and four right angles are squares. The fault here is that the differentia does not exclude instances of the genus "closed plane figure" that are not squares, such as rectangles shaped like football fields. This fault is easily remedied by limiting the differentia with the word *equal*.

A square is a closed plane figure with four equal sides and four right angles.

In this case the definiens is not too broad, for every figure to which it refers is a square.

As an example of a definition that is too narrow, consider this one.

A thermometer is a glass instrument for measuring temperature.

Here the definiens places thermometers in the genus of "glass instruments." It thereby excludes thermometers not made of glass and hence is too narrow. The defect is easily remedied by removing the word *glass* from the description of the genus.

In some instances a definiens is too broad in one respect and at the same time too narrow in another. Here is an example.

A thermometer is an instrument that is calibrated in degrees Fahrenheit.

This definition has a definiens that is too narrow, for it fails to include in its reference thermometers calibrated according to other scales. At the same time, it is too broad, for it includes in its reference devices such as thermostats and oven dials. The definiens overlooks the fact that instruments calibrated for temperature are used to set temperature as well as to measure it.

In avoiding problems of broadness and narrowness, it helps to be careful in selecting the genus. If we think of thermometers as belonging to the class of glass instruments, we will automatically produce a definiens that is too narrow since this genus excludes some thermometers from the start. On the other hand, the genus we select should not be so broad that differentiation becomes impractical. In the example below, the unnecessarily large size of the genus makes it difficult to differentiate *child* from other immature living organisms.

A child is an immature living organism.

The remedy is to substitute a smaller genus.

A child is an immature human being.

The Definiens Should Not Contain Ambiguous, Figurative, or Obscure Language. Since the purpose of a definition is to describe the meaning of a term clearly and precisely, ambiguous or obscure language is obviously out of place. Although figurative language can aid communication by stating or implying a resemblance, it is not likely to describe meaning accurately and can therefore be misleading. Consider this definition:

An aircraft is a means of transportation that serves as a magic carpet for its passengers.

Here *magic carpet* is used figuratively. Terms such as this might be properly used to amplify the meaning of a definition, but they should not be used in the definition itself because they do not accurately describe the concept being defined. Whether the language of a definition is obscure may depend on the frame of reference. Technical language may be quite clear to one person and completely obscure to another. If a person knows the language of computers, he or she will understand what it means to say that a certain computer has 64K RAM; but another may not know that this language describes the quantity of memory circuits in the computer that are available to the user in operating it. We are often tempted to use this sort of jargon, partly in the interest of brevity and partly because it sounds prestigious, but it should be avoided in definitions; the language of a definition should be selected to communicate rather than to impress.

The Definiens Should Not Be Unnecessarily Negative. Some of the terms we employ are negative in their meaning and hence should be defined negatively. The following definition is an example.

Immutable means the characteristic of not being subject to change.

Here the definiens is appropriately negative because the term being defined signifies the absence of changeability. Too often, however, we are tempted to use negative language to define terms that are not negative in meaning, simply because we cannot quite put our finger on the positive attributes a term signifies or cannot find appropriate language to describe them. The definition below is a case in point.

An undergraduate is a college student who has not completed the requirements for a degree.

The difficulty with this sort of definition is that it tells us what the items the definiendum refers to are *not*, instead of what they are. The meanings of terms that are not negative are much better clarified by concentrating on their positive signification. A better definition would be this one:

An undergraduate is a student enrolled in a course of study aimed at a bachelor's degree or its equivalent.

Good definitions by genus and difference are sometimes difficult to produce. Ideally, the definiendum and definiens should be exactly the same in meaning. When this is achieved, the two can be interchanged in any context without changing what we say or the items to which we refer. Although this ideal is not always attained, we should try to come as close as possible. The resulting clarity both in our systems of classification and in the way we express our thoughts is well worth the effort.

Evaluation and Decision

With any system of classification, the decision to be made in phase 5 is whether to adopt the system as formulated or to continue refining it. Even systems of classification that begin with lexical definitions can be modified by stipulating changes in those definitions so that a more useful ordering of the material results. In fact, a great deal of science and scholarship have developed in exactly this way. When the number of items to be classified is small, as in your personal filing system, the decision is easy. You can simply start using the system and refine it as you go. But when the mass is large and the issue important, the procedures described in Chapter 13 should be used.

Certain hazards in classification should be kept in mind. First, systems of classification are meaningless without their definitions, and definitions must be expressed in language. Definitions are therefore subject to dangers inherent in the symbolic character of language, such as ambiguity or obscurity. Second, a system of classification does not alter the nature of the objects, ideas, actions, or qualities classified. In fact, classificatory systems can be very misleading about the nature of things. The early chemists who thought water was an element were following a tradition that dated from ancient Greece and occupied an important position in their frame of reference. Accordingly, when experiments began to indicate that water is in fact a compound composed of two gases found in ordinary air, many eminent chemists rejected this finding. No less a figure than Joseph Priestley, one of the discoverers of oxygen, resisted to the day he died the view that water is a compound. Finally, systems of classification tend to deceive us into overlooking the fact that, although all members of a given class have certain characteristics, they may also have very significant differences. Anyone who has ever collected stamps knows that differences in design so minute that the average person could not distinguish them can make the difference between a stamp worth fifty cents and a stamp worth fifty thousand dollars.

The hazards and difficulties in systems of classification should not make us overlook their great advantages. The explosion of knowledge in our age has made classification more important than ever in organizing and clarifying it. Systems of classification and definition often appear intimidating and tedious to learn. As a result, we tend to want to pass over them lightly and get to what we hasten to claim are more "important" things. To react in this way is to overlook the fact that workable systems of classification and definition are at the very heart of learning. Trying to learn the information necessary to pass even an elementary course in zoology without the benefit of a classificatory system would be roughly comparable to trying to memorize the Manhattan telephone directory. And when we have trouble using systems of classification, for instance, trouble recognizing different types of argument, the reason is often that we have failed to learn the definitions properly. Only good systems of classification and definition make it possible to organize our knowledge into a coherent whole and to reveal the relationships between the parts.

Exercise 14

Problems 1–6. These questions refer to the following definition: An automobile is a motor-powered vehicle made to carry passengers.

1. What is the definiendum? _____

2. What is the genus? _____

3. What is the differentia? _____

4. What is the definiens?_____

5. Is a bus with a capacity of forty passengers an *automobile* in terms of this definition?

   _____

6. Is a cart powered by an electric motor made to carry two players on a golf course an *automobile* in terms of this definition?

   _____

Problems 7–11. Which rule(s), if any, of definition by genus and difference is (are) violated by the following definitions?

7. Questionable cause is an error in thinking in which it is inferred that one event causes another.

   _____

8. Hasty generalization is a form of reasoning in which a generalization is made about a group on the basis of an inadequate sample of the group.

   _____

9. The gambler's fallacy is an error in reasoning in which one assumes that if a coin has come up heads several times in succession it is very likely to come up tails on the next toss.

   _____

10. Uncertain relationship between premises is a fallacy in which the premises of an argument unsuccessfully grope for one another in the dark.

    _____

11. A fallacy is not sound reasoning.   _____

12. Laws in some states set different speed limits for certain classes of vehicles. Using the method of definition by genus and difference, define *trailers* for the purpose of enforcing the above law.

Problems 13–18. Consider the following set of categories for classifying electronic devices found in the home by the purpose for which they are used.

A. Cooking   **C. Entertainment**

_____   _____

_____   _____

_____   _____

_____

B. Cleaning   **D. Schoolwork**

_____   _____

_____   _____

_____   _____

_____

13. Test this set of categories by inserting the following items in the appropriate blanks above. Assume all the items refer to electronic devices.

Vacuum cleaner Power drill
Pocket calculator Clothes washer
Stereo Oven
Corn popper Television
Home computer Paint sprayer
Dishwasher Blender
Radio Pencil sharpener
Toaster

14. What class should be added?

_____

15. Which of the classes are not mutually exclusive?

_____

16. Is the overlapping of these classes due to the nature of the things to be classified or a flaw in the system of classification?

_____

17. Would an ice-cream maker fit into any of these categories? _____

18. If not, how would you deal with this problem?

_____

Chapter 15

Categorical Propositions

- **Relationships Between Classes**
- **A-Form Propositions**
- **E-Form Propositions**
- **I-Form Propositions**
- **O-Form Propositions**

Precise and accurate definitions of terms are an indispensable aid to understanding the meanings of the propositions in which they are employed. But the structure of a proposition also contributes importantly to its meaning, and we have seen that the validity of deductive arguments is determined by structural considerations. Since the next several chapters are devoted to deductive arguments, it is important to have a firm grasp of the structural features of certain types of propositions.

The difference between structural meaning and the meanings of terms may be made clear by considering an example. Suppose the registrar at Wysacki University issues the following order: "All students will register for the spring semester during the first week of December unless their grades are substandard." There are two ways in which this order may be misunderstood. First, the words themselves may be misunderstood. "Substandard" grades may be defined differently in the different colleges of the university and may even differ from one program to

another within a college. In order to avoid confusion and enable students to respond appropriately to the registrar's order, the various units of Wysacki University should make clear to the students what is meant by substandard grades.

Second, this order can be misunderstood if the linguistic structure of the proposition in which it is stated is misused or misinterpreted. The registrar's order can be written in hypothetical form as follows.

If a student's grades are not substandard, *then* he or she will register during the first week of December.

This proposition contains two structure words, *if* and *then*, which identify the antecedent and consequent, respectively, and state the relationship between them. The consequent is to be observed by any student who satisfies the antecedent by having grades that are not substandard. But it is not stated that no student with substandard grades may register; indeed, nothing at all is said about what procedures students with substandard grades are to follow. First-year students, for example, might be permitted to register anyway, on the ground that no student will be dropped from the rolls of Wysacki on the basis of a single semester's bad performance. Now suppose that Gordon Smythe, a junior with substandard grades, notices that a freshman whose grades are even lower is registering. If he does not understand the meaning conveyed by the structure of the registrar's proposition, he may wrongly conclude that he may register also, even though his dean has informed him that his grades are substandard. If Smythe draws this conclusion, he will have added a probably erroneous meaning to the registrar's order, a meaning not conveyed by its structure.

The structure of certain propositional forms is clear and unequivocal. When they are misunderstood, the fault lies with the person interpreting them rather than with the proposition. These propositional forms can be useful as a kind of second language into which we can translate propositions to see what they really mean. We have already studied the hypothetical propositional form in Chapter 3. We turn now to the **categorical** form, which is especially useful for making general statements and employing systems of classification.

Relationships Between Classes

Whereas a hypothetical proposition states a relationship between an antecedent and a consequent, a categorical proposition names or describes two classes and states a relationship between them. For example, the proposition "All whales are mammals" names two classes, whales and mammals, and states a relationship be-

tween them. Given accurate definitions of the two classes, the relationship between them is clear and unequivocal to anyone who understands this form of proposition. Almost any idea can be stated as a categorical proposition, although some awkward twisting of language may be necessary.

Categorical propositions occur in four different forms. When an idea is correctly stated in one of these, there can be no reasonable doubt about the meaning—assuming we understand the structure of the particular form being used. A full grasp of these forms sharpens our understanding of language and strengthens our powers of reasoning.

A-Form Propositions[1]

An A-form proposition names two classes of objects or ideas and declares that the relationship between them is **total inclusion**—that all of one class is included within the other. Two familiar classes of people having this relationship are Baptists and Protestants. We can express this relationship in a categorical proposition.

All people in the class of Baptists are included in the class of Protestants.

As long as we fully understand that we are talking about classes, we can shorten the statement as shown below, with the parts marked.

Quanti-fier	Subject term	Connective	Predicate term
All	Baptists	are included in	Protestants

---

[1] The four forms of categorical propositions take their names from the first two vowels in each of the Latin words *AffIrmo* and *nEgO*, which mean "I affirm" and "I deny."

Note that in a categorical proposition, the **subject term** names one class, and the **predicate term** names the other. The **connective** describes the relationship between the classes. The connective is accordingly not treated in logic as being part of the predicate term. The **quantifier** indicates how many of the members of the class named by the subject term are included in the class named by the predicate term. Because the relationship signified by an A-form proposition is *total* inclusion, the quantifier must be the word *all* or some word meaning *all*.

Since we will be dealing with many such categorical propositions, let us adopt a shorthand system to save writing. Let us use the symbol < to mean *is* or *are included in*. We can now write our proposition thus.

All Baptists < Protestants.

Now let us take a close look at what the relationship of total inclusion means. To do so let us introduce a system of simple diagrams that will show what we mean.

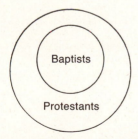

Our diagram is analogous to a map of a county within a state, with the Baptists the county and the Protestants the state.

Note that the symbol for inclusion (<) does not have the same meaning in logic and mathematics. In logic it expresses a relationship between classes; it means only that every member of the subject class is included in the predicate class. It does not necessarily mean that there are any additional members of the predicate class. Precisely the same point applies to the circle diagram. It is only analogous to a map, not exactly like one. If the meaning of the diagram above were exactly like a map, we could assume that there is some territory in the state that is not in the county—in this case, that there are some Protestants that are not Baptists. We cannot make this assumption logically, however, because it does not follow deductively from the proposition with which we began. To say that all Baptists are Protestants is to say nothing whatever about whether there are any Protestants of other denominations. It happens to be true that there are, but that is not stated in the A-form proposition. This can be seen by realizing that other A-form propositions represent perfect definitions by genus and difference, in which the classes referred to by definiendum and definiens are precisely the same. For example, it is true that all squares are equilateral rectangles, but false that there are any equilateral rectangles that are not squares.

The four statements below summarize the meaning conveyed by the linguistic structure of an A-form proposition.

1. Anything in the subject class *is* in the predicate class.
2. Anything outside the subject class *may* or *may not be* in the predicate class.
3. Anything in the predicate class *may* or *may not be* in the subject class.
4. Anything outside the predicate class *is not* in the subject class.

Both in understanding categorical propositions and in dealing with syllogisms that employ them, we need to know one other important detail. The terms of a categorical proposition may be either distributed or undistributed. The terminology is somewhat unfortunate, but it has been used by logicians for a long time. The two words have no meaning except in terms of the relationship between the two classes named in the proposition.

A term is **distributed** when it accounts for all the members of the class insofar as its relationship to the other class is concerned. The term Baptists is distributed because we have put 100 percent of the Baptists within the class of Protestants. If Robinson is a Baptist, he has to be a Protestant. The *subject* terms of A-form propositions are always *distributed*.

A term is **undistributed** when it accounts for less than all the members of a class insofar as its relationship to the other class is concerned. The term Protestants is undistributed because we do not know the relationship between all Protestants and Baptists. Jameson can be a Protestant without being a Baptist. The predicate terms of A-form propositions are never distributed.

Now we can add to our shorthand system by using the symbols **d** for distributed and **u** for undistributed. We may state our proposition in our complete shorthand system thus:

d   u
Baptists < Protestants.

Before reading further, test your understanding by writing shorthand propositions accurately expressing the relationship you believe to exist between the following pairs of classes. (You will find the answers at the end of the chapter.)

1. Virginians—Americans.

2. Citizens—voters.

E-Form Propositions

An E-form proposition names two classes and declares that the relationship between them is total exclusion—that the two classes are entirely separate. Two familiar classes having this relationship are blue jays and robins.

We can express the relationship in a categorical proposition this way:

The entire class of blue jays is completely excluded from the class of robins.

But this statement is wordy, and if we remember that we are talking about classes, we can shorten it to the form below.

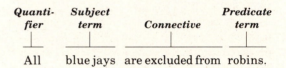

Quanti- fier	Subject term	Connective	Predicate term
All	blue jays	are excluded from	robins.

For our shorthand system let us adopt the symbol ⊀ to mean *is* or *are excluded from*. We can now write our proposition thus:

All blue jays ⊀ robins.

The circle diagram for this relationship appears below.

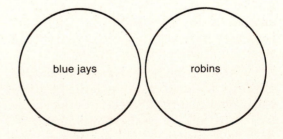

The diagram is exactly analogous to a map of two different states. Anything in one state cannot be in the other. Anything not in one state may or may not be in the other, for it could be in a state not shown.

In an E-form proposition, *both* terms are *distributed,* for we know the relationship of 100 percent of each class to the other. If a certain bird is a blue jay, it cannot be a robin, and vice versa. Stated in shorthand, our proposition becomes

$$\begin{array}{ccc} d & & d \\ \text{Blue jays} & \text{⸁} & \text{robins.} \end{array}$$

E-form propositions are frequently expressed by using the word *no* in a double role: as quantifier and to signify the exclusion relationship. Thus our E-form proposition can also be read as "No blue jays are robins."

Before reading further, test your understanding by writing shorthand propositions expressing accurately the relationship you believe to exist between the following pairs of classes.

3. Professional people—doctors.

4. College graduates—illiterates.

I-Form Propositions

An I-form proposition names two classes and states that at least a part of the subject class is included within the predicate class. You run into this relationship when you start calling your friends for a date and find that the first two or three you call already have dates. The classes are *my friends* and *people who have dates*. You do not yet know the complete relationship between the classes: for all you know, the rest of your friends may have dates, or none of them may. All you know is that some of your friends have dates. Ex-

pressed wordily, your proposition is as follows:

Some of the people in the class of my friends are included in the class of people who have dates.

Expressed more economically, it is

Quanti-fier	Subject term	Connective	Predicate term
Some of	my friends	are included in	people who have dates.

Here is the circle diagram.

The circles overlap to show that some friends have dates. The analogy to a map no longer holds, for a map drawn this way would indicate that some of your friends are in the territory of people who have dates and some are outside that territory. But all you know is that some of your friends are within the territory of people who have dates—you know nothing about the location of the rest of your friends. You cannot conclude from this diagram that some of your friends do not have dates. That may turn out to be true, but it does not follow from the proposition with which you began. Thus there is a question that some of your friends do not have dates. That may turn out to be true, but it does not follow from the proposition with which you began. Thus there is a question mark in the area of the diagram that refers to friends who do not have dates. The territory covered by both circles is shaded to show that the part of the class of friends we do know about is within the territory of people having dates. Another important point concerns the degree of overlap there must be between the circles before we may use the word "some." That is, how many of your friends must have dates before we say that "some" of them do? The answer is that in logic we use the word *some* to mean that *at least one* member of the subject class belongs to the predicate class as well. If just one of your friends has a date, we are permitted in logic to say that some of your friends are included in the class of people having dates. Thus the extent to which the circles overlap is unimportant; we are concerned here only with whether there is overlapping, not with how much.

In an I-form proposition *both* terms are *undistributed,* for we do not know the relationship of all of either class to the other. If I know only that Sharon Davis is a friend of yours, I do not know whether she has a date; if I know only that Alice Jones has a date, I do not know whether she is a friend of yours.

Your proposition is stated in shorthand thus:

$$\overset{u}{\text{My friends}} < \overset{u}{\text{people who have dates.}}$$

It is important to note that a single I-form proposition is not sufficient to state the complete relationship between two overlapping classes, such as mushrooms and edible plants.

$$\overset{u}{\text{Mushrooms}} < \overset{u}{\text{edible plants.}}$$

The I-form proposition above states only that at least some of the members of the mushroom class are included in the edible plant class. If we interpret this proposition to mean that some edible plants are not mushrooms, we are reading into the proposition a meaning that is not conveyed by the proposition's structure.

Before reading further, test your understanding by writing shorthand propositions accurately expressing the relationship you believe to exist between the following pairs of classes.

5. Courses you took last semester— courses you flunked. (You have just received your grades; all are Bs.)
6. College professors—people who use big words. (You are sitting in your first college class. The professor has just said, "Absences lacking plenary justification by a physician will not be tolerated.")

O-Form Propositions

An O-form proposition names two classes and declares that the relationship is **partial exclusion**, that is, at least a part of the subject class is outside the predicate class.

You encounter this relationship when you try to borrow money from your friends and the first ones you ask will not lend you the money. Your classes are *my friends* and *people who will lend me money*. You do not know the complete relationship between the classes: for all you know, the next friend you try may lend you the money, or it may be that none of them will. All you know is that some of your friends will not lend you money. Expressed wordily, your proposition is as follows:

> Some of those in the class of my friends are excluded from the class of people who will lend me money.

Expressed more economically, it is

Quanti-fier	Subject term	Connective	Predicate term
Some of	my friends	are excluded from	people who will lend me money

Here is the circle diagram.

The circles overlap to show the possibility that some friends *might* lend you the money, and a question mark is put in the overlapping territory to show doubt whether such overlapping is reflected in the facts. The part of the circle for friends outside the other circle is shaded to show that we know some friends are outside the circle of those who will lend you money.

As in the case of I-form propositions, logicians permit themselves to use O-form propositions provided *at least one* member of the subject class is excluded from the predicate class. Thus if even one of your friends refuses to lend you money, logic permits the statement that some of your friends will not lend you money.

In the O-form proposition, the *subject* term is *undistributed,* because we do not know the complete relationship of the subject class to the predicate class. If I know only that your proposition is true and that Joe Smythe is your friend, I do not know whether he will lend you money.

The *predicate* term is *distributed.* When part or all of one class is excluded from another, it is excluded from *all* of the other class. If some of your friends will not lend you money, then those friends, the only ones of whom the proposition speaks, are excluded from the *entire* class of people (if any) who will lend you money. Accordingly, the predicate term of the proposition, "people who will lend you money," accounts for the entire class to which it refers, satisfying the definition of distribution.

Stated in shorthand, your proposition is

$$\overset{\text{u}}{\text{My friends}} \nmid \overset{\text{d}}{\text{people who will lend me}}$$
money.

Note the important difference between I- and O-forms. The I-form guarantees that at least one member of the subject class is within the predicate class; the O-form guarantees that at least one member of the subject class is outside the predicate class. Neither of these forms, however, guarantees the truth of the other form. It is true that the statement that some of your friends will lend you money is sometimes taken as suggesting that some of your friends will not lend you money, and vice versa. But this is strictly a matter of the connotations these propositions tend to acquire in practical settings, not part of their literal meaning. When some members of a given class are included in another while others are not included, it takes both an I-form and an O-form proposition to express the complete relationship. Neither will suffice alone.

Now check your understanding of categorical propositions by writing shorthand propositions accurately expressing the relationship you believe to exist between the following pairs of classes.

7. College students—people expected to read books.

8. College students—eighth-grade students.

9. Residents of your dormitory—psychology majors. (You have learned that two residents of your dormitory are psychology majors; you know nothing about the others.)

10. Residents of your dormitory—people who have B averages. (You have just learned that at least one resident of your dormitory does not have a B average; you know nothing about the averages of the others.)

11. Residents of your dormitory—people who have B averages. (You now know that ten of the residents of your dormitory have B averages and that the others do not.)

Answers to Self-Check Questions

Page 216:

             d   u
1. Virginians < Americans.

        d   u
2. Voters < citizens.

Page 217:

        d   u
3. Doctors < professional people.

             d   d
4. College graduates ✦ illiterates.

Page 218:

             d   d
5. courses taken last semester ✦ courses flunked.

       u   u
6. Professors < users of big words.

Page 220:

        d   u
7. College students < people expected to read books.

        d   d
8. College students ✦ eighth-grade students.

          u   u
9. Residents of your dormitory < psychology majors.

         u   d
10. Residents of your dormitory ✦ people who have B averages.

         u   u
11. Residents of your dormitory < people who have B averages;

         u   d
Residents of your dormitory ✦ people who have B averages.

Exercise 15

Problems 1–14. Each problem requires three answers:

1. Identify the parts of the proposition by drawing a bracket over the part and writing Q for "quantifier," S for "subject term," P for "predicate term," and C for "connective."

2. On the line provided, write the proposition in shorthand form.

3. Draw a circle diagram for the proposition.

Problem 1 has been worked as an example. Do not change the meaning of the proposition stated; your task is to state the proposition, not your belief, in shorthand and diagrammatic form.

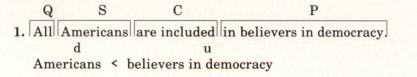

```
        Q      S          C                  P
1.  ⌈All⌉⌈Americans⌉⌈are included⌉⌈in believers in democracy.⌉
        d                u
    Americans  <  believers in democracy
```

2. All metals are denser than water.

_____

3. All fascists are excluded from believers in individual freedom.

_____

4. No modern automobiles are powered by steam engines.

_____

5. Some failures are excluded from failures because of indolence.

_____

6. Some electricians are not good insurance risks.

_____

7. Some paintings by Van Gogh are included in masterpieces.

---

8. Many so-called leaders are merely figureheads.

---

9. Every case of infection is accompanied by fever.

---

10. Re-examinations are never given at Wysacki.

---

11. Some habits of thinking do not improve decisions.

---

12. All perceptions are subject to error.

---

13. All generalizations are based on samples.

---

14. Thinking that is not creative is not effective.

Chapter 16

Immediate Inference

- Conversion
- Obversion
- The Square of Opposition
- The Importance of Immediate Inference

Let us now consider the simplest types of deductive argument involving categorical propositions. These are **immediate inferences**, or arguments in which a conclusion is drawn from a single premise, without reference to evidence from any other source. By studying immediate inferences, we can increase the skill with which we use and interpret language, and prepare ourselves to deal with the more complicated sorts of argument we will see later. As we noted in Chapter 3, when the decision-making cycle follows a deductive pattern, phase 4 (testing tentative conclusions) includes testing inferences for validity. Thus, besides aiming to improve our facility with language, this chapter will focus on determining the validity of immediate inferences. As always in the discussion of deduction, however, we must not forget that even a validly drawn conclusion is no more reliable than the premises on which it is based.

Conversion

As with all deductive arguments, the validity of immediate inference depends entirely on the meaning conveyed by the **structure** of proposition. An important structural feature of categorical propositions is that the relationship between classes that they express runs from left to right. That is, members of the subject class are always included in or excluded from the predicate class. One type of immediate inference, which is not always valid, involves inferring from a categorical proposition a relationship that runs in the opposite direction. This kind of inference is called **conversion** and is achieved by interchanging the subject and predicate terms. For example, if you interpret the proposition "No statesman puts votes ahead of duty" to imply that no one who puts votes ahead of duty is a statesman, you have made an immediate inference by converting the original proposition. The proposition that results from the conversion is the **converse** of the original. The converse has the subject of the original proposition for its predicate and the predicate of the original for its subject.

Whether an inference by conversion is valid or not depends on the particular form of the proposition that is converted. The rule is simple: **if a conversion is valid, no term in the converse can be distributed unless it was distributed in the original proposition.**

The basis for this rule is the fact that in a valid argument any information contained in the conclusion must be implicit in the premise or premises. When we convert a proposition, the resultant proposition is the conclusion of an argument. If a term is distributed in the conclusion, then information is presented about all members of the class to which it refers. Thus, for the conversion to be valid, the premise must also contain information about all members of the class, which it cannot do unless the term in question is distributed there as well.

E- and I-Form Propositions Can Be Validly Converted. For example, from the premise that all mammals are excluded from the class of insects we can validly infer that all insects are excluded from the class of mammals. Similarly, from the proposition that some men are students we can validly infer that some students are men. Written in our shorthand, these inferences are as follows:

$$\text{Given:} \quad \overset{d}{\text{Mammals}} \; \cancel{k} \; \overset{d}{\text{insects.}}$$

$$\text{Converse:} \quad \overset{d}{\text{Insects}} \; \cancel{k} \; \overset{d}{\text{mammals.}}$$

$$\text{Given:} \quad \overset{u}{\text{Students}} \; < \; \overset{u}{\text{men.}}$$

$$\text{Converse:} \quad \overset{u}{\text{Men}} \; < \; \overset{u}{\text{students.}}$$

Note that in neither case is there any term distributed in the converse that was not distributed in the original proposition. Thus our rule for validity is satisfied. Note too that the result of converting an E-form proposition is another E-form proposition, and the result of converting an I-form proposition is another I-form proposition. Consequently, each of our resultant propositions could be validly converted again, returning us to the proposition with which we began. Since this reverse operation is also valid, E- and I-form propositions are **logically equivalent** to their converses. That is to say, the E-form proposition and its converse can validly be inferred from one another, and the same is true of the I-form proposition and its converse. Although there may be a difference in emphasis between the given proposition and its converse, there is no difference in logical meaning.

O-Form Propositions Cannot Be Validly Converted. Consider the example below.

$$\text{Given:} \quad \overset{u}{\text{Animals}} \; \cancel{k} \; \overset{d}{\text{mammals.}}$$

$$\text{Converse:} \quad \overset{u}{\text{Mammals}} \; \cancel{k} \; \overset{d}{\text{animals.}}$$

In this example, we can easily tell from our knowledge of the relationship between the two classes that the conversion is invalid. Knowledge of the subject matter is not necessary, however, for the term *animals* is undistributed in the given proposition and distributed in the converse. Thus the converse makes a claim that is not justified by the evidence.

A-Form Propositions Cannot Be Validly Converted. Consider the propositions below.

Given: Pennsylvanians $\overset{d}{<}$ $\overset{u}{}$ Americans.

Converse: Americans $\overset{d}{<}$ $\overset{u}{}$ Pennsylvanians.

Obviously the inference is invalid, for the given proposition does not state a relationship of *all* Americans to Pennsylvanians, while the converse does. Note that *Americans* is undistributed in the original but distributed in the converse.

Obversion

Obversion consists in changing the predicate term of a proposition from positive to negative, or vice versa, and changing inclusion to exclusion, or vice versa. The two changes offset each other, and the proposition they produce, called the **obverse**, differs in tone from the original but not in logical meaning.

Given: Sloops $\overset{d}{<}$ $\overset{u}{}$ boats.

Obverse: Sloops $\overset{d}{\nless}$ $\overset{d}{}$ non-boats.

The above example illustrates obversion for an A-form proposition. The first thing to notice about it is that the inference to the obverse is valid. If all sloops are boats, then all sloops are excluded from the class of non-boats. Unlike the case with conversion, **obversion is a valid operation for all four types of categorical propositions.** We can validly obvert A-, E-, I-, and O-form propositions if the changes we make in the given proposition meet the definition above.

The second thing to note about the above example is that the proposition produced by obversion is not of the same form as the original. This is another difference between obversion and conversion. Conversion always produces a proposition of the same form. But when we obvert an A-form proposition we get an E-form proposition, and vice versa; and when we obvert an I-form proposition we get an O-form proposition, and vice versa. Finally, we should note that since obversion is always valid the obverse of any proposition can validly be obverted again, returning us to the proposition with which we began. This shows that any categorical proposition is **logically equivalent** to its obverse.

Sometimes what purport to be inferences by obversion fail to satisfy the definition given above. This occurs most commonly because of attempts to avoid awkward expressions when seeking a negative term to replace the predicate in the proposition to be obverted. Ideally, negative terms should be formed by prefixing *non-*to the predicate of the given proposition. But although this is easy enough when the given predicate is a single noun like "boats," it is not so easy in other cases. Consider the example below.

Given: Good people $\overset{d}{\nless}$ $\overset{d}{}$ people who live to be old.

Faulty Obverse: Good people $\overset{d}{<}$ people who die young.

Here the predicate to be negated is "people who live to be old." Now suppose we had tried to negate it by speaking of "non-people who live to be old." If you think about the literal meaning of this expression, you will realize that our obverse would then have said that all good people are non-people and that they live to be old—hardly the meaning of the proposition given to be obverted. Faced with this type of problem, we are often tempted to obvert propositions by changing the predicate to an antonym, or phrase with an opposite or contrasting meaning. That is what the above example does. Nevertheless, the example constitutes a **faulty obversion** because there is a change in meaning from the given proposition to the purported obverse. The given proposition asserts that the good die before they get old; it does not prohibit them from living to be middle-aged. But the faulty obverse asserts that the good die while still young, before reaching middle age. Thus, as is often the case, this faulty obversion is invalid because the conclusion goes beyond the information in the given proposition. One way to avoid this problem is to form the negations of predicate terms that use more than one word by putting parentheses around the entire phrase and then prefixing it with "non-." The resulting expression may be a bit cumbersome, but it can be read as the true negation of the original predicate term. Faulty obversions can then be avoided.

		d		d
Given:	Good people	⨍	people who live to be old.	

		d		
Obverse:	Good people	<	non- (people who live to be old).	

It is worth noting that not all faulty obversions are invalid. Suppose the given proposition had read: "Good people die young." If we change it to read "Good people do not live to be old," we would have a case of faulty obversion since dying young is not the equivalent of not living to

be old. But although this faulty obverse is not the equivalent of the given proposition, it follows validly from it: if the good die young, they cannot live to be old. Where faulty obversion produces an invalid inference, we may speak of the **fallacy of faulty obversion**; otherwise we have a faulty obversion, but no fallacy.

In a true obversion, the subject term of the given proposition is never changed. In the example below, the subject term has been changed, and the obversion is faulty.

	d		u
Given:	Logicians	<	wise people.

	d		d
Faulty Obverse:	People who are not logicians	⨍	wise people.

This kind of faulty obversion is always invalid because the original information in the given proposition is limited to the class described by the subject term. In the above example, the information in the given proposition is limited to logicians; nothing whatever is said about people who are not logicians. In reading poetry, it is permissible to draw inferences from what is not said; in logic such inferences are unreliable.

It is worth noting that immediate inferences of conversion and obversion can be performed in sequence. Consider the following example:

	d		u
Given:	Thieves	<	parasites.

	d		d
Obverse:	Thieves	⨍	non-parasites.

	d		d
Converse of the obverse:	Non-parasites	⨍	thieves.

Chains of immediate inference like this

can be useful for logical purposes, especially when, as in this case, the original proposition cannot be validly converted.

Propagandists and advertisers often exploit people's ignorance or carelessness about drawing inferences from propositions. For example, an advertiser may make this claim: "Every bar of Satin Soap contains lanolin." Assuming the advertiser is telling the truth, this statement involves no fallacy. But it may tempt you to commit a fallacy by invalidly converting it to "All bars of soap that contain lanolin are bars of Satin Soap" or by invalidly obverting it to "No soap that is not Satin Soap contains lanolin."

The Square of Opposition

The operations of conversion and obversion both involve changing terms in categorical propositions. There is another set of immediate inferences that do not call for such changes; rather they involve A-, E-, I-, and O-form propositions with exactly the same subject and predicate. You will no doubt have noticed that an A-form proposition such as "All cats are mammals" is in a way the opposite of its corresponding O-form proposition, "Some cats are not mammals." Because these propositions are opposed to one another, if you know it is true that all cats are mammals, you can infer that it is false that some cats are not mammals. This is a valid immediate inference and just one of the group of such inferences we are about to discuss. In order to understand such inferences, we must first be clear about the different ways in which categorical propositions with the same subject and predicate can be opposites.

If we use the letters S and P to stand for subject and predicate, the four forms of

categorical propositions may be represented symbolically as follows:

$$\text{A-form: } \overset{d}{S}s < \overset{u}{P}s$$

$$\text{E-form: } \overset{d}{S}s \nless \overset{d}{P}s$$

$$\text{I-form: } \overset{u}{S}s < \overset{u}{P}s$$

$$\text{O-form: } \overset{u}{S}s \nless \overset{d}{P}s$$

Now suppose we were presented with a group of four propositions, one of each of these forms and all with the same subject and predicate. If so, each of our four propositions would oppose or contrast with each of the others in a different, specific way. Following a tradition of many centuries, we can represent these relationships on the following diagram, called the *square of opposition*.

Figure 16.1 Square of Opposition

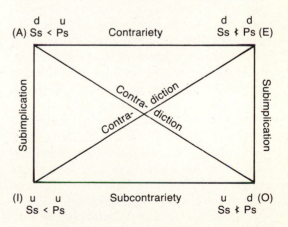

As you can see, each of the four types of categorical propositions appears on the diagram, and each is joined to each of the others by a line. The line symbolizes the type of relationship between them. In all, there are four relationships to be considered.

Contradiction. Two propositions are **contradictories** when they cannot both be true, and cannot both be false. **Contradiction** is a very strong logical relationship because whenever we know that one of a pair of contradictories is true we can infer validly that the other member of the pair is false and whenever we know that one of the pair is false we can validly infer that the other is true. The pairs of propositions joined by diagonal lines on the square of opposition, namely the A- and O-forms and the E- and I-forms, are contradictories. Accordingly, to know the truth value of one member of a pair is to be able to infer the falsity of the other, and vice versa. Given that all cats are mammals, it follows that it is false that some cats are not mammals. On the other hand, if it were false that all cats are mammals, it would have to be the case that at least some cats are not mammals. On the other hand, if it were false that all cats are mammals, it would have to be the case that at least some cats are not mammals. We get the same type of result if we begin with the O-form proposition. If it were true that some cats are not mammals, then it would be false that all cats are mammals. On the other hand, given that it is false that some cats are not mammals, it follows that all cats are mammals. If you think through an example involving E- and I-form propositions, such as "No cats are dogs" and "Some cats are dogs," you will see that all of the same deductive relationships hold.

Incidentally, the relationship of contradiction does not hold only between propositions that have the A- and O-, or E- and I-forms. Any proposition, categorical or not, can be contradicted simply by denying it. "If it rains, we will get wet" and "It is false that if it rains we will get wet" are contradictories. It would be wrong, therefore, to define contradiction as a relationship between A- and O-, or E- and I-form propositions. Such a definition would be altogether too narrow.

Contrariety. Two propositions are **contraries** when they cannot both be true, but can both be false. Only two of the propositions on the square of opposition, namely the A- and E-forms, share this relationship. Unlike the case with contradiction, the relation of **contrariety** permits a valid inference only when we know that one of the propositions is true; nothing follows about the other when one is false. Thus, if you know it is true that all students are people who study hard, you can validly infer that it is false that no students are people who study hard. But knowing it is false that all students are people who study hard, you cannot validly infer that no students are people who study hard. That may be the case, but it may also be that some students study hard and some do not. Your evidence simply does not tell you which is the case. The situation is the same if we begin with an E-form proposition. Knowing it is true, we can validly infer that the corresponding A-form is false; but knowing the E-form is false, we can infer nothing about the A-form. You will see this if you think it through in terms of an example, such as "No professors are millionaires."

As with contradiction, it is not the case that only A- and E-form propositions are contraries. If you consider the matter, you will realize that "Lincoln's beard was black" and "Lincoln's beard was blond" are contraries.

Subcontrariety. Two propositions are **subcontraries** when they cannot both be false, but can both be true. Among other types of propositions, I- and O-form propositions share this relationship. Consider the pair of propositions "Some logicians are music lovers" and "Some logicians are not music lovers." If you knew that one of these propositions was false, you would be able to infer that the other is true. If it is false that some logicians are music lovers, then it has to be true that at least some logicians are not music lovers, for in fact none of them is. On the other hand, knowing one of a pair of subcontraries is true permits no inference about the other. If you know that some logicians are music lovers, you are unable to infer that some logicians are not music lovers. That may be the case, but it may also be the case that all logicians are music lovers. You simply do not know.

Subimplication. When two categorical propositions differ only in their degree of generality, the more general one logically implies the less general one. This relationship obtains between the A- and I-form propositions, and between the E- and O-forms. Consider the propositions "All crows are scavengers" and "Some crows are scavengers." These two categorical propositions contrast only in their degree of generality. The former is a general statement about all crows; the latter is less general since it speaks only of at least one crow. Given that all crows are scavengers, we may validly infer that at least some are. By contrast, if we know only that some crows are scavengers, it does not follow that all are. If such a thing did follow, it would never be possible to commit fallacies of hasty generalization. Suppose, on the other hand, that we know it to be *false* that even some crows are scavengers. We could then deduce validly that it is false that all crows are scavengers. Thus, **when the less general proposition is false, it follows that the more general one is false also.** Again, however, the converse relationship fails. If we know it is false that all crows are scavengers, we cannot validly infer that it is false that some are. You will find that these relationships also hold between E- and O-form propositions if you check by using an example such as "No students are professors" and "Some students are not professors."

We may now summarize the inferences that can be made validly using the square of opposition. The table below tells what can be inferred validly about the other three propositions given the truth of one of them and given the falsity of one of them. Once again, you will find it easier to understand these relationships if you think them through using an example of your own devising.

Table 16.1 Valid Inferences from the Square of Opposition

Given	Validly Inferred	Undecided
A-form true	O-form false (by contradiction) E-form false (by contrariety) I-form true (by subimplication)	
E-form true	I-form false (by contradiction) A-form false (by contrariety) O-form true (by subimplication)	

Table 16.1   Cont'd.

Given	Validly Inferred	Undecided
I-form true	E-form false (by contradiction)	A-form O-form
O-form true	A-form false (by contradiction)	E-form I-form
A-form false	O-form true (by contradiction)	E-form I-form
E-form false	I-form true (by contradiction)	A-form O-form
I-form false	E-form true (by contradiction) A-form false (by subimplication) O-form true (by subcontrariety)	
O-form false	A-form true (by contradiction) E-form false (by subimplication) I-form true (by subcontrariety)	

The Importance of Immediate Inference

Many people are intimidated by the subject of immediate inference when they first begin to study logic. The sheer number of inferences that can be made using a single categorical proposition or its denial as a premise is surprising, and there are too many of them for most of us to master by simple memorization. Rather, immediate inferences must be mastered by learning the logical concepts on which they are based, and these concepts tend to be more abstract than most that we employ in our daily lives. But the importance of immediate inference cannot be overemphasized. A clear understanding of it is a vital steppingstone to dealing with more complex arguments and hence is crucial to effective thinking. When thinking goes wrong, the mistake often begins with an invalid immediate inference.

A classic example concerns invalid conversion of propositions. Suppose you are told that to be eligible for a certain scholarship a student must have a B average or better. This requirement can be expressed in the A-form proposition "All students eligible for this scholarship are students with a B average or better." But if you conclude from what you are told that any student with at least a B average, yourself for example, is eligible for the scholarship, you have in effect invalidly converted this A-form proposition. There may be a number of other conditions that you would have to meet in order to qualify. Invalid conversion of A-form propositions occurs frequently and is always a mistake. From "All Ss are Ps" it simply does not follow that all Ps are Ss.

Other common mistakes fail to respect relationships on the square of opposition. Suppose your instructor announces to the class after an examination, "Some of you passed." Since I-form propositions are often stated in contexts where the speaker believes the corresponding O-form proposition is true as well, you might conclude from the instructor's remark that some people in the class did not pass. But this does not follow from what was said, nor need it be true. Perhaps everyone passed, and the instructor is simply concealing the fact that he or she has not yet graded all the exams. There is no denying that in some contexts the statement of one of a pair of subcontraries may be taken to suggest that the other is true as well. But even where this can be inferred, the inference has to be based on more evidence than the simple statement that was made. Logical thinking has to be based on what propositions state, not what they suggest.

Finally, consider what often occurs when someone states a generalization with which another disagrees. The person who disagrees often tries to refute the first generalization by trying to defend its contrary. For example, if someone claims that all headwaiters are insolent, an opponent, especially one who is a headwaiter, might try to refute this claim by arguing that no headwaiters are insolent. But general claims are difficult to prove, and no such claim need be defended in order to show the falsity of "All headwaiters are insolent." The proper way to refute a generalization is by arguing not for the contrary but for the contradictory. It is a lot easier to show that some headwaiters are not insolent than to show that none is. Relationships on the square of opposition often dictate the basic strategy that an argument must follow if it is to succeed. When these relationships are misunderstood, a lot of effort can be wasted.

Mistaken immediate inferences can be easily overlooked or forgotten in the course of lengthy discussions. We should work, therefore, to make skill at immediate inference second nature to our thinking. The reward is well worth the effort.

Exercise 16

Problems 1–4. Assume that the italicized proposition in each group is true. Evaluate each of the other propositions in the group, using the letter T if it can be validly inferred to be true, F if it can be validly inferred to be false, and U (undecided) if its truth or falsity cannot be validly inferred from the italicized proposition.

1. *All students like to sleep late.*

    (a) No students like to sleep late. _____

    (b) Some students like to sleep late. _____

    (c) Some students do not like to sleep late. _____

    (d) All persons who like to sleep late are students. _____

    (e) No persons who like to sleep late are students. _____

2. *Some professors like to tell jokes.*

    (a) All professors like to tell jokes. _____

    (b) Some people who like to tell jokes are professors. _____

    (c) Some professors do not like to tell jokes. _____

    (d) Some students like to tell jokes. _____

    (e) No professors like to tell jokes. _____

3. *Some doctors are not surgeons.*

    (a) All doctors are surgeons. _____

    (b) No doctors are surgeons. _____

    (c) Some doctors are surgeons. _____

    (d) Some surgeons are not doctors. _____

    (e) Some medical students are not surgeons. _____

4. *No old persons are drafted.*

    (a) All old persons are drafted. _____

(b) Some old persons are drafted. _____

(c) Some old persons are not drafted. _____

(d) No persons who are drafted are old. _____

(e) All persons who are drafted are young. _____

Problems 5–8. In the next four groups , assume that the italicized proposition is false.

5. *Some dictators do not restrict liberty.*

(a) All dictators restrict liberty. _____

(b) Some dictators restrict liberty. _____

(c) Some dictators do not restrict liberty. _____

(d) No dictators restrict liberty. _____

(e) Some persons who restrict liberty are not dictators. _____

6. *Some women are indispensable.*

(a) No women are indispensable. _____

(b) Some women are not indispensable. _____

(c) No persons who are indispensable are women. _____

(d) All women are indispensable. _____

(e) No men are indispensable. _____

7. *All tugbeets are dragdites.*

(a) Some tugbeets are dragdites. _____

(b) Some tugbeets are not dragdites. _____

(c) No tugbeets are dragdites. _____

(d) All dragdites are tugbeets. _____

(e) Some dragdites are not tugbeets. _____

8. *No nabberocks are pearlgates.*

    (a) No pearlgates are nabberocks..   ———————

    (b) No nabberocks are pearlgates.   ———————

    (c) Some nabberocks are not pearlgates.   ———————

    (d) Some nabberocks are pearlgates.   ———————

    (e) All nabberocks are pearlgates.   ———————

Problems 9–10. Write in logical shorthand. (1) the obverse of the given propositions and (2) the converse of the given proposition if it can be validly converted.

9. Some students are inattentive at lectures.

    (1) _____

    (2) _____

10. Some students are not mature.

    (1) _____

    (2) _____

Chapter 17

Categorical Syllogisms

- **Structure**
- **The Four-Terms Fallacy**
- **The Fallacy of Faulty Exclusion**
- **The Fallacy of Undistributed Middle**

- **The Fallacy of Illicit Distribution**
- **Constellations of Terms**

As was said in Chapter 3, a syllogism is a deductive argument that has two premises and a conclusion. Syllogisms constitute perhaps the most important type of argument used in deductive decision making; hence it is important to gain a thorough understanding of the various forms they can take. We have already studied the hypothetical form. We turn now to the categorical. This chapter will focus on the principles of validity for categorical syllogisms. As with the principles governing immediate inference, these rules need to become almost second nature to us, for deductive thinking tends to proceed so quickly that only the development of sound habits of thinking can guarantee its effectiveness.

Structure

A categorical syllogism consists of two categorical propositions used as premises and a conclusion in categorical form drawn from the premises by deduction. Here is an example.

	Quantifier	*Middle Term*	*Connective*	*Major Term*
Major Premise:	All	things created by humans	are included in	things subject to error.
	Quantifier	*Minor Term*	*Connective*	*Middle Term*
Minor Premise:	All	books	are included in	things created by humans.
	Quantifier	*Minor Term*	*Connective*	*Major Term*
Conclusion:	All	books	are included in	things subject to error.

As you can see, each of the propositions in this argument is a categorical one, with a quantifier, two terms, and a connective signifying a relationship of inclusion or exclusion between the classes the terms signify. But while there is a grand total of six subjects and predicates in the three propositions, the syllogism as a whole uses only three terms. This is because each proposition in the argument has a term in common with each of the other propositions. This fact forms the basis for the designations of "Major" and "Minor" given in the example. It works this way. The **major term** is defined as being whatever term is the predicate of the conclusion; the **minor term** is whatever term is the subject of the conclusion. The premise in which the major term appears is by definition the **major premise**, and the premise in which the minor term appears is by definition the **minor premise**. The remaining term, or the term that appears in both premises, is the **middle term**. When logicians write out syllogisms for logical analysis, they follow the convention of writing the major premise first, the minor premise second, and the conclusion last. But this is only a convenient practice used in logic; as we saw in Chapter 2, arguments in ordinary discourse observe no such niceties. A categorical syllogism is valid only when its structure closes all possible loopholes, so that the relationship between classes claimed by the conclusion is guaranteed by the relationships set up in the premises. A natural human tendency is to rate a syllogism as valid when we like its conclusion and to rate it as invalid when we dislike the conclusion. Clearly, effective thinking requires a better system.

All possible loopholes in a categorical syllogism are closed only when it meets four rules of validity. If the syllogism violates a single rule, it is invalid and its con-clusion, though possibly true, is not reliable. The remainder of this chapter describes a procedure for applying these four rules. When we have had sufficient practice in using it, we can eliminate or consolidate some of the steps. Eventually we should be able to check a simple syllogism in a few seconds, but in the beginning the long way around is best.

The first step in this procedure is to write the syllogism in logical shorthand. The syllogism above would be written this way.

$$\overset{d}{\text{Things created by humans}} < \overset{u}{\text{things subject to error.}}$$

$$\overset{d}{\text{Books}} < \overset{u}{\text{things created by humans.}}$$

$$\therefore \overset{d}{\text{Books}} < \overset{u}{\text{things subject to error.}}$$

When a syllogism is correctly written in shorthand, it is relatively easy to determine whether it meets the four rules of validity, which are discussed in the following sections.

The Four-Terms Fallacy

The next step in our procedure is to determine whether the syllogism meets the first of these four rules. If the syllogism is valid, it must follow the rule below.

A valid syllogism must have exactly three terms, each used exactly twice to refer to the same class.

If the syllogism violates the rule in any way—by having four terms, by using one term only once or more than twice, or by using the same term to refer ambiguously to different classes—it is invalid. This error is called the **four-terms fallacy.**

We can see the reason for this rule by

studying the valid syllogism above. Its conclusion relates the minor term ("books") to the major term ("things subject to error"). Whatever relationship a conclusion describes, it has to be guaranteed by the premises. When valid, categorical syllogisms guarantee the relationship between the major and minor terms through the "mediation" of the middle term ("things created by humans"). One premise describes the relation of the major term to the middle term, and the other describes the relation of the minor term to the middle term. If a syllogism fails to do exactly this, it contains a loophole and is invalid. In order to do this, it must contain exactly three terms, each used exactly twice. There is no other way. The four-terms fallacy corresponds in some respects to the fallacy of uncertain relationships between premises in hypothetical syllogisms.

Now suppose your instructor tells you that you are wasting time in college because all who flunked this course are poorly motivated and you made the lowest grade in the class. If you are unwilling to accept this allegation, you must attack either the premises or the validity of the argument. Let us test it for validity first. The instructor's premises are written in shorthand below.

$$\overset{d}{\text{People who flunked}} < \overset{u}{\text{poorly motivated.}}$$
this course

$$\overset{d}{\text{You}} < \overset{u}{\text{made the lowest grade in the class.}}$$

You can see the four-terms fallacy in this argument without bothering to write the conclusion. The minor premise introduces a new term ("you"), but it does not clearly relate this term to either term in the major premise. Even if you did make the

lowest grade in the class, it is not necessarily true that you flunked the course. Perhaps everybody passed. (Incidentally, you will have noticed that the term "you" is distributed. This is because it refers to a single individual.)

Now suppose that when you call attention to this fallacy your instructor changes the syllogism to the version below.

$$\overset{d}{\text{People who flunked}} < \overset{u}{\text{poorly motivated.}}$$
this course

$$\overset{d}{\text{You}} < \overset{u}{\text{people who flunked this course.}}$$

$$\therefore \overset{d}{\text{You}} < \overset{u}{\text{wasting time in college.}}$$

The minor premise does its work perfectly by relating "you" to people who flunked the course, but the conclusion violates the rule. For this syllogism to be valid, the conclusion must relate "you" to the "poorly motivated." Instead, it relates you to those "wasting time in college," which is quite a different class. Although in categorical analysis we call this a four-terms fallacy, you will recognize this particular example as a non sequitur. The instructor's syllogism would have been valid if he or she had merely accused you of being poorly motivated. Of course, the accusation may still be false. If it is, then one of the instructor's premises is false, for valid arguments with true premises cannot yield false conclusions.

In writing syllogisms in shorthand, we must be very careful to identify and state the classes accurately. Otherwise, we may accept a fallacious syllogism like the one below.

Smoke is a nuisance.

Bill and Rita smoke.

Therefore Bill and Rita are nuisances.

The four-terms fallacy becomes obvious when the premises are correctly written in shorthand, for "smoke" and "smokers" are not the same class.

$$\begin{array}{cc} d & u \\ \text{Smoke} < \text{nuisances.} \end{array}$$

$$\begin{array}{cc} d & u \\ \text{Bill and Rita} < \text{smokers.} \end{array}$$

The Fallacy of Faulty Exclusion

Suppose your employer gives you an argument you do not like. Since it is often easier to destroy an argument by showing it to be invalid than by disprovng a premise, you test it for validity. When you write the argument in logical shorthand, it looks like this.

$$\begin{array}{cc} d & d \\ \text{Professionals} ɨ \text{break appointments unnecessarily.} \end{array}$$

$$\begin{array}{cc} d & d \\ \text{You} ɨ \text{professionals.} \end{array}$$

$$\begin{array}{cc} d & u \\ \therefore \text{You} < \text{break appointments unnecessarily.} \end{array}$$

You can quickly see that this argument meets the four-terms rule, so the next step is to check it using the second rule of validity, stated below.

> **A valid syllogism must have no exclusions, or exactly two, one of which must be in the conclusion.**

You would be justified in tactfully suggesting to your employer that she be more logical, for her syllogism contains the fallacy of faulty exclusion by having exclusions in both premises.

The reasons for the rule on exclusion are easy enough to see. Two exclusions in the premises prove nothing because the third term is not linked to anything. In the example above, "you" is linked in no way to "people who break appointments unnecessarily." Now suppose that your employer changes her argument to this.

$$\begin{array}{cc} d & d \\ \text{Professionals} ɨ \text{break appointments unnecessarily.} \end{array}$$

$$\begin{array}{cc} d & u \\ \text{You} < \text{professionals.} \end{array}$$

$$\begin{array}{cc} d & u \\ \therefore \text{You} < \text{break appointments unnecessarily.} \end{array}$$

Although your employer is now being more conciliatory, you can still chide her for faulty logic. This syllogism also breaks the rule on exclusions. The premises actually prove the opposite of the conclusion. Thus if there is one exclusion in either premise, the conclusion must also contain an exclusion. Otherwise the syllogism contains the fallacy of faulty exclusion.

The Fallacy of Undistributed Middle

Suppose you park overtime, and the traffic officer makes the unpalatable accusation in the syllogism below.

$$\begin{array}{cc} d & u \\ \text{Criminals} < \text{lawbreakers.} \end{array}$$

$$\begin{array}{cc} d & u \\ \text{You} < \text{lawbreakers.} \end{array}$$

$$\begin{array}{cc} d & u \\ \therefore \text{You} < \text{criminals.} \end{array}$$

This syllogism clearly passes the first

two tests for validity. The next step, therefore, is to test it by the third rule, stated below.

In a valid syllogism, the middle term must be distributed at least once.

The middle term must be distributed at least once because it is the middle link in the chain of argument. Look at the valid syllogism on page 237. "Things created by humans" is the middle term because it is the term that appears in both premises. In the major premise, all "things created by humans" are included in the class "things subject to error." In the minor premise, "books" are included in "things created by humans." Thus the middle term links "books" and "things subject to error" as surely as a town is linked to a state because it is in a certain county in the state. Note that the middle term is distributed in the major premise.

Now look at the impolite police officer's syllogism. The middle term is "lawbreakers." But this link has a gap in it. Even if you knew nothing whatever about the two classes in the major premise, you know from the structure of the proposition that the second class, "lawbreakers," is possibly, even probably, larger than the first class, "criminals." Proving that you are a lawbreaker does not prove that you are a criminal, for the same reason that living in a certain state does not prove that you live in a certain county. Now note that the middle term is *undistributed* in *both* premises. Thus the syllogism violates the rule and is invalid.

Now suppose you recklessly point out to the officer that this logic is unworthy of his or her profession, and suppose the officer changes the syllogism a bit, as shown below.

$$\overset{d}{\text{Lawbreakers}} < \overset{u}{\text{criminals.}}$$

$$\overset{d}{\text{You}} < \overset{u}{\text{lawbreakers.}}$$

$$\therefore \overset{d}{\text{You}} < \overset{u}{\text{criminals.}}$$

The fallacy of undistributed middle has been eliminated. But before you let your self-concept be damaged by this syllogism, compare its major premise with the one in the officer's original argument. Both major premises are classificatory statements. The first is generally accepted; the second is not.

These two syllogisms illustrate a problem we frequently encounter: depending on the structure of the premises, the evidence in hand gives us either an invalid syllogism with reliable premises or a valid syllogism with unreliable premises. In these situations, we cannot afford to throw away the evidence in syllogisms with undistributed middle terms, for these syllogisms are like hypothetical syllogisms with affirmed consequents. The conclusions are not proved, but the probability that they are true is increased.

When either or both of the premises are expressed in statistical terms, the probability that the conclusion is true can sometimes be estimated with a fair degree of accuracy. Consider the following example.

Twenty-four per hundred thousand Americans will be killed in motor-vehicle accidents next year.[1]

You are an American.

Therefore you will be killed in a motor-vehicle accident next year.

The middle term, "Americans," is undistributed in both premises (in the major

---

[1] Based on National Safety Council data.

premise because the quantity referred to is less than all; in the minor premise because it follows inclusion). Thus the argument is invalid. But the probability that it is true on this evidence alone, assuming that the premises are true, is easily computed: it is the probability that any given American will be killed in vehicular accident this year, or $24/100,000$. Although this probability is low, it is still high enough to justify a decision to drive carefully.

The Fallacy of Illicit Distribution

It is not enough to check only the arguments we dislike. We should be particularly careful in checking arguments we like to offset our natural tendency to accept them. Consider the syllogism below.

$$\overset{d}{\text{Stupid people}} < \overset{u}{\text{swallow propaganda.}}$$

$$\overset{d}{\text{Logic students}} \nless \overset{d}{\text{stupid.}}$$

$$\therefore \overset{d}{\text{Logic students}} \nless \overset{d}{\text{swallow propaganda.}}$$

It meets the test of all three rules studied so far. But there is one more rule.

In a valid syllogism, every term distributed in the conclusion must be distributed in the premise in which it appears.

Note that this rule applies only to distributed terms in the conclusion. The minor terms, "logic students," is distributed in the conclusion; it meets the rule because it is also distributed in the minor premise. The major term, "people who swallow propaganda," is also distributed in the conclusion, but it is undistributed in the major premise. Thus the rule has

been violated, and we have the fallacy of *illicit distribution*.

The reason for the rule is easy to understand. The essence of validity is that the conclusion must never go beyond the evidence actually stated in the premises. The conclusion above claims that 100 percent of those who swallow propaganda are accounted for with respect to logic students. Yet the major premise accounts for only some of those who swallow propaganda, because this latter class follows inclusion. It is possible, even probable, that some people who swallow propaganda are not stupid, and some of these people could, alas, be logic students.

Consider another example.

$$\overset{d}{\text{Students}} < \overset{u}{\text{alert.}}$$

$$\overset{u}{\text{Women}} < \overset{u}{\text{students.}}$$

$$\therefore \overset{d}{\text{Women}} < \overset{u}{\text{alert.}}$$

Note that the term "women" is distributed in the conclusion, but not in the minor premise. The minor premise puts *some* women in the class of students, and these women are certainly in the class of the alert if the major premise is true. But the conclusion claims that *all* women are in the class of the alert. Had it modestly claimed only that some women are alert, it would have followed validly.

Consider another example, using the same major premise.

$$\overset{d}{\text{Students}} < \overset{u}{\text{alert.}}$$

$$\overset{d}{\text{Sophomores}} < \overset{u}{\text{students.}}$$

$$\therefore \overset{u}{\text{Sophomores}} < \overset{u}{\text{alert.}}$$

This syllogism does not violate the rule. Given these premises, the conclusion could validly claim that all sophomores are alert. But there is no law of validity that prohibits claiming too little. Claiming too little may waste evidence, but it never invalidates an argument. The laws of validity prohibit only claiming too much.

Constellations of Terms

Let us now return briefly to our example of failure to distribute the middle term.

$$\text{Criminals} \overset{d}{<} \overset{u}{\text{lawbreakers.}}$$

$$\text{You} \overset{d}{<} \overset{u}{\text{lawbreakers.}}$$

$$\therefore \text{You} \overset{d}{<} \overset{u}{\text{criminals.}}$$

In considering this example, you may have been inclined to think the error in the argument was that the major term—the predicate of the conclusion—was not used as the predicate of the major premise. This, however, cannot be made a requirement for validity, for consider the following example.

$$\text{Dogs} \overset{d}{\nless} \overset{d}{\text{cats.}}$$

$$\text{Cheshires} \overset{d}{<} \overset{u}{\text{cats.}}$$

$$\therefore \text{Cheshires} \overset{d}{\nless} \overset{d}{\text{dogs.}}$$

If you check this argument by the rules, you will see that it is valid. There are also valid syllogisms in which the minor term, that is, the subject of the conclusion, appears as the predicate in the minor premise. Here is one.

$$\text{Birds} \overset{u}{\nless} \overset{d}{\text{robins.}}$$

$$\text{Birds} \overset{d}{<} \overset{u}{\text{animals.}}$$

$$\therefore \text{Animals} \overset{u}{\nless} \overset{d}{\text{robins.}}$$

Finally, there are cases of valid syllogisms in which the major term is the subject of the major premise and the minor term is the predicate of the minor premise, such as the following.

$$\text{Dogs} \overset{d}{\nless} \overset{d}{\text{cats.}}$$

$$\text{Cats} \overset{u}{<} \overset{u}{\text{pets.}}$$

$$\therefore \text{Pets} \overset{u}{\nless} \overset{d}{\text{dogs.}}$$

The lesson to be drawn from these examples is obvious. **There is no restriction on the positions the major and minor terms must have in their respective premises.** In illustrating the rules for validity, we confined our attention mostly to arguments in which the major term is the predicate of the major premise and the minor term is the subject of the minor premise. This order of terms is the one most commonly encountered in ordinary discourse, so it is best for purposes of illustration. But syllogisms with terms in this more normal arrangement are no more likely to be valid than syllogisms with terms in the other constellations.

As with all deductive arguments, we must remember that validity is only part of the story of reliability as regards categorical syllogisms. To produce a reliable conclusion, a deductive argument must not only be valid but also have reliable premises. Nevertheless, there is no greater asset an argument can have than to be deductively valid. Arguments having this feature provide us with the tremendous advantage that, unlike inductive arguments, they cannot lead us from truth into error. Thus the principles of validity for categorical syllogisms deserve our close attention, the more so since the categorical syllogism is a powerful tool for analyzing complicated arguments, as we shall see in the chapters to follow.

Exercise 17

Problems 1–9. In the space provided, rewrite each syllogism in categorical shorthand. Then analyze it using the rules for validity and write in the blank the number of the appropriate statement from the key list.

Key List

1. The syllogism contains the fallacy of four terms.
2. The syllogism contains the fallacy of faulty exclusion.
3. The syllogism contains the fallacy of undistributed middle.
4. The syllogism contains the fallacy of illicit distribution.
5. The syllogism meets all rules and is valid.

1. No good students neglect their studies.

   He neglects his studies.

   Therefore he is not a good student.

   _____

2. All violent persons must be restrained.

   John often does not know when to stop.

   Therefore John must be violent.

   _____

3. All surgeons have steady nerves.

   Sheila is not a surgeon.

   Therefore Sheila does not have steady nerves.

   _____

4. Some Southern senators oppose a school prayer amendment.

   Senator Linseed is a Southern senator.

   Therefore Senator Linseed opposes a school prayer amendment.

   _____

5. All good tests are difficult.

All tests on deductive reasoning are difficult.

Therefore all tests on deductive reasoning are good tests.

_____

_____

_____

_____

6. All industrialists are capitalists.

Most industrialists are not politicians.

Therefore politicians are capitalists.

_____

_____

_____

_____

7. All radicals are communists.

All progressives advocate changes.

Therefore all progressives are communists.

_____

_____

_____

8. Some difficult courses are not worthwhile.

All difficult courses are time-consuming.

Therefore some time-consuming courses are not worthwhile.

_____

_____

_____

9. Most good blockers are star players.

All our backfield men are good blockers.

Therefore some of our backfield men are star players.

_____

_____

Chapter 18

Categorical Syllogisms in Ordinary Discourse

- **Interpreting Categorical Propositions**
- **Finding the Parts of Syllogisms**
- **Putting Arguments into Logical Form**
- **Missing Propositions**

Nearly all our examples in the last three chapters have been arranged in neat packages. Categorical propositions have been clear as to which of the four forms they exemplify and their terms easily recognizable. The syllogisms have had their premises and conclusions neatly identified and in the standard order, and the terms used in the different propositions have been clear in their relation to one another. Our purpose has been to learn how our tools work before applying them to the more involved arguments we encounter daily in textbooks, editorials, speeches, and even ordinary conversation. The logical features of the propositions that may be found in such contexts are often not as clear as they are in the textbook examples. Moreover, arguments in ordinary discourse are seldom stated simply or with premises and conclusion conveniently arranged in order. Often the basic structure of an argument is concealed in several paragraphs or pages, and the careless thinker is tempted to accept the conclusion offered rather than take the trouble to pick out and analyze the argument. Those who would deceive us do not advertise the fallacies in their arguments. It is important, therefore, that we learn how to deal both with nonstandard categorical propositions and with syllogisms in their natural surroundings. Without doing so, learning rules for validity would be like buying good tools and never learning how to use them.

Interpreting Categorical Propositions

The standardized forms of sentences we used in introducing categorical propositions have the advantage of clearly exhibiting the important logical features of these propositions. The quantifier is explicit, the relation of inclusion or exclusion specified, and the subject and predicate terms are given in their usual order and in the form of nouns or noun phrases. We may think of these sentences as expressing the **logical form** of categorical propositions. Ordinary English sentences that express categorical propositions can deviate from these forms in several ways. We have already seen some of the more obvious and simple ones. Few sentences use the connectives "are included in" and "are excluded from." We are more likely to hear "All cats are mammals" than to hear "All cats are included in the class of mammals." E-form propositions are more likely to be expressed not by a sentence such as "All cats are excluded from the class of dogs," but rather by "No cats are dogs." As was noted in Chapter 15, the word *no* does double duty when E-form propositions are expressed in this way. It acts as a quantifier and also tells us that the relation between subject and predicate is one of exclusion.

Another common variation is that whereas our logical forms use a noun or noun phrase to express the predicate many sentences in ordinary discourse do not. Sometimes predicate adjectives are used, as when we are told "All logicians are intelligent" instead of "All logicians are intelligent people." At other times, the predicate is expressed in part by the main verb. Thus we might hear "All lions eat meat" as opposed to "All lions are meat-eaters." These variations usually present no difficulty. When they do, as, for example, when we wish to obvert "Some predators do not eat people" to "Some predators are non-people-eaters," it is usually an easy enough thing to recast the predicate as a noun or noun phrase, provided we are willing to accept a bit of awkwardness.

Finally, we have had occasion to note that the singular pronoun "you," should be understood as distributed because it refers to a single individual. The same applies to all singular pronouns, to proper names, and to any other expression that refers to a single object, person, idea, or quality. Thus, "The Sears Tower is a skyscraper" should be interpreted as stating an A-form proposition, and "The person who did this is not an arsonist" should be taken as stating an E-form proposition. They should be expressed in logical form as follows.

$$\overset{d}{\text{The Sears Tower}} < \overset{u}{\text{skyscrapers.}}$$

$$\overset{d}{\text{The person who did this}} \nless \overset{d}{\text{arsonists.}}$$

We have not yet encountered a number of other types of English sentences that deviate from logical form. Of these, five types tend to give special trouble and hence deserve special attention.

One type can be easily identified by the presence of any one of the following structure words or their equivalents: *only, none but, none except,* and *alone.* The effect of these expressions in a sentence is to reverse the normal order of terms in the proposition expressed. Most English sentences that express categorical propositions follow the same order our logical forms do in stating the subject first and the predicate second. Sentences using the expression listed above are different. All the following sentences have the same meaning.

Only students may attend the concert.

None but students may attend the concert.

None except students may attend the concert.

Students alone may attend the concert.

To state in logical form the proposition these sentences express we would have to reverse the order of the terms. For to say that only students can attend the concert is *not* to say that all students may attend. Some may be excluded for one reason or another. Perhaps students on disciplinary probation are not eligible for tickets. But to state any of the above sentences *is* to say that all persons who may attend the concert are students. Thus in order to translate the above sentences into logical form, our rule must be to **use the A-form and reverse the original order of the terms.** The proper translation for all four of the above sentences is shown below.

d   u
Persons who may attend < students.
the concert

The second troublesome type of sentence resembles those considered above in stating the predicate first. It differs from the first type in having an easily identifiable structure instead of easily identifiable key expressions: a descriptive word or words, stated first, constitute the predicate, followed by the verb and subject. The following sentences illustrate this type.

Ill lay Larry Stein.

Blessed are the meek.

Foolish are they who reason from false premises.

In logic, these sentences are dealt with in the same way as the first group. We use the A-form and reverse the original order of the terms. The proper translations for our examples are as follows.

d   u
Larry Stein < people who lay ill.

d   u
Meek people < blessed people.

d   u
People who reason < foolish people.
from false premises

In the third type of problematic sentence, the subject and predicate are given in the normal order. These sentences may be identified by their use of the expressions *all but, all except,* and *unless,* or words that have the same meaning. In ordinary English, these expressions have a negative meaning that always attaches itself to the subject of the sentence. When we translate the sentence into logical form we must be careful to make the first term (the subject term) negative and avoid the error of attaching the negative meaning to the connective, which expresses the relationship between the subject and predicate terms. The following sentences illustrate this third type.

All but Carlos came to the party.

Everyone in the class except Marie preferred to postpone the test.

Unless excused, everyone must attend class.

When expressing them in logical form, we need only **retain the A-form** (since subject and predicate are in the normal order) **and make their first terms negative.**

$$\overset{d}{\text{Persons who are not Carlos}} < \overset{u}{\underset{\substack{\text{persons who} \\ \text{came to the} \\ \text{party.}}}{}}$$

$$\underset{\text{who are not Marie}}{\overset{d}{\text{Persons in the class}}} < \underset{\text{to postpone the test.}}{\overset{u}{\text{persons who preferred}}}$$

$$\underset{\text{excused}}{\overset{d}{\text{Persons who are not}}} < \underset{\text{must attend class.}}{\overset{u}{\text{persons who}}}$$

Sentences with *unless* sometimes cause needless confusion because *unless* can be in almost any position in the sentence. The example above, for instance, could also be stated, "Everyone must attend class unless excused." We need only remember that the word or words immediately following *unless* form the first term of the logical proposition and must be negated.

The precise meaning conveyed by the expressions *all but, all except,* and *unless* is often a subject of controversy. Very likely when we state that "All but Carlos came to the party," we mean to suggest that Carlos was the only one of those expected at the party who did not come. But logic is a discipline concerned with literal meaning, and all that is guaranteed by our stating this sentence is that all persons other than Carlos came to the party; strictly speaking, no information whatever about Carlos himself is conveyed. In the second example cited above, it is possible that Marie was the only member absent at the time the class's opinion was determined, and to assume that she preferred *not* to postpone the test would be unwarranted. The propositions conveys no information about Marie or her preference; it merely states the preference of all members of the

class other than Marie. No matter how reasonable the belief may seem to us that something about Carlos or Marie or the excused is conveyed in these three propositions, we should understand that the structure of the proposition actually conveys no such information. In important matters, we should assume that the strict logical meaning is all that is conveyed.

Finally, note that *all but* and *all except* must never be confused with *none but* and *none except*—their meanings within sentence contexts are vastly different, as we have seen.

A fourth type of troublesome sentence involves the O-form (partial exclusion). Every expression of partial exclusion in ordinary English must be made by means of one of the following structures (or an easily identifiable variant); they are cited in the order of their frequency in everyday usage.

Some Ss are not Ps.

Not all Ss are Ps.

All Ss are not Ps.

It is false that all Ss are Ps.

Properly understood and used, all these sentences express partial exclusion.

$$\overset{u}{\text{Ss}} \nleftarrow \overset{d}{\text{Ps}}$$

At first glance, we may be tempted to assume that "Not all Wysacki professors are entertaining" and "All Wysacki professors are not entertaining" are E-form propositions, expressing total exclusion. But suppose two first-year students at Wysacki form these statements from their own experience. Let us assume that they have their classes together and that they notice from the beginning that all but one of their professors conduct lively classes, tell reasonably good jokes, and have a refreshing and upbeat approach to their subject. One professor, however, though perfectly competent, has a workaday classroom style and displays little or no humor. After a few weeks of classes, one of the students may say to the other, with some regret, "Well, not all Wysacki professors are entertaining." The other may reply, "You're right. All Wysacki professors are not entertaining." Obviously, having decided that one professor does not qualify as being entertaining, the two students are conveying to one another their view that at least one Wysacki professor is excluded from the class of entertaining professors. The truth is that most of the confusion that arises regarding sentences of these types occurs in the written forms. In our speech, stress and pitch patterns will usually make the meaning clear. If, in speech, one stresses the *all* in "*All* Wysacki professors are not entertaining," probably no one would miss the partial exclusion, the only meaning logically conveyed.

Similarly, if we insert the same subject and predicate in the last O-form example cited above ("It is false that all Wysacki professors are entertaining"), the meaning conveyed must be that at least one Wysacki professor is *not* entertaining. The denial of an A-form proposition is always logically equivalent to the corresponding O-form proposition. Hence, in logical form,

$$\overset{u}{\text{Wysacki professor}} \nmid \overset{d}{\text{entertaining professors.}}$$

The last of our five kinds of troublesome sentences expressing categorical propositions are those that contain the expressions *few* and *a few*. When we state

that "Few people are truly brave" we seem to be expressing partial inclusion (I-form), but what we mean—and also what we are conveying—is that "Most people are not truly brave," or partial exclusion (O-form). By the same reasoning, what we mean and convey by "Few people are not truly brave" is that "Most people are truly brave," or partial inclusion (I-form). Our rule, therefore, is that when we transform sentences containing *few* into logical propositions, we must **use the partial quantifier (some) and change the relationship between the terms (the connective).** The propositions below illustrate the rule.

Ordinary English	***Logical Form***
Few children smoke.	$\overset{u}{\text{Children}} \nmid \overset{d}{\text{people who smoke.}}$
Few adults do not drive automobiles.	$\overset{u}{\text{Adults}} < \overset{u}{\text{people who drive automobiles.}}$

The expression *a few* differs in meaning from *few,* for it simply indicates the quantifier *some*. Hence when we transform any sentence containing *a few* into logical form, our rule is **to use the partial quantifier (some) and to keep the original relationship between the terms (the connective),** as shown in the following examples.

Ordinary English	***Logical Form***
A few officials are corrupt.	$\overset{u}{\text{Officials}} < \overset{u}{\text{corrupt people.}}$
A few diamond cutters are not patient.	$\overset{u}{\text{Diamond cutters}} \nmid \overset{d}{\text{patient people.}}$

Finding the Parts of Syllogisms

Let us now turn to the problem of analyzing categorical syllogisms found in ordinary discourse. The first step in dealing with such arguments is to pick out their structure. It is usually best to look first for the conclusion. If we mistake the major premise for the minor premise, it is still possible to analyze the argument correctly, but if we mistake the conclusion for a premise, we may analyze *an* argument correctly, but not the one we started with. It is hardly fair to use the evidence given in an argument as the conclusion of the argument.

As we saw in Chapter 2, the conclusion is whatever proposition the person offering an argument is attempting to prove. In the formal statements of arguments that logicians use, the conclusion is given last. But we have seen that in ordinary contexts the conclusion may appear anywhere in the argument. People who believe they have a sound argument and wish to present it fairly often state the conclusion first so that the hearer or reader can check the evidence as it is presented. Sometimes the conclusion appears near the middle of the argument, with introductory material at the beginning and with evidence stated after, or both before and after, the conclusion.

The words and phrases most often used to introduce conclusions and premises, also studied in Chapter 2, are listed below for review. Careful attention to them makes it possible to pick out the conclusions and premises of many arguments. It must be remembered, however, that such expressions are not always used. Arguments in which the conclusion is stated first seldom contain conclusion indicators. There are also cases where no expressions indicating either conclusion or premises occur, and we must rely on the context of our general knowledge in picking them out. If you are still uncertain how to deal with these problems, you may find it helpful to reread Chapter 2.

Conclusion Indicators	*Premise Indicators*
Therefore	Since
So	For
Hence	Because
Thus	As
Consequently	For the reason that
As a result	As shown by
It must be	As demonstrated by
Indicating that	Inasmuch as
Suggesting that	
Proving that	
Showing that	
Demonstrating that	

In order to recognize the structure of categorical syllogisms, we have to be able to isolate their premises and conclusions within larger contexts in which other information is given and other claims are made. Suppose you read in the newspaper that the following argument was given by a Soviet leader in a speech to the Supreme Council of the Soviet Union. The sentences have been numbered for convenience.

1. The news of the past week proves again that America is a warmongering nation, bent on universal destruction. 2. The American government has announced that it will develop new laser weapons, capable of destroying guided missiles in outer space. 3. These weapons will enhance the Americans' first-strike capability by making them safe from counterattack. 4. Warmongering peoples can be recognized by the fact that they build up their arms. 5. In that way they hope to threaten into submission the peace-loving countries of the world. 6. The development of these new weapons is only one of many steps by

which America is intensifying the arms race. 7. They are constantly increasing their military might. 8. This latest provocation leaves no doubt as to American intentions.

Although this particular argument is fictitious, it is of a depressingly familiar type, which no doubt has existed at least since the invention of the bow and arrow. In a world pervaded by fear of foreign domination, it might convince many people. But in addition to some misuses of evaluative language, it contains a basic fallacy.

We can begin our search for the fallacy by locating the conclusion. In this argument, the speaker has stated the conclusion in the first sentence and alluded to it again in the last sentence for emphasis. It is that America is a warmongering nation.

The next step in analyzing an involved argument is to locate the premises, which lie among the other propositions that have been stated. When, as in this case, the argument is a categorical syllogism, a useful aid in locating the premises is examining the terms in the conclusion. We will be able to recognize the major premise by the fact that it contains the predicate of the conclusion; we will recognize the minor premise by the fact that it contains the subject of the conclusion. The best rule to follow is to try to locate the major premise first. Since the conclusion is "America is a warmongering nation," the major premise will contain the term "warmongering nations," or some expression that for practical purposes means the same. Sentence 4 contains the term "warmongering peoples," which is virtually equivalent to "warmongering nations," and conveys the general claim that all warmongering nations are nations that build up their arms. Thus Sentence 4 qualifies as the major premise.

We have now identified the conclusion and the major premise, as shown below.

Major Premise:	All warmongering nations are nations that build up their arms.
Minor Premise:	
Conclusion:	America is a warmongering nation.

The minor premise is now easily identified. If the four-term fallacy is to be avoided, this premise should contain the two terms that have been used only once: "America" and "nations that build up their arms." Although nearly all the sentences given contain some reference to America or Americans, only one contains a term that is for practical purposes equivalent to "nation that builds up its arms." This is Sentence 7, which can be restated for the purposes of this argument as "America is a nation that builds up its arms." Sentence 7, then, gives the minor premise.

Putting Arguments into Logical Form

Once the parts have been identified, the next step is to write the argument in logical form. To do so, we translate each proposition into logical form, and place the major premise first, the minor premise second, and the conclusion last. The argument above refers to the classes of warmongering nations and nations that build up their arms and to the class composed of the single member America. Shown in logical shorthand, the categorical syllogism it presents is as follows.

d		u
Warmongering nations	<	nations that build up their arms.

d		u
America	<	nations that build up their arms.

d		u
America	<	warmongering nations.

The fallacy in this argument is now clearly exposed: the middle term is not distributed. This argument, like many others, loses its effect once its skeleton is exposed.

There are a number of pitfalls to be avoided in analyzing naturally occurring categorical syllogisms. Perhaps the most common one stems from a tendency many of us have to hear or read others as arguing reasonably or as agreeing with our beliefs when in fact they do not. Because of this tendency, we are likely to translate propositions with which we do not agree into propositions with which we do agree and to translate invalid arguments into valid ones. To avoid this problem, we must be careful to preserve the logical meaning of premises and conclusions in translating them. At the same time, both premises and conclusions should always be interpreted in the context of the whole argument. There is no rule of logic or rhetoric requiring that a term be stated in exactly the same words in the two places it appears in a syllogism. In fact, terms are frequently stated in different words for the sake of variety in expression. Thus it is often necessary to "edit" premises and conclusions in order to avoid introducing fallacies that were not there originally. The argument considered above illustrates one way in which the need for editing may arise. Sometimes the same class is referred to by more than one expression in an argument. When this occurs, we should choose a single conve-

nient expression for referring to the class and use it throughout the argument. Thus instead of speaking of "nations that build up their arms" in the major premise and "nations that increase their military might" in the minor, we chose to use just one of these expressions. Either one would have worked.

Another kind of statement that may need editing is illustrated by the following syllogism. If you think about it, you will see that it is perfectly valid.

All except aliens are eligible.

None of these applicants is an alien.

Therefore all these applicants are eligible.

Suppose now that we wish to represent this argument in logical form. Since the propositions are already in the correct order, we might begin simply by representing each proposition in the logical form it most closely resembles.

	d		u
Persons who are not aliens	<	eligible persons.

	d		d
These applicants	∤	aliens.

∴ These applicants < eligible persons.

Note, however, that this result is not satisfactory. For while the original argument is valid, this form appears not to be. It seems to contain two fallacies: four terms (persons who are not aliens, persons who are eligible, these applicants, and aliens) and faulty exclusion.

The reason for this problem is that we have thus far considered the propositions only in isolation from one another. When we begin in this way, we must always remember to consider how the terms in the propositions we produce may be related. In particular, we should be on the lookout for pairs of terms that, for the purpose of the argument, may be taken to differ only in one of them being positive and the other negative. This occurs in the argument above. The term "aliens," which is the predicate of the second premise, can be viewed as the negative of "persons who are not aliens," which is the subject of the major. When this situation arises, the pair of terms can always be made to match by some process of immediate inference. In the present case, for example, we can get the terms to agree by obverting the second premise.

$$
\begin{array}{ccc}
\text{d} & & \text{u} \\
\text{Persons who are not aliens} & < & \text{eligible persons.}
\end{array}
$$

$$
\begin{array}{ccc}
\text{d} & & \text{u} \\
\text{These applicants} & < & \text{persons who are not aliens.}
\end{array}
$$

$$
\begin{array}{ccc}
\text{d} & & \text{u} \\
\therefore \text{ These applicants} & < & \text{eligible persons.}
\end{array}
$$

Note that in performing this obversion we have transformed the second premise from an E-form proposition to an A-form. Thus we have not only gotten rid of the fourth term, but also removed the negation that seemed to make the argument an instance of faulty exclusion. Thus our original argument can now be seen to be a valid categorical syllogism.

The lesson to be drawn from this example is that syllogisms that appear invalid on first effort at translation will sometimes turn out to be valid once their terms are brought into agreement through immediate inference. As we saw in studying immediate inference, this is because each of the four basic forms of categorical proposition has at least one proposition of another basic form to which it is logically equivalent. Thus, bringing the terms of a syllogism into agreement may require performing immediate inferences on one or more of the propositions it

contains. Obviously, in doing this kind of "editing," we must be careful to perform only valid immediate inferences. Otherwise we will change the logical meaning of the propositions and misrepresent the argument.

We frequently encounter arguments containing categorical propositions that have plural subjects but no quantifier. In dealing with propositions of this kind, a decision must be made about whether the subject term is meant to be distributed or not. The problem is illustrated by the following pair of propositions.

Squirrels are rodents.

Squirrels are in the attic.

As you can see, the grammar of each of these propositions does not by itself indicate whether the term "squirrels" is distributed. Nevertheless, it is easy to see that in the first proposition the term is distributed, because this proposition is a classificatory statement and hence applies to all squirrels. Thus this statement should be interpreted as "All squirrels are rodents." By contrast, the second proposition should be taken as saying "Some squirrels are in the attic," for its predicate is a property some squirrels have and others lack. It is important to interpret such propositions correctly when they appear in arguments. Otherwise we are apt to see fallacies where none exists. The following argument is a case in point.

Squirrels are rodents.

This animal is not a rodent.

Therefore it is not a squirrel.

As a rule, the context in which propositions with missing quantifiers occur helps us decide whether the subject is distributed or not. When the context fails to make the matter clear, it is usually advisable to be conservative and consider the term undistributed. Otherwise we may base a decision on what amounts to a hasty generalization. In giving arguments of our own, we should always supply a quantifier to avoid being misunderstood.

Missing Propositions

We often omit propositions from arguments because the context makes clear what the missing proposition is to be. Missing propositions are an especially frequent phenomenon in categorical syllogisms found in ordinary discourse. Since any of the propositions in a categorical syllogism shares each of its terms with one of the other propositions, it is always possible to omit a proposition without omitting any terms. Thus stylistic considerations, such as brevity and avoidance of repetition or pedantry, often lead to one of the propositions being left out. Unfortunately, there is another motive as well. Sometimes those who would deceive us leave out a proposition because the argument is more convincing without it. Arguments with propositions missing are called **enthymemes.**

The missing proposition may be the conclusion.

> My opponent in this race believes in government ownership of basic industry, and the Communists believe in government ownership of basic industry. Now, my friends, you may draw your own conclusion about my opponent.

If the speaker had stated the conclusion he or she is suggesting, we could destroy the argument by pointing out the undistributed middle. But since the conclusion is not stated, we can blame only ourselves if we credulously jump to it. This trick often works, perhaps because we are so flattered by being trusted to draw the conclusion that we forget all about logic. Careful thinkers cultivate the habit of resisting suggested conclusions until they have tested them for validity.

The missing proposition may be a premise. Even without help from outsiders, we can and do deceive ourselves with missing premises. There are assumptions behind nearly every decision we make, even though we often fail to recognize them. When we reason from an assumption without realizing it, the assumption is in effect a missing premise. Therefore, even when an argument is our own, we need to know what the premises are, for otherwise we cannot judge the argument for reliability. Whenever careful thinkers encounter an argument with a missing premise, they try to recover the premise for examination. Suppose you hear the following argument in a political campaign.

> Senator Levine is a critic of the present administration. Clearly, therefore, she is a promoter of progress.

We may never know what this speaker was actually assuming, but we can find out the minimum he or she had to assume to make the argument valid. We can do this by trial and error, but a better way is to analyze the syllogism backward. The first step is to write the known parts in the appropriate syllogistic form, beginning with the conclusion. As you can see, the conclusion in this case is the second of the two propositions given, which says that Senator Levine is a promoter of progress. The next step is to determine whether the premise that has been supplied is the major or the minor premise. If it is the major premise, it will contain the predicate of the conclusion; if it is the minor, it will contain the subject of the conclusion.

The premise given in this argument is the minor premise since it contains the term "Senator Levine" which is the subject of the conclusion.

Major Premise:

	d	u
Minor Premise:	Senator Levine <	critics of the present administration.

	d	u
Conclusion:	Senator Levine <	promoters of progress.

The major premise needed to make the argument valid can now be supplied by using the rules of validity for categorical syllogisms. One of the terms in the major premise must be the middle term, which is the term not stated in the conclusion, namely, "critics of the present administration." The other term must, of course, be the major term, "promoters of progress."

The relationship between terms in both minor premise and conclusion is inclusion. Therefore the relationship in the major premise must also be inclusion; otherwise the argument would violate the faulty exclusion rule.

The middle term, "critics of the present administration," must be distributed at least once. Since the relationship in the major premise is inclusion, only the subject term can be distributed. Thus "critics of the present administration" must be the subject term.

By elimination, the predicate term in the major premise must be "promoters of progress." Because it follows inclusion, it must be undistributed. This same term is undistributed in the conclusion and may

therefore be undistributed in the major premise. The major premise needed to make the argument valid is now clearly revealed.

	d		u
Critics of the present administration	<		promoters of progress.

You will note that this major premise is a sweeping general statement. We could prove it false merely by finding a single critic of the administration who does not promote progress. The argument was more convincing without the major premise.

Since we are trying to find the minimum assumption needed to make the argument valid, **we should never make a term distributed unless necessary.** Sometimes either term may be put in the subject position. If both terms in the missing proposition must be distributed, requiring an E-form proposition, it will not matter which of the terms is put first since the E-form is validly convertible. The same holds for the I-form proposition, which we should use when neither term has to be distributed.

Sometimes an enthymeme cannot be made valid with any premise we can supply. An example would be an argument with a term that is distributed in the conclusion but undistributed in the stated premise. All such enthymemes should be considered invalid.

When decisions we have made prove to be "bad," it is a good idea to try to remember our reasoning and test it by this system. It may be that we were reasoning from an unstated premise that, had we been conscious of it, we would not have accepted as a fact.

Obviously, categorical syllogisms are not the only deductive arguments found in ordinary discourse. We have already seen that hypothetical syllogisms may be used, and there are other types of syllogisms we have still to consider, as well as a number of argument forms that are too advanced for this text. Nevertheless, categorical syllogisms can be used to analyze an astonishing number of the arguments we encounter in everyday life. Learning how to use them is therefore an important step toward effective thinking.

Exercise 18A

Problems 1–20. Write the following sentences in the logical form for categorical propositions.

1. A few people are cowards.

2. All except English majors may take this course.

3. Only the brave deserve the fair.

4. Long is the road to Paradise.

5. All models have gyrosteer unless manufactured this year.

6. Not all teams have winning streaks.

7. None except Elizabeth's friends is welcome here.

8. Few men earn more than the president.

9. All that glitters is not gold.

10. All but the first group of passengers was quarantined.

11. None but the lonely heart can know my sadness.

_____

12. It is completely untrue that all musicians gossip.

_____

13. Commanders alone are entitled to make such decisions.

_____

14. Happy are the sounds of children playing.

_____

15. Horses are not carnivores.

_____

16. Horses are found in circuses.

_____

17. Only a fool would believe that.

_____

18. All but the most skeptical considered his position sound.

_____

19. A daring general was Julius Caesar.

_____

20. Conscience doth make cowards of us all.

_____

Exercise 18B

Problems 1–10. Translate these syllogisms into logical form and analyze them for validity. State the fallacy or fallacies involved in every invalid case.

1. Diligent are they who work harder than their friends.

    John does not work harder than his friends.

    Therefore John is not diligent.

    Fallacy _____

2. Few teachers are free from financial worry.

    All physicians are not teachers.

    Therefore all physicians are free from financial worry.

    Fallacy _____

3. Only women may bowl today.

    Carmen is a woman.

    Therefore she may bowl today.

    Fallacy _____

4. Not all sixteen-year-olds are sweet.

    Nancy is sixteen.

    Therefore Nancy is not sweet.

    Fallacy _____

5. All but those who have seen an adviser must make an appointment today.

    Jamaal is among those who have not seen an adviser.

Therefore he must make an appointment today.

Fallacy _____

6. None except freshmen may use the pool today. _____

   Mary may use the pool today. _____

   Therefore Mary is not a freshman. _____

   Fallacy _____

7. A few lazy students do not prepare for class. _____

   Eric prepares for class. _____

   Therefore Eric is not a lazy student. _____

   Fallacy _____

8. All Wysacki students are not A students. _____

   Yvette is an A student. _____

   Therefore Yvette is not a Wysacki student. _____

   Fallacy _____

9. One should study at least two hours for each credit hour, unless he or she is exceptionally brilliant. _____

   I am exceptionally brilliant. _____

   Therefore I should not study at least two hours for each credit hour. _____

   Fallacy _____

10. All trees are not maples. _____

    Only plants can be trees. _____

    Therefore it is false that all plants are maples. _____

    Fallacy _____

Exercise 18 C

Problems 1–8. Translate these syllogisms into logical form and analyze them for validity. State the fallacy or fallacies involved in every invalid case.

1. Most good political speakers would not use this story. Since Davis used it, he must not be a good political speaker.

   _____

   _____

   _____

   _____

2. No temperamental people ever learn to accept criticism gracefully. But Wythe is not the least bit temperamental, so we can conclude that she knows how to accept criticism gracefully.

   _____

   _____

   _____

   _____

3. It is clear that some of Riley's arguments are deceptive, for all fallacies are deceptive and some of Riley's arguments are fallacies.

   _____

   _____

   _____

   _____

4. Only the brave deserve the fair and no one who is not brave has ever conquered Everest, so anyone who has conquered Everest deserves the fair.

   _____

   _____

   _____

   _____

5. According to the laws of physics, water must be lighter than air, for water contains hydrogen, and certainly hydrogen is lighter than air.

_____

_____

_____

_____

6. This plant must be certified, because all certified plants have been inspected, and this plant has a tag showing that it has been inspected.

_____

_____

_____

_____

7. A few squirrels have gotten into our attic. Since only mammals can be squirrels, it follows that some of the animals in our attic are mammals.

_____

_____

_____

_____

8. No persons other than children of deceased firemen are eligible for this scholarship. It follows that Cheryl is eligible since she is the daughter of a deceased fireman.

_____

_____

_____

_____

Problems 9–12. State whether each of the following enthymemes can be validly completed or not. If an enthymeme can be validly completed, supply the missing premise. If it cannot be validly completed, state which fallacy it commits.

9. All students are not geniuses, since all Nobel Prize winners are.

_____

10. Only swimmers can be lifeguards, so Johnson cannot be a lifeguard.

_____

11. No one but a fool would believe that, so some Wysacki professors are fools.

_____

12. Only students on scholastic probation are not allowed to preregister, so I suppose I'll have to wait until spring to register.

_____

Chapter 19

Alternative and Disjunctive Syllogisms

- **Structure of the Alternative Syllogism**
- **Affirming an Alternative**
- **Denying an Alternative**
- **Structure of the Disjunctive Syllogism**

- **Affirming a Disjunct**
- **Denying a Disjunct**
- **Combined Alternative and Disjunctive Syllogisms**
- **Uncertain Relationship Between Premises**

To complete our study of syllogisms, we must consider two more types, the alternative and the disjunctive. Although more limited in their applications than the categorical or the hypothetical syllogisms, they serve a necessary purpose. You have doubtless used them hundreds of times without realizing it, and mostly with success. Nevertheless, there is an ambiguity affecting these syllogisms that at times leads us to make mistaken inferences. Learning about alternative and disjunctive syllogisms alerts us to the ambiguity, thus sharpening our skills at using and interpreting language. It also puts us in a position where we need never again make errors in the use of these types of argument.

Structure of the Alternative Syllogism

Suppose a doctor is treating a sick patient and can think of only two diseases that would account for the patient's symptoms, malaria and rheumatic fever. The doctor expresses this knowledge in the following proposition.

> Either the patient has malaria or he has rheumatic fever.

In this proposition the words *either* and *or* constitute the connective. Taken together, they express the relationship between the two parts of the proposition stated. The question is, what is this relationship? To answer this question, we must consider the ambiguity referred to above.

In ordinary English, the expression *either . . . or* is a classic case of an expression that has two quite distinct and clearly specifiable meanings. Sometimes it is used to mean that *at least one and maybe both* of the possibilities cited are true. Fully expressed, its meaning is "Either . . . or . . . and possibly both." On other occasions this connective is used to mean that *one, but not both,* of the possibilities cited is true. Fully expressed, its meaning is "Either . . . or . . . but not both."[1] As with any expression having more than one meaning, which meaning the connective has on a given occasion depends on the intention of the speaker. Since the speaker's intention is not always clear, we as logicians are often faced with a problem of ambiguity. We have to decide how to interpret propositions that use the connective "either . . . or."

Fortunately, there is an easy way out of this problem. Of the two meanings cited, the first is the weaker one because, as we shall see, it permits fewer valid inferences than the second. In logic, we must always guard against interpreting propositions too strongly. Otherwise we are likely to accept as valid an inference that was not intended by the speaker or writer whose statement we are using as a premise. Accordingly, we shall always interpret the connective "either . . . or" in the first of the two senses given above. On this approach, the words "either . . . or" limit the possibilities to two; **they do not prohibit both possibilities from being true at the same time.** This is the safest approach for avoiding fallacies.

Let us now return to the doctor's statement. A good doctor would be sensitive to the possibility, however remote, that the patient being treated is suffering from both diseases that are possible. Hence the statement given above was probably intended to mean "Either . . . or . . . and possibly both." In any case, we will interpret the statement this way since that is the safest logical course. Taken in this way, the doctor's statement constitutes what we shall call an **alternative**

---

[1] Not all languages contain this ambiguity. In Latin, for example, the word *vel* is used to signify "either . . . or . . . and possibly both" and *aut* is used to signify "either . . . or . . . but not both."

proposition. The two possibilities cited, that the patient has malaria and that he has rheumatic fever, are called **alternatives**, from which the proposition gets its name. The logical form of this proposition may be expressed as follows.

	Alternative 1		*Alternative 2*
Either	the patient has malaria	or	he has rheumatic fever.

Alternative propositions may occur as the major premise of an **alternative syllogism**. The minor premise may be of two kinds: (1) it may declare that one of the alternatives is true, or (2) it may eliminate one alternative by declaring it false.

Affirming an Alternative

Suppose you are a medical technician working for the doctor in our example. You run a test and find that the patient does have malaria. You now have a minor premise that affirms the first alternative, that is, declares that the condition described by the first alternative is true.

	Alternative 1		*Alternative 2*
Major Premise:			
Either	the patient has malaria	or	he has rheumatic fever.

Minor Premise: He has malaria.

Given these premises, it is invalid to conclude that the patient does not have rheumatic fever. On the only safe interpretation, the doctor's statement is an alternative proposition and does not rule out the patient's having both diseases; it merely asserts that the explanation of his symptoms is limited to the two diseases. As a matter of fact, the patient could have both. Affirming an alternative is an invalid form. Note that in the example above the second alternative is affirmed by the minor premise. It does not matter which alternative is affirmed—the principle is the same.

Consider another example.

	Alternative 1	Alternative 2
Major Premise:		
Either	the tank is empty	or	the ignition is faulty.

Minor Premise: The ignition is faulty.

One might be tempted to conclude that the tank is not empty. This conclusion would have some probability, but it would be invalidly drawn because the major premise declares only that one of the two alternatives must be true. It says nothing whatever about the probabilities that both could be true. Any estimate of the probability that the conclusion is true must be based on evidence not in the premises.

Remember, The words *either . . . or* limit the possibilities to two; they do not prohibit both possibilities from being true at the same time.

Denying an Alternative

The other possibility for the minor premise is to deny one of the alternatives by declaring that the condition or situation it describes is not true.

	Alternative 1	Alternative 2
Major Premise:		
Either	the tank is empty	or	the ignition is faulty.

Minor Premise: The tank is not empty.

Conclusion: The ignition is faulty.

Certainly if the possibilities stated by the major premise are limited to two, one of which is demonstrated to be false, then the other must be true. The inference is valid.

Denying an alternative is a *valid* form. As in the hypothetical syllogism, a valid form permits only one conclusion. Before we rate an alternative syllogism valid, we must check the conclusion to see that it is the proper one. To be validly inferred, the conclusion must declare that the other alternative (the one not eliminated by the minor premise) is true. The principle is the same, regardless of which alternative is denied. Any other conclusion is a non sequitur.

Alternative syllogisms are particularly prone to weaknesses in the major premise. In the example above, the major premise is actually a listing of two alternative hypotheses. When we reason in this way, we may be limiting ourselves to just two possible explanations because we can think of no others. Unfortunately, the fact that we can think of only two hypotheses does not make our premise reliable. Although our focus in this chapter is on validity, we should never forget that a validly drawn conclusion is no more reliable than the premises on which it is based.

Structure of the Disjunctive Syllogism

The disjunctive form of syllogism is the complement of the alternative form. The major premise of a disjunctive syllogism names two possibilities and declares that the two cannot exist together. These two possibilities are called **disjuncts** because they are completely separate. If one is true, the other cannot be. You can see this in the disjunctive premise below.

	Disjunct 1		Disjunct 2
The patient cannot both	be well	and	have a fever.

The words *cannot* and *both* assert that these two disjuncts cannot occur together. There are only two possibilities for the minor premise: (1) it may declare that one of the disjuncts is true, or (2) one is false.

Affirming a Disjunct

The minor premise may affirm one of the disjuncts by declaring that it is true in the particular case involved.

		Disjunct 1		Disjunct 2
Major Premise:	The patient cannot	be well	and	have a fever

Minor Premise: The patient is well.

Conclusion: The patient cannot have a fever.

The argument is *valid*; since the patient cannot be well and have a fever at the same time and since he is declared to be well, he cannot have a fever. Should a clinical thermometer show the patient's temperature to be 105°, then there is something wrong with the premises or with the thermometer, for the argument is valid. The argument will always be valid when the minor premise affirms one disjunct and the conclusion denies the other.

The principle is the same regardless of which disjunct is affirmed. Given the major premise above, should the minor premise declare that the patient has a fever, we can validly conclude that the other disjunct is not true: the patient is not well. Any other conclusion would be a non sequitur.

Denying a Disjunct

The minor premise may also deny one of the disjuncts by declaring that the condition or situation it describes is not true in the particular situation involved.

		Disjunct 1		Disjunct 2
Major Premise:	The patient cannot	be well	and	have a fever.

Minor Premise: The patient is not well.

No conclusion can be validly derived from these two premises. The major premise does not guarantee that the patient has to be either well or feverish. The patient may be ill with or without a fever.

Denying a disjunct is an *invalid form.* The major premise prohibits both disjuncts from being true at the same time; it does not guarantee that either one of them is true. There may be, and often are, many other possibilities. It does not matter which disjunct is denied. No conclusion follows.

Combined Alternative and Disjunctive Syllogisms

Suppose your adviser tells you, "You must take either Math 120 or Math 130, but you cannot take both." Notice that this statement combines the essential elements of alternative and disjunctive propositions. It says that either of two alternatives must be satisfied but that both cannot be. Thus the sense of this statement is precisely the strong sense that, as we noted earlier, statements using only the connective "either . . . or" sometimes have in everyday discourse. The difference is that in this case no guesswork is involved. Your adviser has made it explicit that exactly one of the two alternatives described must be satisfied. When it is **explicitly stated** that either of two alternatives, but not both, must be satisfied, we may form syllogisms that employ the combination of alternation and disjunction as the major premise.

	Alternative- Disjunct 1		Alternative- Disjunct 2
Either	take Math 120	*or*	take Math 130,
		but not both.	

Since this premise combines the function of alternative and disjunctive propositions, any minor premise that clearly affirms or denies either alternative-disjunct will yield a validly drawn conclusion. Not just any inference will be valid, of course. If the minor premise affirms one alternative-disjunct, the conclusion must deny the other; if the minor premise denies one alternative-disjunct, the conclusion must affirm the other. Otherwise the conclusion is a non sequitur.

Note again that in logic we never consider a proposition to have the alternative-disjunctive form unless the structure words (or their equivalents) for both alternative and disjunctive propositions are present. This is somewhat inconvenient at times since there are situations in which our frame of reference tells us that propositions using only the connective "either . . . or" are meant to be alternative-disjunctions. Thus if you are looking for your roommate and Carlos Williams tells you, "He is either in the library or in the lab," you would probably be safe in assuming that Carlos would not have missed the fact

that your roommate cannot be in both places. All the same, it is best to follow the procedure we use in this book, and treat all propositions using only the connective "either . . . or" as alternative propositions. Besides reducing disputes over uncertain meanings, this procedure helps keep us aware of options we might otherwise overlook in decision making. Thus if you are told, "Either you continue your education or you join the armed forces," consider it an alternative form. Your frame of reference may tell you that you cannot do both, but your frame of reference could be wrong. There may be ways you do not know about for continuing your education while in the armed forces. Similarly, propositions containing only the structure words for disjunctive form should not be taken to be alternative as well. Should your professor declare, "You cannot stay in my class and refuse to prepare your assignments," you are not entitled to consider her declaration a combination form. She has nowhere said that you have to do either.

In reasoning from our own premises, we should cultivate the habit of saying and thinking exactly what we mean. If we believe a situation presents only two choices, both of which cannot be true together, we should put in the "either. . .or" and the "not both." Putting in the words may at times save us from serious error by making us realize we are reasoning from a false assumption.

Uncertain Relationship Between Premises

In alternative and disjunctive syllogisms, as in hypothetical ones, the minor premise must clearly affirm or deny one of the possibilities of the major premise. Otherwise the syllogism is invalid, no matter what the form.

Suppose your professor gives you this major premise in combination form: "Either you turn in an acceptable term paper by Tuesday and pass the final or you fail the course, but not both." Should I learn only that you turned in a term paper and passed the final, I am not entitled to conclude that you passed the course, for my information does not clearly affirm all conditions set forth by the first alternative-disjunct. I do not know that the term paper was acceptable or that it was turned in by Tuesday. On the other hand, if I know that you did not pass the final, I can conclude that you failed the course, because I have sufficient information to deny that first alternative-disjunct.

Alternative and disjunctive syllogisms are valid only under the conditions summarized below.

The Major Premise Says	And the Minor Premise	And the Conclusion Declares
either . . . or, or words to that effect	clearly denies one alternative	the other alternative true
not this . . . and this, or *not both,* or words to that effect	clearly affirms one disjunct	the other disjunct false
either . . . or, but not both, or words to that effect	clearly affirms one alternative-disjunct	the other false
	clearly denies one alternative-disjunct	the other true

Exercise 19

Problems 1–8. In these problems,

    a. write in the blank the number of each statement from the key list below that applies to the item.

    b. following this number, write V if the argument is valid or I if it is invalid.

Key List

1. An alternative is affirmed.
2. An alternative is denied.
3. A disjunct is affirmed.
4. A disjunct is denied.
5. An alternative-disjunct is affirmed.
6. An alternative-disjunct is denied.
7. The relationship between premises is uncertain.
8. The form is valid but the conclusion is a non sequitur.

1. Either he is seriously injured or his wind is knocked out.
   His wind is certainly knocked out.
   Therefore he is not seriously injured. _____ _____

2. You cannot break training and still play on our team.
   You broke training.
   Therefore you cannot play on our team. _____ _____

3. She cannot know the facts and be prejudiced too.
   She is not prejudiced.
   Therefore she must know the facts. _____ _____

4. Either the radiator is clogged or it has sprung a leak.
   But it is not leaking.
   Therefore it must be clogged. _____ _____

5. Either she lacks the ability or she is not studying.
   We know that she is studying hard.
   Therefore she must lack the ability. _____ _____

6. He cannot fail to satisfy his needs and still be happy.
   He is not happy.
   Therefore he is failing to satisfy his needs. _____ _____

7. Either her fever must break soon or she will die.
   Her fever is definitely breaking right now.
   Therefore she will recover completely. _____ _____

8. Either John is broke or he would have sent me a present.
I did not receive a present.
Therefore he is broke. _____ _____

Problems 9–16. If the premises in the following problems yield a validly drawn conclusion, write it in the blank. If not, write the name of the fallacy.

9. One cannot be registered in both the Lower Division and the College of Business Administration. Jacobson is not registered in the Lower Division.

_____

10. This snake is either a deadly coral snake or a harmless milk snake. It does not have the coloration sometimes found on the milk snake.

_____

11. He is either a Rotarian or a Kiwanian but not both. He is not a Rotarian.

_____

12. Either he is an elusive runner or he has unusual speed. He is certainly not an elusive runner.

_____

13. She is either the Wysacki softball coach or the chairperson of the physical education department. She is the Wysacki softball coach.

_____

14. Either the rain must stop before noon or the game will have to be postponed. The Weather Bureau has predicted showers for the afternoon.

_____

15. It cannot be that she was innocent of evil intentions and still aware of the consequences of her act. This evidence proves that she could not have been aware of the consequences of her act.

_____

16. This man's behavior is such that we can be sure that he is either guilty of a crime or shielding someone who is guilty. The evidence makes it clear that he is not guilty of a crime.

_____

Chapter 20

Complex Syllogistic Forms

- **Dilemmas**
- **Chain Arguments**
- **Syllogisms Within Syllogisms**
- **Deductive-Inductive Arguments**

We have now studied four basic types of syllogisms: hypothetical, categorical, alternative, and disjunctive. Categorical syllogisms are characterized by the fact that all their propositions are categorical ones, in which one class is totally or partially included in or excluded from another class. The other types of syllogisms can be characterized by the type of logical relationship expressed by the structure words used to form the major premise. In the hypothetical syllogism, this relationship is conditional: the major premise states that the consequent is true on condition that the antecedent is true. In the alternative syllogism, the major premise states two possibilities and declares that at least one of them is true. In the disjunctive type, the major premise states two possibilities and declares that at least one of them is not true. There are other types of propositions besides those we have studied, but if we thoroughly master these, we can handle a great many others with little difficulty.

Propositions of the kinds we have studied can be put together in a huge variety of combinations, and we cannot even begin to study all of them. Fortunately, it is not necessary to do so. A careful study of two of these combinations will enable us to deal with most of the complex deductive arguments we encounter. The techniques of analysis we have studied so far must be modified to make them applicable to some of these combinations.

Dilemmas

Deductive arguments can be composed of a mixture of propositional types. One such mixture is the **dilemma**. Dilemmas may occur in several varieties. In common speech, however, the word is normally used to refer to a situation in which there are only two choices, both of which are unpleasant. This variety of dilemma is composed of a mixture of hypothetical and alternative propositions. The major premise is a pair of hypothetical propositions; the minor premise and the conclusion are alternative propositions. Consider the student who has wasted time during the semester, and comes to the end of the term with insufficient time to prepare adequately for all his or her examinations. If the student distributes study time about equally among his or her courses, the result will be low grades in all of them. If, on the other hand, the student devotes enough time to some courses to make good grades in them, he or she will fail other courses. The consequences of both choices are undesirable. Our student now has the major premise of a dilemma.

> If I study all courses about equally, I will make low grades in all of them; if I study some enough to make good grades, I will fail others.

The student does not yet have a complete dilemma, for this premise does not state that either choice is required. But if the student reasons that one or the other choice has to be made, he or she now has this minor premise:

> I must either study all courses about equally, or study some enough to make high grades.

This minor premise affirms the antecedents of both hypotheticals and forces this unpalatable conclusion:

> I must either make low grades in all courses or fail some of them.

The student can be said to be caught on the "horns" of a dilemma, for choosing either antecedent means being "stuck" by its consequent. Since this variety of dilemma is valid, the only possible attack is on the reliability of the premises.

One way to attack the premises of a dilemma is to "break a horn," that is, to choose one of the antecedents without in-

curring the consequent attached to it. Consider the following dilemma in which a congressman might find himself.

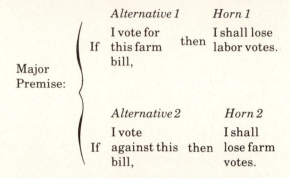

Major Premise:

Alternative 1   *Horn 1*

If I vote for this farm bill, then I shall lose labor votes.

Alternative 2   *Horn 2*

If I vote against this bill, then I shall lose farm votes.

Minor Premise: But I must either vote for or vote against this bill.

Conclusion: Therefore, I must lose labor votes or farm votes.

Should the congressman choose the first alternative by voting for the farm bill and still keep the labor votes by convincing his constituents that his position is sound, he would break the first horn. Note that in so doing he would demonstrate that the first hypothetical of the major premise is false. He might break the second horn by voting against the bill without losing the votes of farmers by convincing them that the passage of the bill was not in their best interests.

The congressman might avoid the unpleasant consequences described in the dilemma above in another way. According to the minor premise, he is restricted to two choices, voting for and voting against the bill. He might, however, be conveniently ill or out of town on the day of the vote, or he might pair his vote with another member of Congress, thereby choosing neither alternative and avoiding both consequences. Should he do so, he would be **escaping between the horns**, which may be defined as finding a possibility not included in the minor premise. In so doing, of course, he is demonstrating this premise to be false, for it stipulated that the two choices mentioned were the only possible ones.

The dilemma form should be avoided whenever possible in decision making because there is a serious psychological hazard inherent in it. Suppose you find yourself in a situation like one that occurred in a hotel in Atlanta, where a fire originating in the basement swept flames and deadly gases through most of the structure, which was supposed to be fireproof. You are trapped in a room on the thirteenth floor. If you try to escape through the halls of the building, you know that you will be burned to death unless the gases kill you first. If you try to escape by jumping from the window, you know that you will be smashed on the pavement below. You now have the major premise of your dilemma. If you add a minor premise that limits your choices to jumping or going into the hall, you tend to fix your attention on the terrible consequences of your two choices instead of on finding a better solution. As you think about the horns of your dilemma, your fears are likely to rise higher and higher and make you less and less able to think constructively. Many people in this particular fire apparently did just that and lost their lives by jumping, by feeble attempts to reach the stairways, or by decision by indecision, hesitating in their rooms until overcome by the deadly gases. Cooler heads in this same episode escaped between the horns of the dilemma. They neither jumped nor went out through the halls. Instead, they stopped the cracks around their doors with newspapers or cloth to keep out the gases, opened their windows for fresh air, and quietly waited to be rescued by the firemen.

A situation in which we find our-selves thinking that we must choose between two evils should become an automatic stimulus for repeating the five-phase cycle, with special emphasis on forming other proposals for action. Even if we can find no third alternative, we can usually find some way of mitigating the undesirable consequences of at least one of the choices.

Chain Arguments

Syllogisms can be combined to form a chain of reasoning with any number of links.[1] Here is an example:

All insects are invertebrate animals.

All mosquitoes are insects.

All anopheles are mosquitoes.

Therefore all anopheles are invertebrate animals.

Since this argument has three premises, it is not a syllogism. Nevertheless, you can see that it is valid, and the procedure for analyzing syllogisms can be utilized to prove that it is. The problem of analyzing arguments with more than two premises is analogous to computing complex probabilities. We found that we could work complex problems in probability with simple procedures merely by dividing the problems into installments and then working each installment separately. Similarly, the procedures we have studied for analyzing syllogisms can be applied to arguments with more than two premises

---

[1] This type of argument is sometimes called a *sorites*, a term that derives from the Greek word *soros*, meaning "heap."

simply by analyzing these arguments in installments.

For the first installment, let us analyze the first two premises in the argument above. They yield a valid conclusion, as shown in shorthand below.

>   d   u
> Insects < invertebrate animals.
>
>   d   u
> Mosquitoes < insects.
>
>   d   u
> ∴ Mosquitoes < invertebrate animals.

Now let us use the valid conclusion above as the major premise of a second installment, using the original third premise as the minor premise. We get the following.

>   d   u
> Mosquitoes < invertebrate animals.
>
>   d   u
> Anopheles < mosquitoes.
>
>   d   u
> ∴ Anopheles < invertebrate animals.

Thus all the evidence necessary to make the conclusion valid is explicitly stated in the premises.

In the example above, the premises are arranged in a descending order of magnitude, with the predicate of the first premise referring to the largest class, and the subject of the last premise referring to the smallest class. In the example below the premises are arranged in an ascending order.

All residents of Precinct 5 are residents of the city.

All residents of the city are residents of the county.

All residents of the county are residents of the state.

All residents of the state are residents of the United States.

Therefore all residents of Precinct 5 are residents of the United States.

This argument is more easily analyzed backward, using the last premise as the major premise of the first installment, as shown below in shorthand.

>   d   u
> Residents of the state < residents of the
> United States.
>
>   d   u
> Residents of the county < residents of the
> state.
>
>   d   u
> ∴ Residents of the county < residents of the
> United States.

The conclusion above then becomes the major premise of the second installment, as shown below.

>   d   u
> Residents of the county < residents of the U.S.
>
>   d   u
> Residents of the city < residents of the county.
>
>   d   u
> ∴ Residents of the city < residents of the U.S.

In turn, the conclusion above becomes the major premise of the third installment, which shows that the conclusion is valid.

Chains of hypothetical premises can be analyzed in installments too, using the rules of the hypothetical syllogism. Consider the example below.

If the defendant is guilty, then he had the murder weapon in his posession.

If he had the murder weapon in his possession, he must have stolen it.

If he stole the murder weapon, he must have been in Chicago on December 11.

He was seen in South Bend on December 11.

Therefore the defendant cannot be guilty.

This example is invalid because the fourth premise (He was seen in South Bend on December 11) is in uncertain relationship with the third premise.

Chain arguments should be handled with care. They are no stronger than their weakest link, and the conclusion follows only if all the syllogisms in the chain are valid. Furthermore, the conclusion is reliable only if every premise is reliable. Consider the following chain argument.

> 1. Perhaps the greatest misfortune to befall the Carter administration was the failure of an attempt in 1980 to rescue by military force a group of Americans being held hostage in Iran. 2. The operation was to be carried out by helicopter and involved a stop at an abandoned airstrip in Iran to refuel the helicopters. 3. Because of a sandstorm in the area, two of the helicopters malfunctioned and a third, while attempting to lift off from the airstrip, collided with the tanker plane from which it had refueled. A number of personnel were killed, and the rescue attempt had to be abandoned. 4. If there had been no sandstorm in Iran, no mishaps involving the helicopters would have occurred. 5. If these mishaps had not occurred, the mission would have proceeded. 6. If the mission had proceeded, the hostages would have been rescued. 7. If the hostages had been rescued, Jimmy Carter would have been perceived as a hero. 8. If he had been perceived as a hero, he would have been elected to another term as president. 9. Therefore if there had been no sandstorm in Iran, Jimmy Carter would have been elected to another term as president.

The chain argument begins with sentence 4 and ends with sentence 9, which is the conclusion. Note that the conclusion simply combines the antecedent of the first premise with the consequent of the last premise. Since the consequent of each premise after the first one affirms the antecedent of the premise preceding it, the argument is valid. But the conclusion of the argument is far from reliable. The conclusion of a chain argument is unreliable unless *all* the propositions in the chain are reliable. In this argument not one of them is reliable, for each speculates about what the consequences would have been if a particular fact related to the rescue attempt had been different. This type of reasoning, known as "hypothesis contrary to fact," is fallacious. It will be discussed more fully in Part 4.

We learned in our study of probability that the greater the number of events that must occur, the lower is the probability. Similarly, the greater the number of premises in a chain argument, the lower is the probability that all links are valid and that all premises are reliable.

Syllogisms Within Syllogisms

Some arguments contain syllogisms within syllogisms. Consider the following argument.

> 1. This tax cannot serve the best interests of the country as a whole and at the same time discourage the development of heavy industry. 2. All military experts of any reputation assert that heavy industry is essential to national defense. 3. Had this tax not discouraged the development of heavy industry, our capacity for making steel would have increased by at least 5 percent during the past year. 4. Instead, it

has dropped by 2 percent. 5. This tax cannot be in the best interests of the country as a whole.

The conclusion of this argument is sentence 5 (This tax cannot be in the best interests of the country). The major premise is sentence 1 (This tax cannot serve the best interests of the country and at the same time discourage the development of heavy industry). Sentence 2 presents evidence in support of the major premise and is not a part of the skeleton of the argument. The minor premise in this argument is not stated. However, sentences 3 and 4 constitute the premises of a valid syllogism within the main syllogism.

This tax had not discouraged the development of heavy industry.	⊃	our capacity for making steel would have increased by at least 5 percent during the past year.

Our capacity has dropped by 2 percent.

The minor premise clearly denies the consequent and yields this validly drawn, though unstated, conclusion: this tax discouraged the development of heavy industry. This unstated conclusion is the minor premise of the main argument, as in a chain syllogism. Thus the argument contains enough information to yield a validly inferred conclusion: this tax cannot be in the best interests of the country.

Deductive-Inductive Arguments

Deductive reasoning and inductive reasoning are frequently combined. Consider the argument below, which might be made by a prosecutor in summing up the evidence in a murder trial.

1. If the defendant fired the fatal shot with malice aforethought, then she is guilty of murder in the first degree. 2. Reliable witnesses have testified that the defendant owned the murder weapon, that her fingerprints were on it when it was found at the scene of the crime, and that she was seen leaving the scene of the crime shortly after the fatal shot was fired. 3. Reliable witnesses have also testified that the defendant had a powerful motive and that she had several times threatened to kill the deceased. 4. There can be no reasonable doubt that the defendant fired the fatal shot and did so with malice aforethought. 5. The defendant is therefore guilty of murder in the first degree.

Sentence 1 states the law under which the defendant is being tried. It serves as the major premise, sentence 4 is the minor premise, and sentence 5 is the conclusion. Note, however, that sentence 4 actually states a hypothesis, which is supported by sentences 2 and 3. If the hypothesis is true, the defendant is clearly guilty. The issue, then, is whether the hypothesis is sufficiently reliable to be rated true beyond reasonable doubt. This is the decision the jury must make.

There is nothing logically wrong with combining deductive and inductive reasoning. In fact, many of our decisions involve a combination of both. It is important to know the difference, however, because the methods of testing are quite different. Deductive inferences are always tested for validity, using the rules appropriate to the particular logical form involved. Inductive inferences are tested for reliability by methods appropriate to the particular type of inference, which were covered in earlier chapters.

Since even the conclusions of valid deductive arguments are no more reliable than the premises on which they are based, testing deductive arguments requires assessing the reliability of their premises. Up to a point, premises can be tested for reliability by deductive inference from other premises. Ultimately, however, this process reaches a premise or premises that must be tested by inductive methods or not tested at all. The vast majority of our knowledge, therefore, is in the end based on induction and so is not absolutely certain.

Since this is so, people who insist on basing all decisions on absolutely certain premises find themselves beset by many difficulties. Too often they fall prey to decision by indecision. In other cases, they are prone to rate premises as more reliable than they are, often on the ground that they are "scientific," or reflect some recently introduced and hence fashionable point of view. When people who insist on certainty make mistaken decisions, as inevitably we all do, they may feel unjustified guilt about the error. Moreover, the ability of such people to solve problems by creative thinking tends to be narrowly circumscribed, for they are apt to reject promising hypotheses, causal principles, and proposals for action. If uncertainty bothers us, we should try an exercise in creative thinking and consider how uninteresting, unchallenging, and downright unpleasant a world of absolute certainty would be.

Exercise 20A

Problems 1–3. These problems refer to the following situation:

Joe Smythe's father wanted him to be a doctor. He told Smythe, "If you go into engineering, I won't give you a dime to finance an education." Blythe, his fiancée, did not want to be a doctor's wife. She threatened, "If you go into medicine I won't marry you."

1. Smythe's situation can be stated as the major premise of a dilemma. Write it below.

_____

2. Write below the minor premise necessary to make his situation a dilemma.

_____

3. Write below the conclusion of his dilemma.

_____

Problems 4–8. Select from the key list below the statement which describes the method used to solve the problem.

Key List

1. Breaking the first horn
2. Breaking the second horn
3. Escaping between the horns
4. Accepting the consequences of an alternative

4. Smythe went into medicine but persuaded Blythe to marry him anyway.

_____

5. Smythe went into business and married Blythe.

_____

6. Smythe went into engineering and persuaded his father to pay part of his educational expenses.

_____

7. Smythe went into medicine and remained a bachelor.

_____

8. Smythe went into a new field of research known as engineering medicine, married Blythe, and kept his father's support.

_____

Problems 9–16. Analyze the following chain arguments. If the argument is valid, write V in the space provided; otherwise write the name of the fallacy involved.

9. If Dale values learning, she is studying tonight.
   If she is studying tonight, she is in the library.
   She does value learning.
   Therefore she is in the library now.

   _____

10. Nothing that hurts other people is moral.
    Nothing that improves the mind hurts other people.
    Studying effective thinking improves the mind.
    Therefore studying effective thinking is moral.

    _____

11. All persons who deserve to pass study faithfully.
    All persons who study faithfully study thirty hours per week.
    All Beta Beta Betas study thirty hours per week.
    Therefore all Beta Beta Betas deserve to pass.

    _____

12. This policy will not improve education.
    All policies that improve education improve society.
    All policies that improve society are good.
    Therefore this policy is not good.

    _____

13. If it rains during the game, we cannot pass effectively.
    If we cannot pass effectively, our offensive team cannot score.
    If we cannot score one touchdown, we will lose.
    If we lose, we will be very unhappy.
    It is certain to rain during the game.
    Therefore we will be very unhappy.

    _____

14. All medicines are exempt from the sales tax.
    All drugs prescribed by doctors are medicines.
    Some alcoholic beverages are prescribed by doctors.
    Therefore some alcoholic beverages are exempt from the sales tax.

    _____

15. No people who choose the wrong career are happy in it.
    All people who chose a career for which they are not qualified have chosen the wrong career.
    All people who are weak in mathematics and chose engineering as a career have chosen a career for which they are not qualified.
    Therefore no people who are weak in mathematics and who chose engineering as a career will be happy in it.

    _____

16. If you do not study this term, your grades will be poor.
    If your grades are poor, you will be put on probation.
    If you are put on probation, you will lose your scholarship.
    If you lose your scholarship, you will have to drop out.
    If you drop out, you will be unable to finish your education.
    Therefore if you do not study this term, you will be unable to finish your education.

    _____

Exercise 20B

Problems 1–4. Strip the following arguments down to essentials and rewrite them in hypothetical, alternative, or disjunctive form, as indicated by the structure words in the argument. Then analyze them by the rules for the form of syllogism you have used. Use the key list to indicate your evaluation of the argument. Write the number of your choice in the blank.

Key List

1. Denied antecedent
2. Affirmed consequent

3. Affirmed alternative
4. Denied disjunct

5. Uncertain relations
6. Non sequitur
7. Valid

1. Wysacki students cannot leave town every weekend and still do justice to their studies. Washington must do justice to his studies, for he never leaves town.

_____

_____

_____

_____

2. Her absence from meetings can be accounted for in only two ways. Either she is very busy, or she has lost interest in the club. I can assure you that she has been exceedingly busy studying for exams ever since Christmas. You can stop worrying that she has lost interest in the club.

_____

_____

_____

_____

3. This man should not be hired. If he were a graduate of Wysacki, he would be well educated, but he never attended Wysacki, so he cannot be well educated. If he is not well educated, he should not be hired.

_____

_____

_____

4. When Smythe found a burglar in his home, he leaped out of an upstairs window and ran for help. Had he had any common sense, he would have called for help instead of performing such a dangerous feat. Consequently, we can see that Smythe is not a person of common sense.

_____

_____

_____

_____

Problems 5–12. Analyze the following arguments, from which the conclusion has been omitted. If the premises yield a validly drawn conclusion, write it in the space provided. If they do not yield a validly drawn conclusion, write the name of the fallacy.

5. Only if the present administration succeeds in balancing the budget can it claim in the next election to be the party of economy. It is now certain that the administration will succeed in balancing the budget.

_____

6. Unless a student is willing to work at analyzing involved arguments, he or she cannot hope to improve significantly in thinking ability. These problems you are trying hard to solve are involved.

_____

7. In selecting a modern automobile, one may choose a car with the speed, comfort, and roadability desirable on the highway or one with the agility and short turning radius needed in city traffic. No one car provides both. The Urbancar has unusual agility and a very short turning radius.

_____

8. John Stuart Mill argued that if a belief is not grounded in conviction, it is likely to give way to the slightest of arguments. Many of our beliefs, on which we base our most important judgments, are not based on conviction at all but are carelessly and unconsciously adopted.

_____

9. During the presidential campaigns, many people listen only to the speeches that are favorable to the side for which they intend to vote. If one takes one side of an issue without examining the evidence for the other side, he or she has no adequate ground for taking either side.

10. If a press association releases a news report without checking it, it runs the risk of being inaccurate; if it takes the time to check the report, it runs the risk of having a competitor release the report. Obviously, however, the press association must either release the report without checking it or delay it for the time necessary to check it.

11. Scouts reported that whenever State's star passer intended to carry the ball on a sweep around left end, he unconsciously put his hand on his left knee. At a critical point in the game, with State on Wysacki's eleven, the Wysacki captain noted that the passer was resting his hand on his left knee.

12. Those who are ignorant of the facts in a case should never criticize a judicial decision. Most reporters, however, are not ignorant of the facts.

Part Four

Ineffective Thinking

Chapter 21

Faulty Assumptions

- **Straw Man**
- **Argument from Ignorance**
- **Hypothesis Contrary to Fact**
- **Irrelevant Conclusion**
- **False Analogy**

- **Composition**
- **Division**
- **Circular Argument**
- **Accident and Cliché Thinking**
- **Inconsistency**

We have now examined a number of techniques of both inductive and deductive reasoning. Used with care, they can do much to help us become effective thinkers and decision makers. Obviously, however, not all thinking is effective. Part of the task of developing our powers of reasoning is to become familiar with some of the more common types of fallacies so that we will be able to recognize and avoid them in our own thinking. In studying induction and deduction, we have had occasion to note some of these errors. Our task here in Part Four will be to examine a number of other fallacies that frequently interfere with effective thinking and decision making.

You will recall from Chapter 3 that as the term is used in logic a **fallacy** is an error in reasoning. Fallacies come in all sorts of varieties, and logicians are not entirely agreed on their taxonomy. It is common, however, to distinguish between formal and informal fallacies. The first are

generally spoken of only in contexts of deductive reasoning: a **formal fallacy** occurs when an argument that is intended to be deductively valid fails to be so because of a defect in its structure. We have discussed the formal fallacies in the chapters on deduction; denying the antecedent, affirming the consequent, undistributed middle, and faulty exclusion are all examples of formal fallacies. The notion of an informal fallacy is broader; such fallacies may occur in either deductive or inductive contexts, and arguments that commit formal fallacies often commit informal ones as well. An **informal fallacy** is an error in reasoning involving the *content* of an argument: the information or strategy the argument employs is such that a reasonable person ought not to be convinced by it. Hasty generalization and questionable cause are among the informal fallacies we have already encountered. Those that remain to be considered are numerous, and the mistakes they involve constitute such a complicated array that any attempt to divide them into distinct categories is bound to involve a certain amount of arbitrariness. Informal fallacies can, however, be loosely grouped under various headings, and doing so is helpful for learning them even if the classification that results is not entirely adequate. The group of fallacies we shall consider in this chapter may be understood as involving faulty assumptions. They are types of argument that include or are based on mistaken or inadequate assumptions, either about the subject at issue or about what would constitute a reliable argument for a particular conclusion concerning it.

Straw Man

In our study of induction, we saw that when we are trying to decide among competing hypotheses or causal principles, it is useful to try to eliminate all but one. A similar tactic is useful in many contexts of argument. By trying to eliminate views that we consider mistaken, we prepare the way for correct conclusions to emerge. There is, however, a temptation to which many of us succumb in pursuing this tactic. When we dislike a certain view, we often base our objections to it on false or exaggerated assumptions as to its nature or consequences. That is, we tend to misrepresent positions with which we disagree in order to refute them more easily. When we do so, we commit the **straw man** fallacy.

An opponent of straw is easier to attack than one of flesh and blood, and an opponent's position is easier to demolish with the evidence available if we present it in exaggerated form. The more extreme we can make an opponent's position appear, the more successfully we can attack

it. Opponents of the Equal Rights Amendment got a great deal of mileage out of the argument that if the ERA passed, we would no longer be able to have separate men's and women's rest rooms in public places. It is easy to argue that one should have separate men's and women's rest rooms. But when the consequences of the ERA were portrayed in this way, they were extended by exaggeration, and proof against the extended proposition is not the same as proof against the original one.

Similarly, if a student says frankly to his professor, "I'll admit I haven't put in the time on this subject that I should have," and the professor answers in annoyance, "How do you expect to get good grades when you admit that you don't study?" the professor's question includes a clear exaggeration of the student's admission. For the student did not admit that he didn't study at all—only that he didn't study as much as he should have. The exaggeration makes it possible for the professor to rebuke the student more severely than he deserves.

Or if a student told by her academic adviser that she will be required to take a certain course should reply impatiently, "From what you say, a student doesn't have any choice in what she takes at this university," she would be extending the adviser's statement. If the extension went unchallenged, the student could easily build on it a forceful set of arguments against an arbitrary and narrow, but perhaps nonexistent, curriculum.

Successful use of the straw man fallacy often depends on the audience's not having a clear understanding of the specifics of a particular issue. The approach is particularly common in congressional debates, where both sides wish to impress the voters as having won. When the primary objective is to win an argument, one tends to interpret an opponent's position in the worst possible light, and straw man is an easy method of doing so. Thus in a debate over a new tax bill, one party might propose a slight increase in taxes in the lower income brackets. The opposing party might then attempt, deliberately or otherwise, to argue against the proposal as though it were designed to take bread from the mouths of wage earners. It is much easier to argue effectively against the proposal when it is interpreted in terms of this exaggerated and derogatory assumption.

Since the voters are unlikely to know much about exactly what effect the proposed taxes will have, they may be willing to accept the exaggeration as a fact. Similarly, when you argue against or permit the discussion to continue on the straw man version of your position, you in effect accept this version, and thereby increase the difficulty of making your original point. The defense against the straw man, therefore, is to restate immediately exactly what your position is and not be lured out on a limb. Also, when we become angry in an argument, we tend to become reckless and more readily take up the gauntlet in favor of the exaggerated issue instead of the original one. For that reason, some arguers deliberately irritate or anger their opponents before setting up a straw man. Thus defense against this fallacy also requires a cool head.

Argument from Ignorance

Sometimes people try to support a claim by citing the lack of evidence to the contrary as proof that the claim is justified. At other times they try to attack a claim by citing a lack of evidence for it. Either tactic is fallacious because logically lack of evidence is not evidence. I cannot de-

cide that drinking three cups of coffee upon awakening each morning is good for me because no one has ever demonstrated conclusively that it isn't; nor can I decide it is bad for me because no one has ever shown it to be good. This fallacy is called **argument from ignorance**, or **argumentum ad ignorantiam**. To commit it is in effect to assume that the burden of proof is all on our opponents and that as long as they cannot convince us we have to be right.

Arguments from ignorance sometimes arise in scientific contexts. The thalidomide tragedy of the 1950s and 1960s illustrates the hazard. The drug thalidomide was put on the market on the basis that since it did not appear to cause any harmful effects it had no such effects. Not long after, however, harmful effects made themselves known, in the form of severe defects in the children of women who had taken the drug during the critical first two months of pregnancy. What happened in this case was that in testing the drug investigators had failed to form and test a crucial causal principle: that thalidomide might cause defects in the unborn. Had all possible causal principles as to harm the drug might cause been formed and tested, it would have been reasonable to conclude that thalidomide was harmless. But by overlooking a critical possibility, investigators were misled. Many arguments from ignorance result from a failure to consider a wide enough range of ways in which evidence might arise.

One very common instance of argument from ignorance concerns values. It begins with the claim, usually unsupported, that no one has ever been able to produce a convincing proof that there is an objective right or wrong. On this basis, it is concluded that values are a relative matter: what is right or wrong is simply what each society or individual believes to be right or wrong. And it is suggested that since this is so we should be equally tolerant of all systems of value. One fallacy in this argument is obvious. Even if, as the premise claims, proof for objective values is lacking, it does not follow that no such proof will someday be produced. If one wishes to claim that one has no obligations beyond those his or her conscience dictates, what is needed is a proof of that claim, not the observation that opposite claims have not been proven. Moreover, the further conclusion that, since values are relative, we ought to be tolerant, does not follow either. What follows is something a good deal more unsettling: namely, that we should tolerate those whom our conscience tells us to tolerate, and be intolerant toward those against whom it counsels intolerance. This second mistake is an instance of the fallacy of irrelevant conclusion, which is described later in this chapter.

It is worth noting that the premise of the above argument speaks not just of proof but of "convincing proof." Someone who argues from ignorance can often enhance the argument by minimizing or belittling evidence to the contrary, claiming that there is no "real" evidence against his or her position, or that the contrary has not been proven "sufficiently." When the surgeon general's first report detailing the relationship between cigarette smoking and lung cancer appeared, the tobacco companies took out full-page ads in popular magazines, claiming that no one had ever "proven conclusively" that cigarette ingredients led to lung cancer and implying that therefore they did not. Since induction can never produce a "conclusive proof" of *anything*, the statement used as evidence was technically correct. But it certainly misrepresented the massive sample in the surgeon general's report.

The principle that in American courts those accused are to be presumed innocent until proven guilty may seem to be an argument from ignorance, but in fact it is not. There is a difference between legal innocence and actual innocence. Legal innocence means that not enough evidence has been found to convince a jury "beyond the shadow of a doubt" that the accused has committed the crime. Many guilty persons have been declared innocent by law simply because there was not enough evidence to establish guilt. It would be possible to base our court procedures on the opposite assumption—that every suspect has to prove his or her innocence. But then a guiltless defendant might be convicted because he or she could not do so. In Scottish law there is a third possible verdict that seems to take into account the possibility of argument from ignorance. This third verdict, "not proven," is reached when there is enough evidence to create a grave suspicion that the accused is guilty but not enough to prove guilt beyond a reasonable doubt. The effect of this verdict is to publicly discredit the defendant, although it does not result in imprisonment.

Arguments from ignorance are often used concerning the existence of hard-to-demonstrate phenomena, such as flying saucers, ghosts, and so on. Here as in many other cases, the argument may be used by both sides—there are flying saucers because no one has been able to prove they don't exist; there are no flying saucers because no one has been able to prove that there are.

The best defense against arguments from ignorance is to remember that the absence of evidence for a given view supports competing views only to the extent that the thoroughness of the investigation has reduced the probability that such evidence exists.

Hypothesis Contrary to Fact

The fallacy of appeal to ignorance frequently occurs because it is wrongly assumed that all reasonable hypotheses have been formed and tested. Another fallacy, **hypothesis contrary to fact**, occurs when we form hypotheses that run counter to what we know to be the facts and then speculate loosely about their consequences. The faulty assumption here is that we can easily tell what would have happened in a given situation if only one circumstance had been different.

If you lost a job because of cutbacks in federal programs mandated under the Reagan administration or if you were no longer eligible for a student loan, you might conclude, "If only Reagan had lost the election to Carter, then I would still have my job (or my loan)." Unfortunately, your reasoning would commit the fallacy of hypothesis contrary to fact. Note that this argument does not commit the questionable cause fallacy: Reagan was at least a considerable part of the cause of these cuts. But the antecedent of your statement describes something that did not happen, and we can seldom be sure what would have ensued had a particular event been different. Had Carter won, he also might have decided that your particular program was unnecessary. Congress might have insisted on cuts in the student loan program. Your job might even have been supplanted because of a different and more ambitious program requiring personnel with other training.

Given just one change in circumstances, any number of things might happen; we cannot assume that one of them would be inevitable. The fallacy can easily be seen in a classic example of hypothesis contrary to fact: if Marie Curie hadn't left a photographic plate in a drawer with some pitchblende, the world today would not have radium. She might well have discovered it later, or someone else might have discovered it.

A hypothesis contrary to fact should be tested for reliability just as any other hypothesis. Consider the example below.

> If Smythe had not dropped that pass in the end zone, Wysacki would have won.

If we know also that this play was the last one in the game, that there were no infractions of the rules by the offense on this play, and that Wysacki was no more than five points behind, this hypothesis deserves a rating of highly probable. If, however, we know that the play occurred late in the second quarter, the reliability of the statement is low: if Wysacki had scored at that point, the situation during the remainder of the game could have been quite different.

Hypotheses contrary to fact are common in the political arena. One still hears claims that:

> If the Democrats were in power between 1928 and 1932, there would have been no depression in the early 1930s.

> If the Republicans had been in power between 1932 and 1944, the United States would not have been involved in World War II.

And there is little that is new under the political sun:

A Republican administration never would have made the mistake of getting us into Vietnam.

A Democratic administration would have found a way to cope with the unemployment of the early 1980s.

All these propositions involve hypotheses contrary to fact. The Republicans *were* in power from 1928 to 1932 and the Democrats from 1932 to 1944. It was under the Kennedy administration that the United States entered the Vietnam conflict, and Ronald Reagan took office in 1980. The propositions are unreliable because the consequents do not necessarily follow from the antecedents. We can only speculate about what would have happened had the other party been in power. The depression might have been avoided, or it might have been worse. The United States might or might not have been involved in World War II and Vietnam. The Carter administration may have been unable to handle the country's economic problems.

The hypothesis contrary to fact is commonly used in rationalizing. "If I had not been tired, I would not have made that mistake." On the other hand, committing this fallacy can cause unjustified guilt feelings. When you make a decision that has unfortunate consequences, it is easy to conclude that if you had not made the decision, your situation would now be good. Many a parent has needlessly shouldered blame for something that happened to his or her child. As we noted in Chapter 1, perfect thinking is impossible. We should not blame ourselves for a regrettable decision if the procedures for effective thinking were followed reasonably well.

To avoid the pitfall of hypothesis contrary to fact, we always need to qualify the consequent with an appropriate phrase indicating the probability, such as "might have," or "possibly would have."

Irrelevant Conclusion

The term **irrelevant conclusion**, though it is the most common name for this fallacy, is somewhat misleading since a great many other fallacies involve irrelevance. The real nature of this fallacy is more aptly conveyed by its Latin name, **ignoratio elenchi** (literally, "ignorance of the kernel"), which signifies missing the point of an argument or a body of evidence. Frequently, a person who commits this fallacy is only partially familiar with the subject at issue or anxious to reach a conclusion to which the evidence has only an indirect or partial relation. As a result, he or she brings forth evidence that would support one conclusion, but uses it to support another. For example, a prosecuting attorney may use pictures of a murder victim and graphic descriptions of the crime as evidence. This evidence does indeed support the conclusion that the crime was a terrible one. But the fallacy of irrelevant conclusion is committed if one is asked to infer from this evidence that the accused is guilty, for it is wrongly assumed that evidence that supports the first conclusion also supports the second. The kind of evidence necessary to establish guilt would be altogether different. Nevertheless, the fallacious argument may be effective, for the jury may swallow the assumption: they may be so horrified by the pictures that they vote "guilty," in the belief that such a terrible crime needs to be punished.

The fallacy of irrelevant conclusion, like so many others, is often committed by proponents of a piece of legislation in an attempt to get the bill passed. "Aren't factories polluting the atmosphere at an alarming rate? We need Senator Sludge's antipollution Bill." "Isn't there evidence of a coming gas shortage? Vote for the gas and oil deregulation bill sponsored by Congressman Profitt." It is easy enough to prove that pollution is dangerous, and it may be easy to prove that there is a coming gas shortage. But what the proponents of these bills need to do, if they are to avoid the fallacy of irrelevant conclusion, is to demonstrate that their bills are the best answer to the problems in question rather than simply assume that they are.

Let us look at an example closer to home. Suppose Wysacki University has just built a new dormitory complex and for the first time in its history has enough room for all students to live on campus. The question arises, should all students except those who live with their parents be required to live in a dormitory? A university official might argue that students often have housing problems, that every student needs a safe and inexpensive place to live, and that consequently all students should be required to live in the dormitory. The official has committed the fallacy of irrelevant conclusion. He has failed to show that the dormitory does indeed provide such a place, that other forms of housing do not, and that, besides providing every student with a safe and inexpensive place to live, the college has the right to make him or her live in it.

As can be seen from the various examples, this fallacy may be partly an emotional appeal. The arguer may whip up enthusiasm or instill horror by demonstrating an easily supported thesis, such as that murder is terrible or pollution is dangerous, and then transfer the emotions to secure acceptance of another conclusion. But not all irrelevant conclusions involve emotional appeals. Suppose you design a new home computer, which has features decidedly superior to those of other machines on the market. If you conclude on this basis that your computer will be a commercial success, you have committed the fallacy of irrelevant conclusion. Your competitors' products may be cheaper to manufacture, better advertised, and backed by a stronger company name. Commercial success neither requires nor is guaranteed by a superior product.

The way to counter the fallacy of irrelevant conclusion is simply to point out that an unjustified conclusion has been drawn and to insist that evidence be provided for the full range of facts bearing on the dispute.

False Analogy

"What, prove the existence of God? Does one light a candle to see the sun?"

In writing, an analogy can make vivid a thesis that would take pages of dull explanation to clarify. And we shall see in Part Five that consideration of analogies can provide an investigator with suggestive and valuable new hypotheses. As the above example illustrates, analogies can also be used to argue for conclusions, in this case the existence of God. An argument by analogy occurs whenever it is argued that because two or more things are similar in some respects, they are similar in other respects as well. The above example also illustrates, however, that arguing by analogy can be extremely hazardous. The reason is that such arguments are only as good as the underlying assumptions of overall similarity on which they are based. Too often the similarities in the items being compared are too remote to permit a reliable conclusion, or crucial differences between the items are overlooked. When this happens, the fallacy of **false analogy** is committed. The example given illustrates this error, because the similarity between God and the sun is simply not close enough to permit a conclusion about whether proofs of his existence are either necessary or available.

Some arguments by analogy are clearly stronger than others. If I have bought three pairs of shoes of the same brand and style and they have all worn well, I have some grounds for assuming that if I buy a fourth pair, they will wear well also. I need not generalize that all shoes of this brand and style are good; my sample is too small for that. But given that another pair would most likely be made of the same kinds of materials and would be manufactured according to the same design specifications, by much the same process, and subject to much the same controls, I have good reason to risk the relatively small investment of buying another pair.

On the other hand, consider the following argument:

Don't drink the water! Look at what water does to pipes—it rusts them. Consider what it must do to the sensitive lining of your stomach!

Now I am judging that the human stomach is similar enough to pipes in its materials, molecular structure, and resistance to corrosion that water will damage it. Such a degree of similarity does not exist, nor have I any serious reason to suppose it does. Most arguments by analogy fall somewhere between the case of buying shoes and that of drinking water as to reliability. That is to say, the strength of their conclusions tends to vary from probable to unlikely.

Certain factors will increase the strength of an analogy, and others will decrease it. Thus our judgment as to an analogy's strength may change as we gather evidence. If you receive an A in English 101, you have some grounds for expecting a high grade in English 102. Factors that would increase the reliabil-

ity of your conclusion would include high grades in other English courses, and a high degree of similarity of content between English 101 and 102. Circumstances that would decrease the reliability would include significant differences in content (for instance, English 101 might be a course in literature and 102 in composition), or in teachers (perhaps 102 has a teacher with a reputation for giving low grades).

Most analogies used as sales pitches overlook obviously relevant dissimilarities. Consider this advertisement:

Your television is a delicate and complicated mechanism. You should select your serviceman with the same care you would use in selecting your doctor.

The advertisement argues, in effect, that since the human body and a television set are alike in that both are delicate and complex, they must also be alike in that both require the same degree of concern on our part in selecting professional care. The weakness is, however, that although the two are alike in some respects, they are significantly different in others, including both their *degree* of complexity and their importance. The complexity of a television bears no comparison to that of a human body, nor is it subject to as many maladies. Moreover, a television can be replaced. Our bodies cannot, at least as yet. Thus the latter require considerably greater concern.

Defense against false analogies is best achieved by pointing out the relevant differences between the two items that are being compared. The relevant differences are those that make the conclusion less likely than it is claimed to be. Thus, in regard to whether water will corrode your stomach as it does pipes, it is relevant that your stomach is not made of metal and that your body can repair damaged tissue. It is not relevant that stomachs and pipes are different in shape. Nor is it relevant that stomachs are not pipes, for all analogies involve things that differ in one way or another. The question is whether the differences count in a clearly recognizable way against the conclusion.

Composition

Suppose that your university has hired an architect to draw up plans for a new student center, and the famed Charles Wwrong combines in his design the best features of Gothic, Renaissance, neoclassic, and modern styles, believing that the building as a whole will have the excellence of the individual features of each style. Of course, the new student center will be a very strange place indeed, for it will have as its guiding conception a fallacy of **composition**. This fallacy is committed when it is assumed that because the parts of an organized whole have a certain characteristic the whole will have that characteristic or that a statement that is true of the members of a class individually will be true of the class collectively. Charles Wwrong's planning of the new student center commits the first of these types of mistake. While each of the styles of architecture mentioned might produce a building of great beauty and utility, combining all of them in one structure would result in a monstrosity.

It is the element of organization in wholes that makes composition a special danger. In general, the greater the degree of organization involved, the less likely it is that the whole will retain the characteristics of the parts. A team composed of the four best golfers at Wysacki is likely to defeat a team composed of the next best four because in golf the members of the team perform as individuals. There is little organization as far as actual play is concerned. On the other hand, a soccer team composed of the best players in the world brought together to play just one game would be less likely to defeat the World Cup champions because a soccer team functions as an organized whole rather than as individuals.

It is far from true that an organized whole necessarily has the characteristics of its component parts; indeed, sometimes it may have characteristics exactly the opposite of those of the parts. A stone wall, for example, may be graceful and pleasing to the eye although every stone in it is rough and crude. Individual flowers used in a decorative scheme may be especially pretty, but the arrangement may give a total impression of ugliness. Every residence in a community may in itself be most attractive, yet the community as a whole may not be so; the various types of architecture may not harmonize, or the houses may be too closely packed or otherwise badly located in relation to one another.

Another form of the fallacy of composition occurs when it is argued that something that is true of the members of a group individually must be true of the group taken collectively, as in this example: all human beings are mortal, and hence the human race must someday die out. It is clear that the mortality of each individual is not enough to establish that the human race must someday come to extinction because there could be an infinite progression of finite individuals. It is only rarely the case that the characteristics of the members of groups apply to groups taken collectively. Thus the set of numbers is not a number, and though every member of your English class may be wearing socks today, it hardly follows that the class as a whole is wearing socks.

Superficially, composition resembles the fallacy of hasty generalization, but in fact it is quite different. Hasty generalization involves reasoning from a *sample* to a *greater number* of instances and saying that because a few members of a group have some characteristic the larger number must have it also. But it is still the *individuals* in the larger group who are said to have the characteristic in question, not the group taken as a whole. If you keep this difference in mind, you will find that you can distinguish the two fallacies without difficulty.

It is fallacious, then, to assume that the whole necessarily possesses the characteristics of its parts or that what is true of members of a group separately must be true of the group.

Division

Exactly the reverse of composition is the fallacy of **division**. Division is the assumption that what is true of an organized whole is necessarily true of each part or that what is true of a group collectively must be true of each of its members. Consider this argument.

> Big, gas-guzzling cars are vanishing from the American scene. That old Buick over there is a big, gas-guzzling car. Therefore that old Buick over there must be vanishing from the American scene.

Here a characteristic that belongs to a group—that of big, gas-guzzling cars—is mistakenly applied to a member of the group. Taken as a class, cars of this kind are indeed vanishing. In fact, however, the old Buick in this example may be around for a good many years. Moreover, if it does "vanish," it will not be in the

gradual way that the class of big gas-guzzlers here is said to be vanishing. Gradual disappearances can happen to a class of cars, but not to the individual cars that make up the class. Thus the conclusion of the above argument does not follow from the premise given.

More commonly encountered examples of division go from organized wholes to their parts, saying that the characteristics of one belong to the other. But the characteristics of wholes need not be the same as those of their parts. We may have an outstanding team without any individual stars. Our political system is based on a belief in the wisdom of the electorate, but it would be an error of division to conclude that every voter is wise. If we were to argue that a person is a good lawyer because he or she belongs to a good law firm, that a person is a democratic person because he or she is a citizen of a democratic country, or that another is a communist because he or she is a citizen of a Communist country, we would be committing the fallacy of division.

We are likely to be mistaken if we assume that the parts necessarily possess the characteristics of the whole, or that what is true of a group collectively must be true of its members individually.

Circular Argument

Circular argument, which is also sometimes called **begging the question**, occurs when the conclusion we are trying to prove is assumed in our premises. This may happen either in a single argument or in a chain of arguments aimed at establishing a conclusion. For example, suppose we say, "John had an antipathy for soccer because it was a game he did not like." This argument begs the question because its premise is really just a restatement of the conclusion using somewhat different language. The argument is, of course, valid, for every proposition follows from itself. But this argument does not increase the reliability of the conclusion; only if we had already accepted the conclusion could we be satisfied with it as a premise.

In more extended examples, we may link a series of propositions together in such a way that the same statement is used as both evidence and conclusion, while conveying the illusion that a significant logical progression is occurring. If we argue that we need more automobiles on the road because we need more money from gasoline taxes so that we can build more roads in order to have more automobiles, we have completed a circle without proving anything. We have in effect argued that we need more automobiles because we need more automobiles. Our reasoning is analogous to that of the three fools, each of whom tied his horse to another's, thinking that he had thereby secured his own horse.

Circular arguments are to be rejected for reasons analogous to those for avoiding circular definitions. Just as we can learn nothing about the meaning of a word if it is used to define itself, so also we cannot establish a proposition as reliable by using it to prove itself. Nevertheless, circular arguments can be seductive in lengthy and loosely organized discussions, thanks to human forgetfulness. It is easy to fail to realize that a proposition given as a conclusion a few minutes or pages ago is now being served up as evidence for itself. To locate this fallacy, as well as many others, it is helpful to outline the argument, keeping track of all the logical connectives and structure words, so that we know exactly what is supposed to prove what.

Accident and Cliché Thinking

Earlier we studied the fallacy of hasty generalization; in that fallacy, the evidence was a small or biased sample from which a general conclusion was drawn. The opposite of hasty generalization is the fallacy of **accident**. This fallacy involves beginning with a sweepingly general statement and then applying it to a case or cases in which special or "accidental" circumstances make the general statement inapplicable. Thus while hasty generalization involves going from the specific to the general, accident involves going from the general to the specific. What makes this fallacy possible is that a great many general statements are employed largely for the sake of convenience and are not meant to apply literally to every case that appears to fall under them. For instance, you know that narcotics are addictive. But if you break your arm wrestling and refuse the doctor's codeine analgesic on the basis that narcotics are addictive, you are committing the fallacy of accident. Certainly narcotics are addictive. But if you are taking a carefully measured dose of codeine for a specific purpose under a doctor's supervision, you will in all probability not become an addict.

Just as hasty generalization is sometimes confused with composition, so also accident tends to be confused with division. Again, however, this is strictly a matter of appearance, for the two fallacies are quite distinct. Consider the following pair of arguments.

Hunters mistakenly shoot hundreds of persons annually.

Smith is a hunter.

Therefore Smith mistakenly shoots hundreds of persons annually.

Citizens have the right to freedom of speech.

Therefore journalists should be allowed to publish libelous stories.

The first of these arguments is a fallacy of division, because its first premise applies to hunters taken as a group, not to hunters as individuals. The second argument is a fallacy of accident because its first premise applies to *each* citizen, not citizens taken collectively. If you were deceived into thinking the first argument is a fallacy of accident, the reason is probably that its first premise begins with the plural noun "hunters" and so appears to be a general statement. In fact, however, this statement is not general at all, for it is about only one thing, namely the class of hunters taken as a unit. Learning to distinguish fallacies of division from fallacies of accident is relatively easy once we realize that plural nouns and noun phrases sometimes refer to classes as units and at other times refer to the members of the class. A good way to tell the difference is to try inserting a quantifier such as "each" or "every" in front of the plural noun. Statements that are intended to refer to groups collectively usually have little plausibility when this is done. No one is likely to believe that every hunter mistakenly shoots hundreds of persons a year.

A great many fallacies of accident result from accepting clichés as blanket truths and applying them without caution to everyday decisions and inferences. Proverbs, maxims, aphorisms, and familiar quotations have a special persuasiveness. Because they are pithy and often in rhyme, they are easily remembered. Many of them have the prestige of age; some are almost as old as civilization itself. But using them uncritically as premises in decision making is illogical.

First, many clichés are stated in figurative language and have no precise meaning. Suppose you are trying to decide whether to sell a stock for a small profit or hold it in the hope that you can make a larger profit later. If you decide to sell your stock on the ground that "a bird in hand is worth two in the bush," you may be committing a fallacy of accident. The real issue is whether the stock is more likely to go up or down. When you have decided this question, you have no need for the cliché. But if you make your decision in terms of the cliché, you are probably overlooking the real issue.

Second, clichés are usually oversimplifications. It is true in some situations that "haste makes waste," but in other situations "he who hesitates is lost." In some situations it is true that "nothing ventured, nothing gained," but in others it is "better to be safe than sorry." The real issue is whether the particular situation calls for haste or caution. Unfortunately, clichés are so persuasive that we tend to act on the first one that occurs to us, without considering the real issue.

Third, clichés often state as truth what are only unproved general statements or causal principles. "Like father, like son" is true only sometimes and in some respects. "Early to bed and early to rise" does not necessarily make one "healthy, wealthy, and wise."

Finally, clichés often express value judgments that may be good in isolation but are incompatible with other values one holds. "Better to be safe than sorry" seems to be a sound value principle. But if this cliché is interpreted to mean "never take any risk," it would be incompatible with another value most of us hold, according to which achievement in areas where the probability of success is low is especially praiseworthy. In a somewhat different vein, "Hitch your wagon to a star" can be pernicious in the value system of people who tend to judge themselves by excessively high standards.

Cliché thinking should not be confused with the use of trite language. Consider the statement "If you don't study more, you will fail this course as surely as the sun will rise tomorrow." The words "as surely as the sun will rise tomorrow" are a cliché in the sense that the language is trite. But the statement is not a case of cliché thinking because the cliché is not used as a premise. The remedy for cliché thinking is to translate the cliché into an ordinary general statement, free of imagery, rhyme, and persuasive language, and then determine whether this statement is reliable and whether it applies to the specific case at hand. For example, "where there's smoke, there's fire" can often be translated into "all rumors are based on fact." Is this true? Obviously not, for many rumors begin when one person's speculation is repeated by someone else as though it were true. Thus, if you hear rumors about some new policy at your college that will affect you, it is much more sensible to check out the facts than simply say to yourself, "Where there's smoke, there's fire," and assume the rumors are true.

Inconsistency

The fallacy of **inconsistency** involves reasoning from premises that are contradictories or contraries or in conflict to at least some degree. Obviously, no reliable conclusion can be drawn from a pair of propositions like these below:

All social welfare programs are bad.

Some social welfare programs are not bad.

The reason is that each of the propositions undercuts the other. Hence any argument that employed one of them as evidence would be undermined by the evidence the other provides. The result is that no conclusion can be defended in a convincing way.

Yet people argue from such pairs of premises all the time. Consider the alumnus who contends that Wysacki lost the football game because of bad breaks. He points to a Wysacki fumble late in the game that led to the winning touchdown by the opposition and argues that fumbles are bad breaks. When reminded that a fumble by the opposition led to Wysacki's only touchdown, he argues that this fumble was not a bad break because hard tackling by Wysacki caused it. The alumnus is arguing from contradictory propositions: "All fumbles are bad breaks" and "Some fumbles are not bad breaks." Similarly, a business person who favors regulation of freight rates but opposes price control on the ground that it involves governmental influence in free enterprise is arguing inconsistently, for presumably regulation of freight rates is also a form of price control and it is certainly a form of governmental influence.

Inconsistency often appears in governmental responses to social problems, partly because experts often disagree on the best approach to take and partly because measures adopted at different times are meant to satisfy different constituencies that have opposed philosophies. For example, many people favor liberal programs of aid for the unemployed and for families below the poverty level on the basis that no one in a country as wealthy as the United States should starve and that many people find themselves in poverty due to circumstances beyond their control. Others prefer much more stringent welfare programs, on the ground that this fosters self-sufficiency and reduces opportunities for people to exploit such programs out of laziness. Obviously, any government that tried to please both extremes would be basing its decisions on inconsistent premises, for it cannot have programs that are both liberal and stringent. Yet it often appears that government tries to please both factions, at times with paradoxical results. Not long ago, for example, many students could qualify to receive food stamps while people who were far less privileged were denied such aid.

When inconsistencies occur in social settings, they often stem from conflicting values held by different segments of society. When this sort of conflict occurs, it may be possible to achieve a balance between the two values, though this may not be the best course in all cases. Needless to say, each of us can experience conflicts in our own values also. Procedures for resolving conflicts in value systems are discussed in Chapter 31.

When you encounter cases where this fallacy is committed, it is useful to point out the inconsistency in the position being taken. Your opponents may be able to produce a qualified assertion that clears up the discrepancies, or they may not. In either case, the fallacy will be exposed. And when someone tells you that "you cannot have it both ways" or "you cannot have your cake and eat it too," you should start to examine your premises, for you are being accused of inconsistency.

Two points are worth noting by way of concluding. First, the evidence cited in a fallacy is not always completely extraneous. The reasons given in a fallacious argument may provide some evidence for the reliability of the conclusion, or they may provide none at all. But even when it has some relevance, the evidence provided in a fallacious argument is never enough to cause us to accept the conclusion on a rational basis. Second, the presence of a fallacy in an argument does not *disprove* the conclusion. The conclusion may be true anyway; the fallacy only indicates that the particular evidence cited doesn't justify the conclusion drawn from it. Thus, if you find that two of your fellow students in your logic class are accounting majors and your major is also accounting, you will be making a hasty generalization if you decide that the other twenty students in the class are accounting majors too— but in fact they may be. And if you ask them all and find out that they are actually all majoring in accounting, your initial conclusion will still have been reached by hasty generalization. But that fact does not make it incorrect. Indeed, to think that because someone is guilty of fallacy his or her conclusion must be wrong is to *commit* a fallacy, one of argument from ignorance. For to think this is to assume that since the conclusion has not been proven true it must be false.

Suggested Supplementary Reading

Alex C. Michalos, *Improving Your Reasoning* (Englewood Cliffs, N.J.: Prentice-Hall, 1970).

S. Morris Engel, *With Good Reason: An Introduction to Informal Fallacies* (New York: St. Martin's, 1976).

Exercise 21

Problems 1–7. These problems refer to the lettered statements below. Assume that all observational claims contained in these statements are true.

A. *Abrams*: "I nominate Thompson for president of the Wysacki student body."

B. *Bacon*: "I nominate Willoughby the Wallaby, our school mascot."

C. *Clarendon*: "Don't be ridiculous. Willie is a kangaroo; he can't be president."

D. *Dexter*: "I agree with the nomination of Willie. He is at every athletic contest, supporting the team. Besides, he's been here for years, and represents Wysacki at a lot of public functions. No one can prove he hasn't earned the nomination. Therefore he deserves it."

E. *Foster*: "I'm for Thompson. Willie may be the mascot of the Wysacki Kangaroos, but he's not a student. Regulations state clearly that the president of the student body has to be a student."

F. *Bacon*: "But if he were a student, Willoughby would have been president long ago, so why not nominate him now?"

G. *Grimes*: "I'm for Willie. Thompson has already been student body president, and he wasn't effective. With Willie we can be sure it will be a different story. He's a wallaby. Therefore he represents new blood."

H. *Clarendon*: "You people are just making a game out of this. You can't seriously believe Willoughby will make an effective president when he isn't even human."

I. *Dexter*: "What do you mean, he's not human? Willie the Wallaby eats, drinks, and sleeps just like you do. He's affectionate, communicative, and feels joy and pain just like Abrams over there. I don't see where the problem is."

J. *Clarendon*: "The problem is that if we put Willie in an important position like the presidency, we'll just make ourselves a laughing stock."

K. *Dexter*: "Well if you don't think Willoughby the Wallaby is important, why don't we just get rid of him as school mascot, too? Is that what you want?"

1. Which statement defines the issue? _____

2. Which statement(s) introduce(s) relevant evidence and contain(s) no fallacy?

   _____

3. Which statement illustrates the straw man fallacy? _____

4. Which statement illustrates argument from ignorance? _____

5. Which statement illustrates hypothesis contrary to fact? _____

6. Which statement illustrates faulty analogy? _____

7. Which statement illustrates irrelevant conclusion? _____

Problems 8–13. These problems refer to the statements below.

L. *Edwards*: "There's another reason for supporting Willoughby the Wallaby for student body president. The wallaby is a vanishing species in these parts. We'd better get him elected before he disappears."

M. *Clarendon*: "I've had about enough of this. I don't see how we can have efficient student government with a kangaroo as president of the student body."

N. *Bacon*: "But all the people presently involved in the student government will remain, and every one of them has a reputation for efficiency. If those who make up the government are efficient, we can be sure the government will be, too."

O. *Grimes*: "Not only that, but having the confidence of the student body always makes for an effective student body president, and Wysacki students all have great confidence in Willie."

P. *Dexter*: "One thing certain is that Willoughby will win the election if he's nominated. He's bound to win, because he's certain to get more votes than any other candidate."

Q. *Abrams*: "Thompson is still my candidate, and I plan to support him to the end. However, given the views of the other members of this committee, I say let's make it unanimous. Willoughby the Wallaby, for president!"

8. Which statement contains no fallacy? _____

9. Which statement illustrates the fallacy of accident? _____

10. Which statement illustrates composition? _____

11. Which statement illustrates division? _____

12. Which statement illustrates circular argument? _____

13. Which statement illustrates inconsistency? _____

Problems 14–31. Write in the blank the name of the specific fallacy that is most prominent in each problem.

14. If Thomas Jefferson had lived two hundred years earlier, he would have been burned at the stake.

_____

15. "My roommate tells me that he enjoys reading only good books."
"How does he know when they are good?"
"He says that if they're not good he doesn't enjoy them."

_____

16. Her father can't get around well and has trouble seeing. Therefore she should put her father in a nursing home.

_____

17. *Speaker who advocates a society almost completely planned and administered by a central government:* "Let the government manage your affairs so that you may have more time to enjoy liberty and freedom to do as you wish."

_____

18. "Whaddaya mean, 'quark'? You ever see one? Smell one? Hear one? Taste one? Feel one? Can you give me any proof there is such a thing? Well, that just goes to show there isn't."

_____

19. *Professor:* "One should do unto others as he would have them do unto him. If I were a student, I would want to receive an A in this course. Therefore I should give all my students As."

_____

20. *Incumbent:* "You wouldn't change surgeons in the middle of an operation. Why change governors in these days of constant crisis?"

_____

21. Students at Wysacki spend over two million dollars a year on books. That explains why they have so little spending money. After all, two million would be a crimp in anyone's budget.

_____

22. If I had eaten a good breakfast this morning, I wouldn't have slipped on my son's roller skate, I wouldn't have hit my head on the bowling ball, and I wouldn't be lying here in the hospital.

_____

23. Chez Smythe has the smallest kitchen of any restaurant in Micronesia. Therefore Chez Smythe is a very small restaurant.

_____

24. It would be no crime to divert the Nile or Danube from its course, were I able to effect such purposes. Where then is the crime of turning a few ounces of blood from its natural channel?

David Hume, "On Suicide,"

_____

25. This argument is fallacious. You can tell it is fallacious because it is not valid. It is not valid because it contains a fallacy.

_____

26. *Student:* "Dad, send money."

Father: "Are you kidding? Don't you know money is the root of all evil?"

_____

27. The claims of the health food people about the American diet are ridiculous. You can't do construction work on a cup of yogurt and a handful of lentils.

_____

28. One Nazi explained to another in 1938 that Germany had to go to war in order to acquire more living space for her crowded population. Moreover, the German birthrate had to be increased greatly to furnish future soldiers and to populate the conquered living space.

_____

29. You cannot afford to be without the Grutz Slicerblender! So economical—just ten dollars down and a dollar a week forever!

_____

30. By far the greatest cause of fatalities among young adults is drunken driving. The drinking age should therefore be raised to twenty-five.

_____

31. At the beginning of a chess game, the pieces on the board occupy thirty-two squares. But there are only sixty-four squares on a chess board. Therefore there must be only two pieces on the board when the game begins.

_____

Chapter 22   Neglected Aspect

- **Oversimplification**
- **The Black-or-White Fallacy**
- **The Argument of the Beard**
- **Misuse of the Mean**
- **Half-truths**
- **Decision by Indecision**

A number of informal fallacies involve a failure to attend to important evidence. Such fallacies may be grouped under the general heading of **neglected aspect.** We commit a fallacy of this type whenever we fail to consider evidence or factors that are both relevant and significant to the issue at hand. The results are always harmful, for even when fallacies of neglected aspect do not lead us completely astray in our thinking, they diminish the effectiveness of the arguments by which we might convince others.

Sometimes failure to consider an important part of the evidence can lead to a totally false conclusion. For example, a person who reads of a number of fatal accidents in airplanes and decides, upon this evidence alone, that travel by plane should be prohibited has neglected significant aspects of the question, namely, the great advantages of air transport and the relatively low rate of accidents per million miles traveled. Even in the most careful investigation, there is always the possibil-

ity that one may fail to take into account all the relevant factors.

Many a superficially plausible argument fails to hold up when the overlooked evidence comes into view. If someone should argue that reckless driving benefits society as a whole because it furnishes employment to automobile mechanics, ambulance drivers, doctors and nurses, undertakers, and insurance people, it would be immediately clear that one important factor was being overlooked—one that we would not agree to leave out—the value of human life. But sometimes the hidden factors are less obvious. A gun-control proponent, for instance, might argue that since there is gun control in Vermont and not in Alabama and there are far more murders in Alabama, gun control must work. His or her opponent might argue that relevant factors in number of murders have always included number of related individuals per square mile and median age of a population and that since Alabama has more related individuals and a generally younger population, it is natural that more murders would be committed there than in Vermont. The determination of relevance and importance of a given piece of information requires analytical subtlety, and the costs of overlooking relevant factors can be great. Suppose, for example, that someone who is in the market for a motel discovers one for sale that seems to be a bargain. Records for a period of years show consistently high profits and low maintenance costs. Yet within a year after our hypothetical business person purchases the motel, the profits disappear and the value of the property plummets because a long-planned freeway has been built two miles away from the motel. Failure to consider this discoverable aspect of the truth has led directly to an expensive mistake.

The fallacy of neglected aspect can occur in all phases of the decision-making cycle. In phase 1 we can commit the fallacy by defining the problem so narrowly as to exclude an important part of it. In phase 2, like the motel purchaser, we can fail to gather essential information. In phase 3 we can fail to take into account essential information in forming tentative conclusions. In phase 4 we can fail to apply essential tests for validity or reliability.

In phase 5 we can fail to see the consequences of a proposed action, particularly its long-range consequences. Consider the college halfback who, while in college, studied just enough to stay eligible for football and win glory on the field. When his eligibility for college football ran out, he dropped out of college and entered professional football. His career in professional football was successful for ten years, after which he was released because he had become too slow. At this point he made a painful discovery: the world has little use for thirty-two-year-old former halfbacks. When he tried to find

another satisfying career, he found the doors closed because he lacked sufficient education. When he tried to return to college, he was told that his academic record was so bad that he could not possibly graduate.

It is clear that fallacies of neglected aspect are not easy to avoid. Gathering and properly considering all significant aspects of an issue requires both time and hard work. None of us has a frame of reference sufficiently complete and accurate for recognizing and properly interpreting all aspects of all issues. Moreover, we are psychologically predisposed to commit these fallacies. We have a natural tendency to overlook or to refuse to see or to refuse to believe significant evidence that threatens the self-concept. A high degree of susceptibility to fallacies of neglected aspect may amount to a refusal to deal with reality.

Our best protection against the neglected aspect fallacies includes careful research, openmindedness, and awareness of the kinds of factors that may be overlooked. When we must counter arguments that involve neglected aspect, it is usually best to call attention to the neglected aspect and point out its significance.

Oversimplification

There are a number of specific forms of neglected aspect. One of these is **oversimplification**, which occurs when we think of or describe a situation as though it involved only a few significant facets, whereas in truth it involves a complex of many significant facets.

An inadequate frame of reference almost inevitably leads to oversimplification. To people whose knowledge of national and international affairs is limited to newspaper headlines and a few radio and television newscasts, solutions to major problems may seem relatively simple. Their understanding of complex problems may be compared to the view they would have of a forest while flying over it at an altitude of fifteen thousand feet. They could see the forest but not the trees. They may think, for instance, that the inflation problem could be quickly solved by freezing all prices and all wages at the present level. It is easy to fail to realize that it would be impossible to freeze prices of imported raw materials and consumer goods and that price freezes tend to lead to shortages of needed items. Oversimplification is not limited to the uninformed, however. The specialist who has vast knowledge of his or her own field may be relatively ignorant in other areas. Specialists in all areas related to human behavior tend to oversimplify human behavior by attaching too much importance to one particular facet and neglecting many others. For example, the economist tends to attach too much importance to economic motives, the biologist to explain too much of human behavior in terms of heredity, the sociologist to attach too much importance to environment, and the psychologist to exaggerate the importance of childhood experiences.

Our self-concept often encourages oversimplification. It is important to the self-concept that we see ourselves as able to cope with our environment. But coping with our environment requires that we first understand it, and few of us have both the frame of reference and the reasoning skills necessary to understand accurately all the significant aspects of our experience. Hence some of our interpretations of the world are necessarily oversimplified.

Another cause of oversimplification is our fondness for the dramatic. Sportswriters, for example, tend to describe athletic contests in terms of the performances of one or two star players. A football game in which the most dramatic play was a pass from the star quarterback to the star end may be described as though these two players won the game by themselves. Baseball games are often described as though they were won by the pitcher. A wise coach or manager tries to offset this oversimplification by stressing the contributions of other members of the team.

Even if we could eliminate the influence of subjective factors, we still could not eliminate oversimplification. Our views of some situations are necessarily oversimplified because we do not have time to gather and consider all the relevant and significant information.

Oversimplification frequently results from efforts to be concise. Radio and newspaper headlines, which must be concise, are likely to be oversimplifications whenever they deal with complex subjects. Introductory textbooks usually contain some oversimplifications, too, for it is difficult to present a complete and balanced picture of a subject without confusing the beginning student with a mass of detail.

Chronic oversimplifiers are easy to spot. They have a breezy, self-assured way of speaking and hold strong opinions on every possible subject. They are fond of such expressions as "That's the situation in a nutshell"—as if any complex situation would fit into a nutshell. To protect ourselves from oversimplification, we should cultivate the habit of being suspicious of simple explanations of, or solutions to, complex problems. When we must counter arguments containing oversimplification, the best defense is to point out the significant neglected aspects.

The Black-or-White Fallacy

Another specific form of neglected aspect, the **black-or-white fallacy**, stems from the fact that many objects or qualities cannot be divided into discrete categories. Instead, they are spread over a continuum from one extreme to the other, just as paint can vary in an infinite number of shades between black and white. In some respects, for instance, all students can be definitely categorized. Every student is an in-state student or an out-of-state student, a freshman or an upperclassman, a full-time student or a part-time student. On the other hand, students range on a continuum of academic ability and performance all the way from very good to very bad, and it is difficult to divide them into separate and distinct categories. In principle, an experienced instructor sees a very significant difference between A students and B students, but in practice he or she finds that many of them are in a gray zone between the two categories.

We commit the black-or-white fallacy when we suppose that in a given situation there are only two alternatives when in fact there are more than two. This fallacy is sometimes called the **false dilemma**, since a dilemma is a situation in which one faces two alternatives. We are particularly vulnerable to this error when the two alternatives we have in mind are opposite extremes. For between opposites or extremes there are frequently intermediate positions, neutral points of view, or moderate courses of action. Items that are not white are not necessarily black: they may be any shade of gray. Deeds that are not evil are not necessarily good: they may be neutral in moral significance. Water that is not hot is not necessarily cold: it may be tepid.

The black-or-white fallacy is particularly bad in phase 5 of decision making, for it may lead us into taking extreme action when more moderate action would be wiser. Suppose a freshman who is working thirty hours a week gets poor grades at midterm. She may decide that she must either drop her job or quit school and work full-time. In fact, she might be able to work twenty hours a week, cut out her Wednesday night breaks at the Chicken dance hall, and raise her grades considerably.

Greater than average susceptibility to the black-or-white fallacy may indicate immaturity. Children in early experiences with people are unable to make discriminating judgments. People to them tend to be either all good or all bad. The fairy tales and television programs designed for their entertainment abound in angelic heroines and hideous villains. Many individuals fail to outgrow these childhood tendencies. In later years they yearn for the security of childhood and tend to forget the bruises and burned fingers suffered because they failed to understand their environment.

To protect ourselves from the black-or-white fallacy, we should cultivate the habit of forming a number of tentative conclusions and proposals for action. And when we are faced with any either-or situation, we shoud ask, "Why not neither? Why not both?"

The Argument of the Beard

Another specific form of neglected aspect, the **argument of the beard**, also stems from the fact that most objects or qualities range on a continuum from one extreme to the other. In a sense, the argument of the beard may be considered the opposite of the black-or-white fallacy. We are guilty of black-or-white reasoning if we fail to admit the possibility of a middle ground between extremes. We are guilty of the argument of the beard if we use the middle ground, or the fact of continuous and gradual shading between two extremes, to raise doubt about the existence of real differences between such opposites as strong and weak, good and bad, and black and white. The gradual shading between extremes may blind us to significant differences. The fact that we cannot determine the exact point at which white ceases to be white does not prove that there is no difference between white and black.

The very name of the fallacy is derived from a classic example. Think how difficult it would be to decide just how many whiskers it takes to make a beard. Surely one whisker is not sufficient. Possibly even twenty-five are too few. Then let us say that three hundred and fifty whiskers make a beard. Why not three hundred and forty-nine? Three hundred and forty-eight? And so on. We would have trouble determining an exact minimum. Does this fact mean that there is no difference between having a beard and not having one?

The commission of this fallacy reveals an inability to distinguish or acknowledge small differences even when they are of real significance. Seeing such differences is frequently difficult, especially in a field in which we are not well informed, and students will therefore occasionally charge their instructors with "splitting hairs." Usually, though, the instructor is simply insisting that the student must keep struggling with a subject until he or she can grasp the distinctions essential to an understanding of it. Learning to see close distinctions is a very important part of becoming educated.

Unhappily, in many practical affairs we must make arbitrary distinctions on the basis of small differences. Suppose the scores of 101 students are evenly distributed between zero and 100, and the instructor draws the line so that the lowest passing score is 60. Someone with a score of 59 might contend that one point should not make this much difference. If the instructor agrees, however, that drawing the line between 59 and 60 is not justified, then where is the line to be drawn? How is any line to be drawn at all? And if the instructor shirks responsibility for drawing the line, will he or she not ultimately be treating the students with zero and 100 as if there were no difference between them? We commit the argument of the beard whenever we dispute the legitimacy of drawing lines simply because the difference between the items on each side of the line is small.

This is not to say that all statements to the effect that a little difference will not matter contain this fallacy, for there are many situations in which a little more or less actually does not matter. When you are putting sugar in your coffee, it is true that a little more or less won't matter *one time*. But if you are on a diet and argue that having an extra half a teaspoon of sugar in every cup won't matter, then you are committing the fallacy. The little difference per cup may accumulate into a large difference in your caloric intake.

The argument of the beard is especially tempting in situations where we wish to deceive ourselves. It is a heaven-sent gift for a person who is looking for a way of rationalizing his or her behavior. The citizen who thinks that a little bit of cheating on income taxes won't make any difference, the student who argues that a small amount of dishonesty on an exam is harmless, the teacher who cuts corners in class preparation on the grounds that none of his or her lectures are perfect any-way, are all guilty of this fallacy.

We may guard against the argument of the beard by reminding ourselves that an accumulation of even small differences may bridge the distance between great extremes. When we are tempted to argue or believe that just a little will not make any difference, we must consider whether the difference involved could be cumulative.

Misuse of the Mean

There is yet a third way of neglecting the aspects of a continuum between extremes. When we believe or argue that a position near the center is sound solely because it is near the center of the continuum, we commit the fallacy **misuse of the mean** (the word "mean" is used here in a general sense; it does not necessarily refer to the statistical mean). We would commit this fallacy if we argued that the ideal speed on the highway is forty miles per hour because it is between the extremes of the poky driver and the speed maniac. There are at least four flaws in such reasoning. First, the ideal position may vary with circumstances: forty miles per hour may be too fast in congested traffic and too slow on an interstate highway. Second, it is not enough merely to show that the position is somewhere between the extremes; we must also show that it is the right position. One may drive faster than the poky driver and still be driving too slowly. Third, a position is not necessarily wrong because it is extreme. The poky driver's speed may be about right in a fog. Many ideas we now cherish were once considered extreme. Finally, the location of the middle position depends on how the extremes are defined. If driving at ten miles per hour is defined as one extreme and eighty miles per hour the other, then the

center of the continuum is forty-five. But if the extremes are defined as twenty and sixty, then the center is forty. In short, the fact that a position is near the center is not sufficient evidence to establish that it is sound.

Misuse of the mean often appears as a device of persuasion. In political campaigns each party frequently tries to define the extremes in such a way that its own position appears to be near the center. Candidates often describe their political views as "moderate," wishing to avoid rejection by either liberals or conservatives and to capture the votes of all those who consider their own views "middle of the road."

Misuse of the mean is frequently involved in compromises. Suppose the members of an organization are divided over the qualifications for membership. One faction advocates very high and rigid qualifications while the other faction advocates moderate ones. To assume that a compromise position is the best solution without reference to the actual merits of the case is to commit the fallacy. While compromises may often be necessary and desirable in a democratic society, we should never assume that a position is sound merely because it is a compromise. Parties to a dispute often begin by making unreasonable demands in the hope that the eventual compromise will be nearer to what they want. A good defense against misuse of the mean as a device of persuasion is to point out the merits of another position on the continuum.

The distinction between the black-or-white fallacy, the argument of the beard, and misuse of the mean on the one hand and oversimplification on the other can be explained in terms of an analogy—like the difference between a straight line and a spider web. The black-or-white fallacy, the argument of the beard, and misuse of the mean involve failure to consider different points on a straight line. Oversimplification, on the other hand, involves failure to consider significant parts of a spider web. The former involves differences in degree; the latter involves omissions of many kinds.

Half-truths

Witnesses in court must swear to tell the truth, the whole truth, and nothing but the truth. The requirement to tell the whole truth is included in the oath because just a part of the truth can be as misleading as a completely false statement. The omission of a single fact may lead to a totally erroneous conclusion. For instance, in a trial following a disastrous wreck at a railroad crossing, a trainman testified that he had signaled by vigorously waving a lantern. He demonstrated dramatically to the jury the manner in which he had waved it. After the trial, the railway's attorney commended him for the effectiveness of his testimony. The trainman wiped some perspiration from his brow and said, "Whew, I was awfully afraid that other lawyer would ask me if the lantern was lighted!"

The type of neglected aspect illustrated in this anecdote is the **half-truth**, a statement that, although true as far as it goes, creates a false impression because one or more significant, relevant facts are omitted from the statement.

For purposes of deception, the half-truth is often more effective than a lie. It is therefore a favorite device of confidence artists and propagandists. A lie is dangerous to the propagandist because being caught in a lie often means losing one's audience's confidence. But a half-truth is hard to expose. In fact, a skillful propagandist can frequently use the half-truth

in such a way that it is difficult to prove that he or she was telling anything but the truth. Indeed, what is said in a half-truth is true—it is simply not the whole truth.

An especially tricky and subtle variety of half-truth is sometimes called **card stacking.** The evidence given appears to be fair to both sides, but in fact the evidence is carefully selected to make one side of the argument much more convincing than it would be if the whole truth were told. During the Vietnam war, for example, makers of documentaries selected scenes according to how they felt about the war, so that viewers often could hardly believe they were seeing portrayals of the same war. A lot of false come-ons used in promotional campaigns also involve card stacking. Sellers of time-share condominiums, for instance, may send you a card that reads, "Congratulations, Mr. Fillin! You have won either a Cadillac or a camera!" You find that you must drive for two hours and sit through two more hours of intense hard-sell to learn what you have won—which turns out to be a camera you could have bought for $3.98, if you had wanted one. After you get home, you turn over the card and read the fine print, which tells you your chances of getting the car—one in seventeen million. Finally, consider a program that was once presented on Moscow television entitled "A City Without a Soul," a documentary film on New York City. As reported by the Associated Press, the film showed the buildings of Rockefeller Center and the financial district, even though Soviet cameramen usually avoid photographing buildings in the West. Also shown were "photographs of Harlem, blind beggars, dirty streets, and unemployed men lining up for compensation payments." Much attention was given to shops selling pornographic magazines, but there were no views of food stores. "Even the Easter parade on

Fifth Avenue was shown. No mention was made of Easter, though. The announcer merely said that once a year traffic is stopped so that women can show their hats."

Card stacking is present in almost all advertising. Business firms can hardly be expected to spend their advertising budgets to inform the public of the faults in their products. The distinguishing characteristic of the half-truth is one-sidedness. An argument may involve neglected aspect in its general or specific forms without being one-sided. The half-truth is always one-sided. Usually, though not always, the half-truth is used as a device of persuasion: the situation is deliberately distorted by the selection of evidence.

To avoid being victimized by half-truths, we should cultivate the habit of being suspicious of one-sided arguments.

Decision by Indecision

In trying to avoid fallacies of all kinds, we must beware of stumbling into the pitfall of decision by indecision by permitting time and events to make decisions for us. Decision by indecision may itself involve a kind of neglected aspect. For as long as we hesitate to act on a tentative conclusion because it seems insufficiently reliable, we are acting in a way that in effect ignores the evidence in favor of the tentative conclusion. A doctor treating a patient with symptoms of Legionnaires' disease, for instance, cannot afford to put off treating the patient until conclusive evidence of Legionnaires' disease is found. Waiting for the results of tissue cultures and tests of antibody reactions could easily result in loss of the patient. The doctor must act on his or her tentative conclusion by prescribing the appropriate treatment.

It should be noted that taking no action in a situation is not necessarily decision by indecision. On some issues there may be a clear-cut position of neutrality; during a general war, for example, a country may decide that its national interest requires that it join neither side. The very act of deciding not to take sides is itself a decision; it is a deliberate choice, not a failure to make a choice. If, however, the nation remains neutral through a lack of resolute policy and its responsible officials by default allow the turn of international events to make their decisions for them, then these officials are guilty of decision by indecision.

Decision by indecision on the part of Adolf Hitler had a vital effect on the outcome of World War II. In the early fall of 1942, the German Sixth Army occupied a salient extending into Stalingrad, many miles in front of the main German lines. Although the Germans held much of the city, it continued to be defended with almost incredible sacrifice by Soviet troops, as well as by women and children fighting with sticks, stones, and bare hands. Early in September, the German general staff urged Hitler to withdraw the Sixth Army to the main lines. Hitler refused to do so. Several weeks later German military intelligence warned Hitler that the Soviets were preparing a massive offensive designed to encircle and destroy the Sixth Army. At this point it could probably have been withdrawn from the salient. But Hitler did not believe the warning and waited for the situation to clear up.

While evidence of the impending Soviet offensive continued to mount, Hitler continued to hesitate. Military evidence indicated that the middle of November was the latest possible date for the Sixth Army to withdraw. Still Hitler hesitated. The Soviet offensive began on November 19, and within a few days it succeeded in surrounding the Sixth Army. The Sixth Army still had a chance to fight its way back through the loosely organized Soviet forces cutting it off from the main German lines. But Hitler publicly ordered it to advance. It was not until early December that Hitler was finally persuaded to permit the Sixth Army to fight its way out of the trap. In the intervening days, however, the Soviets had strengthened their position, and the attempt failed.

Even at this late hour, some of the Sixth Army might have been saved. General Zeitzler suggested an emergency airlift of supplies, together with a massive attempt by forces from the main German lines to cut through the encircling Soviet forces. Again Hitler hesitated for weeks. He finally decided in January to make the attempt, but it was too late. Consequently, the entire Sixth Army was lost. Of the 330,000 well-equipped and well-trained men, only 5,000 survived as prisoners of war. By not deciding until it was too late, Hitler had in effect decided to sacrifice the Sixth Army. Many military historians believe that the loss of this army marked the turning point of the war, for Germany never again recovered the political and military initiative.

Many people try to avoid decision by indecision by acting on impulse and then seeking evidence to convince themselves that the decision was sound. There is a better way, as we shall see. It is wise to recognize that you cannot always be right. Dr. A. Lawrence Lowell, at one time president of Harvard University, was fond of saying, "There is a Harvard man on the wrong side of every question." If your self-concept includes a view of yourself as a person who never makes a mistake, you are extremely vulnerable to decision by indecision: the fear of having to admit to yourself that you have made a mistake

will make you hesitate to make a decision.

Hitler's self-concept was apparently an important factor in his decisions by indecision. German propaganda had pictured Hitler as a military genius who could do no wrong. Apparently Hitler began to believe his own propaganda. A year or so before the disaster at Stalingrad, he arbitrarily wrested total direction of the armed forces from his general staff, stating flatly that "where the German soldier sets his foot, there he stays." When the Sixth Army first entered Stalingrad he announced prematurely that the city had fallen and that this was an irretrievable disaster for the Soviets. Hitler might have avoided the disaster at Stalingrad and saved his own pride, too, had he been able to be objective in his appraisal of the situation. But the threat to his self-concept was so great that he was totally unable to recognize the truth.

Although the results are not always undesirable, decisions by indecision are always bad from the point of view of effective thinking. To the extent that you let time or events make your decisions, you are letting time or events be the master of your fate. Furthermore, decisions made by using the procedures of effective thinking will prove to be sound much more often than those made by indecision. Habitually following three procedural rules is helpful in avoiding decision by indecision.

Put First Things First. There is not enough time in any one day to consider carefully and thoroughly every decision that must be made on that day; some decisions by indecision are inevitable. It is therefore desirable to spend your thinking time on the more important decisions. For instance, if you need to decide on the same day whether to apply to a certain graduate school and what to wear at a costume party you are planning to attend that evening, it might be wiser to spend your time finding out about the graduate school and settle for whatever costume you are able to throw together at the last minute.

Set a Time Limit for Making the Decision. In many situations you can determine fairly accurately when the deadline is. For example, the catalog of the graduate school you are considering may give an application deadline. When you know the approximate date, you can apply the five-phase cycle as thoroughly as possible and act before the deadline.

Carefully Weigh the Alternatives. To do so, you can use the procedures described in previous chapters, especially those concerned with evaluating proposals for action. Then act within the deadline. According to Dr. Lowell, the mark of an educated person is "the ability to make a reasoned guess on the basis of insufficient information." To which we might add that the mark of a courageous person is the ability to act on a reasoned guess when not to act would be decision by indecision.

Exercise 22

Problems 1–6. These problems refer to the following statements made at a committee meeting.

A. *Abbot:* "This committee has been charged with the responsibility of revising the academic rules for continued enrollment at Wysacki."

B. *Baker:* "Under our present rules, a student is put on probation if his or her grade-point average for the preceding term is below 1.7. I don't think there should be any probation. A student is either good enough to stay in or not good enough."

C. *Clark:* "I don't think we should eliminate probation. After all, there is no significant difference between averages of 1.70 and 1.69."

D. *Davis:* "If we eliminate probation and suspend all students who fail to maintain a certain average, we would suspend many students whose averages have dropped temporarily because of illness or other factors beyond their control. A probationary period would give them a chance to catch up."

E. *Elton:* "It seems to me that the whole purpose of the rules is to make students study. If we set high standards, the students will meet them. I think we should suspend all students who fail to maintain a 2.0 average."

F. *Ferguson:* "Making students study is only part of the reason for the regulation. We also want to provide advance warning to the student when his or her performance is unsatisfactory."

1. Which statements define issues?   _____

2. Which statement contains a definition of an issue that illustrates oversimplification?

   _____

3. Which statement illustrates the black-or-white fallacy?   _____

4. Which statement illustrates the argument of the beard?   _____

5. Which statement is a proper defense against the general fallacy of neglected aspect?.

   _____

6. Which statement is a proper defense against the fallacy of oversimplification?

   _____

Problems 7–13. These problems refer to the statements below.

G. *Elton:* "I still think we should change the rules to require a minimum average of 2.0. They adopted this rule at Farmington College five years ago. Since then the student body average has risen from 2.3 to 2.9, and the percentage of students suspended did not increase."

H. *Clark:* "True enough. But I happen to know that the enrollment dropped sharply after the first year of the new rule, and the faculty solved the problem by lowering the grading standards."

I. *Abbot:* "We seem to have a difference of opinion. Some of you seem to favor keeping the present requirement at 1.7, and others favor raising it to 2.0. I propose that we raise the requirement to 1.85."

J. *Clark:* "There's nothing magic about 1.85. Why not 1.8 or 1.9?"

K. *Davis:* "Before we take any action on this issue, I think we should ask the Registrar to analyze the effect this proposal would have had on the students last term."

L. *Elton:* "If we do that, it would be too late to change the rules until next year."

M. *Davis:* "I move that we retain the present rules for another year. During that time we can make an adequate study of the matter."

7. Which statement contains a half-truth?　　　　　_____

8. Which statement illustrates a proper defense against a half-truth?

_____

9. Which statement calls attention to the danger of decision by indecision?

_____

10. Which statement illustrates a means of avoiding decision by indecision?

_____

11. Which statement illustrates misuse of the mean?　　　_____

12. Which statement illustrates a proper defense against misuse of the mean?

_____

13. Which statement illustrates the method of testing a tentative solution by predicting its consequences?

_____

Problems 14–15. Write in the blank the name of the specific fallacy of neglected aspect that is most prominent in each item.

14. *Irate parent:* "Don't give me all that stuff about the stiff competition at school. I've told you and I'll tell you again that all you have to do to make good grades is study three hours a night."

_____

15. *Politician:* "Chaos and confusion have developed around this and related issues. We can eliminate the confusion by clarifying the issues and by sound reasoning. The issue, uncomplicated by red herrings and smoke screens, is whether we favor giving the defense department the increase it asks for or giving it nothing at all."

_____

Chapter 23

Pitfalls in Language

- **The Problem of Communication**
- **Lifting Out of Context**
- **Equivocation**
- **Amphiboly**

- **Misuse of Evaluative Words**
- **Obfuscation**
- **Hairsplitting**
- **Complex Question**

The procedures of thinking we have discussed in this book are carried out largely through the medium of language. Even those parts of our reasoning that are not verbal often must be articulated when we wish to convince others of our conclusions or to translate our ideas into action. There are, however, a number of ways in which the articulation of reasons can mislead or deceive. Therefore attention to language and the pitfalls it presents is necessary if we are to become effective thinkers. Trying to think without understanding these pitfalls would be like trying to navigate a great river without understanding how the constantly changing currents create eddies and shoals.

The Problem of Communication

As we saw in Chapter 14, language is a means of communicating through symbols with agreed-upon meanings. We are able to communicate as well as we do because our frames of reference contain common elements. We know similar things and we know how to symbolize those things in language. By the same token, however, we can fail to communicate accurately when our frames of reference lack certain information. Most of us have experienced the frustration of picking up a book on a subject we thought interesting only to find the vocabulary of the book so unfamiliar that we could not understand what was said. The same problem can occur in the college classroom. Many students find college difficult at first because before they can do well they have to master the vocabulary of the field in which they wish to study. Moreover, even when our vocabulary is large enough and precise enough for effective communication, we sometimes misuse it. If we are careless in choosing our language or use words too advanced for our listeners without defining them, we can fail to make ourselves understood even though we have the knowledge to do so. We can also confuse or mislead an audience by using terms that have more than one meaning or by shifting the meaning in the course of the discussion. Thus accuracy in communication requires that we be conscientious in both developing and employing a sensitive understanding of language.

The difficulties of accurate communication are compounded by the imperfections and inaccuracies of language itself. First, words and phrases in common usage do not always have exact meanings. We may say that we "love" mother, country, friend, and stewed rutabagas, and refer to a distinctly different feeling in each instance. A student might say to a friend, "I have to go to the dentist this week," and mean that he has an appointment for a root canal on Tuesday or that his tooth is bothering him and he must find time to see about it. Possibly the greatest variations in meaning are to be found in words that denote emotion, such as *love, hate, fear, anger,* and so on, but many other categories of words have inexact meanings.

Second, many ideas are relative. For example, an object can be said to be cold or hot only in relation to some standard. Most residents of southern Florida or southern California would consider a day "cold" on which the temperature drops into the forties, whereas an Eskimo visiting either of these areas would doubtless consider it "hot." Science would never have made the progress it has with so imprecise a system for describing gradations of temperature. Gabriel Daniel Fahrenheit is listed in the dictionary because he devised a precise standard for measuring temperature and a system of symbols for expressing various temperatures.

Third, the meanings of words are constantly shifting. As new bodies of knowledge develop, ways of symbolizing the new knowledge must also be developed. Sometimes they are new words and expressions, sometimes they are borrowings from other languages of both the past and the present, and sometimes they are simply old words or new combinations of parts of them used with new or additional meanings. The vocabulary of the computer age is an example. *Hardware* used to refer to such things as hammers and pliers, screws and nails; now it evokes thoughts of keyboards, monitors, and printers. Besides changes in meanings, hundreds of words like *megabyte* and *modem* have simply been invented to describe things that did not exist a few years ago. Every science has its own jargon, which expands as the science progresses, but since computers have invaded American households, words from the language of computer science have found their way into everyday vocabulary.

Because language is shifting and indefinite in meaning, it is easy to make errors in expressing the arguments by which we seek to justify our conclusions. Some problems with language are inevitable, for no matter how precise our vocabulary and sophisticated our syntax, we cannot always say *exactly* what we mean. Not all of the pitfalls of language constitute errors made in innocence, however. There are also fallacies and other abuses that may be employed deliberately to mislead others. Let us consider some abuses of language that can occur in contexts of argument.

Lifting Out of Context

Many words and phrases do multiple duty. The word "bolt," for instance, has twenty-nine definitions as a noun and two as a verb in *The Random House Dictionary of the English Language;* in addition, there are combinations such as "bolt boat" and "bolt action" listed separately. A man described as "hit by a bolt" might have been struck down by lightning or hit be a piece of metal; he could have been conked by a hundred yards of cloth wrapped around a paper spindle, or metaphorically, he could have been suddenly enlightened. We can know the intended meaning only by knowing the context in which the statement was made. At times the same word or phrase gets used with two distinct meanings in the same context of argument, in such a way that the conclusion that is being argued for is supported only misleadingly. When this happens, a **fallacy of ambiguity** occurs. Several of the pitfalls of language involve fallacies of ambiguity.

Fallacies of ambiguity are sometimes committed by lifting words or statements out of context, as those who would deceive us often do. Consider the example below.

Review in a news magazine: "Sheldon Smelley's new novel is a tremendous flop! Supposedly 'the suspense-packed story of an Arctic expedition,' the only real suspense was whether the reviewer could last through a first reading of this silly drivel. The only spellbinder is the nauseating front cover, a close-up of an explorer who has fallen into. . . ."

Jacket blurb: "Hear what an outstanding critic says: 'tremendous . . . ! . . . real suspense . . . a first . . . spellbinder. . . .' "

By selectively quoting the reviewer in this way, the jacket advertisement changes the reviewer's meaning in an effort to get the reader to buy the book, thereby committing the fallacy of **lifting out of context.**

In other instances, lifting out of context does not change meaning as much as it simply ignores part of what the speaker or writer had to say. There is not, strictly speaking, a fallacy of ambiguity in this sort of case, but the misrepresentation of evidence that results can be every bit as misleading. The example below illustrates this use of lifting out of context.

Laboratory report: "Our tests of Drain-Free show that it will positively remove the grease from the trap of a kitchen sink, even though the trap is completely clogged. Unfortunately, this product also removes the metal in the plumbing."

Advertisement: "Laboratory tests show that Drain-Free will remove the grease from the trap of a kitchen sink, even though it is completely clogged."

Although direct quotation adds verisimilitude, lifting out of context can be accomplished by a paraphrase, as shown in the example below.

Medical writer: "Doctors are concerned about the increasing number of Americans who are exposing themselves to malnutrition by following reducing diets. It is estimated that some fourteen million Americans are starving themselves in order to lose weight."

Politician: "We must support the antipoverty program. Doctors are concerned because fourteen million Americans go to bed hungry."

Lifting out of context may easily occur through carelessness rather than intent to deceive. We should never repeat a quotation without checking the original context, for the distortion of meaning in quotations, like the distortion of truth in gossip, tends to increase as it is passed on from person to person. Whenever we quote another person, we should be careful that the meaning we convey is accurate.

Since the result of selective quotation is often a half-truth, lifting out of context frequently counts as a form of card stacking. To avoid being misled by this device, we need to check our sources carefully. If a quotation is given as part of an argument or evidence is presented that derives from the testimony of others, we need to check the original context to be sure the source has not been misrepresented.

Equivocation

A word is used equivocally when it is used in more than one sense in the same context. Multiple meaning enriches literature, especially poetry, by providing it with ambiguities and resonances. The pun is often the stuff of wit and humor, as in this little tale: "Knott and Shott fought a duel. Knott was shot and Shott was not. Was it better to be Shott or Knott?" In this sort of case, we are expected to see the shifts in meaning and if not laugh at them, at least groan or scratch our heads. We are supposed to recognize the word play; we are all in on the trick.

In other cases, double meanings can deceive. In contexts of argument, to exploit double meanings is to commit the **fallacy of equivocation.** This occurs when an inference is drawn by using a word whose meaning has been deliberately or inadvertently shifted in the course of argument. For no logical progression of thought can occur if the terms are used first in one sense and then in another. The very fact that an inference is drawn indicates that we are expected to take the word in one sense only; we are not supposed to spot the equivocation. For example, most of us will grant the premise that a person ought to do what is right. Let us also grant that a person has the right to eat as much as he or she wishes. But anyone who concludes, or asks us to conclude, that a person ought therefore to eat as much as he or she wishes is committing the fallacy of equivocation, for the word

"right" does not have the same meaning in the two premises. With words whose meanings are complex, words like *democracy* and *fair play,* it is especially easy to fall into equivocation. This fallacy may also involve the figurative use of words. It has been argued that the Taft-Hartley law is a slave labor law and that slave labor is prohibited under the Constitution. The catch here is that the term *slave labor* is first used figuratively and then literally.

When equivocation occurs in categorical syllogisms, formal analysis will disclose a fallacy of four terms. A careful definition of terms is the best protection against equivocation.

Amphiboly

Very similar to equivocation is amphiboly, which consists in more than one meaning being signified due to ambiguous grammatical construction of a sentence. Here, the ambiguity is founded upon syntax, rather than the different dictionary meanings a word or phrase may have. The sentence, "He told his father he was a fool" is grammatically ambiguous. There is no way of telling for certain whether the second "he" refers to the same person as the first "he" or to the father. Yet the writer of the sentence obviously meant to refer to one or the other, but not both. Consider the headline, "Professor Rakes Leaves." Is a certain Professor Rakes leaving, or is some professor simply out in his front yard raking leaves? The answer is probably the former, since leaf-raking professors are hardly headline material. (The possibilities here are endless—Professor Summers in Europe, Professor Falls Ill, and on and on.) Such syntactically ambiguous constructions leave open the possibility of the **fallacy of amphiboly**, which involves moving from the intended meaning of a sentence to another meaning which is unintended but grammatically possible. Imagine that Joe Smythe reads an announcement that says, "Officer Williams of the Wysacki Police Department will give a speech on violent crime in the College Auditorium tonight." If Joe assumes that there will be a lot of violent crime in the auditorium that evening and that therefore he had better stay away, he has committed the fallacy of amphiboly. It is true that amphiboly is rarely found in serious argument. It is occasionally used in a deliberate and obvious way in advertising to attract attention. We should avoid making amphibolous statements accidentally because they call attention to themselves and away from the point we are trying to make. They may also confuse our audience. If you advertise, "four-poster bed—ideal for antique lover," you never know what may show up.

Misuse of Evaluative Words

We come now to a pitfall of language that involves not ambiguity, but the fact that much of our language has **evaluative**, as well as literal, meaning. We use words to evaluate, as well as to symbolize, objects, actions, qualities, and ideas. The common items of our experiences can often be referred to by a number of different words that can be arranged in a sequence running from derogatory through neutral to laudatory. For example, the house in which you live can be called a "shack," a "domicile," or a "mansion." Unfortunately for accurate communication, the precise position of these words on the continuum is a function of the individual's frame of reference: one person's mansion may be another's shack.

Evaluative words are *misused* when they cause a false evaluation of the ob-

jects, actions, qualities, or ideas to which they are applied. Misuse of evaluative words is perhaps the most common, and also the most pernicious, of the pitfalls of language. It has three principal varieties.

Misuse of Labels. Words are commonly used as labels for classes of objects, actions, or ideas. For example, the word *desert* is used to designate a category of land that is dry, barren, and sandy. Using words as labels for categories can be very helpful both in communication and in thinking—as long as the labels are accurate. But words that function as labels are **misused** when they mislead. Suppose a real estate promoter buys a tract of land in the desert and divides it into parcels fifty feet wide and a hundred feet long. If the promoter advertises these plots for sale as "small desert plots," he or she has correctly labeled them. The label "Desert Acres" would, however, be misleading; it connotes considerable size, since an acre contains 43,560 square feet. If the promoter used the term "Green Acres" or "Shady Acres," he or she should be prosecuted for fraud. Note that the evaluative qualities of words used as labels change with the context. The name "Desert Acres" applied to a sanitorium located in the desert for the treatment of patients requiring dry air does not deceive; the same name applied to home sites of five thousand square feet located in the desert does deceive.

Prestige Jargon. Just as people acquire reputations from the company they keep, words acquire evaluative meanings from the contexts in which they are frequently used. For example, because of the prestige of science, words used normally in scientific contexts acquire a prestige of their own. We tend to assume, therefore, that objects, actions, or ideas described in language that appears to be technical or scientific are more important or of higher quality than the same objects, actions, or ideas described in common language. Those who would deceive us into exaggerating the value of something take advantage of this unreliable assumption by using prestige words instead of common ones. In the advertising world, false teeth become dentures, vitamin pills are multivitamin supplements, and toothpaste is a dentifrice.

The use of technical words is not necessarily inappropriate. Such words are proper when they promote accurate and economical communication. But when they are used to impress the hearer, rather than to convey a thought exactly, the fallacy of misuse is committed. Beauty products are often purchased on the ground that they contain collagens, amino acids, oils from miscellaneous glands, and other ingredients the buyer may not be able to identify precisely. These ingredients may do little or nothing for the effectiveness of the product, but they sound good. Nor does all prestige jargon come from the dictionary. There are people who make their living by coming up with new terms for everything from laundry products to automobile suspensions, terms that are designed to sound technical or scientific. Often the main use of such terms is simply to exploit the prestige attached to science rather than to describe anything of scientific interest.

Name Calling. The evaluative characteristics of words can be used to put individual persons or groups of persons in an unfavorable light. This principle was pointed up by Bertrand Russell in what he described as the "conjugation" of an "irregular verb."

I am firm.

You are obstinate.

He is a pig-headed fool.

It is all too easy to put people in a bad light by calling them uncomplimentary names. Derogatory ethnic names represent the most obvious sort of name calling. To any civilized listener, they cast more of a slur on the user than on the group he or she wishes to abuse. Almost as obvious are references to political liberals as "commie radicals" and to conservatives as "right-wing fascists." And there are any numbers of terms for negative reference to religious, professional, and other groups. Perhaps nothing destroys intelligent and informed discussion more effectively than the use of such language. More than a few people during the 1960s attended discussions on the Vietnam war only to leave in disgust when it became apparent that the level of name calling on both sides had gotten so high that little or no agreement could conceivably be reached. When name calling dominates a discussion, the aim is almost invariably to condemn rather than convince.

To avoid being victimized by the misuse of evaluative words, we should cultivate the habit of looking behind evaluative language. Pasting the label "caviar" on a can of sardines does not change the contents of the can. An ordinary flashlight is still an ordinary flashlight, even though described in pseudotechnical jargon as an "electronic illuminator." Calling a political opponent a "fascist" does not make him one. If we catch ourselves stereotyping any group—thinking in terms of "dumb sorority girls" or "illiterate athletes" or "screwball radicals"—we should forget the group and consider the individuals who compose it. It won't take long for us to find the 4.0 student in the sorority, the Rhodes scholar among the athletes, or the pragmatic and reflective person on the political left.

A rose by any other name would smell as sweet only if we react to the rose instead of the linguistic symbol. Hence we should cultivate the habit of avoiding the misuse of evaluative language in our own thinking. Whenever we are not certain whether evaluative words are accurate or relevant, we should translate them into neutral ones. If you think of your academic adviser simply as a "paper pusher" whose sole purpose is to make sure you fill all the requirements for a degree, you may underrate his or her advice. Furthermore, your negative attitude may carry over to a course you have to take, leading you to profit less from it than you might. On the other hand, if you think of your adviser as your "mentor," you may begin to react as though he or she is wiser than is actually the case. Your attitude may make you credulous about your courses. The antidote is to refer to him or her by a neutral term such as "adviser," at least until it is clear that a more strongly evaluative term is deserved.

Obfuscation

Words may be used to conceal or to obscure as well as to enlighten. The weakness of a questionable argument may be difficult to detect if the structure of the argument is concealed in a mass of words that convey little or no meaning. For this reason, a person may appear to deal with an issue without actually doing so, simply by using an excessive number of words. It is often easier to avoid taking a stand on an issue in a thousand words than in fifty. **Obfuscation**, then, consists in using language to hide the truth, either by throwing up a smoke screen of meaningless generalities or by using terms and phrases unfamiliar to the audience.

Consider the statement of a politician trying to avoid committing himself on the issue of federal aid to education: "I firmly believe that every citizen is entitled to the best possible education. In fact, it is my unalterable conviction that it is the solemn obligation of each generation to endow its youth with the knowledge of the noble achievements of the human species and to make these endowments equally without regard to race, creed, sex, color, or region. I also hold that the burden of providing these rights and privileges should be equitably allotted among those most capable of assuming the burden." The politician has made it clear in his first sentence that he favors education. Does he favor federal aid to education? One cannot tell. As we might expect, obfuscation is frequently combined with diversion (see Chapter 24) and prestige jargon.

Or consider the case of a columnist who dismisses an opponent's view as "pure Lysenkoism." Only readers with the right scientific training or a thick dictionary could know that he is alluding to the theories of a Soviet biologist that heredity is not based on genes and that acquired traits are inherited. And even once this is known, it need not be clear in what way the opponent is supposed to be a Lysenkoist.

Obfuscation is often effective in argument because the mind refuses to trace the meaning through the maze of words and tends to assume that significant meaning is there because the language is impressive. If we are favorably impressed by a speech but are unable to remember what was said, the use of obfuscation may be the explanation. We can guard against obfuscation by reducing wordy passages to their simplest elements and barest meaning.

Hairsplitting

You have probably heard discussions which did not seem to be going anywhere because the point of the argument had somehow been set aside and the participants were making tiny, unnecessary distinctions concerning things only tangentially related to the main issue. Quibbling of this sort can be called **hairsplitting**—a laborious attempt to distinguish separate classes when whatever is being separated should not, or perhaps even cannot, be divided, or when the division is irrelevant. Essentially, the hairsplitter tries to make an issue out of something trivial. Varieties of hairsplitting include arguing over the meaning of a word when there is no reasonable doubt about its meaning, making unreasonably fine distinctions, or wrangling about trivial points in such a way as to obscure the real issue or the important evidence. In nearly all cases of hairsplitting, what is going on is simply an attempt to evade the real subject at hand.

Let us look at some illustrations. The social committee of a civic organization announces a date for the organization's annual picnic. In the event of rain, the committee says, the picnic will be held a week later. One of the members, who does not wish to miss the picnic but who finds it inconvenient to go at the appointed time, sincerely hopes that rain will cause a postponement. On the day of the picnic, although there is no serious threat of rain, there is a very light scattering of raindrops—not enough to settle the dust. This member then calls the chairperson of the committee and insists that the picnic be set for the following week, for, as he says, "It's been raining." His effort to interpret the scattering of raindrops as "rain" in the sense intended by the committee is hairsplitting.

A student preparing to demonstrate a proposition in geometry draws some circles on the blackboard. A fellow student argues that the demonstration cannot proceed because the circles are not perfectly drawn. This argument is hairsplitting, for technical perfection in the drawing of the circles is not essential to the success of the demonstration.

The loser of an election bet walks from his home to Washington, D.C., a distance of over five hundred miles, to satisfy the terms of the bet. But when the winner learns that the loser had been obliged at one point to cross a river by ferry, the winner grumbles, "He was supposed to walk every foot of the way." This trivial complaint, considered in the light of a five-hundred-mile hike, is hairsplitting.

Although hairsplitting is not an uncommon fallacy, it is important to realize that some subtle distinctions are very significant, and some labored precision is purposeful. If you arrive at 2:01 for a dentist appointment set for 2:00 and your dentist says, "Sorry! You're late—I can't take you," you could justly accuse him of hairsplitting. However, if a government committee spends a week deciding that the poverty level is $10,000 for a family of four, and hence that families making $10,001 or more are not eligible for government benefits, the committee is setting a purposeful boundary. You can argue that the limit is too low, but you cannot accuse the committee of hairsplitting. Because of the importance refined thinking can have, we should be careful to confine such accusations to cases where it is clear that the real issues are being lost or avoided.

In true cases of hairsplitting, the issues being discussed have little or no relevance to the real issue, which is decided by other factors. Discussions that involve hairsplitting tend to be like those in which obfuscation is employed: little or no real progress is made. The difference is that the obfuscator tends to trade in generalities and undefined terms whereas the currency of the hairsplitter is overprecision and a penchant for exact definition. In both cases, the effect is to divert attention from any meaningful approach to the real issue.

The retort, "So what?" is a natural and often effective response to hairsplitting. A more tactful defense is to point out how unimportant the point under discussion is to the main issue and to try to lead the discussion back to what counts.

Complex Question

The structure of language often allows us to build into a question a presumption that involves accepting a conclusion. When the person of whom such a question is asked accepts the question as phrased, he or she falls into a trap. The classic example of complex question is apt to be found in old gangster movies. A bank has been robbed, and the police haul in a prime suspect, seat him at a table and shine a bright light on his face. "All right, Rocky," says the gruff lieutenant, "what did you do with the money you stole?" But Rocky is too smart for them. "What money?" he says.

The first of these two questions is a **complex question**: it assumes an answer to a prior question that wasn't asked. Had Rocky not given the reply he did, he would have accepted the presumption that he had committed a robbery. A number of complex questions work like the one in this example. They can be especially effective when they invite a yes or no answer, for either can be incriminating. "Have you stopped cheating your way through

Wysacki?" ("Yes. That is, no. Hey! I've never cheated!")

A slightly different type of complex question involves connecting two ideas that should be kept separate. "Would you give your support to a screwball liberal?" ("A liberal, perhaps; a screwball, no.") "Are you going to allow a Republican lackey of big business into the White House?" ("A Republican, maybe; a lackey of big business, no.") As in these examples, such questions often employ name-calling epithets. In other cases, the effect can be similar to that of the black-or-white fallacy, in that alternatives are presented as unreasonably limited. "Which would you like, low taxes and inflation or high taxes and loss of prosperity?"

Closely related to complex questions are what are known in legal language as "leading questions." Leading questions have the effect of directing the listener to give a certain sort of answer, usually a yes or no, as in these examples: "You haven't studied your lesson, have you?" (No); "You worked hard on this problem, didn't you?" (Yes); "You haven't seen the defendant before today, have you?" (No); "You and the witness are close friends, aren't you?" (Yes). Complex questions presuppose the answer to some other question. A leading question makes a presupposition about what the answer to the question itself is to be. Leading questions can seriously distort the testimony of a witness, and courts of law have strict rules to prevent attorneys from asking them.

Since complex questions introduce illicit assumptions into the discussion, their use may also be considered a fallacy of faulty assumption. The best defense against a complex question is to point out the hidden question whose answer is presupposed and to answer the parts of the complex question separately.

Exercise 23

1. What does *score* mean in the context of this sentence: "The conductor must have forgotten the score"?

   _____

2. What does *score* mean in the context of this sentence: "The quarterback must have forgotten the score"?

   _____

3. Arrange the following words on the continuum below: *car, jalopy, limousine.*

   Derogatory _____ Neutral _____ Laudatory _____

Problems 4–17. Supply the name of the most conspicuous fallacy or device of persuasion in the problems below.

4. Instead of writing "Between seventy-five and one hundred people heard a speech last evening by Senator Smythe at the Evergreen Gardens near the Southside City Limits," a reporter wrote, "A crowd of suckers came to listen to a political hack last evening in that rickety firetrap that disfigures the south side of town."

   _____

5. *Laboratory report:* "We find that Tanka Tea has 3.246 milligrams of caffeine per pound. Two other brands tested had 3.2467 and 3.248 milligrams respectively. For all practical purposes the difference in caffeine content of these three brands is insignificant."

   Advertisement: "Drink Tanka Tea. It will let you sleep. An independent laboratory reports that Tanka contains less caffeine than any other brand tested."

   _____

6. The rock concert was supposed to start at 1:00. Well, here it is 1:01 and it hasn't started yet. I don't guess there'll be any concert. I suppose I'll just have to demand my money back and go home.

   _____

7. *Excerpt from a piece of literary criticism:* "Despite the insistent, denotative matter-of-factness at the surface of the presentation, the subsurface activity of *Hearth and Sea* is organized connotatively around two poles. By a process of accrual and coagulation, the images tend to build around the opposed concepts of Home and Not-Home. Neither, of course, is truly conceptualistic; each is a kind of poetic intuition, charged with emotional values and woven, like a cable, of many strands. . . ."

   _____

8. *Title of a country and western song:* "Lord I need somebody bad tonight 'cause I just lost somebody good."

_____

9. Feeling that Lincoln's administration was not taking a strong enough stand against slavery, a contemporary newspaper denounced "this albino administration, and its diluted spawn of pink-eyed patriots."

_____

10. *Book review in the New York* Bugle: "The only mystery about this mystery is where the mystery is. It is about as subtle as a gangster with a tommy gun and about as electrifying as the shock of a flashlight battery."

   Book jacket: "New York *Bugle:* 'This mystery . . . is . . . subtle . . . electrifying . . .' "

_____

11. The people who have contributed most to the growth of America have been progressive people. Americans should therefore support the Progressive party.

_____

12. *Salesman for a lock company:* "Can you afford to continue to run the risk of having your office accessible to prowlers?"

_____

13. Being in love is no illness, and no illness is worse than cancer. Therefore being in love is worse than cancer.

_____

14. *Politician:* "When you ask me if I favor the special bond issue for roads, I reply that I have always been for better roads. They are the arteries of our commerce. They are the pathways to progress. And yet I would not deem it wise to bankrupt ourselves even to pay for better roads. This is a serious question—so serious that I think each person should think it through for himself or herself. That is one of the glories of our American way of life—that each person has a right to determine which way he or she shall vote."

_____

15. *Advertisement:* "Lowtemp Antifreeze consists of a specially inhibited, concentrated methanol base to which has been added esterol, a new organic solvent that makes the metal in your radiator rust resistant."

_____

16.   Here the Red Queen began again. "Can you answer useful questions?" she said. "How is bread made?"

   "I know that!" Alice cried eagerly. "You take some flour—"

   "Where do you pick the flower?" the White Queen asked. "In a garden or in the hedges?"

   "Well, it isn't picked at all," Alice explained, "it's ground—"

   "How many acres of ground?" asked the White Queen. "You mustn't leave out so many things."

   Lewis Carroll, *Through the Looking Glass*

_____

Chapter 24

Irrelevant Appeals

- **Appeal to Pity**
- **Personal Attack**
- **Poisoning the Well**
- **Appeal to Force**

- **Misuse of Authority**
- **Bandwagon Argument**
- **Meaning from Association**
- **Diversion**

The last group of fallacies we have to consider may be placed under the heading of **irrelevant appeals**. Characteristic of these types of argument is that they seek to exploit the emotions or values of an audience in order to lead discussion away from pertinent issues and evidence. Consequently, the question being discussed is apt to be settled on irrelevant grounds. This is not to say that considerations having to do with values and emotions are never relevant to effective thinking. On the contrary, decisions among alternative courses of action have to be based on evaluation of the consequences of the proposals for action that have been developed. Thus a student's decision to follow a certain curriculum in college will be based in part on the value he or she attaches to the career to which it leads. Similarly, reflective awareness of our emotions is often required if we are to think and act effectively. If, for example, you enjoy being around children, that would be a reason in favor of pursuing a

career in teaching or child care. By contrast, if being around people who are sick tends to make you depressed and morose, you should probably think twice about pursuing a career in medicine. Though, of course, these are not the only factors to consider, they should be taken into account. But while sound decisions often require reasoned consideration of values and emotions, there are other occasions where these factors impede effective thinking. Decisions made under the sway of emotion tend to be unsound, and if we allow our values to deflect our attention from relevant issues and evidence, our conclusions are likely to be unreliable. Skillful propagandists can manipulate the feelings and attitudes of an audience so that it will accept conclusions that discount or run counter to the weight of evidence. This may be achieved simply by stirring up emotions to the point where the audience forgets to examine the evidence closely. Alternatively, the manipulator may raise an issue about which the audience has strong feelings, hoping to sidetrack the discussion or perhaps to lead the audience to transfer a positive or negative reaction from one target to another. Or the audience may be induced to confuse people with issues. Irrelevant appeals come in an immense variety, and only the more common types have specific names. In this chapter, we will take up eight major types of irrelevant appeal.

Appeal to Pity

If a person attempts to win assent to a conclusion by appealing to your sympathy instead of presenting solid evidence, he or she is committing the fallacy known as **appeal to pity**, or **argumentum ad misericordiam**. This kind of argument is frequently heard in courtroom trials, when an attorney for the defense ignores the relevant facts and tries to elicit favorable consideration for his or her client by playing upon the sympathy of the jury.

Although evaluative words may be important in appeals to pity, they are not essential; a play on sympathy can be achieved without the use of words. The attorney for the defense may, for example, bring into the courtroom the poorly-dressed wife of the defendant, surrounded by pathetic children in rags, and thus say in effect to the jury, "If you send my client to the electric chair, you make a widow of this poor woman and orphans of these innocent children. What have they done to deserve this?" Attorneys may even attempt to win acquittal for a client by generating sympathy for themselves—for instance, by appearing tired and haggard on the day they give their final summation or by suggesting that the judge has not allowed them a fair chance to present their case. More than one court case has been

won because the jury did not want to see the defense attorney lose. All such appeals are irrelevant because they have nothing to do with the issue to be decided, namely, whether the defendant is guilty or innocent.

Argumentum ad misericordiam is by no means confined to the courtroom. A driver who has been stopped for speeding may emphasize his or her poverty-stricken condition to the police officer and the fact that medical expenses for a parent in the hospital make paying a traffic fine an unbearable burden. Students having academic problems have been known to employ a similar tactic: "I've had a terrible semester, Professor Flunkmore. I received Fs in two other courses, and unless you raise my C in this course to a B, I won't have enough grade points to stay in school."

That appeals to pity are often fallacious does not mean that one ought never to make decisions in which sympathy plays a part. Sympathy is a perfectly good reason for contributing to charity, for example.

Personal Attack

The fallacy of **personal attack**, or **argumentum ad hominem**, is generally based on the assumption that anything that discredits a person discredits his or her views. Thus, instead of attacking directly a position with which we disagree, we may attack the person advancing the position, supposing that, if we can show something to his or her personal disadvantage, it must follow that the view he or she upholds is also objectionable.

If we are suspicious of the results announced by a research scholar and give as our reason that these results are not to be relied upon because the scholar was recently a principal figure in a notorious scandal, we are using an ad hominem argument. We may decline to accept someone's suggestion because she uses questionable grammar. Or we may object to a plan for civic improvement because we know that the originator of the plan is cruel to his family. The irrelevance of these reasons is not hard to see.

Under some circumstances the reputation of a person may be relevant to the reliability of that person's statements. In a courtroom, for example, the character of witnesses is important because their testimony will be discredited if it can be shown that they are untruthful or dishonest. But we must not assume the defendant is guilty as charged just because he or she is notoriously dishonest. The worst scoundrel in town need not be guilty of any particular offense, and even someone with an unsavory reputation may tell the truth on a witness stand. To determine just how much a person's character is relevant to a specific issue requires careful analysis. In court this is the responsibility of the judge and the jury.

It is important to note that a slur on a person's character is not necessarily an instance of argument directed against the person. To constitute a fallacy of personal attack, the slur must be irrelevant to the issue in hand. In a political campaign, for example, the issue is the candidate's character and qualifications for the office sought. An attack on a candidate for the position of road commissioner on the ground that he or she has been convicted of accepting bribes is relevant to the issue. On the other hand, attacks on his or her family background or religion are instances of ad hominem argument unless it is clearly shown that these matters are relevant to the responsibilities of the office of road commissioner.

We may best defend ourselves against the fallacy of personal attack by showing that the attack is irrelevant to the issue. To avoid committing the fallacy ourselves, we should be careful that any criticism we make of the person involved is relevant to the issue.

Poisoning the Well

Poisoning the well is a fallacy similar to personal attack, but it has the additional dimension of placing not just a particular opponent but anyone associated with a certain position under a cloud. This fallacy gets its name from the fact that if a well is known to be poisoned no one will want to drink from it. Poisoning the well involves putting a negative label on all who hold a certain position in order to discredit the position itself. To see how this tactic differs from a simple ad hominem argument, consider the following example.

Suppose that the issue in question is whether ROTC should be compulsory. And suppose Colonel Abernathy has stated that ROTC should be compulsory in order to provide an adequate reserve of trained officers. One might try to discredit Colonel Abernathy's argument by pointing out that he has been divorced twice and is not, therefore, a successful family man. This would be a clear case of ad hominem argument, for Colonel Abernathy's family life is irrelevant to his qualifications to speak on the issue of compulsory ROTC.

Suppose, however, that someone argues that anyone who advocates compulsory ROTC is a fascist. This is a clear case of poisoning the well because not just the colonel but anyone else who wishes to defend compulsory ROTC has received a pejorative label. Arguments of this kind have four potential effects, all undesirable from the point of view of effective thinking. First, this kind of argument may have the effect of ad hominem with respect to any contrary argument: any argument for compulsory ROTC is labeled in advance as coming from a fascist. Yet little or no evidence is given to justify this label. Second, putting the label of fascist on those who argue on the other side of the issue also puts the label of fascist on compulsory ROTC itself, with little or no evidence to justify it. Third, arguments of this kind can have the effect of deflecting the discussion onto irrelevant issues—in this case, the issue of what counts as fascism. This is the so-called red-herring effect, which is discussed below. Finally, this kind of argument tends to shut off rational discussion of the issue by intimidating those who might wish to argue on the other side. This effect is more psychological than logical: opponents are forced to remain silent or to take a position labeled as contrary to their own self-concept.

In resisting this fallacy, it is helpful to keep in mind that people who use it may feel too insecure about their position on the issue to consider contrary evidence. Direct and logical counterarguments are unlikely to have any effect on such opponents; hence little is likely to be gained by continuing a private discussion. In a public discussion, however, serious harm may be done if the use of poisoning the well is permitted to go unchallenged. In such a situation a two-part defense should be used. It should be pointed out, as tactfully as possible but as forcefully as necessary, that the person using the device is guilty of name-calling and trying to intimidate his or her opponents. Then attention should be recalled to the real issue in question.

Appeal to Force

When reason fails to persuade, or sometimes instead of attempting to persuade through reason, people may use force or coercive threats to win agreement or compliance. This practice is called **appeal to force**, or **argumentum ad baculum**.[1] Needless to say, threats are often very effective persuaders. On the lowest level, the robber uses this technique when he points his gun at you and says, "Your money or your life"—and it would be unwise of you to point out his logical fallacy. In other cases, parents may use the paddle to control the behavior of their children, lobbyists may use the threat of their influence to try to get members of Congress to change their votes, and nations may hold impressive military maneuvers near the border of a neighboring country in times of tension or when international agreements are being negotiated.

While such devices are often effective, they are always logically irrelevant and may be dangerous to human and to international relations. We should never lose sight of the fact that, even when submission or use of counterforce may be deemed necessary, such solutions do not persuade by use of reason, and create resentment and bitterness.

What we should do when faced with an appeal to force depends on the circumstances. Sometimes we may oppose the threat effectively with reasonable ar-

---

[1] *Baculus* is the Latin word for "stick" or "staff," hence this tactic is also called the argument of the club.

gument; at other times it may be necessary to submit or to combat force with force.

Misuse of Authority

In Chapter 6 we discussed how to evaluate authorities as sources of information. Many of the decisions we make have to be based on evidence from authorities, for the simple reason that we have neither the time nor the skills to find out everything for ourselves. Thus if the professional meteorologist on your local television channel announces that tornadoes have been sighted in your area, you would be well advised to take cover immediately and not postpone action until you see one yourself. However, appeals to the testimony of authorities are not always appropriate to the case at hand. When they are not, the fallacy of **misuse of authority**, or **argumentum ad verecundiam**, is committed.[2]

Misuse of authority comes in two forms, the first of which is the more common. It occurs when an authority is appealed to for testimony on matters outside his or her field of competence. Usually, the authority is a person known not only to specialists, but also to the general public, so that he or she has a certain "celebrity" status. Because we accept the authority's expertise or eminence in one area, we are tempted to accept his or her opinion on other matters as well, and the fallacy exploits this temptation. The case may be one in which a nuclear physicist has strong opinions on the value of vitamin C, or a renowned pediatrician supports a certain approach to foreign policy, or a specialist in education backs a specific theory regarding the genetic basis of intelligence, or an entertainer or sports star promotes his or her candidate for president. You would not want to accept any of these people as authorities on the subjects in question because their education, training, and accomplishments are not in these areas. Neither should you accept other people's appeal to the eminence of these authorities to support the views described. Obviously, authorities are as entitled as anyone else to hold and foster views in areas where they lack expertise. But that they hold such opinions makes these opinions no more reliable than would the testimony of any ordinary individual.

An important instance of this type of misuse of authority occurs in testimonial commercials and advertisements. Distinguished and famous people of all types are quoted or pictured in advertising as endorsing, preferring, or recommending the product being advertised. The object is to try to bring about a transfer of the consumer's respect from the person to the product so that they will buy it more readily. People who do testimonials are often carefully selected to fit certain attitudes. Athletes are selected to endorse razor blades; drunkards are hardly ever presented as endorsing alcoholic beverages.

The second type of *argumentum ad verecundiam* occurs when the issue at hand is one we are expected to settle on its own merits, rather than on the basis of the testimony of others. Here the reliability of the authority does not matter: we are still misusing authority if we act as though the testimony of another settles the issue. Sometimes cases of this type involve subjects on which even the experts disagree. For example, no amount of testimony from mathematicians can settle the issue of

---

[2] *Verecundia* is Latin for "modesty."

whether Goldbach's conjecture that every even number is the sum of two primes is correct, for no proof of the conjecture is known as yet. In other cases, the requirement that we not rely on authorities is a product of the setting. In your chemistry lab, for example, you would not be allowed to produce solutions to your experiments using as your only evidence the fact that your textbook says this is the right answer; you are expected to perform the relevant tests yourself. In the same way, a philosopher at a meeting of a professional society would be ridiculed if he tried to settle a philosophical question simply by appealing to the authority of a famous philosopher such as Aristotle or Descartes; nor could a physicist gain acceptance for a certain interpretation of quantum mechanics if her only argument were that Einstein endorsed the view in question.

To guard against the first form of misuse of authority, you should check the credentials of authorities according to the criteria listed in Chapter 6. To guard against the second, you should be aware to what extent the circumstances in which a discussion occurs require that the evidence used be drawn from the facts concerning the issue at hand rather than from the views of experts.

Bandwagon Argument

If we don't have the authority of prestigious or famous people to invoke, we can always appeal to the authority of the mob. This fallacy is called the **bandwagon argument**: it occurs when a position is deemed correct because everyone, or nearly everyone, agrees with it, or deemed incorrect because it is widely rejected. In many instances, bandwagon arguments are used to rationalize misdeeds. Thus a person might claim that it is all right to falsify an income tax return because "everyone does it"; or a student might rationalize dishonesty on an examination because "everybody cheats a little bit." Young people sometimes show a fondness for the bandwagon argument in negotiating with their parents. A rock concert a hundred miles away has to be attended because "the whole school is going"; a new fashion in clothing is acceptable because "everybody's wearing them." In all these cases, "everybody" turns out to be a lot fewer than the meaning of the term would require: there are a few known cases, a bunch of supposed ones, and then a whole lot of people who for some reason or another do not count. Nevertheless, bandwagon arguments can be effective, especially on parents who do not want their children to suffer the pain of not being accepted by their peers. Effective or not, however, such arguments are fallacies. The agreement of all the world does not make a proposition true or a proposal for action acceptable; nor does universal rejection make the proposition or proposal incorrect.

Bandwagon arguments sometimes appear in philosophical and religious contexts. It may be argued, for example, that there must be a God because human beings have always believed there was, or that a certain moral practice is wrong because it has always been viewed as such. Politicians are anxious to achieve a bandwagon effect in their campaigns for election. As election day approaches, they are apt to cite any public opinion poll they can find that indicates they are gaining support—and to ignore or discount any evidence that voters are drifting to other candidates. The bandwagon argument is also a popular advertising tool. Any product that can be advertised as the best-selling or "most popular" item of its kind is likely to gain more buyers simply by virtue of the popularity it is already perceived to have.

The bandwagon fallacy is easily avoided if we refuse to allow our thinking to be dictated by considerations of popularity and general agreement and keep our attention on the real merits of the case at hand.

Meaning from Association

A number of irrelevant appeals may be grouped under the heading **meaning from association**. Like misuse of authority, this tactic aims at effecting a transfer of attitudes in the minds of the audience. An idea or product or person is presented to the audience in association with other concepts or things to which the audience can be expected to react either positively or negatively. The hope is that the positive or negative reaction will then transfer to the items in question.

For example, suppose a political speaker talks of a candidate he supports in the following terms: "It is only fitting that the foundation of my candidate's support is in the Midwest—that bastion of home, family, and traditional values." Here, the speaker tries to elicit a positive reaction from his audience that he hopes will transfer to his candidate. Alternatively, he might try to associate an opposing candidate with a person or idea he expects voters to condemn, thereby damaging that candidate's image in voters' minds.

Advertising, too, takes advantage of meaning from association. Commercials for automobiles often try to associate the product with things expected to gain the approval of potential buyers. If, for exam-ple, the car is sporty and aimed at youthful buyers, it may be presented as driven by someone young, lively, and attractive, accompanied by an equally attractive person of the opposite sex, cruising along the beach or through the mountains at a somewhat excessive speed. Obviously, buying the car will not make anyone more attractive, nor will it allow him or her to assume the lifestyle the advertisement associates with the automobile. But if the car can be associated with a fast and fun-filled life in a potential buyer's mind, he or she may become the next customer.

Appeals such as the above are fairly easy to spot because the product being sold is associated directly with things that appeal to the audience. In other cases the appeal can be quite subtle and operate through symbols aimed at the subconscious. For example, a television commercial for life insurance may present you with a spokesperson who putters around the garden while telling you about his or her insurance coverage. The garden really doesn't need work: everything is in good health and well trimmed, and there is not a weed to be seen. As for the spokesperson's house, it is in perfect repair and probably newly painted. Moreover, it is set against a protective background of trees, most likely evergreens. The lawn is in beautiful shape, and the place is surrounded by an unobtrusive but sturdy picket fence. The viewer is unlikely to realize it, but every detail of this scene symbolizes life and security—the very things a potential insurance customer is looking for. If the person in the commercial has all this and insurance too, why shouldn't you?

Meaning from association is sometimes called **appeal to the people** because it plays on standard popular beliefs and values. People tend to value tradition and so may buy overpriced stainless steel flatware because it has "an authentic Victorian pattern." People value patriotism and so may pick up a red, white, and blue box of almost anything. People respect the rich and famous and so may vote for a political candidate who is pictured in the paper with millionaires and sports stars. Kissing a few babies does not hurt either. Using the product or accepting the candidate gives one the sense of participating in something he or she values—even though reason will tell us that one margarine is not more patriotic than another and babies don't understand politics.

Guarding against the fallacy of meaning by association is not that difficult when the appeal is obvious, as it often is. What is needed is a willingness to analyze the associations that have been presented before making any kind of decision. Where symbolic approaches are used, the task can be more difficult because the nature of the appeal may not be obvious at all. Guarding against subtle forms of meaning by association requires understanding how symbols affect our thinking. Some understanding of the effect of symbols can be gained through the study of literature or art or by reading a book on the subject. In any case, when we find that a speech or advertisement has swayed our opinion without presenting any convincing argument, we should be cautious about making any decision. Meaning by association may be at work in our thinking.

Diversion

Sometimes it is possible to exploit the concerns and attitudes of listeners in such a way as to distract attention from the main issue, and lead the discussion onto irrelevant and unproductive paths. This practice is called **diversion**. Usually, diversion does not convince an audience of anything, but it is an important propaganda device, for it obscures the issue and may prevent any decision from being reached. Often the person using diversion is trying to forestall a decision on an issue, and thereby gain time to put other persuasive devices into play. In other cases, the diversion is not intentional, but the digression that results still obscures the real issue and needlessly prolongs discussion. Diversion can be accomplished in a number of ways; we will consider two of them.

Red Herring. This maneuver gets its name from the trick of throwing tracking dogs off a scent by drawing a smoked (hence red) herring across the trail they are following and leading them in a different direction. Suppose you do not like the direction a discussion is taking but are unable to change the subject directly. You may be able to lead the discussion off track simply by raising an issue of importance to other participants in the discussion. If their concern is strongly enough aroused, they will turn their attention to the new issue and the discussion will digress, as it does in the following dialogue.

Chairperson: "Is there any further discussion of the motion to pay a dividend of 2 percent on common stock for the last quarter?"

Cranston: "What are we going to do about the competition from Amalgamated Widget?"

Chairperson: "It may affect our ability to pay dividends in the future, but it had little effect on last quarter's profits."

Dawson: "Cranston has a point. Amalgamated has been cutting into our market, and International Contrivance looks like they're about to do the same."

Chairperson: "Yes, but. . . ."

Evans: "I've been concerned about this problem, too. Maybe we should deal with it now, before it gets out of hand."

Chairperson: "Well, what strategies have you been working on?"

In this case, the chairperson's first statement defines the issue clearly: whether to pay a dividend of 2 percent on common stock. Cranston has another issue in mind, which turns out to be one of general concern. Although the chairperson tries to keep the discussion on track, others take up the new scent and race off in a new direction. In the end, even the chairperson has to go along. This is a clear instance of the red-herring effect, for whether Cranston intends to do so or not, his maneuver of raising the issue of competition leads the discussion into a digression. Note, too, that the digression would probably not have occurred if fears about competition had not been aroused. The red-herring tactic works best when the new issue arouses strong feelings in listeners. If they are neutral or unconcerned, they will probably stick to the issue at hand and refuse to be sidetracked.

Misuse of Humor. When properly used, humor can promote effective thinking. Since our concentration span is limited, we are better able to follow a serious or complex argument if the speaker or writer permits us to relax for a moment with a bit of humor. Humor may also help to relax tensions when emotions are running too high. If the humor used is related to the issue in hand, it is less likely to divert attention from it.

But humor can also be used to divert attention from an issue, disrupt effective thinking, and so prevent decisive action. Suppose that a school board is holding a public hearing on its proposal to consolidate two rural schools. In the audience are the parents of the children that attend the schools who are concerned about their children's welfare and suspicious of the proposal. Members of the board make effective arguments for consolidation by pointing out the advantages to the children of a larger school—until an opponent of the proposal makes this little speech. "All this reminds me of a remark in *Following the Equator:* 'In the first place God made idiots. This was for practice. Then He made school boards.' " The audience bursts into uproarious laughter, and the school board is not able again that night to draw attention back to the educational advantages of consolidation. Note that like the red-herring tactic, this use of humor plays on the feelings and values of the audience. Parents are usually disposed to resist changes in the school situation of their children, and by holding the board up to ridicule, the opponent of the proposal enables the parents to ignore the proposal, at least for the time being. But of course the issue at hand remains to be decided, even though the focus of the discussion is now lost. Effective decisions are unlikely in this sort of situation.

When we are trying to reach a decision, we should guard against diversion by reminding ourselves of the issue at hand and asking ourselves whether the points raised are relevant. When others introduce diversionary material, either innocently or deliberately, the best defense is a tactful suggestion that the discussion return to the issue.

There are many ways in which those who are willing to exploit the emotions and values of an audience can cloud an issue and encourage decisions based on irrelevant considerations instead of a clear understanding of the evidence. If we learn to recognize the fallacies discussed above, we have made a start at resisting such tactics.

Exercise 24

Problems 1–16. Identify the irrelevant appeal that is most prominent in each passage.

1. *Child, to teammates:* "It is not my turn to play goalie! And if you insist that it is, I'll just take my hockey ball and go home."

   _____

2. Tempus Fugit watches must be the best watches because they outsell every other brand.

   _____

3. I know "Practical Reason" is an easy course because Hugo Narr told me so. Old Hugo knew all about courses; too bad he flunked out last semester.

   _____

4. Platinum Gold champagne—Only the best people drink it. Not just anyone can afford it.

   _____

5. How can you support socialized medicine? Anyone who advocates governmental takeover of a competitive system is a communist.

   _____

6. *Advertisement:* "You may *feel* certain, but can you *be* certain you are not offending? Only if you use Certain deodorant can you be certain. . . ."

   _____

7. Don't bother reading Dr. Fume's discussion of the dangers of smoking. He can't be serious—after all, he smokes like a chimney himself.

   _____

8. What do you mean, this laboratory doesn't need a new quigometric idomatizer? Remember last year at this time it was you who insisted on buying all those isothones, and half of them haven't even been unwrapped yet.

   _____

9. *Political speaker:* Ladies and gentlemen, we must return Senator Phyllis Buster to her post in Washington in the next election. In addition to the fact that she sacrificed a lucrative career in law to enter public service, she has recently suffered the tragedy of losing a daughter in an automobile accident.

   _____

10. The findings of science do nothing to undermine religious belief. No less a physicist than Einstein himself testified that his discoveries only strengthened his religious convictions.

   _____

11. *Advertisement:* "At last, all the garbage is on the truck . . . bring on the beer! Hey, what the heck? Belly Light? You expect me to drink that wimpy stuff? No, I never tasted it but———" (pop top snaps) "Ah-h-h-h-h! This is *real* beer! Have a Belly Light!"

_____

12. *Opponent of Mothers Against Drunk Driving:* The MADD spokesperson argues that there has been an increase in the number of deaths involving drunken driving. Unfortunately, there has been a nationwide increase in all kinds of crime; this country is suffering from a general loss of respect for the law. . . ."

_____

13. You cannot accept that author's portrayal of life in underdeveloped countries. He later committed suicide, so he must have been maladjusted when he wrote his analyses.

_____

14. It should be clear to you that the pollution bill has no merit, Senator Rodriguez. I would like to remind you that I represent a lot of votes; industry contributed greatly to your holding that senate seat, and you will soon be campaigning for re-election.

_____

15. The objections of opponents to our foreign policy in Latin America should be dismissed. The policy was adopted only after long and careful study, and anyone who opposes it is guilty of disloyalty to our nation.

_____

16. Find three fallacies of irrelevant appeal in the letters-to-the-editor column of your school or local newspaper. Be ready to discuss the basis for your identifications.

Part Five The Human Element

Chapter 25   Creative Thinking

- **The Creative Breakthrough**
- **Preparation**
- **Incubation**
- **Persistence**

- **Mechanical Methods**
- **Analogies**
- **Adversity**
- **Practice**

We have now considered both effective and ineffective thinking. We have studied a number of techniques and principles designed to assist us in reaching reliable conclusions, and we have seen how to recognize and avoid the most common fallacies that occur when thinking is ineffective. The methods we have discussed have general applicability: any individual can employ them to good effect in his or her own thinking. However, there is also a deeply personal dimension to thinking, for depending on our personality, the ways in which we approach the tasks of decision making can vary dramatically. Thus it is important for us to focus not just on decision making, but on the decision maker as well. Here in Part Five, we will discuss those aspects of decision making in which personality and individuality play an important role and the ways in which our individual personality can affect our reasoning.

One area in which the individual personality tends to assert itself strongly is creative thinking. The importance of creative thinking has been extolled repeatedly in this book. Without it, the human condition would be little better than it was forty thousand years ago. Every idea that has led to the improvement of our lot or to the advancement of civilization has been the product of creative thinking. The oldest ideas we use daily—that most food is better cooked, that clothing keeps us warm, that the earth is round—were once unknown. Someone with a creative cast of mind had to produce these ideas, and we too must think creatively in our careers and in our daily lives. That the products of creative thinking bear the individual stamp of the thinker who produces them is most apparent in the arts, but it holds true in other areas as well. We all have our preferred ways of approaching problems and tend to favor particular sorts of solutions. Even in the sciences, particular investigators favor different ways of explaining phenomena, and this affects the tentative conclusions they form. Creative thinking in the sciences is an especially worthwhile object of study because in science, as in most circumstances of daily life, not just any solution to a problem will do. Some individuals appear to have a special facility for coming up with right answers where others fail or give up in frustration. When this occurs, the solution that the individual produces can become the foundation for a whole field of study.

A case in point is that of Archimedes, the Greek mathematician, who was once given a problem to solve by Hieron, king of Sicily. Someone had made a crown for the king and had claimed that it was of pure gold, but Hieron thought that there might be silver in it. Could Archimedes help him? The mathematician thought for days, but nothing came to mind until one day when he was stepping into his bath and noticed the water overflowing. It occurred to him then that since silver is lighter than gold the total volume of the metal in Hieron's crown would be greater if the crown were made of a mixture of silver and gold than if it were made of an equal weight of gold alone. The difference in volume could be recognized by placing first the crown, and then an equal weight of gold, into a vessel of water, and checking to see if there was a difference in the amount of overflow. If the crown was gold, the crown and its weight in gold would displace the same amount of water. If there was silver in the crown, it would displace an amount of water somewhere between that displaced by its weight in gold and that displaced by its weight in silver. According to the story, Archimedes leapt from the tub and ran naked through the streets, shouting, *"Eureka!"* which means, "I found it!" (Perhaps this incident was the origin of the expression "flash of inspiration.") From his bathtub insight, Archimedes developed his whole set of principles of flotation, explaining why boats float and rocks sink; the theorems he developed in the second century B.C. were highly original for their own time and are still very much in use today.

The example of Archimedes shows something of how creative thinking works, and brings up two significant questions: What exactly happened to Archimedes in his bath? How can we get this same thing to happen to us? These questions are difficult to answer because there are no rules that will guarantee our discovering new solutions to problems. Some scientists, for example, might achieve insights through reading James Bond novels while others might manage better by making exhaustive lists of all the possibilities they can think of. But even though no procedure will guarantee our reaching new insights, this does not mean that creative thinking is entirely dependent on raw talent. Some people have more of this talent than others, but there are ways of facilitating insights, methods of opening the mind so that when we come to the third phase of decision making we are ready to take an inductive leap rather than hover frustrated on the brink.

The Creative Breakthrough

We do not always approach decisions creatively, nor is it always necessary to do so. When we encounter a problem, we tend first to try to deal with it by familiar methods. In using the five-phase cycle, the first tentative conclusions we form in phase 3 are usually the easiest to reach. If these work, of course, there is no need to look further. Most of us have too many problems to warrant wasting time on those for which we can reach satisfactory solutions without great expenditure of effort. But if the usual methods for finding solutions do not work, we have to go further; we have to try for a creative breakthrough.

The very term "creative break-through" shows a difference between how we view creative thinking and how we view critical thinking. Critical thinking is patterned in terms of logical rules, and leads to a predictable outcome. But there are no logical rules that determine the results of creative thinking, and precisely because what is discovered in a creative breakthrough is new, it cannot be predicted in advance. Moreover, there is a certain passive element in creative thinking. For although there are methods that can help lead us to a creative break-through, the breakthrough itself is something that "happens." That is why, as in the case of Archimedes, we so often speak of the solution to a problem as "occurring to" someone. To get a better idea of how breakthroughs come about, let us consider another case, about which more of the details are known. In the warmer parts of the United States, the health and sometimes the lives of mammals can be threatened by screwworm flies. In the late 1950s, the damage done by these pests to the cattle industry alone was estimated as high as $25,000,000 each year. Screw-worm flies lay hundreds of eggs in open wounds of animals. Within hours the eggs become larvae, which burrow deep into the wound and feed on blood and tissue. Unless the infested wounds are treated, the pests can kill an animal within ten days.

In 1938, two young entomologists in the Department of Agriculture, Edward F. Knipling and Raymond C. Bushland, were assigned the problem of developing a chemical treatment for screwworm wounds. The definition of the problem assigned to Knipling and Bushland was quite conventional. It did not take them long to solve the problem as defined, for they could do so by following paths familiar to well-trained entomologists. They soon developed a chemical treatment that, if applied to the wounds in time, would save the animals' lives. But the two scientists were not satisfied with this conventional solution. All too often infected animals were not found in time; treating the wounds was too much like setting up a hospital to treat people injured in automobile accidents instead of trying to eliminate the accidents. They decided that the only satisfactory solution was to get rid of the insects. In making this decision, they were redefining their problem.

Knipling and Bushland presumably first tried to adapt conventional methods of killing insects to the problem of exterminating the screwworm fly. But no conventional methods were practical. With chemical insecticides, there would always be survivors that would rebuild the population within a short time. A totally new approach was needed, and finding it required a high order of creative thinking. Knipling and Bushland worked hard on the problem for some time, but their efforts seemed fruitless until suddenly a revolutionary hypothesis popped into Knipling's mind—that screwworm flies could be eliminated by sterilizing the males. Even though a method of sterilizing the flies still had to be found, Knipling's hypothesis may be described as a breakthrough, for in forming it he broke through the boundaries of his knowledge.

Our knowledge of how such creative breakthroughs come about is very incomplete; indeed, it is doubtful that Knipling himself knows exactly how he came to form his revolutionary hypothesis. In general, however, the creative process seems to consist of searching the frame of reference, selecting certain items from it, combining them in a way that has new implications, and then seeing these implications. Knipling apparently combined the following items of information.

1. The life cycle of the screwworm fly is short, lasting only two or three weeks.

2. Only a small reduction in the rate of reproduction would significantly reduce the population within a short time.

3. Female screwworm flies mate only once.

4. Research on the sterilization of insects had been started about 1916.

Creative breakthroughs seem easy—once they have been made. In fact, people responsible for creative breakthroughs often wonder afterward why it took them so long. The idea they have produced makes such good sense that they are inclined to believe they should have thought of it right away. Unfortunately, creative breakthroughs are not nearly as easy as they seem to be after they have been made, for a breakthrough requires that three conditions be met. The first is obvious, but it is often overlooked: the necessary ideas or information must be available in the frame of reference. That is why breakthroughs in science are usually made only by trained professionals. It is doubtful that Knipling would ever have formed his revolutionary hypothesis had he not known that female flies mate only once.

The second condition is that the necessary items of information have to be put together into a combination that has implications for the problem at hand. This in turn requires that the right items of information be selected. The difficulty of reaching combinations of ideas that have creative value can be seen in the light of the theory of probability. As a well-trained entomologist, Knipling doubtless knew thousands of items of information potentially relevant to the elimination of insects. To keep our arithmetic in bounds, however, let us assume that Knipling's frame of reference contained only 1,000 items of information of possible relevance. It so happens that 41,417,124,750 different combinations of four items each can be formed from 1,000 items. It seems unlikely, therefore, that Knipling happened to combine these 4 items purely by chance. Yet neither could he have selected them with the purpose of reaching precisely the breakthrough he did. For he did not yet know what the breakthrough was to be.

The third condition for a creative breakthrough is perhaps the most mysterious of all. Even after reaching a combination of ideas that have useful implications, these implications have to be *seen*. It would not be impossible even for a trained scientist to look at the four facts Knipling assembled and fail to recognize the crucial implication that screwworm flies could be controlled by sterilizing the males. That implication can be recognized only by creative insight, for it does not follow from the four facts listed by any pattern of deductive inference. Rather, it seems to lurk in these facts, awaiting the investigator whose mind's eye is sharp enough to see it. Even a competent mind could miss it, just as a competent mind can miss a word suggested by a clue in a crossword puzzle. Once the solution has been recognized, however, it may well seem obvious—and the creative breakthrough may in retrospect appear easy.

It should be noted that creative breakthroughs vary widely in the degree of creativity involved. The invention of the telephone, for example, involved a high degree of creativity. The invention of the dial system was somewhat less creative and the invention of push-button telephones was still less so. The degree of creativity involved in a breakthrough depends on how new the tentative solution that is produced is to the person making the breakthrough. What may be routine thinking to one person may be a creative breakthrough for another. Nor are creative breakthroughs made only by brilliant scientists and other trained professionals. They are as much a part of ordinary life as they were of the lives of Einstein and Edison. A student who, in writing a term paper, forms a hypothesis that is new to her has made a creative breakthrough, even if a million other people have thought of the hypothesis before. The same applies to a student who comes up with a new method that enables him to study more efficiently. All of us must make creative breakthroughs if we are to achieve our potential as individuals. And while there is no recipe that will guarantee a creative breakthrough, studies of creative people in all walks of life indicate that the probability of a breakthrough can be greatly increased by following certain procedures.

Preparation

Creative breakthroughs rarely occur to people who have not prepared for them. At the very least, proper preparation requires completing the first two phases of the decision-making cycle. Phase 1 identifies and analyzes the problem that the creative breakthrough is to solve. Unless this phase is carefully carried out, creative thinking is left without a proper target.

Phase 2 supplies information not already in the frame of reference. For example, when Knipling and Bushland first started work on the problem of eliminating the screwworm fly, they did not have the necessary information in their frames of reference. Since they did not know exactly what information they would need, they undertook an intensive study of the life cycle of the screwworm fly. In the same way, the investigators of Legionnaires' disease had to collect a vast amount of data, since there were so many ways in which the illness could have been caused.

In most cases, proper preparation also requires a serious effort to complete phases 3 and 4 of the cycle. Usually the first tentative conclusions that occur to us in phase 3 are the obvious or familiar ones. But when the problem at hand requires a creative breakthrough, the testing done in phase 4 will show that none of these conclusions is satisfactory. What is more, the tests performed are likely to turn up further important information. Joseph McDade would never have discovered the cause of Legionnaires' disease unless a number of more familiar types of causal explanations had been formed and tested. The new information we gain by carrying out these phases can be most helpful because forming additional hypotheses becomes more and more difficult as we move away from the routine and familiar. It is not at all unusual for people who make creative breakthroughs to have formed tentative conclusions until they felt they could not possibly think of another one and to have tested many of these conclusions and found them wanting. Indeed, it is at this point that noncreative thinkers usually give up in frustration and settle if they can for some routine solution that is less than satisfactory. The creative thinker, on the other hand, knows that creative breakthroughs are rarely easy and treats frustration as a spur to greater effort.

Incubation

When an attempt to think of all possible solutions does not produce a creative breakthrough, an incubation period—a period of time during which conscious attention is turned away from the problem in hand—is indicated. The experience of creative persons indicates that breakthroughs occur more readily during times when conscious attention is focused on some other subject or at least is directed away from the frantic reviewing of unacceptable solutions that frustration often engenders. The explanation seems to be that information is brought into unusual and suggestive combinations by the "unconscious" rather than by the "conscious" mind. We do not yet know exactly what this "unconscious" mind is, but we can be reasonably certain that much of our thinking goes on below the conscious level. We all remember many instances when we could not recollect a fact, such as a telephone number, a date, or a name, only to have it pop into consciousness later when we were thinking of something else. Most of us, too, recall instances in which the solution of a problem eluded us for a time and then came to us suddenly minutes, hours, or days after we had stopped thinking about it. Apparently, when we consciously seek a new or unusual tentative conclusion, we tend to stay in familiar channels. But when we permit the unconscious mind to roam the frame of reference, free from restraint by the conscious mind, it is often able to break out of familiar channels and see connections that elude a conscious search.

While the operation of the unconscious mind is still a mystery, the experiences of many creative people indicate that we can learn to make it an invaluable adjunct to effective thinking. The procedure for using the unconscious mind seems to consist of two steps: (1) preparation, as described above, and (2) an incubation period in which the unconscious mind is allowed to work on the problem

free from direction or restraint by the conscious mind. Creative people use many different methods of providing this incubation. They may go fishing, or play golf, or take a nap, or take a walk, or take a leisurely shower, or deliberately turn their attention to something else.

Barbara McClintock, who in 1983 received a Nobel Prize for her work in genetics, once found her way past a major obstacle by removing herself from the laboratory situation. At Stanford University she was attempting to grasp the meiotic cycle of chromosomes in fungi, and had spent days in her laboratory fruitlessly looking through her microscope. She says, "I got very discouraged, and realized that there was something wrong—something quite seriously wrong. I wasn't seeing things, I wasn't integrating, I wasn't getting things right at all. I was lost." So she left the lab, took a walk, and found a bench under the eucalyptus trees where she could sit and think. She sat for a half hour and then jumped up to rush back to the laboratory. She had found her solution.[1] She attributes the breakthrough to "intense, subconscious thinking." Connections that were inaccessible in the lab became clear under the eucalyptus trees.

Sleep appears to provide one of the more effective incubation periods. Many professional writers follow a set routine. In the morning they write. In the afternoon they prepare for the next morning by deciding what topic to develop next and by reading on the subject. During the evening they go into an incubation period by relaxing in various ways. Many college students discover that they can solve

---

[1] Evelyn Fox Keller, *A Feeling for the Organism: The Life and Work of Barbara McClintock* (San Francisco: W.H. Freeman and Co., 1983), p.115.

homework problems with less effort and time if they struggle with them just before going to bed. Frequently the solutions will come to them before they have finished breakfast.

Of course, the unconscious mind must be given adequate time to come up with a solution. Students who wait until the last minute to start working on term papers are likely to find that the ideas will not come. A much more productive procedure is to start work on the term paper as soon as possible so that the unconscious mind can have time to work on the information gathered. How long an incubation period must be is unpredictable. Sometimes the breakthrough occurs after only a few minutes of incubation. Sometimes it requires days, weeks, or even years.

Persistence

Providing an incubation period may not be enough; persistent effort may also be needed to overcome the blocks to creative breakthrough. Some of these blocks are emotional; they include fear of rejection, difficulty in breaking away from patterned thinking, and fear of taking a risk. Often the only way past such blocks is continued and unremitting effort. Occasionally, the block can be identified and dealt with, but usually the impediment is clear only in retrospect, if then.

We have already seen one example of outstanding persistence in the work of the scientists who investigated Legionnaires' disease. Knipling and Bushland also worked long and hard at their problem before Knipling thought of the hypothesis that screwworm flies could be eliminated by sterilizing the male flies. And this creative breakthrough was only the beginning. A lot more persistence would be needed to show that Knipling's hypothesis

was correct. For one thing, a practical method of sterilizing the flies still had to be found and would require another creative breakthrough. Knipling and Bushland worked at this problem for a decade before developing a method that seemed promising enough to test. Another difficulty had to be faced as well. Any new idea is likely to threaten somebody's self-concept and therefore to meet resistance. When Knipling first discussed his revolutionary hypothesis with other entomologists, some of them laughed outright at the very idea. Knipling persisted in the face of criticism and failure until 1950, when he read an article by Dr. H. J. Muller, a world-famous geneticist, describing experiments in which fruit flies were sterilized by overdoses of x rays. Even then Knipling had trouble getting sufficient scientific and financial support to complete the project. Bushland, who was committed to another project, could work on the method of sterilization only on weekends.

Knipling's and Bushland's perseverance were to be put on trial yet again. The whole hypothesis was first tested on Sanibel Island, two miles off the coast of Florida. Although the population of screwworm flies on the island was greatly reduced, the procedure did not eliminate them. Hordes of fertile flies migrated from the mainland and rebuilt the population. Knipling and Bushland had to wait two more years before the overall hypothesis was proved in a test made in Curaçao. Several years after this test, the method was used with spectacular success in Florida and later in the southeastern United States. After eighteen years of intermittent effort, Knipling and Bushland had found a solution that satisfied them.

As this case illustrates, it is not enough simply to persist until an initial creative breakthrough is reached. Creative thinking will usually be wasted unless the ideas that result are developed, tested, and shown to be sound. The time required for a creative breakthrough to be brought to fruition can be long indeed. The history of science contains more than one case of a correct theory being proposed and rejected, only to be revived, sometimes centuries later, and seen to be correct. Perhaps the most outstanding example is that of the astronomer Aristarchus of Samos, who in the third century B.C. proposed that instead of the sun going around the earth, the earth actually went around the sun. He was, however, unable to convince others; indeed, we would not even know of his proposal had it not been recorded as a curiosity by other ancient writers. Eighteen hundred years were to pass before the proposal would be revived by Copernicus, and developed into a systematic theory.

One reason for the initial lack of success of many creative breakthroughs is that, as in the case of Knipling and Bushland, it takes time to accumulate enough evidence to demonstrate that the new approach is superior to existing ones. In addition, the ideas reached initially in a creative breakthrough often require modification and refinement before their fruitfulness emerges. Even the theory of celestial movement developed by Copernicus was not superior to its Ptolemaic rivals in the accuracy with which it predicted the movements of the planets. Only after the theory was revised by Kepler to make the paths of the planets elliptical rather than circular was the Copernican approach able to claim greater accuracy than the Ptolemaic one. Kepler's task was not easy; it took long and intense effort to find a version of the Copernican theory that would work. By the time Kepler's results finally appeared, Copernicus had been dead for over sixty years. And even

then the resistance of academic and religious authorities to the new science had still to be overcome. That resistance was to culminate in the trial of Galileo, which was still more than twenty years in the future.

Fortunately, the creative breakthroughs that are needed to solve the problems of daily life seldom require the amount of persistence that can be demanded in science. Even so, the most patient effort can sometimes fail to result in a breakthrough. When this happens, the reason may be that the problem has not been correctly defined. In this case, the next step is to begin again with phase 1. Sometimes a breakthrough can be precipitated by redefining the problem in such a way as to combine two seemingly separate problems. Suppose Kathy Collins has two problems. She needs money to stay in college, and she needs to test a hypothesis that she should prepare for a career in hospital management. She can deal with the two problems separately by taking a part-time job off campus and talking to an adviser about hospital management. But these solutions to the two problems may not be altogether satisfactory. The time spent on the part-time job will reduce the time she has available for testing her hypothesis about hospital management. Furthermore, the wages she earns in the part-time job may be relatively low, and the experience may be of little value. Suppose, however, that she combines the two problems into a single one, which she defines as being to find a job that will give her the necessary income as well as the experience that will help her test her hypothesis. This new definition is a kind of breakthrough in itself, for it leads Collins directly to a solution—find a part-time job in a hospital.

On other occasions, the creative breakthrough does not come because the necessary information is not in a person's frame of reference. If, after redefining the problem, the breakthrough does not come within a reasonable period of time, it is desirable to return to phase 2 and do more study in the area we are investigating. Sometimes we fail to collect the necessary information because the tentative conclusions we have formed have misguided our search. When this occurs, it may be necessary to make a broader search for information without reference to tentative conclusions. It is often helpful to examine solutions to other, related problems, for one of these may contain an important clue. Sometimes a creative breakthrough will not come until we have thoroughly immersed ourselves in a subject. You may find, for instance, that your term paper won't take shape because you haven't yet read enough to be able to structure it. The prospect of returning to the study phase may seem discouraging at this point, especially if you believed that your research was sufficient. In fact, however, a solution may be more quickly achieved by returning to an earlier phase in the cycle than by persisting in a later one for which we are not yet prepared.

Mechanical Methods

Sometimes despite careful and accurate definition of the problem and adequate information, the mind fails to combine the necessary items and nothing happens. In these cases it may be possible to use mechanical methods to jog or prod the mind into taking a new direction. Putting items of information into suggestive combinations is analogous to putting together a large jigsaw puzzle that forms a picture you have not seen. Your procedure, at least until you can see a picture emerging, must be mechanical. You can simply select a piece at random and systematically try the other pieces until you find the one that fits. After a period of frustration in using this procedure, a kind of creative breakthrough may occur. For instance, you may suddenly realize that one of the things portrayed in the puzzle is a mountain. You then can begin looking for pieces that might picture mountainous terrain. What you have done, in effect, is to think of a better system.

Systematically combining items is not creative thinking, of course, but it can precipitate creative thinking by forcing the mind to put items into unfamiliar combinations. Suppose you are confronted with this problem. Three boxes identical in weight and appearance are presented to you. You are given the following information: (1) one box contains two white marbles; (2) one contains two black marbles; (3) one contains a white and a black marble; (4) each box is labeled to show the contents (WW, BB, WB), but the labels have been switched so that every box is incorrectly labeled. You are to receive $2,000 for correctly identifying the contents of all three boxes, but you must pay $1,000 for each marble you inspect, and you must pay a fine of $10,000 if you incorrectly identify the contents of any box. You define your problem to be to make the maximum profit.[2]

Obviously you have to begin by taking a marble from one of the boxes. You could select the box at random, but if you did so you would have violated one of the rules of effective thinking set forth in Chapter 13, for you would have executed a proposal for action without having first tested it. A better procedure would be to list the boxes you might try first, together

---

[2] Adapted from "Mathematical Games," Martin Gardner. Copyright © 1957 by *Scientific American, Inc.*, p. 154. All rights reserved.

with the consequences. The box you should try first, of course, is the one that will give you the most information. The three possibilities and their consequences are tabulated below.

Box Opened First	Consequence		(Information Gained)
WW	Marble white	$\supset$	this box WW or WB.
	Marble black	$\supset$	this box BB or WB.
BB	Marble white	$\supset$	this box WW or WB.
	Marble black	$\supset$	this box BB or WB.
WB	Marble white	$\supset$	this box WW or WB.
	Marble black	$\supset$	this box BB or WB.

So far your procedure has been mechanical rather than creative, but it has laid the foundation for creative thinking. For you can readily see from the tabulation above that you will lose money unless you can find a better method. You will have to remove both marbles from the first box and at least one marble from another box before you can be sure of the contents of all the boxes. But try applying your creative ingenuity to the problem. Is there anything in your frame of reference that could give you a new slant on the situation?

The example above is unusual in that the number of possible combinations is small. Generally, when we try to list the possibilities we discover that there are too many—that we will never solve the problem unless we find a shortcut. Even so, this discovery moves us closer to the breakthrough, for it gives us a clearer idea of what the problem is.

Analogies

We saw in Chapter 21 that arguing for the reliability of conclusions on the basis of analogies can be risky. As a source of **tentative** conclusions, however, analogies are extremely useful; hence considering them can often lead to a creative breakthrough. Analogies are **partial resemblances between two or more objects, ideas, or processes**. Analogies provide a link between the known and the unknown. When the problem in hand closely resembles another problem with which we have dealt successfully, we usually encounter little trouble in forming tentative conclusions. We can easily see the analogy between the two problems, and the analogy suggests the tentative conclusions. The police routinely use analogy in solving crimes. One type of analogy they use involves the M. O., that is, the criminal's method of operation. If a safe has been cracked by the skillful use of an acetylene torch, they search their records for other instances of safe-cracking in which an acetylene torch has been skillfully used. All criminals in the police records who have been known to crack safes in this manner are automatically suspect until investigated.

When the decision making cycle stalls because we cannot think of a satisfactory tentative conclusion, searching for analogies may be a useful method of precipitating a breakthrough. The search for analogies should begin by comparing the problem in hand with other problems like it. If this fails, the search should be widened to include situations that bear a less obvious relationship to the problem in hand.

Archimedes' body being lowered into a tub might not seem relevant to the question of how to determine the authenticity of gold. But, his mind preoccupied with the question, Archimedes saw himself as an analogy. If he displaced a given amount of water, other bodies would displace a certain amount, depending on their density. Once he saw the relationship between himself and gold, he was able to return to the problem of Hieron's crown with a potential solution in mind. It is doubtful that Archimedes was consciously looking for this analogy, but considering all similar situations, even those that only remotely resemble the problem, is one way to facilitate a creative breakthrough.

An especially interesting use of analogy occurred during the second national census of the United States in 1910. The census turned out to be much more complicated than expected and to require more personnel than were available. It looked as though the data could not possibly be collected within the allotted time. In an effort to keep track of information in more streamlined ways than they had done before, the conductors of the poll looked at a simple machine that had been devised to keep track of the various colors of wool in a woven pattern. The machine consisted basically of a flat board with holes through which the various wools were strung. It occurred to the beleaguered conductors that information might be "sorted" in a similar way, and a simple calculating machine was constructed on the same principle. The machine turned out to be one of the forerunners of the modern computer.

The analogy between lines of information and strands of colored wool is quite subtle, but it turned out to be extremely useful. Often, therefore, it is important to pursue analogies carefully. Even though a conscious search for analogous situations may fail, it can have the effect of getting the unconscious mind to take up the search for more subtle analogies, which may eventually lead to a breakthrough.

Adversity

Though few of us enjoy adversity, it may ultimately facilitate creative breakthrough. An old proverb runs, "Necessity is the mother of invention." A problem or need or lack can lead to a significant discovery, as it did for Archimedes. In our own lives, a failure can lead to much greater success. Many of our most important technological developments have resulted from efforts to overcome adversity. Sonar, developed in World War II to detect enemy submarines, is now widely used to find fish and keep small boats off reefs. Another example is radar. Once used only for military purposes, it is now an invaluable aid in air traffic control and the tracking of satellites; it also helps provide early warning of dangerous weather.

What is seen as adversity by one person is often viewed by another as an advantage. The first Spanish explorers to come to the Grand Canyon saw only an impediment, a huge, ugly gash in arid terrain that blocked their way north. They turned away disgruntled, and one wrote in his diary that he doubted anyone would ever return to this unprosperous place. Others, needless to say, have seen matters differently. What the early explorers viewed as a nuisance is now perceived as perhaps the pre-eminent scenic wonder of the world. The canyon still blocks the way north, but it is visited by millions annually, who contribute to a thriving local economy. Personal adversity, too, can carry the seeds of later advantage. There have been failed scientists who became great musicians, and failed musicians who became great scientists. Thousands of students have experienced the desolation of failing in the curriculum they chose upon entering college, only to be forced by the failure into a field in which their true talents could express themselves. When we experience adversity, therefore, we should try to turn it to advantage. Even if this proves difficult, the effort often enables us to reduce the adversity by attacking the problem creatively.

Practice

Practice is as effective in learning to think creatively as it is in developing powers of critical thinking. The difference is that effective practice is harder to get. There are as yet few sets of useful exercises, and it is pointless to try to practice creative thinking by beginning with problems that are too large. Trying to produce a new solution to the problem of unemployment, a new physical theory, or a new philosophical perspective is for the beginner as foolhardy as it would be for a person who knows nothing of mountain climbing to attempt the Matterhorn. Failure is all but inevitable, and the result can be a crushed spirit of adventure. The place to begin is with the small and familiar problems of daily life.

One exercise that can be especially useful as practice is forming and testing hypotheses about factors in your life that may have inhibited your creative thinking. Recognizing these factors will make it easier to offset them. You may find some of them in your education, both past and present. A teacher of a large class may be unable to identify creative thinking, much less encourage it. Because a large mass of subject matter must be covered in a limited time, the teacher is likely to fall into the habit of following standard channels. He or she may discourage the expression of divergent opinions in class discussion because diverging opinions would lead away from standard channels and impede coverage of the required subject matter.

Another inhibiting factor is emphasis on grades. Although some teachers do encourage creative thinking and reward it with higher grades, teachers with large classes often find it impossible to do so. To reward creative thinking, the teacher must decide whether the student's diverging answer is an instance of creative thinking or merely an indication of ignorance, and this takes time. Hence students are likely to conclude that the best way to make high grades is to memorize and regurgitate. Students who would like to do their own thinking often feel that they do not have time to learn the assigned material and think about it too.

Thus students who would like to develop their abilities in creative thinking may experience a conflict in values. In the face of this conflict, some students give up creative thinking and concentrate on grades; others become disinterested in college and drop out.

This conflict is easily resolved. An excellent way to practice creative thinking is to relate the subject matter of different courses such as literature and history, or logic and computer science. In this way you can increase your skill in creative thinking by putting subject matter into new combinations, and you can increase your resources for creative thinking by enlarging your frame of reference. You can improve your grades at the same time. When you relate subject matter from different courses, you make it much easier to remember. You can do better on examinations by increasing your skill in using information you do have to substitute for information you do not have. Furthermore, your courses will become more interesting and therefore easier to study.

When you are working to produce a creative solution to a problem, you should base your procedures on the factors we have discussed. List all the solutions you can think of; then go back to the problem and think of some more. Consider all the analogies to the situation you can find, getting more and more subtle and far-fetched in your parallels. Alternate periods of intense focus with times of incubation, when you get as far as possible from the problem. Take notes when a hazy half-solution occurs to you; the solution may clarify itself later, when you look over the notes. Above all, don't give up.

In practicing creative thinking, it is important not to move to phases 4 and 5 too quickly. Creative ideas are often imperfect in their original form. If you are too quick to apply the tests of critical thinking, you may destroy a potentially good idea before it has time to develop. Copernicus's theory of astronomy had to be refined by Kepler before it succeeded. Knipling's orginal hypothesis was incomplete because it did not include a method of sterilizing the male screwworm flies. If he had been too critical of his hypothesis at this point, he might have abandoned it.

On the other hand, constructive criticism of new ideas is essential to their development. A good rule to practice is to give the imagination freedom to range over the frame of reference unchecked by critical thinking until a new idea is formed. Then this idea should be subjected to constructive criticism designed to improve or refine the idea rather than to determine whether it is useful. A new idea should not be abandoned until after a serious effort has been made to develop it.

It should never be forgotten that creative and critical thinking are two sides of the same coin: one is of little use without the other. If we cannot create new ideas, we are condemned to following the crowd. But if we act on creative ideas without first subjecting them to careful testing and evaluation, we will make mistakes for which circumstances or the crowd, or both, will punish us. Many child psychologists believe that children are naturally creative but that their creative abilities are stifled during childhood when their creative ideas lead them to make mistakes for which they are punished by their parents, by their peers, or by circumstances. The child's trouble comes from lacking the critical skills and knowledge to balance natural creativeness. Critical thinking, if properly applied, need not restrict creativity at all, for it enables creative thinking to proceed safely. The motto of the effective thinker is: be bold and adventurous in forming tentative conclusions; be careful and thorough in criticizing them.

Suggested Supplementary Reading

Arthur Koestler, *The Act of Creation* (New York: Dell, 1977).

James L. Adams, *Conceptual Blockbusting*, 2nd ed. (New York: Norton, 1979).

Exercise 25

Problems 1–4. Answer each problem before reading beyond it.

1. In the problem of the three boxes, what item of relevant information has not been used?

   _____

2. Complete the tabulation below, using *all* relevant information given.

Box Opened First	Consequence (Information Gained)	
WW	Marble white ⊃ this box is	_____
	Marble black ⊃ this box is	_____
WB	Marble white ⊃ this box is	_____
	Marble black ⊃ this box is	_____
BB	Marble white ⊃ this box is	_____
	Marble black ⊃ this box is	_____

3. From which box should you remove the first marble?   _____

4. What is the minimum number of marbles you must examine in order to be sure of the contents of all three boxes?   _____

Problems 5–6. These problems are based on an actual incident that occurred at the library of Stanford University.

   You are a librarian at a major university library. A pipe has broken and several hundred valuable books have been soaked by the water. Until they can be properly dried, you must preserve the books against mildew, which could hopelessly ruin them in a day or so.

5. What analogy is there between your problem and that of preserving fresh vegetables from spoiling?

   _____

6. What should you do to keep the books from being damaged by mildew?

Problems 7–10. The remaining problems concern the case of the *Marine Sulphur Queen* introduced in Exercise 13. In March 1963 the Coast Guard conducted a formal inquiry into the disappearance of the *Queen*. Evidence introduced included the following propositions.

1. The *Queen* was a World War II tanker converted to carry molten sulphur. She had 15,000 tons aboard when she left Beaumont, Texas, on February 2, 1963.

2. Cracks in the hull of the *Queen* were patched in February and October, 1962.

3. Despite the fact that the *Queen* carried three separate radios, the last radio contact with her was on February 3, when she was 230 miles southeast of New Orleans.

4. The *Queen*'s normal course would have taken her through a severe storm.

5. Between February 8 and 11, planes flew for five hundred hours searching Atlantic and Gulf waters for the *Queen*. No trace of her was found.

7. Write two specific hypotheses that explain what happened to the *Queen*.

(1) _____

_____

(2) _____

_____

6. On February 20, an American shrimp boat reported that Cuban planes fired rockets near it when it passed through the Florida straits.

7. On February 20 and 21, flotsam and life preservers from the *Sulphur Queen* were found in waters off Miami, Florida.

8. The report of the Coast Guard included the following sentence: "The condition of the life preserver indicated that it had been used by a crew member and that the crew member subsequently drowned and slipped out of the preserver or was attacked by a predatory fish."

8. Write a specific hypothesis that takes into account all the evidence above and yet leaves the *Queen* still afloat.

_____

_____

9. The conclusion reached by the Coast Guard was that the *Queen* sank off the east coast of Florida after an explosion or structural collapse. On the basis of all the above evidence, rate the reliability of this hypothesis.

_____

10. Suppose that you are an investigator for an insurance company that has insured the lives of many of the *Queen*'s thirty-nine member crew. On March 30, the day before you planned to leave for a vacation in the Bahamas aboard your new boat, you are ordered by your company to investigate the possibility that some of the *Queen*'s crew may still be alive. Write below a plan for investigating this possibility that, if accepted by your company, will turn this seeming adversity into an advantage.

_____

_____

Chapter 26

Need-Directed Thinking

- **Needs and Thinking**
- **Physiological Needs**
- **Needs of the Self-concept**
- **Intellectual Needs**
- **Balanced Satisfaction of Needs**

If human beings were mere thinking machines that ground out accurate answers solely on the basis of data fed into them, the study of effective thinking could be confined to procedures which, when systematically applied, lead to reliable conclusions. But we are not thinking machines. We are biological organisms, fostered and raised within communities with which we interact through our entire lives. In addition, each of us has a unique personal point of view, structured in terms of needs and values that vary from person to person. As a result, the decisions each of us makes are influenced not simply by the information available to us, but also by subjective factors. Any study of procedures of thinking that does not embrace a study of these subjective factors is certainly incomplete and possibly even dangerous. For procedures of thinking are like the devices of technology; they can be put to bad uses as well as good. We have already examined a large array of fal-

lacies that can undermine effective thinking. Fallacious reasoning would be a serious enough problem if it were used only to mislead others. Unfortunately, we sometimes use it also to mislead ourselves.

When we face problems, especially personal ones in which strong feelings are involved, we may easily forget efficient procedures of thinking. When this occurs, we tend to use logic to justify the conclusions we want to reach rather than to reach conclusions that are truly reliable. We are highly sensitive to evidence that supports our favored views and adept at using this evidence to construct arguments which, to us at least, are convincing. We are equally good at ignoring evidence contrary to our pet views and at discounting the evidence we cannot ignore. For example, we may be quick to make the hasty generalizations we want to make and just as quick to apply all the logical tests to generalizations we do not like. Obviously, to engage in such tactics is to be guilty of a failure of objectivity. Used in this way, logic is little more than a facade: its purpose is to justify building false or unreliable propositions into our frame of reference rather than taking the risk of searching for reliable ones. Such failures of objectivity are not infrequent, and they introduce distortions into the personal point of view, thus decreasing our ability to think effectively. In order to avoid these distortions, we must first come to understand the needs that underlie the personal point of view and influence its development. That is the business of this chapter.

Needs and Thinking

It is sometimes claimed that we only seek truth to satisfy our needs. Whether this is so depends on whether one defines the category of needs broadly enough to include intellectual needs as well as practical ones. In any case, it is certainly true that a great deal of thinking is in response to the practical needs that each of us has. A model for the way needs affect us can be found in the way we respond to biological needs. Life is not a static thing but a dynamic, ongoing process. This process has to be kept in constant equilibrium by continual adaptation to changes in the organism and its environment. When physiological processes are disturbed, or when any of the elements necessary for life are inadequately supplied, the organism experiences a need to have its equilibrium restored. The need can manifest itself in a number of ways, including hunger, thirst, pain, or other forms of tension or stress. When a need is experienced, the organism acts to satisfy it. Only when the need has been satisfied and equilibrium approached do the tension and stress to which it gives rise diminish.

What holds true in the realm of the physical applies to other areas as well. If we feel that others do not respect us enough, that loved ones are withholding their affection, or that friends and co-workers are not cooperating with us, we are apt to be saddened, hurt, or angered. These emotions are manifestations of psychological needs we have. Indeed, much of our behavior occurs in response to needs that are at least in part psychological. Even activities that seem trivial and involuntary, such as daydreaming, occur in response to unsatisfied needs. When you find yourself daydreaming in class instead of listening to the professor, you may be responding to a need to solve some problem not connected with your studies or to a need to get away from class because you are doing poorly in the subject or to any number of other needs you may not be conscious of at the time. On some occasions the need is an intellectual one. Perhaps you already know the material the professor is covering and require subject matter that arouses your curiosity.

None of our needs will just "go away." Rather, they must somehow be met or they will continue to make us distressed and unhappy. And for humans at least, the satisfaction of needs is not automatic or instinctive; we have to think to satisfy them. Even the mundane business of getting enough nourishment and sleep can require considerable planning, as any college student facing final examinations knows. We have to budget our time to allow for meals, decide what we will eat, and in many cases learn how to cook it. We have to plan time to rest each day. Over the long term, we must have the financial means to keep ourselves fed, clothed, and sheltered. For most of us this entails making sure we are employed, which may in turn require the acquisition of skills that involve highly sophisticated thinking. In complex societies, then, even satisfying the basic needs of life can be an involved project to which the ability to think effectively is indispensable. We also have to think in order to satisfy psychological needs. From our earliest years we calculate how to win our parents' approval, gain the friendship of others, and secure a satisfying self-concept. The project of satisfying psychological needs continues throughout our lives, and we are often preoccupied with it. Books about how to attract members of the opposite sex and how to secure positions of social prestige and influence have been with us for a long time. In recent years, however, there has been an explosion of "self-help" books that promise to assist us in satisfying our every psychological need. They are found on virtually every bookrack we pass, a fact that testifies to the amount of thinking many of us devote to understanding and meeting our psychological needs.

In order to understand how needs affect our thinking, we must first have some understanding of what our needs are. For the sake of convenience, we may divide needs into three categories: physical, psychological, and intellectual. These categories are, of course, closely interrelated. A need in one category may give rise to a need in another, and the same activity on our part is often directed at satisfying needs in all three of these categories at once. Thus, though we will discuss the categories separately, we should remember that they are actually not nearly as distinct as they may seem.

Physiological Needs

Our most fundamental needs—the first of which we are aware and among the first that must be satisfied—stem from our nature as biological animals and have to do with the maintenance of physiological equilibrium. This category includes: (1) the maintenance of body chemistry by providing a constant supply of air, water, and suitable food, by eliminating waste materials, and by keeping body temperature within a narrow range; (2) response to sex drives; (3) the avoidance of pain; (4) protection from external danger; (5) activity and rest, in proper balance.

Physical needs influence thinking in obvious ways. Students find it increasingly difficult to keep their minds on what the professor is saying when the classroom gets too warm, when they become thirsty, or when lunch time approaches. The idea of eating raw fish would normally be repulsive, but if we were stranded long enough on a life raft without food, we would come to regard raw fish with the same enthusiasm most of us have for T-bone steak. After spending a day in strenuous activity, we yearn for rest, but after enough rest, we yearn for activity. You would probably be less inclined to turn to the job of cleaning your room after washing your car than after doing your homework.

At times we ignore physical needs in order to satisfy others, as when an athlete endures the pain of training in an effort to achieve the satisfaction of excelling in a sport. By and large, however, physical needs tend to take primacy over others. When physical needs are not met, especially for a sustained period, all other needs tend to be subordinated in the attempt to meet them. For the homeless, for example, life may become a search for food and shelter in which everything encountered is evaluated in terms of its potential to satisfy these needs. One sociologist found that in the United States it was often harder to find a place to sleep than to find food; thus the homeless spend their days searching for a means of sleeping that night in as little discomfort and personal danger as possible.

Needs of the Self-concept

When a child emerges from its mother's womb, it is not first fed, or cleaned up, or properly dressed. It is first held. This phenomenon illustrates both the close relationship between physical and psychological needs and the fact that we have psychological needs from the time we first enter the world. A newborn baby is not just cold but also upset, and its comfort is from the beginning an emotional matter as well as a physical one. Physical and psychological needs remain intimately associated through the first months of life. To be held and fed satisfies the need for affection as well as for nourishment, and infants do not immediately distinguish the two. They will, at least for short periods, be calmed by affection when they are hungry and by food when they are in need of attention. But the distinction is soon learned. By the age of eighteen months, children know when they want food and when they want to be played with and do not confuse the two. Along the way, a lot has happened. The child has learned to distinguish the objects and persons in his or her environment and to understand some of their characteristics and behavior. He or she has developed likes and dislikes, based on experiences of what satisfies or frustrates wants, and so has the beginnings of a system of values. Finally, the child has begun to develop a self-concept, which will affect his or her decisions from this time on. Beginning at this age if not before, a large number of

our psychological needs can be understood to center on the development and maintenance of a satisfactory self-concept.

As we saw in Chapter 1, the self-concept is the picture each of us has of the kind of person he or she is. Much of the self-concept is made up of information about ourselves, our personal histories, projects, abilities, and so on. But the most important feature of the self-concept is that it is heavily laden with the value judgments we make about ourselves. Most of the information in it is bound up with our assessments of our own worth or lack of it. Early in life, our evaluations of ourselves are based primarily on how others react to us. If Algernon Smythe plays quietly with his toys and eats all his dinner, he is "good little Al." But if he satisfies his hunger by eating the dog's food, or his curiosity by pouring his grape juice into the fish tank, he is "bad Al! naughty!" As we develop, however, the picture becomes far more complicated. Our sense of personal worth is dependent on our satisfying a complex set of needs, not all of which impel us in the same direction. Some of the needs of the self-concept reflect our dependence on the people around us, while others manifest a drive to be independent and self-sufficient. Still other needs relate strategies for dealing with the conflicts to which needs in the first two groups give rise.

Affection. Our psychological dependence on others is first manifested in the need for affection, which exists in children from birth. In early childhood, the need for affection is focused on our parents, on whom we depend for the satisfaction of most of our other needs. It is primarily from our parents' reaction to us that we form our initial conceptions of our worth. As we develop, the focus of this need broadens to include others. But its strength is undiminished. In fact, it seems that we can adequately sense our own value only through the high value placed on us by another's affection. The need for the deep affection of at least one other person continues throughout life.

The persons whose affections we crave most strongly are those toward whom we feel affection. Thus we strive to please our parents, to charm members of the opposite sex whom we find attractive, and to make friends with people we like. When the need for affection is frustrated, we tend first to languish and then to become hostile. Infants who receive little or no affection in the first months of life tend to be listless and dispirited; if the deprivation persists, they may, in later years, be cold, aloof, and suspicious, or even downright sociopathic. A similar situation holds with sexual relationships. An infatuated person who finds that his or her overtures of friendship elicit little or no response may languish and experience self-doubt. Still worse is the situation where efforts to establish friendship are rebuffed or where an initially favorable reaction is followed by rejection. In this sort of case we tend to feel betrayed and to react accordingly. The person to whom we were once attracted we may now find distinctly unattractive. The complimentary remarks and positive judgements we used to make may be replaced by hostile criticism. Almost nothing wounds us more deeply than having our affection rejected, and betrayal is the surest recipe for turning love into hate.

Approval. Just as a child needs parental affection, so he or she needs to feel secure in their approval. Indeed, to children the two are probably much the same, since parents tend to demonstrate approval of their children's behavior by showing affection and to withhold affection when they disapprove of their behavior. But affection and approval are not the same thing, for we can have affection for people of whom we disapprove and approve of people for whom we feel little or no affection. Affection is an emotional attachment; approval occurs when one person judges another to be worthy of respect or admiration. Each of us needs parental approval during childhood, for our sense of our own worthiness depends heavily on our early perceptions of parental attitudes. In time the need for approval spreads from parents to playmates and schoolmates, and eventually to friends, neighbors, and associates. This need continues to influence behavior and thinking in a marked way all through life.

As with affection, we tend to seek most the approval of those of whom we ourselves most approve. Students who feel they are studying under the best professor on campus will often spend long hours on term papers and projects, even if it means neglecting other courses. The same students, in a course in which they feel the professor is incompetent, may themselves do incompetent work even if they find the subject interesting. Also, it is possible to deceive ourselves as to how much approval we feel toward others. If you profess to hold someone in little regard, yet find yourself trying to impress him or her, it is worth re-examining your evaluation of that person. Right or wrong, it is probably a lot higher than you think.

Individuals whose need for approval is unsatisfied tend to seek attention. In fact, they will do so even if, paradoxically, the kind of attention they are getting indicates disapproval rather than approval. The reason is that even disapproval is better than nothing. We feel more important if we are disapproved of than if we are ignored, for even disapproval tends to demonstrate that we are a force to be contended with. For this reason children who cannot get the attention of their parents in any other way may misbehave until they are punished. For though the punishment indicates disapproval, it is a form of attention. Similarly, adults will sometimes seek the spotlight even though they have to make fools of themselves to do so.

Group Acceptance. An important consequence of the need for approval is our need for group acceptance. Human beings function not just as individuals but as members of various social units. Others are more likely to approve of us if we are accepted in groups to which they belong, and our own sense of identity is enhanced if we feel accepted in the social groups to which we aspire. Thus it becomes important to us to achieve acceptance in our family, school, profession, and neighborhood. Children have trouble satisfying this need when they are rejected or kept on the fringe of "popular" school groups. The problem is especially common with children who are frequently moved from one school to another. Before they can win acceptance in any group at all, they must start over in a new one. As a result they may come to feel that they are inferior in some important way. Many first-year students in college who made fine academic records in high school do less well in their college studies because they are too busy getting accepted by the "right" groups.

Our needs for approval and group acceptance constitute important impulses toward conformity. Like ourselves, other individuals tend to disapprove of behavior too different from their own. Accordingly, gaining approval and group acceptance often requires tailoring our behavior and ideas to the standards of others. At times, this can happen quite subconsciously. If you attend college in an area of the country more conservative than that in which

you grew up, you may well find that your views become more conservative with time. Alternatively, if you are well established in a liberal group, you may find yourself disapproving of conservatives and being more or less uncommunicative toward them. Tendencies of this kind appear lamentable, but they are perfectly human and they have a brighter side. If you find friends and associates who value objectivity and originality, you will be encouraged, even if you are unaware of it, to steer a course between the various extremist options that confront you.

Autonomy. The three needs discussed so far are expressions of our dependence on others, for their satisfaction depends ultimately on how others respond to us. We can do much to encourage others to give us affection and approval, but we cannot force them to do so. The need for autonomy is of quite a different kind. Rather than expressing dependence on others, it is a need to rise above that dependence and to establish ourselves as self-sufficient individuals, unique in our own right and, as far as possible, in control of our own destinies. Children display this need when they insist on climbing into their high chairs rather than being lifted or on walking through shopping malls and across intersections without holding anyone's hand. The need for autonomy is a powerful force. Even two-year-olds don't want to be "babies."

Failure in almost any enterprise is apt to frustrate our need for autonomy. Students who are failing in their studies are likely to be unhappy not just because they are jeopardizing career goals and spending effort with no reward, but also because their sense of autonomy is suffering. They are not just failing their courses; they are also failing to demonstrate mastery over their own situation.

The need for autonomy is also likely to assert itself when our needs for affection and approval go unsatisfied. A spurned suitor says, "I never needed her anyway," and students who fail to gain acceptance into fraternities, sororities, or other social groups may console themselves by pointing to the independent path they will be taking. Such protestations may sound pretty hollow, especially when first made, but they do point up the fact that what fails to satisfy one psychological need may often satisfy an opposite one.

Achievement. Closely related to the need for autonomy is our need for achievement. We demonstrate mastery over our situation through our accomplishments, such as the production of goods and services or the acquisition of knowledge or skills. To be able to build a house, repair a car, or teach a third-grade class enhances our self-concept not just because it helps gain the approval of others, but because it makes us feel productive and independent. The same applies to the achievements of learning: to gain an intellectual grip on the world is in itself an important accomplishment, for we are intellectual as well as physical beings, and it paves the way for further achievements in which knowledge is applied to the satisfaction of other needs.

The achievements we value most vary with our age, culture, and social circumstances. Children must master the skill of walking and learn a language. Adults have a greater variety of goals from which to choose and will aim at different achievements depending on their circumstances. Among the Manus of New Guinea, who live in huts built on stilts in shallow lagoons and wrest their living mainly from the sea, there is a high premium on mastering the arts of swimming, canoeing, and fishing. In the environment of an American college, on the other hand, one can do quite well without any of these accomplishments; what matter are academic success, skill in organized athletics, leadership abilities, and so on. Thus the achievements we value are in part socially determined. Another important factor is our own native abilities. We are inclined to value most those achievements that come most naturally to us and in which our natural talents are displayed to best advantage. Thus people of high intellectual talent tend to consider achievements in learning and the arts to be most important; those of a more practical bent prefer technological achievement.

It should be apparent that there is a tension between our needs for autonomy and achievement and our needs for affection, approval, and group acceptance. Full autonomy, if it could be achieved, would require that we be completely free of dependence on others. This would mean not only meeting our physical needs without others' support, but also not depending on others psychologically. However, to the extent that we require the affection and approval of others—and all of us require both—we cannot be complete masters of our situation and so cannot be fully autonomous. This is true because, first of all, we cannot force others to love or approve of us. Rather, these needs can be satisfied only by our submitting ourselves to others for their evaluation, an act which in itself runs counter to our need for self-sufficiency. Moreover, efforts to make ourselves acceptable to others usually involve giving up some autonomy. We make ourselves acceptable by conforming to the demands of others and acting in ways calculated to satisfy them rather than us. Life frequently presents us with situations where to satisfy our needs for affection and approval we must deny our need for autonomy, and vice versa. Some students, for instance, choose a college curriculum out of need for parental or social approval and not because it suits their own abilities and career preferences. Another example is the student who, because he fears the disapproval of parents and professors, works hard at his studies rather than at becoming what he would like to be—namely, the best pocket billiards player on campus. Obviously, it is not always clear how these conflicts should be resolved. Certain other psychological needs may be viewed as arising from the conflict between our needs for affection and approval on the one hand, and for autonomy and achievement on the other.

Prestige. The conflict can be lessened if others admire and approve of us because of our achievements. The need for prestige, which we all have, is a need for this kind of approval. When we gain such approval, the conflict between dependence and autonomy is reduced because the two are partly harmonized: we receive approval for the very accomplishments that contribute to our autonomy. Thus the prestige of a college degree derives from the fact that the degree signifies both a higher level of learning and competence and the increased autonomy that they bring. We should not forget, however, that in our need for prestige our dependence on others is actually reasserting itself. In seeking prestige, we often conform to standards that do not suit us and aspire to tastes we do not have. Thus we have the miserable premed student who could be making a fortune selling hardware, the country club golfer who would rather be bowling, the bored but loyal concert goer who can't tell Haydn from Bartok, and the professed gourmet who sends you to the worst restaurant in town.

People in whom the need for prestige is strong but unsatisfied may react in a number of ways, many of them counterproductive. They may become overly demanding, and seek special consideration from employers and others in positions of influence. They may at times downgrade the accomplishments of others, or try to surround themselves with friends and colleagues whose accomplishments are few, thus becoming a big frog in a little pond. At the same time, however, they may be deeply anxious to please and willing to carry far more than their fair burden of work. Their problem is a difficult one because, like affection and approval, prestige depends on evaluation by others. It cannot be forced, and any attempt to do so is likely to result in less prestige rather than more. In the end, seeking prestige is not a very useful way of bridging the gap between dependence and autonomy.

Expanding the Self-concept. A better strategy is to expand the self-concept, which we can do in two ways. One is to raise the standards we set for ourselves. The self-concept, like the process of biological adaptation, is dynamic rather than static. We set up an ideal self-concept and try to make the real one match it. Then, as the real approaches the ideal, we tend to raise the ideal. Thus a self-concept that is satisfactory today will not be so tomorrow unless new and higher goals have been set and striven for. The need for this sort of growth is part of the force that drives us ceaselessly to achieve something better— better jobs, better housing, better clothes, better social relationships. The standards by which we measured our worth yesterday are too low today; hence we raise them and then strive to meet the higher standards. In this way we are less at the mercy of others in gaining approval. For the higher our standards, the more likely others are to approve and the more likely we are to value ourselves independently of their judgment.

But raising our standards is not enough; we must also expand the area of the self-concept. If the self-concept is limited strictly to one's own interests, the opportunities for enhancement are similarly limited. Moreover, when we limit our interests in this way, we tend to become more and more ingrown. Like a small town cut off from the outside world, we shrink and shrivel instead of growing and become mired in suspicion and petty eccentricity. We are called selfish, and others react accordingly by withdrawing approval and affection. On the other hand, when we expand our interests to include those of others, we become like a town at a busy commercial crossroads, which grows and prospers through contact with the outside. We become outward-looking and are described and reacted to by others as unselfish. Then our sense of personal worth gains from their approval.

Expanding the area of the self-concept is accomplished by **identification**, that is, by looking at ourselves as though we were in the place of others and sharing their feelings and needs, successes and failures. We identify with the characters of movies and plays when we feel sorrow over their sufferings and exult in their triumphs. We also identify with others in real life, and doing so is an important means of personal growth. Children identify strongly with their parents and hence try to do things their parents would do or would approve of doing. This identification can remain strong throughout life and is one of the reasons children often follow in their parents' career footsteps or try to accomplish goals their parents had but were unable to accomplish. We also identify with friends and associates, members of our social group, our spouses, and our own children. When we do so, our self-concept expands to include theirs: their needs become our own, and when they succeed or fail, we do so as well.

Expanding the area of self-concept is a strategy without equal for bridging the gulf between dependence and autonomy. This is because expanding the self-concept makes the well-being of others a part of our own well-being. Thus our sense of autonomy no longer depends on pursuing narrowly selfish goals; rather, it becomes possible to achieve autonomy in part by furthering the success of others. At the same time, we are less dependent on others for strictly personal approval, for if they are accepted, we are accepted. Thus a parent takes pride in a child's good grades and beams at his or her graduation. Friends rejoice in each other's success, and students and alumni say "we won" when all they did was sit in the stands and yell. Obviously, the process of identification increases immeasurably our opportunities for self-enhancement and offers ways of achieving prestige that do not exclude other people. It might seem that it also would increase our risk of suffering from injury. But this does not seem to happen. People with an expanded self-concept are better able to stand disappointment or injury to what they love. It is those with a shriveled self-concept who run the greatest risk—perhaps because they have so little they can ill afford to lose any of it.

Service to Others. The need to expand the area of the self-concept and the need to give service to others are reciprocally related. Obviously, if we expand the self-concept to include others, we will want to act in ways that satisfy their needs and help them to achieve their goals. But at the same time acting in these ways helps expand the self-concept because by making service to others our goal we associate their well-being with our own. Thus we have the father who reluctantly agrees to help coach his son's little league team, only to become so involved in boys' sports that they turn into the consuming interest of his life. You may well remember occasions in your own life when out of a sense of duty you took on some seemingly onerous task of service to others, only to find that you enjoyed it immensely. It is not only more blessed to give than to receive, but also more enhancing to the self-concept. Thus we need to give approval as well as receive it, to improve the world as well as to profit from it, to respect and protect the rights of others as well as to receive protection. By these means we strengthen our security in feeling that we are valuable and worthy members of our society.

Conformity to Conscience. Another need that manifests a way of coming to grips with the tension between autonomy and dependence is the need for conformity to conscience. **Conscience** may be defined as the sense each of us has of the moral value or disvalue of our own conduct. It is the vehicle through which our system of values is brought to bear on our own behavior. During our formative years, conscience develops mostly through the incorporation into our thinking of values we received from others. Later, it may assume a more individualistic character, for conscience is not a static collection of "shoulds" and "should nots." It is a dynamic critical faculty that grows and changes as we do. Eventually, it comes to reflect the judgments we reach as individuals about the value of persons, things, and actions. But whether the values embedded in conscience are received or are products of individual thought, they become very much our own once they are adopted, and are seldom easily dislodged. Conscience plays two important roles in

our thinking. First, as we shall see more fully below, the values that make up our conscience help us decide between conflicting needs and conflicting ways of satisfying them. Conscience makes us more aware of when a particular course of action will either further or violate the well-being of ourselves or others and hence is an aid to effective decision making in practical situations. Second, conscience acts as a moral judge of our behavior. When we do something we consider wrong, we feel guilty and unworthy. On the other hand, when we do something we consider right, we feel valuable and deserving of praise. The combination of these reactions lessens the tension between our needs for autonomy and achievement on the one hand, and affection and approval on the other. In order to avoid guilt, we will be inclined to choose means to autonomy that accord with the well-being of others as well as our own. At the same time, our dependence on others is lessened, for even if our actions do not elicit their respect and approval, we will have the respect and approval of our conscience.

The voice of conscience is strong, and it is impossible to maintain a satisfactory self-concept without following it reasonably well. The punishments society is able to inflict on us when we violate accepted standards of behavior are seldom more effective than the punishment we inflict on ourselves when we violate our own standards. The disapproval of others is damaging only if we have respect for them and it can be escaped completely if our deeds go unnoticed. Not so with our own disapproval. Self-disapproval is always damaging, and although we can try to ignore or rationalize feelings of guilt, we cannot escape them. We can only drive them into our subconscious mind, where they will become even more damaging. Thus the need to satisfy our consciences is strong, and much of the thought that goes into decision making is aimed at choosing courses of action that accord with what we understand to be proper values.

Intellectual Needs

Not all of our psychological needs relate directly to the maintenance of a strong and viable self-concept. Besides the needs of the self-concept, we have **intellectual needs**—needs that manifest the fact that we are rational, thinking beings. These needs are, of course, related to those we have already discussed, for by satisfying our intellectual needs, we often put ourselves in a better position to satisfy physiological needs and needs of the self-concept. But intellectual needs also have independent standing, for they are manifestations of what distinguishes us most from other beings: our rationality. In this respect, there is a parallel between physical and mental activity. We require physical exercise not just because it strengthens the body for work, but because it heightens our general sense of well-being and fulfillment. The same is true of exercising our mental capacities: it is important not just for solving practical problems and preparing us for life, but because of the satisfaction we achieve simply by using our minds. Intellectual needs may be understood to fall under three major headings: the need for knowledge, the need for an effective value system, and the need for beauty. As with the needs we have already discussed, however, we must remember that these categories are closely related, and any attempt to separate them is at least partly artificial.

Knowledge. All human beings are infected with an intense curiosity about what is, a curiosity that distinguishes us from the lower animals. The most striking and uniquely human dimension of this curiosity is our concern about metaphysical issues having to do with the origin of the universe, our place in it, and our ultimate destiny. On a less profound level, we need to know how the universe functions and to form causal principles about the things in our experience that will explain and give order to the bewildering array of phenomena surrounding us every moment of our lives. And, of course, we need to know about the objects and persons that make up our immediate environment. We want to understand how our friends think, how the devices of technology work, even such mundane facts as how our neighborhood is laid out and how our clothes are made. We find out about most simpler things when we are young, and then we take them for granted. We forget about the intense fascination we experienced as children even in learning our way around our rooms.

The need to know can be satisfied only by truth, and this need is strong enough in many people to mitigate the effects of other needs on thinking. Some people will go loveless or hungry to find things out, just for the sake of knowing them. Many a college student makes large personal sacrifices in order to attain an education. Even people who appear to have personal gain as their first priority in life will often harbor a fascination for history, politics, or some branch of science. The importance of this phenomenon may go unrecognized because we tend to think of the search for knowledge as something that goes on only in colleges and universities. In fact, it goes on wherever anyone picks up a newspaper, rummages through old family photographs, or opens the hood of a new car. It is far from true, however, that our need for knowledge always overrides other needs; on the contrary, it can be diminished or even submerged by them. People who suffered personal deprivation in childhood may suppress natural curiosity in a drive to achieve wealth. Scientists in whom the need for prestige is a powerful force have at times knowingly ignored evidence against their theories or concocted evidence in favor of them. In other cases, evidence against views to which our self-concepts are tied may simply be missed or be seen but not understood. The need to know is, however, the foundation of pure science and of our efforts to gain an intellectual grip on the world and the circumstances with which it confronts us. Thus it is important that we be able to recognize when other needs are impeding the satisfaction of our need to know and that we learn to counteract them.

By satisfying our need to know, we develop resources to satisfy other needs as well. The scientist studying the DNA structure of viruses may contribute to the development of a cure for some form of cancer, a cure that will both benefit others and make the scientist rich and famous. Similarly, a successful college student increases his or her ability to satisfy needs for prestige and social acceptance, as well as the physiological and other needs of the family he or she may eventually have. But knowledge is not always sought as a means to these further ends. In many cases, practicing scientists are simply trying to understand our world. Regardless of its practical applications, the scientist is apt to view his or her work as "basic research," which is simply an effort to expand our knowledge. The scientist's motivation is the the same as that of a child who puts aside toys or candy to watch the garbage collectors dump the cans into the immense machine on wheels. Intellectual fascination also plays an important role in the lives of most college students. Even in the most practically oriented curriculum, it is doubtful that the average student could withstand the labor and frustrations of four or more years of study simply on the promise of a more comfortable life sometime in the future. Experienced teachers know that the question, "What is this stuff good for anyway?" a question often heard in college classrooms, is usually not a manifestation of any special practical concern on the student's part. Rather, it is nearly always a manifestation of frustration at having studied some body of material and failed to understand it. When we understand, the satisfaction of our need to know is usually enough to keep us going, and we let the practical applications take care of themselves.

Values. As we have seen throughout this book, the culmination of many processes of thinking is a decision, usually to take some practical action or other. In order to make decisions, we must have values. This is so for two reasons. First, when we make a decision, we feel that the action we will take is up to us, in the sense that it is not automatically determined by our needs and the situation in which we find ourselves. We are not inanimate objects that react to forces exerted upon them in blind and unthinking ways. Rather, we make **choices** as to how we will respond to the stimuli that affect us. At the same time, however, we do not wish to make **arbitrary** choices—choices that have no rational foundation and could just as easily and reasonably have gone the other way. If we choose to study rather than go out socially, to enter one profession instead of another, or to live in the South rather than the North, we want to have a good reason for our choice. Reasons for choices are provided by our values. We choose to study because we think it is more important, to enter a certain career because we value the accomplishments it offers more highly than others, and so on. When we make such choices, we believe that we have other options but that our choices are the best ones, that is, the most valuable ones, and in this way our actions are made rational rather than arbitrary.

The second reason that we need values is related to the first. We have already seen that we are subject to a complex and bewildering array of needs, and these needs inevitably compete against one another. If our physiological needs are not at least minimally satisfied, they will prevent us from satisfying any others. All of us struggle to balance our needs for acceptance and autonomy, and all of us look for time to satisfy intellectual needs as well. The only way to deal effectively with the many needs that confront us is to establish a hierarchy among them. That is, we must determine which needs we will give priority and how the priority may have to vary depending on the situation. This is what values are for. By developing a system of values, we determine the extent to which we will seek physical comfort and wealth, the extent to which we will seek acceptance, the extent to which we will seek knowledge. When our needs conflict—for example, when our need for success tempts us to ignore our loved ones' needs for affection—our system of values helps us settle the conflict. Indeed, it is our system of values that gives our lives meaning, purpose, and direction. Without it, our activities would be chaotic and contradictory, and our lives without systematic goals. Thinking itself would be without any purpose except to describe the world, for we would be without the means of finding our way through life in an orderly fashion.

An adequate system of values is, then, a vital need for all of us since it enables us to make particular decisions in a rational way and to blend all our decisions into a unified and coherent pattern of life. Moreover, in developing a system of values, each of us forms his or her own conscience. We thus put ourselves in a position to satisfy the important need of conformity to conscience and thereby enhance our self-concept. Our system of values has much to do with the kind of person each of us is and manifests itself in nearly all our actions. That is why our value system is a major component in our personal point of view. The development of a sensitive and finely tuned system of values is a lifelong enterprise; we shall have more to say about it in the next chapter.

Beauty. Finally, each of us has a need for beauty—not so much to possess it as to experience it and, at least on some occasions, to create it. This need appears early in children, and parents instinctively provide for it with crayons and coloring books, bedtime stories, and the like. It is a need that stays with us throughout our lives—a fact that is often overlooked because we tend to associate beauty only with the fine arts. But the need for beauty extends to nearly every phase of our lives: we surround our homes with flowers, admire the lines of our new car, put posters and prints on our walls, and drive others crazy with our stereos. Beauty is especially associated with leisure. The mountains of Colorado are generally regarded as a prime vacation spot because when people seek rest and refreshment, they treat beauty as an important—perhaps the most important—component of the experience they wish to have. And, of course, many people spend much of their leisure time reading novels, enjoying concerts, plays or films, or participating in artistic activities themselves. Beauty affects thinking in a number of ways: it increases our sense of order, provides a means of emotional expression, broadens our experience, and stimulates our own creativity. We can, of course, live without beauty, but not very well. People whose lives lack the experience of beauty tend to be dull, unimaginative, and resentful of their environment. In fact, to live in ugly surroundings can be, and often is, damaging to the self-concept, for we tend to view our environment as expressing our selves. The need for beauty is, then, a deeply pervasive force in our lives, a force whose impact is often greatly underestimated.

Balanced Satisfaction of Needs

We have spoken in this chapter of a large number of needs, both physiological and psychological. There is virtually no human activity that cannot be viewed as aimed at satisfying some need, and the complex interrelations and tensions among our needs make the project of satisfying them difficult indeed. In order to have a happy and fulfilling life, we have to satisfy at least a good many of our needs. Attention to a few at the expense of all the others will not work. At times, of course, certain of our needs may predominate. Physiological needs are the most fundamental because unless they are satisfied at least in a minimal way we die. The paramount need of someone who is drowning is for air—he or she has no time to be concerned with matters of the intellect or of self-enhancement. It would be a mistake, however, to think that physiological needs dominate most people's thinking. On the contrary, most of us are fortunate enough to have worked out fairly reliable

ways of satisfying our physiological needs. Thus, even if we have to work hard earning a living, our minds are free a good deal of the time to work on satisfying psychological needs.

Among psychological needs, the needs of the self-concept are closest to our hearts. Satisfying these needs adequately requires a lot of effective thinking. As we have seen, the needs of the self-concept tend to conflict with one another, and so much careful thought is required to bring them into harmony. This problem is compounded by a second difficulty—namely, that few of us understand ourselves well enough to know in every case the needs that are affecting us. In response to tension or frustration, we may try to satisfy the wrong need, thereby making the problem worse. For example, in our highly competitive culture, it is possible to strive so hard for success that we neglect family and friends. When our unsatisfied need for affection manifests itself in feelings of frustration and lack of fulfillment, we may fail to realize the true cause and relieve our sense of inadequacy temporarily by striving even harder for success. In some cases, the true cause of our unhappiness goes unrecognized until serious harm has occurred. We also react to threats to future satisfaction of our needs. For example, most people experience anxiety when a new supervisor takes over in their place of employment. If they are unable to please the new boss, a great many of their needs could go unsatisfied. The same thing can occur when students sign up for a course and fail to get the teacher they expected. When we find ourselves uneasy or unhappy without knowing why, an unsatisfied need or a threat to the future satisfaction of some need may be the cause. The procedures of effective thinking are useful both in identifying the need or the threat and in finding a way to satisfy the need or deal with the threat.

Of all our needs, however, intellectual needs are the most useful and fulfilling ones to satisfy, for then we enrich our personal point of view, which is both fulfilling in itself and makes us better able to deal with our other needs in an informed and effective way. By satisfying our need for knowledge, we develop a frame of reference, which provides the factual information we must have in order to live. By satisfying our need for a system of values, we develop a hierarchy for the satisfaction of needs and thus can satisfy them in a conscientious and coherent way. The information and values that we develop with regard to ourselves constitute our self-concept, which plays a role in all we do. Thus the three main components of the personal point of view are developed precisely by satisfying our intellectual needs. And since the personal point of view is something without which we could not think at all, it is the first prerequisite for effective thinking and decision making. We shall have more to say about the development of the personal point of view in the next chapter.

Exercise 26

Problems 1–5. Use the key list below to identify the need or needs you think are most likely to be manifesting themselves in the following situations. Since any attempt to interpret the motives of others must be considered speculative, answers may vary, but you should be ready to explain your choices.

Key List

1. Affection	7. Expanding the self-concept
2. Approval	8. Service to others
3. Group acceptance	9. Conformity to conscience
4. Autonomy	10. Knowledge
5. Achievement	11. Values
6. Prestige	12. Beauty

1. Anne Appleton spends whatever time she can listening to classical music, although none of her friends enjoys this type of music and, in fact, she has never known a friend or had a family member who did.

   _____

2. Betty Baker is a Phi Beta Kappa, cocaptain of the women's softball team, and president of a campus service organization. She is highly respected as an able and conscientious person but has no intimate friends. To the surprise of everyone, she eloped with the driver of a pizza truck.

   _____

3. Charley Carter had the choice of acting behind the scenes and being the most powerful student on the campus or being elected to a high office in which he would be a figurehead. He chose the latter.

   _____

4. Della Dakin chose to work her way through Wysacki rather than live with her parents and attend a college near home.

   _____

5. Ed Easterton was working hard to win a national contest for the best original essay in political science, the rules of which prohibited the use of any quotations. While searching for material, he found a brilliant article in an obscure foreign journal. He appropriated the best passages from the article by simply leaving off the quotation marks.

   _____

6. Frank Flanagan, in the same situation, decided that it would be better to present some of the ideas in the article in his own words, giving credit to the author in a footnote.

   _____

7. Gail Grangerford was studying for her math test when she read that Pythagoras stated that the odd numbers were male and the even numbers female. She abandoned her studying to find out why.

_____

8. Harriet Huang declined to run for president of the student body, even though she would almost certainly have won, because she wanted to devote her time to her premedical studies.

_____

9. After Huang declined to run, Ira Ireland also declined, because he was too busy conducting the campus drive for funds for research on the causes of leukemia.

_____

10. Janice Jones realized that she could not both associate with her friends and win the election for freshman senator. She values her friends highly, so she decided to forget about the election.

_____

11. Karl King writes a sports column for the campus newspaper. The student body was up in arms over an incident occurring in the homecoming game in which players of the rival school had repeatedly piled on the star quarterback. King thought it would be better to forget the matter, but in his column he advocated breaking off athletic relations with the rival school.

_____

12. Lynn Lee, in applying for membership in a social club, wrote down that she spends her Sunday afternoon "visiting with friends," instead of revealing that she actually visits the art museum.

_____

13. Mort Murray is short of cash, but he returned the extra $10 the supermarket checker accidentally gave him.

_____

14. Neil Narrow has a good grade-point average, but he never takes a course unless he has been assured by friends that the course is easy.

_____

15. Olivia Olesky is in a difficult curriculum in engineering and has only one free elective to take in her senior year. She signs up for a course in ethics for professionals.

_____

16. Consider a major decision you have made recently, and, using the key list, identify the needs you were meeting in taking that action. Rank the needs in their order of importance. How successful was your action in meeting these needs?

Chapter 27

The Personal Point Of View

- **The Organization of Experience**
- **Value Systems**
- **The Importance of Culture**
- **The Individual Character of Thinking**

Of all newborn creatures, human infants have the most complex set of needs to be met and are least able to meet them without the ministrations of others. From our earliest days, we must learn to get along in a vastly complicated material and social universe. In the first weeks of life, our drives are almost completely instinctive and directed at satisfying basic physiological needs, along with the primitive need for affection and love. Our early behavior is likewise relatively simple. As newborn infants, about all we can do when hungry or uncomfortable is squirm and squall until someone comes to relieve the stress.

But with our first breath in this new universe, we begin to interact with the surrounding physical and social environment and to learn new, more complex methods of satisfying needs. Gradually, through trial and error, we achieve more and more control over our bodies and environment, learning to call others, roll over, sit up, and so on. In so doing, we start

to develop a personal point of view: a fund of understanding about the world and primitive values about how best to get on in it.

The Organization of Experience

We begin organizing our experiences as soon as we are born, by learning to discriminate objects, discern the footsteps of others, and so forth. By so doing, we develop the beginnings of a frame of reference. What enables this frame of reference to grow by leaps and bounds, however, is our learning to use language. To be sure, we could not use words as meaningful symbols unless we already had at least a fumbling grasp of the things to which they refer. To a child with no understanding whatever of what a book, a bird, or a bottle is, these words can have no useful meaning. All the same, learning language is an indispensable aid to developing our frame of reference since, except for proper names, many of the terms in language signify abstract concepts that apply to more than one situation. Learning language therefore helps us to think abstractly and thus extend our experiences to new and untested situations. A child who has been fed food that is too hot has had an unpleasant experience and may hesitate to eat the same food again. However, once the child has learned that the word for this unpleasant experience is "hot," he or she may learn without direct experience that the stove is "hot," and so come to associate the stove with hotness in general. The child can then be suitably cautious with other food that comes from the stove.

In learning language we also learn concepts, many of which have existed in our culture for countless generations and have withstood the test of time. There is no word in any language that combines just pears, pilots, and pitchblende into one category, and for a very good reason: such a category would be totally useless. But children do not know this, nor do they understand in any systematic way what concepts can be used to form reliable general statements and causal principles. By learning language, they learn useful categories from others and are able to avoid confusion and frustration. Thus we do not teach our children to holler "Parent!" when they want a particular parent's attention, but rather to call "Mommy!" or "Daddy!" In this way, they are more apt to achieve success in getting the attention they want. If this sort of point seems trivial, we should remember the problem, alluded to in Chapter 14, of the early chemists who thought water was an element and metals were compounds. Their system of categories was so askew

that they were unable to understand the phenomena of chemistry in useful ways. Unlike today's children, they had no one to teach them the correct categories and had to go through the long and difficult process of developing the right ones on their own.

Finally, learning language helps us extend our frame of reference because once we have the words in hand to express some concepts, we are able to learn others by the use of definitions. Thus we become possessed of more and more numerous and sophisticated categories by means of which to order our experience, and are able to develop our frame of reference more deeply and thoroughly.

We use concepts to develop our frame of reference by connecting them with one another in propositions which we understand to express truths about the world. Many of these propositions are simple descriptive statements about the things in our experience. Others are causal judgments about single cases, such as Algernon Smythe's judgment that the bump on his head was caused by running into a particular piece of furniture. It is when we get to the level of general statements, however, that the propositions making up our frame of reference become most useful. For example, experience in getting along with a particular person is useless for getting along with others unless we generalize from it in some way. You would probably have considerable trouble in doing your work to the satisfaction of your college professors unless you had already drawn certain general conclusions from your experience with high school teachers, such as "Teachers like to have assignments turned in on time." General statements often turn out to be inexact or to have exceptions, of course, but even when this is so, they are usually more helpful than no general statement at all.

Foremost among the general propositions that help us find our way in the world are causal principles. Early in life, the aid of others is very useful in helping us understand the causal principles at work behind our experience. No amount of suffering with stomach pains brought on by eating green apples will suffice to make a child stop eating green apples until he or she has come to understand the experience as exemplifying the causal principle that eating green apples causes stomach pains. The usefulness of this principle in thinking is increased when it is further generalized to cover the eating of all unripe fruit. As we grow older, we come to rely more and more on our own abilities in forming general statements and causal principles. But as the earlier chapters of this book have shown, doing so can be a treacherous business. Considering information gained from others in forming such principles is a standard procedure for any effective thinker. Indeed, that is one of the reasons why we have universities. Even the most sophisticated scientists and philosophers will readily admit that they would be lost without access to the community of inquiry that a university represents, and the information it generates.

Among the beliefs that make up our frame of reference are propositions about ourselves and the kind of person we are. In childhood these are based almost entirely on the way others treat us and on what they say to and about us. Later such beliefs become more independent but the reaction of others is always important in their formation. These propositions form the informational component of our self-concept. The other component consists of the value judgments about ourselves contained in our value systems.

Value Systems

We have noted that values are an immensely important force in our lives. They lend rationality to the particular decisions we make, form our consciences, and establish for us a hierarchy among the various needs we have. Each of us has a system of values that sets the goals we seek to attain in life and the preferred means for attaining them. And of course both the goals and means vary from person to person. Some people value wealth above knowledge; others value knowledge above wealth. Still others will sacrifice both to gain prestige in the eyes of their peers, and a few will suppress all these needs in the interest of service to others. As to the means by which we achieve our goals, some people will deceive and manipulate others in the interest of financial gain—by selling defective goods, for example, or by false advertising. Others will go out of their way to make sure a potential customer knows the bad as well as the good points of a product to be sold so that no deception takes place. Obviously, we do not always adhere to our values: all of us do things that we believe to be wrong and that we think manifest our weaknesses rather than our true values. All the same, our values are among the most powerful influences over our behavior and a dominant factor in deciding the sort of person we become. The difference between the values we truly hold and those to which we only do lip service is to be found in our conduct, especially when it falls into consistent patterns.

The factors that shape our values are many and varied. Some values come to us quite naturally. No one has to teach a child to value affection or to disvalue physical discomfort; these values emerge in the ordinary course of affairs, as a product of the child's needs. Our needs remain a powerful influence on our values throughout our lives, but their effect is not the same on everyone. In part, this is because needs differ in strength from person to person. People in whom the need for acceptance is strong tend to place a high value on conformity and to avoid controversy. Those with a greater need for autonomy place little value on conformity and treat controversy as a valuable chance to establish their own views over those of others. Our values also vary depending on our particular circumstances and chosen projects. Children tend to value snow because it offers a chance at a day off from school and some fun sledding. Over-the-road truckdrivers tend to feel differently about the matter. Two different people in the clubhouse of a golf course may perceive a steady rain in much the same way and yet react quite differently because of different value systems. The confirmed golfer may react negatively because he places a high value on playing golf. The greenskeeper, on the other hand, may be pleased by the rain because he places a high value on healthy grass.

By far the most important influence on our values is the training and advice we receive from others, along with the example they set for us. Our training in values begins before we learn to walk, when our parents caution us about dangers, scold our misconduct, and encourage our acceptable behavior. We learn early what things are ours to play with and enjoy and what things are not. We are taught how to behave toward our siblings, toward our elders, and toward strangers. The process continues throughout life. When we start school, we do not first learn how to read, write, and count. We first learn the rules and the penalties for violating them. The same process is repeated in high school and college, and in the work place. Almost every setting in which we find ourselves contains a prescribed pattern of conduct and means for its enforcement. In addition, we constantly receive information and advice about acceptable values from friends, the media, religious institutions, advertisers, and others. Obviously, these sources are often far from agreement with one another, and they will sometimes even contradict themselves. Nor does their advice always square with the goals toward which our needs and personal circumstances impel us. The process of sifting and selecting among the values with which we are presented can be difficult, and the results are not always satisfactory.

One problem is that we sometimes adopt and pursue values without fully understanding what they are or how they are best observed. For example, two people may place a high value on religion and may be members of the same church. To one, keeping the letter of the law may be the most important part of religion; this individual may be careful to attend services each week and keep the church's rules scrupulously, but may fail to practice religious principles in daily life. Another may be more careless about the specific rules but practice the spirit of his or her church's teaching with warmth and generosity. Again, two students at the same college and with the same major may value education highly. But one may give priority to doing assignments well and receiving good grades as a reward and never give a thought to going beyond the demands of the syllabus; the other may consider the spirit of inquiry the essence of education and, while not neglecting assignments, go at times in directions the instructor did not suggest and does not reward. In adopting values, it is important to have a full appreciation of what they are; we need to understand exactly what makes the thing being valued worthwhile.

A second problem in forming value systems is that we may adopt a set of values that is too narrow and confining. Obviously, we have to give the satisfaction of some needs priority over satisfying others, but if we are too one-sided about our choices, we can become as one-dimensional as our values. To satisfy the need for knowledge at the expense of physical activity is to miss an important source of enjoyment and perhaps suffer from ill health as well. On the other hand, satisfying the need for physical activity to the exclusion of any intellectual endeavor eventually leads to an impoverished life, one in which we would lack the concepts needed to make experience meaningful. In short, balanced satisfaction of needs requires a balanced system of values, which in turn requires discerning judgment. What makes this problem especially important is that once adopted, our values tend to perpetuate themselves and to exclude others. Thus a person who values music, or baseball, or cooking will tend to learn more about it, and thus come to enjoy it more and value it even more highly. By contrast, if these things are disvalued, they will remain unfamiliar, with little chance of being either understood or appreciated. This phenomenon is one of the reasons why we may tend to get a bit "stodgy" as we grow older. The antidote is to try to develop a balanced set of values early in life.

There is a reciprocal relation between one's value system and one's self-concept. If we value contributing to the welfare of others, we are apt to picture ourselves as people who do so. By the same token, if we see ourselves as contributing to the well-being of others, we are likely to set a higher value on occupations where we could do so rather than on occupations that merely produce material wealth. Value judgments are frequently evaluations of experience that help to maintain and protect the self-concept.

Certain values promote effective thinking. Following the New Testament principle "The truth shall make you free" may help one become a more effective thinker by providing motivation for the necessary effort. Certain value judgments held by scientists have contributed to the progress of modern science. It is said that Thomas Edison strove to overcome such obstacles as lack of support by fellow scientists, financial difficulties, and repeated failure of experiments with the electric light bulb because he believed that brighter light would benefit humanity.

On the other hand, values can lead to self-deception. The value judgments we wish to uphold frequently conflict with our immediate desires. Suppose that you want to be an artist but your parents want you to be an engineer and will help with your college expenses only if you study engineering. Your parents are thwarting you, and you may be tempted to retaliate by thwarting them. Suppose further that your values include the Commandment "Honor thy father and thy mother...." Your all-too-human desires are now in conflict with your values. If you are tolerant enough of your own feelings to recognize them honestly, you are likely to realize that retaliation would damage your sense of personal worth and to seek a more constructive solution.

But you can satisfy the desire to retaliate and protect your self-concept too—temporarily. You can retaliate by flunking out of college and can protect your self-concept by deceiving yourself about your motives. You can make yourself believe you really meant to succeed in college but failed through circumstances beyond your control. Thus you can have your cake and eat it—for a while. But the price is high, for when you deceive yourself, you distort your frame of reference and thereby blur your view of reality.

The system of value premises we use in making decisions largely determines what kind of people we will become. When the values are sound and reasonably consistent, the system gives life meaning, purpose, direction, and richness. But when the judgments in a value system are unsound or in conflict with each other, it is all but impossible to make sound decisions, and life seems without purpose or direction.

When life seems to lack meaning or purpose or we feel unhappy much of the time, it is worth testing the hypothesis that our value system is at fault. Unless we are perfect, some of the principles in our system are unsuitable or even false. We may have chosen to satisfy certain needs over others, and made the wrong choices. Some students decide that friendship is more important than academic achievement, only to wind up flunking out and missing both. Some of the value judgments associated with our self-concepts may have been derived by faulty reasoning from childhood experience. For example, based on childhood failures, some people mistakenly believe that they are too clumsy to enjoy anything athletic and therefore fail to meet their need for physical activity. Or they may underrate their intellectual abilities. Not a few students who have perfectly good ability in mathematics are deeply intimidated by the subject and consider themselves to be no good at it. They refuse to take any mathematics courses and so limit their opportunities both for understanding the subject and for rewarding careers. Unsatisfactory values may also be derived from other people. We tend to trust the value judgments of people we admire, but their judgments may not be correct or suited to the circumstances of a particular individual. Still other value judgments may be fine in themselves but unsatisfactory for a particular individual because they conflict with other values in his or her system.

Today's college student is confronted with perhaps the most disturbing array of conflicting values of all time. The many roots of American culture have made it the most richly varied in the world and perhaps the most inconsistent. The rapid social change of our era is adding new values that conflict sharply with older and more traditional ones. For almost every value precept you can think of, there is a contradictory one. Consider the conflict between the principle that we ought not to hold grudges and the principle expressed by the saying "Don't get mad, get even." They are patently at odds, yet both are embedded in our culture.

Other inconsistent values relate to conformity. We are exhorted not to be sheep, unthinkingly following others and doing as they do. The *Organization Man* is by now as much a term of contempt as it is the title of a book. But the very path of conformity that we are urged to avoid leads to another cluster of values we are told to pursue: "The day is past when you can get ahead on your own. Teamwork is what counts. Learn to fit—cooperate, be a good team player." Nonconformity reaps penalties as well as praise in our society; conformity earns both contempt and rewards. The fact that we often speak of "doing lip-service" to our ideals is an acknowledgment that we sometimes proclaim one value but practice a contradictory one.

It is up to each of us as individuals to decide which of the many conflicting values presented to us are worth building into our value systems. Indeed, the degree of our maturity is characterized—can to some extent even be measured—by the degree to which we make ourselves responsible for our own standards and accept responsibility for the actions to which they give rise. Nor should it be supposed that decisions about values are strictly arbitrary. Paradoxical though it may seem, the very procedures of thinking that have brought such progress in science are responsible, at least in part, for confusion and conflicts in value systems. Because new techniques of counting and measuring have been important in science, we tend to feel that *only* things that can be counted or measured are worth thinking about. From this notion has grown perhaps the great fallacy of our age: since value cannot be readily counted or measured, value judgments cannot be evaluated or tested.

It is true that value cannot be weighed and measured with the precision of the laboratory. But to assume from this fact that value judgments cannot be evaluated at all is a non sequitur. One of the main theses of this book is that certain procedures of thinking can be as valuable in developing a satisfactory system of values as the methods of science have been in dealing with the physical world. We shall take up the problem of testing value judgments in Chapter 31.

The Importance of Culture

By culture we mean the complex body of knowledge, beliefs, customs, laws, morals, and arts in which each of us is immersed as a member of society. It should be apparent from the last two sections that the in-

fluence of culture in shaping the personal point of view is immense. All of us have some beliefs and values that are derived immediately from personal experience. For the most part, however, these are narrowly focused on our own circumstances, such as a child's belief that the stove is hot or that eating a certain kind of candy is a pleasant experience. Once we get to the level of generality, it quickly becomes apparent that an accurate and effective set of beliefs and values would be impossible without the support of culture. Most of the beliefs and values we have are acquired directly or indirectly from the culture in which we find ourselves. And even those that are not so acquired are usually made possible by cultural influences and shaped by them.

To see that this is so, imagine the situation in which you would find yourself if, by some fortuitous circumstance, you had been able to survive from birth without the aid, or even the presence, of other people and so had been subject to no cultural influences whatever. We can only speculate on the amount of knowledge you could require, for it would all have to be by trial and error and induction. Living in such isolation, you would have no one to teach you a language; hence your system of categories for ordering experience would have to be built from scratch, and your capacity for abstract thought would be vastly impaired. You would have a hard time conceptualizing your observations and storing them so as to build a fund of knowledge upon them. Certainly, you would not have the knowledge and skills needed to maintain your life in a comfortable way. You would be lucky to be able to find an overhanging rock to sleep under, some insects to eat, and clean water to drink. Your situation with regard to values would be equally primitive. What values you might have would probably be confined to matters that concerned the satisfaction of immediate bodily needs. If you were to encounter another person in the same circumstances as yourself, you would have no idea that this person had any rights or that you were obligated to constrain your conduct toward him or her in any way at all. Perhaps it would be possible to work out a way of getting along, but the relationship would most likely amount to a tense stand-off, marked by competition and conflict. There is a good chance that one of you would simply kill the other. In all, then, your life without the aid of the culture would approximate what the English philosopher Thomas Hobbes called the "state of nature"—a state, he said, in which the life of man is "solitary, poor, nasty, brutish and short."[1]

It is largely with the aid of culture that we are able to rise above the level of the other animals, for only culture, by providing for the interchange of ideas and experience, makes it possible for us to utilize the knowledge and values of others in expanding and articulating our own frame of reference and value system. This is not an automatic process or even an easy one. What is presented to us as knowledge is always incomplete and sometimes false or inconsistent. And we have seen that our cultural environment is riddled with many conflicting values among which we all must decide. But despite the challenges and confusion of living in a culture, there is no denying that we would be little more than animals without it.

The culture in which we find ourselves molds and shapes us, for the price of access to a culture is always some degree of conformity. If society is to maintain itself so

that it can provide individuals with the tremendous advantages of living in a culture, it must to some extent regulate their behavior. By prohibiting individuals from assaulting their neighbors, society provides freedom to walk the streets without carrying weapons. By inducing people to enter specialized occupations, it provides individuals with the necessities of life at a smaller cost in time and effort, thus freeing their time and energy for developing their other individual capacities. By setting up schools and libraries, together with rules and regulations for their use, it makes available to individuals the experience accumulated by billions of people in thousands of years. Through its culture, society controls the behavior of individuals. The manners, morals, customs, and beliefs of the culture in which individuals live become the propositions by which they run their lives.

Some of these propositions are taken over directly. The individual hears them from other people, or reads them, or observes other people following them, and simply adopts them without examining them critically or seeking evidence to support them. These propositions may be of minor impact, for instance, "On Sunday one has the main meal at midday," or of major, significance, for example, "One of America's most important rights is the right to own guns." These propositions may never be questioned by the person accepting them. This is not to say the propositions are right or wrong. The point is that they are adopted from the culture without actual evidence.

Other propositions are adopted from the culture through **introjection**, the process by which we react to incidents and to other persons as though they were within ourselves. In early development, when children first begin to make value judgments about themselves, they encounter one of the most frustrating facts of human

---

[1] Thomas Hobbes, *Leviathan,* Michael Oakeshott (New York: Macmillan, 1962, p.100.

life—that the satisfaction of organic needs frequently conflicts with the maintenance of a satisfactory self-concept. When, in response to hunger, Al Smythe steals cookies from a neighbor's kitchen, he finds the action pleasant because it satisfies an organic need. But when his mother scolds him by calling him "naughty" or "bad," he may infer that he is not loved or lovable when he steals cookies. Now he has two conflicting evaluations of his action, one from his own senses and one from his mother. Because of strong identification with his mother, he may introject his mother's evaluation of his action, just as though he himself had found the action bad by his own experience, that is, he takes over from his mother a cultural prohibition, despite the contrary evidence of his own senses and despite the fact that he understands nothing of property rights.

The culture is not only a shaping influence, but also a part of the environment to which individuals must adjust. For the manners, customs, and morals of the culture often stand between us and the satisfaction of our needs. If we satisfy our need for food by throwing a brick through the bakery window and helping ourselves, we risk being put in jail. Assuming that we have absorbed the culture's moral prohibition against stealing, we may also be punished for our act by our conscience. The culture, too, is the only source of satisfaction of such needs as approval and prestige. By attaching approval or prestige to certain activites and discredit or shame to others, a community can prod individuals into approved behavior. It can, for example, induce a busy business person to give to the management of a charity drive time and energy worth hundreds of dollars. It can force us to wear uncomfortable clothing on a hot day. It can even control our thinking to some degree, for it is uncomfortable to think thoughts not approved by one's culture. We all find our desires in conflict with our culture on some occasions. Yet to be happy, we must live in reasonable harmony with our culture. Such conflicts can be satisfactorily resolved, but high-grade thinking is necessary.

The culture also helps to account for differences in thinking, for no two of us are exposed to exactly the same cultural influences. Cultural patterns differ, sometimes sharply, between families, neighborhoods, social groups, communities, regions, and nations. Different fraternities and sororities on the same campus often manifest different values. Different corporations can have different "corporate cultures": one may do business in a brash and aggressive way and another may be low-keyed and patient. Different areas of the same country may vary in political outlook, manners, and pace of life. The kind of person you become is in many ways dependent on the "style" of the groups with which you associate, your career environment, and your geographical location.

All in all, culture has a hand in virtually everything you think, in your taste in food and books, your ambitions, your moral code, your political opinions, and your beliefs about health, wealth, and happiness. It is hard for most of us to realize the full impact of cultural influences on us, for we have always been subject to them. Like fish that have never been out of water, we do not know what it is like to exist in a different element. One of the best ways to realize how much culture has influenced you is to become acquainted with one that is different from your own. You can do this by reading anthropological studies of primitive cultures.[2] Or if time and finances permit,

---

[2] Such as Margaret Mead, *Growing Up in New Guinea* (New York: Morrow, 1976).

you can visit another culture and directly observe the differences between its collective values and those of your native culture. Immersing yourself in another culture can be hard at first, but it will give you new perspectives on your own. Many nations that we would consider at least as civilized as our own are less materialistic, more settled politically, and offer a slower pace of life. Others are highly energetic, moving aggressively toward a higher standard of living, and deeply involved in world affairs. Experiencing such contrasts is an indispensable aid to deciding which of your own values you would like to export and which would be better superseded by values imported from elsewhere.

The Individual Character of Thinking

As powerful as culture is in shaping the individual, it cannot eliminate individual differences. This is in part because culture itself is not a seamless fabric; it presents us with a number of perspectives on the world and a profusion of values, among which we must decide. Besides, no two of us live in exactly the same circumstances. We grow up in different homes, attend different schools, and follow different careers. As a result, each of us is exposed to culture in a unique way: each individual sees some aspects of it more clearly than others and is affected by parts of the culture that do not affect others. Finally, each of us is a unique individual, both physiologically and psychologically, and the beliefs and values we develop have to be tailored to fit our particular needs and aspirations. Thus each of us develops a uniquely individual personal point of view. The particular frame of reference we develop reflects our individual circumstances; we all have beliefs others do not have and know about some things more intimately than others do. We have not only value systems that reflect our individual training and are oriented to the satisfaction of our particular needs, but also highly individual self-concepts, composed of the beliefs and values that we frame about ourselves. The particular personal point of view each of us develops profoundly affects the decisions we make and stamps them as our own.

The personal point of view functions as a selector of experience. We are physically incapable of observing more than a fraction of what goes on about us at any given time. At a football game, we can watch the ball or the scoreboard or the officials or the star halfback or the plane flying overhead, but we cannot pay attention to all of them at the same instant. At any one time, one aspect of the scene is the foreground and the rest is the background.

The foreground is selected primarily on the basis of needs. That is why different individuals observe different aspects of the same scene. At the football game, the scout concentrates on the tactics of the team; the spectator who has bet on the outcome concentrates on the progress of the ball; the fashion editor concentrates on what the spectators are wearing; and the policeman on duty keeps half his attention on the game while he scans the crowd for signs of undesirable action off the field.

Incidents in the background of the scene may, of course, impinge on our attention if the stimulus is strong enough. The scout may be distracted by a fight between spectators. But in general what is in the background makes little impression; it does not as a rule become part of the individual's experience.

Each proposition that becomes a part

of our frame of reference tends to set the pattern for the selection of other propositions. For example, children who are rewarded by parents for being agreeable are likely to incorporate into their self-concepts the proposition that they are agreeable persons. This proposition leads to the adoption of the value premise that it is good to be agreeable. From then on the children will most likely resist ideas that are incompatible with this value premise. Children who resent parental interference are likely to resent authority in any form. Children who are punished severely by parents or by experience for being venturesome may adopt the proposition that it is better to be safe than sorry and may become less and less venturesome as time goes by. Children who succeed in their attempts at self-assertion may adopt the proposition that nothing is gained unless something is ventured and so may grow into aggressive business executives. Thus, by directing the selection of experience, the personal point of view channels its own development, choosing among alternative or incompatible modes of thought and experience. This is one of the ways in which each of us develops into a unique personality.

The personal point of view functions as much more than a selector of experience. In another role, it serves as the agency through which needs are recognized, interpreted, and translated into thought and action. It serves, so to speak, as chairperson of the Committee on Need Satisfaction. And like a good committee leader, it tries to keep the thinking relevant to the issue at hand. The relevant issue at any given moment is the most pressing need of that moment. We do not concern ourselves with needs of the past or future unless they are manifesting themselves in the present. When you are trying to solve a problem in chemistry, the only logically relevant factors are those having to do with the problem. But while you are thinking about the problem, you may suddenly recall that you have only one day left in which to register for the coming semester. If your next chemistry class is not until next week, you may forget all about chemistry and begin planning your next semester's schedule. Thus your perception as to which situation most requires attention determines what you think about.

By focusing our attention on certain experiences and needs, the personal point of view controls the subject matter of our thinking. It also exerts a strong influence on the observations we are able to make about the subject matter at hand, as we saw in Chapter 6. Furthermore, the personal point of view exerts a strong influence on the inferences we draw from the information at our disposal.

Suppose you know these facts: Arthur Mason has not returned from a fishing trip in the Gulf of Mexico. It is now Tuesday morning and Mason was due back late Monday afternoon. He left the dock alone Monday morning in a sturdy skiff, powered by an outboard motor. He carried a spare motor. No storms have occurred in the area. Mason was an expert swimmer and boatman. He was emotionally depressed, having recently learned that the severe pain in his abdomen was caused by an incurable cancer. He was heavily in debt. He carried an insurance policy of a hundred thousand dollars.

A number of plausible hypotheses might be formed to explain the information in hand. Mason has met with an accident; he is lost; he is still out fishing, not caring any longer about his business; he has committed suicide. In general, you will tend to favor the hypothesis most congenial to your personal point of view. The owner of a helicopter, eager to demonstrate its usefulness in rescue work, would probably favor the hypothesis that Mason is lost. Since Mason's insurance policy is invalid in case of suicide, the insurance agent might favor the suicide hypothesis. Mason's friends would probably prefer any hypothesis to that one. If you had recently urged Mason not to go fishing in the Gulf alone, you might favor the hypothesis that he is lost or has had an accident.

The personal point of view also influences the significance we attach to the facts. The insurance agent might pick as most significant the facts that no storm has occurred, that Mason is an expert boatman and swimmer, and that he carried a spare motor, and interpret these facts as ruling out any hypothesis except suicide. Mason's friends, on the other hand, might attach little importance to these facts, reasoning that anyone could have an accident or get lost. The owner of the helicopter might reason that these facts are significant in supporting the hypothesis that Mason is still alive and in need of rescue. One reason for forming the habit of setting up rival hypotheses and testing the supporting facts by appropriate criteria is that these measures help to overcome the bias of our personal point of view.

Perhaps the most important of all the roles played by the personal point of view is that of evaluator of experience. It is the Bureau of Standards by which experience is judged to be desirable and hence to be repeated or undesirable and hence to be avoided. The value system provides the standards used. Is reading a mystery story a waste of time or a desirable relaxation? Is the current fad in popular music really music or mere noise? Our opinion depends on our value judgments. Sometimes, our personal interests color our judgment. When four tacklers gang up on the ball carrier and slam him to earth, whether the play was "good football" or "unnecessary roughness" may depend on which team we favor.

Thus to some degree we create the world in which we live. We react to reality not as it is but as it appears to us through our personal points of view. We can no more see reality independently of this personal point of view than we can listen to a broadcast of a football game independently of the radio announcer. If the announcer is skillful and accurate, we get a reasonably accurate picture of the game. Similarly, if we have an adequate supply of accurate propositions, we get a reasonably accurate and workable view of life. But if the propositions in the personal point of view are inadequate or inaccurate, poor thinking is inevitable. We will use erroneous propositions that increasingly misrepresent the world until we cannot tell what is truth and what is distortion. In the next chapter, we will examine some ways in which our personal point of view can lead us to distort reality.

Exercise 27

Problems 1–15. Indicate whether the following statements agree with the hypotheses presented in this chapter by writing T for true or F for false in the blank.

1. We must learn a language before we can think at all.   _____

2. Language helps us organize experience into usefully defined categories.

   _____

3. We sometimes adopt values that are too broad and ill-defined to be satisfied adequately.

   _____

4. It is impossible to perceive reality except in terms of one's personal point of view.

   _____

5. Value judgments determine to a large extent which experiences we seek and which we avoid.

   _____

6. The propositions that make up the personal point of view are always consistent with each other.

   _____

7. Once a proposition has become a part of the personal point of view, it is never changed or abandoned.

   _____

8. Our self-concept is determined completely by information we receive from others.

   _____

9. Which hypotheses we favor in explaining our experience is influenced by our personal point of view.

   _____

10. The influence of culture begins after we leave the family circle.   _____

11. When our values appear to conflict with those of our culture, we should always follow our own values.

   _____

12. Sometimes one need is satisfied at the expense of others.   _____

13. Most of the propositions making up the personal point of view are derived by induction from experience.

   _____

14. Culture helps to promote adaptation and at the same time is the source of many problems of adaptation.

_____

15. Cultural differences can be noted between groups on the same college campus.

_____

Problems 16–20. Suppose that the University Senate at Wysacki is voting on the issue of whether to let men and women share the same dormitories. Given below is information about the personal points of view of a number of members of the senate. Using this information, make a reasoned guess about how each would vote on the issue.

16. Colonel Abernathy will retire next year after 35 years of teaching military science at Wysacki. He doesn't much like the changes he has seen in the university over the years.

_____

17. Betty Blake is a senior, one of the two students in the University Senate. She is active in liberal causes and takes her position as student representative very seriously.

_____

18. Carl Crary, the other student, is a straight-A engineering major who wishes he had never gotten involved with the senate because it takes too much time. College is for learning, he says.

_____

19. Professor Dan Drake is just out of graduate school. He always wears sandals, even in December. He is tremendously popular and always seems to be accompanied by a group of students.

_____

20. Professor Ellen Evans is chairperson of the Language Department. She has often been heard to say that only through communication can different groups demythologize one another and learn to live in harmony.

_____

Problems 21–25. Now suppose that each of these individuals surprises you and votes the opposite way from what you had predicted. Write a value proposition for each that is not inconsistent with the original description and explains the unexpected vote.

21. Abernathy _____

22. Blake _____

23. Crary _____

24. Drake _____

25. Evans _____

Chapter 28

How We May Distort the Evidence

- **Self-Defense**
- **Mechanisms of Self-Defense**
- **Sophistical Defense**
- **Avoidance**
- **Distraction Devices**

- **Rationalizing**
- **Repression**
- **Projection**
- **Evaluating Defense Mechanisms**

All of us would have more success in dealing with the world if we could be thoroughly trained in the techniques of effective thinking before birth. Obviously, however, this cannot be done. We have to learn to think at the same time as we are drawing conclusions about ourselves and the world—conclusions based on very limited experience. The result inevitably is error and distortion in our frames of reference and value systems. Moreover, once these shortcomings enter the personal point of view, they tend to direct our thinking in ways that perpetuate them. We are in the game of thinking from the very beginning, and for keeps. None of us can step outside his or her personal point of view, compare it with reality, and introduce the corrections necessary for more accurate thinking. Rather, we must correct it from within, and must base the cor-

rections on evidence that is both limited and filtered through the very frame of reference we are trying to correct. Thus the evidence itself is at times distorted, for our frames of reference incline us to view the world as we expect it to be rather than as it is. As a result, error in our personal point of view cannot be completely avoided. We cannot remove all the flaws in our frames of reference, make our value systems completely consistent, and operate from a totally sound self-concept. We can, however, be aware of the various ways in which distortions and false propositions gain our acceptance. Awareness of the ways in which it is possible to manipulate experience so that we can see the things we wish to see and avoid seeing the things we wish to avoid is an important aid in minimizing the errors in our thinking.

Self-Defense

The fundamental motive behind many distortions of evidence is to protect ourselves. Suppose, for example, that a man thinks of himself as broad-minded and liberal but cannot accept the fact that his daughter has a live-in boyfriend. He may try to distort the evidence so that his attitude does not seem inconsistent—he may find imaginary faults in the boyfriend, for instance, and claim that he disapproves of the relationship because of the young man's character. But all along, the truth is that on this subject, at least, he is not nearly as broad-minded as he thinks. Similarly, someone who prides herself on her ability to stay calm in situations of danger may refuse to accept the fact that she has acted irrationally in a crisis. If so, she may continually replay the scene in her mind, with slight changes in each replay, until she is "remembering" the event in such a way as to reflect much less discredit upon herself. Shakespeare has a good example of this sort of distortion in *Henry IV, Part I*. Prince Hal and Falstaff, his fat, drunken friend, plot a robbery along with some others. After Falstaff and the others carry off the robbery, the prince and another friend disguise themselves and rob the robbers. Later, Falstaff and Poins, his companion in the first robbery, describe the second robbery to the prince.

Falstaff: . . . Four rogues in buckrom let drive
    at me—
Prince: What, four? Thou saidst but two even
   now.
Falstaff: Four, Hal. I told thee four.
Poins: Ay, Ay, he said four.
Falstaff: These four came all afront. I made
   me no more ado but took all their seven
   points in my target, thus.

The two assailants grow to four, then seven, then eleven, then fourteen; finally, the prince makes Falstaff face the truth:

Prince: Mark now how a plain tale shall put
   you down. . . . we two set on you four, and
   with a word, outfaced you from your prize,
   and have it. . . . And, Falstaff, you carried
   your guts away as nimbly, with as quick
   dexterity, and roared for mercy . . . as
   ever I heard bull-calf.

Since we don't have an inner truthteller, a Prince Hal in our heads to bring us back to earth, it is usually possible for us to distort and misrepresent the evidence. As in the above examples, we may do so to protect our good opinions of ourselves. But we also frequently distort evidence to protect *poor* opinions of ourselves. The records of clinical psychologists are filled with cases of individuals who damage their lives by refusing to give up harmful and false beliefs about themselves. The reason for this phenomenon is that a harmful belief or a negative value judgment can be as central to our self-concept as any other, so that a threat to it is a threat to our whole personality, and to our whole pattern of life. Many of us have too low rather than too high an opinion of ourselves but refuse to surrender it because though painful, it is familiar, and to give it up would be to give up our sense of security.

Distortion of reality can vary in degree from slight misperception to total delusion. In general the more important a proposition is in the personal point of view, the more zealously it is defended. The propositions making up the personal point of view interlock like the stones in an arch. When a major proposition is threatened, the whole structure is threatened, just as the arch falls if the keystone crumbles. A boy who has adopted the belief that his father does not love him tends to resist or ignore evidence to the contrary. Even though he would like to be loved, abandoning his belief would undermine his whole personal point of view. A major proposition about one's abilities, even though unfavorable, will usually be defended vigorously, whereas a minor proposition about how to play chess may be abandoned readily. Your boss, for example, may readily accept your suggestion about how to improve his golf and yet be offended at your suggestion about how to run his business.

A girl who has dismantled the family alarm clock may interpret her father's comment that she cannot put it back together as meaning that she lacks mechanical ability. This she may generalize and introject as "I have no mechanical ability." Later, when she succeeds in repairing the chain on her bicycle she interprets the incident in the light of her previous generalization, attributes her success to sheer luck, and fails to recognize it as evidence that she does have mechanical ability. Later still, when she goes to college, she may reject the evidence of vocational tests that she has high ability in engineering and choose a less suitable career.

In general, the less sure we are of ourselves, the more defensive we are likely to be. For example, an instructor who is confident in his or her ability will usually not hesitate to acknowledge a mistake made in class, for the mistake will not be perceived by the instructor as a threat to his or her position. But an instructor who is insecure may argue vigorously even over some minor point, feeling that he or she cannot afford even the smallest defeat. Also, we can be sure of ourselves in one area but unsure in another. A person with broad business experience but little knowledge of the arts may feel at ease in a sophisticated discussion of economics, but uncomfortable in a discussion of poetry or music.

Mechanisms of Self-Defense

If we were perfectly objective, we would not be threatened by evidence contrary to the propositions we have accepted. We would carefully evaluate the evidence and correct or replace the propositions. When we encountered difficult practical situations, we would deal with them directly and realistically. Or, if our realistic perception of a situation indicated we could do nothing constructive about it, we would accept the situation and adapt to it. But none of us is perfectly objective. There can be a great deal of evidence in our environments that would be threatening if clearly perceived and accurately interpreted. Instead of dealing directly with this evidence, we sometimes resort to various mechanisms of self-defense by which we ignore or distort or misinterpret the evidence so as to avoid or minimize the threat. At times we combine several of these mechanisms. It is possible to use them without realizing that the situation is threatening. Even when consciously aware of the threat in a situation, we may be unaware at the time that we are using defense mechanisms. Let us examine some of the more important of these mechanisms. It is often easier to observe them in others than in ourselves, but the effective thinker will learn to recognize his or her own characteristic defense mechanisms so as to minimize their negative effects.

Sophistical Defense

When we find an idea threatening, we can defend ourselves against it with a device named after the Sophists, who acquired a reputation for teaching dishonest tricks of argument to young Athenians. This device uses the procedures of effective thinking not to establish truth, but simply to win whatever dispute is occurring. In general, it is based on the faulty assumption that if one can find, or pretend to find, flaws in the way an argument is presented, one is entitled to dismiss the conclusion. This, of course, is false. An argument in favor of capital punishment, for example, may be riddled with violations of reason, or at least may be so poorly presented that we can claim it is unreasonable. But this would not show that capital punishment is wrong. To show that, we would have to come to grips with the issues rather than just pecking away at our opponent's argument.

If we practice sophistry, we avoid considering the possibility that a threatening proposition is true, and instead start hunting around for flaws or seeming flaws in its presentation. If the proposition is a hypothesis, we can counter by claiming that some other hypothesis, yet to be discovered, might account for the evidence in a more satisfying way. If it is a general statement, we can convince ourselves that it is based on a loaded sample. If it is a causal principle, we can point to the ever-present possibility of questionable cause. If someone criticizes us, we can use a whole array of logical tricks. We may attack our opponent's objectivity: "He is prejudiced and uninformed." We can pretend to be persecuted: "She has always had it in for me." And so on. The trouble with sophistical defense is that it keeps us from dealing with the real issue, thus necessitating more maneuvers. When we find ourselves vigorously attacking an idea, it is well to make sure we know the real reason we dislike it.

Avoidance

If a situation is threatening, one can consciously and deliberately avoid it by **removing oneself from the situation.** For example, if you are unprepared for your next class, you can cut it. By so doing you make it likely that you will be even more unprepared for the next class, but you temporarily escape the threat of embarrassment or bad grades. One of the easiest ways to avoid a threatening situation is to look the other way. If you were chairman of the student honor system, the knowledge that wholesale cheating was going on would be a threat to your self-concept as an effective official. If you suspected that wholesale cheating was occurring in a course you were taking, you could look the other way by keeping your eyes glued to your own paper. By so doing you could minimize the threat, for it is less threatening to suspect than to know. But you would not solve the real problem, and sooner or later conscience or public scorn might catch up with you.

When we have an unpleasant experience in front of us, we can avoid it by **forgetting** it. So many people routinely forget dentist appointments that dentists take steps to prevent this defense mechanism, by telephone reminders, waiting periods before rescheduled appointments, and the like. If we are ashamed of something we have done, we can forget it as we would a telephone number we no longer need. What we do not remember does not bother us—at the moment. Forgetting, of course, is not necessarily self-defensive. We may forget the matter simply because it is of no importance to us, like the telephone number. But if the things we forget tend to be unpleasant ones, we may be intentionally avoiding them.

If an idea is sufficiently threatening, we can keep it entirely out of consciousness by **perceptual defense.** We may shift the spotlight away from the threat and keep it so deep in the background that it is not perceived at all. Suppose that you have strong feelings of loyalty to your football team and strongly negative feelings about poor sportsmanship. When you see the fist of one of your players start toward the face of an opponent, you may shift your attention elsewhere before you can perceive the act of slugging. Thus many of the neglected aspects in our observations are self-defensive maneuvers. The remedy, in part, is to practice and take pride in being an accurate and objective observer. The remedy for forgetting unpleasant duties or appointments is to keep reminders of them around so that at least we will have to work harder to forget them.

Distraction Devices

Avoiding an unpleasant situation is easier if we employ a distraction device to keep our attention elsewhere. Thus we may find it easier to ignore a toothache if our attention is absorbed by a movie. A student who dreads studying for a biology test may distract her attention from it by playing a few rounds of bridge after supper. Someone forced to spend the Christmas holidays away from home may avoid confronting his loneliness by becoming absorbed in work. If these devices are insufficient, we can try a stronger distraction, for the list of distraction devices is endless. The stereo, television, and work are only the obvious ones. There is also the long-delayed skiing trip, the suddenly felt need to give one's home a thorough cleaning, and the intense craving for a dish that will take five hours to cook.

Up to a point, distraction devices are beneficial. You may find, for instance, that listening to music takes the anxiety out of studying for finals or that it is easier to do your calculus after a couple of burritos. But when we find ourselves seeking diversion excessively without knowing why, self-deception is probably involved, and we should search for the real reason. Some distraction devices, like alcohol and narcotics, are notorious for making life harder rather than easier to deal with, and excessive use of any distraction device involves much wasted time. There are, of course, lots of distraction devices that appear in contexts of reasoning, and we can use them on others as well as ourselves. A great many fallacies of relevance are distraction devices.

Rationalizing

Sometimes we are ashamed of the motives behind our actions. For example, an instructor may wish to give only objective examinations in a course because he finds grading essays too much work. If the instructor gives only objective tests for this reason, he will suffer a loss of self-esteem—it is painful to acknowledge that one is lazy. It is possible, however, to give only objective examinations and avoid acknowledging the true motive by **rationalizing**, that is, substituting acceptable reasons for the real reasons behind the action. It is easy to find acceptable reasons for most actions, even if the reasons are not our own. Thus the instructor may argue, "The students cannot write well enough to handle essays and the subject matter is too complicated. There are too many students in the class. And I will be able to devote more time to research if I spend less time grading papers." Rationalizing comes in several brands.

One is known as **sour grapes.** You cannot reach the grapes? "They were sour anyway." You failed to make Phi Beta Kappa? "I wouldn't want to be known as a bookworm." You failed to get a job for which you applied? "Well, now I don't have to waste time traveling to and from work every day. And besides, the boss there is a real jerk."

Another popular brand of rationalizing is called the **sweet lemon.** Is that car you bought a lemon? "But it is a sweet lemon. Even if it does break down every other day, it has many virtues. It is comfortable, the tires are good, and it has more prestige than cheaper models."

Still another is **excuse making.** Did you fail the course because you did not study enough? "It wasn't all my fault. I was in the infirmary three days early in the semester. I lost my book. And I had a headache the day of the final."

A similar one is **blaming others.** "It wasn't my fault I failed. The instructor didn't teach me anything, and besides he had it in for me." One trouble with this one is that we may cause hostility if our remarks get back to the person blamed.

A worse form of rationalizing is **criticizing others.** We can raise our own relative position by tearing down our competitors with criticism. Or we can use it to rationalize jealousy. Suppose Mr. Flack's neighbor has a new Mercedes whereas Mr. Flack's car has seen better days. Jealousy is not an acceptable reason for hating one's neighbor, so Flack finds better reasons: his neighbor is too ostentatious, spends all his money on himself, is a social climber, and is selfish to boot. Engaging in invective may make Flack feel better whether his neighbor has these faults or not—as long as Flack can convince himself that he has. Criticism of others is not necessarily self-defensive; we may have other motives or adequate evidence for the criticism. But when we use it to rationalize our own shortcomings, we deceive ourselves about our motives, make false appraisals of others, and often alienate both those we criticize and those to whom we complain. When we find ourselves critical of others, it is well to seek our real motive.

Rationalization is bad for thinking on three counts: (1) it is habit-forming, since it is easier to make excuses than to face the issue squarely; (2) it eases the pain without removing the cause, and if we make excuses for our failures without correcting the cause, we are likely to experience other failures as well; and (3) by obscuring motives, it tends to make behavior irrational. Excessive rationalizers are nearly always poor decision-makers because they are unable to face up to their own feelings about things. Because they make poor decisions, the issues they are trying to evade tend to become more painful with time and hence still more difficult to face. The way to prevent this from happening is to try to deal with troublesome issues as they arise, so that the cycle of rationalization cannot get started.

Repression

When a threatening idea is too serious to be dealt with by the devices already mentioned, we can repress it, that is, we can block it from entering consciousness. In effect, we lock the evidence away in a closet because we cannot face it. This method is similar to forgetting, except that often the offensive material is not fully recognized and conceptualized before it is rejected. Hence, it is very hard to catch ourselves at repression. Consider the case of Mrs. Smythe, who during her college years was the best tennis player at Wysacki. Every two weeks or so, Mr. Smythe asks her to join him in a doubles match against his employer and the employer's wife. Mrs. Smythe really doesn't like the idea. For one thing, none of the other three players is up to her level of competition. Also, she doesn't much care for either the boss or his wife and still less does she respect the idea of her husband trying to curry favor in this way. All the same, she wants to be a good sport and to help her husband out if she can, so the match is held regularly. It seems, however, that whenever Mr. Smythe's employer is situated directly across the net from her, Mrs. Smythe tends inadvertently to slam the ball directly at him. Once the match even had to end early because the boss's eye was swollen shut. Mrs. Smythe is embarrassed by these occurrences and doesn't know why they happen. She refuses to admit to herself that the real reason is boredom and disgust on her part. In fact, she would deny that she feels either of these emotions. Instead, she combines repression with rationalization and blames the errant shots on her worry that little Algernon may be harassing his babysitter back at the house—and sincerely believes this to be the real reason.

Repression is perhaps the most pernicious of all self-defensive maneuvers. In the first place, it tends to spread. Even though repressed, the threatening idea is still there—in the closet. To keep it out of consciousness, we must avoid contact with ideas which might force it into consciousness through association. We may, for example, be unable to remember names associated with the repressed idea. To keep the evidence securely locked in the closet, we must also lock up things closely connected with it. This requires further self-deception and distortion of reality, which

enlarges the area of self-defensiveness. When we find ourselves using any self-defensive device without quite knowing what we are defending against, repression may be at the bottom of it.

In the second place, repression reduces the control of thinking over behavior. We cannot use in thinking the evidence we have hidden from ourselves. The result is behavior that we can neither understand nor approve. Evidence locked in the closet by repression seems not to lie quietly—the inner tension is still there. And tension that is not allowed expression seems to increase in pressure like steam in a boiler. When we repress the idea causing the tension, we block or inhibit the normal expression or release of the pressure. So it builds up and breaks out somewhere else.

For instance, it is normal for young adults to feel both love and hostility toward their parents, who may be trying to retain control at the same time their children are trying to become independent. But the young people may repress the hostility instead of recognizing it. Feeling that it is wrong to harbor resentment against their parents, they may experience tension without recognizing the cause. They may release the tension, without knowing why, by expressing hostility toward someone who reminds them of the parent. Or hostility can break out in some other way. If parents are overly ambitious for their children who are students, the students can respond indirectly by failing courses without having the faintest suspicion of the real reason for their poor work. College counselors can testify to the frequency with which repressed hostility toward parents seems to be at the bottom of poor college work.

Finally, repression is hard to deal with. It is hard to correct unsatisfactory or hurtful behavior without knowing the cause, and repression keeps the cause hidden. The essential step, therefore, is to induce oneself to admit the repressed idea to consciousness. In serious cases of repression, this step may require the help of others.

Projection

When we possess a trait we wish not to face, we can not only repress it but project it as well. That is, we can repress the recognition of it in ourselves and transfer it to other people, as the movie projector transfers to the screen the image on the film. Thus, if an executive mistreats subordinates and cannot face the fact, he or she can bury the fault more deeply by finding it in others: they overwork their staff, pay inadequate salaries, and browbeat new employees. The truth of the accusations does not matter. When we project, we need little evidence.

Projection is a strong and dangerous form of psychological self-protection. In the first place, it breeds intolerance. People who recognize their own faults are usually tolerant of those same faults in others; but people who are projecting their faults are notoriously intolerant of those faults in others. In the second place, projection leads to aggression. When we repress a fault, we cannot attack it in ourselves, but we can release the tension by attacking others. Such behavior is typical of the fanatic who viciously attacks a certain sin wherever it can be found—and the fanatic finds it everywhere. Sexual problems are particularly prone to being projected. The play *Tea and Sympathy* by Robert Anderson gives a typical example of this kind of projection: the macho headmaster of a boy's school who spends much of his time ferreting out homosexuals

turns out to have such tendencies himself—which, unrecognized and not dealt with, have made him into a homophobe.

Projection is hard to deal with because it springs from unconscious motives. Perhaps the best practice is to think twice before criticizing others. We should also think twice before concluding that others are projecting. Not all people who criticize others or attack what they consider evil are projecting. They may have other and more acceptable reasons. Clues that indicate the probability, but not the certainty, of projection are intolerance, unreasonableness, hatred, and extremely aggressive attack.

Evaluating Defense Mechanisms

Some use of defense mechanisms is inevitable. None of us can live so well that there are no painful elements in our lives. Mental suffering can be much harder to bear than physical suffering. Without defense mechanisms, all of us would have difficulty maintaining a satisfactory self-concept. But, like powerful drugs, they can become addictive and destructive, and thus their use must be controlled. No hard and fast rules for their use can be established, for whether a given device is helpful or harmful depends on a highly complex relationship between the individual and the situation. However, the two following criteria will prove useful.

A Defense Mechanism Can Be Considered Helpful or Harmful According to Whether It Promotes or Interferes with Adaptation Over the Long-run. Suppose you find yourself unprepared for approaching examinations. As you survey the work yet to be done and the time left to do it in, you may become so disturbed as to be unable to concentrate. At this point, you may use a distraction device such as going to see a movie, thereby escaping the situation and forgetting your problem temporarily. If you return to your studies the next day refreshed and able to concentrate, presumably the distraction device has helped you solve your problem. But if you enjoy the escape so much that you start spending most of your time at the movies, the distraction device is making the solution of your problem more difficult, if not impossible.

The More Self-deception Involved in a Defense Mechanism, the More Likely It Is to Be Harmful. Suppose you convince yourself that being unprepared for examinations is not your fault. Perhaps you decide that your instructors are hostile and overly demanding and that your adviser erred in suggesting a course load that was too heavy. Let us imagine, however, that in so deciding you ignore the facts that other students in your courses are not having trouble and that your course load is no heavier than theirs. Blaming others may ease the pain for the moment, but the problem is still there: the examinations must still be faced, and the penalties for failure are still the same. By deceiving yourself about the causes of your problem, you have made it more difficult to remove those causes in the future. The problem may be that you have devoted too much time to extracurricular activities or to working to help meet your expenses. You may simply have failed to study enough during the semester, thinking you would be able to catch up at the end. Or your course of study may not be suited to your abilities. Whatever the true cause, it is important that it be recognized and dealt with, or it is likely to recur the following semester, with still more painful consequences. The longer we blind ourselves to the realities of life, the more difficult it becomes to deal with them. While some self-deception is inevitable, it can be carried to the point where one becomes unable to deal with reality at all.

Any improvement we can make in our ability to think soundly will reduce our reliance on defense mechanisms. The more personal problems we solve, the fewer we will have left to hide from. The more accurate our frame of reference, the less we will need to distort or ignore reality in order to protect false propositions.

Exercise 28

Problems 1—20. Write in the blank the name of the defense mechanism probably used in each of the following cases.

1. *Adam Able:* "I would have had my term paper in on time, but my roommate is always playing loud rock music, and when I went to the library to get away from him and get some work done, I bumped into a tree in the dark and broke my glasses, so. . ."

_____

2. *Betsy Bridge:* "I don't see how you can give a student a low grade on a test like this, Professor Peachpit. There are at least three misspellings on the first page alone, and a number of the questions have no punctuation at the end of them."

_____

3. *Carl Carson:* "The thought of tomorrow's calculus test is getting me down. I think I'll try to cheer myself up by taking in the triple horror show at the drive-in."

_____

4. Doreen Davis was shocked to find that she would not be able to register for her final semester in college until she paid 53 parking tickets she had acquired over the years. She said she knew she had received a few, but had no idea there were so many.

_____

5. *Ed Esteban:* "I do not sing off key! The people in the congregation who say that can't carry a tune."

_____

6. Everyone wonders why Fay Fenton always criticizes others for being cheap, when Fay never spends a dime if she can avoid it.

_____

7. Gary Greenberg has met a new girl on campus and feels he should tell his high school sweetheart about the situation. But whenever he picks up a pen to write to her, he ends up first drawing pictures on the paper and finally doing something else.

_____

8. Hal Harrington dislikes his literature professor for being rigid and authoritarian. When Hal coaches the third-grade soccer team, however, he makes the children toe the line and is unable to tolerate the least bit of horseplay.

9. *Isobel Innes:* "This apartment may be expensive and far both from my school and my job, but it certainly is quiet here. With so many of the other apartments vacant, I can get my studying done without interruption."

10. John James doesn't remember that he was badly bitten by a German shepherd when he was four. He only knows that he hates large dogs and doesn't care for people who own them.

11. Karl Klaus was dropped by two girls recently, and although his religion has always been lukewarm, he is considering becoming a monk.

12. Lois Larsen is failing most of her courses, but she spends most of her time and all the money she can scrape together on her hobby of skydiving. She says she'll study next semester.

13. Murray Miller was one of the candidates dropped from the football squad after the first week of practice. He said, "I've changed my mind about football. It takes a lot of time that I can spend better."

14. Ned Nott, who was also dropped from the squad, went home every weekend when a football game was played on campus.

15. Ollie Olsen was dropped, too, and offered this explanation: "I had a run of bad luck. Every time the coaches looked at me I was playing against the first string. Also, I hurt my leg and couldn't go at full speed. I played wishbone in high school and didn't have time to adjust to the pro-style offense."

16. Patty Pensek has long been a Democrat. When a number of newspapers began to criticize the Democratic administration, she complained: "Republicans control most

of the newspapers. They put Democratic mistakes on the front page and leave out Republican mistakes."

17. Quincey Quimby comes from a family that has voted Republican for two generations. When a news magazine began criticizing Republican policies, he canceled his subscription.

18. Rona Roark's fiancé was killed in an accident. Rona is now carrying the maximum academic load and participating in dramatics and student government.

19. Sally Siegfried did not look forward to telling her roommate that she broke the headphones to the stereo. Just before her roommate came in, Sally left to return a book to the library.

20. Tad Treetopper's hatred of the police is well known. His father, a very strict disciplinarian, happens to be a police captain, but Tad believes he has only positive feelings toward his father.

Chapter 29

Dealing with Emotions

- **Emotions and Physiology**
- **Emotions and Thinking**
- **Anxiety**
- **Feelings of Insecurity and Inferiority**

- **Guilt**
- **Depression**
- **Coping with Stress**
- **Expert Help**

Have you ever, under the stress of excitement, made a decision so foolish that you wondered later how you made it? Have you ever become so panic-stricken while making a speech or taking an examination that you could not remember material you knew well? Have you ever become angry in an argument and made rash statements that you later regretted? Have you ever tossed and turned all night, replaying to yourself an angry encounter with someone and considering radical courses of action, only to realize the next day that the issue was too trivial to lose sleep over? These responses show how emotions can sometimes overrule effective thinking and lead to irrational and destructive behavior. We are all aware of occasions when we have overreacted to situations we perceived as threatening, and made regrettable decisions. It is useful to analyze how emotions affect our decision making. This will enable us to control the role emotions play in our decisions and help us make choices that reflect our rationally considered, long-term values rather than the passions of the moment.

Perhaps more than any other type of experience we have, emotions display the close linkage between mind and body. When our emotions are aroused, we experience intensified feelings about some situation. We may feel elation over some success, fear over an impending failure, grief over the death of a parent or friend. These feelings have both a physiological and a psychological side. An athlete who senses victory is likely to experience both a surge of energy and thoughts of the rewards success will bring. Faced with failure, he or she may experience fatigue and baleful thoughts of the criticism that will follow defeat. Understanding emotions requires understanding both the physiological and psychological effects to which they give rise.

Emotions and Physiology

The pattern of physiological changes and the degree to which they occur vary according to the intensity of the emotion and the type of situation. When the feelings involved are mild, the physiological changes are correspondingly slight. In mild fear, for example, the changes include increase in pulse rate, blood pressure, and rate of breathing. Though physiological, these changes actually constitute a good part of what happens when we speak of an individual as being "psyched up"; their effect is that the individual has the energy to work longer and more intensely and is thus better able to deal with the situation that causes the fear.

When feelings are strong, however, the accompanying physiological changes are extensive. In strong anger or fear, the changes have the effect of preparing the body for a fight. Suppose that on a camping trip you suddenly find yourself surrounded by a forest fire, and interpret the situation as a critical threat to your life. You would probably experience strong fear, and automatically and instantly, your body would begin to put into effect a pattern of extensive changes.

Under strong fear, the adrenal glands begin to release adrenalin into the bloodstream, stimulating the heart to greater activity and thereby increasing circulation. The circulatory system begins to redistribute the blood supply, taking it away from stomach and intestines, where it is not needed at the moment, and sending it to the big muscles of arms and legs, where it will be needed. The liver begins to pump glycogen into the bloodstream, providing a quick source of extra energy. Rate of breathing increases, and the spleen dispatches large numbers of additional red corpuscles into the bloodstream, enabling the lungs to extract more oxygen from the air. Meanwhile, the pupils of the eyes dilate a little, admitting more light. The hair bristles. Blood-clotting hormones appear in the blood, providing some protection against bleeding to death in the event of a wound. One is prepared either to run or to fight. But one is not prepared to think, for the redistribution of the blood supply tends to decrease the supply to the higher brain centers and to leave them undernourished.

In grief or despair, the pattern may be quite different. Suppose you have your life's savings invested in a small manufacturing plant. You have failed to renew your insurance, and the plant is destroyed by fire. At the moment you can see no way to start again. Presumably, you would experience feelings of despair. The resulting physiological changes would probably have the effect of lowering energy rather than mobilizing it. They would include a reduction in pulse rate, blood pressure, breathing, appetite, and muscular strength. The general numbness of body and mind that results makes the blow easier to bear, and since nothing can be done at the moment anyway, no surge of energy is called for.

The pattern of physiological changes varies, then, with the emotion we experience. Moreover, both these changes and their psychological effects can be intensified and prolonged by our own perception that we are experiencing the emotion in question. When we are happy about something, we tend to become even happier when we realize that we are happy; likewise, the experience of our own sadness tends to make us sadder still. Actors know about this reaction, and often use it consciously to help themselves assume the appropriate emotions for the parts they play. But the reaction occurs quite normally even when we are not conscious of it. That is why we are sometimes able to ease emotional upheavals in ourselves by not dwelling on them and instead putting our minds on something else.

Emotions and Thinking

The importance of emotions to a rich and full experience of life should not be underestimated. Without happiness, love, and the emotions that go with aesthetic experiences, life would be empty indeed. Moreover, even our negative emotions, such as anger and fear, are vital to our very survival. An individual incapable of anger would be at the mercy of others; someone incapable of fear would be unable to summon reserves of energy for emergencies and would lack the survival skill of knowing when the only thing to do is turn and run. Negative emotions also help us in many other situations: fear of failure makes us strive harder to achieve our goals; remorse over our misdeeds impels us to try to do better. But although we cannot do without emotions, they are often more of a liability than an asset to effective thinking, especially when they are strong.

Sometimes mild emotions promote sound thinking. The physiological changes they involve increase mental alertness and endurance. Students can often study longer, harder, and more effectively when they experience mild anxiety over an examination. A person who must make a speech is apt to do a better job if he or she is a little worried about success. Under the influence of mild emotions, you can probably write better poetry or better term papers or be more persuasive in a discussion.

On the other hand, even mild emotions tend to hamper sound thinking if

they intensify self-defensive behavior. When our primary interest is to defend ourselves, we become more alert to methods of defense than to the truth and may be tempted to use whatever weapons seem necessary. Thus, if you have just received what you think is an unfair grade on a test, it would be best to allow your emotions to subside before going to see your instructor. Otherwise, you may be too angry to make an effective case that the grade is unjust and hence have no chance of convincing your instructor to change it. Or you may use self-deceptive mechanisms to blind yourself to your instructor's views on the matter and hence be unable to learn from his or her explanation of the grade, no matter how correct it may be.

Strong emotions, especially fear and rage, are about as useful in thinking as lighted matches in a dynamite factory. Excessive emotion interferes with effective thinking in at least five ways.

First, strong emotion **interferes with learning.** Students who are deeply fearful of academic failure find themselves frantically reading words but retaining little meaning. Physiologically, they are on an emergency footing: they have plenty of energy and can study for many hours without seeming to tire. But they are unable to learn, partly because their heightened energy state makes them rush from one sentence to the next without absorbing any meaning.

Second, strong emotion **inhibits recall**. Students who are too fearful of failing an examination often "draw a blank": they are unable to recall much of what they actually know while taking the examination, even though they can easily remember the material once the examination is over.

Third, strong emotion **narrows and distorts perception.** When we are afraid, we tend to perceive only those elements in the situation that stimulate our fear. Walking alone at night, we perceive every sound as a mugger's footsteps. We focus so intently on those "footsteps" that we fail to perceive the policeman on the other side of the street. When we are angry, we tend to perceive only those elements in the situation that feed our anger. A person who is angry at his or her spouse tends to perceive all of the spouse's bad behavior and none of the good.

Associated with the narrowing of perception is the inhibition of creative thinking, especially the formation of rival hypotheses. Critical thinking is also inhibited. We become prone to most of the fallacies of thinking, especially hasty generalization and neglected aspect. For example, when we feel threatened by another person, we are likely to exaggerate a particular flaw we find in that person and then generalize it to his or her whole character. Then we are tempted to extend this generalization to the person's family and even to his or her associates.

Fourth, strong emotion **hinders concentration.** When we interpret a situation as critical, we tend to become so concerned with the threat that we are unable to concentrate on the problem. We are like a person trying to work a difficult problem in calculus while suffering from a severe stomachache. Many students are unable to concentrate while preparing for examinations because their thoughts continually drift toward the painful consequences of failure. People who suffer from stage fright are prevented from concentrating on a speech because they are too busy worrying about how the audience will react to them; they stutter and stammer and forget the words they planned to say. Thus fear may help bring about the very things we fear.

Finally, strong emotion **reduces the control of behavior by thought.** Under strong emotional tension, we feel an urge to do something immediately, even if it is wrong, rather than wait until we can consider the situation in the light of accumulated experience. We tend to act first and think later—and later we are likely to have a lot of thinking to do to get out of the mess caused by our impulsive behavior.

Anxiety

Some emotional states, such as fear and anger, tend to be short-lived; others last longer. An example with which we have all had some experience is anxiety, or lingering apprehension. Anxiety is like fear in that the accompanying physiological changes prepare us for action. But it differs from fear in two respects. Fear is a reaction to a perceived danger in one's immediate situation whereas anxiety is likely to be focused on remote situations, usually in the future. And whereas fear usually subsides when the stimulus has been removed, anxiety is a persisting state of tension.

Within limits, anxiety, like fear, promotes adaptation. When we have experienced a difficult situation, we often feel anxiety that we will encounter it again. Anxiety is an unpleasant state, and we will go to great lengths to get rid of it. Hence we are driven to learn how to avoid difficulties in the future and to take measures for dealing with anticipated emergencies before they occur. Thus students who are anxious enough about final examinations may study throughout the semester to prepare for the anticipated emergency.

Like other forms of emotion, however, anxiety is harmful when excessive. If we spend a good deal of time worrying about things that are unlikely to happen, our anxiety level is too high and may be interfering with the effectiveness of our thinking and decision making. Anxiety may be directed toward a specific type of situation, such as speaking in front of a group or flying. Specific phobias like these may lead us to avoid activities that arouse them, thus depriving ourselves of experiences that are otherwise enjoyable and valuable. Some people allow anxieties to restrict their activities more and more until they are virtually paralyzed; such severe anxiety often requires years of therapy to resolve. On the other hand, anxiety may be general and relatively unfocused. Even so, it makes us tense and defensive and may eventually lead to serious health problems.

Clearly, anxiety, when excessive, interferes with adaptation. The overanxious person is so concerned with relieving the pain of anxiety that he or she tends to deal with the anxiety itself rather than its cause. Students who are reasonably anxious about examinations may study conscientiously all semester. But if they are overanxious, they may find the temptation to escape through distraction devices all but irresistible. Then, as the examination period approaches, the anxiety mounts. It may become so acute that effective study becomes impossible, and attempts to study only convince the student that he or she knows very little. In the end, the only escape may be to withdraw from college or enter the infirmary with an illness that is psychologically caused. Excessive anxiety is at the bottom of many psychosomatic illnesses, for it keeps its victim in a chronic state of emotional stress.

There are many ways of dealing with anxiety, depending on its symptoms and causes. In general, the more specifically focused anxiety is, the easier it is to cope with. Suppose, for example, that you have a fear of speaking before a group. Therapists often treat specific phobias by gradually increasing the dosage of exposure to the feared situation—a kind of psychological desensitizing. If you are afraid to give speeches, you might try giving your speech to your roommate first and then to a few friends. You may then be better prepared to give the speech in class, your anxiety considerably diminished by having experienced the preliminary, less threatening situations. Also, you will be more confident about the speech itself because you are more familiar with it. Often, specific anxieties can be overcome without our ever knowing what originally gave rise to them. A person who fears flying may be able to get over the problem by getting on and around planes at every opportunity, until the situation of flying becomes almost commonplace and is no longer a cause of anxiety. When severe, however, phobias tend to resist self-help measures and can be alleviated only through professional counseling.

Less focused anxiety is more difficult to deal with, since it is not centered on any one type of situation or experience. Often, generalized anxiety arises from problems or experiences that have been repressed and may be difficult to uncover. Frequently, the problem is one of deep-seated insecurity or of feelings of inferiority.

Feelings of Insecurity and Inferiority

Like anxiety, feelings of insecurity and inferiority affect everyone. The conditions of our lives are shifting and uncertain, and none of us performs up to his or her standards at all times. Feelings of insecurity and inferiority may, however, be based on false premises, and when they are, they can get out of hand. This is especially the case when the premises are repressed and thus concealed from conscious awareness. Then, along with generalized anxiety, insecurity and a sense of inferiority can affect a person's whole approach to life, limiting both experience and achievement.

Excessive insecurity may be defined as an unduly pessimistic personal point of view. Because of this pessimism, insecure people are predisposed to be more sensitive to potential threats and to interpret situations as more threatening than they are. Thus they fall easy prey to anxiety. They are unduly fearful that they will lose their jobs and be unable to sustain themselves and their loved ones. They worry about losing the affection and approval of those whose love and admiration they desire. They are concerned that they will fall into ill health, and so on. The insecurity may be limited to one area of need or it may extend to all.

Excessive insecurity is often responsible for poor decisions and rash actions. Insecure people are especially prone to self-defensive thinking and behavior. They tend to be unwilling to adopt a course of action unless it has a very high probability of success. They are intolerant of criticism, take every setback as a crushing defeat, and are likely to be troubled by anxiety and guilt. They may become excessively fearful with little cause and overreact to the threat, either by anger and aggression or by fleeing from it. They are likely to interpret the remarks of others as critical even when no criticism is intended and to meet even mild criticism with a sharp rebuttal or by breaking off the conversation. Insecure people seldom enter risky occupations. They will reject exciting but uncertain careers in which they could have been brilliantly successful for dull but secure ones in which they

will never be happy. Students who are excessively insecure about their college work may study long hours and strive compulsively to meet every requirement to the letter. Or they may not study at all since failure is easier to accept if one never tries to succeed.

Should we find ourselves suffering from insecurity—and *suffering* is the appropriate word—the first step is to find the false propositions in our personal point of view. Insecurity may originate in some severe emotional shock. It may be intensified, if not caused, by the discovery that the premises by which we have guided our life no longer work. Students from small communities or rural areas often feel insecure in the strange new world of a large college.

The most probable cause, however, is likely to be something that occurred in childhood. If our parents were inconsistent, so that we never knew quite how to behave in order to stay in their good graces, or if they were themselves insecure or in conflict, it would be only natural for us to become pessimistic about getting and keeping the affection of those most important to us. If when we were children our parents were hard pressed to pay the rent, we may feel economically insecure no matter how much money we have in the bank. If in childhood we found it very difficult, if not impossible, to satisfy the standards set for us by parents, teachers, and others in authority, we may have difficulty feeling secure about the tasks we take on later in life.

Finding the cause is itself an aid in overcoming insecurity. When we find the cause, we can almost always see immediately that it springs from a hasty generalization, based on instances that are too few and no longer representative of our life as a whole.

The rest of the remedy is to correct the

general claim. Complete correction will be difficult, but any progress we can make will increase our happiness. A number of procedures should prove helpful. The first is to make a realistic appraisal of what we can expect from the world. We can hardly feel secure if we set our standards of security too high. We are hardly justified in expecting everyone to love us exclusively or in believing that we can succeed in all we attempt or that we can keep everything in our present situation exactly as it is.

Our appraisal of what to expect from the world will be more accurate if we deepen and broaden our understanding of other people. When we understand them, their behavior will seem less inconsistent and capricious. When we are better able to predict their behavior, we will be more able to deal with them successfully. By learning what to expect of other people, we become less likely to make impossible demands of them and to experience frustration when these demands are not met.

Insecurity is often tied to deep-seated feelings of inferiority. Of course, knowing that there are some things we cannot do very well is a necessary part of honest self-appraisal. But the correlation between actual incompetence and feelings of incompetence is quite low. Sometimes even the ablest people feel incompetent to cope with life. They are suffering from inferiority feelings, which amount to a chronically unsatisfactory self-concept.

Like insecurity, feelings of inferiority often arise from faulty generalizations about oneself; hence, the first step in dealing with them is to search out the experiences on which the generalizations are based. Once again, childhood is a good place to look. If our parents punished us in such a way as to make us feel unworthy of their love or pushed us to achieve goals which were beyond our capacity or com-

pared us unfavorably with our brothers or sisters, we are likely to suffer the pangs of inferiority feelings. If our parents overprotected us by giving us everything we needed without effort on our part, solving all our problems, and shielding us from trouble, we may suffer from inferiority feelings in adulthood because we have failed to gain experience in running our own life. Once the apparent cause of feelings of inferiority has been found, we can begin the process of improving our self-concept. But we should not expect to finish the job in a day.

The next step is to make a careful appraisal of our own assets and liabilities. A person suffering from inferiority tends to discount evidence of success and dwell on evidence of failure, especially recent evidence. Thus a student who has a good academic average may suffer out of all proportion because of one poor grade, ignoring the fact that his or her average is still good. The problem, therefore, is to make new generalizations about oneself which take into account *all* the evidence.

Another necessary step is to revise our goals to make them consistent with our abilities. Persons suffering from inferiority feelings tend to set their goals impossibly high, on the theory that only earth-shaking achievements will vindicate them before the world. They thereby condemn themselves to almost certain failure and new scars on their already battered self-concepts. A counselor can help with this step. By administering a battery of tests and making a thorough study of a person's record, he or she can give a more objective appraisal of that person's abilities than the person could give unassisted. Striving to achieve goals for which we lack the ability is an almost certain way of intensifying feelings of inferiority.

Finally, the individual struggling with feelings of inferiority needs to set about achieving goals in a realistic way. If we expect to achieve great things overnight, failure will reinforce our sense of inferiority. The solution, therefore, is to set small, modest, short-term goals and to strive to achieve them. By so doing, we gradually build up a balance of success. We also reduce emotional stress by using our energy in constructive effort.

Guilt

If by careless or drunken driving you caused injury or death to others, you would doubtless suffer from guilt and remorse. Such feelings are inevitable when we perform actions we believe are wrong; they are the means by which conscience punishes us when we violate our own moral codes, as all of us sometimes do.

As long as the punishment fits the crime, guilt feelings are indispensable to society. No number of laws and police could hold society together were it not for the fact that individuals suffer from guilt feelings when they violate their codes and anticipate more guilt feelings when they are tempted to violate them again. Within limits, guilt feelings also aid adaptation. People with poorly developed moral codes and no tendency toward remorse have a high probability of spending most of their lives in jail. But the punishment does not always fit the crime. As innumerable clergy and counselors have observed, those who suffer most from guilt feelings are frequently the least guilty. The correlation between guilt feelings and real guilt is low, if not actually negative.

When guilt feelings are excessive, as they often are, they tend to prevent rather than promote adaptation. Feelings of guilt are extremely painful, for they imply a belief that one is unworthy of love and respect. Persons afflicted with guilt will

go to great lengths to be rid of the pain. In extreme cases, they may spend a lifetime trying to atone for a minor offense. Upon occasion, people in middle age mail to supermarkets payment—with interest— for candy bars they stole as children or take out large ads in newspapers to apologize for a childhood insult. Others seek to reduce the guilt by some form of self-punishment, such as denying themselves certain pleasures and comforts. Or, as some psychologists believe, they may unconsciously court accidents as a means of self-punishment. They may also try to excuse themselves from blame by mechanisms of self-deception. If all else fails, they may repress the knowledge of the guilt. But then it is only driven underground; the person still feels guilty but does not know why. Persons afflicted with guilt frequently find it difficult to do anything constructive about the situation, partly because pathological guilt tends to carry with it the assumption that one can never be forgiven, and partly because they fear making another mistake that would only add to their guilt. The result is that the stress continues and pervades their entire personalities. When combined with feelings of inferiority, as is frequent, guilt feelings constitute a very difficult problem.

When we make a mistake for which we feel guilty, it is important to face the issue squarely and deal with it as soon as possible. Otherwise, we will suffer unnecessarily, and we make take some unwise action or resort to self-deception. If the mistake has injured someone, we can relieve guilt by making appropriate reparation. If circumstances do not permit direct reparation to the person injured, a good substitute is to do a good turn for someone else. And certainly we can use the mistake as a lesson to help us avoid future mistakes. The past cannot be undone, but in matters of conscience, as in any other, past experiences can be used to make a better future.

Depression

Another emotional problem that is often caused in part by false premises in the frame of reference is depression. Depression, like the other psychological tormentors described above, strikes us all at one time or another as we encounter disturbing or painful events. But if the depression does not lift with time, or if it continues for an extended period without apparent cause, then it is time to view it as a problem and try to deal with it. Severe depression that includes suicidal thoughts, whether it occurs in ourselves or others, should always be viewed as a reason for seeking professional assistance. Students who commit suicide—and there are many every year—often need not have been lost but for the fact that their threats to kill themselves were dismissed by their friends and associates as idle talk. Low-grade depression, on the other hand, may subside with the aid of effective thinking techniques, leaving the sufferer wondering why he or she didn't recognize the problem and take action against it before.

A mixture of insecurity and anxiety often figures in depression. Depression is experienced as feelings of unhappiness, apathy, and pessimism. The depressed person may be fatigued and irritable much of the time. Nothing seems worth the effort; the cards seem to be stacked against him or her. The depressed person is especially vulnerable to the fallacy of decision by indecision because he or she lacks the energy to make resolute decisions and feels that things will turn out badly anyway. When they do, often because the individual has not taken the trouble to gather enough information and develop viable proposals for action, he or she feels even more manipulated by fate and even more depressed. Positive events are interpreted by the depression sufferer in the most negative possible way. Eeyore, the donkey in A.A. Milne's classic children's story, *Winnie the Pooh,* illustrates the typical attitudes of depression: he always feels overlooked, unwanted, unappreciated, uncelebrated—even though all the other animals regard him as their good friend.

As with other long-term emotional problems, dealing with depression requires searching through the frame of reference and value system for the false propositions that underlie feelings of unacceptability and worthlessness. In cases where depression arises from insecurity, it can be dealt with in part by discarding the old parental and environmental "tapes" in our subconscious that continually play bad news. Another important step in dealing with depression is to take a more active role in directing our lives. This requires developing proposals for action that promise to lead us to our objectives and then acting upon them. In so doing, it is important not to cheat our value system; going against our own values only leads to guilt feelings, which in the end intensify, rather than alleviate, depression. Dealing with depression also requires attention to the physical side of the mind-body dependency by treating physical illnesses promptly and getting plenty of exercise. A regular program of exercise gives us more energy, which we can then apply to both mental and physical tasks. In general, the self-help technique for depression involves taking a more active part in one's life. As it becomes clear to the depressed person that his or her actions do make things happen, the depression dissipates.

Coping with Stress

We have seen that emotional stress can have powerful and pervasive effects on our thinking and hence that emotions need to be controlled as responsibly as possible. Another reason for controlling emotions is that, especially when prolonged, emotional stress can be damaging physically as well. Even a short outburst of anger, for example, has effects that stay with us for a while. Only seconds are required for the physiological changes associated with anger to take place, but hours, days, or weeks may be required to restore the bodily economy to normal. Usually, the tension of emotions persists until the disturbing situation has passed or has been dealt with. When the situation is a prolonged one and the emotional stress is intense enough, serious physiological impairments can occur. The connection between prolonged stress and ulcers is long established; emotional disturbance is also suspected of causing or contributing to heart trouble, asthma, allergies, high blood pressure, diseases of the colon, and a host of other disorders. Of course, the dependency works the other way, too. If a person's thyroid gland is not functioning properly, he or she may suffer symptoms of depression or even schizophrenia. Diabetes can cause mental problems, especially if unrecognized. More than one patient has been treated for a psychiatric disorder while the real cause, a physical disease, went unnoticed and unchecked. On the whole, however, physical problems are more likely to result from emotional problems than to cause them.

In addition to the damaging effects of emotional stress on our thinking, then, we also have reasons of health for bringing our emotions under control. Control does not mean elimination; there are times when we should be afraid or angry, times when we should be mournful, and times when we should feel remorse. If we did not experience these emotions in some contexts, our frame of reference would be giving us a false picture. Responsible control of emotions means becoming emotional in the right way, in the right amount, and at the right time but not allowing emotions to dominate our thinking. Achieving control over emotions is a twofold enterprise. First, we have to learn to withstand the outbursts of emotion that occur in particular situations and are likely to dominate or rule out effective thinking and decision-making for the duration of their intensity. Second, we have to learn to deal with long-term emotional problems, which arise from deep-seated inaccuracies in the personal point of view that distort our thinking.

The first of these enterprises is the easier one, for the procedures for dealing with onslaughts of emotion in particular circumstances are nothing more than rules of common sense. Yet they require our attention and effort to be put to use, for common sense is precisely what often deserts us when emotional storms occur.

Avoid Tension-producing Stimuli. One of the most effective means for controlling emotional outbursts is not to let them start. If we know that we tend to become angry, fearful, or morose if certain subjects are discussed, it is wise to avoid such discussions until we find out the source of the problem. Students who know that they tend to panic at examination time should try to take a schedule of courses that will not result in their examinations coming all at once. Many emotional difficulties can be avoided simply by avoiding the situations that produce them. If we are already in a state of stress, a distraction device may prove useful. For example, a person experiencing grief over the death of a friend may find it helpful to keep occupied or to take a brief vacation in new surroundings.

Recognize the Symptoms. We usually know when we are terrified or furious, but we sometimes fail to recognize the symptoms of anxiety and other forms of excessive emotional stress. These include insomnia, sweaty palms, lack of concentration, excessive hostility or irritability, and a feeling that one must constantly hurry. There is, of course, considerable variation among individuals, and in situations where emotion is appropriate symptoms like these need not indicate an unacceptable level of stress. We require more tension for an athletic contest than for studying and decision making. Nevertheless, these symptoms usually indicate that emotions are running high and are apt to affect behavior.

Get Rid of Excess Energy. When our tension level is high we may find ourselves unable to think effectively about a situation until we can use up some of the excess energy generated. In such a situation, the remedy is to burn up some of the energy with relaxing forms of exercise. For example, students who are so keyed up that they cannot study may find that a game of tennis, a swim, or a long walk can reduce their tension level sufficiently to enable them to work more effectively.

Reinterpret the Situation. The secret of real emotional control lies in our interpretation of the threatening situation. Before we can react to any situation, we must first interpret it, and as Montaigne said, "A man is hurt not so much by what happens, as by his opinion of what happens." If we suspect that our emotional reaction is inappropriate or excessive, a reinterpretation of the situation is called for. Reinterpreting a situation is really a matter of setting up alternative hypotheses that will explain our experience in a way that is less threatening than the hypothesis that is responsible for our emotional reaction.

Consider the case of Bill Biltmore, who throughout his upbringing was allowed little independence. When he entered college, Bill's parents brought him to the campus, selected his room and his roommates, told him what courses to study, paid his fees for the semester, gave him $100 for pocket money, and instructed him to write for more when that ran out. Bill's grades for his first semester were low. Now, at the beginning of his second semester, his parents hand him a check for his expenses for the semester, tell him that he will receive no more, let him get back to the campus by himself, show no interest in what courses he will take or where he will room, and make no comment about his low grades.

Bill might conclude that his parents are furious because he made low grades. But these facts could be explained by three other hypotheses: (1) his parents are too occupied with other matters to give him their usual attention; (2) they are disappointed with his grades and believe he will do better if left on his own; (3) they now have enough confidence in him to let him manage his own life. The habit of setting up rival hypotheses is a good one to cultivate, especially in interpreting personal matters. We will often discover that we have interpreted a situation inaccurately and that our fear or anger was not justified.

An important aid to objectively reinterpreting a situation is to try to describe it to oneself in emotively neutral language. As we saw in Chapter 23, evaluative terms often have the power to stir our emotions and sway our judgment. These should be avoided, especially in first efforts at reinterpreting emotion-producing situations. Moreover, words often acquire the power to stir emotions quite apart from their standard evaluative meaning. Suppose that you have an employer whom you dislike intensely. And suppose that this person often addresses you as "friend" and then criticizes or insults you. Through this experience, the word "friend" could acquire the power to stir your anger even in quite different contexts. When a real friend addresses you as "friend," you might find yourself irritated even though you know what your friend means. Thus the same term may have quite different emotional meanings for different people. To avoid reacting emotionally to a situation, we should cultivate the habit of thinking about the situation in terms that have neutral meanings for us.

Take Constructive Action. Constructive action in response to a threatening situation will usually reduce the stress level. We often find ourselves in situations where we cannot possibly do everything we should do in time to meet some deadline. The constructive procedure is to do the most important things first. In this way we can use the energy generated by our emotions to deal with the threatening situation. Suppose you are unprepared for an examination you must take within a day or two. If at this late hour you try to learn all the minutiae the examination might cover, every topic you try to learn becomes a tension-producing stimulus and your tension level is apt to rise higher and higher. A more constructive approach to the problem would be to study the main topics first.

Avoid Rash Decisions. Excessive emo-

tions may cause us not only to exaggerate the situation, but also to make rash decisions. When our emotional level is high, it is advisable to postpone making important decisions until our emotions have subsided or until we must act to avoid decision by indecision. When we must make a decision before our emotions have subsided, we should carefully follow the procedures for forming and testing proposals for action discussed in Chapter 13. Since the actions we may take under the influence of emotions are likely to be extreme, we should try to find proposals for action that will not be disastrous if our interpretation of the situation proves wrong. We should also keep in mind the fact that emotions tend to make us forget the long-term values experience has taught us. For example, when someone has hurt us, our anger may make us momentarily value striking back. Later, when our anger has subsided, we may realize that we have allowed the wrong value proposition to guide our behavior.

When the measures just described fail to keep our emotions within desirable limits, the trouble may stem from distortions in our frame of reference arising from repressed and long-forgotten experiences. As we have seen, it may be possible to discover false and damaging propositions on our own, and there are many books available that can be useful for dealing with deep-running personal problems. Discovering the basis of our emotional difficulties on our own is, however, a difficult project. Experiences too painful to remember are hard to recover, and the very distortions that lead us into emotional problems are apt to color and twist our efforts to frame useful hypotheses to explain our problems. When our decisions seem to be consistently bad and we are unable to reason clearly about our problems or to take constructive action to alleviate them, an expert's help in identifying the offending propositions can be useful.

Expert Help

A large part of the difficulty in solving our own problems is in seeing all the relevant evidence in a clear and objective way. When we try to find the propositions that lead us into difficulty, we are apt to underrate the importance of some experiences and overrate that of others and to cling to unsound value judgments rather than analyze them objectively. Professional counseling is aimed at helping us overcome these problems. Although methods differ according to the school of thought to which a counselor belongs, most professional counselors have one practice in common: they help us solve our problem, but they do not solve it for us. Their aim is not to lecture us about our false beliefs but to help us bring to light the relevant propositions, so we can examine and begin to modify them.

One approach to counseling is especially worth considering because it advocates an objectivity and tolerance that we can also apply ourselves in bringing submerged feelings to the surface. As the psychologist Carl Rogers describes this school of thought, the counselor operates from the premise that we are all capable of making our own decisions. The counselor makes no attempt to judge anyone, accepting each patient as he or she is, without blame or praise. The counselor has only one purpose: to give complete and sympathetic understanding, by thinking about the patient's problems as he or she does. The counselor tries to adopt the patient's frame of reference, to see the patient through the patient's own eyes, and to act as a sensitive and accurate sounding board for what he or she says.

When the patient makes a statement, the counselor rephrases it in accurate, matter-of-fact language without a trace of criticism, and in a friendly tone of voice. When we hear our value judgments, hypotheses, and other propositions repeated to us in this way, we can more easily see the inaccuracies in them.

Advocates of this method of counseling believe the secret of its effectiveness lies in the atmosphere of the interview. Most of us have friends to whom we feel we can talk freely on some subjects because they will understand us. But we hesitate to discuss other subjects with them because we fear they will not understand or will have a personal reason for wanting us to think in some particular way. But an effective counselor tries to understand a patient in *all* respects and to exclude his or her own interests. This enables the person to become less self-defensive and to strip away self-deception, so that he or she can admit the relevant evidence to consciousness and correct the errors in it.

Many avenues of professional counseling are available, and we are fortunate that in our time the stigma once attached to seeking psychological counseling has all but disappeared. In some circumstances, clergy can be effective counselors, and many are trained in counseling techniques. In addition, psychiatrists and psychologists can be consulted, either individually or in group therapy sessions. The psychiatrist, as a physician with additional training in treating mental disorders, treats serious psychological problems with both medicine and therapy. Many colleges have their own psychiatrists, who operate through the campus health center. Other colleges provide referral systems that allow students to obtain low-cost psychiatric help through their health-service fees. A psychologist has a graduate degree in psychology and may have additional clinical training in therapy. He or she helps patients see their problems more realistically and find ways of solving them. Often the psychologist helps the patient use a variant of the five-phase decision-making cycle to alleviate personal problems. The psychologist does not dispense medicine. Most colleges now have at least one psychologist to counsel students, and many have full-fledged counseling services. Group therapy may be led by either a psychiatrist or a psychologist; in group therapy, a small group of people, often with similar problems, help one another to work out their problems. Some colleges with counseling services offer group therapy to their students. Therapy groups are also led by psychologists in private practice. Students who believe they need professional advice in solving their problems should begin by finding out what their school has to offer by way of counseling services. If nothing is available, they may wish to consult a professional counselor on their own.

Suggested Supplementary Reading

Carl R. Rogers, *On Becoming a Person* (Boston: Houghton Mifflin Co., 1961).

Exercise 29A

Problems 1–17. Indicate whether the following statements agree with the hypotheses presented in this chapter by writing in the blank T if true or F if false.

1. The physiological changes occurring with emotions usually follow the same pattern and reach about the same degree.

    _____

2. The physiological changes occurring with strong anger include an increase in blood supply to the higher brain centers.

    _____

3. How one feels about a situation may depend more on his or her interpretation of it than on the situation itself.

    _____

4. Emotions have no beneficial effects on thinking.

    _____

5. Even mild emotions can interfere with objectivity.

    _____

6. Fear and rage interfere with sound thinking by fixing one's attention on the threat rather than the remedy.

    _____

7. Under the influence of strong emotion, one is more likely to invent rival hypotheses.

    _____

8. Emotions tend to make one more susceptible to the fallacy of oversimplification.

    _____

9. We are sometimes unable to think clearly at the very time we most need to do so.

    _____

10. Strong emotions broaden the field of perception.

    _____

11. A strong resolution not to have emotions is an effective means of controlling them.

    _____

12. The emotional tensions of anxiety usually disappear as soon as the threatening situation has passed.

_____

13. Anxiety tends to make one exaggerate the significance of unfavorable evidence.

_____

14. Insecurity is usually the result of a realistic appraisal of one's total situation.

_____

15. The ambitions of a person suffering from a sense of inferiority are usually too modest.

_____

16. It is wise for a depressed person to get more rest and let others control his or her life.

_____

17. To deal with guilt, one should discard one's value system and invent new values that correspond to what one feels like doing.

_____

Problems 18–24. Write your answers to the following questions in the space provided.

18. You and your neighbor have a common lawn and no fence between your houses. Because you have been ill, you have neglected to mow your side of the lawn, and the grass has grown quite high. Finally your neighbor mows both your side and his. If you conclude that he has tired of seeing your ugly lawn and has meddled in your business, what defense mechanism have you possibly used?

_____

19. Write another hypothesis to explain your neighbor's behavior.

_____

20. List two emotional influences that might have led to your first conclusion.

_____

21. You are slightly late for a job interview because you tripped on a discarded beer can and fell, tearing your clothing. You think you have the damage patched up. But while you are waiting, one of the secretaries whispers something to the other, and the two suddenly start laughing. List two emotional influences that might lead you to conclude they are laughing at you.

22. What are two self-defeating actions that might result from your drawing this conclusion?

_____

_____

23. What would be another hypothesis to explain the secretaries' behavior?

_____

24. What is the advantage of your not assuming the laughter is directed at you?

_____

Exercise 29B

Problems 1–12. Answer each question before reading beyond it. Use all the evidence presented up to and in the question, but do not use evidence presented in later questions.

You teach freshman English at Wysacki University. You have noticed that the themes turned in by Jack Cratchit are unusually poor. Not knowing that Cratchit was out for football, you are surprised when he starts at quarterback in the first game of the season. On the first play from scrimmage he fumbles the snap and is downed. After a six-yard loss then he throws a wild pass that is almost intercepted. On the next play, he calls for a quarterback sneak, which gains three yards. At that point the coach takes Cratchit out of the game.

1. Rate the hypothesis that Cratchit's intelligence is low.

_____

The following Monday afternoon you drop by the practice field and find Cratchit working out with the kicking team, covering punts. When you comment to the coach, he replies, "I can't understand it. He's the smartest quarterback prospect we've had in a long time." The next morning you look up Cratchit's entrance record. He barely graduated from high school, but his scores on intelligence tests place him only slightly below the genius class.

2. Rate the hypothesis that Cratchit's intelligence is low.

_____

3. Write a rival hypothesis to explain Cratchit's poor performance, in high school, in English, and in football.

_____

The following week your class is making speeches. When you call on Cratchit, he mumbles that he is unprepared. You invite him to come to your office for a conference. When he explains that he simply does not know anything to make a speech about, you shift the conversation to football. In response to a question, he gives you a brilliant exposition of the respective advantages of the wishbone and pro-style systems of offense. After some urging, he agrees to make a speech about football at the next class. He cuts the next class. The following day you go to the second freshman game. Cratchit plays brilliantly on the kicking team.

4. List the antecedents common to all instances of poor performance by Cratchit.

_____

5. Rate the hypothesis that Cratchit's poor performances are due to laziness.

_____

6. Write a rival hypothesis to explain why Cratchit did well on the kicking team but not at quarterback or in schoolwork.

_____

When Cratchit cuts class again on Monday, you send for him. He explains that he cut class because he could not make a speech.

7. What defense mechanism has he used?

_____

When you ask Cratchit why he played so much better on the kicking team than at quarterback, he replies, "It was the wool jersey I was wearing at quarterback. Wool makes me itch and gives me the willies. They gave me a nylon jersey when I played on the kicking team."

8. What fallacy has he apparently committed?

_____

You explain to Cratchit that he has fine prospects as a student and that you would like to help him improve. He replies, "It's no use, Prof. I'll never be able to apply myself."

9. Write the faulty general conclusion Cratchit seems to have drawn about himself.

_____

You ask Cratchit about his ambitions. He replies, "I'd like to be a surgeon, but I'd have to go to medical school. I guess I'll play pro ball until I'm too old and then open a restaurant." You say, "You really like football that much?" His reply is, "I'm not crazy about it. I'd rather be a surgeon. But playing football is the only thing I can do well, so I guess I'll stick to it."

10. Write a hypothesis to explain why Cratchit does not want to go to medical school.

_____

You tell Cratchit that you will excuse him from making speeches if he will take a medical aptitude test. He agrees, "O.K., Prof., but you know I'll flunk it." The test shows Cratchit to be at the ninety-eighth percentile among college freshmen. When you explain the significance of the test to Cratchit, he replies, "Well, I've read a lot on subjects related to medicine, and I guess I've learned a few things. But I don't have the ability to apply myself to studying medicine."

11. What is the inconsistency in Cratchit's thinking?

_____

You tell Cratchit that with his ability he should have made a good record in high school. He replies, "Yeah, all my teachers told me that, but they didn't understand. When I was five the doctors thought I had rheumatic fever, and they kept me in bed for a year. I may not even have had it, because the docs say my heart is O.K. Anyway, the year was half over when I started to school. I started behind and I never caught up. I guess that's part of the trouble. But I'm not as smart as they think, either. My parents were always disappointed in my grades."

12. Write a rival for Cratchit's hypothesis about his behavior.

_____

Chapter 30

Psychological Blinders

- **Mindsets**
- **Thought Habits**
- **Attitudes**
- **Stereotypes**

- **Displacement**
- **Identification**
- **Failure to Listen**

In Chapter 28, we considered a number of mechanisms of self-defense by which we are able to distort, ignore, or avoid facts that we do not wish to admit into our experience. There is another cluster of psychological pitfalls that to some degree affect our thinking. With this group, the dominant theme is not so much self-defense as oversimplification. The world of experience is both complex and challenging, and we are regularly presented with situations that call upon us to rethink our beliefs, refine our values, and find new and more effective means of reaching our goals. We tend, however, to resist doing so. In part, the reasons for this are laziness and fear of the unfamiliar. The main reason, however, is simply that each of us is naturally conservative about his or her own personal point of view. Since we must rely on our frame of reference and value system to understand and deal with any situation we face, it is only natural for us to hope that the beliefs we have already developed are correct, that the values we already hold are adequate, and that tried

and true courses of action will prove successful in the future. As a result, we sometimes oversimplify: we miss the significance of new evidence or fail to see when new strategies of action are demanded. We may think of the mental tendencies and mechanisms by which we oversimplify as **psychological blinders.** They manifest close-mindedness in our thinking; used excessively, they can produce an adult with the mind of a child.

Mindsets

A **mindset** is a tendency of the human mind to view a situation in a certain way despite contrary evidence. Sometimes mindsets result in perceptual errors. Suppose that as you approach a busy traffic intersection you notice that the traffic light for your lane is green. While entering the intersection you focus your attention on other cars and you fail to notice that the light has changed even though you have been looking in the general direction of the light. If you have an accident or get a traffic ticket, a mindset is the villain. Mindsets account in part for our tendency to perceive what we expect to perceive. If we are looking for a diamond ring lost in the grass, we might mistake shiny dewdrops for the diamond because it is what we expect to see. If we are waiting for a friend to get off a plane, we may mistake anyone with a remotely similar appearance for the friend.

Mindsets extend well beyond the perceptual level. The damage a mindset can do is dramatically illustrated by the sinking of the *Titanic* on her maiden voyage in 1912, with the loss of 1,513 lives. Designed to be the safest ship afloat, the *Titanic* was equipped with a double bottom and sixteen watertight compartments. A mindset that the *Titanic* was unsinkable seems to have been largely responsible for the disaster.

The ship carried lifeboats sufficient for only one third of the passengers, and no assignment of passengers was made to these boats; nor were any drills held. The *Titanic* was unsinkable.

Three days out of Queenstown, the ship received its first wireless warning of icebergs in the steamer lanes. A few hours later another message about icebergs was received, but the wireless operator was too busy with his accounts to bother recording the message. The *Titanic* was unsinkable.

That afternoon another warning came in. This time the operator sent it to the Captain, who glanced at it casually and handed it without comment to the managing director of the White Star Line. By 9:30 that night at least five warnings of icebergs had been received and the *Titanic* was nearing their reported location. But no precautions were taken other than to warn the lookouts to be alert. The owners wanted a speed record; the *Titanic* steamed ahead into the darkness at twenty-two knots. The *Titanic* was unsinkable.

The pride of the White Star Line had yet another chance. At 11:30 p.m. the wireless crackled with a message from the *Californian:* "Say, old man, we are stuck here, surrounded by ice." But the mindset held, and the *Titanic*'s operator replied, "Shut up, shut up, keep out. I am talking to Cape Race; you are jamming my signals." The *Titanic* steamed ahead at twenty-two knots—unsinkable.

Ten minutes later the lookout spotted a giant iceberg dead ahead. Officers on the bridge did what they could to avoid the crash, but it was too late. The collision ripped a hundred-yard gash in the ship's double bottom. Although the watertight doors were closed immediately, the bulkheads not already damaged gave way, one by one. The great ship was settling by the bow, doomed.

The loading of the lifeboats went slowly and badly, in part because the passengers would not believe that so safe a ship could sink. The boats left the ship with nearly five hundred passengers less than capacity. At best there would have been room for no more than a thousand. Even so the casualties might have been few if help had come in time. Distress calls were sent out within minutes after the collision, and the ship did not go down until more than two hours later. A number of ships raced to the scene, in spite of the ice. But they were too far away to save the fifteen hundred who did not get into the lifeboats. Meantime, the *Californian* was lying within sight of the *Titanic,* possibly no more than five miles away. Her radio operator did not hear the *Titanic*'s wireless calls; he had gone to bed shortly after being told to "shut up." Some crew members did see the *Titanic*'s lights and rocket signals but did nothing more than try to communicate with the unknown ship by blinker. Testimony in the investigation of the disaster showed that the sea was calm and the night clear, and that the *Californian* might easily have pushed through the ice field to rescue most if not all of the passengers. Perhaps the *Californian*'s officers, too, had a mindset.

What makes mindsets difficult to control is that in following them we think we are being realistic when in fact we are not. Once we become aware that a mindset is dictating our thinking, it is often easy enough to shed it. We become more aware of our mindsets if we pause now and then to evaluate the course we are pursuing. The recommended technique is to set up rival hypotheses about other courses we might follow, giving more attention to contrary than confirmatory evidence, in order to offset our natural tendency to persist in the old course. For example, students should take stock at least once a semester to see whether they are following the academic program best for them. Many a student has graduated before realizing that he or she has pursued the wrong curriculum, though evidence available as early as the freshman year may have indicated that a change of program was desirable. The practice of re-examining goals and methods of achieving them can be overdone, of course, for if we become too anxious to avoid mindsets, we will fall into decision by indecision. The trick is to steer a middle course between the Scylla of "he who hesitates is lost" and the Charybdis of "look before you leap."

Thought Habits

First cousin to the mindset is the **thought habit,** a tendency to persist in a particular method of attack on a problem. Thought habits are not necessarily undesirable. On the contrary, making thought habits of the procedures of effective thinking is an excellent means of improving our decisions. But a thought habit becomes a handicap when it does not work. For example, despite failure in college, some students persist in using the study habits they acquired in high school. Some who depended on cramming in high school continue the practice in college. When they fail, instead of trying a new method, they merely cram harder. Unfortunately, a method that has been successful in one set of circumstances may not work as well in others.

The cure for this psychological blinder is to interpret failure as signaling a need for creative thinking. One way to avoid having to cram is to schedule regular study hours. If a student keeps missing the scheduled hours, he or she should set up a reward system for keeping them. Whenever an unsatisfactory grade is received, the student should examine his or her methods and try to pinpoint the cause. The next step is to set up alternative proposals for action, and in doing so, to consider analogous situations and try new approaches. Many problems are solved by trial and error anyway, and the more new methods we try the more likely we are to find a good one. It is desirable from time to time to test even successful methods by setting up rival hypotheses. We may find still better ones.

Attitudes

An **attitude** is a persisting state of readiness to react favorably or unfavorably, affirmatively or negatively, toward a stimulus, according to one's system of values. Sometimes capable students waste time in college because they have acquired an unfavorable attitude toward study. Even before knowing what an assignment is, they are prepared to react to it unfavorably, as being a useless, unpleasant task that will interfere with more desirable activities. A professor must present very convincing evidence to persuade such students that the assignment is worth doing. On the other hand, students who have acquired a favorable attitude toward study are prepared in advance to react to the assignment as an opportunity for self-improvement. The stronger this attitude, the more evidence will be required to persuade them that the assignment is not worth doing.

Another damaging attitude regarding study has it that only assignments that can be understood as directly relevant to one's planned career are worth doing. This attitude is harmful partly because, ironically enough, it damages one's career opportunities. No individual can predict what he or she will be doing, say, fifteen years after graduation; by that time, the professional responsibilities of many college graduates involve little or nothing for which they undertook specialized training in college. Moreover, a number of recent studies indicate that a general education enables one to advance farther in the business world than a narrowly specialized one. But the worst feature of this attitude is that it is cynical and exploitative toward education itself. A student who views learning simply as something to be used for personal advancement, instead of as a source of personal growth as well, will grow very little. Students who are able to put aside this psychological blinder find that the seemingly least "relevant" assignments are often the most enriching and sometimes even that they related to the planned career after all.

Many attitudes are never put into words; in fact, we are often unaware of our attitudes and their influence on our think-

ing. We would probably condemn some of our attitudes if we expressed them as value judgments and critically examined them. One such attitude is hostility to authority. This attitude usually begins with resentment toward a parent or some other figure in authority and may then be generalized to cover all forms of authority. Persons afflicted with this attitude act as though they believe that all authorities are always wrong. Hence they tend to reject ideas they associate with authority. They have, in effect, closed their minds to certain ideas. The cure for this attitude is not reverence for authority; on the contrary, reverence for authority is the opposite mistake, since authorities are far from being always right. A better solution is to analyze and evaluate ideas in terms of their own merit rather than in terms of their sources.

Attitudes are usually backed by some degree of emotion. Consequently, when an idea encounters a strong attitude, we are likely to react to it with a certain amount of emotion. When this occurs, there is always a danger that emotion will override critical scrutiny. If the attitude is favorable, we may react to it as to a long-lost friend; if the attitude is negative, we may put the idea through a Spanish inquisition and burn it at the stake. Obviously, effective thinkers must learn to curtail both these tendencies.

This is not to say that all attitudes are hazards to thinking. Like other persisting tendencies of mind, they are indispensable. They help us plot our way through unknown waters. We would have no time for anything else if we had to decide how to react to every stimulus. If all our attitudes were sound, all would be well. The trouble is that they are often in conflict with our basic goals and needs. When such conflicts occur, the conditions of life tend to become unsatisfactory, making it necessary to examine our attitudes and values. But we should not be sensitive only to failure and harmful attitudes on our own part. Our successes in life can be as indicative of healthy and useful attitudes as failures are of harmful ones.

Suppose, for example, that a recent college graduate who is highly successful at dealing with others in her personal life experiences a number of conflicts with her fellow workers when she enters her first job. If she considers her success in her ordinary dealings with people, she may realize that it is due to the fact that tolerance and warmth come naturally to her when pressure to succeed is low, because she places a high value on friendship and communication. If she then tries to treat personal relationships on the job as she does other friendships, her new attitude may lead to more successful business dealings and reduced stress. Thus reflection on our successful attitudes often leads to solutions to problems.

Stereotypes

Mindsets, thought habits, and attitudes all have a profound influence on our relations with other people. In our highly mobile society we must deal with many people about whom we know nothing. A thought habit all of us resort to in some degree is classifying people according to personality types and dealing with them as instances of the type instead of as individuals. Up to a point, this thought habit helps in getting along with people, for it enables us to generalize past experience with people and use it in dealing with strangers. How helpful this thought habit is depends on how accurately we type people and how readily we recognize that they are individuals.

But dealing with people by personality types may be a serious pitfall when the types become **stereotypes**, that is, oversimplified, relatively fixed, and identical conceptions of all persons in a category. We form many kinds of stereotypes: according to races and nationalities, such as Scots and Russians; occupations, such as professors and sales people; physical types, such as redheads and fat people; regional types, such as southerners and northerners; and so on.

Stereotypes usually involve a cluster of personality traits that are assumed to go together. The conventional stereotype of college professors includes impracticality and unworldliness, as well as absent-mindedness. Another stereotype pictures women as passive and fuzzy-minded, with no understanding of finances, an uncanny ability to manipulate men, and a tendency to be emotional. The opposite stereotype portrays men as aggressive and ambitious, obsessed with sports, domineering toward women, and overly protective of their own egos. Some stereotypes are derived from our personal experiences with people; others we receive from our culture—through parents, teachers, friends, or the media.

Even if stereotypes were accurate, which they are not, their use would be hazardous. We tend to stereotype people on the basis of some superficial clue, such as dress or mannerisms. Once we have "typed" a person, the stereotype becomes a mindset. Despite contrary evidence, we continue to treat the person in terms of the traits of the stereotype and expect him or her to behave in accordance with them. We expect all French people to be refined and sophisticated and anyone who is Irish to have the "gift of gab." Such mindsets as these keep us from coming to know people as individuals. Thus some professors tend to deal with students (and students with professors) as though they were all carbon copies, despite wide differences among members of the class.

Stereotypes are often reinforced by strong attitudes on our part, which increase our readiness to act toward individuals in accordance with the stereotype they have been put into, whether the action is warranted or not. When the attitudes are strong, we label the class with emotional words, such as the derogatory terms often used to refer to different races and nationalities. Stereotypes have a powerful effect in sustaining social prejudice and injustice.

The antidote for stereotyping is the same as for other faulty generalizations. We should remember that differences among individuals classified in a stereotype are frequently greater than differences between stereotypes. We should be constantly alert to see that our classifications do not become fixed and that we revise them as new evidence becomes available. And we should stop dealing with people in terms of classifications as soon as we have enough knowledge to treat them as individuals.

Displacement

One type of response to frustration is a desire to destroy the object that blocks us from reaching our goals. But this is frequently impossible or unwise—the frustrating object may be too big or powerful. But the tension demands release, and we may be tempted to take it out on some less dangerous object. This reaction is known as **displacement**, the transferring of aggression from the object that provoked it to one less capable of retaliation. A boy whose father has punished him dares not express his resentment by kicking his

father in the shins; so instead, he may kick the innocent cat. A student who is angry at her teacher for not allowing her to make up a missed examination may fly into a rage with her roommate over some trivial incident; the roommate, in turn, may work off resentment by snapping at the cashier in the cafeteria.

Displacement is often an unconscious phenomenon. For instance, an individual may not wish to admit negative feelings toward his or her father, who is a military man and so may hate the military without knowing why. Similarly, people who as children were punished by their parents unless they kept their rooms perfectly neat may tend in later life to be litterbugs and to leave messes everywhere—except, of course, their rooms.

Displacement may take a form that is the opposite of the fallacy of personal attack. If the person who has frustrated us is too big or powerful to attack directly, we can attack his or her ideas. You can see displacement in operation in almost any session of Congress. It is against congressional etiquette for political enemies to come to blows on the floor, though they sometimes do. But no rule prohibits voting against a measure because it is favored by one's opponent and justifying the action by plausible argument.

Displacement often has the effect of cutting off one's nose to spite one's face. A student can indirectly attack an instructor he does not like by refusing to study or to take any interest in the instructor's course. But his grade in the course goes on *his* record, not the instructor's. A student council member can express her resentment against a fellow member by refusing to cooperate in any project he proposes. But it is *she* who gets the reputation of being an obstructionist. Or she can oppose a suggestion made by someone she wishes to attack and find herself upholding a position her own reason tells her is wrong.

Dealing with displacement requires three steps. One is to remember that when we are angry or frustrated we are inclined to vent our emotions on anyone or anything available. The second is to offset this tendency by making a special effort to be tolerant, especially toward innocent bystanders, when we are upset. The third is to use constructively the energy generated by anger or frustration before it explodes in the wrong place.

Identification

Identification is another mental process which, though generally desirable, conceals a pitfall. By identifying with others, we acquire understanding of and sympathy for them and thus expand our self-concepts. The pitfall is our tendency to accept uncritically the ideas of those with whom we have identified. At times we borrow our ideals, attitudes, and stereotypes from these people without stopping to question whether they are right or wrong, true or false. We behave as though we were playing to a grandstand in which the people with whom we have identified are sitting. Thus students may pattern their behavior and beliefs after that of their professors, coaches, or other students whom they admire. Sometimes the ideas we adopt through identification are sound; in other cases we adopt false or inconsistent ideas.

The way to avoid the damaging consequences of identification is to examine critically all ideas before accepting them and to be particularly careful about adopting the ideas of those we admire. As citizens in a democracy, it is our duty, as well as our right, to think for ourselves. Citizens invite a dictatorship if they fall into the habit of adopting uncritically the ideas of their leaders, no matter how worthy the leaders or their ideas may be.

Failure to Listen

A final type of blindness to which we all are subject is the failure, or the inability, to listen carefully to others and hear what they are attempting to tell us. As a result, we sometimes react to a distorted perception of what others think and feel. We may believe that we disagree with someone about an issue, only to find out later that the dispute was merely verbal and arose because we failed to understand the other person's meaning. Or we may rush off to fight an injustice that doesn't exist or ignore one that does—all because we do not listen properly.

The harmful consequences of failure to listen are reinforced by the nature of language itself, which, as we noted when we discussed pitfalls in language, is not rigid or uniform. We may not have the same understanding another speaker of English has of a given word or phrase. Consider the word *humanism,* for instance. One person may think of this word as meaning "devotion to the humanities." He or she may think of humanism as a very good thing indeed. Another might use the word to refer to classical learning and have no strong feelings about it. A third individual might use the term to refer to a philosophy in which man is the measure of all things in a godless universe, and this individual might consider "humanism" a very dangerous influence. Anyone who looked up the word in the dictionary would find that all three uses are acceptable, but the three people involved would have a hard time understanding one another in a discussion of "humanism."

One reason for failure to listen may be sheer intellectual laziness. We often fail to realize how much we have to think in order to listen well, and, of course, thinking is hard work. But the biggest reason for inability to listen is our tendency to be so preoccupied with our own thoughts that we have no time to listen carefully or to try to understand what other people mean by the words they are using. We are too busy evaluating what we think is being said in terms of how it affects us or interpreting it as confirming our beliefs about the speaker, or thinking about whatever we plan to say ourselves in a moment. Mindsets play a part, too; we expect others to say particular things in particular circumstances, and we tend to hear them as saying the things we expect. Many of us talk much better than we listen and pay a price for our inattentiveness in misunderstandings and missed information.

Of course, we can be lazy speakers as well as lazy listeners and not even try to convey accurate information in what we say. We may expect our listeners to do most of the work of communication. When this happens, we simply compound the problem others may have in listening. Although excessive precision is to be avoided, it is important to cultivate the habit of speaking accurately and the vocabulary to do so.

The cure for failure to listen is to try when others are speaking to put ourselves into their frames of reference and to see matters exactly as they do. When it is important that a statement be understood clearly, we should rephrase it in our own words and ask the speaker if that is what he or she means. If there is any doubt, we should keep trying until agreement is reached that the position has been expressed accurately. People who follow this practice are usually regarded as sympathetic and understanding listeners, and they make fewer mistakes. Many seemingly irreconcilable differences of opinion are not differences of opinion at all, but merely differences in wording.

Exercise 30

Problems 1–9. These questions refer to the lettered problems below.

Rick and Nick are having a few beers in the Star Bar. An article on the front page of a discarded newspaper catches Rick's eye.

A. *Rick:* Hmmm. It says here that doctors often choose to terminate lives by "pulling the plug" when they believe the case is hopeless and no further treatment would be useful. I think this is wrong.

B. *Nick:* Why? (Another beer here, waiter.) Somebody has to make such decisions.

C. *Rick:* Because doctors are pledged to try to save lives always. Read the Hippocratic oath they take. (Another for me, too.)

D. *Nick:* Look, there isn't enough equipment to treat everyone, and who could decide whom to treat better than doctors? There are lots of old people who are just hanging on by machines. These people have finished their lives; they don't even want to hang around———

E. *Rick:* Hey! Lots of old people find their lives very satisfying, even if they're sick! After my uncle had three heart attacks, he still taught me———

F. *Nick:* Aw, he's an exception. Anyway, doctors know what they're doing. It's not like some janitor was making the decision.

G. *Rick:* You can't trust doctors! They can be greedy and calculating—and make life-or-death decisions on the basis of what's in it for them. I had an uncle who was a doctor, and he was practically a crook. What we need is socialized medicine.

H. *Nick:* Doctors are the noblest human beings on this earth! My old man is a doctor, and I'm going to be one, too. Socialized medicine—don't you know that's what they have in Russia? What are you, some kind of Communist?

I. *Rick:* You dumb jerk, they have socialized medicine in England too. You wouldn't call them—

J. *Nick:* You Communist!

K. *Rick:* You $#%@$#%!!

Sounds of scuffling, crashes; shriek of sirens.

1. Which speech(es) illustrate(s) stereotypes?   _____

2. Which speech(es) illustrate(s) displacement?   _____

3. Which speech(es) illustrate(s) identification?   _____

4. Which speech(es) illustrate(s) failure to listen?   _____

5. What is Rick's mindset about doctors?

6. What is Nick's mindset about doctors?

_____

7. What is Rick's attitude toward socialized medicine?

_____

8. What is Nick's attitude toward socialized medicine?

_____

9. Which of the fallacies described earlier in this book do you notice in the above dialogue?

_____

_____

Problems 10–14. Identify the psychological blinder probably involved in each of the following cases.

10. Ashford Askroth did not enjoy his trip home. His semester report had preceded him, and his father greeted him with a tongue-lashing about his poor grades and the announcement that he could not take his car back to college. That night he quarrelled with his girl, and the next day he had a bitter argument with his best friend over a trivial issue.

_____

11. When Askroth got back to the campus, he resolved to double his efforts to make good grades. He had been studying only two hours or so the night before a test. He resolved to study a minimum of four hours the night before each test.

_____

12. As Bosley Boskom drove through barren country late one night, he mused, "What a mess I'd be in if the weak coil on this heap conked out now!" A moment later his motor sputtered once and stopped dead. "That's it," thought Boskom. He walked eight miles to the nearest town but could not get a new coil until morning. When he got back to his car, he found that a wire on the distributor had come loose. He could have fixed the trouble easily the night before.

_____

13. Christine Crayder took a job as credit manager for a large store in a cosmopolitan city. She was told by her predecessor, "Don't trust the Bolkonians; they'll cheat you out of your eye teeth." Crayder followed the advice, turning down all requests for credit from Bolkonians. When she lost her wallet containing a considerable sum of money, it was returned to her intact by a young Bolkonian.

_____

14. Evelyn Eversole admired her professor of literature, whose favorite novel was _Tom Jones_. Even though Eversole had never read the book, she always included it in her list of great novels of the world. When she did attempt to read it, she never made her way beyond the first volume.

_____

Chapter 31

Understanding and Refining Values

- **Values and Decision Making**
- **Discovering Value Premises**
- **Criteria**
- **Classifying Values**
- **Modifying Value Systems**
- **Value Conflicts**

Let us now consider how the procedures of effective thinking can profitably be applied to perhaps the most important of all areas of thinking—developing and refining one's value system. The importance in life of a sound and viable system of values can hardly be overestimated. We saw in Chapter 13 that practical decisions are based on an evaluation of the various courses of action under consideration. Even the most routine and habitual actions we perform frequently arise out of judgments we once made as to the value of those actions. Thus our values enter into virtually every phase of our waking lives. In Chapter 26 we saw that by deciding on courses of action in terms of our values we keep our actions from being arbitrary, establish a hierarchy among our needs, and lend unity, coherence, and overall purpose to our lives. Also, since our judgments

about what actions are right or wrong make up our conscience, developing a suitable system of values is indispensable to living in peace not just with others but with ourselves. In all, the system of values we develop is perhaps the most important factor in determining what we are and will become as persons. If we wish to guide our own development, instead of leaving it to chance or to the forces to which we are constantly exposed, we ourselves must select the value premises by which we intend to live.

All of us sometimes base decisions on value premises we would reject if we examined them carefully. Many of our values were originally accepted uncritically from our parents and from our culture. Although most of the values the average person accepts as a child prove reasonably sound when put into practice, there are nearly always a few that should be discarded or modified. Moreover, even if all our values were sound when we a-dopted them, which is unlikely, some modification is usually necessary as our circumstances change. The values that were suitable for you when you were six years old are not altogether suitable for a college student, and the values that are suitable for you now will not be altogether suitable twenty years from now.

Thus a critical assessment of our values from time to time would seem essential. The five-phase cycle of decision making will apply with appropriate modifications to this enterprise as well as it does to other tasks of effective thinking. Suppose, then, that you decide to undertake an assessment of your values. For phase 1, let us define the problem: to examine your value system and make appropriate modifications in it so that you may become more nearly the person your own reasoned reflection indicates you should be. The objective of phase 2 in this use of the cycle is to determine what values make up your present system. To facilitate taking stock of your values, it is helpful to understand something of the nature of values and how they function in decision making.

Values and Decision Making

A **value judgment** is a statement about the worth of an object, experience, idea, or action. When we judge that pleasure is good, that obeying the law is right, or that a certain sunset is beautiful, we are saying that the item in question is a worthy thing to be admired, praised, or sought after. By contrast, when we say that pain is bad, that robbing banks is wrong, or that a flood-ravaged town is an ugly mess,

we mean that the thing in question is a fit object of dislike, distaste, or avoidance. There are several kinds of value judgments. Some concern the sort of life it is best to have and the kind of experiences that are most worth seeking; others involve morals, that is, the types of conduct it is best to pursue or avoid; still others have to do with aesthetics, that is, with determining which things are beautiful or sublime and which are ugly or trivial. Needless to say, these categories are not completely independent. Thus we may judge that the good life should include moral action, that it is wrong to destroy what is beautiful, and so on. Finally, some value judgments are highly specific whereas others are more general. Thus you may judge that a person with your particular talents should pursue a particular career, but not that everyone should. On the other hand, you may think that human sacrifice is never justified and therefore should not be practiced in any circumstances.

The value judgments we make in deciding on particular courses of action are often based on more general value judgments that serve as **value premises** in a deductive inference. To see how value premises function in decisions, let us consider a case like the ones dealt with in Chapter 13, where it is necessary to decide between competing proposals for action that must be evaluated in terms of their consequences.

Suppose you are faced with this problem. You are coming to the end of your freshman year, and although your grades have been good, you have not taken the number of courses needed to let you graduate in four years. You are six credits behind. Your problem is to decide what you will do in the summer months. You consider two proposals for action: the first is to attend summer school, and the second is to work full time and save money through the summer. As you will remember from Chapter 13, proposals for action can be evaluated by forming hypothetical propositions for each proposal, in which the proposal serves as the antecedent and the consequences of the action proposed are attached as consequents. Suppose that your consideration of the consequences of your two proposals for action produces the following results.

Proposal for Action		Advantages	Disadvantages
Attend summer school	⊃	I will make up 6 credits	but I will not be able to afford college in the fall.
Work full time for the summer	⊃	I will be able to afford college in the fall	but I will still be 6 credits behind.

As you can see, your consideration of the consequences of your two proposals for action has disclosed that if you attend summer school you will be unable to meet your expenses for college in the fall. Thus even though going to summer school will enable you to make up the six credits needed to put you on schedule to graduate, the price would be that you would be forced to drop out of college in the fall. At this point, you are ready to decide between the two proposals for action you have formed, and the decision is obvious. For even though attending summer school will temporarily put you on schedule to graduate, you will ultimately wind up further behind: you will lose the fifteen credits you could earn in the fall. Accordingly, you decide to take a job for the summer.

The final phase of your decision-making process in this example can be summarized in terms of categorical syllogisms. Notice that in deciding to take a job, you make two value judgments: you judge that going to summer school would be a bad course of action, and you judge that taking a job would be a good course of action. Both these judgments are based on more fundamental value judgments that, though never explicitly stated, serve as premises in your reasoning. Fully expressed, the syllogisms that summarize your final determination of your situation are as follows:

Major Premise:	Any action that ultimately postpones my graduation is bad.
Minor Premise:	My attending summer school is an action that will ultimately postpone my graduation.
Conclusion:	My attending summer school is bad.
Major Premise:	Any action that ultimately furthers my progress toward graduation is good.
Minor Premise:	My working for the summer ultimately furthers my progress toward graduation.
Conclusion:	My working for the summer is good.

As you can see, then, the value judgments that support your decision to take a job for the summer are based on more general value judgments, which serve as premises in deductive reasoning. These value premises in turn may be based on still more fundamental ones and hence form part of a structured whole. That is why our values constitute a system rather than a loose collection of unrelated judgments.

Note also that the conclusions of both of the above syllogisms are highly specific: each refers to a particular course of action proposed to deal with a particular problem faced by a particular person, yourself. A similar problem faced by another person, or by you in different circumstances, need not have the same solution. Value judgments must always take into account the relevant details of the case at hand. But if you trust your judgment at all in this case, you would presumably think that anyone else in the *same* circumstances would, or at least *should*, make the same decision. That is why it is possible for us both to give and to seek advice about values; we always assume that the facts of the case (including, of course, the relevant facts about the individuals it involves), and not capriciousness, should determine our value judgments.

Finally, note that each of the major premises in the above syllogisms seems quite general. The second syllogism contains the premise that any action that ultimately advances your progress toward graduation is good. Presumably, you do not believe anything quite this general, for you would make exceptions to this principle. For example, although cheating on examinations might help you graduate, you would not want to do it if your value system also includes the proposition that cheating is wrong. Very often, value judgments that appear to be quite general have implicit exceptions attached. Failure to be cognizant of these exceptions leads to many fallacies of accident. The exceptions represent ways of dealing with potential conflicts that might arise between values, by giving one value precedence over the other. Thus your exception to the principle that anything that helps you graduate is good is a way of dealing with conflicts between the value of honesty and the value of graduating; where a conflict occurs, you will give the former value precedence over the latter.

Discovering Value Premises

Discerning what value judgments make up your own system of values is a rewarding task but not always an easy one. The value system of the average adult contains thousands of value judgments, and the interrelations among them are incredibly complex. This need not be a problem if you wish to examine your values on a particular subject, such as sex or going to college. But if you wish to consider your value system as a whole, the sheer number of propositions involved will be too great to manage. Even if you could bring to light your entire system in all its detail, which is at best unlikely, the resulting mass of data would be too immense and too complicated to deal with effectively. In order to understand your complete value system, you need to develop a representative sample of the judgments it contains and study their interrelations. You may then be able to discern conflicts in your values and places where modifications in your system may be in order.

Accumulating a representative sample of your values requires discernment. You can begin to develop such a sample simply by writing down propositions that came to mind. Or you might try to examine your conduct, and the reasoning on which it is based, over a certain period of time. If you choose a short period of time such as a day, some of your more specific values will come to light. Your behavior over longer periods, or during times when you were acting in particularly trying circumstances, may disclose some of the more general and fundamental value-propositions that guide your life. But whatever your method for developing a sample, there are several problems against which it is important to be on guard.

First, many of the value propositions that guide our decisions are implicit rather than explicit, partly because we habitually act in certain ways in certain situations without thinking about the values involved. For example, conscientious students do not, as a rule, debate with themselves every day whether to prepare their assignments: they habitually do their work without giving much thought to the matter. The value judgments that underlie habitual actions may originally have been formed long before the action became habitual and so be hard to recall. Moreover, as the example of the preceding section illustrates, even when we do reason about our actions, the underlying value premises on which we base particular judgments are often left unstated. In other words, our reasoning about values often takes the form of an enthymeme in which we are not even fully aware of the general value principle we are following.

In such cases, the techniques for analyzing deductive arguments can be used to recover the missing value premise. Suppose, for example, that you decide it is a waste of time to study a certain chapter because learning it will not affect your grade. In this case, your reasoning takes the form of an incomplete categorical syllogism:

Minor Premise:	Studying this chapter is a task that will not affect my grade.
Conclusion:	Studying this chapter is a waste of time.

If you remember the technique for dealing with enthymemes that was covered in Chapter 18, you will see that either you are reasoning invalidly here or you are employing an unstated major premise that is affirmative and distributes the middle term. This is your underlying value premise:

Major Premise:	Any task that will not affect my grade is a waste of time.

You may protest that, as stated, this premise is too general, for you only apply it at times when you are faced with examinations or behind in your assignments or the like. And provided you are not rationalizing, that may be true. Nevertheless, analysis of your reasoning above shows that even if such restrictions are attached to it, this value proposition forms a part of your system of values. Leaving it out of your sample simply because you do not like the way it sounds may result in a biased sample.

A second problem you might encounter in developing a representative sample of your values is that the value premises underlying our decisions often occur at the beginning of chain arguments on which the decision is based. Here is an example.

Activities that promote efficiency are good.

Activities that promote health promote efficiency.

Exercise promotes health.

Playing tennis is exercise.

Therefore playing tennis is good.

Although the example is a simple one, it shows that we must sometimes trace back through several links in a chain of reasoning in order to find the underlying value premise. This makes it harder to uncover our value premises, for at times it is difficult to trace the chain backward more than a few steps, especially if the action is a habitual one. Compounding the problem is the fact that many of our decisions are made not so much to achieve desirable consequences as to prevent undesirable ones. Thus the value proposition that guides our behavior is often a negative one about a proposal for action that we rejected rather than a positive one about a proposal we accepted and acted upon.

A third problem is that it is easy to deceive ourselves into believing that we follow one value premise when actually our behavior is based on a different one. In some instances we may have changed our thinking so gradually that we fail to realize we are no longer following the original premise. Suppose, for example, that upon retiring Grandfather Smythe takes up golf to improve his health. At first he plays a few holes at a time and walks for the exercise. Gradually, however, he becomes more interested in golf and less interested in exercise. In order to play more holes he buys a golf cart and confines his walking to the distance from the cart to his ball and back. Then he begins to find pleasure in defeating his friends. To improve his game, Grandfather Smythe takes lessons. To add spice, he begins to wager a dollar on the outcome of each hole. Eventually, Grandfather Smythe "plays" golf as seriously as he once worked at his business. If he continues to believe that he plays golf for exercise and recreation, he has changed his value premise without realizing it.

Finally, we often hide our real values from ourselves in order to protect our self-concepts. Consider the case of Grandmother Smythe, who had a strict upbring-

ing. Grandmother Smythe professes to believe that children should be dealt with firmly and makes no secret of her views. "Lax discipline," she says, "is a form of neglect." She attributes most of today's social ills to the failure of parents (and grandparents, too) to take a strong hand with children and set them on right paths early in life. However, she exhibits not a trace of strictness in her dealings with her grandson Algernon, who is her pride and joy. She brings him presents regularly. When little Al has a temper tantrum and breaks one of the presents, she simply replaces it with another. When Grandmother Smythe babysits for Algernon, he is allowed to stay up as late as he pleases and can watch anything he wants on television. If he wants a cake, Grandmother Smythe will bake one, and she bootlegs candy for him despite his parents' express wishes to the contrary. She admires his every accomplishment, defends his every misdeed, and on the whole is as indulgent toward him as anyone could be. When it is pointed out to her that her actions do not reflect her claimed values, Grandmother Smythe has an explanation. "Well," she says, "a grandmother can be forgiven a weakness for her grandson. Besides, Algernon is a nice boy, and his parents are so busy they can't always give him the attention he deserves." At this point, you should begin to suspect that Grandmother Smythe is rationalizing, and that while she likes to think of herself as a firm disciplinarian, she does not really espouse the value proposition that children are to be dealt with strictly.

The procedure for testing hypotheses described in Chapter 5 is useful for telling whether we are following the values we claim to uphold. It can be applied to one's own case or to that of someone else. The procedure is first to form the hypothesis that the person in question follows a certain value proposition and use this hypothesis as the antecedent of a hypothetical proposition.

Grandmother
Smythe follows
the value proposi-
tion that children   ⊃
should be dealt
with strictly.

Next we add one or more consequents that follow from this antecedent.

The children in
Grandmother
⊃ Smythe's neigh-
borhood should
consider her a pret-
ty tough customer.

The next step is to test the consequent to see whether it is true. Suppose we do and find out that precisely the opposite is the case. "Old Mrs. Smythe is nice," they say, "she has us in for ice cream all the time." In addition, we hear stories about baseball-shattered living room windows that were fixed with never a word to the parents of the batter; we notice the trampled rose bushes where the neighborhood children cut through Grandmother Smythe's property, and so on. Based on this evidence we can conclude that Grandmother Smythe's values about children are a good deal different from what she says they are.

Since the value propositions we conceal from ourselves are the ones most likely to give us trouble, we should make a special effort to uncover our hidden values. Once we have developed a reasonably representative sample of our values, we can begin to evaluate them and modify them in the ways our evaluation indicates to be necessary.

Criteria

When the five-phase cycle is used to assess and refine a value system, the objective of phase 3 is to form criteria for assessing the system. The question of what criteria a system of values needs to satisfy in order to be adequate is a vexing one, especially in our own, skeptical age. It is frequently claimed that among philosophers and laypersons alike there is a vast disagreement about values, that values differ radically from age to age and from culture to culture, and that objective standards for resolving these differences are lacking. Certainly, familiar scientific techniques seem to be inapplicable. Furthermore, people who develop and espouse what they claim are objective standards are viewed with suspicion; it is often thought that to espouse such standards is to try to impose one's own view on others, to engage in judging them, and to attempt to deprive them of autonomy in directing their lives. In the end, it is sometimes said, what is right is simply a matter of what one's culture says is right or what one's own beliefs indicate.

Though this is not the place for a treatise on value theory, there are a few considerations that can help you in dealing with this issue. First, it is important not to overemphasize the differences in the values various people hold. A comparison of your values with those held by a person living in a remote village in New Guinea would certainly reveal differences. But they would not be nearly as great as the differences between your beliefs and those of the village dweller about the workings of the physical world. The same point applies historically. The values defended by moral philosophers today do not differ vastly from those defended by the Greeks—something that can hardly be said of contemporary science as compared with Greek science. Indeed, experts in value theory tend to disagree about the foundations of values more than they do about particular value judgments of the kind likely to make up most of an individual's value system. There is, to say the least, widespread agreement that it is wrong in normal circumstances to build a personal fortune by robbing others and that other things being equal it is not a wholesome thing to throw grandma down the well. Finally, when experts do disagree about particular values, their disagreement is likely to be as much about the relevant facts of the case at issue as about the values involved. Abortion is a case in point: one's stand on whether abortion is right or wrong depends in part on one's view of whether a fetus is human in any sense that would give it moral status. The latter issue is in part a factual one, since settling it requires determining what characteristics of human beings lead us to accord them moral rights and when evidence of these characteristics first appears during the individual's development. These are not, of course, the only questions relevant to the morality of abortion. The rights of others, especially the mother and the father, need to be considered, and there are other problems as well. Nevertheless, a satisfactory resolution of the factual issues involved would make the issue of right or wrong easier to contend with.

Second, although the resolution of value conflicts may not be a matter for empirical science, it does not follow that there are no standards by which this can be done. There is in any case the standard of logical consistency, as we will see, and it is also possible to articulate other standards that are useful in assessing one's value.

Third, a person espousing what he or she claims are objective standards for assessing values is not, by doing so, necessarily trying to impose his or her values on others. Besides, to espouse such standards is to invite reasoned debate, which makes it possible to respect the autonomy of others. Only when reasoned consideration of values is abandoned does personal autonomy tend to be overridden. In the end, we do have to live with one another, and when hope of rational persuasion is abandoned, propaganda and force are all that remain.

Fourth, if we treat values as ultimately relative, whether to culture or to personal belief, it becomes difficult if not impossible to develop reasoned values of our own. For if culture is the arbiter of values, we have no choice but to follow its dictates. If, on the other hand, individual belief is the arbiter, there can be no grounds for preferring one belief to another. Progress in developing our own values requires that we reject both of these alternatives and try to ground our values in reasoned reflection on human nature and on the circumstances in which we must act.

Finally, however the issues regarding the foundations of values are to be resolved, one's life has to be lived here and now; it will not wait until philosophers and anthropologists solve all their problems. Consequently, we must move ahead and exercise our reason as best we can in developing criteria by which to assess and modify our value system. We will find the accumulated wisdom of the human race, as expressed in philosophy, literature, and other fields of knowledge, helpful in this. Also, one can ask of one's value system that it observe standards of logical consistency and promote effective thinking in practical situations. The criteria listed below are some of those that have been found most helpful for assessing values. Since ultimately each must choose his or her own values, you may wish to add further criteria to the list.

A Value System Should Include a Proposition That States Major Goals in Life in Terms of What You Understand to Be Life's Meaning and Purpose. Propositions of this kind play a fundamental role in value systems since they serve as premises from which many other value judgments are derived. People's beliefs about the fundamental purpose of life may be derived from religion, from other cultural influences, or from their own thinking about their life experiences. In most cases all these sources play a role.

A Value System Should Provide a Basis for Decision Making in All Areas of Life. We make so many decisions every day that we seldom have time to examine all the values involved. If we do not have a fairly comprehensive body of value premises to draw on, we tend to fall victim to decision by indecision or be forced to make decisions with little or no attention to the values involved. Your values need not and should not try to dictate a solution for every value problem you will have to face, but they should provide enough of a foundation to guide your thinking in familiar circumstances and get your thinking started when the circumstances are unfamiliar.

A Value System Should Provide for Reasonably Balanced Satisfaction of Needs. As we have noted before, to attain this goal it is necessary that values establish a hierarchy among our needs and set standards for deciding when the satisfaction of one need will take precedence over others. Though there is considerable variety in such standards, any viable system of values must reflect the fact that we are not free to satisfy our physical desires or to express our emotions without restraint, especially where others are concerned. Also, since our self-concept is developed in relation to other people, and in particular by expanding it to include the interests of others as well as our own, we cannot in the end avoid holding ourselves responsible for the effects of our action on other people. Thus value propositions that give us a free rein in our behavior toward others must ultimately be judged incompatible with our psychological nature.

A Value System Should Include a Strong Code of Ethics. This criterion follows in part from the one above. It is also required by the fact that in establishing ourselves as autonomous beings we must inevitably compete with others to some extent. If we were not guided by ethical codes, life would be as chaotic as an ice hockey game without rules. In life, as in hockey, of course, there are people who appear to be unrestrained by ethics. On the surface these people may seem to be happy. There is no real evidence, however, that they have succeeded in developing and maintaining satisfactory self-concepts. On the contrary, there is much evidence that they suffer from feelings of guilt, insecurity, and general or specific inadequacy.

The Premises in a Value System Should Be Compatible with Each Other. In a manner of speaking, values are like forces that tend to push us in a certain direction. When our values are incompatible, they push us in opposite directions, and hence cancel each other. Incompatible values, then, cannot be simultaneously observed. We will have more to say below about the problem of dealing with conflicts in values.

Our Values Should Be Realistic in Terms of Both Our Own Abilities and the World in Which We Live. Our values should be high enough to bring out our best efforts and thus enable us to fulfill our capacities as best we can. But unreasonably high goals are likely to inhibit rather than further our chances of fulfillment. For example, if you know that you have only average ability as a student, it is pointless for you to feel it your duty to achieve the highest grade-point average in your class. Satisfying your needs requires that you adopt the more realistic goal of simply doing as well as your abilities permit. Similarly, there is no point in adopting the belief that anyone who fails to rise to the top of a major corporation is a failure in life. It is in the nature of organizations that only a few people can possibly achieve such a goal, and the values of a realistic person will take account of this fact. The difficulties that stand in the way of success should not, of course, be used as an excuse for aiming at mediocrity. But if we treat goodness as perfection and badness as anything short of perfection, we commit the black-or-white fallacy and set ourselves up for a life of frustration.

Classifying Values

The objective of phase 4 of the cycle is to test your system as a whole, as well as the individual value propositions in it, by applying the criteria you have selected. For the sake of illustration, let us suppose that until now your thinking about values has not been very circumspect, and the sample of values you have listed includes the following.

1. One should always follow the golden rule.

2. A broad and deep understanding of humanity is an essential part of a good education.

3. Happiness is impossible without money, a lot of leisure time, and spacious and comfortable surroundings in which to live.

4. The most important objective in life is to have a successful career.

5. Knowing the truth is preferable to ignorance or self-deception.

6. The ultimate purpose of human life is to serve God.

7. The most important objective in college is high grades.

8. The best careers are those that pay the highest salaries.

9. T.S. Eliot's poetry is better than Browning's.

10. The major goal in life is balanced satisfaction of needs.

11. The best way to serve God is to enter a religious occupation.

12. The end justifies the means.

The procedure for testing the individual propositions in your value system is to treat them as proposals for action. That is, you should frame each value proposition as a proposal for action, and then predict consequences in terms of the criteria you have adopted for assessing your values. An incomplete test of proposition 8, using this procedure, is shown below.

	Advantages
I follow the premise that the best careers are those that pay the highest salaries. $\supset$	the career I choose will probably satisfy my need for prestige.

Disadvantages

my career may not satisfy my need to contribute to the welfare of others.

I may undertake a career that is unrealistic in terms of my abilities and interests.

Testing individual premises is not enough, however. To assume that a value system is satisfactory merely because the individual premises in it are satisfactory is to commit the fallacy of composition. A thorough assessment of your value system must include an examination of the interrelationships among the premises. The best way to see these interrelationships is to classify them. Since your purpose is to understand your system as thoroughly as possible, you should follow the procedures for forming and testing explanatory systems of classification discussed in Chapter 14. Propositions 1–12, which are listed above in random order, can be classified as shown below.

I. Major goals in life

   A. The ultimate purpose of human life is to serve God.

   B. Happiness is impossible without money, a lot of leisure time, and spacious and comfortable surroundings in which to live.

   C. The most important objective in life is to have a successful career.

   D. The primary goal in life is balanced satisfaction of needs.

II. Areas of decision making

   A. Career

      1. The best way to serve God is to enter a religious occupation.

      2. The best careers are those that pay the highest salaries.

   B. Education

      1. The most important objective in college is high grades.

      2. Knowing the truth is preferable to ignorance or self-deception.

      3. A broad and deep understanding of humanity is an essential part of a good education.

   C. Ethics

      1. The end justifies the means.

      2. One should always follow the golden rule.

   D. Aesthetics

      1. T.S. Eliot's poetry is better than Browning's.

When the propositions in a value system are properly classified, the flaws in the system are much easier to find. The classification above make it clear that the list does not constitute a complete system, for many important areas and subareas of decision making are not covered at all. The entries under ethics, for example, are far from adequate. The two values that concern career threaten to be incompatible with each other and are incompatible with one or more of the major goals. The first proposition classified under education is incompatible with the other two. The two principles classified under ethics are also incompatible. A person who tried to follow all of these values would have to move in three or four directions at once.

Modifying Value Systems

When the decision-making cycle is being used to assess and refine your value system, the objective of phase 5 is to decide what changes should be made. You may feel, for example, that some of your values need modification. If so, the modifications should be made with caution. Quick and radical changes of important principles should be avoided: since the propositions in a system are interrelated, a radical and ill-considered change in any one of them may disrupt the entire system. Instead, you should think through the effects that a change in one of your values may have on others, the conflicts it is apt to generate, and so on. Doing so will help you to determine whether a new value proposition you are considering is acceptable or not according to the criteria you have adopted. A classification of a sample of your values will probably reveal gaps. Trying to fill in these gaps will not only help you find some of your hidden values but also indicate areas needing further creative and critical thinking.

Value Conflicts

Unless you are an exception, a thorough analysis and classification of the propositions that make up your value system will reveal conflicts. Unresolved conflicts between important values can be a serious impediment to effective thinking. At the very least they tend to lead to indecision or to a failure to carry out decisions once we have made them. This in turn can result in a good deal of emotional tension and anxiety. In addition, we may sometimes try to deal with our seeming inability to act by doing something rash and impulsive, which in itself may be damaging. Furthermore, whatever impulsive action we take is likely to accord with one of the conflicting values and cause problems by running counter to the other. Conflicts that are allowed to continue unresolved often wind up being simply repressed and can lead to long-term personality disorders that affect mental health as well as our ability to think effectively.

Sometimes what appears to be a conflict in values is not a conflict at all. Suppose, for example, that you believe something like proposition 1 in the category of career values in the above outline—namely, that a religious occupation is the highest calling a person can have. Suppose also that you have no plans to enter such an occupation but instead are studying to become a nuclear engineer. It does not follow that there is any conflict whatever in your values, for there is nothing in your belief about the value of entering a religious occupation that requires everyone to do so. Many other careers are valuable too, and you may have correctly decided that your own abilities and interests best suit you for nuclear engineering. Thus to say that a proposition expresses a value is not necessarily to say it expresses an obligation. Alternative values can often be pursued without conflict.

Genuine value conflicts occur in several types. In one sort of case, the conflict is not between the values themselves but occurs because they cannot both be put into practice at once—usually, because of limitations of time, space, energy, or money. If you elect a course in psychology, you may have to omit some other course. If you participate in college athletics, you may not have the time or energy to earn high grades in a difficult curriculum. If you marry, you may have to give up college, or reduce your standard of living, or require more time to graduate. None of these cases, however, requires that you give up one of the value propositions that lead to the conflict, for the values themselves do not contradict each other. Instead, you need to employ the skills of effective thinking to deal with the practical problem your competing values present.

Suppose that your conflict is between marriage and completing your college degree. Your first step should be to put your creative skills to work to find a proposal for action that will enable you to achieve both goals. Failure to find such a proposal for action does not necessarily mean that you must sacrifice one of your goals forever. Doors that are closed today may be open tomorrow. The next step, therefore, is to decide which value can be better postponed while you continue to seek a means of achieving it. It is far better to satisfy one and postpone the other than to remain in a state of indecision, thereby accomplishing nothing. Having to postpone a goal is not necessarily a disadvantage. For example, a study of college records shows that many students who had to interrupt their college educations for military service made much better academic records after returning to college. Many of these students returned to college with more definite goals and with a clearer understanding of the value of a college education.

Another and more difficult conflict occurs when our ethical values conflict with the value we attach to the satisfaction of various needs. In fact, there is a double conflict in many such cases, for many of the moral principles we espouse are reflected in laws and other rules of society. For example, most people value honesty, and society has laws against theft, embezzlement, and the like. In addition, there are social prohibitions against deception, ruthlessness, and shady dealing, which, though not a part of law, influence our behavior. At the same time, however, all of us require a certain amount of material and financial success to meet our basic needs, and we value the things money can buy even if they are luxuries rather than necessities. Furthermore, society is somewhat two-faced about material success: although we are not supposed to climb over others, we are rewarded with approval and prestige if we can achieve a competitive advantage over others by making more money or rising to higher positions. Thus the value we attach to material success and prestige can often conflict with the rules of behavior that exist both in our conscience and in our culture.

Sometimes people try to resolve such conflicts by cheating on the rules. But such a course is fraught with danger, for when we start to cheat, we may initiate a cycle of erosion in our ethical code. To ease our conscience we may rationalize the action or dismiss it as trivial and unimportant. But this only makes it easier to bend the rules again the next time a similar situation appears. If we do bend them, we have to justify our behavior again, and the more often we do so, the more distorted our view of our own conduct becomes. This kind of downward spiral has brought tragic ruin to many a promising and useful career. The cashier convicted of embezzling half a million dollars of the bank's funds probably started by "borrowing" a few dollars and never expected to take more or to get caught.

A better way to proceed when you encounter conflicts between ethical and social rules and the satisfaction of your needs is to examine carefully both the need and the method by which you propose to satisfy it. Have you exaggerated the need? Will its satisfaction place demands on you that you cannot meet? Would a more modest degree of success be more rewarding in the long run? When you have determined your minimum need, the chances are that you can find a way of satisfying it without violating the rules of society or conscience. If you cannot achieve a particular goal, perhaps you can find a substitute goal that will satisfy the need. For example, if your need is for security and you lack the ability to amass a fortune, you may be able to satisfy the need by being careful of your personal finances and by finding a job in which your responsibilities make it unlikely that you would be dismissed. We should beware of fixing on one particular method of satisfying a need, for most can be satisfied in many ways.

But even if we concentrate on abiding by ethical principles, we sometimes get into dilemmas because the principles themselves appear to be at odds. Perhaps the most troublesome value conflicts are of this kind, for in them it seems we can follow one moral rule only at the expense of another, and so must inevitably violate our conscience. Suppose that you have a friend with a serious drug problem. On the one hand, you may perceive it as your duty to report the case to the authorities, so that your friend can receive the help he or she needs; on the other, one of your moral principles may be that the autonomy of others is to be respected, even in cases where they use it to harm themselves. If you turn your friend in, you violate the

latter principle; if you do not, you violate the former. Either way, you lose.

When analysis reveals that the conflict lies between two rules of conduct, the next step is to examine the conflicting rules. As we have seen, many value propositions have implicit exceptions attached; when this is so, a simple statement of the rule often amounts to an oversimplification. For example, your rule that the autonomy of others is to be respected may carry the proviso that it does not apply when others use their autonomy to injure themselves seriously and permanently. Hidden exceptions like this can often be used to establish when one rule is to take precedence over another in guiding your conduct. Alternatively, it may be possible to introduce modifications in the rule in light of the particular circumstances of the case at hand. Perhaps means are available for helping your friend that would not expose him or her to public reproach. Rigid rules often fail to produce good results in particular cases because each problem has its own complexities. In any case, you should not assume that you must abandon completely one of a pair of rules of conduct simply because they appear to conflict. Effective thinking will often disclose ways to resolve the conflict at much less expense.

Similar considerations apply to cases where value propositions that articulate major goals in life are seen to conflict. Consider propositions C and D listed above under the category of major goals in life. As stated they certainly conflict: a successful career and balanced satisfaction of needs cannot both be the most important thing in life. Usually, however, incompatible values like these two can be reconciled without abandoning either completely. This pair can be made compatible by subordinating the goal of career success to the larger goal of a balanced satisfaction of needs. If achieving a *reasonable* amount of success is made a means of satisfying some needs instead of a primary goal, most, if not all, of the conflict is removed.

If an analysis of conflicting value propositions reveals no error in your interpretation or application of them, test them by Kant's rule of conscience: "Act as though the maxim of your action were by your will to become a universal law of nature." What would happen if everyone followed the rules in question? What course of conduct would you approve for someone else in the same situation? It will often happen that one of the two conflicting value propositions will fail to meet this test, and you can revise it accordingly. But beware of rationalizing. You cannot make an exception of yourself on the ground that your intentions are good.

A thoughtful assessment and modification of your value system is not easy, but wisdom and happiness may be the rewards. It is the only way to be or become the person *you* choose to be.

Exercise 31A

Problems 1–9. These questions refer to the following statements made by Susan Knight, a sophomore engineering student.

   A. I would hate to miss the lecture on the impressionist painters, but I should study for my calculus test tomorrow.

   B. The lecturer is a world-renowned expert on my favorite topic.

   C. I may never have a chance to hear him again.

   D. My average in calculus is 89 going into this test, and it is the last test.

   E. I have not studied much for this test; if I do not study tonight, I will probably make a C on the test, and possibly a D.

1. What are the implicit values struggling for supremacy in this set of statements?

_____

_____

2. If Susan's situation is thought of as a dilemma, what are the unpleasant consequences she must choose between?

_____

_____

3. What value is Susan affirming over the other if she chooses to go to the lecture?

_____

4. If Susan has a straight-A average so far in her college studies, might this fact affect her choice? Why or why not?

_____

_____

5. Suppose Susan does choose the lecture, which of the following statements would then be inconsistent with her value system?

   a. Self-enrichment is important only when it doesn't interfere with getting good grades.

   b. If a rare opportunity comes by, you should take it even though it may cost you something.

c. It is important to study and get good grades.

_____

6. Suppose Susan reasons thus: if I stay home and study, I *may* get an A in calculus; however, if I go to the lecture, I will hear the lecture. How might such reasoning affect her choice?

_____

7. Suppose that another alternative materializes. A good friend from high school, whom Susan hasn't seen in two years, suddenly turns up. She is in town for that evening only and wants Susan to spend the time with her. What third value proposition is Susan following if she puts aside both calculus and lecture and spends the evening with her friend?

_____

8. Susan now has three unpleasant consequences to avoid. What is the third?

_____

9. Is there any possible way of avoiding more than one of the unpleasant consequences?

_____

Exercise 31B

Problems 1–4. These problems refer to the following set of values recommended by Polonius to his son, Laertes, who is about to depart for France (*Hamlet*, Act 1, Scene 3).

A.   Give thy thoughts no tongue,
   Nor any unproportion'd thought his act.

B. Be thou familiar, but by no means vulgar:

C. Those friends thou hast, and their adoption tried,
   Grapple them unto thy soul with hoops of steel,

D. But do not dull thy palm with entertainment
   Of each new-hatch'd, unfledg'd [colleague].

E.   Beware
   Of entrance to a quarrel, but being in,
   Bear't that th' opposed may beware of thee.

F. Give every man thy ear, but few thy voice,

G. Take each man's censure, but reserve thy judgment.

H. Costly thy habit as thy purse can buy,
   But not expressed in fancy, rich, not gaudy,
   For the apparel oft proclaims the man.

• •

I. Neither a borrower nor a lender be,
   For loan oft loses both itself and friend,
   And borrowing dulleth th' edge of husbandry.

J. This above all: to thine own self be true,
   And it must follow, as the night the day,
   Thou canst not then be false to any man.

1. Classify these value propositions by writing the appropriate letter in the outline below. A proposition may be entered in more than one category.

   I.   Major goals in life (in terms of meaning and purpose)

   _____

   II. Success in personal dealings

   _____

III. Educational goals

_____

IV. Ethics

_____

V. Aesthetics

_____

VI. Procedures of thinking

_____

2. Are the propositions above compatible with human nature? If not, explain why.

_____

_____

3. Are the propositions above mutually compatible? If not, explain why.

_____

_____

4. What is your evaluation of the above set of propositions as a value system?

_____

_____

Problems 5–6. These problems refer to the value propositions below.

K. "The vocation of every man and woman is to serve other people."

   L.N. Tolstoy

L. Power and wealth: these alone are worth the striving.

M. "Fear God, and keep His commandments: for this is the whole duty of man."

   Ecclesiastes

N. "Man's highest blessedness,
   In wisdom chiefly stands."

   Sophocles

O. "... that best portion of a good man's life,
His little, nameless, unremembered acts
Of kindness and of love."

William Wordsworth

P. "... any man's death diminishes me, because I am involved in mankind; and therefore never send to know for whom the bell tolls; it tolls for thee."

John Donne

Q. "A thing of beauty is a joy forever."

John Keats

R. "One ought to seek out virtue for its own sake, without being influenced by fear or hope, or by any external influence. Moreover, in that does happiness consist."

Diogenes Laertius

S. "Act as though the maxim of your action were by your will to become a universal law of nature."

Immanuel Kant

T. "So act as to treat humanity, whether in thine own person or in that of another, always as an end, never as a means."

Immanuel Kant

5. Which, if any, of the value propositions above are mutually imcompatible?

_____

_____

6. If you followed proposition L, what needs would be unsatisfied?

_____

_____

Problems 7–10. These problems refer to value propositions A–J as well as K–T.

7. Classify value premises A–T by writing the appropriate letter in the outline below. A premise may be entered in more than one category.

I. Major goals in life

_____

II. Success in personal dealings

_____

III.   Educational goals

_____

IV.   Ethics

_____

V.   Aesthetics

_____

VI.   Procedures of thinking

_____

8. What is your evaluation of the propositions classified above as a value system?

_____

9. List below the letters from any of the propositions that you believe should be omitted.

_____

10. Write below a proposition you believe should be added to the system.

_____

Exercise 31C

1. Write below a representative sample of the value propositions you believe you live by.

A. _____

B. _____

C. _____

D. _____

E. _____

F. _____

G. _____

H. _____

I. _____

J. _____

2. In the space below marked "Conclusion," state as a categorical proposition a decision you have made recently. In the space marked "Minor Premise," state a categorical proposition describing the immediate situation that led to the decision. Then derive the value premise necessary to make the conclusion valid.

Major Premise: _____

Minor Premise: _____

Conclusion: _____

3. In the space below, list the categories you would use in classifying your own values (all lines need not be used).

I. _____

II. _____

III. _____

IV. _____

V. _____

VI. _____

VII. _____

VIII. _____

IX. _____

X. _____

4. Classify the propositions you listed in problem 1 by writing the letter for each proposition after the appropriate category above.

5. Evaluate the propositions so classified as a value system.

_____

_____

_____

6. What propositions would you omit or modify to improve the system?

_____

_____

_____

7. What propositions would you add?

_____

_____

_____

Part Six

The Argumentative Essay

Chapter 32

The Planning Stage

- **Choosing a Topic**
- **Gathering Information**
- **Forming a Thesis**
- **Testing Your Thesis**
- **Evaluating and Deciding**

Besides applying the principles elaborated in this text to your everyday decision making and problem solving, you should find them useful in guiding your writing of argumentative essays—essays that range from letters to the editor to book-length treatises or, more commonly, class-assigned papers. Let us therefore close our study of creative and critical thinking by discussing the argumentative essay. This chapter will present an approach to planning an argumentative essay; this approach is based on the principles of the five-phase decision-making cycle and is intended to clarify and order your thinking about the paper you will write. The approach is not a step-by-step procedure for planning an essay. It is a procedure which, by reminding you of the principles of effective thinking, will help you to choose a topic, gather relevant information, formulate an arguable thesis statement, and test and evaluate the thesis. Planning the essay constitutes the thinking stage that precedes the writing stage (though of course you will continue

to think as you write and you will often need to write to see what you think).

The present chapter treats essay writing as a form of open inquiry; that is, you begin the project without a preset thesis to prove. As you go through the phases of the decision-making cycle, you close in on your topic by applying the principles and techniques of effective thinking so that your final paper will be logically sound as well as rhetorically persuasive. By the time you have followed the procedures described in this chapter, you will have a topic chosen, source materials gathered, a solid thesis statement written, and a tentative overall structure for your material outlined.

The next chapter will present strategies for writing the essay and convincing your audience. Although these topics are presented separately and in two chapters, in actuality they are linked. We tend to think about these elements almost simultaneously as we write. When, for example, we are thinking about how to choose a topic and formulate a thesis statement, we are also thinking about the audience to whom our paper will be addressed and the techniques for arguing our case. These chapters are connected in another way, too. The decision-making approach outlined in this chapter applies the thinking skills presented earlier in this text to clarify, order, and sharpen our thinking about the topic or the problem we face; the argument we build on those principles demonstrates the conclusion we have reached. The rhetorical skills discussed in the next chapter enable us to communicate that argument and to persuade our readers to share our conclusions. But in spite of these links, the topics have been separated in the discussion so that we could focus on each element and its contribution to the writing of an effective argumentative essay.

If we consider the steps preliminary to writing a paper as an example of decision making, we can apply the five-phase cycle as follows: recognizing and defining the problem becomes choosing a subject to investigate; gathering information is just that, collecting and appraising possible sources of evidence; forming tentative conclusions becomes assessing the solidity of the tentative structure; and evalustructure for the essay; testing tentative conclusions becomes assessing the solidity of the tentative structure; and evaluation and decision become the finalizing of plans for the project. You are then ready to consider which writing techniques would be most effective for your particular audience.

Choosing a Topic

As you recall, the first phase of decision making is the recognition of a problem. Writing a paper is a problem, whether "problem" is defined broadly or narrowly;

in this case, part of the problem will be defined for you by the instructor and the assignment, but the rest of the definition will be up to you. Aside from approximate length, you may be given no limitations at all except that the paper be argumentative. In this case, you will want to choose a topic that you will benefit from investigating and that you will be able to discuss knowledgeably after you have done your research.

If the subject area is not limited by the instructor, you will want to search your frame of reference and your present interests to find a topic that makes maximum use of what you already know. Your major may provide such a topic. If you are studying law enforcement, you may already have read about polygraph tests and find that their use interests you but that you have some questions about their reliability. You might then think of the polygraph as a possible topic. A psychology major might be interested in behavior modification. An education major might be interested in the standardized tests, such as SAT and GRE, which are used to determine entrance into colleges and graduate schools. None of these topics—the polygraph, behavior modification, or standardized tests—would be an appropriate final choice for a paper topic. Each of them is far too broad, and a six- or eight-page paper on one of them could provide only the most superficial coverage. But settling on a general topic area is an important first step. For many people it is this first step that proves a major stumbling block—when no topic comes to mind, they are paralyzed by indecision and keep putting off further work on the project, hoping that an inspiration will come from the blue. If you are in this situation, you should reread the chapter on creative thinking and take active steps to facilitate that inspiration. Otherwise, it may not come or may come too late to allow you to complete the project in time.

If your major fails to provide a topic, your present occupation may. A paramedic may believe that people in her field do not receive adequate training. A cafeteria worker may be angry that health regulations do not seem to be enforced. A clerk in a department store may believe that the policies concerning shoplifting applied by his retail chain encourage the practice rather than curtail it. Job "pet peeves" can become topics for lengthy research papers as well as for letters to the editor. Moreover, there is always a chance that researching a job-related topic will provide you with information that you can put to practical use to improve your situation and that of your coworkers.

You may also find it valuable, as well as interesting, to choose a topic concerning your school. This kind of project can be especially rewarding because you can make a genuinely original contribution to the body of knowledge available on the subject—even in the course of investigating the issue to write a short argumentative essay. This area of topic possibilities has the additional advantage of naturally engaging your interest; you are apt to be eager to find out about changes in your school that might affect you. Has some new policy recently been implemented that has caused controversy? Perhaps you are a junior liberal arts major and you have just been informed that before you graduate you will have to complete a course in computer literacy. Let us suppose further that you and a number of liberal arts majors are very unhappy about this requirement. You might want to do some research into the reasoning behind it. The research you do might help you write a convincing argument against the requirement. On the other hand, it might change your mind and help you write an essay that would convince your fellow students to accept the course as a good thing.

One way to find a good campus topic is to visit the office of the school paper and scan the newspapers for the past couple of years. There you will find descriptions of major changes in policy and student and faculty reactions to these changes. You will also find leads to legal documents and government proceedings that relate to the issue. You will find the names of key officials to interview and may also find the results of opinion polls on the issue.

Of course, the nature of the assignment will help lead you to subject areas, even if your instructor has made no specific rules about topics. Are you expected to do primary research, interview people, take polls or surveys, describe from direct personal observation? If so, a local topic would be best. If all your research is to come from secondary sources, then you are not limited to what you can "get your hands on." Still, writing about what you know well often works best. And if primary research is optional, you may find that it is very valuable and that it is this sense of direct involvement on your part that makes the difference between a mediocre paper and a good one.

If you are choosing your own topic, there is something to be said for avoiding the old overused argumentation topics like gun control, euthanasia, abortion, or capital punishment. The chances of your coming up with an original essay on one of these topics are slim. Moreover, these topics are sometimes chosen because they sound like good argumentation topics rather than because they are of real interest to those who choose them. If you are truly committed to a topic on which a great deal has been said, then find a new slant: is there a particular gun control law presently before your state legislature? Argue its merits and defects. If euthanasia is your consuming interest, try to find a recent case with an unusual slant and argue the merits of that case. When choosing a topic, remember that the fact that much has been written about a certain subject usually does not make researching it easier. Rather, it usually makes the problem of selecting and evaluating evidence more complex and difficult.

If the topic is assigned, then see how much leeway you have within the assignment to make the greatest use of your knowledge and experience. It is important, however, to stay within the limits of the assignment. If the instructions are not distributed in written form, take them down carefully when the professor gives them and make sure you understand them. If you have doubts about whether your planned topic fits the assignment, ask the professor. You might also consult with the instructor if you cannot think of a topic. He or she may tell you some of the topics that have produced the most successful essays in the past, and this list may direct your thinking along fruitful lines. Remember that an overall topic, important as it is to have found one, is not the final step in defining the problem. You must also limit and slant your topic so that the final essay will have both unity and direction.

Some topics can never produce successful essays because they are too broad or ill-defined to allow thorough discussion. The best result the writer can then hope for would be a rhetorical, inspirational piece—a nice editorial, perhaps, but a poor research paper. It is to be assumed that you are writing for readers whose intelligence you respect and who are unlikely to be seduced by fallacies and propaganda devices. Therefore, if you are writing a sustained argument, you will want to make your topic narrow and well

focused enough so that you can write a convincing essay with solid evidence to support your claim.

Suppose that you have decided to write about nuclear energy because there are plans to build a nuclear reactor not too far from your city and protest groups have formed. You do not believe that the dangers these groups are describing in their pamphlets and letters to the editor are as serious as the protesters claim. So you decide to write a research paper supporting the claim that nuclear power is basically safe.

At the library, you discover that there are a number of books available on the topic, as well as hundreds of journal articles devoted to the topic of nuclear energy. It occurs to you that saying anything about the safety of nuclear energy in two thousand words or so is going to be difficult if not impossible. What do you do next?

You might try browsing through some of the articles to see how others have slanted or narrowed the topic to suit their audiences. You will probably find the most rewarding articles among those at the highest level of your understanding of the issue. That is, you may find little that is of use in an essay on nuclear energy in *The Reader's Digest*, and you may also not find an analysis in a journal intended for nuclear physicists very helpful. An article in *Science*, however, might provide what you need. Just looking at the titles of recent articles might give you some help. For instance, you might find a whole cluster of articles about Three Mile Island, and you might decide to limit your subject to that. Or you might find that there is more information than you had expected about the plans for the nuclear reactor that originally sparked your interest and conclude that this particular project would afford you the chance to do both primary and secondary research.

In any case, an overabundance of information should be taken as a definite signal that you need to narrow the topic, whereas a lack of information may mean that you need to redirect the topic or broaden it slightly—or simply look further. If your subject is a legal issue, such as a proposed raising of the drinking age in your state, you may find a great deal of valuable information in the proceedings of the state legislature. Other issues may involve using the *Congressional Record* as a source. Government documents of any sort are often strangely indexed and hard to use, but your librarian should be able to help you.

While looking over others' arguments, you should pick out their theses carefully and evaluate these claims by the means described in this book. You should be able to recognize the various kinds of evidence other writers offer in support of their claims and to pick out the fallacies and other devices they use to persuade. Identifying the weaknesses in the arguments of others should help you think of ways to strengthen your own.

Ideally, your topic definition will produce a clearly limited topic and a controlling direction for your essay. In defining your project, you will need to keep in mind the three general rules for defining problems from Chapter 1. The topic should not be so broad that it cannot be supported uniformly and in depth. The topic should not be so broad that it cannot be supported uniformly and in depth. The topic should not be so narrow that available resources are quickly exhausted. (Narrowness of topic is rarely a problem, however.) The defini- a conclusion without examining the evidence. For instance, if you are concerned with the campus parking problem, you would not want to come up initially with the thesis that the parking problem should be solved by building more parking lots. This may or may not be your ultimate solution to the parking problem, but beginning with it would prevent you from investigating other options—closing off the central campus to cars, for instance, or restricting parking permits—that might prove to be more feasible. Your final topic should be something that stirs your interest and about which you have a reasonably open mind so that your research becomes a true investigation.

Gathering Information

As you are defining your problem, you will also need to be gathering information. What you learn about your topic will help direct your "slant," or approach, to the problem, and the direction you give your final project will also be affected by what kind of supporting material is available to you. Of course, information gathering goes on throughout the course of decision making and has its impact on every step; this is also true of writing a paper.

Sources of information fall into two basic categories, primary sources and secondary sources. Often the best-researched papers use a combination of both types. **Primary sources** include interviews, surveys, letters, eyewitness accounts, personal observations, experiments you participated in, and so on. You may find it quite exciting to conduct direct research, and doing so may give you a personal connection with your project that will bring originality and life to it. In addition to primary sources, you may consult **secondary sources**—other researchers' findings and accounts. Some subjects and some assignments require only primary research or only secondary research. You may be asked, for instance, to determine how the students on your campus feel about the proposal to do away with senior exemptions from final exams and to support your position on the issue with your findings. This project would employ primary research entirely. On the other hand, you might be assigned an issue like handgun control and discover that only secondary sources are available.

To find sources of primary materials, check your own knowledge and experience for connections with the project. Do you know anyone who is a genuine authority on the subject? If so, call or write for an interview. If you have chosen a job-related topic, you might try to find out other people's opinions on the subject. Let us say that your employer has recently instituted a four-day work week and that the switch has not proved successful. You might take a poll of your fellow workers to see how they feel about the change. (Of course, in such a case, you'd want to conduct your research in such a way as to make sure your employer does not think you are meddling.)

On-campus issues provide a great variety of primary sources. You might demonstrate that students have a misconception of the campus police by taking a poll demonstrating that students believe the campus police spend 90 percent of their time giving tickets and then obtaining university records that show that in fact the police spend 10 percent of their time ticketing. This evidence could be part of a research paper demonstrating that campus security should be allotted a larger percentage of the university budget. It is possible that in a class or in your job you have actually participated in experiments that support your claim. Their results would also be primary evidence, even though you may not have been the only one involved in conducting the experiment.

Although there are many ways you can have direct contact with your subject matter, probably the two most common sources of primary information for student papers are interviews and polls. Therefore these sources merit comment on the most effective ways of using them.

People, of course, are a most useful resource—professors in the field your project involves, company officials, members of city councils, spokespersons for groups concerned with your issue. You will avoid the fallacy of appealing to false authority if you carefully check the credentials of those whose views you quote or cite and if, when possible, you check their facts with other sources. There are two benefits from actually speaking with those involved with your issue. First, personal contact with those who have devoted time and energy to investigating the issue will probably increase your level of involvement with the question and hence your ability to do a good job. Second, these individuals may be able to refer you to other important sources of information. Sometimes experts in a field will have access to as yet unpublished information that they may be willing to share with you.

It is important to prepare for the interview carefully because you may not get a second chance to speak with the interviewee, which makes it essential that you obtain the information you need under the rather constrained circumstances of the interview. Of course, it is far better to speak with someone in person than over the telephone. Set up the interview far enough in advance to allow for adequate preparation. Study the interviewee's experience carefully so that you can ask specific questions. Set up a list of questions that relate to your project, and if feasible, write them in order of priority, so that if the time allotted is shorter than you think or your interview is derailed somehow, you will have the most important information. Take brief notes during the interview about the answers to each question but do not try to write down everything said. Instead, jot down a few phrases that will remind you of the substance of the answer. If you get facts or figures, though, take the time to write them down exactly; and do the same if your interviewee says something you might like to quote directly. You should try to be extremely diplomatic in interviewing, so as to elicit the most positive response. As soon as the interview is over, sit down in a quiet place and sort out the responses. At this point write down everything you remember of the interview.

Another possible source of primary information is the poll or survey. Of course, this source would not be appropriate for all projects. It would be appropriate if you are concerned with a campus issue for which student opinion or student experience would be relevant. If you are arguing, for instance, that the new procedures adopted by the campus placement office are faulty and do not help students get jobs, then it would certainly be relevant to take a survey of students using the placement service to see if they have had problems and, if so, what kind of problems. It would be even better if you could find students who had gone through both the old and the new procedures. However, if you are arguing that the typical American diet is inadequate, it would not give you much useful evidence to discover that most of the first hundred people you run across agree with you. You would be committing the bandwagon fallacy if you offered the results of this survey in support of your thesis.

Before taking any kind of survey or poll, reread Chapter 8 on generalization and be sure to use correct sampling techniques. Phrase the questions you will ask carefully, to avoid bias in the questions themselves. One mail poll recently asked, "Do you want pornography presented to your children in their elementary school classrooms?" The poll was attempting to establish that sex education in the schools should be discontinued, but the questions were phrased in such a way that some respondents might not even be able to identify the issue. The promoters of the poll also asked for a contribution to their organization with the response; thus, since only those in sympathy with their aims would return the questionnaires, the results would be completely unreliable. In your questions, make sure that the issue is clearly and neutrally presented and that the answers will fall into unequivocal categories. When you summarize the results of the survey, include both the raw numbers and the percentages and make sure the breakdown of the figures is clear. You may find it convenient to make up tables, graphs, or bar or pie charts to represent your results. Such graphics often add interest to the presentation by breaking up the blocks of information and presenting the material in a more interesting format. To make up interesting graphics from your results, you might want to consult a technical writing journal. If you have computer experience you may already be prepared to represent your information in graphic form. Two suggestions are worth keeping in mind: (1) be sure the chart you have created is absolutely clear, with labels at all relevant points; and (2) make your material even more accessible by providing a caption for each chart. The caption should explain exactly what the chart demonstrates. Someone browsing through your paper should be able to figure out what the charts mean without having to sift through the text.

Secondary sources are many and varied. To start with, there are those old standbys from grade school and high school, encyclopedias and dictionaries. Many researchers do not sneer at encyclopedias, because good ones (such as the *Encyclopaedia Britannica* and the *Encyclopedia Americana*) often have good brief bibliographies at the ends of the articles, and the articles themselves may provide solid background material. Books on the topic are found by consulting the card catalogue in your library. Generally, you can tell that if you can find several entire books on your topic, you probably need to narrow it further.

The most valuable sources for most current argumentation topics will be articles in journals. These may be found by consulting *The Readers' Guide to Periodical Literature*, the *Social Sciences Index*, the *Humanities Index*, or the index to journals in your particular field. *The Readers' Guide* is the index to popular journals, such as *Time* and *Newsweek*, and will not help you find technical or scholarly articles. Newspaper articles may sometimes be used as evidence, although these articles are often too superficial to provide solid information. Some newspapers, such as *The New York Times*, are indexed. Most fields have their own specialized reference tools, such as dictionaries, indexes, encyclopedias, and bibliographies, that will help you find materials; there are also guides to reference books to tell you what is available in your field. Specific topics will lead you in other directions for secondary source material: laws under consideration, for instance, may lead you to the *Congressional Record* or to the proceedings of your state legislature. It's a good idea to ask your librarian to help you on your initial library source hunt. In addition, more and more university libraries have various computerized systems to help you find materials. Your librarian will know exactly what is available and how to use it.

As you collect sources, you will find it convenient to keep track of each one on an index card. Your instructor may have specific instructions for what should go on these cards. If not, you may want to include all the data you would need to use in the final bibliography (author, title, journal, date, volume and issue, and page numbers) and a sentence or two about the contents of the article. If you keep this information on cards rather than on a list, you will be able to alphabetize the list easily, will have no problems with adding or dropping entries, and will know at a glance whether a particular article is relevant to your topic as you finally defined it.

When you have taken stock of all your personal connections with the topic, and have made a general survey of the literature available, it is time to formulate your thesis statement.

Forming a Thesis

The next phase of the decision making process, forming tentative conclusions, can be adapted to the formulating of thesis statements. These theses may then be tested like hypotheses and modified or even replaced as the principles of effective thinking dictate. Let us imagine that a proposal has been made to require that a computer literacy course be taken by all majors in your field of study. Let us imagine also that your first reaction—a "gut reaction"—is negative; you think that there are enough requirements in your field already and an additional one would be just an annoyance. The first thesis that you generate, then, may be something like this: "The proposed requirement for a course in computer literacy for liberal arts majors should not be instituted." Next, you derive some consequences of your thesis in order to subject it to preliminary testing. Let us suppose that you produce this hypothetical statement: "If the proposed course should not be instituted, then it would not provide significant and lasting benefits to the students." You proceed to test the consequent of this statement for reliability.

Looking over the material for the proposed course, you find that it will cover basic computer terminology, word processing, simple graphics, and information about how computers operate, among other things. You do find some points against the course: it would be expensive, and it would have to replace an elective. But these points do not relate directly to the consequent you are testing. The more you study the course proposal, the more you begin to suspect that the course would indeed provide important benefits to the student. Indeed, it occurs to you that had you taken it it would have helped you write the essay about it. As you read about how similar courses operate at other universities, you become convinced that the course would be a valuable addition to your curriculum. Therefore you discard your thesis as disproven and form another: "The proposed required course in computer literacy for liberal arts majors should be implemented as soon as possible." Once more you derive consequences: "If the course should be required, it would have lasting benefits for the students who take it." You have already found some evidence that the skills provided by the course would be useful to students while still in college as well as to job seekers. You decide to proceed with your second hypothesis.

Testing Your Thesis

Once you have chosen a thesis, another and more thorough way of testing it is to settle on a tentative plan for the paper. If the thesis is well-chosen, you should be able to find a logical breakdown of points and subpoints. The arrangement of ideas you devise now may not be the final structure of your paper. But if you cannot come up with any meaningful pattern, then you may still need to make some adjustments in the thesis itself, although you will probably not need to go to the extreme of discarding it.

Let us assume that in your paper supporting the computer literacy course requirement you have a number of areas you wish to cover. You think the paper should include a description of the course, the history of such courses, the need for the course, and the desire for the course. You also wish to answer the most cogent objections to the proposal. How might you arrange this material? What kind of outline would be most useful to you in preparing the essay?

First, your introduction poses a problem: how do you interest your audience, whom you conceive to be students, faculty, and administrators of your university, in the topic? You might look over computer literacy courses offered in other colleges. If you find that the best-known colleges all offer such courses, you might begin with that point. It is true that you would be opening with an emotional appeal by exploiting the prestige of these colleges, but it is also true that these institutions would have a certain amount of genuine authority as to what constitutes a good course. Descriptions of the course contents in the various catalogues might give you other ideas about how to begin in such a way that you could capture your audience. Your scratch sheet might then contain the notes for your planned introduction and your thesis, which would follow the introduction.

Considering your goals for your paper and your projected subtopics, then, you might come up with an arrangement something like this:

Introduction: Within the past few years, a number of well-known universities have instituted computer literacy courses. An excellent course in computer literacy has been proposed here, but so far it has not been initiated because of the controversy it has caused. (Note that these comments are not your introduction, but a summary of your planned introduction.)

Thesis: The proposed course should be initiated without delay.
   I.   The course was thoroughly researched and carefully outlined by a committee of experts.
  II.   The skills provided by the course would prove invaluable.
     A. They would give job seekers an advantage.
     B. They would be useful to students.
 III.   Students and faculty for the most part want the course.
 IV.   Objections to the course are without foundation.
     A. It need not be as expensive as opponents fear.
     B. It need not crowd other courses out of the curriculum.

Conclusion: No more time should be lost before putting this new program into practice.

You now have a structure for your paper and a place to put all the information you have collected so far, as well as hints on where to look for further information.

Evaluating and Deciding

You are ready now for the final stage of the decision-making process—to decide whether to commit yourself to the project or to modify or even abandon it. At this point you should look over the work you have done so far and consider the thesis statement you have finally chosen, the resources that are available to you, and the tentative structure for the essay. It is useful to ask yourself three questions:

Are the Relationships Between the Points in the Outline Clear? If not, revise the outline. It may be that you have some interesting information that does not fit into the project as you have conceived it, and you may have to leave the material out. It may be that there is an apparent logical overlap or gap in the outline. For instance, suppose that you have planned to argue that marijuana should not be legalized because it creates various problems for the user and society. You have a tentative structure something like this:

Thesis: Marijuana should not be legalized.
   I.   It causes physical problems.
  II.   It causes psychological problems.
 III.   It causes moral problems.
 IV.   It causes social problems.
  V.   It leads to harder drugs.

Your critical examination of this tentative structure should reveal a number of weaknesses. How do psychological problems differ from moral problems, exactly?

Don't the categories of physical and psychological problems overlap with that of social problems? When we discuss marijuana's tendency to lead to harder drugs, aren't we considering all four of the other categories again? It would seem that the entire project requires rethinking and redirecting.

Is the Project Limited Enough in Scope so that You Will Be Able to Complete It in the Time Allotted and with the Material Available? An important factor here is accessibility of information. Often students conceive of challenging projects that require such items of information as pamphlets from government agencies or interviews with hard-to-reach people. When the material turns out to be delayed in arrival or unavailable, the project suffers because the weight of the evidence is lessened. It is wise not to count on material you do not know is available to you at the time you decide on your project.

As You Look at the Outline as Objectively as Possible, Does It Seem to You to Be the Skeleton of an Interesting, Relevant Essay? Would You Want to Read the Essay? This can be the most important question of all, since your essay is supposed to be convincing to others. If you do not think it represents a valuable and interesting contribution to discussion, perhaps you should rethink your topic.

If these questions are answered in the affirmative, it is time to write. The next chapter will discuss strategies for writing the essay and convincing your audience to accept your point of view.

Exercise 32

Problems 1–3. Consider that you have been assigned to write an eight-page argumentative essay on a topic of your choice falling within these general categories.

    a. Gun control

    b. Campus regulations

    c. The income tax

    d. The military draft

    e. Separation of church and state

1. Derive three different thesis statements that you could then test for suitability to the assignment.

2. Now go to the library and test according to the suggestions in this chapter the three thesis statements for the topic you find most interesting. Rate the thesis statements from 1 (best) to 3 (worst) and be prepared to explain your evaluation to the class.

3. Using the best thesis statement you have devised, write a rough outline for a paper.

Problems 4–5. Narrow down five of the topics and write tentative thesis statements for them. Then go to the library and find three sources of information on each topic.

4. Consider the following topics.

    a. Chemical castration of sex offenders

    b. The nuclear reactor at Commanche Peak

    c. Sterilization of the mentally retarded

    d. "Deprogramming" of religious cult members

    e. Using laetrile to treat cancer.

    f. Parents denying children medical treatment on religious grounds

    g. Opening adoption records to adoptees

    h. Allowing or prohibiting liquor on your campus

    i. Legalizing homosexual marriages

    j. Raising the drinking age to twenty-one by federal law

    k. Permitting parents to educate their school-age children at home

    l. Requiring grade schools to provide bilingual education

5. Write a tentative outline for the best thesis statement you devised in answer to problem 4.

Chapter 33   The Writing Stage

- **Determining Your Purpose**
- **Analyzing Your Audience**
- **Choosing Your Tone**
- **Putting It All Together**

- **The Introduction**
- **The Exposition**
- **The Body**
- **The Conclusion**

In using the five-phase approach to planning your essay, you will have considered the general dimensions of your argument. You will have thought through the thesis of your paper and formulated an arguable thesis statement; you will have done some primary and secondary research; and you will have tested the viability of your hypothesis and established a tentative structure for your essay. You will have had to do a considerable amount of writing to accomplish all this. By now you probably have a rough outline for your paper, as well as notes on the various sources you have consulted. You may even have experimented with possible beginnings or endings for your paper. In any case, the thinking and writing you have been doing has probably given you some tentative but more or less consistent ideas about the audience for the paper, the tone you might take in arguing, and the purpose of the paper. In this chapter we will discuss some of the skills of argumentation that can help you make a convincing argument.

Whereas the principles discussed in the last chapter provide an approach to thinking about and preparing your essay,

the principles discussed in this chapter offer a strategy for writing your essay. Again, they do not constitute a step-by-step plan but are interrelated concepts to consider as you write.

Determining Your Purpose

Why are you writing? There are so many reasons you might have for writing an argumentative essay that it would take more than a chapter just to list them. You might be writing a letter to the editor of the local paper attempting to influence public opinion in favor of a proposed new park. You might be writing a letter to your dean attempting to convince him or her that although your grade point average is below the level ordinarily required for continued enrollment, the circumstances surrounding your case are unusual and you ought to be allowed to remain in school. If you have children in school, you might be writing to your state representative asking him or her to vote against the proposed lengthening of the school day. You may even be writing to the governing board of your college attempting to convince the board to raise needed revenue by some other means besides doubling the tuition. And, of course, you might be writing to fulfill any number of class assignments that specify an audience or a goal.

Deciding what kind of approach to take and how to present your evidence requires that you determine precisely what your purpose is in writing your paper, exactly who is your intended audience, and how you should represent yourself to this audience. For example, consider the letter to the dean. Your purpose is clear: to convince the dean that you should be allowed a semester to build up your grade point average to an acceptable level. Because you are the student with a favor to ask and the dean is the dean, there are probably a few approaches you would automatically rule out: you probably would not start with a few jokes, for instance, or assume that the dean was close-minded toward members of your group, Omega Omega Omega fraternity, and needed to be educated. You would avoid a gimmicky approach with a punch line. Instead, you would try to impress the dean with your conscientiousness and industry, as well as with the weight of the evidence you cite to demonstrate that you didn't get that 1.5 from negligence but because of overwhelming pressures and interruptions. You might try to cite evidence of your abilities under normal circumstances. On the other hand, if you were writing a letter to the campus newspaper with the intention of stirring up a little unrest, you might choose gimmicks and punch lines. For instance, a controversial group recently asked that students show support for it by wearing jeans on a certain day. The response included a letter requesting that students show nonsupport for this group by wearing clothes on that day. There was little of logic or substance in the letter of response, but its writer achieved his purpose.

Questions you might ask to help you define your purpose include the following:

1. Do you want your readers to take some kind of action as a result of your argument? Do you want them, for instance, to vote for someone? To write to their senators? If you want them to take action, what will the action cost them? The more you are asking of your readers, the stronger your argument will have to be.

2. If you are not trying to influence your readers to do something, what are you trying to convince them to think? Are you trying to get them to accept something new? To become concerned about something they had not previously perceived as a problem? Is your argumentative essay a first step in influencing belief so that later calls for action might be more likely to be heeded?

It is often useful to write out a definition of purpose so that your objective can be used in connection with your audience analysis to help determine your tone. Your statement of purpose may be very similar to your thesis statement, for example, "I want to convince students to accept rather than fight the new computer literacy course requirement" or "I want to convince the Faculty Senate that it ought not abolish the traditional senior exemption from final exams." Having such a sentence written out may help to eliminate ambiguities in the conception of the project. Remember, though, that you do not want to use your statement of purpose as your thesis statement because such statements are not rhetorically effective. "In this paper I want to convince you to support the proposed handgun control law" is too obvious and blunt to evoke interest and does little to establish the reader's confidence in you. After such an opening, only those readers who already have an active interest in the issue are likely to continue reading.

By this point it should be clear that purpose, tone, and audience are all interrelated in such a way that they are difficult to discuss separately. Analysis of your audience may cause you to change your purpose slightly. For instance, if you find that your readers are all fervent opponents of gun control, you might decide it would be better to try to get them to soften their position somewhat than to attempt to convince them to go out and vote for a gun control law.

Analyzing Your Audience

If Senator Slick, who was running for re-election, was chosen to give a speech at your college, he would probably not give the same speech he just gave to a fundraising dinner for him or the one he gave to a group of veterans at a VFW post. His goal in all three cases might be similar: to encourage support for his re-election effort. But the three audiences would have different expectations and preconceived ideas. If the senator was at all aware of public speaking techniques—and most successful politicians are very aware of these techniques—he or his speech writers would analyze his audience carefully before deciding what tone to take with them.

A number of factors should be considered in analyzing an audience, whether it consists of editorial readers, toastmasters, or classmates in philosophy. At the present time, you are probably using these suggestions to help you write an assigned essay, and so are writing for an audience consisting of your instructor and perhaps another group he or she has designated. You might be asked to address your peers on a campus issue, for instance, or to write to your legislative representatives in an attempt to influence them to raise or lower the drinking age. The important thing to remember is that you are not just arguing your case, but arguing it for someone who will judge your argument; the more clearly you can picture this judge, the more effective your presentation is likely to be. Perhaps the most important and most easily accessible factors concerning your target audience are age, education, socioeconomic background, attitude toward the subject under discussion, and special interest. Of course, these factors are interrelated and help to shed light on one another. It may help to fill out a brief audience-analysis form before beginning to write. Such a form might include the following points.

Age. How old is your audience? Will your readers be of various ages, or mostly of one age group? Many writers find that the easiest audience to address consists of their own age group because their language and style is most natural to this group. If your readers are younger or older than you are, you may make certain assumptions about their interests and beliefs; but beware of any attempt to speak to them in "their language." Lyndon Johnson once gave a speech to a college audience in which he incorporated slang his daughter Lynda had collected as part of a research project, but the slang turned out to be slightly outdated and Johnson found his audience looking at him and one another oddly.

Education. What is your audience's educational level? If you are addressing college students, you know that they are in the process of preparing for a career and are interested in any social, political, economic, or other factors that might affect that choice or their chances for success in their chosen field. You may also assume that they have a certain level of vocabulary and certain kinds of general knowledge. You cannot assume the background of shared experience that would exist in an audience who had been through the Second World War together, nor can you assume much about their political leanings, unless you have the additional knowledge that you are writing for or speaking to students from a conservative or liberal-minded school.

In addition to the general educational level of your audience, you will want to ask how much knowledge they would be likely to have of the topic at issue. If your topic is something related to nuclear energy, you may find that your readers include many who have fairly strong opinions on the topic without having any solid knowledge about it. If this is the case, your task may be tricky—you will have to provide information without appearing patronizing. It is often difficult to figure out how much information a given audience needs on a topic. If you give too little, the readers or listeners may be confused; if you give too much, they may feel talked down to. Sometimes it helps to read an article on the issue in a publication intended for the same general audience, in order to determine how seasoned writers go about informing their readers.

Socioeconomic Background. Socioeconomic background may be more or less important depending on your subject and the other facts you know about your audience. If you are writing a letter to local property owners about a bond issue, for instance, your awareness of their financial stake in the issue may aid you in finding the right words and facts to convince them. Even if you know only that you are addressing a rich audience or a poor one, your knowledge may help you avoid strategic errors in presentation.

Attitude. Awareness of your audience's attitude toward the issue is crucial, and mainly this factor determines the tone of your presentation. If your readers are already sympathetic to your point of view, they will receive your proposal warmly and will even overlook inadvertent fallacies and propaganda devices that would be immediately apparent to the opposition. This does not mean that you should use fallacies in your argument, but it does mean that it is hard to alienate an audience that shares your view. If your readers are neutral, you will have to be more factual and more convincing. Overtly emotional appeals are likely to sound phony. You will want to collect solid, reliable, and relevant evidence to support your claims. If your readers are actively hostile, you will have a considerably harder time. Rational argument rarely changes the minds of opinionated people, who are likely to take the attitude "I've made up my mind. Don't confuse me with the facts." Your best chance may be to spend considerable time and effort warming up the audience and then suggest a position that is really only a first step toward the final position you wish them to accept. If you are addressing people whom you know to be militantly antiwelfare, for instance, and you wish them to do an about-face and support enlarged welfare programs, you might first attempt to get them to accept the idea that in some extreme cases welfare is necessary. You may do more to open their minds if you make a very modest point and then let them explore the implications of this new direction later than if you state exactly what you mean right away and alienate them.

Of course, if you know that your audience has particular common interests—if, for instance, you are addressing a group of nurses or feminists or police or musicians—then you can use your knowledge of their common concerns to plan your approach. And, of course, you have a special advantage if something in your audience's background or field of interest coincides with something in yours.

Throughout this discussion of argumentation, suggestions are based on the assumption that you are writing for educated, neutral readers, attempting to convince them to accept your position on a topic on which they are fairly well informed. This is the sort of audience that requires convincing argumentation, with careful attention paid to providing solid evidence and avoiding fallacies and evasions.

Choosing Your Tone

Considering your audience and learning everything you can about your potential readers or listeners will help you decide what approach to take with them—humorous or serious, formal or casual, technical or nontechnical. In essence you are deciding what kind of individual, or **persona**, will be addressing them. You are already aware that as a writer you have different personae for addressing different people—the letter you write to your best friend from high school, who quit school to join the army, about your first week in college won't seem to represent the same person as the one you write to your rather formal, tradition-minded aunt or uncle. You do not falsify anything

in either letter; you just choose the language and the particular details that seem appropriate in each case—your friend would be interested in some of your experiences, your aunt or uncle in others. Thus the traditional definition of *persona* as a mask may be slightly misleading. The persona is not a misrepresentation but more an edited version of yourself as a writer; just as we tend to alter our behavior and our language slightly depending on our companions, we select the writing voice most suitable to this or that group of readers. In the case of the paper you plan to write, your actual audience, of course, will be the instructor who made the assignment. But you should not try to play up to what you believe to be his or her beliefs or prejudices; instead, you should consider him or her as one of the general class of intelligent, informed readers.

When you are determining what sort of persona to adopt for an argumentative paper, you will need to ask some questions: Do these readers need a serious, direct approach or a humorous one? What about figures and statistics—how can I make them convincing and not boring? What about emotion—how much is too much? If I use rhetorical devices, can I keep them from sounding pompous? The answers to these questions may be based on the material you have collected about your audience.

If your essay is intended for our imagined neutral, educated audience, you should assume you have conscientious readers who must be treated with respect. You will want to use sound reasoning and solid evidence rather than persuasive emotional devices. Often a generally sound piece of argumentation will begin with a case or instance that might be labeled an emotional appeal; once attention is caught, however, the author will support his or her claims with solid evidence throughout the paper. You will have written an essay to be proud of if you can convince your readers to accept your point of view, as opposed to manipulating them into agreeing with you. Manipulation may cause a temporary compliance on the part of your readers, but they are likely to "wake up" sooner or later and become permanently alienated.

In writing for the audience we have defined, you might keep the following guidelines in mind:

1. You should use the highest level of vocabulary that is natural to you. You should not look up less familiar words in a thesaurus or use words that you believe your audience might use but you ordinarily would not.

2. You should present your thoughts in complete sentences and fully developed paragraphs. Often, each paragraph between the introduction and the conclusion will include a transition linking its thought to the preceding paragraph, a topic sentence, and evidence supporting your topic sentence. Above all, avoid adopting a breezy editorial style and throwing out one paragraph of sweeping statements after another. Your goal is to uphold a position, not merely to state one.

3. You should try to achieve at least the appearance of neutrality in language. Avoid "buzz words" and catch phrases like "law-abiding citizen," "taxpayer," "defenders of civil liberties," and so on. These tags sound good enough to those whose jargon they are, but others may find them glib and empty, or even offensive.

For guidance in achieving the appropriate tone, it might be useful to ask yourself the question: if I were neutral on the topic, what kind of presentation could be used effectively with me?

Putting It All Together

Your purpose, tone, and audience must be considered in determining how the material is to be arranged in your final essay. However, there are some general principles that hold true for most argumentation papers, especially the longer ones (essays of a thousand words or longer). Usually, you begin with an **introduction**, which establishes rapport with the reader, establishes the tone, and introduces the topic of your paper. This introduction is followed by a section that we might call the **exposition**, which provides background information needed for understanding your argument; this section is, in a sense, a secondary introduction. The subsequent portion of your paper, the main **body** of it, presents your evidence and refutes the opposition's point of view. In the **conclusion**, you may recapitulate your main points or make recommendations for action (or do both), or you may simply pick up an image or anecdote from the early portion of your paper to provide a sense of closure. The reader should always feel that his or her experience of your essay has been gracefully rounded off; all your points should fall into place. The reader should not feel that the writer had more to say but arbitrarily stopped or that he or she "ran out of gas," like novice speakers who conclude their first speeches with ". . . and, well, I guess that's about it."

The Introduction

The hardest part of the essay to write is the introduction, partly because it is of such importance. You gain or lose your readership with your introduction. You probably remember sitting in the dentist's waiting room leafing through journals, reading the first sentence or first paragraph of half a dozen articles, until you finally found an introduction interesting enough to overcome your feelings of apathy or apprehension and draw you into the article. You may have even been grateful to the unknown author when the nurse called your name and you realized that you had been so involved with the mating habits of coyotes or the reasons for taking vitamin C that you didn't even think about the dentist for half an hour. Because the introduction is crucial and hard to write, some writing texts suggest that it be left until last, on the theory that when you write it you will know exactly what to introduce. However, sometimes a vivid introduction is the first thing that occurs to you, and you do not want to abandon it. You should then write the introduction first, but keep in mind that introductions, like everything else you write, are subject to revision.

If you find the introduction difficult to write, keep in mind its goals:

1. It must interest readers and draw them into the essay.

2. It must dispose readers favorably toward the writer and his or her point of view.

Your introduction may attract the readers' interest by any number of means. It may point out that they have something to gain from accepting your position, draw a contrast between what most people think about an issue and what you will demonstrate to be the truth, provide an image or anecdote that produces an emotional effect, or point out an odd, little-known fact about a familiar situation. The introduction may also win reader approval in various ways. You do not need to adopt a first-person point of view, that is, to introduce yourself to the reader, to win favorable response. You may win approval by your careful choice of persona and tone. In some cases, a slow, relaxed introduction may be the best choice; in others, a brisk, more direct approach would be preferable. However, you usually need some kind of lead-in material to win reader acceptance. Only very rarely is it a good idea to jump right into your topic.

Consider the following two partial introductions to student papers. The assignment was to research the campus parking problem, come up with a feasible solution, and argue for the solution with solid evidence. The length of the essay was to be about fifteen hundred words.

> Have you ever been late to class because you haven't been able to find a place to park? If so, then you are aware of the parking problem on this campus.

> The cover of Alfred Stegall's new book on the history of this university gives us a nostalgic view of Houston Hall in 1860, when it was the center of campus activity. To me, though, the most noticeable feature of the photograph was the large number of horses tied to trees and stakes, blocking both the road and the main entrance to the university. It would seem that even in 1860 there was a parking problem on this campus. . . .

The first introduction leaps into the issue. It does show a connection between problem and reader, but it does so in an obvious and unoriginal way. And what about those who in fact have not been late to class because of parking problems? A reader who is not already vitally interested in the parking problem is likely to think "ho-hum" and turn elsewhere. In general, the "Have you ever——?" approach may alienate some readers because they may feel patronized and lectured to and may lose others because they haven't ever. The second introduction uses the device of citing a little-known fact to stir up interest, and even the reader who normally rides the shuttlebus may keep reading. Throughout the essay, but especially in the introduction, freshness is important to reader appeal. Therefore you should avoid bland statements and clichés. Clichés may be worn-out figures of speech ("The heartbroken mother watched the yellow school bus bear the apple of her eye to his new school twenty miles away") or slogans associated with a cause ("When guns are outlawed, only outlaws will have guns").

It should be added that an overly long introduction is no better than an abrupt one and may be worse. Having too much introductory material makes the argument itself seem sketchy and anticlimactic. Writers using a long introduction tend to promise or imply that they will do many important things in the essay and then fail to fulfill these promises. In some cases the introduction takes such a long time to get to the point that the reader has begun to wonder if it ever will. Although it is impossible to give a rule for how much of an essay should be devoted to introducing the topic, many well-balanced essays devote around 10 percent of their length to the introduction.

You should, then, make your introduction original and compact but not abrupt. You should establish in it the tone you will take throughout the essay.

The Exposition

Often the second section of your argumen-
tative essay provides background information necessary to the understanding of your position and your evidence. If you are arguing for a proposed handgun control law that is under consideration in your state, you might begin with some startling statistics on violence and handguns and then state your position on handgun control at the end of this introduction. The second section might then be an explanation of the particular law you are supporting, describing its source, its provisions, and its present status, that is, what stage it is in now on the road to enactment. The expository section usually produces a slight drop in interest, making it doubly important to capture the reader with the introduction.

This expository section may contain information on the history of the issue, the nature of the controversy, and the present state of the matter. It may also include definitions of unfamiliar terms necessary to the understanding of the argument. It should not be long; it is very easy to bore readers at this stage. If you have too much exposition, you should see if it is possible to combine some of the expository material with the evidence you are giving in the body of your essay. It is often possible to combine the introduction and the exposition in such a way as to maintain interest, especially if your readers are already fairly familiar with the issue and do not need a great deal of informing.

The exposition should be smoothly introduced and linked to the introduction. Consider the following portion of an expository section:

To understand the depth of the parking problem, it is useful to look at its causes. The enrollment at this university has doubled in the past ten years while available parking spaces have increased only by 20 percent. The dramatic increase in the number of students has far outstripped available dormitory space; now 70 percent of students live off campus, as opposed to only 30 percent in 1973. More students off campus means more cars on campus: 35 percent of students had cars registered in 1973, while 85 percent have them now. The net result of all this is a city-planner's nightmare.

The student writer of this essay began with an image of the situation and an anecdote illustrating the problem. He then led into the body with some information about the causes of the problem. When he set up his proposed solution, he referred to the information given in this section.

The main question to ask in deciding what to put into this section is, what do my readers need to know to understand my argument? If no additional information is necessary, you may provide some informative material that is useful and relevant to round off your introduction and lead the reader into the body of the essay.

The Body

The body is the argument itself: the specific reasons you give to support your thesis and the evidence you give to support these reasons. In the body of your paper you will probably also present and refute the opposition's view. If you do not do this, your essay may appear thin and one-sided to your readers, who will naturally think of the most obvious objections to your position.

It is important that your essay proceed in a well-organized fashion, so that its parts seem appropriately and logically placed and the essay as a whole is a well-crafted piece of work. When you were planning the essay, you devised a tentative structure for it as a means of testing the viability of your thesis. But by now, you have collected your evidence, and you probably have found that your initial outline is either too sketchy or not quite appropriate in some way. Perhaps what you had intended to be your major argument has been superseded by stronger ones, or perhaps you found in your investigation that one of your pieces of evidence was unsound and had to be discarded. Now you need to revise your plans so as to find the most effective arrangement of your reasons and evidence. Some ways of organizing the body of your paper are by the weight of the evidence, by the familiarity of the argument, by the chronological sequence of the evidence, and by the significance of the objections to your position. There are a number of other ways to arrange evidence; it is important not to choose at random from a list of possibilities but to find a clear principle of organization that suits your purpose and your material.

Arguments organized on the basis of the weight of the evidence proceed from the weakest to the strongest argument; since people tend to remember best what comes last, this method has the advantage of making the most convincing material the most memorable. Besides, if you give your most significant material first, you may initially impress your readers, but the later evidence will suffer by contrast, and your readers quite likely will be left feeling that you did not have much of an argument after all. If you do not give equal space to your major points, it makes sense to develop your most important (and last) one at greatest length.

Another direction a paper might take is to lead the reader from known to unknown territory. If you have some arguments with which the reader is already familiar, these might be good to start with. Through them you may establish a rapport with the reader, which will facilitate the acceptance of your new arguments.

Still another technique is to give evidence from a historical perspective. This method may work well if you are trying to convince your readers of some sort of causal connection concerning which a series of studies have been done. For instance, if you are trying to convince readers that vitamin C has curative properties, you might want to trace the history of medical studies of this vitamin. Of course, chronological arrangement works only when the more recent evidence supports your own thesis rather than the opposition's.

If the prevailing opinion seems to be contrary to your thesis, you may wish to structure your essay around the major objections to your thesis. A paper entitled "Common Myths About Welfare," for instance, might take up and systematically demolish the stereotypes some people hold about the typical welfare recipient. This kind of structure, which tends to work best in shorter papers, makes the entire essay a rebuttal argument. Rebuttal arguments are usually most effective when factual and unemotional in tone, which gives the essay the appearance of answering myth with fact and emotion with reason. However, you should be careful to state your opponent's views fairly and not to commit the "straw man" fallacy by reducing the other side of the story to an easily destroyed caricature of the position.

Let us consider a possible problem of organization and some solutions. Perhaps the literature course requirement is to be dropped from your major, which is a technical one, in favor of another technical course. Your position is that this change is a poor one. In your preliminary research, you find some evidence that many employers prefer to hire those with broader backgrounds and that people with narrow educational backgrounds tend to have more trouble adjusting to changes in jobs later in their careers. You also find studying literature personally rewarding and you think that eliminating such electives locks students into a curriculum too early in their college career. The original rough outline that you worked out while planning the paper was something like this:

Thesis: The engineering department should not abolish the literature requirement.

I.   The study of literature is rewarding.
II. Many employers don't want narrow specialists.
III. People who have studied a rigid curriculum have more trouble changing jobs later after beginning their careers.
IV. Rigid curricula lock students into majors too early.

You were not particularly happy with this outline because the divisions were so broad and there didn't seem to be any particular reason for the arrangement of topics, but you thought you would fix that later. Now it is later. What can you do with this material?

You might try arranging it from the least to the most significant argument. If you do this, however, you may have some trouble: how do you rate significance in this case? It may be that in fact you consider the rewards of studying literature the reason of greatest significance, but think that you will be able to find the least solid evidence to use as support for this point. When this is the case, you probably want to avoid arrangement by significance. You might want to consider a semi-chronological arrangement:

I. The study of literature is rewarding (immediately and permanently).
II. Excluding literature and other electives locks students into majors before they know enough to make sound decisions.
III. Excluding literature does not please employers.
IV. Education that is limited to the technical and practical handicaps those who want to or must change careers.

Now the material reflects the order in which a student going through college would encounter the issues. In reading over your plan, it may occur to you that what you are really arguing is that narrowness in education makes for limitation of potential and narrowness in life; the immediate issue of the abolition of the literature requirement is only an example. You will want to write your final essay with both the immediate and the broader issues in mind.

Once you have a meaningful strategy of arrangement, you may want to make out a detailed outline listing your subpoints and showing how you plan to handle the opposition's views, or you may want to go ahead and write the body of your paper, hoping that your interest and enthusiasm will help you structure it. There are any number of possibilities for effective arrangement; what is important is that you recognize the need for a principle of organization and find one that suits your project. For a 150-word editorial, you might simply ask a provocative question and answer it. For a 3,000-word essay demonstrating that the local airport should not be enlarged to enable jets to land, you might work out a pattern of reasons and replies as formal and complicated as a minuet.

The Conclusion

The conclusion should re-establish reader rapport, remind the reader of your main point, and provide a sense of psychological closure. The kind of conclusion you write will, of course, depend greatly on the nature of the project. If the essay is a long one, you may wish to recapitulate your main points. If the essay is short, you will not want 'to conclude by summarizing, since the reader is unlikely to have forgotten the thread of your argument in the space of a few moments. Some common ways of concluding an argumentative essay are by summarizing, by picking up the image or anecdote from your introduction, by making recommendations, and by speculating about the effects of general acceptance (or rejection) of your hypothesis. This last method must be used with caution because some such conclusions are vague and windy. Conclusions to avoid include excessively repetitious summary, introduction of another topic, and sudden shifts in tone or direction. Consider the conclusions of two brief essays arguing that seniors should be allowed to keep their traditional exemption from final exams:

It is clear from the survey results that 90 percent of the students are strongly in favor of the senior exemption. The interviews make it equally clear that forcing seniors to stay and take exams would put them at a definite disadvantage in the job race. Therefore arise, students! Combat this danger to your security and tradition! Take action before it is too late!

. . . thus the final exams that the faculty favor so strongly are not being given almost 60 percent of the time anyway. To require students to work around the many problems that would arise as a result of the policy change when finals are actually being given less than half the time seems unfair if not ridiculous. It is clear that the problems associated with requiring degree candidates to take finals far outweigh any gains that might result.

The first example demonstrates the awkwardness of an attempt to shift to direct address at the end of an argument. The second example uses a general restatement of thesis, but it does so smoothly and so provides a sense of closure. It is hard to generalize about effective conclusions, however, because what will work and what will fall flat depend completely on the rest of your essay.

Although the suggestions made in these two chapters apply most obviously to class-assigned essays, the argumentative uses of the skills acquired in studying effective thinking techniques are limited only by your imagination. You may use these techniques to marshal your arguments in midnight bull sessions, to convince your parents that your change in major is justified and worthwhile, to write a grant proposal enabling you to go study chimpanzees in Kenya. If you enjoy writing, you may want to experiment with satire and sarcasm in letters to the editor, or to express your point of view in plays or poems. Ability to write convincingly is a great boon in helping to satisfy psychological and intellectual needs—needs for autonomy, approval, prestige, and even sometimes for beauty and truth.

Suggested Supplementary Reading

Hans P. Guth, *New Concise Handbook* (Belmont, Calif.: Wadsworth, 1984). For grammar.

Kate L. Turabian, *A Manual for Writers of Term Papers, Theses, and Dissertations* (Chicago: University of Chicago Press, 1973). For form.

Exercise 33

1. For your planned major paper, answer each of the following questions about your intended audience. If your intended audience is your instructor, answer the questions about the group of which he or she is most representative.

   a. What age are your intended readers?

   b. What is their approximate educational level?

   c. What kinds of occupations are represented among them?

   d. Why would they want to read your article?

   e. What general attitudes are they likely to share?

   f. What do they know about this particular issue?

   g. How does this particular issue affect them?

   h. What opinions are they likely to share about this particular issue?

   i. What position do you wish them to adopt concerning this particular issue?

   j. What advantages would they find in adopting this position?

   k. What types of appeals are likely to offend this audience?

   l. What types of appeals are likely to work especially effectively with this audience?

   m. Name a journal into which you can imagine your completed article fitting.

   n. Name a journal for which your completed article would be totally inappropriate.

   o. List the factors you share with your intended audience.

   p. List the factors which separate you from your intended audience.

   q. What kind of material would make the best introduction to your essay, considering the audience as you have defined it?

   r. What kind of conclusion for your essay would best suit this particular audience?

2. Consider the following ten thesis statements, each of which is intended for a paper of about one thousand words. Criticize each according to the principles in the last two chapters. Then choose three of the weakest and rewrite them to eliminate the problems you found.

   a. The campus police should be abolished.

   b. Abortions should be freely available to everybody.

   c. The FDA keeps useful medicines from the public for too long.

   d. Requiring motorcyclists to wear helmets interferes with Constitutionally guaranteed freedom.

e. Students should be required to vote in their hometowns and not permitted to vote where their colleges are located.

f. If guns are outlawed, only outlaws will have guns.

g. Parents should be allowed to choose their children's textbooks.

h. People should always be good citizens.

i. Hosts should be legally responsible for acts committed by drunken guests.

j. Public education should be provided for the children of illegal aliens.

3. Go to the library and find an argumentative essay intended for an educated audience. Outline the essay. Evaluate the thesis statement, the use of support, and the introduction and conclusion.

4. For the topic you have chosen for your major paper, write two different introductions using two different methods of getting reader interest. Evaluate the introductions.

5. Find two argumentative essays on the same topic—preferably your paper topic—that are intended for different audiences. List ten differences in structure, tone, type of evidence, and so on.

6. Write a one-paragraph editorial intended for readers of a local newspaper in which you try to get the readers to do one of the following:

a. Pass an open-container law (a law making it a misdemeanor to carry an open container of an alcoholic beverage in one's car).

b. Ban nonreturnable bottles.

c. Raise taxes to expand the library.

d. Build a wave pool in the town park.

e. Pass a leash law.

f. Get their dogs vaccinated.

g. Allow a rock concert in the town park.

h. Prohibit a rock concert in the town park.

7. On your chosen topic, write a brief essay in which you state and refute one of your opponent's major claims.

Index

Your Opinion of This Book

The authors and editors of *Creative and Critical Thinking* would like to know your opinion of the book. Your comments will help us not only in improving the next edition of the text but also in developing other books. We would appreciate it if you would take a few minutes to respond to the following questions and return the form to: College Marketing, Houghton Mifflin Company, One Beacon Street, Boston, MA 02108

Please tell us your overall reaction to the text.

	Excellent	Good	Adequate	Poor
1. Was it written in clear and understandable style?	_____	_____	_____	_____
2. Were difficult concepts well explained?	_____	_____	_____	_____
3. How does the general interest level of this book compare to other college books?	_____	_____	_____	_____
4. Were the Exercises useful in testing your understanding of the text?	_____	_____	_____	_____
5. What is your overall evaluation of the book?	_____	_____	_____	_____

6. Please cite examples to illustrate any of the above ratings: _____

_____

_____

7. Were there any chapters or examples that you particularly liked or disliked?

If so, what were they and why? _____

_____

_____

8. Were there any topics that were not covered that you believe *should* have been?

_____

_____

_____

9. Did you find the chapters on the "Human Element" helpful to you in thinking about the decisions that you face in your own life? Why or why not?

_____

_____

10. Do you feel that your general thinking procedures have been improved by studying

this text? _____ Yes. _____ No. Please comment: _____

_____

_____

_____

11. Please check one of the responses and complete the information requested.
I read _Creative and Critical Thinking_ as part of

_____ an undergraduate course called _____

in the department of _____.

_____ a graduate course called _____

in the department of _____.

I am majoring in _____ at (identify school) _____

_____.